D1518856

A Companion to Nietzsche

Blackwell Companions to Philosophy

This outstanding student reference series offers a comprehensive and authoritative survey of philosophy as a whole. Written by today's leading philosophers, each volume provides lucid and engaging coverage of the key figures, terms, topics, and problems of the field. Taken together, the volumes provide the ideal basis for course use, representing an unparalleled work of reference for students and specialists alike.

A Companion to Nietzsche

Edited by
Keith Ansell Pearson

Blackwell
Publishing

BLACKWELL PUBLISHING
350 Main Street, Malden, MA 02148-5020, USA
9600 Garsington Road, Oxford OX4 2DQ, UK
550 Swanston Street, Carlton, Victoria 3053, Australia

First published 2006 by Blackwell Publishing Ltd

1   2006

Library of Congress Cataloging-in-Publication Data

A companion to Nietzsche / edited by Keith Ansell Pearson.
      p. cm. — (Blackwell companions to philosophy ; 33)
   Includes bibliographical references and index.
   ISBN-13: 978-1-4051-1622-0 (hardcover)
   ISBN-10: 1-4051-1622-6 (hardcover)
   1. Nietzsche, Friedrich Wilhelm, 1844–1900.   I. Ansell Pearson, Keith, 1960–   II. Series.

   B3317.C619 2006
   193—dc22

                                                                        2005024906

A catalogue record for this title is available from the British Library.

Set in 10/12.5pt Photina
by Graphicraft Limited, Hong Kong
Printed and bound in the United Kingdom
by TJ International, Padstow, Cornwall

The publisher's policy is to use permanent paper from mills that operate a sustainable forestry policy,
and which has been manufactured from pulp processed using acid-free and elementary chlorine-free
practices. Furthermore, the publisher ensures that the text paper and cover board used have met
acceptable environmental accreditation standards.

For further information on
Blackwell Publishing, visit our website:
www.blackwellpublishing.com

This volume is dedicated to the memory of the lives and work of Wolfgang Müller-Lauter (1924–2001) and Jorg Salaquarda (1938–1999)

Contents

Notes on Contributors

Christa Davis Acampora is Associate Professor of Philosophy at Hunter College and the Graduate Center of the City University of New York. She is the author of numerous articles on Nietzsche, and she is the co-editor of *A Nietzschean Bestiary: Becoming Animal Beyond Docile and Brutal* (2004).

Keith Ansell Pearson is Professor of Philosophy and Director of Graduate Research at the University of Warwick. He founded the Friedrich Nietzsche Society (UK) in 1990 and has served on the editorial board of *Nietzsche-Studien* since 1997. He is the author of several books, including *Nietzsche contra Rousseau* (1991), *Viroid Life: Perspectives on Nietzsche and the Transhuman Condition* (1997), *Germinal Life: The Difference and Repetition of Deleuze* (1999), *Philosophy and the Adventure of the Virtual: Bergson and the Time of Life* (2002), and *How to Read Nietzsche* (2005). He is the editor of several books, including *Nietzsche and Modern German Thought* (1991), *The Fate of the New Nietzsche* (with Howard Caygill, 1994), *Deleuze and Philosophy* (1997), *Bergson Key Writings* (with John Mullarkey, 2001), and Blackwell's *The Nietzsche Reader* (with Duncan Large, 2005). His books and essays have been translated into various languages, including Chinese, Italian, Portuguese, Spanish, and Turkish.

Babette E. Babich is Professor of Philosophy at Fordham University, New York City, and Adjunct Research Professor of Philosophy at Georgetown University. She is the founding editor of the journal *New Nietzsche Studies* and Executive Director of the Nietzsche Society in the US. She is author of *Words in Blood, Like Flowers: Philosophy and Poetry, Music and Eros in Hölderlin, Heidegger, and Nietzsche* (2005), and *Nietzsche's Philosophy of Science: Reflecting Science on the Ground of Art and Life* (1994). She is contributing editor of several collections, including *Habermas, Nietzsche, and Critical Theory* (2004), *Nietzsche, Theories of Knowledge, and Critical Theory* (1999), and *Nietzsche, Epistemology and the Philosophy of Science* (1999).

Daniel Came is Lecturer in Philosophy at Birkbeck College, University of London. He has published articles on Nietzsche, aesthetics, and the history of philosophy and is the editor of *Nietzsche and Ethics* (2006).

Maudemarie Clark is George Carleton Jr. Professor of Philosophy at Colgate University. She is the author of *Nietzsche on Truth and Philosophy* (1990), of the entry on

Nietzsche in the *Routledge Encyclopedia of Philosophy*, and of many articles on Nietzsche. She is also co-editor of Nietzsche's *Daybreak* (Cambridge, 1997), and co-translator and co-editor of Nietzsche's *On the Genealogy of Morality* (1998). Her most recent publication is "Nietzsche's Post-Positivism," co-authored with David Dudrick, in the *European Journal of Philosophy* (2004). She and Dudrick are currently working together on a book tentatively titled *Nietzsche's Magnificent Tension of the Spirit*.

Daniel W. Conway is Professor of Philosophy at the Pennsylvania State University. He is the author of *Nietzsche's Dangerous Game* (1997) and *Nietzsche and the Political* (1997). He is also the editor of *Nietzsche: Critical Assessments of Leading Philosophers*, in four volumes (1998) and co-editor of *Nietzsche, Philosophy, and the Arts* (1998).

Christoph Cox is Associate Professor of Philosophy at Hampshire College, Amherst, Massachusetts. He is the author of *Nietzsche: Naturalism and Interpretation* (1999) and co-editor of *Audio Culture: Readings in Modern Music*. He serves on the editorial board of *Cabinet* magazine and writes regularly on contemporary art and music for *Artforum* and *The Wire*.

David Dudrick is Assistant Professor of Philosophy at Colgate University. He is the author of "Foucault, Butler, and the Body," in the *European Journal of Philosophy* (2005), and of "Nietzsche's Shameful Science," forthcoming in *International Studies in Philosophy*. He is also co-author, with Maudemarie Clark, of "Nietzsche's Post-Positivism," in the *European Journal of Philosophy* (2004). He and Clark are currently working together on a book tentatively titled *Nietzsche's Magnificent Tension of the Spirit*.

Volker Gerhardt is Professor of Practical Philosophy and Legal and Social Philosophy at the Humboldt University Berlin and a member of the Berlin-Brandenburg Academy of Sciences. He is the author of many books, including *Pathos und Distanz* (1989), *Vom Willen zur Macht. Anthropologie und Metaphysik der Macht am exemplarischen Fall Friedrich Nietzsches* (1996), *Der Mensch wird geboren. Kleine Apologie der Humanität* (2001), and *Kant. Vernunft und Leben* (2002). He is the editor of numerous books on Nietzsche, Kant, political philosophy, aesthetics, and epistemology.

Robert Guay is Visiting Assistant Professor at Barnard College. He has published essays on Nietzsche in the *European Journal of Philosophy* and *Metaphilosophy*.

Kathleen Marie Higgins is Professor of Philosophy at the University of Texas at Austin. She is the author of *Nietzsche's "Zarathustra"*, *Comic Relief: Nietzsche's "Gay Science"*, and *What Nietzsche Really Said* (with Robert C. Solomon), and books on music and the history of philosophy. She is the editor of *Reading Nietzsche* (with Robert C. Solomon), *The Cambridge Companion to Nietzsche* (with Bernd Magnus), and books on erotic love, ethics, aesthetics, and world philosophy.

Christopher Janaway is Professor of Philosophy at the University of Southampton, and was previously Professor of Philosophy at Birkbeck College of the University of London. He is the author of several works on Schopenhauer and aesthetics, and editor of *Willing and Nothingness: Schopenhauer as Nietzsche's Educator*. He is currently completing a book on Nietzsche's *Genealogy of Morals*.

Laurence Lampert is Professor of Philosophy at Indiana University Indianapolis. He is the author of *Nietzsche's Teaching: An Interpretation of "Thus Spoke Zarathustra," Nietzsche and Modern Times: A Study of Bacon, Descartes, and Nietzsche, Leo Strauss and Nietzsche*, and *Nietzsche's Task: An Interpretation of "Beyond Good and Evil."*

Paul S. Loeb is Professor of Philosophy at the University of Puget Sound. He is the author of numerous articles on Nietzsche and is currently completing a book about *Thus Spoke Zarathustra*.

Jill Marsden is a Senior Lecturer in Philosophy at Bolton Institute. She has written articles on various aspects of Nietzsche's philosophy and is the author of *After Nietzsche: Notes Towards a Philosophy of Ecstasy* (2002).

Elaine P. Miller is Associate Professor of Philosophy at Miami University in Oxford, Ohio. She is the author of *The Vegetative Soul: From Philosophy of Nature to Subjectivity in the Feminine* (2001), as well as articles on Nietzsche, Kant, Hegel, and Irigaray. She is also the co-editor of *Returning to Irigaray* (forthcoming).

Gregory Moore is Lecturer in German Studies at the University of St Andrews. He is the author of *Nietzsche, Biology, and Metaphor* (2002) and co-editor with Thomas Brobjer of *Nietzsche and Science* (2004).

Diane Morgan is Lecturer in Cultural Studies at the University of Leeds. She is the author of *Kant Trouble: Obscurities of the Enlightened* (2000), and is currently working on a book project "Cosmopolitics and the Future of Humanism."

Nuno Nabais is Professor of Philosophy at the University of Lisbon. He is the author, in Portuguese, of *The Metaphysics of the Tragic: Studies on Nietzsche* (1998), *The Evidence of Possibility: The Modal Question in Husserl* (1999), and *The Genealogy of the Sublime: From Kant to Deleuze* (2005).

Robert B. Pippin is the Raymond W. and Martha Hilpert Gruner Distinguished Service Professor in the Committee on Social Thought, the Department of Philosophy, and the College at the University of Chicago. He has been a fellow at the Wissenschaftskolleg in Berlin and the winner of the Mellon Distinguished Achievement Award in the humanities. He is the author of several books, including *Kant's Theory of Form, Hegel's Idealism: The Satisfactions of Self-Consciousness, Modernism as a Philosophical Problem*, and *Henry James and Modern Moral Life*. A collection of recent essays, *Die Verwirklichung der Freiheit*, was published in 2005.

Peter Poellner is Senior Lecturer in Philosophy at the University of Warwick. He is the author of *Nietzsche and Metaphysics* (1995), and of numerous articles on Nietzsche and phenomenology. He is currently completing a book *Value in Modernity*.

James I. Porter is Professor of Classical Studies and Comparative Literature at the University of Michigan. He is the author of *Nietzsche and the Philology of the Future* and *The Invention of Dionysus: An Essay on the "Birth of Tragedy"* (both 2000). He is the editor of *Constructions of the Classical Body* (1999), *Before Subjectivity? Lacan and the Classics* (with Mark Buchan; special issue of *Helios*, Fall 2004), and *Classical Pasts: The Classical Traditions of Greece & Rome* (2005). His current projects include *The Material*

Sublime in Greek & Roman Aesthetics and *Nietzsche and the Seductions of Metaphysics: Nietzsche's Final Philosophy*.

John Richardson is Professor of Philosophy at New York University. He is the author of *Existential Epistemology: A Heideggerian Critique of the Cartesian Project* (1986), *Nietzsche's System* (1996), and *Nietzsche's New Darwinism* (2004). He is the co-editor with Brian Leiter of the collection *Nietzsche* (2001).

Richard Schacht is Professor of Philosophy and Jubilee Professor of Liberal Arts and Sciences at the University of Illinois. His books include *Alienation, Hegel and After, Nietzsche, The Future of Alienation, Making Sense of Nietzsche*, and, with Philip Kitcher, *Finding an Ending: Reflections on Wagner's Ring*.

Gary Shapiro is Tucker-Boatwright Professor in the Humanities and Professor of Philosophy at the University of Richmond. He is the author of *Nietzschean Narratives* (1989), *Alcyone: Nietzsche on Gifts, Noise, and Women* (1991), *Earthwards: Robert Smithson and Art after Babel* (1995), and *Archaeologies of Vision: Foucault and Nietzsche on Seeing and Saying* (2003). His current projects are concerned with European philosophy and environmental aesthetics.

Herman Siemens teaches modern philosophy at the University of Leiden, the Netherlands. Since 1998 he has been working together with other Nietzsche scholars on the *Nietzsche Dictionary* project, based at the University of Nijmegen. At the same time he has been conducting research into Nietzsche's concept of the *agon*, a cultural and ethical ideal of limited conflict derived from Greek antiquity.

Robin Small teaches at Auckland University, New Zealand. He is the author of *Nietzsche in Context* (2001), and *Nietzsche and Rée: A Star Friendship* (2005). He is the editor of *A Hundred Years of Phenomenology* (2001) and *Paul Rée: Basic Writings* (2003). He has also published articles on Hegel, Marx, Husserl, and Kafka.

Robert C. Solomon is Quincy Lee Centennial Professor and Distinguished Teaching Professor at the University of Texas at Austin. He is the author of more than 40 books, including *The Passions, In the Spirit of Hegel, About Love, A Passion for Justice, A Short History of Philosophy, Ethics and Excellence, The Joy of Philosophy*, and *Not Passion's Slave*. His most recent book is *Living with Nietzsche: What the Great "Immoralist" has to teach* us. He is the co-editor of *Reading Nietzsche* and co-author of *What Nietzsche Really Said* (both with Kathleen Marie Higgins).

Andreas Urs Sommer is a Lecturer in Philosophy at the University of Greifswald, Germany. He has been a Visiting Research Fellow at Princeton University and a Visiting Fellow at the Institute of Germanic Studies, School of Advanced Study, University of London. He is the author of several books, including *Der Geist der Historie und das Ende des Christentums. Zur "Waffengenossenschaft" von Friedrich Nietzsche und Franz Overbeck* (1997), *Friedrich Nietzsches "Der Antichrist." Ein philosophisch-historischer Kommentar* (2000), and *Die Hortung. Eine Philosophie des Sammelns* (2000). He has also edited several volumes, including *Im Spannungsfeld von Gott und Welt* (1997), *Existenzphilosophie und Christentum. Albert Schweitzer und Fritz Buri. Briefe 1935–1964* (2000), and *Lohnt es sich, ein guter Mensch zu sein? Und andere philosophische Anfragen*

(2004). He is co-editor of the letters of Franz Overbeck (*Werke und Nachlass*, volume 8, forthcoming).

Henry Staten is Lockwood Professor in the Humanities and Adjunct Professor of Philosophy at the University of Washington, Seattle. He is the author of *Wittgenstein and Derrida* (1986), *Nietzsche's Voice* (1990) and *Eros in Mourning: From Homer to Lacan* (2002).

Paul J. M. van Tongeren is Professor of Philosophy at Radboud University Nijmegen, the Netherlands, and at the Katholieke Universiteit Leuven, Belgium. He is the author of *Reinterpreting Modern Culture: An Introduction to Friedrich Nietzsche's Philosophy* (1999) and chief editor of the *Nietzsche Dictionary*.

A Note on References to Nietzsche's Works

With the exception of *Kritische Studienausgabe* (*KSA*) and *The Will to Power* (*WP*), where only one edition of each exists, the contributors to this volume have used different editions and translations of Nietzsche's texts. Where no details of Nietzsche's texts are given at the end of an essay this is because the contributor has relied exclusively on their own translations. References to *KSA* are not given in chapter bibliographies to avoid unnecessary repetition; references appear extensively throughout the volume. When citing from the German editions of Nietzsche's works contributors have sought to provide reference to an English source where available. Unless stated otherwise, references given throughout the text are to aphorism and section numbers, not page numbers, for example *GS* 54, *BGE* 36. A reference to *KSA* gives first the volume number followed by the note number (e.g. *KSA* 9, 11[141]). Where a text by Nietzsche is divided into chapters or parts with separately numbered sections, these are cited by an intermediate roman numeral – for example, *GM* I. 12, *Z* II – followed by title of the particular discourse. *Twilight of the Idols* is cited by the abbreviation (*TI*) followed by the title of the particular chapter and then section number, for example, *TI*, "Expeditions of an Untimely Man," 14. The third chapter of *Ecce Homo* contains parts with separately numbered sections on Nietzsche's books, and these are referenced as, for example, *EH*, "BT," 3, *EH*, "Z," 2, and so on.

The following system of abbreviations has been used throughout the text:

Books Published by Nietzsche or Prepared for Publication by Nietzsche

A	*The Anti-Christian*
AOM	*Assorted Opinions and Maxims* (volume 2, part 1, of *Human, All Too Human*)
BGE	*Beyond Good and Evil*
BT	*The Birth of Tragedy*
CW	*The Case of Wagner*
D	*Daybreak*
EH	*Ecce Homo*
GM	*On the Genealogy of Morality*
GS	*The Gay Science*

HH   *Human, All Too Human* (this refers to volume 1 only)
NCW   *Nietzsche contra Wagner*
TI   *Twilight of the Idols*
UM II   *The Uses and Disadvantages of History for Life* (second *Untimely Meditation*)
UM III   *Schopenhauer as Educator* (third *Untimely Meditation*)
WS   *The Wanderer and his Shadow* (volume 2, part 2, of *Human, All Too Human*)
Z   *Thus Spoke Zarathustra*

Unpublished Essays and Books

HC   "Homer's Contest"
PTAG   "Philosophy in the Tragic Age of the Greeks"
TL   "On Truth and Lies in a Non-Moral Sense"

Posthumous Selections from Nietzsche's Notebooks

LN   *Writings from the Late Notebooks*
WP   *The Will to Power*. Ed. and trans. R. J. Hollingdale and Walter Kaufmann. New York: Vintage Books, 1967

German Editions of Nietzsche's Works and Letters

In referring to Nietzsche's works in German the vast majority of contributors have utilized the following edition:

KSA   *Sämtliche Werke. Kritische Studienausgabe*, 15 volumes. Ed. G. Colli and M. Montinari. Berlin and New York: Walter de Gruyter, 1967–77; Munich: Deutscher Taschenbuch Verlag, 1980.

KSA Nachlass Volumes

Over half of this edition of Nietzsche's works is made up of posthumously published notebooks or *Nachlass*.

Volume 1 includes both Nietzsche's first-published text, *Birth of Tragedy* (1872), and *Nachlass* writings of 1870–3, including pieces cited by contributors in this volume such as: "On the Pathos of Truth" (pp. 755–61), "Homer's Contest" (pp. 783–93), *Philosophy in the Tragic Age of the Greeks* (pp. 799–813), and "On Truth and Lies in a Non-Moral Sense" (pp. 873–91).
Volumes 2–6 cover the texts and materials Nietzsche published or prepared for publication during his lifetime.
Volume 7 = *Nachlass* 1869–74
Volume 8 = *Nachlass* 1875–9

Volume 9 = *Nachlass* 1880–2
Volume 10 = *Nachlass* 1882–4
Volume 11 = *Nachlass* 1884–5
Volume 12 = *Nachlass* 1885–7
Volume 13 = *Nachlass* 1887–9
Volume 14 = the editors' commentary on volumes 1–13

Other References to Nietzsche's Works

The following are occasionally referenced:

BAW *Friedrich Nietzsche, Werke und Briefe. Historisch-Kritische-Gesamtausgabe.* Ed. J. Mette and K. Schlechta. Munich: Beck, 1933– .

GOA *Friedrich Nietzsche, Werke. Grossoktav-Ausgabe*, 19 volumes. Ed. E. Förster-Nietzsche, Peter Gast, et al. Leipzig: Naumann/Kröner, 1894– .

KGW *Werke. Kritische Gesamtausgabe*, ca. 40 volumes. Established G. Colli and M. Montinari, continued by W. Müller-Lauter and K. Pestalozzi. Berlin and New York: Walter de Gruyter, 1967– .

KSB *Sämtliche Briefe. Kritische Studienausgabe Briefe*, 8 volumes. Ed. G. Colli and M. Montinari. Berlin and New York: Walter de Gruyter; Munich: dtv, 1986.

A Note on Translated Essays

The essays by Volker Gerhardt, Nuno Nabais, Andreas Urs Sommer, and Paul van Tongeren have been translated by Colin King, Christopher Rollason, Carol Diethe, and Thomas Hart respectively. Each essay was further refined and edited by the editor.

A Note on Cross-References

A system of cross-referencing has been deployed throughout the volume to help readers quickly identify relevant essays. Only essays outside the section in which a particular essay appears are cross-referenced; readers should consider examining all the essays in any given section where an essay they wish to consult appears. A number of essays in the volume could have been placed in more than one section. The decision where to place an essay was done on the basis of its overriding theme and where it would gain its greatest pertinence. Several constructions of this volume were possible. Although the final construction is a piece of artifice, it has not been put together in an arbitrary fashion.

Chronology of Nietzsche's Life and Work

1844 Friedrich Wilhelm Nietzsche born in Röcken (Saxony) on October 15, son of Karl Ludwig and Franziska Nietzsche. His father and both grandfathers are Protestant clergymen.

1846 Birth of sister Elisabeth.

1849 Birth of brother Joseph; death of father due to "softening of the brain" following a fall.

1850 Death of brother; family moves to Naumburg.

1858–64 Attends renowned Pforta boarding school, where he excels in classics.

1862 Writes his first philosophical essays on fate, history, and freedom of the will under the influence of Ralph Waldo Emerson.

1864 Enters Bonn University to study theology and classical philology.

1865 Follows his classics professor to Leipzig University, where he drops theology and continues with studies in classical philology. Discovers Schopenhauer's philosophy.

1867–8 Military service in Naumburg, until invalided out after a riding accident.

1868 Back in Leipzig, meets Richard Wagner for the first time and becomes a devotee. Increasing disaffection with philology: plans to go to Paris to study chemistry.

1869 Appointed Extraordinary (Associate) Professor of Classical Philology at Basel University and teacher of Greek at the associated grammar school. Awarded doctorate without examination; renounces Prussian citizenship and applies for Swiss citizenship without success (he lacks the necessary residential qualification and is stateless for the rest of his life). Begins a series of idyllic visits to the Wagners at Tribschen, on Lake Lucerne. Gives inaugural lecture "On Homer's Personality." Meets the historian Jacob Burckhardt and the theologian Franz Overbeck.

1870 Promoted to full professor and gives public lectures on "The Greek Music-Drama" and "Socrates and Tragedy." Composes sketches for a drama on the philosopher Empedocles, which anticipates many of the themes of *The Birth of Tragedy*. Participates in the Franco-Prussian War as volunteer medical orderly, but contracts dysentery and diphtheria at the front within a fortnight. Spends Christmas with Wagner and present at the first performance of the *Siegfried Idyll* at Tribschen.

1871	Nietzsche works intensively on *The Birth of Tragedy*. Germany unified; founding of the Reich. Nietzsche granted his first period of leave of absence from his university "for the purpose of restoring his health."
1872	Publishes *The Birth of Tragedy out of the Spirit of Music*. Lectures "On the Future of our Educational Institutions"; attends laying of foundation stone for Bayreuth Festival Theatre. Gives Cosima Wagner Christmas present of "five prefaces to unwritten books," which include "On the Pathos of Truth" and "Homer's Contest."
1873	Publishes first *Untimely Meditation: David Strauss the Confessor and the Writer*. Drafts the essay "On Truth and Lies in a Non-Moral Sense" but refrains from publishing it.
1874	Publishes second and third *Untimely Meditations: On the Use and Disadvantage of History for Life* and *Schopenhauer as Educator*. Relationship with Wagner begins to sour, and makes his last private visit to him in August. They do not see each other for nearly two years.
1875	Meets musician Heinrich Köselitz (Peter Gast), who idolizes him and becomes his disciple. Attends a spa in the Black Forest seeking a cure to his violent headaches and vomiting.
1876	Publishes fourth and last *Untimely Meditation: Richard Wagner in Bayreuth*. Attends first Bayreuth Festival but leaves early and subsequently breaks with Wagner. Further illness; granted full year's sick leave from the university. Spends time with Paul Rée in Sorrento where both write and where he also meets Wagner for the last time.
1877	Travels alone in Italy and Switzerland; arrives back in Basel and resumes teaching duties.
1878	Publishes *Human, All Too Human: A Book for Free Spirits*, which confirms the break with Wagner and who declines to read the book.
1879	Publishes supplement to *Human, All Too Human, Assorted Opinions and Maxims*. Finally retires from teaching on a pension; first visits the Engadine, summering in St Moritz.
1880	Publishes *The Wanderer and his Shadow*. First stays in Venice and Genoa.
1881	Publishes *Daybreak: Thoughts on the Prejudices of Morality*. First stay in Sils-Maria. Composition of notes and sketches on "the thought of thoughts," the eternal return of the same. Sees Bizet's *Carmen* for the first time and adopts it as the model antithesis to Wagner.
1882	Publishes *The Gay Science*. Spends time with Rée in Genoa, travels to Rome where he eventually meets with Lou Andreas-Salomé and becomes infatuated with her. Salomé spurns his marriage proposals. By the end of the year Nietzsche realizes he has been abandoned by Rée and Salomé and is physically and emotionally exhausted.
1883	Publishes *Thus Spoke Zarathustra: A Book for Everyone and No One*, Parts I and II (separately). Death of Wagner. Spends the summer in Sils and the winter in Nice, his pattern for the next five years. Increasingly consumed by writing.
1884	Publishes *Thus Spoke Zarathustra*, Part III.

CHRONOLOGY OF NIETZSCHE'S LIFE AND WORK

1885	*Thus Spoke Zarathustra*, Part IV, printed but circulated to only a handful of friends.
1886	Publishes *Beyond Good and Evil: Prelude to a Philosophy of the Future*. Sketches out plans for a *magnum opus* in several volumes entitled *The Will to Power: Attempt at a Revaluation of All Values*, which he continues to work on into 1888.
1887	Publishes *On the Genealogy of Morality: A Polemic*.
1888	Begins to receive public recognition: Karl Spitteler publishes first review of his work as a whole in the Bern *Bund* and Georg Brandes lectures on his work in Copenhagen. Discovers Turin, where he writes *The Wagner Case: A Musician's Problem*. Completes, in quick succession, *Twilight of the Idols, or How to Philosophize with a Hammer* (first published 1889), *The Antichristian: Curse on Christianity* (first published 1895), *Ecce Homo, or How to Become What You Are* (first published 1908), *Nietzsche contra Wagner: Documents of a Psychologist* (first published 1895), and *Dionysus Dithyrambs* (first published 1892).
1889	Suffers mental breakdown in Turin (3 January) and taken by Overbeck to the university clinic at Basel where the diagnosis is "progressive paralysis" or general paresis (the diagnosis cannot be taken as fact); later transferred to the university clinic at Jena. *Twilight of the Idols* published 24 January, the first of his new books to appear after his collapse.
1890	Discharged into the care of his mother in Naumburg.
1894	Elisabeth founds Nietzsche Archive in Naumburg (moving it to Weimar two years later).
1895	Publication of *The Anti-Christian* and *Nietzsche contra Wagner*. Elisabeth becomes the owner of Nietzsche's copyright.
1897	Mother dies; Elisabeth moves Nietzsche to Weimar.
1900	Nietzsche dies in Weimar on 25 August.

I am grateful to Duncan Large for allowing me to use his now standard Chronology of Nietzsche, which I have amended and enlarged.

1

Friedrich Nietzsche: An Introduction to his Thought, Life, and Work

KEITH ANSELL PEARSON

Friedrich Nietzsche (1844–1900) exerted an extraordinary influence on twentieth-century thought and continues to be a major source of inspiration for work being done today in all the branches of philosophical inquiry. Nietzsche was first and foremost an intellectual revolutionary who sought to change the way we think about existence and how we actually live. To this end he constructed new tasks and projects and put forward new ways of interpreting and evaluating existence.

Nietzsche's philosophical legacy, however, is a complex one. Nietzsche aptly characterized his manner of doing philosophy when, in a letter to a friend, he spoke of his "whole *philosophical heterodoxy.*"[1] Most of his texts are aphoristic in style, his meaning is deliberately enigmatic, and he plays all kinds of tricks on his readers. One commentator, Eugen Fink, has argued that the metaphors and images that abound in Nietzsche's writings must be translated into *thoughts* if we are not to hear in them only an opulent, overloaded, and loquacious voice.[2] In spite of his heterodoxy and the difficulties presented by his philosophical style, Nietzsche's influence on modern trajectories of thought has been enormous and he continues to be utilized for important philosophical ends. His ideas exerted an influence on almost every important intellectual movement of the last century, including existentialism, structuralism, and post-structuralism. Aspects of his thought have had an influence on major philosophical figures in both North America and Great Britain, including Stanley Cavell, Richard Rorty, and Bernard Williams. Today he is the subject of a wide array of philosophical treatments, having been adopted by philosophers both of so-called "analytical" persuasions and so-called "continental" ones. Philosophical appreciation of Nietzsche has perhaps never been in a healthier state. Today there are lively debates over every aspect of his thinking, and sophisticated academic studies of his ideas are published on a regular basis.

This volume showcases the full range of work currently being done in the area of Nietzsche studies and appreciation. This includes close textual analysis and exegesis, the treatment of *Nachlass* material, clarification of aspects of his core doctrines and concepts, including some of the most difficult aspects, the consideration of Nietzsche's ideas in relation to fundamental philosophical problems that continue to occupy the attention of philosophers, and critical engagement with these ideas. The volume profiles contemporary thinking on Nietzsche's unpublished material and published texts and reflects trends in recent scholarship, such as the renewed focus on Nietzsche's naturalism and interest in his philosophy of time, of nature, and of life. There are instructive treatments of Nietzsche in relation to both established philosophical projects, such as phenomenology, and new ones, such as geophilosophy. The aim of the volume is essentially twofold: to illuminate core aspects of Nietzsche's thinking and to show the continuing relevance for philosophy of many of his ideas and projects and tasks. By way of an introduction to the essays that follow I wish to offer a synoptic guide to Nietzsche's thought, life, and work.[3]

Early Life and Thought

Friedrich Wilhelm Nietzsche was born on October 15, 1844 in Röcken, a tiny village near Lützen in Saxony. His father was a Lutheran pastor and was to die only five years after Nietzsche's birth as a result of softening of the brain. The experience of death, of its brute eruption into life and the violent separations it effects, took place early in Nietzsche's life, and the deaths of both his father and his brother Joseph (who was to die before his second birthday) continued to deeply affect Nietzsche throughout the course of his adolescent life and into maturity.

On the death of his father Nietzsche's family, which included his mother, his sister Elisabeth, and two unmarried aunts, relocated to Naumburg. Nietzsche began learning to play the piano and composed his first philosophical essay, "On the Origin of Evil." In 1858 he entered Pforta school in the Saale valley and was a student at this famous boarding school for six years. During this formative period of his youth he developed a love of various writers and poets, including Friedrich Hölderlin and Lord Byron. It is also during this period that he composed his first essay in classical philology and isolated pieces of philosophical reflection, such as "Fate and History."

On his fifteenth birthday Nietzsche declared that he had been "seized" and taken over by an "inordinate desire for knowledge and universal enlightenment." In an autobiographical fragment dated 1868/9 he reveals it was only in the final stages of his education at Pforta that he abandoned his artistic plans to be a musician and moved into the field of classical philology. He was motivated by a desire to have a counterweight to his changeable and restless inclinations. The science of philology on which he chose to focus his labors was one he could pursue with "cool impartiality, with cold logic, with regular work, without its results touching me at all deeply" (Nietzsche's mature approach to the matter of knowledge could not be more different!).[4] When he got to university Nietzsche realized that although he had been "well taught" at school he was also "badly educated"; he could think for himself but did not have the skills to express himself and he had "learned nothing of the educative influence of women."[5]

In October 1864 Nietzsche commenced his undergraduate studies in theology and classical philology at Bonn University. He attended the lectures of the classicist Friedrich Ritschl, who was later to play an influential role in securing Nietzsche's professorship at Basel. In his first year of university life he underwent the rite of passage offered by a duel and began his journey of alienation from his mother and sister by refusing to take communion. In 1865 he moved university to study just classical philology, following his teacher Ritschl to Leipzig. He speaks of his move from Bonn to Leipzig in a letter to his sister Elisabeth dated June 11, 1865, where he states that if a person wishes to achieve peace of mind and happiness then they should acquire faith, but if they want to be a disciple of truth, which can be "frightening and ugly," then they need to search. In his second year of university he discovered Schopenhauer, who suited his melancholic disposition at the time, and in 1866 he found a veritable "treasure-chest" of riches in Friedrich Albert Lange's magisterial study *History of Materialism*. In 1867 Leipzig University awarded him a prize for his study of Diogenes Laertius and he spent the third year of his university studies in military service.

In early 1869 Nietzsche, who had recently begun to feel disaffected with his chosen subject of study and research, was appointed to Basel University as Extraordinary Professor of Classical Philology (he was to apply for the Chair in Philosophy a few years later when it became vacant, but was not successful). Nietzsche assumed the role and duties of a professor at the age of 24 without completing his dissertation or postgraduate thesis.

Although Nietzsche often criticized the discipline of philology he had been trained in for its scholasticism and pedantry, the importance it places on the arts of reading and interpretation deeply informed his work. He repeatedly stresses the importance of knowing how to read well. He presents himself in untimely or unfashionable terms as a friend of slowness (*lento*) and as the teacher of slow reading. The contemporary age is an age of quickness; it no longer values slowness but seeks to hurry everything. Philology can be viewed as a venerable art that demands that its practitioners take time so as to become still and slow. More than anything it is an art that teaches one how to read well, which consists in reading slowly and deeply, and with the aid of which one looks and sees in a certain and specific manner: cautiously, observantly, "with doors left open" and "with delicate eyes and fingers" (*D*, preface, 5). Nietzsche believes that reading should be an art, for which rumination is required. He stresses that an aphorism has not been deciphered just because it has been read out; rather, an art of interpretation or exegesis needs to come into play. On Nietzsche's specific art of the aphorism see the essay by Jill Marsden (chapter 2).

Nietzsche had made the personal acquaintance of Wagner in November 1868 in Leipzig, and he made his first visit to the composer and his mistress (later wife) Cosima von Bülow at their house "Tribschen" near Lucerne not long after his arrival in Basel in April 1869. Between 1869 and 1872 Nietzsche would make over 20 visits to Tribschen. Nietzsche became a devotee of Wagner and considered himself to be in the presence of genius. This devotion did not last, and in his later writings he approaches Wagner as a case study that offers instructive lessons in how to read the signs and symptoms of pathological modernity (*CW*, preface).

In 1870 and 1871 Nietzsche lectured on topics, such as Socrates and tragedy and the "Dionysian world-view," that would form the basis of his first book, *The Birth of Tragedy*. He had the intimation that he was about to give birth to a "centaur" with art, philosophy, and scholarship all growing together inside him. In the Franco-Prussian War Nietzsche served for a few weeks as a medical orderly, but was invalided out when he contracted dysentery and diphtheria himself; on his return to Basel he began to suffer from insomnia, and he was to suffer from serious bouts of ill health and migraine attacks throughout the rest of his life. He wrote most of *The Birth of Tragedy* while on convalescent leave from his university, in 1871, and it was published at the beginning of 1872. Upon its publication Nietzsche's book met with vehement rejection by the philological community, and after being rejected by his mentor, Ritschl, Nietzsche had to admit that he had fallen from grace and was now ostracized from the guild of philologists. In 1873 Nietzsche worked on various projects, such as "Philosophy in the Tragic Age of the Greeks," the essay "On Truth and Lies in a Non-Moral Sense," and his *Untimely Meditations*. Nietzsche planned several dozen of these but only four actually materialized, and he regarded the whole exercise of writing them as a way of extracting everything he saw as negative in himself.

The Birth of Tragedy begins by defining two competing but also complementary impulses in Greek culture, the duality of the Apollonian and the Dionysian. The first takes its name from Apollo, the god of light (*der Scheinende*, the shining one), dream, and prophecy, while the second takes its name from Dionysus, the god of intoxication and rapture (*Rausch*). While Apollo is associated with visible form, comprehensible knowledge, and moderation, Dionysus is linked with formless flux, mystical intuition, and excess. Furthermore, while the Apollonian world is one of distinct individuals, the Dionysian world is one where these separate individual identities have been dissolved and human beings find themselves reconciled with the elemental energies of nature. Through Dionysian rapture we become part of a single, living being with whose joy in eternal creation we are fused. In artistic terms, Apollo is the god of the plastic or representational arts (painting and sculpture) and has a strong association with architecture, while Dionysus is the god of the non-representational art of music. One of the innovative aspects of Nietzsche's argument in the book is the way it contests the idealized image of the Greeks which had been handed down and which depicted ancient Greek culture as a culture of serenity and calm grandeur. Nietzsche seeks to show that the calm Apollonian surface of Greek art and culture is the product of a long and complex wrestling with the tragic insights afforded by the Dionysian state. In Nietzsche's argument the monumental achievement of the Attic tragedy of the fifth century BC, contained in the work of tragedians like Aeschylus and Sophocles, amounts to a fusion of the Apollonian and the Dionysian. Nietzsche's book is a search for an adequate knowledge of the union between the two artistic powers (a union he calls a "mystery") and of the origin (*Ursprung*) of Greek tragedy.

Nietzsche's first book was a striking debut. Although it has several core ideas, the most fundamental thesis of the book is that "only as an aesthetic phenomenon are the world and existence eternally justified." But just how is this "aestheticist" conception of the world to be heard and understood? What kind of "justification" is intended? The essay by Daniel Came seeks to clarify the status of the unorthodox insight at the heart of the book. Came takes issue with the charge often leveled against Nietzsche's position that it rests on a radical immoralism by arguing that, in fact, it has no moral implications. Furthermore, the "justification" of existence that is sought is epistemically neutral in the sense that it does not claim that existence is *actually* justified through aesthetic affirmation. Nietzsche affirms art because it embraces the need for illusion and semblance, as opposed to morality that seeks to deny the necessity of the perspectival and of interpretation, as well as its own implication in appearance and semblance (see *BT*, "Self-Criticism," 5). An aesthetic affirmation of existence is only a problem for the moral view of the world that shuns all forms of illusion. From the "dangerous" perspective of the moral view of the world an artistic metaphysics is to be judged as something arbitrary, idle, and fantastic ("Self-Criticism," 5).

Another important issue about Nietzsche's first book concerns the nature and extent of Schopenhauer's influence on it. In recent years Nietzsche studies in the English-speaking world has begun to develop a more scholarly appreciation of this issue, with the result that the questions are now posed and considered in a much more incisive and nuanced manner. Schopenhauer's metaphysics rest on dividing the world into two fundamental dimensions: will and representation. He borrows the expression *principium individuationis* (principle of individuation) from scholastic thinking and uses it to denote the phenomenal world of time and space as that which gives us a plurality of coexistent and successive things (this is the world of representation and of individual things). By contrast, the will is the thing-in-itself and outside the order of time and space (this is to name the world's real or genuine character). Because it also lies outside the province of the principle of sufficient reason (that which explains why something is what it is at a specific time and place), the will is equally groundless and can be said to be primordially "one" (not simply one as either an object or a concept). In their coming to be and perishing away individuals exist only as phenomena of the will (conceived as a "blind, irresistible urge"). Schopenhauer, in *The World as Will and Representation* (vol. 1, section 28), views the expression of the will in phenomena in Platonic terms: "the will is indivisible and wholly present in every phenomenon, although the degrees of its objectification [. . .] are very different". Schopenhauer goes on to talk of the crystal, the plant, the animal, and man as examples of objectified will. Each species of life and every original force of inorganic nature has an empirical character, but this character is nothing more than the phenomenon (manifestation) of an underlying intelligible character, namely, an indivisible will that is outside time.[6]

Although Nietzsche's argument in *Birth of Tragedy* relies heavily on the terms of Schopenhauer's metaphysics it does not simply replicate them. Apollo is conceived as the "transfiguring genius" of the *principium individuationis* through whom "redemption in appearance" (*Schein*) can be attained. Dionysus, by contrast, stands for the bursting apart of the spell of this *principium* that provides the path to the innermost being of things. Nietzsche finds something "sublime" in the way the pleasure to be had from the "beauty of appearance" can be experienced through the Apollonian (*BT* 1). A different kind of sublime is opened up, however, through the Dionysian and the breakdown of cognitive forms it inaugurates (it is the sublime of "horror"). The play between the two opposing forces gives rise in Nietzsche's text to a series of tensions between the one and the multiple, the sub-phenomenal and the phenomenal (the intelligible and the empirical realms), the desire for eternal life and the heroic trials of individuals. But Nietzsche gives equal weight to the two forces or powers, and he does not follow Schopenhauer in simply arguing for a mystical suppression of the will; rather, in the text we find Nietzsche attempting a justification of the plane of appearance and semblance (*Schein*) itself.

The essay by Nuno Nabais (chapter 5) contains valuable insight into Nietzsche's early "Schopenhauerianism" and traces his attempt to break free of it. Nabais provides a highly original interpretation of Nietzsche's thinking on the individual and seeks to account for the philosophical reasons informing his eventual positing of the will to power. Elaine P. Miller has made a notable contribution within English-speaking commentary to the appreciation of the problematic of individuation in Nietzsche, and in her essay (chapter 4) she utilizes her recent research in an effort to illuminate the problem for the reader, including appreciation of the will to power. Miller is concerned with the nature of Nietzsche's interest in a fundamental problem he encountered in Schopenhauer's metaphysics, that of individuation. This encompasses a number of issues that the essays by Nabais and Miller explore, including the character and status of the individual in Nietzsche's thinking. Miller draws attention to the importance of Nietzsche's sketches and outlines for key philosophical work prior to *Birth of Tragedy*, including his dissertation outline of 1868 on teleology and the problem of the organic since Kant and, also from this time, the unpublished essay entitled "On Schopenhauer." In addition she seeks to show the importance of Kant and Goethe for a full appreciation of Nietzsche's thinking on individuation.

In looking back on *The Birth of Tragedy* from the perspective of 1886, Nietzsche locates a "strange voice" at work in the text (an indication that the voice is not straight-forwardly a Schopenhauerian one), the voice of a disciple of a still "unknown god"[7] concealed under the hood of the scholar, the dialectical ill humor of the German, and the bad manners of the Wagnerian. At work in it is a "spirit of memory," one that is bursting forth with questions, experiences, concealed things, and question marks. It is a work which "stammers" its attempt to comprehend the Greeks through the question "What is Dionysian?" Tragedy, for Nietzsche, concerns affirmation and not resignation; it inspires an affirmation of the pains of growth rather than simply reproducing the sufferings of individuation. As he puts it in his self-criticism of 1886, and as a question designed to challenge psychiatry, are there such things as healthy neuroses? Nietzsche continued to remain attached to the Dionysian as a fundamental philosophy of life and he returns to it in the texts of his late period, such as *Beyond Good and Evil* (especially 295) and *Twilight of the Idols*. The Dionysian mysteries symbolize for Nietzsche the primacy of a life-drive, one that he will link with his own doctrines such as the eternal recurrence. In "What I Owe the Ancients" in *TI* he presents the Dionysian as a "faith" in which "the most profound instinct of life," namely, the instinct for its future and eternity, is felt in a religious manner. In the Dionysian mysteries and in the psychological state of the Dionysian the Hellene secures for himself "the eternal return of life" in which the future is consecrated in the past and there is a triumphant "yea-saying" to life over and above death and change. The essays by Laurence Lampert and Christoph Cox focus, albeit in different ways, on the role the figure of Dionysus and the Dionysian play in Nietzsche's philosophy (see chapters 8 and 27).

The Middle Period

1878 proved to be a decisive year in Nietzsche's life with the publication of the first volume of *Human, All Too Human*, a work that is remarkably different in tone and outlook from his previous published writings. With it Nietzsche announces his intellectual independence and his break from both Schopenhauer and Wagner. Wagner was repulsed by Nietzsche's new philosophical outlook and offended by the book's dedication to Voltaire, a figure he reviled for his anti-Christian outlook and whom his wife Cosima held to be a "demon of perversity." In *The Birth of Tragedy* Nietzsche had attacked theoretical optimism and the Socratic faith in knowledge, as well as all forms of realism and naturalism in art (where the emphasis is on environmental and biological determinism and on the exclusion of any dimension beyond the factual and the material). Now, he was inviting his readers to value "little, unpretentious truths," to celebrate the science of physics for its "modest" and "insignificant" explanations, and to lose faith in all inspiration and in any knowledge acquired by miraculous means.

In early 1879 deteriorating health forced Nietzsche to resign from his position at Basel University, which granted him an annual pension. In the course of the next ten years Nietzsche became a veritable European traveler and tourist with periods of residence in Venice, Genoa, St. Moritz and Sils-Maria, Rome, Sorrento, and Nice (where he was to witness an earthquake in 1887).

Nietzsche often likes to present himself as a "good European" unrestricted by established territories, be they geographical or spiritual, and who looks "beyond all merely locally, merely nationally conditioned perspectives" (*EH*, "Why I Am So Wise," 3). He writes as "the last *anti-political* German" and as a trans-national philosopher who wishes to see a "great politics" come into existence that will triumph over the prevailing small or petty politics of the time, which is a politics centered on race, nation, and state. In her contribution, "Nietzsche and National Identity" (chapter 25), Diane Morgan takes this aspect of Nietzsche's thought seriously, but also seeks to redefine the terms in which questions of nationalism and the trans-national are posed, both with regard to Nietzsche's own position on this issue and with regard to contemporary positionings. To date insufficient attention has been paid in the literature to the fertile character of Nietzsche's invocation of a new earth and new peoples to come (see *Thus Spoke Zarathustra*). Gary Shapiro (chapter 26) proposes we read Nietzsche as a "geophilosopher" who maps the possibilities of human thought in terms of territories and spaces, and argues that for Nietzsche the earth is a "text" that we must learn to "read."

Nietzsche's intellectual output in the ten-year period 1878–88 was prolific and his life was ruled by writing. In the summer of 1881 he made his first trip to Sils-Maria in the Upper Engadine, which was to become his regular summer residence. It is at this time that he has the experience and inspiration of eternal recurrence, "6,000 feet beyond man and time," as he was later to express it in *Ecce Homo*. In a letter to Peter Gast from this time Nietzsche speaks of leading an extremely perilous life (intellectually speaking) and of being "one of those machines that can explode." The intensity of his feelings, he confided, made him shudder and laugh, weeping not sentimental tears but tears of joy. Nietzsche would now oscillate between states of euphoria and depression.

It was in the summer of 1881 that Nietzsche also discovered a precursor in Spinoza, to whom he was brought, he said, through the guidance of instinct. The affinity he felt with Spinoza, as he perceived it, was one of a shared set of doctrines (he mentions the denial of free will, of purposes, of a moral world order, and of evil), and the fundamental tendency to make knowledge the most powerful passion.

Daybreak was published in July 1881 and *The Gay Science* followed in 1882. It is in these texts that Nietzsche practices his "cheerful" and transfigurative "philosophy of the morning" and conceives of life experimentally as a means to knowledge. It is in a famous section of the latter work that he has a madman declare that "God is dead. And we have killed him" (section 125). In one section of the book Nietzsche suggests replacing churches with botanical gardens in our busy towns and cities as places of reflection where the godless can go to give expression to the sublimity of their thoughts and see themselves translated into stones and plants (GS 280). In 1882 he met Lou Andreas-Salomé and proposed to her, unsuccessfully, twice. In the early part of 1883 he began work on *Thus Spoke Zarathustra* and was affected by the death of Wagner. Nietzsche would hold alternating views on *Zarathustra*, having serious doubts about it yet regarding it as an epochal work. During all this time Nietzsche's relationship with his sister had been extremely tense and in 1884 he spoke of her anti-Semitism as the cause of a "radical break."

The central teaching of Nietzsche's from his middle period is that of the eternal recurrence (or return) of the same. It is a teaching that has perplexed generations of commentators and readers. It has been extensively treated in the literature in terms of its cosmological, existential, and quasi-ethical aspects. For new insights into the cosmology of eternal recurrence see the essay by Robin Small (chapter 11). Commentators do not agree over the precise significance of the thought or on what role it is playing in his thinking. For some it has tremendous transformational effects; for others, it is simply a means to reveal the type of being that one is and has no such effects (our response to the thought, it is claimed on this reading, is predetermined). In its first published formulation in GS 341 the thought is designed to provide nothing other and nothing less than a shock to our thinking about existence. In this well-known and widely studied aphorism the three principal aspects of the thought appear to be in evidence: the disclosure by the demon of our cosmological eternal recurrence, which we can greet with indifference; the quasi-ethical and practical import of the doctrine, "Do you want to do this again and again?" which is an invitation to become the creator, judge, and avenger of one's own law, and which we cannot be indifferent towards if our desire is to become the one that we are (see GS 335); and the existential test of affirmation, which necessitates becoming well-disposed towards ourselves and life so as to want nothing more fervently than the ultimate eternal confirmation and seal afforded by eternal recurrence. The essay by Paul S. Loeb provides a set of new insights into eternal recurrence and the well-known aphorism 341 of *The Gay Science* (see chapter 10). In his later writings Nietzsche construes eternal return working primarily in terms of a principle of selection. As a new means of cultural discipline and breeding it serves to contest the law of gregariousness that he holds has dominated evolution (natural selection) and history (the will to power of the weakest) to date. The very first sketch Nietzsche wrote of what he called his "thought of thoughts" was for a book in five parts on the return of the same. Ansell Pearson provides a partial translation of this first sketch in his contribution (chapter 13). The teaching addresses us moderns in our singularity: although our piece of human history will eternally repeat itself it is necessary to ignore this insight so as to focus on what is our singular task, namely, to "outweigh" the whole past of previous humanity. Nietzsche states that for us to be equal to this task "indifference" needs to have worked its way deep inside us, and even the misery of a future humanity cannot concern us. The question for we moderns who are experimenting with truth and knowledge is whether "we still *want to* live: and how!"

8

In his contribution John Richardson (chapter 12) also offers fresh insights into eternal recurrence based on a careful working through of Nietzsche's thinking on time and becoming, which is widely recognized to be one of the most important but also one of the most perplexing aspects of his philosophy – perplexing simply because Nietzsche appears to hold contradictory, or at the very least inconsistent, positions and it is extremely difficult to develop a coherent sense of his thinking on this core topic. Richardson attempts to do just this.

Although science is crucially important to Nietzsche's project it is not a question for him of philosophical thinking and questioning being completely subsumed within its ambit. In his early writings we find Nietzsche arguing that although science can probe the processes of nature it can never "command" human beings: "science knows nothing of taste, love, pleasure, displeasure, exaltation, or exhaustion. Man must in some way *interpret*, and thereby evaluate, what he lives through and experiences."[8] The mature Nietzsche comes to the view that science must now inform what constitutes the matter of interpretation and evaluation. However, the disciplines of interpretation and evaluation also require an education in a superior empiricism that knows how to discriminate between noble and base ways of thinking and is able to determine the question of value. Nietzsche writes: "*All* sciences must, from now on, prepare the way for the future work of the philosopher: this work being understood to mean that the philosopher has to solve the *problem of values* and that he has to decide on the *hierarchy of values*" (GM I. 17 "Note"). A core issue in Nietzsche interpretation concerns just how the placement or positioning of questions of value is to be understood, and a concern with this issue informs many of the contributions to this volume. This topic informs, in part, Richard Schacht's contribution (chapter 7) and is at the center of the probing inquiry to be found in the essay by Maudemarie Clark and David Dudrick, which aims to secure some precise insight into the relation between the "will to truth" and the "will to value" (chapter 9; see also Came, chapter 3, Janaway, chapter 18 and Higgins, chapter 22).

Nietzsche has, in fact, his own specific and novel conception of science, what he calls the "gay" science. As Babette E. Babich seeks to demonstrate in her contribution (chapter 6), it is vitally important that we develop an adequate understanding of the sense that science has for Nietzsche and how he seeks to put it to work. The German word Nietzsche uses, *Wissenschaft*, has a quite specific set of meanings and is a much richer term than the English word. The gay science is intended by Nietzsche to mark a new stage in the history of our becoming-human, in which humankind has become mature enough to ask of the world and of itself the most challenging and demanding questions. It seeks to show us that the intellect does not have to be a "clumsy, gloomy, creaking machine" (GS 327). The specific "gravity" of this new gay science stems from that fact that there now takes place a return of the fundamental questions, but staged and encountered in new-found conditions and circumstances: How do we now live? And what do we love? In his notebooks of the 1880s the two projects of "the gay science" and thinking "beyond good and evil" become entwined and subsumed within the more general and wider project of preparing the ground for a "philosophy of the future." In a deep sense, Nietzsche is appealing to something that can be called *over*human. Typically, we conceive of the overhuman in fantastical terms. However, an adequate understanding of its "fantastical" character requires an appreciation of the various tasks that Nietzsche associates with the coming into being of a new and superior mode of existence that will put the measure of the human to the test. This is the concern of the essay by Ansell Pearson (chapter 13; see also Shapiro, chapter 26).

In his writings Nietzsche seeks to combat what he saw as the timid reduction of philosophy to the "theory of knowledge" (*BGE* 204). He draws attention to what he regards as the debasement of the concept of philosophy at the hands of certain "Engländer" – he names Hobbes, Hume, Locke, Carlyle, Darwin, John Stuart Mill, Herbert Spencer (*BGE* 252–3). He speaks of philosophy as entailing "spiritual perception" or vision of "real depth" (*BGE* 252), and argues that true and genuine philosophers are "commanders and lawgivers" (*BGE* 211). Moreover, the philosopher is "*necessarily* a man of tomorrow and the day after tomorrow" who exists in conflict with his "today" and must, therefore, assume the guise of an untimely figure (*BGE* 212). Furthermore, science has its own prejudice, on which Nietzsche comments in *GS* 373. Here he takes to task what he calls the "faith" of "materialistic natural scientists," which rests on the supposition that the world can find an equivalence and measure in human thought and valuations, such as a "'world of truth'."

Nietzsche mainly has in mind here a mechanistic interpretation of the world, one that "permits counting, calculating, weighing, seeing, and touching," and he argues that such an interpretation amounts to "a crudity and naiveté" and might be "one of the *most stupid* of all possible interpretations of the world" as it would be "one of the poorest in meaning": "an essentially mechanical world would be an essentially *meaningless* [*sinnlose*] world." Nietzsche has to be read carefully when he makes this criticism. There are places in his writings where he recognizes the achievement of scientific mechanism; it wins an important victory over the teleological view of the world that would see final or ultimate purposes everywhere. The new science becomes stupid, however, when it seeks to take over and dominate all questions that can be asked of existence. He is keen to protect what he calls the "*rich ambiguity*" of existence, and calls attention to "ambiguity" as a "dictate of good taste [. . .] the taste of reverence for everything that lies beyond your horizon."

This aphorism (*GS* 373) occupies the attention of two explorations in this volume, the essays by Clark and Dudrick and by Cox (see chapters 9 and 27). Cox places its insights and claims in the service of a novel appreciation of the ontology of music, whilst Clark and Dudrick examine the aphorism in the context of its surrounding aphorisms in effort to develop a full appreciation of the complex nature of Nietzsche's empiricism. *Sinn* is an important word in Nietzsche's vocabulary and its philosophical richness has not been fully appreciated in the English-speaking reception of his work. In addition to the essays by Cox and by Clark and Dudrick, those by Volker Gerhardt and Shapiro aim to enrich our appreciation of its significance in Nietzsche's thinking (see chapters 15 and 26).

When we consider the relation between art and science in Nietzsche we also need to take stock of the account of his thinking found in the 1886 self-criticism he prepared for the new edition of *BT*. There Nietzsche speaks of his attempt to grapple with a *new* problem, a "problem with horns," namely "the *problem of science* itself," science grasped as something "problematic" and "questionable" (*BT*, "Self-Criticism," 2). Strikingly, Nietzsche insists that "the problem of science cannot be recognized on its own ground" and proposes, daringly, that the task is to view science "*through the optic of the artist,*

10

and art through the optic of life" ("Self-Criticism," 2; see Babich in chapter 6 below for further insight as well as Cox, chapter 27).

It is customary to divide Nietzsche's corpus into three distinct periods: an early first period of 1872–6 (*Birth of Tragedy* and the four *Untimely Meditations*), a second, middle, period of 1878–82 (the free spirit trilogy comprising *Human, All Too Human*, *Daybreak*, and *Gay Science*) and 1883–5 (*Zarathustra*), and a late, final period of 1886– 8 (*Beyond Good and Evil* and onwards). Many of the ideas that appear in *Human, All Too Human* had been germinating in Nietzsche's mind since 1875/6. Where the first edition of *Birth of Tragedy* was dedicated to Wagner and brought out by Wagner's publisher, taking up the Romantic cause against modern Enlightenment and opposing indigenous German culture to superficial French civilization, the first edition of *HH*, published in 1878, is dedicated to Voltaire and takes up the cause of the Enlighten- ment against revolutionary romantics.

However, it is mistaken to suppose that the move from *Birth of Tragedy* to *Human, All Too Human* amounts to a straightforward shift in his thinking, from a concern with art and metaphysics to a new privileging of science over both. Of the three texts from the so-called middle period, *Gay Science* represents Nietzsche's most mature philosophical position, in which art is praised for teaching us about the "good will to appearance" (*GS* 107). Art always has a wider significance for Nietzsche than is commonly accorded to it. In short, an understanding of art is necessary to a fuller appreciation of the nature and activity of knowing, and *GS* contains many important lessons in how we are to negotiate both the surfaces and the depths of things, the field of appearance and apparentness and the depths sought by scientific knowledge (see the essays by Babich, Acampora, and Cox, chapters 6, 17, and 27).

In the texts that make up this middle period we find Nietzsche seeking to emancipate himself as a thinker and coming to terms with what he regards as the end of metaphysics, an end which now calls into being a new practice of the love of know- ledge. Nietzsche always had sympathies with ancient traditions of materialism and naturalism (Democritus and Empedocles, for example). At the same time, however, he recognized that the tradition of materialism concealed its own metaphysics (Democritus and his atoms, for example)[9] and that, in another sense, metaphysics cannot readily be given up since it constitutes an essential part of the treasure of human tradition and culture. In *HH* 251 he speaks of our health demanding that the two experiences of science and non-science should lie next to each other, self- contained and without confusion: "Illusions, biases, passions must give heat; with the help of scientific knowledge, the pernicious and dangerous consequences of overheating must be prevented" (see also *HH* 222, where he speaks of the scientific man as a further development of the artistic man). A "great culture," he argues, is one in which individuals have the flexibility to pursue knowledge in a rigorous manner while at the same time appreciating the power and beauty of art, religion, and metaphysics (*HH* 278). A higher culture will give the human being a "double brain, two brain chambers [. . .], one to experience science, and one to experience nonscience" (*HH* 251).

Nietzsche's position gives rise to tremendous tensions in his thinking, since it is clear that traditional metaphysics cannot survive the interrogation afforded by the new methods of knowledge and inquiry. The way in which we think about knowledge (epistemology) and being (ontology), as well as our entire understanding of moral concepts and sensations, must undergo a radical transformation.

There are other tensions in Nietzsche's thinking, which run throughout the texts of his middle and late periods, and which center on the role he accords to reason and consciousness in the economy of life, including human life. The essays to be found in part IV, "Philosophy of Mind," illuminate core aspects of Nietzsche's thinking on questions of reason, phenomenal consciousness, and the nature of the subject. Volker Gerhardt (chapter 15) focuses on a well-known and oft-cited formula to be found in a discourse in *Thus Spoke Zarathustra*, where Nietzsche has Zarathustra speak of "the great reason" of the body. Gerhardt aims to show that this reduction of reason to the body is a highly complicated move on Nietzsche's part and cannot be read simply as an instance of his alleged irrationalism. Peter Poellner, who has done seminal work on Nietzsche's relation to phenomenology, seeks to illuminate Nietzsche's thinking on phenomenal consciousness (chapter 16). He shows that, in spite of the widespread depiction of Nietzsche as an irrationalist wedded to a form of psychologism, there are core elements in his thinking on consciousness that anticipate the phenomenological turn in philosophy. Poellner seeks to show just how we can get right the relation between the phenomenological, the scientific, and the metaphysical in Nietzsche's thinking, and our own too. Christa Davis Acampora situates Nietzsche's thinking in relation to the concerns of psychology and the philosophy of mind and seeks to show the complicated character of his naturalism, claiming that it cannot be equated with a scientism (chapter 17; see also Janaway, chapter 18). Acampora's focus is on gaining an adequate comprehension of the "subject" of Nietzsche's moral psychology and in a double sense: just what informs and constitutes Nietzsche's moral psychology? What is the nature of the moral subject presupposed by it?

With *Human, All Too Human* begins Nietzsche's commitment to an examination of the origins of morality, which was now to become a feature of all his work and constitutes one of its most essential tasks. In this text the focus is largely on the origin of moral sensations and on demonstrating the illusory and mythical character of the belief that individuals are free willing centers and originators of actions. Nietzsche endorses as a tenet possessing both frightful and fruitful consequences the insight of his friend Paul Rée that the moral human being is situated no nearer to the metaphysical or intelligible world than the physical man. Nietzsche states that this is an insight that needs to grow hard and sharp with the "hammerblow of historical knowledge" (*HH* 37).

Several essays in this volume illuminate both core and novel aspects of Nietzsche's thinking about ethics and morality, notably the essays by Paul van Tongeren, Kathleen Marie Higgins, and Robert C. Solomon (chapters 21, 22, and 23). The essays by the contributors in part V, "Philosophy and Genealogy" (Robert Guay and Robert B. Pippin, chapters 19 and 20), as well as the essay on Nietzsche and freedom by Herman Siemens which presents important new research (chapter 24), should also be consulted. Christopher Janaway's essay (chapter 18) seeks to illuminate both the specific character of Nietzsche's naturalism and the fundamental differences in the approaches Rée and Nietzsche adopt to questions concerning the origins of morality and moral feelings.

It is also in *Human, All Too Human* that Nietzsche calls for a mode of "historical philosophizing" as a way of eliminating problems of metaphysics (including the thing-in-itself). In section 9 he allows for the fact that there could be a "metaphysical world," but because we cannot chop off our own head all we can ever say of it is that it has a "differentness" that is inaccessible to us. He suggests that the question how our image of the world might be different to the "disclosed essence of the world" is a matter best left to physiology, and what he calls "the ontogeny [*Entwickelungsgeschichte*] of organisms and concepts," to solve (*HH* 10, 16). Nietzsche reflects on how an "ontogeny of thought" will come to show us that what today we call the world is the result of numerous errors and fantasies and part of the development of organic life. This collection of errors and fantasies also constitutes the treasure of a tradition (the "value" of humanity depends upon it), thus giving rise to a necessary conflict between, on the one hand, our reliance on error and our need for fantasy, and on the other the development of science and of scientific truth. Humankind has inherited so many intellectual errors; the challenge facing it now is whether it can be equal to the task of incorporating truth (on this experiment see Ansell Pearson, chapter 13).

The position Nietzsche adopts on philosophical questions and topics in the opening of *Human, All Too Human* finds an echo in the first section of *Beyond Good and Evil* entitled "On the Prejudices of Philosophers." In the opening section of *HH* he focuses on the question of how something can originate in its opposite, and sets up a contrast between "metaphysical philosophy" and "historical philosophy." The former answers the question by appealing to a miraculous source to explain the origin of something held to be of a higher value. The latter, by contrast, which Nietzsche insists can no longer be separated from the natural sciences and which he names as the youngest of all philosophical methods, seeks to show that there are no opposites but that all things arise from and are implicated in a process of sublimation, hence his call for a "chemistry of concepts and sensations." This historical mode of philosophizing gives rise to a number of provocative ideas that have proved seminal in modern thought: that there are no "unalterable facts of mankind," that everything that exists is subject to "becoming," that our faculty of cognition, far from being the transcendental source or originator of our knowledge of the world (the reference is to Kant), has itself become, and that a society's order of rank concerning what it holds to be good and evil actions is constantly changing (*HH* 2, 107). We do not require certainties with regard to the "first and last things" in order to live a "full and excellent human life" (*WS* 16).

Nietzsche is proposing that a fundamental rupture be effected with regard to customary habits of thinking. Concerning the first and last or ultimate things – What is the purpose of man? What is his fate after death? How can man be reconciled with God? – it should not be felt necessary to develop knowledge against faith; rather, we should practice an *indifference* towards faith and supposed knowledge in the domains of metaphysics, morality, and religion. One of the reasons why Nietzsche takes issue with "philosophical dogmatists" of all persuasions – be they idealists or materialists or realists, he says – is that they seek to force us into taking decisions "in domains where neither faith nor knowledge is needed" (*WS* 16). The "greatest lovers of knowledge" will thus practice knowledge in a different way and remain steadfastly and gaily indifferent to the first and last things. In *Beyond Good and Evil* Nietzsche teaches the responsibilities of the "dangerous Perhaps" and argues that it is necessary now to wait "for a new category of philosophers" to arrive (*BGE* 2). These "coming" philosophers will be ones who do not accept at face value the belief of the "metaphysicians" in the "opposition of values." The taste and inclination of these philosophers will be very different from that which has hitherto guided philosophical inquiry.

Most commentators writing on Nietzsche today, be they of an analytical or a continental persuasion, agree in positioning him as a philosophical naturalist. Nietzsche's naturalism is evident in the frequent recourse he has to physiology, to psychology, and to the insights of evolutionary theory, as well as in the way he takes to task our habits of thinking for being mythological, including our reliance on imaginary causes and fictions (such as the "cloddish simplicity" of the idea of free will, *BGE* 21) and the anthropomorphic manner in which we conceive existence in terms of intentions and final purposes. However, while Nietzsche's naturalistic proclivities and commitments have been well established in the literature, the precise character of his naturalism is not so well understood. In the case of a heterodox thinker like Nietzsche it is important we don't make his ideas and projects neatly fit into pre-established philosophical positions. If we respect, and pay attention to, the intricate and subtle character of his thinking we will be more receptive to the challenges it aims to present to our evolved and conventional modes of thought. On how Nietzsche's naturalism can best be configured see in particular the essays by Clark and Dudrick, Acampora, Janaway, Higgins, and Solomon (chapters 9, 17, 18, 22, 23).

The Final Period and Late Writings

In 1888 Nietzsche spent what turned out to be his last summer in Sils-Maria. Earlier in the year he had written to his friend Franz Overbeck that the world should expect no more "beautiful things" from him, just as one should not expect a suffering and starving animal to attack its prey with grace. He confessed to being devoid of a "refreshing and healing human love" and spoke of his "absurd isolation," which made the residues of a connection with people only something that wounded him. He was becoming fully aware that the philosopher who embarks on a relentless struggle against everything that human beings have hitherto revered will be met with a hostile public reception, one that will condemn him to an icy isolation with his books being judged by the language of pathology and psychiatry.

Nietzsche stayed in the city of Turin in April and May of this year. He returned in September and stayed there up to the point of his mental collapse in January 1889. In it he found not a modern metropolis but, he wrote, a "princely residence of the seventeenth century" and an "aristocratic calm" with no "petty suburbs" and a unity of commanding taste. He especially liked the beautiful cafés, the lovely sidewalks, the organization of trams and buses, and the fact that the streets were clean. *The Case of Wagner* was published, and though it received some vitriolic reviews it was also welcomed enthusiastically by August Strindberg. While in Turin in May Nietzsche came across a French translation (carried out in India) of Manu's book of laws, which he thought supplemented his views on religion in a "most remarkable way." In a letter to Carl Fuchs written in Sils in July, Nietzsche says that it is neither necessary nor desirable to argue in his favor, and suggests instead that a more intelligent attitude towards him would be to adopt the pose one would in the presence of a foreign and alien plant, namely, one of curiosity and ironic resistance.

Nietzsche began work on *Ecce Homo: How One Becomes What One Is* on his birthday, October 15. The text was designed as a way of testing the risks that could be taken with "German ideas of freedom of speech," Nietzsche said in a letter to Gast, in which he would talk about himself and his writings with "all possible psychological cunning and gay detachment." The last thing he wanted, he confided, was to be treated as some kind of prophet, and he hoped the book would prevent readers from confusing him with what he was not. In it Nietzsche expresses his preference for French over German culture, including a number of contemporary French writers and novelists that he regards as all "delicate psychologists" (they include Paul Bourget, Anatole France, and Guy de Maupassant, to whom Nietzsche says he feels especially attached). Stendhal, he confides, represents one of the "fairest accidents" of his life. Nietzsche says he prefers this generation of writers over their teachers, such as Hippolyte Taine, whom he regards as having been ruined by German philosophy (*EH*, "Why I Am So Clever," 3).

In December *Ecce Homo* was sent to the publishers and Nietzsche was observed chanting and dancing naked in his room by his landlady. On the morning of January 3, 1889, as Nietzsche was taking a stroll through Piazza Carlo Alberto in Turin, he witnessed a carriage driver beating a horse. He threw his arms around the horse's neck and then collapsed to the ground, losing consciousness. In the course of the next few days he composed a series of dramatic and disturbing letters. He wrote to Gast announcing that the world had become transfigured. To Georg Brandes, his champion in Copenhagen, he wrote that now he had discovered him the great difficulty was how to lose him. To Cosima Wagner he wrote, famously, "Ariadne, I love you"; to Overbeck that he was having all anti-Semites shot; and to Jacob Burckhardt that he was all the names in history. Burckhardt showed the letter he had received to Overbeck, who then traveled to Turin and brought Nietzsche back to Basel. The diagnosis was "progressive paralysis." Nietzsche spent a year in a psychiatric clinic in Jena; in 1890 his mother took him to Naumburg, and, upon her death in 1897, his sister Elisabeth brought Nietzsche to the Villa Silberblick in Weimar and inaugurated the Nietzsche cult. Nietzsche died on August 25, 1900.

One of the greatest ironies of Nietzsche's fate is that his mental collapse should have been followed by the rapid establishment of the "Nietzsche legend" and the "Nietzsche industry." As far as Nietzsche himself was concerned, though, and to speak with Hamlet's last words (one of his favorite quotations), "the rest is silence." What followed the end of his intellectual career was over a decade of mental and physical degeneration before his eventual death at the dawn of a new century that would finally begin to embark on the task of understanding itself with the aid of his work.

Two main features about Nietzsche's late writings can be noted. The first is that they are written as a philosophy of the future and seek to herald this philosophy as an event. The second is that, in contrast to what he saw as the "yes-saying" part of his task carried out in his previous writings from 1878 onwards, they form part of what Nietzsche called the "no-saying" part, such as demanding a revaluation of values and heralding a great day of decision. From this point on, he says, all his writings are fish-hooks and are looking for fish; in other words, they are attempts to seduce (*amor* comes from *amus*, the Latin word for hook).

What turned out to be the final period of Nietzsche's intellectual output dates from 1886 with the publication of *Beyond Good and Evil*, which bears the subtitle "Prelude to a Philosophy of the Future."[10] It is around this time that he began writing a major work that was to consist of four books and to which he gave the working title "Will to Power: Attempt at a Revaluation of All Values." Nietzsche was never to bring this planned *magnum opus* to fruition, but something of its nature can be found in the texts *Twilight of the Idols* (published in 1889) and *The Anti-Christian* (published in 1895 and regarded by Nietzsche as the first book of the transvaluation of all values). It is also in this year that he composed a set of new prefaces to his back catalog of published texts, and many scholars regard these prefaces as among the finest pieces of philosophical self-reflection Nietzsche ever wrote. In 1887 a new edition of *The Gay Science* was published with an added fifth book which began with a discourse entitled "The Meaning of Our Cheerfulness" and in which Nietzsche elaborated upon the significance of the death of God as a "monstrous event" that heralded a new dawn in which all the daring of the lover of knowledge could once again be permitted. He also read Dostoevsky, composed extensive notes on "European nihilism," and published *On the Genealogy of Morality* with its three striking inquiries into the spirit of *ressentiment*, the origins of the bad conscience, and the meaning of the ascetic ideal. In a letter written in December of 1887 to the Danish critic Brandes, the first person ever to lecture on his work, Nietzsche responded favorably to his description of his thinking as an "aristocratic radicalism." However, he regarded it as something of a comic fact that he was beginning to have a subterranean influence among a diverse array of radical parties and circles.

Beyond Good and Evil is said by Nietzsche to be "in all essentials" a critique of modernity that includes within its range of attack modern science, modern art, and modern politics. Where the vision of *Zarathustra* was that of distant things, the vision of *BGE* is focused sharply on the modern age, on "what is *around us.*" However, Nietzsche holds the two projects and tasks to be intimately related: "In every aspect of the book," he writes in *Ecce Homo*, "above all in its form, one will discover the same *intentional* [*willkürliche*] turning away from the instincts out of which a Zarathustra becomes possible." In a letter to his former Basel colleague Jacob Burckhardt dated September 22, 1886, Nietzsche stresses that *Beyond Good and Evil* says the same things as *Zarathustra* "only in a way that is different – very different." In this letter he draws attention to the book's chief preoccupations and mentions the "mysterious conditions of any growth in culture," the "extremely dubious relation between what is called the 'improvement' of man (or even 'humanization') and the enlargement of the human type," and, "above all the contradiction between every moral concept and every scientific concept of *life*."[11] For two accounts of aspects of *BGE* see the essays by Lampert and by Clark and Dudrick (chapters 8 and 9).

Nietzsche intended *Genealogy of Morality* as a "supplement" to and "clarification" of his previous book, *Beyond Good and Evil*. Although in recent years it has come to be prized as his most important and systematic work, Nietzsche himself conceived it as a "small polemical pamphlet," one that might help him sell more copies of his earlier writings.[12] It clearly merits, though, the level of attention it receives from commentators and can justifiably be regarded as one of the key texts of European intellectual modernity. It is a disturbing book, and Nietzsche himself was well aware of the book's character. In *Ecce Homo* he discloses that an "art of surprise" guides each of the three essays that make up the book and admits that they merit being taken as among the "uncanniest" things ever scripted. He then stresses that his god, Dionysus, is also "the god of darkness" (*EH*, "GM").

The preface to the book is crucial for understanding Nietzsche's unique conception of the philosophical project. It begins with the enigmatic statement that we knowers, as we moderns like to think of ourselves, are unknown to ourselves. The preface also makes clear that Nietzsche conceived his project not simply as a contribution to late nineteenth-century naturalism. Nothing less than a "new twist and possible outcome" in the "Dionysian drama on the fate of the 'soul'" (*GM*, preface, 7) is what is to be meditated upon and chewed over in our exegetical reading of this book.

Nietzsche focuses his critique of morality on an issue he claims previous psychologists have not properly touched upon in constructing their genealogies, namely, morality's *value* (he singles out for special consideration the question "value *for what?*"). Rather, they have articulated merely "an erudite form of true *belief* in the prevailing morality," and, as a result, their inquiries remain "a part of the state of affairs within a particular morality" (*BGE* 186), such as the estimation accorded to unegoistic instincts and the utilitarian principle of the happiness of the greatest number. In opposition to the assumption there is a single morality valid for all he maintains that "there is a *hierarchy* between human and human, and therefore between morality and morality as well" (*BGE* 228). Morality is to be held as the "danger of dangers" because it contributes to a situation in which the present is lived at the expense of the future; if the value of values is taken as given and as factual, "beyond all questioning," this will prevent the human species from attaining its "*highest potential power and splendour* . . ." (*GM*, preface, 6). For Nietzsche the human animal is one that "has not yet been established" (*BGE* 62), and he desires a new cultivation of it.

In the entry on *Genealogy of Morality* in *Ecce Homo* Nietzsche tells us that each of the three essays that make up the book contains a beginning that is calculated to mislead, which intentionally "keeps in suspense," while at the conclusion of each essay "a *new truth*" becomes "visible between thick clouds." Each essay begins coolly and scientifically but at the end of each a reckoning is called for, and this demand concerns the future. Several essays in this volume illuminate core aspects of the book, for example, those by Schacht, Acampora, Janaway, Guay, and Pippin (chapters 7, 17, 18, 19, 20). The essay by Higgins (chapter 22) examines some personal aspects of the Nietzschean revaluation of values. Nietzsche is well known for his diagnosis of nihilism to define the modern European condition and for proclaiming himself as the first complete or perfect nihilist. Andreas Urs Sommer (chapter 14) provides an extensive survey of the references to, and definitions of, nihilism to be found in Nietzsche's corpus, and uncovers the influences and sources that informed Nietzsche's working through of the nihilism problem.

Since the publication of his first book, *The Birth of Tragedy*, in 1872, Nietzsche had published on average exactly one new book per year. 1888 saw a marked acceleration in output and he completed no fewer than six books. These are all shorter works and they vary greatly in philosophical scope, in form and in tone. *Twilight of the Idols* and *Ecce Homo* are both works of considerable ambition, providing relatively disparate but highly condensed overviews of Nietzsche's preoccupations throughout his career

KEITH ANSELL PEARSON

thus far; *The Case of Wagner* and *The Anti-Christian*, by contrast, are more narrowly focused polemics on specific themes, "through-composed" single arguments of the kind Nietzsche had not produced since the *Untimely Meditations* a decade and a half before. Two works, *Nietzsche contra Wagner* and the *Dionysus Dithyrambs*, are re-edited compilations of earlier material on which Nietzsche worked at the very end of this *annus mirabilis*, in December 1888 and the first days of January 1889, immediately before his definitive collapse into insanity.

With the benefit of hindsight it is easy to view Nietzsche's works of 1888 as a glorious final flourishing before the descent into darkness, but it should be borne in mind that Nietzsche himself was far from imagining them as any kind of swan-song. On the contrary, he wrote the works of 1888 in high-spirited anticipation of the momentous impact he was shortly to have on the world by publishing a great summation of his philosophical ideas. This *magnum opus* was the project on which he had been working in the background since the time of *Zarathustra* in 1884, amassing a great many preparatory notes towards what he generally referred to as *The Will to Power*. The story of the works of 1888 is intimately bound up with the gradual abandonment of that project – in the course of the year it was retitled and reconceived as *Revaluation of All Values* before being definitively shelved shortly before Nietzsche's mental collapse – but its prospect haunted him till the end. As he was writing the works of 1888, then, Nietzsche considered them products of an interim period, situated between the "philosophy of the future" pronounced by Zarathustra and its fulfillment in the great work to come.[13]

In a letter of September 14, 1888 to his friend Paul Deussen, for example, Nietzsche describes *The Case of Wagner* and *Twilight of the Idols* as "only recuperations in the midst of an immeasurably difficult and decisive task which, *when it is understood*, will split humanity into two halves."[14] Similarly, he begins the foreword to *Ecce Homo* with a justification for writing his autobiography on the grounds that "I must shortly approach mankind with the heaviest demand that has ever been made on it." Janus-faced, though, Nietzsche looked backwards as well: in preparation for the earth-shatteringly affirmative philosophy to come, he was concerned to settle his accounts and draw a line under as many as possible of his philosophical antagonisms, bringing to a conclusion the period of negativity inaugurated by *Beyond Good and Evil*. Not surprisingly, then, the majority of these 1888 works are (like *On the Genealogy of Morality*) polemics, and parodic in intent, less concerned with introducing new themes than with reaching definitive formulations of earlier positions in order to rebuff the staunchest of his philosophical opponents – most notably Wagner, his compatriots the Germans in general, and Christianity.

At an early stage in the composition of *Twilight of the Idols* Nietzsche decided to hold back the majority of his material on Christianity to form the nucleus of a separate text (*The Anti-Christian*), so that "Morality as Anti-Nature" in *TI* is left as the main attack on Christian morality in this text. Following on from the Third Essay of *On the Genealogy of Morality*, Christian morality is here condemned as decadent, anti-instinctual, anti-natural, "inimical to life," even if "we immoralists and anti-Christians" still deem it necessary to uphold it as an enemy (and, to that extent, respect it). In the section of *TI* entitled "The Four Great Errors" Nietzsche argues that we suffer from a "causal drive" which impels us to explain actions in terms of erroneous "inner facts" such as

18

"will," "mind," and "subject" which are but illusions populating our fabricated "inner world." Morality and religion thus belong entirely within "the *psychology of error*." Developing the argument of the Second Essay of *On the Genealogy of Morality*, Nietzsche argues that the mythological idea of "free will" derives from Christian theology's desire to make people responsible for their actions and thus foster guilt, which in turn derives from the ("slavish") desire to blame and punish. Instead, he proposes as his own counter-explanation a kind of fatalism: "*No one* is the result of his own intention, his own will, his own purpose." On Nietzsche's fatalism see the essay by Robert C. Solomon (chapter 23). Morality is a semiotics (in the original, medical sense of the word), a surface phenomenon requiring meta-level interpretation in accordance with a different, superior set of extra-moral values "beyond good and evil."

It is in *Beyond Good and Evil* and *Genealogy of Morality* that we encounter the two most important presentations of the doctrine of the will to power in Nietzsche's published writings (*BGE* 36 and *GM* II. 12). The teaching first appears in his work in the discourse on "Self-Overcoming" in *Zarathustra*, and hitherto in his work he had spoken only of "the feeling of power" (in *Daybreak* and in *GS* 13, for example). It is without doubt the doctrine which now generates the most dispute amongst commentators on Nietzsche's work. Is he propounding with it a new ontology and cosmology of forces and, if so, is he entitled to do so? Some commentators argue that the will to power operates strictly on the level of an empirical psychology, especially human psychology, and are suspicious of treating the will to power as an ontology and cosmology of forces. Others have insisted that the will to power cannot be restricted to the merely empirical or psychological, arguing that it is indeed an ontology and defending Nietzsche's entitlement to one. Commentators suspicious of treating the doctrine of will to power in terms of an ontology argue that there is little basis in Nietzsche for doing so. How coherent is it, for example, for Nietzsche to draw our attention to the anthropomorphic character of our designations of nature (see *GS* 109), and then go on to claim that the world in its essence and in all its aspects is will to power? How can we be sure that in this doctrine Nietzsche does not do what he criticizes the Stoics and other modes of thinking for doing, namely, imposing a subterfuge morality or ideal on nature (see *BGE* 9)? Is the will to power simply a projection of his own evaluative commitments? These are questions that any conscientious reader of Nietzsche must wrestle with, and they continue to exercise the attention of his commentators.

The majority of Nietzsche's most extensive explorations of the world as will to power are to be found in his *Nachlass* material, selections of which are available in English translation in the volume *The Will to Power*. This is a highly unreliable text put together after Nietzsche's death by his sister and her supporters.[15] Although Heidegger is often attacked for placing undue emphasis in his interpretation of Nietzsche on the notebooks, this ignores the fact that he was one of the first to cast suspicion on the volume that bears the title *The Will to Power*. He noted that the *WP* edition gives us a book falsely ascribed to Nietzsche and that it is little more than an arbitrary selection of the notes which predetermines our conception of Nietzsche's philosophy during the period 1883–8.[16]

It might be proposed that the most prudent approach to adopt with respect to the doctrine of will to power is to pay careful and close attention to what Nietzsche says in his published texts about it, and then allow the notebooks from the 1880s to be used only on the basis of connections one can plausibly make between them and the published texts. However, adopting such a transparently sensible approach as this is not without problems, especially when the complex character of Nietzsche's presentation of his philosophy is taken into account. In his 1971 study the eminent German scholar Wolfgang Müller-Lauter drew attention to those places where Nietzsche complicates the issue of how we are to receive his writings, including a note from 1887 in which he says that he does not write for readers but takes notes only for himself. It is on the basis of such disclosures, which can also be found in the published material, that Müller-Lauter defends Heidegger's contentious view that the "real philosophy" of Nietzsche is not to be found in the published texts, which are merely "foreground," but rather in what he leaves behind as his posthumous legacy.[17]

The main questions the student of Nietzsche needs to focus on in engaging with the teaching or doctrine (*Lehre*) of the will to power include: What is its precise status in his thinking? What philosophical work is it doing in his critical thinking? Can it fulfill all the operational and critical tasks Nietzsche assigns to it?

The essays in the final section of this volume will greatly aid the reader and student in gaining a critical purchase on the most salient issues surrounding Nietzsche's "theory" and doctrine of the will to power (see also the contributions by Miller and Nabais, chapters 4 and 5). Recent scholarship has drawn on the pioneering insights of Müller-Lauter, which succeeded in showing the extent to which Nietzsche's doctrine is also bound up with his readings in biology and evolutionary theory (in *BGE* 23 Nietzsche presents the will to power in terms of "morphology and evolutionary theory"). Gregory Moore has done important research on this aspect of Nietzsche's work, and his essay seeks to illuminate some core issues for the reader (chapter 28). In his essay (chapter 29) Daniel W. Conway focuses on a core doctrine of Nietzsche's but one that is also inadequately understood and in fact very hard to get the full measure of. This is Nietzsche's well-known claim that self-overcoming is the very "law of life" (*GM* III. 27), which is also significant for our understanding of the doctrine of the will to power. James Porter wrestles with the most important thorny philosophical issues surrounding Nietzsche's conscientious commitment to the doctrine (chapter 30). Finally, Henry Staten offers a critical engagement with Nietzsche's conception of life as will to power by drawing attention to the way in which his thinking, in his view, overlooks questions concerning *techne* and the social construction of our drives (chapter 31).

Nietzsche bequeaths to us moderns – defined curiously and uncannily as knowers not known to themselves (*GM*, preface, 1) – a unique set of philosophical tasks and projects. Getting the measure of them, and understanding and engaging with the work that they are seeking to do, is the most fundamental task facing the reader of Nietzsche's texts. In the foreword to *The Anti-Christian* Nietzsche tells us what he wishes in the way of his future readers. They include: "new ears for new music," "new eyes for the most distant things," a "new conscience for truths that have hitherto remained dumb," the ability to keep one's energy and enthusiasm in bounds, "reverence for oneself," and "unconditional freedom with respect to oneself." Nietzsche wants his readers to wrestle with his doctrines and thought-experiments and subject them to various tests. He also wants his readers to think for themselves and come to know and appreciate what it means to think.

Notes

1 Letter to Paul Deussen, Sils-Maria, September 14, 1888, in *Selected Letters of Friedrich Nietzsche*, ed. and trans. Christopher Middleton (Indianapolis and Cambridge: Hackett, 1996), pp. 310–11.

2 Eugen Fink, *Nietzsche's Philosophy*, trans. Goetz Richter (London and New York: Continuum Press, 2003), p. 91.

3 Some of the material of that follows is taken from the various introductions that feature in *The Nietzsche Reader* edited by myself and Duncan Large (Oxford: Basil Blackwell, 2006) and from my *How to Read Nietzsche* (London: Granta Books, 2005; New York: W. W. Norton, 2006).

4 See *Selected Letters of Friedrich Nietzsche*, p. 47.

5 Ibid., p. 48.

6 Further insight into Schopenhauer's metaphysics can be found in *The Nietzsche Reader*, ed. Ansell Pearson and Large.

7 The "unknown god" is from Acts of the Apostles 17: 23.

8 Nietzsche, "The Struggle Between Science and Wisdom" (1875), in *Philosophy and Truth: Selections from Nietzsche's Notebooks of the Early 1870s*, ed. and trans. Daniel Breazeale (Atlantic Highlands, NJ: Humanities Press, 1979), p. 141.

9 See *TI*, "'Reason' in Philosophy," section 5. Nietzsche is attacking what he sees as a Parmenidean bias in Western metaphysics, which he locates in Democritus' teaching in which each atom embodies the properties of Being on a small scale (being unitary, indivisible, unchanging, etc.). See also *GS* 112 and *BGE* 12.

10 Nietzsche had been experimenting with the idea of a philosophy of the future as early as 1872 in his "Philosophers' Book," no doubt inspired by Wagner's conception of his art as "music of the future" (*Zukunftsmusik*), which in turn took its inspiration from Feuerbach's "principles of the philosophy of the future."

11 This letter can be found in Middleton's edition of the *Selected Letters*, p. 255.

12 Letter to Peter Gast, July 18, 1887, ibid., p. 269.

13 In *TI* Nietzsche writes: "I have given humanity the most profound book it possesses, my *Zarathustra*: I shall shortly give it the most independent one. –"

14 *Selected Letters of Friedrich Nietzsche*, p. 311.

15 *The Will to Power* was compiled from Nietzsche's notebooks by a group of editors working under Elisabeth's controlling influence. A first edition composed of 483 aphorisms appeared in 1901 and a second edition of 1,067 aphorisms in 1906 (this is the volume we are familiar with in English translation).

16 M. Heidegger, *Nietzsche*, vol. 2: *The Eternal Recurrence of the Same*, trans. David Farrell Krell (New York: Harper & Row, 1984), pp. 152–3. See also the remarks of Maurice Blanchot in his *The Infinite Conversation*, trans. Susan Hanson (Minneapolis and London: University of Minnesota Press, 1993), pp. 137ff.

17 W. Müller-Lauter, *Nietzsche: His Philosophy of Contradictions and the Contradictions of his Philosophy*, trans. David J. Parent (Urbana and Chicago: University of Illinois Press, 1999), pp. 125ff.

2

Nietzsche and the Art of the Aphorism

JILL MARSDEN

Throughout his philosophical corpus, Nietzsche acknowledges that our habits of thought constitute what we *recognize* as thought. Much of what we call "cognition" is for Nietzsche merely re-cognition, the expression of a new insight by means of familiar signs. Shaped by the "habits of our senses" our prevailing judgments and beliefs reinforce our unconscious expectations and it is "by these horizons [. . .] that we *measure the world*" (*D* 117). It is in the context of these constraints – which are simultaneously cultural and physiological – that Nietzsche utilizes the aphorism as a weapon of critique. Nietzsche's aphorisms are escape routes from convictions, byways into the labyrinth of the unforeseen. Deriving from the Greek term *aphorismos*, meaning "definition" (from *aphorizein* to define, from *horos*, boundary), the aphorism emerges in Nietzsche's writings as a new "horizon" for philosophy, that which sets the limit rather than that which is defined *by* a limit. Unlike the categories of knowledge which function by subsuming thought in a limited number of ways, the aphorism is a singular and sinuous form which frames thought like a skin, enclosing yet growing with what it confines. In this respect it does not so much add to existing orthodoxy as indicate new ways in which philosophical activity might yet be possible.

Both conclusive and question-begging, a masterpiece of condensed discontinuity, the maxim aggresses against our ingrained philosophical instincts which favor doctrine over declamation and expansiveness over brevity. It is telling that in pursuing Nietzsche's major ideas – such as the "overcoming of Platonism" or the "revaluation of all values" – there is a tendency for commentators to focus on the "substance" of his texts rather than the materiality of their "form." It would be all too easy to regard his collections of aphorisms as entertaining but incidental "interludes" (*Zwischenspiele*) between the "main acts" of his philosophical compositions (see for example the fourth chapter of *Beyond Good and Evil*, which is entitled "Maxims and Interludes"). However, to do so would be both to dismiss large swaths of Nietzsche's output as philosophically negligible and to ignore the extensive reflections on the "art of the aphorism" to be found in his works. Moreover, one must ask whether it is enough to challenge the dogmas of metaphysics at the level of ideas while continuing to remain uncritical of *stylistic values* at the level of the text.

In what follows, the philosophical value of writing aphoristically will be submitted to scrutiny. The first section aims to consider what Nietzsche understands by "the aphoristic form" and to situate it within his broader experimentation with the material conditions of thought. This is developed in the second section, which considers the specific ways in which aphoristic writing challenges our habits of reading. Building on these reflections we turn in the third section to examine Nietzsche's contentious claim that the Third Essay of *On the Genealogy of Morals* is to be regarded as an "exegesis" of an aphorism. The guiding concern throughout will be to ask what is philosophically distinctive about this mode of philosophical communication and to consider why it might be preferred above more conventional means of expression.

Nietzsche's Understanding of the Aphorism

> The aphorism [*der Aphorismos*], the apophthegm [*die Sentenz*], in which I am the first master among Germans, are the forms of "eternity"; my ambition is to say in ten sentences what everyone else says in a book – what everyone else *does not* say in a book. (*TI*, "Expeditions of an Untimely Man," 51)

The first of Nietzsche's texts to make extensive use of the aphoristic form is *Human, All Too Human* (1878), which interweaves a variety of acerbic, incisive and observational maxims with short paragraph essays of varying length. In its orthodox usage, the term "aphorism" is used to denote a short expression of a general truth or pointed assertion. Strictly speaking, the German word *Sentenz* (translated as "maxim" or "apophthegm") conveys this sense most closely, although Nietzsche often uses the term *Aphorismus* synonymously. His description of *Human, All Too Human* as a "collection of aphorisms" in the preface to *On the Genealogy of Morals* suggests that there may be some justification for taking the term "aphorism" to denote a *style of writing* rather than the classically terse statement; nevertheless, caution is required here. While it seems reasonable to regard some of the longer passages in Nietzsche's works as aphoristic in character (owing to their semantic and stylistic concision and their sharpness of observation) Nietzsche alludes to them simply as "sections" when making retrospective reference to such texts (for example in the preface to *On the Genealogy of Morals* and in *Ecce Homo*). For this reason, although it has become standard practice in Nietzsche scholarship to use the term "aphorism" to describe the vast majority of such numbered pieces, it is unwise to treat all examples of the latter as aphorisms, particularly in essay-length texts such as *On the Genealogy of Morals*, *The Wagner Case*, and *Ecce Homo*, where it would seem more accurate to describe them as chapters. Although it cannot settle the matter decisively, reflection on what makes something "aphoristic" for Nietzsche is of obvious benefit to our inquiry.

Some clues are to be found by tracing the emergence of the aphoristic style in Nietzsche's work. In *Ecce Homo* he identifies the period in which *Human, All Too Human* is written as a turning point in his philosophical development. Partly as a result of a serious decline in his health, partly as a result of reaching the nadir of impatience with his philological labors, Nietzsche abandons what he calls "historical" study in favor of a new focus on diagnostics: "A downright burning thirst seized hold of me: thenceforward I pursued in fact nothing other than physiology, medicine and natural science" (*EH*, "Human, All Too Human," 3). The development of the aphoristic style appears to coincide with this period of "convalescence" from scholarship, marking a "sudden end" to all his "infections" with idealism.[1] The series of books written at this time – *Assorted Opinions and Maxims* (1879), *The Wanderer and his Shadow* (1880) and *Daybreak* (1881) – represent a "supreme kind of recovery" (*EH*, "Human, All Too Human," 4). In their different ways, each is a study in symptomatology and stands comparison with the collection of ancient treatises attributed to Hippocrates, the Corpus Hippocraticum. Indeed, it is generally thought that the term "aphorism" is first used in the writings attributed to Hippocrates.[2] The Corpus Hippocraticum consists of rules and prescriptions for living well, for diagnosing symptoms, and for promoting the art of good health. What is most significant about these "medical" aphorisms is that they came into being as the result of experience and experimentation and in this respect differed from logical axioms or scientific propositions. True, one might find precepts when consulting such a work, but they are as much tools for diagnosis as prescriptions for practice. Just as a novice in the medical arts might turn to the Hippocratic texts seeking edification, the reader of Nietzsche's aphorisms might hope to find maxims by which to live. In each case one is more likely to discover that the said "principles" prompt *self-analysis*, leading to the identification of "symptoms" of a hitherto unrealized malady.

It seems significant that the aphoristic style should be developed in Nietzsche's thought at a time when he is exploring the extent to which ideas can transform and redirect the energies of the body. While it is not obvious whether his sickness at the time of writing *Human, All Too Human* is triggered by depleted enthusiasm for philology or whether the latter is the result of his burgeoning affliction, it is undeniable that sickness gave him the "right" to a "complete reversal of habits" (*EH*, "Human, All Too Human," 4). From this new perspective it is possible to ask *under what conditions* dominant beliefs, perceptions, and value judgments are fostered, a process that Nietzsche describes as psychological critique. Not without its dangers, this method may induce iatrogenic symptoms. As both patient and physician, Nietzsche succinctly identifies the affective investment that one might have in sustaining rather than resolving a potentially morbid state and hence in earnestly acting against one's own agenda: "He who lives for the sake of combating an enemy has an interest in seeing that his enemy stays alive" (*HH* 531). Favoring such motivational analysis over metaphysical specu-lation, Nietzsche starts to recommend ways in which the reader can use his or her own life course as an "instrument and means of knowledge" (*HH* 292).

> However you may be, serve yourself as your own source of experience! Throw off discontent with your nature, forgive yourself your own ego, for in any event you possess in yourself a ladder with a hundred rungs upon which you can climb to knowledge. (*HH* 292)

In this context Nietzsche emphasizes how wrong turnings in life can be invaluable lessons, how one can learn to see the "necessity inherent in the course of culture in general" by recognizing how one's experiments, errors, faults, delusions, passions, love and hope can become part of a "necessary chain of rings of culture" (*HH* 292). The lesson here is to extract from one's affective encounters articles of wisdom that cease to reflect the parochial conditions of their genesis. Their "truth" is not confirmed by *personal* experience because such insights are won by exchanging contingencies for imperatives. In other words, to the extent that subjective testimony is registered in the third person, Nietzsche appears to use the aphoristic form to convey a transpersonal affectivity, uniting the singular and the universal in a unique aesthetic judgment. In this way, the aphorism strikes a powerful chord but the melody is not of our making. Through isolating the impersonal core of raw feeling at the heart of experience, individual testimony becomes a means for the production of something more perfect than itself.

It is in this respect that Nietzsche's aphoristic writing lacks the comforting tenor of "home-spun wisdom." While the maxim or adage is typically characterized as an aptly worded truism or commonplace, in Nietzsche's hands bold assertion is coupled with the expression of uncommon or inverted reasoning to create a novel experiment in the provocation to think. This is increasingly apparent in his later works such as *Twilight of the Idols* in which his adoption of the aphoristic form functions as a malicious dissection of popular psychology, only "curative" by virtue of striking at the heart of established therapeutics. For example, with implicit reference to the old saw that "Idleness is the beginning of all vices" Nietzsche writes: "Idleness is the beginning of all psychology. What? Could psychology be – a vice?" (*TI*, "Maxims and Arrows"). By using the rhetoric of popular morality against itself psychology is presented as a mode of inquiry that prospers through indolence. Accordingly, the self-evidence of "virtue" is called into question. To be idle rather than industrious is to indulge the curiosity of the genealogist who probes the value judgments underlying the habits of our senses. This aphorism, which is the first of the series to follow after the preface to *Twilight of the Idols*, echoes a remark made there about the book being an idle dalliance of a psychologist. Indeed, idleness is the prerogative of the *convalescent* (and Nietzsche tells us in this preface – as in several others – that this text is itself part of a project of recovery). We are also told in the preface, in the form of a maxim, that "the spirit grows, strength is restored by wounding." The reader is left in little doubt that the regimen which will promote well-being will also exploit the capacity for suffering. Nietzsche's choice of the title "Maxims and Arrows" for the opening series of aphorisms in *Twilight of the Idols* suggests a shower of dangerous and targeted insights which will achieve their effects by bypassing the defences of an idling consciousness, viscerally inscribing their mark.

In considering the meaning that the aphorism has for Nietzsche one might look beyond the possible debt to Hippocrates' medical arts and note other prominent aphorists that undoubtedly influenced his style. The notion that an aphorism is "barbed" calls to mind Heraclitus, whose epigrammatic sentences make liberal use of counter-logic and metaphor. The Heraclitean aphorism: "The bow [biós] is called life [bíos], but its work is death" (fragment B 48) serves as a painful reminder that no art of living well is immune from sickness, indeed, life is the arrow which targets itself. It is clear that Heraclitus was a decisive influence on Nietzsche's development of the aphoristic device although in *Twilight of the Idols* he also declares a serious ambition towards "*Roman* style" (*TI*, "What I Owe the Ancients," 1). There he writes that his sense of the epigram as style was awoken on coming into contact with Sallust: "Compact, severe, with as much substance as possible, a cold malice towards 'fine words,' also towards 'fine feelings' – in that I knew myself" (*TI*, "What I Owe the Ancients," 1). In a similar manner, he praises the Horatian ode, which achieves a maximum energy from a minimum use of signs. More immediately, during the period in which *Human, All Too Human* was composed, Nietzsche was immersed in the works of the French *moralistes*, especially Pascal, Voltaire, and Montaigne. Additionally, from La Rochefoucauld he appears to have inherited a love of exaggeration and paradox, and from Chamfort a skill in the art of the short dialog form. It is fair to say that the explicitly psychological observations of the latter thinkers may have fueled Nietzsche's interest in diagnostics and the "arts of living" as much as works of the "ancients." One should also not forget the wry Teutonic incisiveness of Lichtenberg and Schopenhauer, both of whom Nietzsche regarded as exemplars of German prose.

This notwithstanding, there is a limit to how much the intellectual context of Nietzsche's development of the aphorism can tell us about his understanding of its function. It is interesting to note that, in contrast to his predecessors, he does not display a distinctive aphoristic style. Unlike the "bon mot" or fitting remark, the Nietzschean aphorism is not easily culled and quoted ubiquitously. There is no singularity of tone or "signature." Indeed, in a philosophical tradition dominated by argumentation (dialectic, deduction, refutation and counter-refutation) the Nietzschean aphorism proves a difficult item to place. While it frequently takes the form of an assertion and hence dispenses with the need to persuade, its substance may be a partial impression or prejudice. Such aphorisms are compact and severe, displaying a preference for economy of thought and expression, for example: "If one trains one's conscience it will kiss us as it bites" (*BGE* 98). By contrast, other aphorisms are "trembling with passion" and exhibit the acoustic precision more characteristic of poetry than prose (*EH*, "Thus Spoke Zarathustra," 6). Nietzsche says of *Thus Spoke Zarathustra* that here eloquence becomes music: "here all things come caressingly to your discourse and flatter you: for they want to ride upon your back. Upon every image you here ride to every truth" (*EH*, "Thus Spoke Zarathustra," 6). Still other aphorisms map a dialog or set a scene. Examples would include the discourse between the "wanderer" and his "shadow" or the short exchanges *à la* Chamfort between the interlocutors "A" and "B" which figure in a number of Nietzsche's texts.

However, despite the absence of a quintessential Nietzschean form of the aphorism, his writings contain a number of striking reflections on its status and function. In *Thus Spoke Zarathustra* Nietzsche's Zarathustra declares – in a series of aphorisms – that of all writings he loves only that which is "written with blood" for "blood is spirit" and not an easy thing for the "reading idler" to understand:

> He who writes in blood and aphorisms does not want to be read, he wants to be learned by heart.
>
> In the mountains the shortest route is from peak to peak, but for that you must have long legs. Aphorisms should be peaks, and those to whom they are spoken should be big and tall of stature. (Z I, "Of Reading and Writing")

The peak may be the summit of a thought, the apex or high point of meditation. However, it is also the point at which the air is at its thinnest and purest, a dangerous altitude. For Zarathustra, the aphorism is an exalted and ominous thought, far removed from the shallow slogans and chatter of the mass. If to "read" is to participate in the public interpretation of written signs, to "learn by heart" is to reinvigorate those signs by incorporating them into the body. The passage recalls Plato's *Phaedrus* and the arguments made there against writing. When something is learnt by heart it is committed to memory and quite literally becomes part of the sensitive matter of the subject. This may be one of the reasons why Nietzsche favors the aphoristic form over other kinds of writing which make far less of a demand upon the reader. With the aphoristic form memory is cultivated through the impress of stark and pointed assertions. In this respect the notion of writing in blood suggests a brutal mnemonics of pain, but the lodging of maxims and arrows need not be equated with suffering. The incorporation or "ensouling" of aphorisms can occur involuntarily owing to the preconscious tempo of the syntax. Quite simply, one is caught up in the speed of the aphorism – its rhythmic necessity – prior to comprehension. As a result, unlike other kinds of philosophical text, the aphorism can take hold of its host and impose itself on consciousness in its entirety. The question then is simply whether one will return to the aphorism, reflecting on its meaning, or whether it is "remembered" as a formula but not considered in any way.

Although the issue of what constitutes an aphorism for Nietzsche cannot be definitively decided, its role in relation to diagnostics, therapeutics, and the embodiment of thought prompts reflection on the way in which ideas impact upon the senses and the way in which the senses respond to and "evaluate" ideas. For Nietzsche, the "sense" (*Sinn*) that we make of our world is partly determined by our senses (*Sinne*). Our sense perceptions are permeated by value judgments which reflect our needs and desires (*WP* 505). In this respect it is idle to insist that our physiological disposition is unrelated to evaluation. Nietzsche's project of interpreting the physiological value judgments that shape philosophical habits of thought may in part be prompted by his experimentation with different forms of aphoristic writing. What this suggests is that, although our frames of reference may be habitual, it is possible for our senses to become attuned to different conceptual rhythms, to develop senses for new kinds of philosophical thought. With this in mind, we turn now to consider how the aphorism works to disrupt the value judgments that have been "incorporated" in the reading of philosophy, creating new "matter" for thought in the process.

How Aphorisms Reconfigure the "Habits of the Senses"

In books of aphorisms like mine nothing but lengthy, forbidden things and chains of thought stand between and behind short aphorisms; and many among them that would be questionable enough for Oedipus and his Sphinx. I do not write treatises: they are for asses and journal readers. (*KSA* 11, 37[5])

Aphorisms are essentially modular assertions which function independently of narrativity. Although some sequences in Nietzsche's works are both syntactically and stylistically linked – such as the "catechism" section of *The Gay Science* (268–75) and the "questions of conscience" in *Twilight of the Idols* ("Maxims and Arrows," 37–41) – for the most part, the context of the aphorism is no broader than its terms. In fact, taken as a whole, the seams of short aphorisms have a paratactic effect. The constantly broken pace, the apparently inexhaustible fund of topics that follow one after another, and the use of the full range of personal pronouns contribute to the sense of a polyphony of voices or at the very least, "an all-desiring self that would like, as it were, to see with the eyes and seize with the hands of many individuals" (GS 249). This multiplication of senses and affects contributes to the feeling that aphoristic writing speaks *of* and *to* the body but it is not a corporeality which neatly dovetails with an authorial ego – the self which is marked by the grammatical signifier "I." The disorientating effect that these aphorisms have on the reader is experienced as a break with the "spell of definite grammatical functions" which Nietzsche suggests is ultimately "the spell of *physiological* value judgements" (BGE 20).

For Nietzsche, grammar is "the people's metaphysics" (GS 354), the somatically encoded "innate systematism and relationship of concepts" that enables knowledge to function according to the rules of resemblance and recognition (BGE 20). Unanchored from this logic of classification, Nietzsche's aphorisms disrupt its "unconscious domination" (BGE 20). In particular, the short, one-sentence utterance violates the "habits of the senses" by expropriating the reader from the learned passivity that comes from familiarity with the tone, syntax, and subject matter of an author or genre. Crystalline in its definition, uncompromising in its certitude, the aphorism is a species of philosophical punctuation that compels the reader to pause and re-begin. We may feel that we "know" a thing when we can identify its species or locate it in its context, but the aphorism has a stalling effect on the even rhythm of contemplation, forcing thought to take a new line of flight. This has two related physiological effects. First, reading ceases to be a "natural" process and is experienced as a cognitive and sensory dissonance which prompts reflection on its own conditions of production. Secondly, attention is drawn to language's own reality and to the thoughts that *only these* precise terms incant. In each case, acoustically embedded patterns are frustrated, forestalling conceptual expectations and potentially making space for the production of new sensibilities.

This imposition of the materiality of the sign is the ingress of the *body* into philosophy, the irruption of intensity into thought. There has been a tendency in the Western philosophical tradition to regard the body as ancillary to the mind, just as there has been a tendency to regard the rhythm, cadence, color, and image of language as superfluous to the message that words convey. However, it would seem that Nietzsche's goal in crafting the aphorism is to find the tone, phrase, word, or texture that triggers a certain mood or vibration, still more the silence that resounds. Words thus deployed are not linguistic items that disappear beneath the meanings that they carry. On the contrary, in the aphorism words resist the comprehending consciousness which would efface them. For Nietzsche, every style is good which "actually communicates an inner state" and which makes no mistake as to the tempo of signs and gestures (EH, "Thus Spoke Zarathustra," 4). To communicate "what everyone else does *not* say in a book" is testament to his power to use signs to transmit affects without trimming affects down to signs. To this end, he is fulsome in his praise for the Horatian ode, which he characterizes as a "mosaic of words in which every word, as sound, as locus, as concept, pours forth its power to left and right and over the whole," achieving a maximum in the "energy of the signs" through a minimum in their range and number (TI, "What I Owe the Ancients," 1). He further proposes that the art of writing demands skill in attaining in written form the repertoire of expression only strictly available in speech (*WS* 110).

Such claims indicate that the "art of the aphorism" involves the stimulation of thoughts which have never hitherto acquired the shape of "stock" sensations. The distinctive effect of the aphorism is crafted by the very precision of its terms and syntax but, as in poetic utterance, its sense cannot be bartered into common currency by paraphrase. In the second part of volume 2 of *Human, All Too Human* Nietzsche declares that all great art likes to "arrest the feelings on their course" and not allow them to run *quite* to their conclusion (*WS* 136). Great artists are said to be skilled in "avoidance," veering instinctively away from the common phrase or expression that would have naturally imposed itself upon a mediocre writer (*WS* 97). The effect of this writing is such that one catches the flight vector of a thought without it coalescing into a familiar conceptual form or cliché.

To this end, Nietzsche decries the "scientific" habit of imposing a false arrangement of deduction and dialectic upon thoughts arrived at by other, less methodical means.

> One should not conceal and despoil the *facts* of how our thoughts have come to us. The most profound and inexhaustible books always have something of the aphoristic and sudden character of Pascal's *Pensées*. The *driving* forces and evaluations have for a long time lain under the surface; what comes out is effect. (*KSA* 11, 35[31])

To the extent that it emerges without an obvious context of elaboration, the aphorism embodies the spirit of inspiration or sudden illumination. One has the sense of a thought arriving fully fledged in a moment of brilliant insight, marking a striking contrast to the more even tempo of discourse in which revelations have been checked, standardized, and censored. Most significantly, Nietzsche speaks of this eruption of intensity in terms of the effect of latent *evaluations* – value judgments that testify to an established but hitherto hidden style of being. What the aphorism represents for its author – as much as for its reader – devolves on a diagnosis of the habits of the senses to which it owes its origin.

This takes us to the heart of the question of the philosophical *value* of aphoristic expression. What is momentarily glimpsed or made tangible in the aphorism is a mute affective vitality. Experiences which have been "incorporated" (physiologically assimilated or "consumed") give rise to "symptoms" experienced as affects (e.g. feelings of inclination or repugnance) which form the basis of value judgments. Arguably, the effect of these evaluations is transmitted to the reader in advance of the reader–writer circuit of comprehension as it might be understood according to the logic of reflection. This "effect" passes from writer to reader in much the same way as the rhythm of a poem commands a certain expectation and assent. It is in this respect that response to the aphorism is partly determined by our senses. However, if value judgments about what it is to read and process signs are also the product of prior evaluations, our receptivity to new ideas will also in part reflect the needs and desires of our senses.

Here it is imperative to distinguish between different types of reader. Much of what Nietzsche has to say about the "consumption" of aphorisms concerns the value judgments that different protocols of reading express. If responding to an aphorism entails the kind of physiological self-analysis that we discussed in the first section above, it is not surprising that many of Nietzsche's commentators prefer to bypass the short aphorisms or at least to treat them as no different in kind to any other philosophical form. Following Zarathustra's condemnation of the "mob spirit" cultivated by reading we might say that the "reading idler" will be inclined to seek the "shortest route from peak to peak" without suffering the discomforts of negotiating a bleak and jagged landscape. In this connection, Nietzsche comments that the numerous complaints made about the obscurity of Heraclitus are voiced by "readers who skim and race" (PTAG 7). However, citing Jean Paul he goes on to note that it is generally preferable if matters of great profundity are expressed briefly because the light-minded reader is tempted to dismiss them as nonsense rather than translate them into a nonsense that they can comprehend: "For mean, vulgar minds have an ugly facility for seeing in the profoundest and most pregnant utterance only their everyday opinion" (PTAG 7). The irony here is that the reader who wants to philosophize at speed is actually too slow to register the aesthetic momentum of the aphorism and seeks a translation where self-transformation is what is actually required. By contrast, the more discerning reader is left to reflect on the shock of the sudden impact of these striking ideas. Nietzsche declares in the preface to *Daybreak* that he writes in a tempo which reduces to despair every reader who is in a hurry. He recommends an art of reading that abjures imprudent haste: "it teaches to read *well*, that is to say, to read slowly, deeply, looking cautiously before and aft, with reservations, with doors left open, with delicate eyes and fingers" (D, preface, 5).

Arguably, what this indicates is the extent to which our receptivity to ideas has been disciplined by our prior philosophical habits. In this respect, Nietzsche uses the aphorism to manipulate and unsettle embodied assumptions about what it means to "read" and to "digest" philosophy. To simply assume that ideas articulated aphoristically are synoptic utterances to be unfolded and "fleshed out" is to fail to be affected by the unique materiality of their form. If aphorisms are "peaks," the suggestion is that they are the high points of a meditation rather than seed crystals for future doctrines.

> *Against the censurers of brevity.* – Something said briefly can be the fruit of much long thought: but the reader who is a novice in this field, and has as yet reflected on it not at all, sees in everything said briefly something embryonic, not without censuring the author for having served him up such immature and unripened fare. (AOM 127)

Thus defined, the aphorism is a refusal to elaborate, to build. Although it may be the product of "long thought," this particular kind of succinctness is to be regarded as absolute rather than rudimentary. In this regard, Nietzsche cautions against the prejudice that something presented in small pieces is necessarily splintered: "*Against the shortsighted.* – Do you think that this work must be fragmentary because I give it to you (and have to give it to you) in fragments?" (AOM 28). As a fragment the aphorism is a noun that has the force of a verb: it is only fragmentary to the extent that it *fragments* expectations. By failing to supply the "connective tissue" that would impose a semblance of unity on the text, Nietzsche compels his readers to be *active* in their reception of his ideas.

By virtue of its brevity and lapidary precision Nietzsche's aphoristic style constitutes a particular provocation to the reader. While complete in itself, the aphorism seems to command a response. This is most evident when a question is posed, but arguably a good deal of Nietzsche's aphorisms have an interrogatory tone irrespective of the question form. In a note from winter 1876–7 Nietzsche suggests that the maxim awaits a catalyzing power that only the reader can supply:

> A maxim is a link in a chain of thoughts; it requires the reader to restore this chain out of his own resources: in this respect, a great deal is required. A maxim is a presumptuous thing. – Or it is an occasion for caution, as Heraclitus knew. In order to be savoured, a maxim must first be stirred up and mixed with other matter (an example, experiences, stories). Most do not understand that and therefore one can express disturbing things quite innocuously in maxims. (*KSA* 8, 20[3])

The absorption of maxims, like the metabolization of any unfamiliar substance, is something that has to be learnt if it is to release its greatest potential. Experimentation of this order locks out the passive reader, who is capable of assimilating only dull and obvious thoughts. It is notable that the reader is enjoined to call upon "his own resources" in order to link the maxim in a chain of thoughts. A significant contrast is drawn here with the "worst readers of maxims" who attempt to reconstruct a definitive trajectory for the observation in question.

> *Readers of Maxims.* – The worst readers of maxims are the friends of their author when they are exercised to trace the general observation back to the particular event to which the maxim owes its origin: for through this prying they render all the author's efforts null and void, so that, instead of philosophical instruction, all they receive (and all they deserve to receive) is the satisfaction of a vulgar curiosity. (*AOM* 129)

This forensic reconstruction of the path of thought testifies to the popular conception that truth is to be found at the "origin" of a phenomenon. It also betrays a faith in the notion of a "past" that will always exist unchanged despite the probings of the investigator. By contrast, for Nietzsche, the past is that which is actively "produced" in the present according to our current quests and investments. As he notes in *Twilight of the Idols*, the presentiments of danger and disquiet that are stimulated by an encounter with the unknown are rapidly alleviated when something known is posited as their cause (*TI*, "The Four Great Errors," 5). "Explanations" of this comforting kind abolish the sense of enigma that the aphorist has cultivated by aspiring to write without leaving a trace at the scene. Once a case history has been fabricated ideas are ensnared in a structure, their cross-fertilization impeded and their permutations reduced. This is what it means to perpetuate the value judgments that immobilize thought, to remain locked in one's perceptual horizons as if in prison.

By contrast, for the active reader the aphorism, like the arrow, is thought in flight. If we are moved by the aphorism we return to it again and again as something that has the power to move. In thinking aphoristically, philosophical ideas become distilled without becoming static. They become links in chains which are unanchored. Many "lengthy, forbidden things and chains of thought" may stand between and behind short aphorisms, but it is clear that an aphorism does not state in a short form a more lengthy idea that awaits dilution into prose. In being made aware of what our senses are attuned to – and not attuned to – our philosophical horizons begin to adjust. To appreciate this more fully we turn finally to consider Nietzsche's "lesson" on the art of reading an aphorism.

The Art of Exegesis

The preface is the author's right; the reader's is – the postface. (*KSA* 8, 23[196])

Nietzsche's remarks in the preface to *On the Genealogy of Morals* are of particular interest for our study of the aphorism. It is here that Nietzsche indicates what is involved in the treatment of this specific form. In this context, Nietzsche is insistent on the point that his readers take the trouble to acquaint themselves with his other writings, listing relevant sections to earlier works and noting their considerable complexity (*GM*, preface, 4). With respect to *Thus Spoke Zarathustra*, he declares that only those who have been profoundly "wounded" and "delighted" by every word of the text could possibly share in the "halcyon element" out of which it was born (*GM*, preface, 8). Directly after this he remarks:

> In other cases, people find difficulty with the aphoristic form: this arises from the fact that today this form is *not taken seriously enough*. An aphorism, properly stamped and moulded, has not been "deciphered" when it has simply been read; rather, one has then to begin its *exegesis*, – for which is required an art of exegesis [*Auslegung*]. (*GM*, preface, 8)

The reference to "other cases" at the opening of the quotation implies a contrast between *Thus Spoke Zarathustra* and other, more obviously aphoristic, works. However, a clear reference is made to *Thus Spoke Zarathustra* in Nietzsche's next statement – "I have offered in the third essay of the present book an example of what I regard as 'exegesis' in such a case – an aphorism is prefixed to this essay, the essay itself is a commentary upon it" (*GM*, preface, 8). The said aphorism is extracted from the section of *Thus Spoke Zarathustra* entitled "Of Reading and Writing," in which Nietzsche makes the celebrated remarks about aphorisms being "peaks" in high mountains. Interestingly, however, the aphorism selected for the epigram concerns a set of apparently unrelated themes: "Unconcerned, mocking, violent – thus wisdom wants *us*: she is a woman and always loves only a warrior" (Z, "On Reading and Writing"). More interesting still, the Third Essay of *On the Genealogy of Morals* does not explicitly *mention* the aphorism it supposedly explicates, prompting a series of questions as to how the aphorism and its "exegesis" are to be read.

Building on our discussion of the challenges posed to our reading habits by the aphorism, one strategy would be to focus on what Nietzsche might mean by "exegesis." Normally one would expect an "exegesis" or "interpretation" to involve clarification or explication – as implied by the term *Auslegung* – literally a "laying out." However, the notion of "active reading" that we have been exploring in relation to the aphorism works against the assumption that interpretation is simply the task of unfolding a latent "meaning." Indeed, in his assorted remarks on interpretation in *On the Genealogy of Morals* Nietzsche emphasizes the link between interpretation and will to power:

[W]hatever exists, having somehow come into being, is again and again reinterpreted [*ausgelegt*] to new ends, taken over, transformed, and redirected by some power superior to it; all events in the organic world are a subduing, a *becoming master*, and all subduing and becoming master involves a fresh interpretation [*Neu-Interpretieren*], an adaptation through which any previous "meaning" and "purpose" are necessarily obscured or even obliterated. (*GM* II. 12)

To be engaged in the task of interpretation is to find oneself implicated in the process of transformation and renewal. Recalling our earlier discussion of the relationship between ideas and the body, it could be argued that "interpreting" as a continuous and ongoing process involves the recalibration of sensory and conceptual horizons to accommodate new and surprising thoughts. As active readers our intellectual and affective responses to an aphorism cannot be divorced from the aphorism – just as Nietzsche's claim that the Third Essay of *On the Genealogy of Morals* is an exegesis of an aphorism cannot be divorced from its expressed theme: "What Is the Meaning of Ascetic Ideals?" Through diagnosing the ways in which various physiological symptoms have been interpreted, the essay identifies the ascetic ideal as a fundamental demand that life (and suffering) have a meaning. As readers of the essay – and its aphorism – we are compelled to ask *what it means to ask about the meaning* of the ascetic ideal. Just as Nietzsche constantly implicates himself in the diagnosis of asceticism, the reader in pursuit of "meaning" is thereby implicated in the ascetic ideal. Once again, the path to knowledge seems to be fatefully rerouted through the labyrinths of sickness.

However, just as there are different value judgments at work in active and passive reading, there are different regimes of health and sickness that pertain to exegesis and interpretation.

[M]oral evaluation is an *exegesis* [*Auslegung*], a way of interpreting. The exegesis itself is a symptom of certain physiological conditions, likewise of a particular spiritual level of prevalent judgements: Who interprets? Our affects. (*WP* 254)

We remarked earlier that aphoristic writing achieved a kind of anonymity by making tangible the vital continuum or "inner state" from which the anecdotal has been subtracted. The "sense" of the aphorism – as both affect and significance – cannot be assimilated by the active reader without registering a palpable, material difference. The greatest challenge for such readers is to diagnose the physiological conditions – the affective states or style of being – of which Nietzsche's exegesis is symptomatic, something which can only be achieved by analysing *our* responses. Owing to the obvious discomforts of this regimen, the "reading idler" is disinclined to cultivate the art of "reading well," indeed, Nietzsche warns us in the preface to *On the Genealogy of Morals* that the art of exegesis lies beyond the reach of "modern man." Directly after his claim that the Third Essay is a commentary on an aphorism he writes:

To be sure, one thing is necessary above all if one is to practise reading as an *art* in this way, something that has been unlearned most thoroughly nowadays – and therefore it will be some time before my writings are "readable" – something for which one has almost to be a cow and in any case *not* a "modern man": rumination [*Wiederkäuen*]. (*GM*, preface, 8)

33

To ruminate means to "chew again" or to "go over again and again." This is a process distinctively different to commentary or elucidation. Nietzsche suggests that the aphorism is to be assimilated slowly in renewed encounters, "again and again reinterpreted [*ausgelegt*] to new ends, taken over, transformed." At first reading, an affect may be triggered and perhaps an idea begins to develop. However, the process of mulling over and incorporating the aphorism entails that whatever is initially "digested" is "metabolized" or thrown over by new forces. Engaged in this process, the reader is not referring back to a static form that recurs again and again to a reflective consciousness. For the active reader, the sense of the aphorism changes each time it is revisited.

Indeed, time and again in *On the Genealogy of Morals* we are instructed to refer back to Nietzsche's other texts and it is assumed that we will actually do this. If we go back to the section in *Thus Spoke Zarathustra* entitled "On Reading and Writing" from which the epigram is taken we notice a number of ways in which this text and the themes from the Third Essay are linked.

> Who among you can at the same time laugh and be exalted?
> He who climbs upon the highest mountains laughs at all tragedies, real or imaginary.
> [Courageous] unconcerned, mocking, violent – thus wisdom wants *us*: she is a woman and always loves only a warrior. (Z, "Of Reading and Writing")[3]

This key section from *Thus Spoke Zarathustra* is invoked in section 3 of the Third Essay of *On the Genealogy of Morals*, in which Nietzsche contemplates the possibility that Wagner's *Parsifal* is a wanton parody of the tragic itself:

> This, to repeat, would have been worthy of a great tragedian, who, like every artist, arrives at the ultimate pinnacle of his greatness only when he comes to see himself and his art *beneath* him – when he knows how to *laugh* at himself. (*GM* III. 3)

Nietzsche tells us here that it is laughter that kills the spirit of gravity and ultimately we learn in the Third Essay that it is the comedians of the ascetic ideal who are its only effective enemy (*GM* III. 27).

There may be more to this theme of laughter and mockery than is at first apparent. If we return to this text – ruminate on it perhaps – we will notice that Nietzsche has seemingly misquoted his aphorism, missing off the word "courageous" at the start of the sentence and italicizing "us." Such a detail seems significant given that Nietzsche tells us in the same section of "Of Reading and Writing" that the writer of aphorisms does not want to be read but wants to be learnt by heart. Is Nietzsche illustrating Zarathustra's warning that in the long run reading will ruin not only writing but thinking too (Z, "Of Reading and Writing")? Should the reader meditate on what Zarathustra has to say in the passage about *courage* "wanting to laugh"? Or in our earnestness to "decipher" the tantalizing aphorism do we become the object of mockery? After all, since Zarathustra is an *orator* – one who condemns reading and only endorses that which is written in blood – the active reader is obliged to ruminate upon Nietzsche's reasons for offering a reading lesson in the exegesis of an aphorism which is taken from such an overdetermined text.

Ruminating further, the reader notices that the aphorism which forms the "horizon" of the Third Essay is attributed to Zarathustra and not strictly speaking to Nietzsche. In fact, in the final passage of the Second Essay (added at the proof stage) Nietzsche unexpectedly defers his authorial authority to Zarathustra, declaring that he must remain silent or else he will usurp that to which only Zarathustra has a right (*GM* II. 25). This seems significant given Nietzsche's assertion in *Ecce Homo* that the ascetic ideal has flourished hitherto because it has had no competitors: "What was lacking above all was a *counter-ideal – until the advent of Zarathustra. –* I have been understood" (*EH*, "Genealogy of Morals"). The reference to having been understood refers the reader to the end of section 1 of the Third Essay where, to the question of being understood, Nietzsche anticipates the response "not at all," which prompts the task of starting again "from the beginning" (*GM* III. 1). Negotiating these resonances, the reader is obliged to go over the lessons of *On the Genealogy of Morals*, looking "forwards and backwards" to consider the teachings of *Thus Spoke Zarathustra* and the retrospective analysis in *Ecce Homo*. What Nietzsche's instruction in interpreting an aphorism shows us is that we must supply a chain of thoughts fashioned out of our own resources, making the effort to seek out unfamiliar paths "with delicate eyes and fingers."

The fact that the Third Essay of *On the Genealogy of Morals* does not directly expand on the aphorism appended to it now looks less puzzling, especially when one starts to ruminate on the prevalence of the themes of femininity, violence, and the fortunes of wisdom that thread through the text.[4] While the skeptical reader might still insist that the essay is not an exegesis of the aphorism at all,[5] it is worth remembering Nietzsche's warning that it is "ascetic" to believe in an "in-itself" of meaning (*GM* III. 7). Indeed, since the ascetic ideal functions as a comprehensive "system of interpretation" that "permits no other interpretation" beyond its own (*GM* III. 23), the ascetic ideal might be said to embody the value judgments of just such a reader.

Perhaps to be "unconcerned, mocking and violent" is to be liberated from the need to give meaning to suffering – or perhaps at least a different meaning is now possible. Interestingly, Nietzsche implies that historically there is much to learn from the ascetic ideal insofar as it reversed "accustomed perspectives" (*GM* III. 12). As we remarked earlier, as both patient and physician, Nietzsche is able to diagnose the libidinal invest-ment that the spirit might have in "raging against itself for so long": there is a skill to be learnt here, namely knowing how to "employ a variety of perspectives and affective interpretations in the service of knowledge" (*GM* III. 12). Without presuming that it is "noble" or "masterly" to multiply perspectives, perhaps the "warrior" is one who learns how to use philosophy as a weapon to think against oneself. If the "art of reading" involves self-diagnosis of the stakes set by one's own reading (such as the desire to be "correct," to have authority, to trust the stated aims of the author), the active reader may be well advised to "violate" scholarly conventions and learn to laugh at the gravity of the exegete. After all, Zarathustra's aphorism may be an arrow targeted at the reader and the challenge to learn to write with one's blood.

If aphorisms are peaks, their analysis rewards a reading that makes leaps, not one which follows patiently according to a map. As Nietzsche's "exegesis" demonstrates, aphoristic writing prompts a thinking that is alert to subtle cues and responsive to enigma. We are enjoined to chart a non-teleological path of thought, navigating according to the star of inspiration rather than the compass of deduction. For the

35

interpreter of aphorisms, philosophical thinking is a voyage of exploration and its strange continents grow ever stranger as our perspectives grow and shift. Like the ascetic priest we may be unable to avoid ascribing meaning to a text, but our task is one of opening the text to a reading which will trigger a new connection. As in the infectious power of laughter, in the aphorism something is felt which is as yet unexpressed. It is this charge which ignites other thoughts, prompting other associations, which ultimately may stray far beyond the "sense" of the initial aphorism. No longer privileging familiar habits of recognition, we come to trust our peripheral vision, the judgments of our remote receptors, our new sensory horizons.

If philosophy has a tendency to negate problems by representing them as propositions to be conceptually prodded, the aphorism is a bastard species of philosophical assertion, allergic to intellectual resolution. The challenge of aphoristic writing is that the reader will incorporate new values into thought. Nietzsche argues that his writings are permeated by the idea that "every elevation of man brings with it the overcoming of narrower interpretations; that every strengthening and increase of power opens up new perspectives and means believing in new horizons" (*WP* 616). With the aphorism, Nietzsche voyages into the "horizon of the infinite" (*GS* 124). Like a depth charge cast into the body of the reader, the aphorism is a detonator for new philosophical thoughts. Beyond the reader–writer circuit of exchange it is possible to encounter the aphorism as a tool in the creation of new weapons, new bodies, new organs.

See also 3 "The Aesthetic Justification Of Existence"; 6 "Nietzsche's 'Gay' Science"; 15 "The Body, the Self, and the Ego"; 22 "Rebaptizing Our Evil"; 26 "Nietzsche on Geophilosophy and Geoaesthetics"

Notes

I would like to thank Keith Ansell Pearson for his extensive editorial suggestions and advice.

1   Nietzsche is reputed to have told Arthur Egidi that the illness that befell him at this time compelled him to use the briefest mode of expression, hence the choice of the aphorism. See S. L. Gilman and D. J. Parent, *Conversations with Nietzsche: A Life in the Words of his Contemporaries* (Oxford: Oxford University Press, 1987), p. 129.

2   I am indebted to Keith Ansell Pearson for bringing this to my attention. Arthur Danto develops this theme in his essay "Some Remarks on the *Genealogy of Morals*," in R. C. Solomon and K. M. Higgins, *Reading Nietzsche* (Oxford: Oxford University Press, 1988).

3   For consistency with Kaufmann's translation of this section of *Thus Spoke Zarathustra* I have substituted the former for Hollingdale's translation of the passage, which reads "Untroubled, scornful, outrageous – that is how wisdom wants us to be: she is a woman and never loves anyone but a warrior." Interestingly – given the theme of learning by heart – Hollingdale omits to translate *muthig* (courageous) at the beginning of the aphorism: "Muthig, unbekümmert, spöttisch, gewaltthätig – so will uns die Weisheit: sie ist ein Weib und liebt immer nur einen Kriegsmann."

4   Unfortunately it would be beyond the scope of the present essay to explore these associations here. I refer the interested reader to the extensive discussion offered by Kelly Oliver, *Womanizing Nietzsche: Philosophy's Relation to the "Feminine"* (London: Routledge, 1995).

5 Such a position has been argued by John T. Wilcox, "What Aphorism Does Nietzsche
   Explicate in *Genealogy of Morals*, Essay III?," *Journal of the History of Philosophy*, 35, 4 (1997),
   pp. 593–610, who contends that the epigraph from *Thus Spoke Zarathustra* is simply a "motto"
   and that the first section of the Third Essay is the "aphorism" Nietzsche actually submits to
   exegetical analysis. He points out that the structure of the essay as a whole "mirrors almost
   perfectly the structure of that opening from its beginning to its end," that it "repeats almost
   verbatim" and "clearly explains" the set of themes section 1 sets out: in short, "it is exactly
   what a Nietzschean exegesis of a Nietzschean aphorism should be" (p. 606). Our caveats
   about treating all numbered segments as aphorisms notwithstanding, why should we
   assume, given everything Nietzsche says about the difficulty of the form, that an exegesis of
   a maxim should resemble the maxim? Aren't we in danger of confusing an essay synopsis
   with aphoristic succinctness and exegesis with recognition? Without "ruminating" on the
   links that Nietzsche draws with *Thus Spoke Zarathustra* it is easy to see why one might read
   the first section of the Third Essay as a "key" to the whole but the explanation for this
   is simple enough: Nietzsche added it to the printed manuscript after the text had been
   completed (see *KSA* 14, p. 380). If Wilcox's reading is to be preferred, it would mean that
   Nietzsche's essay was an exegesis of an "aphorism" he had yet to write.

Editions of Nietzsche Used

Beyond Good and Evil, trans. R. J. Hollingdale (Harmondsworth: Penguin, 1973).
Daybreak, trans. R. J. Hollingdale (Cambridge: Cambridge University Press, 1982).
Ecce Homo, trans. R. J. Hollingdale (Harmondsworth: Penguin, 1979).
The Gay Science, trans. Josefine Nauckhoff (Cambridge: Cambridge University Press, 2001).
On the Genealogy of Morals, trans. Walter Kaufmann (New York: Vintage Books, 1967).
Human, All Too Human, trans. R. J. Hollingdale, 2 vols. (Cambridge: Cambridge University Press, 1986).
Philosophy in the Tragic Age of the Greeks, trans. M. Cowan (Chicago: Gateway, 1962).
Thus Spoke Zarathustra, trans. R. J. Hollingdale (Harmondsworth: Penguin, 1961).
Twilight of the Idols, trans. R. J. Hollingdale (Harmondsworth: Penguin, 1968).
Untimely Meditations, trans. R. J. Hollingdale (Cambridge: Cambridge University Press, 1983).
The Will to Power, trans. Walter Kaufmann and R. J. Hollingdale (New York: Vintage Books, 1967).

Further Reading

Kofman, S. (1993). *Nietzsche and Metaphor* (1972), trans. D. Large (London: Athlone Press).
Nehamas, A. (1995). *Nietzsche: Life as Literature* (Cambridge, MA: Harvard University Press).
Williams, W. D. (1952). *Nietzsche and the French: A Study of the Influence of Nietzsche's French Reading on his Thought and Writing* (Oxford: Basil Blackwell).

Part I

Art, Nature, and Individuation

3

The Aesthetic Justification of Existence

DANIEL CAME

1 Introduction

Nietzsche spent most of his productive life trying to identify the foundational conditions that invite love of life and protect against world-denying pessimism. During his short philosophical career, the basic attitudes that he evinced on this matter deviated little from juvenilia to mature thought. He always maintained, for example, that the dreadful aspects of the human and natural worlds call for something like a theodicy, a mode of justification that would allow the troubled soul to accept its place in them, and that a justification of existence was all but impossible if one approached life in the perspective of morality, "because life is [. . .] essentially amoral" (*BT*, preface, 5); and with the possible exception of his so-called "positivist" period associated with *Human, All Too Human* (1878), Nietzsche always approached the problem of justification in some measure in terms of art and the concept of the aesthetic.

It was primarily with the project of justification in mind that he conducted his famous re-evaluation of values, that is, his assessment of the value of our "moral" values. In *Twilight of the Idols*, he retrospectively describes his first published work, *The Birth of Tragedy* (*BT*), as his "first re-evaluation of values" (*TI*, "What I Owe to the Ancients," 5; cf. *BT*, preface, 5). What values are being re-evaluated in this text? And how does the re-evaluation in *BT* contribute to Nietzsche's overarching project of justification?

The discussion of this project in *BT* converges on the re-evaluation of the traditionally negative moral valuation of suffering. This essay offers a critical examination of this leading motif in *BT*. I interpret and assess Nietzsche's most important statement on this theme, which occurs twice in *BT* and is repeated approvingly in the "Attempt at a Self-Criticism," the brilliant preface that Nietzsche wrote for the third edition of the book in 1886: namely, the famous claim that "it is only as an *aesthetic phenomenon* that existence and the world are eternally *justified*" (*BT* 5; cf. *BT* 25; *BT*, preface, 5). The claim refers principally to the imposition of aesthetic form on suffering that, left unmediated, would lead only to despair. Beyond this, however, the claim does not lend itself to a self-evident interpretation. How could existence be an "aesthetic phenomenon"? And who said it needed to be "justified"?

Where these questions are concerned, the interpretive process is rendered even more problematical by the rhapsodic style of *BT*, and its immersion in the concepts and categories of Schopenhauer's metaphysics. But in what follows I attempt to cut through the suggestive imagery and questionable metaphysics to what I take to be the core propositions of the text's notion of an aesthetic justification. After initially expounding what I take to be Nietzsche's main target in *BT* – morality and its pessimistic consequences – I seek to elucidate the precise sense of the term "justification" in that work. It is my general contention that when Nietzsche speaks of the aesthetic justifying life, he does not mean that it shows us that life is *actually* justified, but rather that it educes an affectively positive attitude towards life that is *epistemically neutral*.

I then consider what I take to be the pivotal hinge of the notion of an aesthetic justification of existence, specifically, the claim that suffering is a possible object of positive aesthetic evaluation. The claim immediately raises at least two questions: first, is it psychologically possible to view suffering, especially horrendous suffering, as beautiful? And second, if it is possible, could such a vantage point feature in any recognizably human perspective on the world? I answer both questions in the affirmative but argue that an aesthetic standpoint on pain is possible only through a radical falsification and abstraction of the reality of suffering. Nevertheless, I suggest that, on the terms of his conception of justification, this does not render Nietzsche's project of affirmation a failure. That a justification of existence involves falsification matters only to those whose moral view of the world shuns all forms of illusion.

2 The Schopenhauerian Challenge

Why should existence seem to be in need of a justification? Summarily speaking, the need for a justification of existence is engendered by the pessimistic verdict on the value of existence that Nietzsche encountered in Schopenhauer's philosophy. In his major work, *The World as Will and Representation* (*WWR*), Schopenhauer argues by a priori and empirical methods that a careful reflection on the world and human experience shows, as he puts it, that "it would be better for us not to exist" (Schopenhauer 1969: vol. 2, p. 605). This nihilistic judgment follows, Schopenhauer argues, primarily from his account of self-conscious beings as characterized by an incessant and inherently painful willing. According to Schopenhauer, willing is a sufficient condition of suffering, because all willing arises necessarily from a want or deficiency, and to experience a want is to suffer: to live is to will; to will is to suffer; therefore to live is to suffer.

At times, Nietzsche seems to espouse a pessimism as dire as Schopenhauer's, if not the same. Although he does not explicitly refer to pessimism in *BT*, it is the basic premise of the book, enshrined in the "wisdom of Silenus": "What is best of all is utterly beyond your reach: not to be born, not to *be*, to be *nothing*. But the second best for you is – to die soon" (*BT* 3). But Silenus' wisdom is not to be the last word. Nietzsche accepts that human existence is chiefly characterized by an ineluctable and all-pervasive suffering, and that life offers no real opportunity for lasting satisfaction or happiness; but he rejects, or at any rate seeks to resist, Schopenhauer's negative evaluation of life – the judgment that existence itself is undesirable and lacks positive value – which is based on or evidentially supported by the fact of the predominance of suffering in life.

Now, by accepting Schopenhauer's descriptive account of human existence but rejecting his evaluative conclusion, Nietzsche seems to have recognized that the quantity of suffering in the world logically entails nothing about the value of existence. One could hold, that is, that life is a vale of tears without being obliged by any logical consideration to add that it lacks positive value. It is, rather, only in the perspective of certain particular values that the suffering of life points to the devaluation of the world. That is, for the pessimist to experience life as valueless because it is dominated by suffering, his beliefs about how life *ought* to be must already have been armed by specific values. Nietzsche's view is that the values in question are those of traditional morality (*BT*, preface, 5; cf. *BT* 3, 22).[1] Thus he claims in a posthumously published note of the mid-1880s that "the pessimistic condemnation of life in Schopenhauer's work is a moral transfer of the herd's yardsticks to the metaphysical realm" (*WP* 379, translation mine).

Of the yardsticks in question, most salient in the present context is morality's axiological hedonism: its judgment, broadly speaking, that happiness is good and suffering is bad, which is evinced, for example, by its positive evaluation of qualities and dispositions that reduce or limit suffering. Hedonism is plainly a tacit assumption of Schopenhauer's pessimism: it is because the sum of displeasure outweighs the sum of pleasure that it would be better if the world did not exist. But far from being a self-evidently valid axiom, this assumption actually constitutes a substantive philosophical presupposition that is, at the very least, genuinely problematic.

Of course, it is normally thought to matter a great deal whether people are happy or unhappy, and whether they experience pleasure or pain. For Nietzsche, however, this way of thinking is blinkered. "Happiness," he contends in a later work, is "no argument in favour of something"; and "making unhappy" is "no counter-argument" (*BGE* 39) with respect to either truth or value. It is no argument because, first, pleasure and pain are "mere epiphenomena" (*WP* 702) of our physical and unconscious natures and hence "have no [...] metaphysical significance" (*WP* 789); and second, because "life" is (or should be) the sole locus of value, and its preservation, flourishing, and enhancement are ultimately decisive in the determination of value (*BGE* 4).

It is not entirely clear why the epiphenomenal nature of hedonic experience is supposed to rob it of any significance in the evaluation of life. The claim seems to be that the causal dependence of hedonic states on our physical and unconscious natures renders them, at best, of marginal significance to questions of value. But this is clearly a non sequitur: that A causes B does not entail that A is extraneous to the value of C. If Nietzsche were claiming that consciousness were eliminable from a scientific or neurological point of view, then his claim would prima facie be more plausible. For, presumably, the unreality of conscious states *would* preclude such states featuring legitimately in the assessment of the value of reality: the value of A is a function of A's actual properties and effects. But Nietzsche does not think that consciousness is eliminable. Conscious states, he thinks, are epiphenomena of the physical. Therefore, when Nietzsche describes something as epiphenomenal he does not mean to deny that it is real, but only to place it in a certain causal nexus in which it is an effect of some cause but has no causal role itself.

Nietzsche's second argument against hedonism is altogether more powerful. It is a basic axiom of Nietzsche's entire philosophy that what we might call the "life-value" of

DANIEL CAME

a proposition or set of propositions alone is of ultimate significance to its appraisal. This has two distinct applications in his critique of hedonism. First, something might have "value for life" despite not engendering happiness, or perhaps even despite occasioning considerable unhappiness and suffering. Second, the claim that "life" is the sole locus of value entails a general subordination of all other values, including epistemic values, to that of "life." It follows that the truth-value of hedonism is strictly irrelevant to its assessment. Therefore, even if hedonism were known to be true – that is, even if there were some sound theoretical justification for evaluating life and our experience according to hedonistic standards – we should not endorse hedonism if doing so would be detrimental to life.[2]

Nevertheless, one might still claim that, given our ostensive natural aversion to pain, it is reasonable to suppose that a significant predominance of suffering would indeed render life intolerable. This inference may be hostile to "life," as well as deductively invalid, but it is surely based on a natural way of viewing suffering. Moreover, it is this natural way of seeing suffering to which Schopenhauer appeals in his main arguments for pessimism, which he constructs on the basis of a certain naturalistic thesis about the meanings of the terms "good" and "bad." "Good" (*Gut*) connotes "*the fitness or suitableness of an object to any definite effort of the will*," and "bad" (*Schlecht*) "everything that is not agreeable to the striving of the will" (Schopenhauer 1969: vol. 1, sect. 65, p. 360). Suffering, Schopenhauer plausibly argues, is not agreeable to the striving of the will, and therefore by definition is bad. And since the sum of pain overbalances that of pleasure, it follows that human existence itself is bad – and what is bad "ought not to be" (1969: vol. 2, p. 576).

For Nietzsche, it seems, this argument may be valid but it is not sound, for he rejects outright Schopenhauer's definition of "good" and "bad." Far from being constitutive of badness, that which is disagreeable to an agent's willing is necessary for her to attain what her willing is in fact teleologically directed towards – namely, an increase in the experience of power. This, of course, is Nietzsche's psychological doctrine of the will to power, according to which an agent experiences a growth in power in relation to phenomena over which she previously lacked power, phenomena which previously obstructed her willing. The experience of power therefore depends on the overcoming of obstacles. It follows that what is disagreeable to our willing is not only compatible with the human good, but actually constitutive of it.

But this seems a rather tenuous way of averting Schopenhauer's pessimistic conclusion. For one thing, it appears obvious that it works only for very specific situations and forms of suffering. One can see suffering as an obstacle to be overcome if there is a real chance of overcoming it. But in cases of extreme suffering this surely cannot apply. It would be foolish to say to somebody who is terminally ill with cancer that they should welcome their suffering because it provides an opportunity for striving and exertion and thereby the experience of power. Could the 5-year-old girl of whom Ivan Karamazov speaks in Dostoyevsky's novel, hideously beaten by her parents, forced to consume excrement, weeping in dark solitude, begging "gentle Jesus" for rescue, find a trace of solace in this putative side-effect of her suffering? In such cases, Nietzsche's re-evaluation of suffering seems transparently to fail.

On the other hand, the notion that a sense of power is derivable from suffering relates quite readily to someone, like Nietzsche, who is subject to less severe suffering,

44

such as migraine attacks. Indeed, it might be prudent for such a person to construct a theory of value that enables him to live with his condition; to declare, as Nietzsche famously does, that "what does not kill me makes me stronger" (*TI*, "Maxims and Arrows," 8). On such a view, suffering gives one extra strength, since it shows that, in spite of one's affliction, one can in some sense prevail. And it is easy to imagine that, for a person who lives by this dictum, suffering could have a psychologically invigorating effect. Perhaps, then, the right doses of suffering can indeed be administered to good effect. But, again, it would surely be frivolous to suggest that one could embrace overwhelming suffering in the way Nietzsche prescribes. In relation to such cases, Nietzsche's pronouncements on power echo Paul's seemingly hollow words, addressed to the Romans, that "we boast of our afflictions, knowing that affliction produces endurance" (Romans 5: 3).

Can anything be said for Nietzsche's view in the light of extreme suffering? Naturally, its plausibility depends on what we understand "power" to be. If "power" in this case means the power to escape (say) a terminal illness, then clearly there is no power available in that sense. But if "power" means something like the courage to fight the illness, to overcome one's fear and weakness, despite the impossibility of ever winning, then that might bestow some value on one's suffering, even though one's life ends.

It is possible that Nietzsche has it in mind that his doctrine of the will to power is itself a justification of existence.[3] It is very likely that he saw the positive evaluative stance towards suffering made possible by the will to power as having some kind of redemptive capacity. But the value in such a case could only be consolatory, not justificatory. For in his view human beings are constitutionally unable to perceive the world in all its terrible, unfalsified reality. As he asserts throughout his writings, some degree of falsification of life is necessary for us to be functional agents capable of affirmation and self-affirmation. But if there is suffering from which redemptive power cannot be derived, then the will to power cannot be sufficient for a justification of suffering.

3 "Justification"

Before proceeding any further, we must attempt to pin down Nietzsche's intended sense of "justification." His use of this term has a self-conscious echo of the Western theological attempt to justify the ways of God to man; and it is clear that he conceives of his task of justification as a secularized version of this project of theodicy – i.e., as an attempt to vindicate the desirability of life in the face of suffering.[4] In certain forms of Christian theology, such a justification would identify a morally sufficient reason for God's inaction with respect to evil, so that the moral economy of the world would be vindicated. Nietzsche is very clear that it would be about as sensible to attempt to give a moral justification of existence – such as that the world exhibits a perfect balance of retributive justice or a favorable balance of moral good over moral evil – as to try to square a circle (*BT*, preface, 5). But he also seems to reject the whole attempt, exemplified by the theological approach, to discharge the need for a justification by rational or conceptual methods. The old Athenians justified their world aesthetically, by finding beauty even in its most terrible depredations; but we moderns, the heirs of Socrates, can accept only reasoned justifications, typified by the empirical generalizations of science and the universal norms of morality. But it seems that we are wrong, and they were right: rationalism in art and in ethics is doomed to fail even on its own terms.

The cult of intelligibility embodied in morals, in science, in contemporary philosophy, and in realistic art, fails to offer a justification. Hence it is central to Nietzsche's purpose in *BT* to undercut rationalism. This means that he cannot be using "justification" in that work in the scientific/philosophic sense that denotes some kind of conceptual structure, since to do so would clearly subvert his own anti-rationalist agenda. Nonetheless it is not entirely clear why conceptual methods will not work as a mode of justification. One possibility is that Nietzsche thinks that a rational or discursive justification cannot succeed because he thinks that if one reasons *correctly* about the world, one will inevitably come to Schopenhauer's conclusion that life is worthless (Geuss 1999: 107). But since, as we have seen, Nietzsche implicitly regards this conclusion as inferentially invalid, this cannot be right.

Perhaps, then, Nietzsche rejects the notion of a reason-based justification because he denies that "rational thought [. . .] can penetrate to the depths of being" (*BT* 15): if reason is not adequate to the nature of reality, then it cannot reliably assess reality's value, assuming that the value of reality is a function of reality as a whole. It follows that any attempt to justify existence rationally *must* fail, because that would be to attempt to do something that cannot be done with the means one is committed to using. This seems a more likely explanation. But if that is right, how are we to account for Nietzsche's pursuit of a justification on any level? Surely the attempt to justify existence is a hopeless undertaking if the value of existence outstrips our cognitive capacities.

This would be so only if we understood the aim of justification as that of showing that existence is *actually* justified. But if we were to allow for the possibility of a justification that involved no commitments to the ultimate truth about the justificatory status of existence, then our ignorance about whether life is actually justified would be beside the point.

For a justification in the traditional sense to be possible it must be true that:

(a)   the world is *actually* justified, and that
(b)   we can know that (a) is the case.

Nietzsche's position in *BT* with respect to (a) is unclear, but in a roughly contemporaneous notebook entry, he is explicitly skeptical about our prospects for confirming or disconfirming (a): "Neither the metaphysical, nor the ethical, nor the aesthetic significance of existence can be *proven*" (*Philosophy and Truth*, p. 32);[5] he therefore must regard (b) as false. But our inability to verify (a) renders the project of justification futile only if we conceive of that project as operating under certain epistemological constraints. That we cannot know whether the world is justified matters only if we think that we are in some sense *required* to align our evaluative stance vis-à-vis the world with the actual value of existence. It is this supposition of the traditional approach to justification that Nietzsche rejects; not because he thinks that awareness of our true situation is incompatible with a justification of the traditional kind, but because, first, such awareness is not available to us; and second, because the whole demand for a justification to be true is part of a wider system of life-denying, Socratic valuations that Nietzsche explicitly rejects in *BT*.

For these reasons, Nietzsche must be operating with an *epistemically neutral* conception of justification – that is, a conception of justification that involves no commitment with respect to its own truth-value. It seems that for Nietzsche this is the closest approximation to a traditional, full-blooded justification that is possible. But it is important to emphasize that the fact that a successful justification must deal in illusion is not, at least for Nietzsche, to be lamented. An epistemically neutral justification is not to be thought of as a second-rate version of a justification in the traditional sense. For, again, the presence of illusion in a justification matters only to those with a morality that shuns all forms of illusion.

But we may still want to ask how such a justification could ever be successful. How could a justification that does not purport actually to justify existence persuade us that life is an appropriate object of affirmation? That is, how could a justification that does not in fact justify existence still be a justification? Let us first note that a justification for Nietzsche is optative – it is not supposed to issue in anything like a propositional truth. Rather, it is designed to generate in us something like an affectively positive attitude towards life, or life-affirmation (*BT* 1). But to have an affectively positive attitude towards X need not entail having any beliefs about the objective value of X, or even the belief that X has an objective value. I can be positively disposed towards all kinds of things (the taste of muffins, the smell of coffee, etc.) without supposing that my attitude reflects anything about the actual value of the object of my esteem. In such cases, my approbative attitude can be unpacked in terms of a relationship between X and me, and not in terms of intrinsic properties of X or in terms of X's relationship to anybody else.

It is a feature of this kind of attitude that it stays in place when we confront the fact that it is not tied to any objective value property. We do not stop retching when we realize that there is nothing objectively disgusting about a smell of rotten vegetables. No doubt many of our evaluative attitudes are *essentially* connected to beliefs about the objective value of the thing contemplated. But even the most emotionally intense evaluative attitudes can be felt in a way that does not presuppose the existence of objective value properties. So, given that Nietzsche's justification aims to generate life-affirmation in us, and that such an attitude does not necessarily involve entertaining any explicit beliefs about the value of existence, that Nietzsche's justification does not demonstrate the positive value of existence does not militate against it.

In this connection, we should also pay heed to the fact that it is specifically an *aesthetic* justification that Nietzsche is attempting to furnish in *BT*. Both in *BT* and his later writing on aesthetics, it is clear that the value of art for Nietzsche is extrinsic. Art is not valuable per se, but rather because it "makes life possible and worth living" (*BT* 1), by turning the "eternal suffering" and "terror and horror of existence" (*BT* 3; cf. *TI*, "Expeditions of an Untimely Man," 24) "into notions with which one can live" (*BT* 7). It is also clear that Nietzsche is an anti-realist about beauty. In *BT*, for instance, beauty is identified with the act of projecting pleasing Apollonian "semblance" or "illusion" onto the object of aesthetic representation (*BT* 3). Nevertheless, the capacity of aesthetic experience to render its subject-matter affirmable is evidently not weakened for Nietzsche by the mind-dependence of beauty.

47

This, arguably, is because aesthetic qualities do not admit of an appearance/reality distinction. It is constitutive of aesthetic pleasure that the subject is not interested in the objective existence of the object of her attention, but is concerned only with the phenomenology of the experience; and the phenomenology is sufficient for the aesthetic pleasure. Aesthetic pleasure in an object consists in the positive hedonic experience which we connect with the representation of the object. Hence aesthetic pleasure does not take into consideration the objective properties of the object, but only the mere presentation of the object. Our aesthetic interest in an object is purely phenomeno-logical, and whether the phenomenology belongs to external or objective properties of the object is extraneous to the aesthetic attitude. Another way of putting this is to say that a subject's aesthetic pleasure towards an object is a first-order attitude, while her beliefs about the ontological status of the object's aesthetic qualities are constitutive of a logically independent, second-order attitude.

Now although Nietzsche does not explicitly state this view of aesthetic experience, something along these Kantian lines does seem to be implied by his claim that aesthetic representation in general is inherently falsifying: if beauty is illusory, then aesthetic experience *qua* aesthetic experience must be purely phenomenological. And from this it follows that the capacity of art to foster life-affirmation and thereby to justify existence is not destabilized by its inseparability from illusion.

4 The Extension of "Aesthetic Phenomenon"

The next thing to get clear about is the reference of the phrase "aesthetic phenom-enon" in Nietzsche's claim that the world is justified "only as an *aesthetic phenomenon*" (*BT* 5). The claim is ambiguous. It could mean:

(a) it is when the world is depicted in certain works of art that it appears justified, or
(b) it is when we view the world itself as an aesthetic phenomenon – that is, as if it were *itself* a work of art or bearer of aesthetic value – that it appears justified.

These propositions are not inconsistent; hence there is a third reading yielded from their conjunction:

(c) it is only when the world is depicted in certain works of art *or* when it is itself viewed as a work of art or bearer of aesthetic value that it appears justified.

At first sight, Nietzsche certainly seems to endorse (a), but for reasons that straddle two distinct conceptions of the nature of tragic pleasure. Firstly, Attic tragedy is said to depict the necessity of cruelty, suffering, catastrophe, and death – its "Dionysian" content – over which it casts a veil of "Apollonian" beauty, primarily in the form of beautiful speeches and the artistry of the production. The Apollonian elements of the drama offset and dilute the impact of the painful subject-matter, making it tolerable to humans. In tragedy, suffering and beauty coexist, and suffering is "redeemed" by the beauty of its representation, thereby "seducing" the spectator to affirm life. The justificatory effect of tragedy, then, consists, first, in its revealing to us the inherent

48

pain of life and, second, in its capacity to compensate for this pain by casting over it a layer of transfiguring Apollonian beauty.

But this seems to be simply a restatement of the Humean solution to the paradox of tragedy, albeit couched in poetic language and intended to serve an existential rather than theoretical end, and with the happy exclusion of Hume's improbable thesis that in the concurrent experience of two emotions of opposing and unequal hedonic values, the stronger emotion will capture and reverse the strength of the weaker emotion (Hume 1985). Hume maintains that the spectator who responds with painful emotions to the suffering of the tragic protagonist undergoes a painful experience, but that the overall experience includes counterbalancing pleasures, derived from the artistic spectacle, that are concurrent with the painful emotions. Similarly, Nietzsche claims that the experience of tragedy has a dual phenomenology, an affective state involving a positive and a negative hedonic reaction.

However, Nietzsche also claims, more interestingly, that the negative hedonic state is deflected by a second-order positive hedonic state that is not *essentially* related to the Apollonian. Whereas the pleasure associated with the Apollonian is merely concurrent with the negative emotions of the Dionysian, this second pleasure is essentially related to them – indeed it is a pleasure *in* experiencing them. The Apollonian delight is a first-order pleasure in the medium of presentation of the calamity. The second pleasure, by contrast, is essentially related to the painful emotions, it is pleasure in the pain – it is an instance of "the phenomenon that pain begets joy" (*BT* 2). Tragedy, Nietzsche writes at the very end of *BT*, "play[s] with the sting of displeasure [. . .] and by means of this play [. . .] justif[ies] the existence of even the 'worst world'" (*BT* 25).

This is one of Nietzsche's more interesting ideas and it is a shame that he does not give it more explanatory work to do in *BT*. But the idea is proleptic of Nietzsche's more thorough discussion of "the painful voluptuousness of tragedy." Nietzsche came to conceive of what is agreeable in the tragic experience as "the spiritualization of cruelty," that is, the enjoyment in making *oneself* suffer at the sight of the suffering of others (*BGE* 229; cf. *WP* 852).[6] To the extent that this view is present in *BT*, it strikingly prefigures the later will to power doctrine. The "over-abundant enjoyment," the "sweetness," the "voluptuousness" of the experience of tragedy are supervenient upon the cruelty that informs the drama and which cause us to suffer. And the pleasure attendant upon this suffering is the feeling of power that accompanies the recognition that we can expose ourselves to these harsh truths and live with them.

But just as the will to power fails to justify or redeem all instances of suffering, so the prototypical use to which it is put in *BT* does not seem able to do the work required. For as Nietzsche says, the masochistic pleasure derived from the elements of cruelty that inform the drama is itself in some sense dependent upon the Apollonian elements of the drama – even if it is not a pleasure that is taken in those elements. This is implied by his remark that, "not one whit more may enter the consciousness of the human individual than can be overcome again by [the] Apollonian power of transfiguration" (*BT* 25). It follows that there is a maximum value on the suffering that can be rendered Apollonian. Hence, on Nietzsche's own account, tragedy seems constitutively unable to justify suffering in general.

All in all, then, tragedy does not seem to provide a very effective justification of existence. For one thing, it is not real suffering that we affirm when watching tragedy but a disembodied and aesthetically enhanced, and hence falsified, representation of suffering. Second, tragedy appears to justify existence only temporarily, while we are watching the tragedy – and this exhibits a clear tension with Nietzsche's claim that existence is "eternally" justified as an aesthetic phenomenon.

But Nietzsche evidently thinks that tragedy in *some* sense provides a justification. Perhaps, though, what he has in mind is not that tragedy *itself* justifies existence, but rather that the tragic perspective on suffering – the evaluative attitude to suffering elicited in us by tragedy – can serve as a template for our attitude towards real suffering. In other words, it is by seeing the world itself – and hence suffering – through the lens of tragedy that existence and the world seem justified. If this is right, Nietzsche's understanding of the extension of "aesthetic phenomenon" strictly aligns him with (b) above.

But here too Nietzsche runs into serious problems. For what renders the suffering represented in tragedy affirmable is the veil of Apollonian beauty that is spread over it. It is only in the presence of Apollonian artistry that we are able to affirm suffering. One possibility is that Nietzsche thinks that the value derived from the tragic experience outweighs the disvalue of the suffering of ordinary life. Prima facie this seems implausible, but in a culture (such as that of the tragic Greeks) whose dominant values were aesthetic, the fact that tragedy, as a mimetic art form, depends for its subject-matter on real suffering would mean that real suffering were justified indirectly because it makes tragedy possible. If all values are subordinate to art, then that which makes the greatest art possible would have instrumental value at the very least.

Furthermore, it may not be true that the justificatory effects of tragedy are transitory, since that presupposes too sharp a distinction between our experience of art and ordinary life. We do not value works of art only for the experiences they induce in us while we are in direct contact with them. Rather, we value art in some measure because we are able to take something of the aesthetic mindset embodied in the work into our lives. In this way, art is capable of placing our existence in a new and different light. Aristotle, for instance, accepts the possibility that part of the value of tragedy is educative, in the sense that it enables us to feel pity and fear in the right way and towards the right objects, thereby leaving us better disposed towards virtue. Perhaps Nietzsche has in mind something analogous to the Aristotelian view. That is, tragedy might inculcate an aesthetic attitude to suffering that, as it were, one takes from the theatre and into everyday life and applies to real suffering, supplying one's own Apollonian illusion and/or deriving the masochistic pleasure that is derivable from suffering.

It is far from clear, however, what applying our own Apollonian illusion to real suffering would amount to. In tragedy, the justificatory capacity of the Apollonian consists in the beautiful speeches and the artistry of the production that are rarely features of our experience of real suffering. Perhaps, however, a solution is provided by Nietzsche's claim that we enjoy making ourselves suffer at the sight of the suffering of others. But, as we have seen, he holds that not all of life's horrors are tolerable for humans (*BT* 25). Accordingly, the masochistic pleasure derived from real suffering is not sufficient for the affirmation of all suffering. Moreover, if Nietzsche's justification rested solely on the "voluptuousness" of cruelty, it would be unclear why he chooses to characterize it as an *aesthetic* justification.

Can Nietzsche be rescued from these problems? One line of defence against the objection that Apollonian illusions do not attend instances of real suffering depends upon again treating Nietzsche's stance in *BT* as proleptic – that is, as needing to be unpacked using later ideas which are in some sense prefigured by remarks in *BT*. Nietzsche holds, both in *BT* and later on, that artistic creativity occurs in states of intoxication or *Rausch*: "For art to exist [. . .] a certain physiological precondition is indispensable: *intoxication*. [. . .] The essence of intoxication is the feeling of plenitude and increased energy. From out of this feeling one gives to things [. . .] one calls this procedure *idealizing*" (*TI*, "Expeditions of an Untimely Man," 8). Nietzsche also seems to hold that conducive to this condition is the infliction of cruelty upon oneself. The condition of intoxication is characterized by an increase in the feeling of power. And the pleasure of cruelty against ourselves is derived from "the feeling of power over ourselves" (*WP* 802). Hence cruelty against ourselves is a stimulus to intoxication (*TI*, "Expeditions of an Untimely Man," 8). And the condition of intoxication "release[s] artistic powers in us" (*WP* 798), which enable us to "infuse a transfiguration and fullness into things" (*WP* 801).

This notion of transfiguration recurs repeatedly throughout *BT* and features centrally in its conception of the Apollonian. Nietzsche speaks of Apollo as "the transfiguring genius" (*BT* 16), of "the Apollonian power of transfiguration," and describes Apollonian aesthetic qualities as "transfiguring semblance" (*BT* 25). In addition, he understands the Apollonian in general to apply not just to works of art conceived as objects of aesthetic experience, but also to the subject's own psychological identity. Indeed, there is for Nietzsche a significant sense in which all experience is to be considered illusory and hence the product of the Apollonian, since our experience in general may not be supposed to correspond even approximately to the actual nature of reality. Thus understood, it may well be the case that Nietzsche's conception of the Apollonian is sufficiently broad to provide him with the resources to claim that real suffering too is amenable to Apollonian aestheticization.

There still remains, however, the difficulty that not all instances of suffering are amenable to Apollonian aestheticization. But perhaps on the terms of what I have called Nietzsche's epistemically neutral conception of justification, it is not necessary that all suffering is amenable to Apollonian aestheticization. Perhaps, that is, life-affirmation, an attitude that does not necessarily involve the explicit entertaining of beliefs about the objective justificatory status of the world, can be induced in a subject merely by the aestheticization of *some* instances of suffering. It is plausible to think that we might indeed derive "comfort" (*BT* 7) from knowing that at least a large quantity of our suffering has positive aesthetic value. And this comfort might itself be sufficient for life-affirmation and hence a justification. Not all suffering can be transformed and its harshness eradicated by the Apollonian, but to the extent that aestheticized suffering admits of correlation with suffering that is beyond the scope of the Apollonian, our attitude towards the latter profits from this correlation, as our enjoyment in this imagery transfers into our general stance toward anything similar to it.

One may have qualms about the psychological validity of these assertions, but let us now move on and address the contentious issue of whether we actually can see real suffering as beautiful. It is one thing to claim that there can be beautiful artistic

51

representations of suffering; it is quite another thing to claim that real suffering can be beautiful.

5 The Aestheticization of Suffering

The justification of existence that Nietzsche presents in *BT* converges on the identification of tragedy as an agent which re-evaluates pain and suffering in human existence. As such, it is appropriate to position *BT* alongside Nietzsche's later works in which he more explicitly embarks upon re-evaluating that which traditional morality has taught us unthinkingly to assign a negative role in life.

The success of *BT*'s re-evaluative project turns on the credibility (and admissibility) of the ascription of positive aesthetic value to suffering, which seems to be entailed by Nietzsche's claim that the world is to be seen as an "aesthetic phenomenon." The potential for the aestheticization of suffering is decisive in the assessment of Nietzsche's justification. But it is also highly problematic. I want to raise two main questions about this claim: first, is it psychologically possible to see suffering, especially intense suffering, as beautiful? And if it is, could such a vantage point feature in any recognizably human perspective on the world? The two questions are whether we can, and whether we ever should, see suffering as beautiful. I address the first of these in this section and the second in section 6.

In order to determine the plausibility of Nietzsche's claim that real suffering can be beautiful, we need first of all to determine the extension of "suffering" in the context of Nietzsche's justification. What constitutes suffering? Let us first note a distinction between the first- and third-person perspectives on suffering. The distinction relates to the difference between the inner and outer experience of suffering, the interiority of painful experience and the perception of another person's pain. According to this distinction, there is a significant difference between, on the one hand, suffering itself *qua* suffering being beautiful and, on the other, the suffering person being beautiful. In the latter case, the suffering is merely a means to a beautiful end. Clearly this is not sufficient for Nietzsche's idea of suffering itself being beautiful. Surely if we are to grant Nietzsche this claim, we would have to say that it was the intrinsic phenomenology of suffering that is beautiful. If it is suffering viewed from the third-person perspective that is to be beautified, then this would not seem to amount to finding suffering itself beautiful. Such a conception of suffering tends towards the abstract and thus becomes necessarily disembodied. Human suffering, on the other hand, is always the suffering of a particular person at a particular moment in time. So the aestheticization of third-person suffering alone would leave out something quite crucial; what is objectionable about suffering is what it is like from the first-person perspective.

But, having said that, suffering might be a state that presupposes a subject; in other words, it might not make sense to talk about suffering without talking about a subject who suffers. If suffering is essentially tied to a subject who suffers, then, although it may not be logically impossible to specify properties of suffering independently of the subject, it might be phenomenologically difficult. To take a Christian example: the suffering of Christ on the Cross *qua* suffering is not beautiful, but many Christians seem to think that Christ suffering on the Cross *qua* suffering Christ is beautiful. Suffering is necessarily subjective or presupposes a subject; and such a conception of suffering leaves room to blur the distinction between the beauty of the sufferer and the beauty of the suffering, since the suffering *qua* suffering is intrinsically related to a sufferer. The claim is not that a token event of suffering would not be that token event unless it were that token event undergone by that subject; rather the claim is the stronger one that the suffering is made qualitatively what it is, or partly constituted as the suffering that it is, by being the suffering of Christ as opposed to (say) the suffering of Oedipus or the suffering of St. Sebastian. It is partly because these are the sufferings of distinct sufferers that they are qualitatively distinct suffering. If this is right, to find suffering from the third-person perspective beautiful might be sufficient for Nietzsche's claim that we can find suffering itself beautiful.

In any event, the general tenor of his descriptions of suffering in *BT* suggests that it is the pain of others, rather than one's own pain, that is most problematic. It is not the question of how to cope with pain as viewed from the first-person perspective but the question of how to cope with the pain of others that *BT* primarily seeks to answer (*BT* 21; cf. *GS* 338). It is the fact of the predominance of suffering in human life *in general* that stands in need of justification; and this predominance obviously relates most closely to the suffering of others rather than to the suffering of a single human individual.

The ascription of positive aesthetic value to suffering viewed from the third-person perspective is subject to three interpretations:

(a) Suffering itself is beautiful.
(b) Suffering itself is not beautiful, but it is a necessary constituent of the overall aesthetic unity of the world.
(c) Suffering itself is construable as beautiful.

Intuition suggests that (a) is always false: suffering itself is never beautiful. Where beauty and real suffering coexist, we might say, is in the heroic stance in the face of suffering. There is something magnificent in seeing people suffer in a heroic way; even if the sufferer succumbs in the end, as long as he retains his dignity in the face of his suffering it somehow stimulates aesthetic pleasure in us. That (a) is intuitively false does not mean that it *is* false. But to find something beautiful is to take pleasure in that thing. It would be very odd for a person to claim to find a painting beautiful and yet deny that they derive pleasure from it. Suffering is intrinsically painful. Therefore, a person who found suffering itself beautiful would be taking pleasure in pain. Hence there seems to be something slightly paradoxical about the idea of finding suffering itself beautiful.

But perhaps this objection holds on to an old-fashioned notion of beauty. A central part of Nietzsche's enterprise in *BT* seems to be to enrich our notion of the aesthetic, to extend it in such a way that it embraces both pleasure and pain. In any case, even if (a) is really false, this does not mean that Nietzsche does not subscribe to it in *BT*. But since Nietzsche is an anti-realist about beauty, he could not (on pain of inconsistency) subscribe to (a). If beauty is not an objective property, then suffering cannot be objectively beautiful.

One way to make sense of (b) is to say that the world constitutes an aesthetic unity; each feature of the world is a necessary constituent of this aesthetic unity; therefore, each element (even suffering) is justified. The world as a whole exhibits aesthetic order and is all for the best. This fact about the world is not obvious from the viewpoint of an individual human, but this is because we cannot easily overcome our limited human perspective. To see suffering as having positive aesthetic significance consists in seeing the greater whole and transcending the point of view of my own suffering, and appreciating the part that this plays in the "*large-scale economy*" (*WP* 852; cf. *BGE* 23). To adopt the point of view of the universe is to remove myself from my own concerns and take an impartial and abstracted view of things. From this standpoint, I am a part of a greater, cosmic whole; hence I should think of myself as only a part of a larger whole. I should distance and detach myself from my own point of view, and see my situation as merely part of a whole in which my point of view is unimportant.

Even if we could make sense of how we are supposed to attain perception of the whole, we would still find the unhappy situation that we have a peculiarly unsuitable foundation for a justification of existence. The form of Nietzsche's conception of justification is structured around life-affirmation, and the need for a justification is discharged by producing life-affirmation *in us*. But the appeal to the point of view of the universe cannot achieve this. For suppose I did come to have a definite conception of the world as an aesthetic phenomenon from the point of view of the universe; this would still not be relevant to the problem of how to cope with suffering, until it were endorsed through perception from the relevant point of view. But that point of view is my point of view. The point of view of the universe is useless for me unless it is endorsed as part of my outlook on the universe. The criterion of justification is life-affirmation and hence is not objective but relative to individuals.

On the other hand, it might be argued that if the point of view of the universe displays to us an aesthetic structure or pattern, when I come to appreciate it, I will be moved to conform my own perspective to it. Unfortunately, this too fails to give satisfaction. Suppose for the sake of argument that horrendous suffering is partially constitutive of some aesthetically valuable world order. But would knowledge of such a fact in any way undermine the prima-facie reason for supposing that it would have been better if the infant who is cannibalized by her own parents had never been born?

Another way of construing (b) would be to regard suffering as a kind of aesthetic imperfection that enhances the beauty of the whole. It might be thought that, just as an imperfect nose might add to the beauty of a face, so suffering enhances the beauty of the world. However, for an aesthetic imperfection to contribute to the aesthetic value of the whole, the imperfection's negative aesthetic value must be significantly outweighed by the positively valuable aesthetic features of the whole. The imperfection of a nose can only increase the beauty of the face if the rest of the face is beautiful. But suffering seems not only to cancel out but to engulf what ostensibly has positive aesthetic value in the world. Suffering is not like the ugliness of a small patch of color in a painting that is defeated or canceled out by the positive aesthetic value of the whole.

But does Nietzsche himself subscribe to (b)? A strong reason for thinking that he does not is that in an important passage he explicitly states that seeing suffering as beautiful consists in construing instances of suffering as analogous to "musical dissonance" (*BT* 24). It is "music in general," he says, that can illustrate "what is meant by the justification of the world as an aesthetic phenomenon." For the "pleasure engendered by the tragic myth comes from the same native soil as our pleasurable sensation of dissonance in music" (*BT* 24). Now since suffering is analogous to musical dissonance, it follows that, as in music, these dissonances can be pleasurable, and hence justified. What is crucial here is the fact the Nietzsche elucidates the conception of pleasure he has in mind as a mixture of pain and pleasure, or what he sometimes refers to as "Dionysian joy." This is clearly redolent of the kind of masochistic pleasure he claims elsewhere is attendant upon the perception of suffering *itself*. If this is right, it follows that Nietzsche thinks that suffering is construable as beautiful. Suffering is construable as beautiful, rather than itself beautiful, as in (a), because, as we have seen, Nietzsche's anti-realism about beauty precludes him from subscribing to (a). The pleasure is taken in the dissonance itself, it is not taken in something to which the dissonance is in some way related, as would be the case if Nietzsche subscribed to (b).

That the means of aestheticizing suffering results not in its *objective* aestheticization but rather a falsification of suffering through the very process of its aestheticization cannot be an objection to Nietzsche's justification if we are to assess it on its own terms. For, as we have seen, Nietzsche holds that the presence of falsity is not an objection once one has as it were gone beyond the moral valuation of truth which requires us to align our conception of and value judgments about the world with its objective constitution.

6 Concluding Remarks: The Ethics of Aesthetic Justification

To close, I want to consider briefly the objection, leveled against Nietzsche by (among others) Michael Tanner, that not to try to alleviate suffering, but rather to "attempt to see it as beautiful" seems a "monstrous solution" (Tanner 1993: xxiii) to the problem of how to make life bearable. We might augment this with the point that if we find suffering beautiful, should we not only not seek to alleviate it, but rather welcome and perhaps even inflict it?

This latter question is in fact an empirical one, since there is no conceptual connection between finding suffering beautiful and hence affirming it, and the desire to increase the amount of suffering that the world contains. One could find suffering aesthetically valuable, that is, without being obliged by any logical consideration to go out and inflict it. Moreover, in *BT*, Nietzsche does not make any explicit claims about what one should or should not do in the presence of suffering. To view with aesthetic pleasure some instance of suffering does not preclude a more engaged and active response to its ethical import.

But what are the ethical implications of seeing suffering as beautiful? Let us assume that a necessary condition for finding something immoral is that a person feels a certain emotional repugnance towards it. If you think that a child should not be tortured, part of your view being an *ethical* view is that you find it emotionally repugnant. This is not to say with Ayer and Stephenson that the feeling of emotion is sufficient for the moral judgment. But it does seem that they pinpointed a necessary condition for a judgment being moral.

This certainly seems to be in conflict with the pleasure taken in suffering that is entailed by the experience being aesthetic. If the suffering is found to be beautiful, then there is an aesthetic pleasure taken in it. What one would then have to decide in order to determine the ethical significance of finding suffering beautiful is whether those two emotions are mutually exclusive on the psychological level. For them not to be mutually exclusive, it would have to be possible on one level to find the suffering distasteful and yet to take aesthetic pleasure in it. This doesn't seem much more paradoxical than finding the suffering aesthetically pleasurable in the first place. And it is a feature of our response to tragedy that on the one hand we are repelled by the horrors depicted and on the other pleasurably exhilarated. The ambivalence of emotional response, the antithetical pairing of positive and negative emotions, is found in our response to tragedy, and hence presumably could also figure in the response to real suffering.

We might also inquire as to the moral implications of tragedy itself in order to determine the ethics of Nietzsche's position. In tragedy, suffering is not presented as something valuable, as a goal to be pursued, or as a project to be realized. The thought is more that one can cope better with the suffering with which the world is riddled if one adopts a certain sort of stance in relation to it. But that stance does not call on one to go around inflicting suffering on people. Tragedy teaches us that suffering will be central to life whether we inflict it or not. And that is part of Nietzsche's point. The world makes humans suffer necessarily and inevitably as a function of its nature and our nature as finite creatures.

For Nietzsche, the question of whether it is immoral to aestheticize suffering is subordinate to the question of its life-value. Nietzsche's view is a fiercely pragmatic one. Everyone needs to cope with the issue of not being submerged in misery at the amount of suffering in the world. But unless one believes that God is alive and well and expects "eternal beatitude" in the life to come as compensation for earthly suffering, it is unclear how a sensitive spirit could cope with the horrors of life – at least if "cope" here means something like the ability to endure those horrors rather than simply to evade them by (for example) getting drunk or taking various drugs. If, as Nietzsche claims, unmediated experience of suffering is psychologically incompatible with life-affirmation, then perhaps that would obviate the ethical objections to adopting an aesthetic attitude towards suffering. Perhaps to attempt to see suffering as beautiful is the best that can be hoped for in the circumstances. One would therefore reject Nietzsche's proposal at the price of despair.

See also 9 "The Naturalisms of *Beyond Good and Evil*"; 13 "The Incorporation of Truth: Towards the Overhuman"; 16 "Phenomenology and Science in Nietzsche"; 17 "Naturalism and Nietzsche's Moral Psychology"; 21 "Nietzsche and Ethics"; 27 "Nietzsche, Dionysus, and the Ontology Of Music"

Notes

This essay has benefited greatly from input from Tommy Karshan, Stephen Mulhall, Stephen Priest, Vicky Roupa, and Severin Schroeder.

1   For a full discussion of Nietzsche's anti-moral stance in *BT* see Came 2004.
2   Of course, Nietzsche must persuade us that something's life-value is always more important than its truth-value. Nietzsche must independently demonstrate the authority of his

evaluative criterion before he can make claims that we ought to reject something because it fails to meet this criterion. The demonstration is part of the project of the Third Treatise of *On the Genealogy of Morality*, in which Nietzsche argues that to subordinate considerations pertaining to life to epistemological concerns is constitutive of a Christian, ascetic will to truth and hence motivated by a mistaken world-view.

3 Ivan Soll seems to take this view: see Soll 1998: 100–2.
4 I discuss the role of theodicy in *BT* in detail in Came 2004.
5 Cf. Nietzsche's later claim that "the value of life cannot be *estimated*" (*TI*, "The Problem of Socrates," 2). Note the skeptical import of this remark: it is not that life does not have a value, but rather that its value cannot be "estimated." Geuss is therefore wrong to cite this passage as evidence that Nietzsche came to regard the ascription of value to the world as a kind of category error (Geuss 1999: 109).
6 This explanation of why we find pleasure in tragic art effectively resolves the seeming paradox of tragedy. For as Amy Price notes, as "an expression of the attitude of the sufferer to *his* pain," rather than to the tragedy itself, tragic pleasure "does not exhibit the properties of a philosophical paradox" (Price 1998: 386).

Editions of Nietzsche Used

Beyond Good and Evil, trans. R. J. Hollingdale (Harmondsworth: Penguin, 1990).
The Birth of Tragedy, trans. Walter Kaufmann (New York: Vintage Books, 1967).
Philosophy and Truth: Selections from Nietzsche's Notebooks of the Early 1870s, ed. and trans. Daniel Breazeale (Atlantic Highlands, NJ: Humanities Press, 1979).
Twilight of the Idols, trans. R. J. Hollingdale (Harmondsworth: Penguin, 1990).
The Will to Power, trans. Walter Kaufmann and R. J. Hollingdale (New York: Vintage Books, 1967).

References

Came, Daniel (2004). "Nietzsche's Attempt at a Self-Criticism: Art and Morality in *The Birth of Tragedy*," *Nietzsche-Studien*, 33, pp. 37–67.
Geuss, Raymond (1999). *Morality, Culture, and History: Essays on German Philosophy* (Cambridge: Cambridge University Press).
Hume, David (1985). "Of Tragedy," in Eugene Miller (ed.), *Essays: Moral, Political and Literary* (Indianapolis: Liberty Classics), pp. 216–25.
Price, Amy (1998). "Nietzsche on the Paradox of Tragedy," *British Journal of Aesthetics*, 38, pp. 384–93.
Schopenhauer, Arthur (1969). *The World as Will and Representation*, trans. E. F. J. Payne, 2 vols. (New York: Dover).
Soll, Ivan (1998). "Schopenhauer, Nietzsche, and the Redemption of Life through Art," in Christopher Janaway (ed.), *Willing and Nothingness: Schopenhauer as Nietzsche's Educator* (Oxford: Clarendon Press), pp. 79–105.
Tanner, Michael (1993). "Introduction," in *The Birth of Tragedy*, trans. R. J. Hollingdale (Harmondsworth: Penguin), pp. vii–xxx.

4

Nietzsche on Individuation and Purposiveness in Nature

ELAINE P. MILLER

Introduction

In *The Birth of Tragedy* Nietzsche attributes the force of the Apollonian aesthetic to Apollo's dual role as the god of all plastic energies (the individuating god) and as the soothsaying god (*BT* 1). The latter characterization of Apollo is much more familiar than the first to students of Greek mythology. Apollo is well known as the oracular god and the master of harmony. Nietzsche's description of Apollo as the god of plastic creativity reflects the popular nineteenth-century dissemination of the eighteenth-century historian of ancient art Johann Joachim Winckelmann's archaeological work, which depicts Apollo more metaphysically as the symbol of spirit dominating matter (Bonnefoy 1991: vol. 1, p. 437). And the specific portrayal of Apollo as embodying the principle of individuation seems to indicate Nietzsche's preoccupation with Schopenhauer's dualistic, neo-Kantian metaphysics, that, as is well known, divides being into individuated appearance and formless will. Dionysus, the other natural aesthetic force of *The Birth of Tragedy*, represents, of course, the counterpart to Apollo's formative impulse. Nietzsche's study of *The World as Will and Representation*, according to most scholarly and biographical accounts, dominated his thought around the time he published his first book. Nietzsche certainly uses direct references to Schopenhauer and Schopenhauerian vocabulary when discussing Apollo and Dionysus in *The Birth of Tragedy*.[1] Yet is it correct to simply ascribe the linkage of Apollo with individuation to a somewhat uncritical appropriation of Schopenhauerian vocabulary and metaphysics? Are there other sources of Nietzsche's analysis and use of individuation in *The Birth of Tragedy?* Since individuation as a theme survives Nietzsche's disillusionment with Schopenhauer, can we not trace a broader, less derivative genealogy of its centrality to Nietzsche's thought? I will attempt to answer all of these questions and to trace the origins of Nietzsche's interest in individuation to a scholarly endeavor that predates *The Birth of Tragedy* and arguably influences its development to a degree rarely acknowledged, that is, his proposed but never written dissertation and contemporaneous notes on Immanuel Kant and J. W. von Goethe.

If this argument is correct, Nietzsche's discussion of Apollonian individuation and Dionysian collapse of form in *The Birth of Tragedy* can be shown to be linked to his critique of the purely atomistic or mechanical conception of the cosmos as an

58

explanation that may be true but that remains inadequate, and his argument that mechanical explanations need to be combined with organic "fictions" about nature. Such a combination would not imply a mere supplementation of one form of explanation with another, but would reflect a new kind of individuation that would not reflect a simple antithesis of form and "matter." This is a Kantian and Goethean argument, as I hope to show, but it is transformed by Nietzsche into the demand that organic fictions be multiple rather than uniform and unified, in the sense that Goethe had showed actual organisms in fact were. I propose as well as to show how individuation in this new sense, no longer explicitly linked to Schopenhauer's *principium individuationis*, remains an important theme in Nietzsche's works until the very end of his intellectual life, illuminating the very structure of the will to power.

The Dissertation Proposal

In 1868 Nietzsche wrote a letter to Paul Deussen, which his biographer, Curt Paul Jantz, cites as follows:

> The realm of metaphysics, as well as the province of "absolute truth," have been irremediably lowered to the ranks of poetry and of religion. From now on, whoever wants to know something will have to accommodate himself to the relativity of all knowledge: thus, for example, all the great naturalists. Metaphysics may be, for some, one of the needs of the soul, it is essentially edification; on the other hand, it depends on art, notably the art of the composition of ideas. It turns out that metaphysics has no more to do with what one calls "the true, or the thing in itself" than religion or art.
>
> Besides, when you receive my doctoral dissertation at the end of the year, you will find in it numerous passages where this question of the limits of knowledge will be explicated. I have chosen as my subject "The Idea of the Organism in Kant," half philosophical, half natural science. I have almost finished my preparatory work. (Janz 1978: vol. 1, p. 329)

The Kantian and idealist (even Hegelian, in a sense) tone of this description of the relationship between knowledge of nature, metaphysics, religion, and art, however tempered by Nietzschean cynicism about the true nature and necessity of an overarching system, is unmistakable. The passage rings of the "The Oldest Program Towards a System in German Idealism," albeit in the mocking tone of an exposé of the pretensions of certain metaphysics, in line with Hegel's critique of irony in his *Lectures on Fine Art*. In the *Critique of Judgment* Kant argued that metaphysics or synthesis of the many particular laws of nature into an organic whole or system is, after a fashion, one of the needs of the soul. His contention that this whole could only be the product of a "technic of nature" was expanded, by Schelling, into the idea that metaphysics depends on art. And Hegel, Schelling, and Hölderlin together asserted that poetry would bring together what philosophy had sundered and transform the false hierarchies established through religion into a true equality (Krell 1985: 8–13).

Thus Nietzsche's reference to the "thing-in-itself" and its relation to the true reflects not a simple repudiation of Kant but an awareness of the transformations of Kantian philosophy through Fichte, Schelling, and Hegel, rather than through Schopenhauer, who held on to the equation of the True and the thing-in-itself or Will. Nietzsche's choice of dissertation topic is "The Organism in Kant," a crucial part of the third critique taken up by both Schelling and Hegel in order to show that the infinite or absolute is not something over and against the particular but rather that the individual, as Hegel puts it, "in its particular individuality [. . .] has being absolutely *in itself*" (Hegel 1977: 138).

Although Nietzsche eventually gave up the dissertation topic on the idea of the organism in Kant as unsuitable for a philological project, one cannot deny the impact Kant must have had on Nietzsche from early on. The choice of Kant as the subject of a dissertation at a time when Nietzsche had already discovered and read Schopenhauer – and precisely on the notion of the organism in Kant, a topic Schopenhauer hardly mentions in *The World as Will and Representation* – shows us that the well-known representation of the early Nietzsche as entranced by Schopenhauer, and familiar with Kant only through Schopenhauer, is not entirely accurate. Indeed, a set of notes and drafted paragraphs entitled "Zu Schopenhauer," written just previously to the dissertation notes, attests to Nietzsche's early critical stance toward Schopenhauer. In these notes Nietzsche criticizes Schopenhauer for attempting to explain the world according to only one very particular assumption, such that "the thing-in-itself takes on *one* of its possible forms" (my emphasis), an attempt which Nietzsche immediately and decisively evaluates as "unsuccessful" (*BAW* 1:3, p. 352).

Shift to the Critique of Teleology

What was this "one possible form"? To understand, we must first situate Kant and Goethe's critique of teleological judgment and their provisional privilege of the organism with reference to the tradition they were addressing. It was a common practice of late eighteenth-century science to posit final causes in nature. For example, the eighteenth-century Swedish botanist Carl von Linné (Linnaeus) suggested that herbivores were placed on earth in order to control the plant population, predators to limit the herbivores, and human beings to hunt and thus regulate the carnivorous predators. Both Kant and Goethe took umbrage at this kind of reductive theory of purposiveness. What both Kant and Goethe strove to accomplish in intertwining the realms of art and nature, as Kant does in the *Critique of Judgment*, and Goethe in his scientific work, was twofold: first, to discredit unreflectively ontological scientific assumptions of final causes in nature, and second, to reintroduce purposiveness in nature as an *aesthetic* requirement for the creation of satisfactory, i.e. systematic, scientific explanations. We can see Nietzsche's positing of dual *aesthetic forces of nature* in *The Birth of Tragedy* as a transformed successor to this tradition.

In early notebooks from Nietzsche's *Nachlass* we find a draft of Nietzsche's dissertation proposal, composed during his student years in Leipzig, sometime in 1868. Nietzsche entitles the draft "Teleology since Kant"[2] rather than "The Idea of the Organism in Kant," but the two themes are clearly related, as we will see in discussing Kant's *Critique of Judgment*. Appended to this set of notes, which encompasses a 20-page series of drafts of paragraphs, Nietzsche includes a full bibliographical reference as well as numerous direct quotations from Kant's *Critique of Judgment*, in particular from the Critique of Teleological Judgment. Nietzsche begins the draft with a reading list, presumably one he had read prior to what he wrote, since another reading list, with the heading "to be read," follows the unfinished essay. The initial reading list includes Hume's *Dialogues Concerning Natural Religion* and Kant's *Critique of Pure Reason* and *Critique of Judgment*, as well as Kuno Fischer's commentary on Kant (*BAW* 1:3, p. 371).

The first section of the draft, "On Teleology," begins with the observation that optimism and teleology go hand in hand. This theme resurfaces in *The Birth of Tragedy*, where modern science is linked to post-Socratic "Greek cheerfulness," and Kant and Schopenhauer's philosophy is characterized as overcoming the optimism of logic. In the published work, Nietzsche speculates that the Greeks became more and more optimistic and superficial with the dissolution of their culture; he pairs logic and science in general to the equation of knowledge with progress. This gives us a clear indication of the connection Nietzsche would draw between the decline of the Greeks in their move toward theoretical knowledge over tragic wisdom, and the tendency in the science of his day to explain natural phenomena uncritically in terms of anthropocentric purposes (see *BT* 18 and 19).

From the dissertation notes and drafts one learns that Nietzsche's critique of the centrality of purposiveness in natural scientific explanations of his day, and the resulting anthropocentrism of supposedly scientific depictions of nature, draws explicitly on the organic-centered philosophy of Kant and Goethe. Nietzsche criticizes both purely mechanistic and uncritically purposive depictions of natural forces in the manner of both Kant and Goethe. Nietzsche's later use of the language of will to power builds upon the Kantian conception of natural *formative* (as opposed to motive or mechanical) forces to counter atomistic or mechanical cosmologies that reduce being to an aggregate of discrete parts of matter in motion, and to explain how it is that in a world composed of fluctuating energies, we perceive things as interrelating objects. He thus leaves room for a mitigated account of purposiveness in his discussion of individuation as the manifestation of a primordial unity through provisional and fleeting form.

Nietzsche betrays his Kantianism in arguing that it is the constitution of the human cognitive powers that gives the impression of discrete objects that perdure in space and time, although he draws more skeptical conclusions from this limitation of human cognition than Kant would allow. He writes explicitly in 1881:

> We must always remain skeptical with regard to all of our experiences, and say, for example: we can assert the eternal value of no "law of nature," assert the eternal persistence of no chemical quality; we are not finely tuned enough to see the supposed absolute flow of becoming: the perdurant is there only thanks to our unrefined organs which summarize and display that which really does not exist at all. The tree is something new at every moment: we assert form because we are incapable of perceiving the most precise absolute movement. (*KSA* 9, 11[293])

Although Nietzsche's critique in his earliest notes on teleology in nature takes Kant's Critique of Teleological Judgment as its point of departure, he also uses Goethe's scientific writings as a way of adapting Kant's view to his own perspective. Specifically, the debate that Nietzsche sets up centers around the question of whether one understands nature traditionally in terms of a hierarchical progression that categorizes and ranks natural forms (a view that coincides with reductive accounts of purposiveness in the natural science of Linnaeus), or, alternatively, whether one describes natural becoming as the coincidence of force and restraint (formation) such that neither implies a priority over the other. For Nietzsche, like Kant, any "thing-in-itself" can only be thought negatively, in relation to the shapes of appearance or expression of force, and the constitution of the human mind cannot be determined to be either prior or subsequent to the forms that it perceives. For Nietzsche, "form" and "individuation" are other names for "energy" or "force" expressed in particular ways, names that developed dynamically and historically.

Though Nietzsche will use the language of organicism, the organism itself is a name for the most fortuitous coincidence of excess and individuation, or a particular configuration of what is called Dionysian and Apollonian in the early work on tragedy, namely, the organization of forces most conducive to survival. "Organism," for Nietzsche, does not coincide with "individual," for, as he notes early on, citing Goethe, no living thing is really an individual (*BAW* 1:3, p. 376). This caveat works both spatially, in the sense of there being no real physical individual, and temporally, in the sense of a tree, for example, being something new at every moment. Nietzsche writes in 1872, sounding very Hegelian, "there is no *form* in nature, because there is no distinction between inner and outer" (*KSA* 7, 19[144]; *Unpublished Writings*, p. 47; see also Hegel 1977: 160).

Kant's Organicism and Critique of Teleological Judgment

Kant's philosophy of the organism and its link to the possibility of attributing a purposiveness to nature is the ostensible focus of Nietzsche's dissertation project. Kant's technic of nature is informed by the notion of "organism" or "organized being" as the privileged individual that underlies his discussion of teleology as an organizing or systematic force. It is important here to note the connection between teleology and individuation that rests in the figure of the organism. These beings, Kant writes,

> first give objective reality to the concept of a *purpose* that is a purpose *of nature* rather than a practical one, and which hence give natural science the basis for a teleology, i.e., for judging its objects in terms of a special principle that otherwise we simply would not be justified in introducing into natural science (since we have no *a priori* insight whatever into the possibility of such a causality). (Kant 1987: 376)

The perception of organized beings as *self-organizing* allows them to be referred to as natural purposes, according to Kant. A machine, Kant writes, has within itself only a motive force; it requires an external impetus to set it in motion, and if parts are removed from it, it cannot regenerate them nor compensate for their lack by having the other parts help out, much less repair itself (1987: 374). Organisms, by contrast, have within themselves what Kant calls a *formative* force that organizes and propagates itself in a way that cannot be explained through mere mechanism (1987: 374).

Natural purposes, in turn, form the basis for judging nature as a whole teleologically, as a system of purposes (or itself an "organism"). This principle applies only subjectively as the maxim that "everything in the world is good for something or other; nothing in it is gratuitous" (1987: 379), and is a regulative rather than constitutive principle. The principle relies on the peculiarity (*Eigentümlichkeit*) of human understanding, namely, that it cannot rest satisfied with purely mechanical explanations, but must follow the demand of reason that "subordinates such [natural] products [. . .] to the causality in terms of purposes" (1987: 415).

Beyond their internal form, Kant also privileges the form of the natural structures, and of the organism in particular, as the figure that not only justifies the attribution of purposiveness to nature as a regulative ideal, but that also best manifests the nature of the relationship of human cognition to nature. Kant privileges organized beings in nature, stating that they have an "absolute purposiveness" (1987: 217, "First Introduction"). The absolute nature of the purposiveness of the organism, however, has, for Kant, its origin in the human apprehension of it, and not (at least not demonstrably) in itself, a conception that changed in the philosophies of Hegel and Schelling. Insofar as humans cognize nature on the basis of cause and effect or dissection of its parts, Kant implies, natural explanations can be mechanical ones. As soon as one attempts to make any claims about the whole, however, Kant maintains the *absolute necessity* of human cognition proceeding *technically* (from *techne*, or "art"), making the systematicity of nature a subjective aesthetic mandate in which organisms viewed purposively play a central part and indeed provide the figure under which we conceive of nature as a whole.

This requirement relates to the central claim put forward in second edition of Nietzsche's *The Birth of Tragedy* (1886): "To look at science in the perspective of art, but art in that of life" (*BT*, "Attempt at a Self-Criticism," 2). It is clear from Nietzsche's study of teleology in natural science and from various comments interspersed throughout *The Birth of Tragedy*, that when he speaks of "science" (*Wissenschaft*) here, it is not merely in reference to a general term for a certain kind of drive to knowledge that started with Socrates, but also to the practice of natural science of the nineteenth century. In this sense he is reiterating Kant's claim.

Nietzsche begins "Teleology since Kant" by quoting Kant's assertion that the purposiveness of the organic as well as the lawfulness of the inorganic are brought to these phenomena by human understanding rather than inhering in nature. After an introductory set of paragraphs, however, Nietzsche abruptly switches to a polemical mode: "There is no question that is necessarily solved through the assumption of an intelligible world" (*BAW* 1:3, p. 373). What Nietzsche most objects to is the hierarchizing of purposes, ultimately assigning the supersensible world the highest value. Even if we can assign purposiveness to a thing, he writes, the most we can conclude from this is the existence of reason; we have no right to go on to judge this reason as either higher or lower, or to appeal to any purposiveness that is beyond sensibility.

While delegitimizing claims of purposiveness in nature, Kant nevertheless continued to privilege the unknowable. This Nietzsche sees implied when Kant makes a move toward ranking purposes, illegitimate even on his own terms, in claiming, briefly, in the third *Critique*, that the human being is the final cause of nature by virtue of its noumenal nature (Kant 1987: 435). The noumenal status of the human being as *end* and never as *means* – not its erect posture, developed brain, or living habits – led Kant to posit the human being as the creature of highest purposiveness. Thus, Nietzsche claims, Kant ultimately falls prey to the same anthropocentrism in natural science that he wished to critique.

Goethe's Aesthetic Philosophy of Nature

The second part of Nietzsche's dissertation project draft is an engagement with Goethe's natural philosophy. In a passage entitled "Goethe's Attempt," Nietzsche links the structure of metamorphosis to the detachment of the concepts of growth, development, and transformation from the idea of an originary source. Nietzsche writes that the theory of metamorphosis derives the organism from a cause that is undiscoverable, and adds, "this precisely proves that it is the correct human path" (*BAW* 1:3, p. 380). Nietzsche thus uses Goethe to approach and modify Kant's position on teleology and the organism, specifically Kant's attempt to trace, in Nietzsche's view illegitimately, the source of unity ultimately to the human supersensible self, including ultimately the postulate of an overarching coherence in the mind of a god in whom he had previously argued that it was unjustifiable to believe through rational means (see *GS* 335).

Nietzsche notes with appreciation that "Goethe understood the position of the human being in nature, and that of surrounding nature itself, to be more mysterious, enigmatic, and demonic than his contemporaries did" (*KSA* 7, 29[116], p. 684; *Unpublished Writings*, p. 247). Nietzsche was aware of the prevailing practice in eighteenth- and even nineteenth-century studies of nature to assign individual purposes to natural things; in addition, he knew of both Kant and Goethe's critique of teleological science's tendency to trace all purposes back to utility for the human being's needs. Nietzsche admired Goethe for both his acquiescence in the mysterious and impenetrable in nature, for the fact that he was not only a scientist but at the same time an artist, and for Goethe's self-reflective complication of Kant's anthropocentrism. The artist is the one who eschews the desire to ascertain origins in favor of expressing multiple masks of becoming. As in *The Birth of Tragedy*, the Dionysian only comes to appearance through the forms of the Apollonian aesthetic force, yet its meaning is not exhausted in the sum total of those forms, nor can their provenance ever be completely fathomed.

Dionysus is also the god of metamorphosis. After reading Goethe's scientific writings, Nietzsche adopted the terminology of metamorphosis. The overwhelming presence of the god Dionysus in all the notebooks written around the time of *The Birth of Tragedy* and beyond attests to the importance of the idea of metamorphosis for Nietzsche. Dionysus is the god of metamorphosis, whose symbols, the mask, the ivy, and the vine, all exhibit the plant-like characteristics of indefinite sequentiality and unpredictable transformation. Walter F. Otto describes the Dionysian plants in the following way:

> The vine and the ivy [. . .] undergo an amazing metamorphosis. In the cool season of the year the vine lies as though dead and in its dryness resembles a useless stump until the moment when it feels the renewed heat of the sun and blossoms forth in a riot of green [. . .]

[The ivy]'s cycle of growth gives evidence of a duality which is quite capable of suggesting the two-fold nature of Dionysos. First it puts out the so-called shade-seeking shoots, the ascendant tendrils with the well-known lobed leaves. Later, however, a second kind of shoot appears which grows upright and turns toward the light. The leaves are formed completely differently, and now the plant produces flowers and berries. Like Dionysos, it could well be called the "twice-born." (Otto 1965: 153–4)

In 1871 Nietzsche's notebooks are still full of references to Goethe, particularly when Nietzsche is remarking on the power of particular representations of nature, but also when he is explicitly tying together depictions of the structure of nature and of human achievement. For example, Nietzsche writes, among a series of seemingly unconnected notes: "The meaning of *history*: a metamorphosis of plants. Example" (*KSA* 7, 19[212], p. 485; *Unpublished Writings*, p. 66). For Nietzsche, Goethe embodied the capacity to see nature simultaneously with the eye of the philosopher and with the eye of the artist. Nietzsche grants the greatest power to the capacity to see nature aesthetically, a power that Goethe above all possessed: "The cult of nature. That is our most truest experience of art. The more powerfully and magically nature is presented, the more we believe in it. *Goethe on nature*" (*KSA* 7, 9[85], p. 305). This conviction is presented in a most developed way, of course, in *The Birth of Tragedy*, in the guises of both the Dionysian and the Apollonian aesthetic forces of nature.

Multiple Purposivenesses

Kant inaugurated what Nietzsche refers to as "tragic philosophy" or "Dionysian wisdom comprised in concepts" (*BT* 19) in forever cutting the knower off from the thing-in-itself, substituting wisdom for science. Like Kant, Nietzsche recognized the power of the drive to ascertain origins and the need that science and philosophy have to account for the emergence of beings; Nietzsche follows Kant in the conviction that such an explanation reflects the structure of human inquiry rather than any essence of being. Using Kant's language from the third *Critique*, Nietzsche writes in a notebook: "The *philosopher's description of nature*: he arrives at knowledge by poeticizing [*dichten*], and poeticizes by arriving at knowledge" (*KSA* 7, 19[62], p. 439; *Unpublished Writings*, p. 23).[3]

Among the themes that emerge from Nietzsche's discussion of the organism of Kant we may recognize seeds of themes that would dominate his later thought: the principle of metamorphosis interpreted as the perennial self-transformation of becoming informs the concepts of self-overcoming, the eternal recurrence of the same, and the will to power, while the idea of the provisionality of any theory of individuation finds expression in Nietzsche's critique of consciousness, the fiction of the ego, and language formation. Nietzsche assumes that all individual existences are transformative masks for the manifestation of an eternally repeating temporal becoming. A passage from an early notebook states that "every hero is a symbol of Dionysos" (*KSA* 7, 7[81], p. 156). However, Goethean metamorphosis, as Nietzsche understands it, improves on the Kantian technic of nature in that it circumvents the issue of source by positing a constant transformation of everything into everything else. This leads into Nietzsche's solution to the antithesis between mechanistic and organismic views of nature: the idea of multiple purposivenesses, a transformation of Kant's technic of nature, viewed through the lens of metamorphosis.

The sole weapon one could wield against the reductive doctrine of final causes, Nietzsche writes in 1868, would be the discovery of a proof of something that is not purposive. This discovery would prove that even the highest reason (*Vernunft*) has been only sporadically effective, and that there is thus room for multiple lesser "reasons," that there is no *unity* in the teleological world" (*BAW* 1:3, p. 372). Nietzsche proposes an "Empedoclean point of view" in which the purposive is just one case among many, the purposive being the exception rather than the rule. This possibility of simultaneous multiple explanations of nature is a corrective to the limitation that Nietzsche saw in both Kant and Schopenhauer, namely that the thing-in-itself was conceived as only having one possible form. Among other things, "Empedoclean" science would presuppose that, although any underlying "truth" about nature will remain hidden from human understanding, the intuitable components of nature are erratic and arbitrary impulses that can only sometimes be interpreted as rational purposes. The truth of nature thus reveals itself as fully irrational, even if it can occasionally be represented as rational (*BAW* 1:3, p. 372).

The purposive, Nietzsche argues, arose as a particular case of the possible. In other words, life, the root of purposive explanations, evolved as one configuration out of infinite mechanically composed constellations or possibilities of constellations, among which countless others could have been capable of life (*BAW* 1:3, p. 379). Kant denies that life could have originated out of mechanical forces, but, Nietzsche writes, what we can *know* is only the mechanical, even if our understanding organizes itself according to purposiveness. What lies beyond our concepts (Nietzsche, following Kant, considers concepts to be "mechanical") is fully unknowable by Kant's own claim. In terms of our own organization the only knowledge that we are conditioned to understand would indicate a mechanical origin of all things. Thus the purposive explanation involves a creative leap, as well as the elimination of countless accidental details in order to reach the simplicity of the unified and self-enclosed individual. Kant makes this leap, according to Nietzsche, in proceeding from the definition of the organized body as that thing whose parts are purposively connected with each other to the notion of the organism as a purposive being per se (*BAW* 1:3, p. 378), and from there to the comprehensive purposive unity of the natural world as a system. Nietzsche argues that mechanism linked with causality could provide the same explanation for the organism, and that this in itself is enough to set Kant's definition aside (although not enough to embrace a mechanical picture of becoming or any other definitive explanation of the meaning of the organism and of life). Though Kant appears to carefully derive the necessity of systematicity from the perceived parallel structure of our intellect and the self-regulating causality of the organism, his argument ultimately rests, Nietzsche argues, on a *conviction*, rather than a demonstration, that nothing is comparable to the purposiveness and the unity of the organism.

Individuation

What we call "individuals" are actually pluralities, or rather, Nietzsche writes, "individuals" and "organisms" are nothing but abstractions. Nietzsche quotes Goethe to the effect that, although each living thing appears to us to be an individual, there are no unities in nature; each is in fact a gathering or collection (*Versammlung*) of living being (*Wesen*) (*BAW* 1:3, p. 376; see also Goethe 1949: vol. 17, p. 14 and 1988: 64). On this account, and since metamorphosis posits the organism as deriving from a cause that is undiscoverable (*BAW* 1:3, p. 380), one should not try to seek the final cause of inorganic nature because here one can see no individuals, only forces. This means that since, on Nietzsche's view, everything can be traced to "blind forces," one can no longer believe in determinate purposes. By "blind forces" Nietzsche refers not to anything determinately inorganic, but to what cannot be individuated except "mechanically," i.e. through concepts. What is capable of life is formed only through "an endless chain of failures and half-successful attempts" (*BAW* 1:3, p. 381). Since in nature only inorganic forces prevail, things that appear to be purposive are only appearances, and their purposiveness is "our idea" (*BAW* 1:3, p. 381). Organisms manifest only forces that work blindly. Face to face with the unknown, human beings have no recourse except to invent concepts, but these concepts can only bring us to a collection of apparent qualities that will not ever make the leap to a living body (*Leib*). This applies equally to the notions of force, substance, individual, law, organism, atom, and final cause (*BAW* 1:3, p. 383).

To derive the general origin of organic life from observing nature's means of providing for and preserving organisms would not characterize the Empedoclean way of doing science, Nietzsche writes. It is, however, the Epicurean way. By "Epicurean way," Nietzsche is referring to the atomic understanding of being, in which a whole can be derived from a sum of parts, and which allows for an end-point in the endless process of dividing matter. Such an understanding takes an isolatable body as its point of departure. Startlingly, Nietzsche seems to conflate the mechanistic with the organismic view of nature here. To derive the origin of organic life from the empirical observation of the self-preservation of organisms would be equivalent to understanding nature mechanistically, in terms of discrete parts that make up wholes. Nietzsche's line of reasoning proceeds as follows:

> The question is precisely, what "life" is, whether it is just a mere principle of order and form (as with the tragedy), or whether it is something entirely different: against this it must be conceded that within organic nature in the relationship of organisms to each other no other principle exists that does not also exist in inorganic nature. The method of Nature in the treatment of things is equal, she is an impartial mother, equally severe toward inorganic and organic children. (*BAW* 1:3, pp. 385–6)

This passage both echoes and reverses the fragment "Die Natur" that was thought to have been written by the young Goethe. This fragment contains many passages like the following: "[Nature's] children are without number. From none does she withhold all gifts, but upon her favorites she lavishes much and for them she sacrifices much."[4] For Nietzsche, by contrast, Nature has no favorites. It is easy to overlook the strange analogy of natural life to tragedy here, which is only explicable if one looks at the Apollonian/Dionysian birth of tragedy in terms of Nietzsche's concurrent interest in the critique of teleology and the organism in the philosophy of nature.

Nietzsche returns to the question as to whether the force that creates the thing is identical to the force that preserves it. To elaborate on what he has characterized as an "Empedoclean" way of understanding nature, he asks, what is "organism" other than formed life? If the organism's parts are not necessary to it – in other words, if forms other than the organic can be thought of that would equally support life – then one cannot argue that the essence of the organic lies in its form; purposiveness is not reducible to form. On the other hand, one also does not want to say that the organism is mere life without form. Thus, Nietzsche concludes, life has as many different purposivenesses as forms (*BAW* 1:3, pp. 386–7). This relates to Nietzsche's perception of Empedocles' doctrine of movement. Empedocles posited a cosmic vortex, "the opposite of ordered movement" (*KSA* 7, 23[32], p. 552; *Unpublished Writings*, p. 127). In the same way, given Nietzsche's understanding of the relationship between space and time, the organism cannot simply be the result of a single, linear, ordered progression of forms. The polemic against Kant is directed not toward Kant's ultimate conclusion, that purposiveness is brought to nature by human understanding; rather, Nietzsche objects to the assumption that the form organisms have taken follows a singular purposiveness, that we assume that nature was created in the best possible way.

In this claim Nietzsche follows Goethe, who insisted that scientific points of departure conceal as much as they reveal, and must evolve over time, and who advocated a metamorphosis of the scientist parallel to the observed metamorphosis of natural phenomena. Nietzsche got his idea of "multiple purposivenesses," multiple possibilities for understanding nature's tendencies, from reading Goethe. The notion of a whole, in the end, can only be constructed from the point of view of the observer in his or her capacity to synthesize, but this whole has no stability over time.

Rationality and Purposiveness

Nietzsche thus concludes that life is possible under as many forms as there are perspectives. Each of these forms is purposive in a sense, but there are as many types of purposiveness as forms, not one overarching teleology. Nietzsche objects to "rationality" defined as the principle of sufficient reason – the greatest possible narrowing down of a field of possibilities. He writes, "In human life we make a progression in the purposive: we only call it 'reasonable' [*vernünftig*] when a very narrow choice is available. When a person finds the only purposive way in a complicated situation, we say that he is acting rationally. However, when one wants to travel all over the world and follows any old road, one is acting purposively but not rationally." This reductive notion of rationality cannot even begin to touch on the explanation of life: "When we speak of purposive concepts and causes, we only mean: out of a living and thinking thing a form is intentionalized [*intentionirt*], in which it wants to appear" (*BAW* 1:3, p. 387). In other words, "form" always implies a reduction or abstraction of life.

The scientific grasp of life rests ultimately on nothing but static forms conceived as unitary and monolithic individuals. These forms do not comprehend the "eternally becoming" (*ewige Werdende*) that life is. "Forms" are analogous to "individuals," for both words are used to describe organisms conceived as unities in the sense of purposive centers. However, there are unities only for our intellect. If the organism is not an individual, nothing can be, for as Kant showed, nothing more coherent and cohesive exists naturally than self-motivating and self-regulating organism.

Finally, Nietzsche asks whether human beings *need* purposive causes to explain *that* something lives. He concludes that teleology is not necessary to account for life, but only to justify it. We do not need final causes to explain the life of a thing, for " 'life' is something that is entirely obscure, that we can shed no further light on through final causes." Moreover, purposiveness is no absolute notion, but only relative to perspective (*BAW* 1:3, pp. 388–90). Nietzsche thus agrees with Kant that purposiveness lies only in human reflective judgment, but objects along with Goethe to the assumption that a unified purposiveness is the *only* form under which humans can cognize nature. He ends the passage with a question: if "life" as a concept is linked to human consciousness, then what in nature brought about human existence? Did a lack of self-consciousness cause the concept of "life" to arise? Was the notion of life conducive to the formation of self-consciousness? Did it induce human beings to reflect on their position? Humans are unable to approach "life" in general from anything other than a human perspective, in analogy to human life. Even the division into organic and inorganic, then, arises out of human observation of what is similar to and alien to the human being, and the subsequent demand for an explanation that arises from such an examination.[5] Such questions, of course, gain prominence in Nietzsche's later published work, particularly around the time of *The Gay Science* and *Thus Spoke Zarathustra*, but also in *The Will to Power*.

The Legacy of the Dissertation Project in Nietzsche's Later Work

The critique of teleology and the organism in Kant plays itself out in Nietzsche's later thought in multiple and non-systematic ways. Nietzsche continues to focus on the idea of the organism, both positively as a self-regulating purposiveness and self-sufficiency that regulates the way in which we desire, and negatively as an obstacle to a force-centered ontology of will to power. On Nietzsche's view, the fiction of the organism, understood as the natural individual par excellence, formed the basis of the modern account of how consciousness developed and the subsequent belief in the substantiality and individuality of the human ego. Thus Nietzsche's critique of the organic and of teleology cannot be separated from his discussion of consciousness and of language, which he alternately blames for the creation and perpetuation of a subject-centered metaphysics, and excuses for merely manifesting the effects of an already existing conception of subjectivity based on the reification of individuation.

I will focus briefly on three ways in which themes articulated in the dissertation project relate to Nietzsche's later work. First, Nietzsche continues to mock uncritically anthropocentric interpretations of scientific theories, in particular those that posit the human being as the telos of natural being. In the second *Untimely Meditation* Nietzsche repeatedly belittles the attempt to ascertain the purposiveness of nature in a way that recalls Goethe's diatribe against the teleologists of the early nineteenth century (see, for example, *UM II*, 9). In a notebook he used from late 1870 to early 1871, Nietzsche quotes Goethe: "the human never grasps how anthropomorphic he is" (*KSA* 7, 5[39], p. 103). Nietzsche's barbs are not aimed solely at contemporary popular philosophy in this respect, but also, again, at the natural sciences, and particularly at the growing popularity of the theory of evolution, which he took to be the height of anthropomorphic fantasy:

> Contemplation of history has never flown so far, not even in dreams; for now the history of mankind is only the continuation of the history of animals and plants; even in the profoundest depths of the sea the universal historian still finds traces of himself as living slime; gazing in amazement, as at a miracle, at the tremendous course humankind has already run, his gaze trembles at that even more astonishing miracle, the modern human himself, who is capable of surveying this course. He stands high and proud upon the pyramid of the world-process; as he lays the keystone of his knowledge at the top of it he seems to call out to nature all around him: "We have reached the goal, we are the goal, we are nature perfected." (*UM II*, 9)

All the hidden implications for the importance of the human being as the purpose of nature strike Nietzsche as what is insidious about theories that purport to approach nature "neutrally," yet which explain the evolution of human beings as the pinnacle of nature. Nevertheless, Nietzsche still advocates an attentive anthropocentrism that does not reduce the human being to self-evident platitudes, suggesting that it is not possible to practice science without being anthropocentric. In the year 1872–3, Nietzsche's continuing concern with the critique of the self-serving implications of research into nature is reflected in the following note: "All natural science is nothing but an attempt to understand the human being, the anthropological: to be more precise, an attempt constantly to return to the human being by way of the most lengthy detours. The human being swells up to embrace the macrocosm, so as in the end to say, 'in the end, you are what you are'" (*KSA* 7, 19[91], p. 449; *Unpublished Writings*, p. 33). Such an effort, however, assumes from the outset the self-evident nature and the explicability of the human being.

For Nietzsche, by contrast, the "profundity [of the world] is disclosed to [the human being] to the extent that he is amazed at himself and his own complexity" (*KSA* 7, 19[118], p. 458; *Unpublished Writings*, p. 41). An excessive focus on singular origins that tends to privilege the unambiguous, the individual, and the unified, leads to an equal neglect of the question of the meaning and the complexity of the position of the human being in the natural world. Nietzsche mocked natural science's belief that it can circumvent worldviews, subjective projection, theological assumptions, and the like through carefully controlled observation and strictly empirical methods. The notion of objectivity is simply one of many metamorphoses of the human story about nature. Nietzsche advocates a transformed anthropomorphism that would recognize the complexity of this being called human as well as the utter impossibility of coming upon a single universal explanation of what we are. This revised anthropomorphism involves the recognition of the necessary use of masks in explaining any natural phenomenon, not the attempt to do away with masks or a lapse into despair:

> For the tragic philosopher the *image of existence* is made complete by the insight that the metaphysical only appears in anthropomorphic form. He is not a *skeptic*. [. . .] Once it reaches its limitations, the drive for knowledge turns against itself in order to proceed to the *critique of knowing*. Knowledge in the service of the best life. (*KSA* 7, 19[35]; *Unpublished Writings*, p. 13)

The reference to Kant as a tragic philosopher in *The Birth of Tragedy*, together with the advocacy of a "*critique* of knowing," point to an alliance with the Kantian critical project.

Secondly, Nietzsche's critique of the primacy accorded to consciousness forms a parallel discourse to his discussion of teleology and the organism. This is because what Nietzsche criticizes in the privilege accorded to consciousness is the same anthropocentric teleological ideology he sees hidden within it that privileges the human being as the final purpose of the organic. The basis of this hierarchy within the organic, as Nietzsche understands it, is the classification that distinguishes between non-living organic material (minerals), living but unconscious organisms (plants), conscious but not self-conscious organisms (animals), and self-conscious organisms that possess the capacity to articulate their self-consciousness (humans).

Nietzsche's critique of consciousness in *The Gay Science*, published in 1882, is well known. Here he writes:

> Consciousness is the last and latest development of the organic and hence also what is most unfinished and least powerful. [. . .] One thinks that it constitutes the *kernel* of the human being; what is abiding, eternal, ultimate, and most original in it. One takes consciousness for a determinate magnitude! One denies its growth and its intermittences! Takes it for the "unity of the organism"! (*GS* 11)

The passage goes on to say that the advantage of the importance humans accord to conscious thinking has the advantage of *hindering* a precipitous development of consciousness (since it is assumed to already have reached the height of its powers); such a restraint effects the appearance of unity. The illusion of unity, in turn, functions as a protective mechanism in the development of the organism.

Finally, in Nietzsche's notes from the 1880s collected under the title *The Will to Power*, two sections are relevant to the questions we have been considering here. To some readers, the material on "The Will to Power in Nature," subdivided into "The Mechanistic Interpretation of the World" and "The Will to Power as Life," seems oddly out of place in Nietzsche's intellectual corpus. Walter Kaufmann notes that there is no close parallel to this material in Nietzsche's published works (*WP* 332 n. 53). Indeed, without knowledge of the early dissertation proposal, it is hard to see a sustained reflection on the philosophy of nature even in *The Birth of Tragedy*. Given the close connection between the work on tragedy and Nietzsche's early interest in teleology and the organism, however, we can discern in these late notes an abiding interest in the question of the way in which the cosmos is represented. The "will to power" is arguably the way in which Nietzsche strove to mediate between or provide a third position/alternative to the mechanistic interpretation of the world, on the one hand, and the organismic view, on the other.

ELAINE P. MILLER

Nietzsche situates himself in the context of questions that the mechanistic view finds difficult to answer in the first note included in this section:

> Of all the interpretations of the world attempted hitherto, the mechanistic one seems today to stand victorious in the foreground. It evidently has a good conscience on its side; and no science believes it can achieve progress and success except with the aid of mechanistic procedures. Everyone knows these procedures: one leaves "reason" and "purpose" out of account as far as possible. [. . .] Meanwhile, a presentiment, or anxiety is to be noted among select spirits involved in this movement, as if the theory had a hole in it that might sooner or later prove to be its final hole. [. . .] One cannot "explain" pressure and stress themselves, one cannot get free of the *actio in distans* – one has lost the belief in being able to explain at all. (*WP* 618)

Nietzsche goes on to state his view that the concept of force needs to be ascribed an inner will, designated "will to power," which might also be characterized as a "creative drive" (*WP* 619). The human being, and indeed all organic life, is to be thought of in analogy to this force (*WP* 619). The purely neutral and mechanistic forces, such as attraction and repulsion, need to be supplemented with *intention*; a force that we cannot imagine is a mere abstraction (*WP* 627; see also 621).

Such forces are not law-governed or necessary, Nietzsche writes, but we believe them to be so because we need "unities" in order to be able to calculate. Such "unities" are fictions, individuations that we believe to be stable because without them we could not comprehend the world (*WP* 635; see also 624). But we take the notion of a unity or atom from our "ego-concept," what Nietzsche calls "our oldest article of faith" upon which all the rest of our knowledge is predicated (*WP* 635). Again, Nietzsche is making a Kantian argument of a sort, with the aim of overcoming the very gap between theoretical and practical reason that Kant addressed in the *Critique of Judgment*. Nietzsche writes here that will to power is "noumenal," whereas number, motion, unity, and our conception of self are "phenomenal" (*WP* 635), yet he had already considered ways to overcome this distinction (see *BGE* 36). Likewise, he writes that the need to project unity (in this case multiple unities) is a subjective requirement rather than an objective reality, although overcoming this distinction is a key point of the argument.

In his discussion of organic life in *The Will to Power*, Nietzsche reiterates his early assertion of there being no essential distinction between organic and inorganic life. Both are expressions of will to power, although organic life resists domination more strongly and thereby allows will to power to manifest itself more successfully against its resistance (*WP* 656; see also 658). Will to power thus has the *formative* force that for Kant separated organic life from purely mechanical explanations. At the same time will to power is not organic in form; its assimilating and shaping force manifests itself equally in the organic and the inorganic.

Nietzsche is constantly concerned with the representation of nature, which in turn informs the way in which human beings look at themselves and at their position in the world. For the most part this is an unreflective process. In a notebook written in from late 1873 to early 1874 Nietzsche laments, "We are all thoughtless naturalists, and we are fully aware of it" (*KSA* 7, 30[26], p. 741; *Unpublished Writings*, p. 302).

72

Despite the proliferation of "knowledge" about natural phenomena, or perhaps as a result of this plethora of data, we tend to think less and less about the way in which we represent nature as a whole. From the beginning of his academic career, in his thoughts for a dissertation project, and at the end of his intellectual life, in sketching out ideas for an ontology of will to power, Nietzsche was concerned with not just how human beings should live, but how best to think about the natural world that gives rise to human being and ultimately supersedes it. Will to power is another way to conceive of the overcoming of the subjective/objective distinction that Kant struggles with in the third *Critique* in attempting to bridge the gap between nature and freedom. If will to power is not purposive per se, it does have intentionality, and thus it manifests purposiveness as one of its multiple possibilities. Organic life is one possibility, a possibility that in its resistance to incorporation perhaps allows will to power to express itself more richly. But Nietzsche wanted to keep us attentive to the possibility of nature taking on forms that we cannot predict, and which might leave the notion of individuation – and even of ourselves – behind.

See also 13 "The Incorporation of Truth: Towards the Overhuman"; 28 "Nietzsche and Evolutionary Theory"; 30 "Nietzsche's Theory of the Will to Power"; 31 "A Critique of the Will to Power"

Notes

This essay contains significant revision of the material that appeared in Miller 2001.

1 Nietzsche writes that "*in one sense* we might apply to Apollo the words of Schopenhauer when he speaks of the man wrapped in the veil of *maya*: 'Just as in a stormy sea that, unbounded in all directions, raises and drops mountainous waves, howling, a sailor sits in a boat and trusts in his frail bark: so in the midst of a world of torments the individual human being sits quietly, supported by and trusting in the *principium individuationis*.': In fact, we might say of Apollo that in him the unshaken faith in this *principium* and the calm repose of the man wrapped up in it receive their most sublime expression; and we might call Apollo himself the glorious divine image of the *principium individuationis*, through whose gesture and eyes all the joy and wisdom of 'illusion,' together with its beauty, speak to us" (*BT* 1; see also Schopenhauer 1958: vol. 1, p. 416). The Dionysian is described negatively as "the collapse of the *principium individuationis*" (*BT* 1).

2 The *Historisch-Kritische Gesamtausgabe* editors give the date of the unfinished essay, "Die Teleologie seit Kant," as no later than May 1868. Nietzsche's own account of his student years in Leipzig, which goes through Easter 1868, does not mention the work, although he notes a study on Schopenhauer that comes immediately before the teleology essay in the volume. Thus, the notes on Kant's *Kritik der Urteilskraft* and the unfinished essay were probably written sometime in the spring of 1868 (*BAW* 1:3, pp. 371–93).

3 In the *Critique of Pure Reason* Kant defined an "analogy of experience" as "a rule according to which a unity of experience may arise from perception" (KrV, A180 = B223). In the third *Critique* he calls the particular kind of art he is employing "fiction," based on a distinction first made in the first *Critique* between a being of our reasoning (*ens rationis ratiocinantis*) and a being of reason (*ens rationis ratiocinatae*) (Kant 1987: 468), or between an objectively empty concept used merely for reasoning (*conceptus ratiocinans*) and a rational concept that

is a basis for cognition confirmed by reason (*conceptus rationcinatus*) (1987: 396). The former term of each of these distinctions is also called "fiction" or "poetizing" (*dichten*) by Kant (1987: 467). In fiction or poeticizing in this very specific sense, our reason is unable to prove the objective reality of what it posits, but can only use what is posited regulatively for reflective judgment (1987: 396). In the case of considering things of nature as natural purposes, Kant insists that "we do not know whether the concept is an objectively empty one that [we use] merely for reasoning (*conceptus ratiocinans*), or is a rational concept, a concept that is a basis for cognition and is confirmed by reason (*conceptus ratiocinatus*) (1987: 396). We can never know, then, whether the teleology of nature is a fiction or a rational concept. Kant says that we will have to be satisfied with calling it a fiction while we continue to assume that it mirrors the ideas of human reason, since without it we would not be able to cognize nature at all.

4   Goethe copied the passage, actually written by Georg Christoph Tobler, into a notebook found in Goethe 1949: vol. 16, p. 921. In 1828 Goethe rediscovered the fragment and could not recall having written it, although he comments that it "reflect[s] accurately the ideas to which my understanding had then attained" (1949: vol. 16, p. 925).

5   The reading list for the future that follows Nietzsche's essay on teleology includes Schopenhauer's essay *On the Will in Nature*, Schelling's *Ideas for a Philosophy of Nature*, and Schelling's *System of Transcendental Idealism*.

Editions of Nietzsche Used

The Birth of Tragedy, trans. Walter Kaufmann (New York: Vintage Books, 1967).

The Gay Science, trans. Walter Kaufmann (New York: Vintage Books, 1974).

Unpublished Writings from the Period of "Unfashionable Observations," in *The Complete Works of Friedrich Nietzsche*, vol. 11, trans. Richard T. Gray (Stanford, CA: Stanford University Press, 1999).

Untimely Meditations, trans. R. J. Hollingdale (Cambridge: Cambridge University Press, 1983).

The Will to Power, trans. Walter Kaufmann and R. J. Hollingdale (New York: Vintage Books, 1967).

References

Bonnefoy, Yves (1991). *Mythologies*, restructured translation of *Dictionnaire des mythologies et des religions des sociétés traditionnelles et du monde antique*, prepared under the direction of Wendy Doniger, trans. Gerald Honigsblum et al. (Chicago: University of Chicago Press).

Goethe, Johann Wolfgang von (1949). *Gedenkenausgabe der Werke, Briefe und Gespräche*, ed. Ernst Beutler, 24 vols. (Zurich: Goethestiftung für Kunst und Wissenschaft).

—— (1988). *Scientific Studies*, ed. and trans. Douglas Miller (New York: Suhrkamp).

Hegel, Georg Wilhelm Friedrich (1977). *The Phenomenology of Spirit* (1806), trans. A. V. Miller (Oxford and New York: Oxford University Press).

Janz, Curt Paul (1978). *Friedrich Nietzsche: Biographie*, 3 vols. (Munich: Carl Hanser).

Kant, Immanuel (1913). *Kants gesammelte Schriften* (Berlin: Königlich Preußische Akademie der Wissenschaften, 1902– ; Berlin: Georg Reimer).

—— (1965). *Critique of Pure Reason* (1781), trans. Norman Kemp Smith (New York: St. Martin's Press).

—— (1987). *Critique of Judgment* (1790), trans. Werner S. Pluhar (Indianapolis: Hackett).

Krell, David Farrell (trans.) (1985). "The Oldest Program towards a System Program in German Idealism" (1796), *Owl of Minerva*, 17, 1, pp. 8–13. The authorship of this fragment has to this day not been unequivocally established. The fragment is written in Hegel's hand, but contains ideas more often associated with Schelling or Hölderlin; it has variously been attributed to all three writers.

Miller, Elaine (2001). *The Vegetative Soul: From Philosophy of Nature to Subjectivity in the Feminine* (Albany: State University of New York Press).

Otto, Walter F. (1933) *Dionysos, Myth and Cult*, trans. Robert B. Palmer (Bloomington and London: Indiana University Press, 1965).

Schopenhauer, Arthur (1958). *The World as Will and Representation* (1819/1844), trans. E. F. J. Payne, 2 vols. (Indian Hills, CO: The Falcon's Wing Press).

5

The Individual and Individuality
in Nietzsche

NUNO NABAIS

The pessimistic condemnation of life by Schopenhauer is a moral one. Transference of herd standards into the realm of metaphysics. The "individuum" meaningless [. . .] We are paying for the fact that science has not understood the individuum.
(WP 379)

Nietzsche stands in the line of thinkers who attribute ontological primacy to the individual (Aristotle and Leibniz, for example). He declares tirelessly: "There are only individuals" (*KSA* 9, 6[158]). As Leibniz put it in his letter to Arnauld of April 30, 1687, "nothing is truly *one* being if it is not truly one *being*" (Leibniz 1998: 124). Nonetheless, and as is the case with all the other fundamental concepts of Nietzsche's ontology, we will seek in vain in his work for any explicit account of the concept of the individual. The absence of an explicit account of the concept of the individual in Nietzsche has led some commentators to read the theory of the will to power as the negation of a true individuation, in which an undifferentiated continuum prevails. The world is not made up of things but is a single flux of life: a sea with waves but with nothing permanent. Eugen Fink makes the decisive point: "He denies finite and individual being with his fundamental conception of being as becoming. Being does not exist because there is no individuation [. . .] Nietzsche does not deny the phenomenon of individuated being but only its objective significance" (Fink 2003: 150). Contrary to this view, I want to show that Nietzsche does have a theory of individuation. The development of Nietzsche's work over a 17-year period represents a positive search for an adequate conception of the individual.

I will first outline the essential features of the influence of Schopenhauer's theory of individuation on Nietzsche's conception of the individual over the period 1872 to 1885. I will then analyze the new formulation of the problem of individuation and individuality that appears with the theory of the will to power. While the attempt will be made to stress the superiority of the later formulation, I am not suggesting that it can be taken to be the solution to the problem that it is intended to answer. What it does allow for is the suppression of the paradoxes that Nietzsche inherited from Schopenhauer's metaphysics and the laying of a basis for an ethical and ontological justification of the individual existence. This is what my essay seeks to demonstrate.

1 The Individual in the Period Prior to the Theory of the Will to Power

1.1 The paradox of individuality in Schopenhauer

The essential non-correspondence between individuality and individuation is one of the crucial paradoxes of Schopenhauer's metaphysics. Schopenhauer defines the principle of individuation in exclusively spatial and temporal terms: a single individual cannot have two beginnings of existence in time, and, similarly, two individuals cannot occupy the same space simultaneously. He even goes so far as to call space and time the *principium individuationis*, on the grounds that, in his words, "it is only by means of time and space that something which is one and the same according to its nature and its concept appears as different, as a plurality of co-existent and successive things" (Schopenhauer 1969: vol. 1, p. 113). Following Kant, he denies to space and time the character of real determinants of the objects of experience: there is, then, for him no objective principle of differentiation between two individuals, or between two moments of the same individual.

However, in addition to phenomenal individuation, Schopenhauer affirms, for every human being, a real individuality, which is the mark of his uniqueness and the foundation of the identity of his existence in time, beyond the diversity of forms. This individuality is explicitly conceived by Schopenhauer starting out from the model of Kant's concept of the "intelligible character," as employed in the solution of the third antinomy of the *Critique of Pure Reason*, as a means of reconciling the mathematical regularity of phenomena in time with human freedom (Kant 1950: B473/A445). Schopenhauer adopts the Kantian solution, considering it, indeed, to be the point at which critical philosophy becomes the introduction to his metaphysics of the will. But he interprets as a thing what in Kant was merely a law. In fact, he identifies the "intelligible character" as being the will as it manifests itself in each individual. Thus, the thing-in-itself – more than a problematic concept, an ideal correlate of the unity of apperception – manifests itself, in Schopenhauer's view, in an immediate and intuitive fashion in each individual as his will. However – and it is here that the paradox enters – this treatment of the thing-in-itself implies that, as embodied in a multiplicity of particularized wills, it becomes subject to space and time, to the exclusive forms of phenomena.

To the thesis of the unity of the will, as thing-in-itself, beyond the multiplicity of its spatio-temporal embodiments – and this is the central thesis of Schopenhauer's metaphysics of the will – falls, then, the task of superseding the contradiction. From the empirical viewpoint, there is no real distinction between individuals who are numerically distinct; not only this, but the very existence of the multiple is viewed as phenomenal and, as such, a matter of appearance. Consequently, the individual in general is henceforth, paradoxically, considered, on the one hand, as a dual embodiment of the thing-in-itself (as "intelligible character," and as will), and, on the other, as a pure phenomenon. Empirically, then, the individual is not a real particular, and is not endowed with individuality.

What, then, for Schopenhauer, is the real foundation of the individuality of each human individual – which, following Kant, he recognizes as constituting the condition of the possibility of any judgment of imputability, and, therefore, of that individual's ethical nature? His metaphysics provides no answer to this question. Schopenhauer is clearly aware of this when, in one of his last works, he writes: "*individuality* does not rest solely on the *principium individuationis* and so is not through and through mere *phenomenon* [. . .] it is rooted in the thing in itself, the will of the individual; for his character itself is individual. But how far down its roots here go, is one of those questions which I do not undertake to answer" (Schopenhauer 1974: vol. 2, p. 227: "On Ethics" §116). Only from the viewpoint of intelligibility does there exist an absolute criterion of individual differentiation. On the simple level of representation, no distinction exists that is not numerical.

This paradox of individuation has major ethical consequences. For Schopenhauer, precisely because there is no real difference between the multiplicity of individual wills there is no such thing as real difference, the continuing conflict between wills that struggle for their own self-preservation is, essentially, bereft of foundation. From the viewpoint of the thing-in-itself, it is the same will, one and indivisible, that devours itself. It follows that, for Schopenhauer, injustice can be transcended and the plane of appearances superseded only if each subject erases his own individuality and his own individual will and becomes a pure subject of knowledge.

1.2 Individuation, between the aesthetic and the ethical

The works of Nietzsche's first period (1872–6) are profoundly marked by this paradox of individuality of Schopenhauer's metaphysics: they adopt the fundamental distinction between the thing-in-itself and the phenomenon, in much the same way as Schopenhauer, in his fashion (constituting it as the paradigm for a series of oppositions – one/multiple, essence/existence, reality/appearance), had taken it over from Kant. In the first section of *The Birth of Tragedy* Nietzsche clearly sets out the metaphysical principles which are his starting-point: "Philosophical natures even have a presentiment that hidden beneath the reality in which we live and have our being there also lies a second, quite different reality; in other words, this reality too is a semblance [*Schein*]" (*BT* 1). In another passage, he goes so far as to describe this realm of appearance or semblance as devoid of real being (*Wahrhaft-Nichtseiende*), and says that the reality of the dream is that of "the *semblance of the semblance*" (*BT* 4). In Nietzsche's eyes, the empirical individual is, inevitably, doubly unfounded – both in his particular dimension, before the One of the universal will of which he is only an ephemeral manifestation, and in his singular dimension, before his own individuality, his individual essence, which reduces his empirical action to an imperfect and chaotic copy of the intelligible law which it embodies. *The Birth of Tragedy* is constructed through the figures of Dionysus and Apollo and around the opposition between the One and the Multiple. The *Untimely Meditations*, especially the third, *Schopenhauer as Educator* (1874), mark the attempt to transcend the radical non-correspondence between individuality and empirical individuation.

However, like all great disciples, Nietzsche is no mere repeater of his master. These works already adumbrate a process of rupture with Schopenhauer, manifested in the search for a justification of the empirical individual existence: Nietzsche thus breaks not only with Schopenhauer over the definition of the *principium individuationis*, but also concerning the ethical consequences of the absence of a real empirical correlative for individuality. Thus, while admitting that individual existence amounts to an injustice in the face of the One, Nietzsche does not follow Schopenhauer in proposing a process of ascetic negation of the individual will but endeavors to justify the plane of appearance itself, and, therefore, the empirical existence of each individual. If the Dionysian ecstasy represents the state of ascetic fusion with the "primal One" (*das Ur-Eine*), which, as Schopenhauer had said, is attained through the disinterested contemplation of the Whole beyond all individual motivation, that same ecstasy is nonetheless counterbalanced by the figure of Apollo, "the magnificent divine image [*Götterbild*] of the *principium individuationis*," as Nietzsche significantly calls him, who represents the endeavor, through apology for the forms of appearance and dream, to justify the individualized character of human existence. For Nietzsche, the mystery of Greek tragedy lies in the presence within it of that tension between the One, manifested in mystic union with the universe in the Dionysiac delirium, and the multiple, embodied in the characters' struggle for the heroic affirmation of their individuality.

Similarly, in the third of the *Untimely Meditations*, Nietzsche endeavors to justify the empirical existence of each individual, on the basis of an imputed, equally empirical, individuality. He adopts an interior viewpoint, conceiving the individual in both particular and singular terms, starting out from, precisely, his individuality. Right at the beginning, he defines each individual as a "unique miracle," endowed with an absolute "uniqueness." This uniqueness, viewed as, indeed, the "core of his being," is, additionally, conceived in accordance with the model of "intelligible character." This is the "fundamental law" which constitutes the principle of individuality and confers uniqueness on each individual's life-history, since it regulates the form of its manifestation. It is in this context that Nietzsche speaks of the "law" of the "proper self" (*UM III*, 1). However, while he follows Schopenhauer in admitting the inconstant and inauthentic nature of the empirical existence of each individual, Nietzsche does not repudiate that existence: rather, he seeks to imbue it with dignity and intelligibility, by purifying it of its empirical determinations in such a way as to convert it into an exact mirror of the individuality which it incarnates: "Be yourself! The totality of what you are is not what you do, think, desire" (*UM III*, 1).

In both of these works, whether from the viewpoint of individuation or from that of individuality, Nietzsche aims to move beyond the sentence imposed on individual existence by Schopenhauer; nonetheless, he is, at this stage, still the prisoner of the paradigms of the metaphysics of his "educator." If the figure of Apollo embodies Nietzsche's justification of the multiple in retreat from the vertiginous pull of the One, this does not happen in the name of a different conception of individuation; rather, Nietzsche simply invokes the necessity of appearance for life. Nietzsche's solution, since it continues to view space and time as having their origin in the subject of representation, ends up reducing itself to a value judgment: it simply inverts the hierarchical relation between truth and appearance, while failing to question the basic notion of their differentiation.

In the third of the *Untimely Meditations* the continued influence of Schopenhauer's metaphysics means that individuality is seen as contrary to the empirical existence that Nietzsche seeks to justify through it. In contrast to his position from 1885 onwards, the "fundamental law" which defines the individuality of each individual and founds that individual's identity in time is not yet conceived as a serial law which already involves within itself all the stages of the individual's life-history and to which temporality is therefore immanent. Like Schopenhauer, in his 1874 text, Nietzsche conceives individuality as the atemporal rule which manifests itself in a reiterated and circumstantial fashion within the series of events which make up the existence of each individual; since it is unconditioned in its immutability, it is essentially distinct from that existence. The evolution and mutability of each life-history are not contained within the law: they are merely consequences of the diversity of the external conditions that form the empirical framework of its manifestation. Thus, for Nietzsche, the individual can regain contact with his own individuality only by withdrawing his existence from its empirical determinations, transforming each moment of his life-history into an exact expression of his meta-empirical individuality: "In the process of becoming all is hollow, deceitful, vain and worthy of our contempt; the puzzle which man ought to solve, he can only release from being, in being such and not other, in the everlasting. Now he begins to check how deeply he is united with becoming, how deeply he is united with being – an enormous task wells up before his soul: to destroy all becoming, to illuminate all falsity in things" (*UM III*, 4). In this identification with the undying individuality which constitutes the core of that which he is and guarantees his identity in becoming, the individual is reduced to a pure, petrified essence, a disembodied spirit. At the same time the spatio-temporal horizon that is the theatre of his life-history, but condemned as being "vain and deceitful," remains bereft of immanent consistency – not in the face anymore of the One, but of the individual and atemporal law of which it is viewed as a mere sensory manifestation.

The works of this first period do not achieve a positive position on either the individual or individuality. In these writings Nietzsche endeavors simply to invert the ethical consequences of Schopenhauer's paradox of an intelligible individuality to which no empirical individuation corresponds without questioning the underlying metaphysical postulates. The individual remains split between an extrinsic definition (as a particular within a spatio-temporal multiplicity in which all differentiation as such is considered unreal) and an intrinsic definition (as an atemporal individuality which reduces him to an abstract entity) – in other words, split between one differentiation which is purely numerical and another which is real but abstract.

1.3 *The individual without qualities*

The publication of *Human, All Too Human* in 1878 marked an open break with Schopenhauer's metaphysics, and, in Nietzsche's own view, by the same token with metaphysics in general. This break meant, above all, ceasing to accept the distinction between a "world of metaphysics" and a "world of representation." He holds that, although the possibility of a metaphysical world cannot be ruled out, any ontology we could give of it would be purely negative: "an inaccessible, incomprehensible being-other; it would be a thing with negative qualities" (*HH* 9). Nietzsche flatly declares: "we are in the realm of representation [*Vorstellung*], no 'intuition' can take us any further" (*HH* 10). The autonomy he now confers on the forms of space, time, and causality brings in its wake the reality of the *principium individuationis*, which is affirmed against the illusion of the undifferentiated One. Space-time becomes an objective principle of individuation. The individual is no longer seen as a mere phenomenon: "There are only individuals" (*KSA* 9, 6[158]).

The concept of the individual occupies a key position in Nietzsche's works of this period. Nietzsche attempts to determine the historical conditions which permitted the appearance of sovereign individuals who fight for their own individuality, in accordance with the model which he discovers in Italy's "Renaissance man."[1] However, this autonomy of representation compromises the basis of the individuality of each singular being. In fact, to reject the possibility of an unconditioned world constituting the principle of intelligibility of the empirical world means to deprive individuality of the status of an immutable law underlying both the identity of each individual in time and the very internal principle of individual differentiation. On the strict level of representation, the individuality of human action is necessarily diluted by the empirical constraints of a given life-history. Nietzsche goes so far as to argue that the biographical sequence of each individual's life is determined across the long chain of empirical causality in such a fashion that, as he puts it,

> if one were all-knowing, one would be able to calculate every individual action, likewise every advance in knowledge, every error, every piece of wickedness. The actor himself, to be sure, is fixed in the illusion of free will; if for one moment the wheel of the world were to stand still, and there were an all-knowing, calculating intelligence there to make use of this pause, it could narrate the future of every creature to the remotest ages and describe every track along which this wheel hat yet to roll. (*HH* 106)

On the level of representation, any internal law of action disappears. The individual can no longer live according to his own law, can no longer be himself. The only law that remains is that which governs the multiplicity of individual life-histories: the principle of causality which mechanically determines all events within the "wheel of the world" on the basis of their position in the order of simultaneity and succession.

It follows that individuality also ceases to be accessible by means of the closure of each individual on himself. On the strict level of the forms of space and time only external relations exist; in this sense, the "interior" of each particular being is simply the prolongation of those relations, and, in Nietzsche's words, "We have transferred 'society' into ourselves, diminished it, and withdrawing into oneself is no escape from society; rather it is often a meticulous clearing-up and interpretation of our [inner] processes according to the schema of earlier experiences" (*KSA* 9, 6[80]). If representation is maintained to be the sole plane of reality, then numerical difference is henceforth given objective status. The only individual difference now admitted is the numerical, given the refusal of any internal, individual principle of differentiation. The individual is thus condemned to the status of a mere generality, no more than the internal reproduction of the empirical framework within which his existence unfolds. What, then, is the basis of individuality which enables each singular being to construct himself as a person, as an autarkic individual?

Nietzsche's solution is aporetic: since individuality is not a primary datum to be found by each individual within himself, it has to be reconceived as a task to be accomplished. Numerical difference then has to be turned into real difference, through a process by which each individual frees himself of his general features. Nietzsche even declares: "My moral would be ever more to deprive men of their universal character, and to specialize in it, up to a degree incomprehensible for the others to achieve" (*KSA* 9, 6[158]). He now sees individuality as a model to be constructed and realized by each individual: "The point is, however: that each designs his own model-image and actualizes it – the individual model" (*KSA* 9, 6[293]). Nonetheless, this conception of individuality is clearly incompatible with Nietzsche's reduction of all reality to the level of representation, which is governed by mechanical causality. The dynamism implicit in the movement from each being towards his individual model enters into contradiction with the reduction of all causal processes to a single one (that which comes into play in the strict, mechanical enchainment of all events within the "wheel of the world"). This would entail admitting that the real cause of human action could be a tendency towards an individual telos whose existence is merely ideal. Nietzsche himself seems to be aware of this contradiction when he asks: "How does the model relate itself to our evolution? To that which we must necessarily strive for? Is the model at best an anticipation? But why then necessary?" (*WP* 331). In the end, Nietzsche denies any power of causation to the individual model in which he had seen an alternative to the "intelligible character" paradigm. This model is, as he says, no more than "a representation of the ego" (*WP* 331).

The concept of an individual model to be constructed and realized, which had replaced the notion of a fundamental law to be discovered and lived, proves to be no less illusory than its predecessor. Individuality cannot be conceived as something internal to each individual, as the formal cause of the individual's identity in time, because that would entail the existence of a real conditioning relationship between the intelligible plane of the law and the empirical plane of action. The correlative of this position is that, equally, individuality cannot be conceived as something merely external, as something to be attained which, in projective terms and as final cause, can underwrite individual identity. The individual model, as final cause, effectively acquires the same significance on the plane of representation as did the atemporal law conceived as its intelligible formal cause. Nietzsche wishes to remain on the level of representation, rejecting any recourse to "metaphysical intuitions." However, the examination of the real foundation of individuality cannot make any headway at this stage. Schopenhauer, with a view to saving individuality, had reduced the individual to the status of an appearance, by the notion that individuation exists exclusively in the forms of representation. Nietzsche, inverting Schopenhauer's position and guided by the project of justifying individuality within empirical individuation itself, saves the forms of representation by converting them into the sole real plane. However, he thus reduces individuality to an appearance, a mere representation made of itself by an "ego" petrified within the causal chain of events in time. Nietzsche is still the prey of Schopenhauer's metaphysics, even in the form in which he rejects it.

Nietzsche's first attempt to resolve this aporia – this tension between individuality without individuation and individuation without individuality – takes the form of the idea of eternal recurrence.

1.4 Individuality as identity in repetition: the doctrine of eternal recurrence

The image of a long chain of causation or "wheel of the world," within which all events are closely interlinked, led Nietzsche in 1881 to develop the idea of the eternal recurrence. He now concludes that the total series of the world's events cannot have had a beginning in time, nor is it acceptable that it should tend towards any final state; as such, the series must be eternal, in other words it must always have existed and will always continue to exist. Since Nietzsche starts out from the principle that, as the totality of the force of the universe is constant, the number of possible events within the chain of causation is finite, he concludes that becoming is circular: "Up until this moment an infinity has already expired; that is, all possible developments must already have existed. Thus the development of this moment must be a repetition, and also that which generated it, and that which arises from it, and so forward and backward again!" (*KSA* 9, 11[202]). The idea of the eternal recurrence of all events now makes it possible to conceive the basis of the individuality of each individual in a form which is innovative and, at the same time, the locus of a terrible paradox.

We have seen that when he reduces the real to the plane of representation, Nietzsche does not contest Schopenhauer's principle of individuation; he simply considers it as objective, that is, as a real determination of the objects of experience. However, we have also seen how that principle allows only numerical difference, not real difference. Since 1878, Nietzsche had conceived the individual objectively as a particular being numerically distinct from other particular beings, but not in terms of individuality. What constitutes the individual as such is merely the circumstance of not being able to have two different beginnings in time and not being able to occupy two different positions in space at once. On the basis of this continued view of the individual exclusively in terms of his place in the order of succession and simultaneity, Nietzsche concludes that temporal differences are necessarily translated into individual differences: just as a single individual cannot be present simultaneously in two different places, he cannot, by the same token, exist at two different moments. From one instant to the next, he is another. In Nietzsche's words, "there is no individual, in the shortest instant it is something other than in the next, and its conditions of existence are those of innumerable individuals" (*KSA* 9, 11[156]). Eternal recurrence confers individuality on each individual through the simple prolongation to eternity of the spatio-temporal definition of individuation. If time is considered as not only real but infinite, then the individual appears in time endowed with new determinations – he is henceforth defined as the infinite repetition of himself: "All becoming moves itself in the repetition of a determinate number of absolutely identical states" (*KSA* 9, 11[245]). If the identity of the individual is dissolved in time through the unending succession of moments, if he is obliged to become other in every moment, then it is through time that the individual becomes himself at each moment: "Humanity! Your entire life will become like an hourglass, always again turned over and always running out" (*KSA* 9, 11[148]).

Individuality thus appears, no longer as an identity in the continuous order of the linear succession of time, but as an identity in the discontinuous order of repetitions in eternity. If the life-history of each individual is the exact repetition of another series of instants already realized an infinite number of times in the infinite number of circles of the eternal recurrence, then each individual, being different from what he was in the preceding moment and from what he will be in the following moment, is, nonetheless, absolutely identical to himself in every moment, as the infinite repetition of himself. Each event in his individual life-history is endowed with an individuality arising from an eternal and unique model which actualizes itself in him in absolute fashion. Thus, his individuality in each moment, in other words, that which makes each individual exactly the individual he is at that given moment, is the eternal individuality which he incarnates at that moment as a repetition: the individuality of his life-history as a whole is the multiplicity of individualities embodied in the multiplicity of "individuals" which, in their succession, go to make up that same individual's life-history.

The access of each individual to his individuality no longer happens through the mediation of a subtraction from his empirical conditions as a means of becoming a transparent expression of an atemporal law; nor does it occur through the pursuit of an individual model constituting a sublime form. Individuality is no longer conceived as residing either on the hither side of each individual's empirical existence, or beyond it: it is in it, and merges with it in an absolute fashion in each moment. To accede to one's individuality – offered as it is in each moment to each individual as an original given, conferred on him eternally in an immanent fashion – is to reply in the affirmative to the question: "Do you want this once more, and also for innumerable times?" (*GS* 341; *KSA* 9, 11[143]). Individuality takes on the nature of an original given while appearing at the same time as a task. It is what we are and do in each moment, because in each moment we exactly repeat our existence, which is itself an eternal given, conferred on us once and for all. But our individuality also has to be conquered. It is not enough to be: one has to want to be what one is. To take oneself as the individual model to be realized is to make that model coincide with what one is: "To live in such a way that we wish to live once more, and wish to live in eternity! Our task challenges us in every instant" (*KSA* 9, 11[161]).

The idea of eternal recurrence provides a further basis for the individuality of each individual. In Leibnizian terms the difference can be called radical. The past may be infinite, but the number of individuals who are brought into being over time is not. It follows that the genesis of an individual, however distant it may be, is never lost in the depths of time: it can only be prolonged up to the individual himself. Each individual is both the end-point of the long chain of causes which originated in him and the new starting-point of the genesis of his own repetition – that is, the genesis of the infinite number of other individuals whom he repeats and announces, and who are distinguished from him only on the temporal plane, as different occurrences in time of one and the same individuality. This radical individuality is based on the fact that, within a single conjunctural situation, that is, within a complete cycle of actualization of all possible individuals, it is impossible for two indistinguishable individuals to appear. Given the intimate interrelation of all causes, that would mean that both would have had the same genesis – in which case they would not be two, but one and the same individual (either spatially and temporally identical, as a single occurrence of one individuality, or else distinct only in the temporal sense, as different occurrences, in different cycles of recurrence, of a single individuality):

> Whether indeed [. . .] something identical has existed is entirely indemonstrable. [. . .]
> Whether there can be something identical in one total state – two leaves, e.g.? I doubt it:

it would presuppose that there were an absolutely identical generation, and for that we would have to assume that throughout all eternity something identical had endured, despite all alterations to the total state and the creation of new properties – an impossible assumption! (*KSA* 9, 11[202])

The idea of the eternal recurrence furnishes a Leibnizian basis for the principle of the identity of the indiscernible: since his genesis has its roots in eternity and in himself, the individual becomes absolutely unique, and is endowed with a uniqueness which confirms itself in the eternal repetition of himself and of the entire chain of events that culminated in him. Within the idea of the eternal recurrence, individuality is still absolutely conditioned by its place in the order of temporal succession. This does not mean, however, that it is annulled. On the contrary, it acquires new temporal determinations – within each cycle, as a radically individualized and unique genesis; and within eternity, as the infinite repetition of itself in each moment of its existence.

The notion of eternal recurrence finds Nietzsche extracting the most radical consequences possible from his "anti-metaphysical" decision to remain on the plane of representation, refusing the categories of "reason," "beginning," or "finality." Returning eternally on themselves, spatio-temporal relations have become self-subsistent, conferring on themselves, in circular fashion, sufficient reason for the fact that they are what they are rather than something else. In this universe, then, each individual partakes of the privilege of being able to display his *raison d'être* in the fact of existing in a particular space and at a particular time. Nonetheless, the idea of eternal recurrence still requires a complement: it needs to be doubled by an internal perspective on the individuality of each individual. It was precisely such a perspective that Nietzsche attained from 1885 onwards, with the elaboration of the theory of the will to power. I adopt the thesis of Giorgio Colli that it is only in this period that the theory of the will to power makes its appearance in his work because it is only at this time that he deliberately adopts the perspective of metaphysics as a means of endowing the world with the force of an explicative viewpoint, and also because it is only from this moment that he begins to elaborate the fundamental philosophical project to which he gives the name of, precisely, *The Will to Power* (Colli 1980: 151–60).

2 The Individual and Individuality in the Theory of the Will to Power

2.1 The return to metaphysics

The main innovation represented by the theory of the will to power is Nietzsche's abandonment of the plane of representation as the sole means of access to the real. It follows that his principal target is now the mechanistic view of the world – precisely because of its rejection of meta-empirical categories of any kind:

Of all the interpretations of the world attempted hitherto, the mechanistic one seems today to stand victorious in the foreground. It evidently has a good conscience on its side; and no science believes it can achieve progress and success except with the aid of mechanistic procedures. Everyone knows these procedures: one leaves "reason" and "purpose" out of account as far as possible, one shows that, given sufficient time, anything can evolve out of anything else, and one does not conceal a malicious chuckle when "apparent intention" on the fate of a plant or an egg yolk is once again traced to pressure and stress [. . .] one has lost the belief in being able to explain at all. (*WP* 618)

For Nietzsche, the function of mechanics, given its rejection of the categories of "reason" and "end," is confined to describing the visible and formalizing its relations exclusively through the categories of "shock" and "pressure." What is now required is an explicative approach, which can only be attained by questioning the internal processes of all phenomena. Nietzsche thus writes:

> The victorious concept "force", by means of which physicists have created God and the world, still needs to be completed: an inner will must be ascribed to it, which I designate as "will to power," i.e., as an insatiable desire to manifest power; or as the employment and exercise of power, as a creative drive, etc. [. . .] one is obliged to understand all motion, all "appearances", all "laws", only as symptoms of an inner event and to employ man as an analogy to this end. (*WP* 619)

He radically inverts his perspective on the interpretation of the real, abandoning the decision to reject any "intuition" beyond the plane of representation. It is now precisely the internal, that which escapes all representation, which has to become the explicative principle of observable external relations. All movements, all phenomena or laws, will now have to be seen as a manifestation, as a "symptom" of processes of which they are merely an expression: "To the power which transforms itself and always remains the same, belongs an inside, a character type of Proteus-Dionysus, dissembling and enjoying itself in the transformation" (*KSA* 11, 35[68]). What "intuition" can he now invoke to discover force in its internal dimension? As in Schopenhauer, it is the analogy with man which constitutes the "secret passage" to the metaphysical world, the bridge to the "intelligible character" of all phenomena. This analogy will be even more explicitly invoked in *Beyond Good and Evil*, when Nietzsche states:

> Suppose nothing else were "given" as real except our world of desires and passions, and we could not get down, or up, to any other "reality" besides the reality of our drives – for thinking is merely a relations of these drives to each other; is it not permitted to make the experiment and to ask the question whether this "given" would not be sufficient for also understanding on the basis of this kind of thing the so-called mechanistic (or "material") world? [. . .] then one would have gained the right to determine all efficient force univocally as – will to power. The world viewed from inside, the world defined and determined according to its "intelligible character" – it would be "will to power" and nothing else. (*BGE* 36)

2.2 *The discovery of the essence of the world within the individual*

In this return to metaphysics, the definition of the individual plays a twofold part. It is the analogical means of access to the world seen from within; and, since all movements and all phenomena are the result of relations between individual beings, to explain the world from within means to describe individuals in their immanent dynamism. Precisely because of the place it occupies, the concept of the individual is taken as the object of two different descriptive procedures: one leading from the individual as subject of knowledge to the world as named from within, and another aiming to explain the entire visible world by deriving it, as a symptom, from the internal processes discovered in relations between individuals.

To take man as an analogical principle is not merely a methodological decision: it is based on a *de facto* observation. Nietzsche believes that man is condemned to be the primal analogical referent for all interpretation of the world. The theory of the will to power is not to be distinguished from other interpretations of the world by its element of man-as-analogy. The mechanistic perspective itself is none other than a consequence of that analogy – for Nietzsche, the concept of the atom is a projection of the concept of subject/substance on to the smallest structure of the immaterial extension. This means that analogy is no longer a neutral procedure. To take oneself as the first term of the analogy does not guarantee immediate access to the internal processes which govern all phenomena. To start out from man is always to start out from a particular interpretation. The need thus arises for a prior critique of the systems of interpretation of man and their distinguishing marks; only after this can one strive to attain, through man, the internal perspective on the world.

Nietzsche argues that the fundamental error which underlies all interpretations of man, and which man therefore incorrectly projects on to the real, is the error of the individual: "The individual [is] the more subtle error" (*KSA* 9, 11[156]). Does this mean that Nietzsche denies the existence of particular beings, of beings which are numerically distinct and self-subsistent at a given moment in time? This is not the case: what he denies is a specific concept of the "individual" used by man to conceive of himself and, therefore, the world.

> In truth there are no individual truths, but rather mere individual errors – the individual itself is an error. Everything that happens in us is in itself something other, that we do not know: we put intention and background and morality into nature in the first place. – I distinguish, however, the imagined individuals and the true systems of life, of which each of us is one. (*KSA* 9, 11[7])

It is in the name of a new concept of the individual conceived as "system-of-life" (*Leben-systeme*) that Nietzsche now comes to see the notion of the "individual" as the most subtle of errors. Thus, to comprehend the non-imaginary nature of every individual (as "system-of-life"), which constitutes the analogical means of access to the world's internal processes, presupposes a critique of the notion of the "individual" (as an imaginary concept) which man employs to interpret himself, only to falsify himself and, through himself, the world.

What Nietzsche essentially denounces in this imaginary notion of the "individual" is the presupposition of unity. To this he opposes the idea of the individual as a plurality, as "a plurality of animated beings which, partly struggling with one another, partly integrating and subordinating one another, in the affirmation of their individuality, also involuntarily affirm the whole" (*KSA* 11, 27[27]). In turn, the status of an indivisible unity is denied by Nietzsche to each one of the animate beings that make up the plurality which is each individual. He writes: "the very smallest 'individuals' cannot

NUNO NABAIS

be understood in the sense of a metaphysical individuality and atom" (*WP* 704), and again: "there are no durable ultimate units, no atoms, no monads: here, too, 'beings' are only introduced by us" (*WP* 715). To accept the existence of such single ultimate units would, Nietzsche argues, amount to transferring on to the infinitely small the unity and substantial identity which he refuses for the individual as composite whole. To the notion of "atom" or "thing" he now opposes a conception of the "dynamic quanta": "no things remain but dynamic quanta, in a relation of tension to all other dynamic quanta: their essence lies in their relation to all other quanta, in their 'effect' upon the same" (*WP* 635). The essence of these ultimate units is action – an action in which it is impossible to distinguish the agent from the action's effects, since it invariably takes place inside a structure made up of a multiplicity of elements, themselves also active, which simultaneously occupy, in relation to each other, the positions of object and obstacle. To these "dynamic quanta" Nietzsche gives the name of the will to power: they are the primal element of the universe, its homogeneous dynamic, the sea of forces out of which individuation arises.

2.3 Individuality and spontaneity

It is now necessary, firstly, to comprehend how Nietzsche conceives the process of individuation within this sea of forces that he calls the will to power, and, secondly, to analyze the new concept of individuality thus produced.

Within the universe of force there exists an essential continuity between all its forms, which enables a process of continual metamorphosis of one into another. However, this continuum cannot be an undifferentiated whole. Nietzsche conceives it at all moments as exhibiting variations in intensity, with at least two orders of potency (when force accumulates at one point, it dissolves at another). These variations in potency presuppose the existence of points or singularities that constitute both poles of condensation and principles of differentiation; in Nietzsche's words: "Mere variations of power could not feel themselves to be such: there must be present something that wants to grow and interprets the value of whatever else wants to grow" (*WP* 643). Any differences in potency within a dynamic continuum would cancel each other out, were it not for "a certain something," a singularity able to determine that very difference by interpreting it in relation to its own value, its own power of growth, in order to build on it. In the universe of the will to power, then, individuation comes as of right before differentiation.

What is this "something which wants to grow," this minimum element of the universe of force? In the fragment cited above, Nietzsche defines it in terms of two key determinations: the will to growth, and an interpreting being. This definition is bolstered by a spatial perspective: "when A acts upon B, then A is first localized, separated from B" (*KSA* 13, 14[80]). The minimum elements of force are always differently located and establish among themselves a system of co-locations which takes itself as its own referent.[2] Nietzsche further conceives these locations as centers of the movement of the will: "I need initial points and centers of movement, from which the will propagates itself" (*KSA* 13, 14[98]). The minimum elements that make up the totality of the movement of force, and form the internal principle of its differentiation, are conceived on the basis of four determinations: (a) they are differently located;

(b) they exist in a relation of tension with all the other elements; (c) they struggle to achieve their own growth; and (d) they interpret systems of difference in terms of their own value. The main innovation here is to conceive individuality as the principle of differentiation of force, and thence of the process of constitution of individuals as "systems-of-life." If individuation precedes differentiation as of right, then individuation itself must be constituted by individuals endowed with individuality – with an internal quality which enables them to interpret variations in potency and construct them as oppositions. It is thanks to the existence in the universe of a multiplicity of individualized singularities, each with its own individuality, that it is possible to create differences, establish relations of tension between dynamic quanta, and constitute individuals as organic totalities.

How does Nietzsche now conceive the basis of the individuality of each of these singularities? Nietzsche now seems to oscillate between an extrinsic definition (the individual as merely the expression of the system of relations which contains him) and an intrinsic definition (the individual as endowed with immanent qualities which manifest themselves in unconditioned fashion in the relations of conflict which he establishes with all other individuals). On the one hand, he declares: "The properties of a thing are effects on other 'things': if one removes other 'things', then a thing has no properties" (*WP* 557). On the other, he contends that every being is that which it is, constituted in an absolutely individualized form that manifests itself in all its peculiarity in every action vis-à-vis other individuals:

> That something always happens thus and thus is here interpreted as if a creature always acted thus and thus as a result of obedience to a law or to a lawgiver, while it would be free to act otherwise were it not for the "law". But precisely this thus-and-not-otherwise might be inherent in the creature, which might behave thus and thus, not in response to a law, but because it is constituted thus and thus. All it would mean is: something cannot also be something else, cannot do now this and now something else, is neither free not unfree but simply thus and thus. *The mistake lies in the fictitious insertion of a subject.* (*WP* 632)

This indeterminacy concerning the basis of each individual's individuality is the result of the strategic duality that Nietzsche employs to combat the mechanistic interpretation of causal processes. On the one hand, since he wishes to endow the plane of dynamic relations with an explicative perspective, taking those relations as "symptoms" of internal processes, he strives to find an immanent basis for the differentiation between dynamic singularities which can, as of right, precede the system of causal relations and can therefore function as a principle of intelligibility. On the other hand, against the atomism that underlies that same interpretation (which supposes the existence of extensive elements that are indivisible and are endowed with internal properties which are not conditioned vis-à-vis their actions or relations), he stresses the essentially functional nature of each dynamic singularity and, therefore, tends to define it only extrinsically, as a mere pole of convergence of the relations it establishes with other singularities. The conflict is thus linked to the ontological status of the concept of *relation* within the theory of the will to power. Which should be primary as of right – the universe of internally individualized singularities, or the system of relations out of which its properties have been constituted? How can Nietzsche conceive an immanent basis for each individual's individuality without reducing it to an isolated substance that subsists in time beyond its properties or actions? And, conversely, how is it possible to affirm the functional nature of each individual without conferring an autonomous ontological status on *relation* as such?

While not systematic in its scope the solution adopted to deal with the antinomy concerning the ontological status of relation entails: (1) defining all dynamic relations as essentially perspectivist; (2) affirming the superiority of the internal dynamism of each singularity vis-à-vis its external relations.

2.4 The individual and its essential relations: perception and perspective

For Nietzsche, relation is inherent to force; it derives from the fact that "a force can expend itself only on what resists it" (*WP* 694). A force, then, only exists within a *field of forces*. How does this tension between forces establish itself? Is their nature that of pressure, of the shock of contiguity? If so, how are we to comprehend their individuation, the fact that they do not dissolve into a homogeneous mass? Nietzsche argues that if one force is to act on another in a continuous fashion, then it is essential that they remain distinct in terms of location: "when A acts upon B, then A is first localized, separated from B" (*KSA* 13, 14[80]). It follows that forces must necessarily act at a distance – but if they are not contiguous, how can they capture the tensions between them and perceive reciprocal differences of power?

The need to answer this question leads Nietzsche to adopt the thesis of the essentially perceptive nature of all beings. In his words, "Do the various forces stand in relation, such that this relation is bound up with an optics of perception? That would be possible if all being were essentially something perceptual" (*KSA* 12, 5[12]). Each force is related to all the other forces because it perceives them: it is a window on that totality. It is, then, at a distance – in other words, maintaining their co-localizations – that forces attain equilibrium among themselves: "distant forces balance one another. Here is the kernel of perspectivism" (*WP* 637). A dynamic equilibrium among forces is formed out of the play of multiple perspectives, the constant inter-perception of all forces:

> The "effect at a distance" cannot be got rid of: something attracts something else, something feel itself attracted. This is the basic fact: in comparison, the mechanistic representation of pressure and impact is only a hypothesis on the grounds of appearance and the sense of touch. [. . .] In order that this will to power can manifest itself, it must perceive those [other] things. (*KSA* 11, 34[247])

The perception attributed by Nietzsche to all forces or dynamic singularities is not pictorial in character: it is of a purely intensive nature. Each force perceives only differences of power among the multiplicity of forces in relation to which it exists. It is in this sense that Nietzsche claims that there exists a greater perceptive exactitude and clarity in the inorganic world, compared to the organic: "The transition from the inorganic world into the organic is a transition from fixed perceptions of force-values and power relations into perceptions which are uncertain and indeterminate – because a plurality of beings struggling against one another (= Protoplasma) feels itself as opposed to the external world" (*KSA* 11, 35[59]). In the inorganic world, the balance between the forces within a system is stable, since the differences of power have been crystallized; each force therefore has an exact perception of these differences of value and their relations. By contrast, in the organic world, which differs from the inorganic in the sense that each individual is not a mere singularity, differences of power are constantly coming into being, through the structuring or destructuring of internal relations of force; these differences modify the relations of power, at the next level up, between the individual as plurality and the outside world. Each individual's perception is here already the result of the co-possibility of internal perceptions, and even his perception of his own value – on the basis of which he determines his differences of value vis-à-vis other individuals – is uncertain and inexact.

Perception is in its essence not the internal representation of an external given (were that so, the organic world would be the kingdom of the greater clarity, since it possesses systems that permit prolongation and resonance from outside to inside); it is, rather, the regulated, dynamic relation between the totality of singularities in conflict and each one of those singularities. Perception exists because the multiplicity of the elements of a structure expresses itself in each single unit. The more regulated the relation – that is, the more stable the differences of power – the more clearly will each singularity perceive, or, rather, express within itself, the multiplicity with which it enters into relation. Thus, if Nietzsche defines relation as the result of the perceptive nature of each force, it follows reciprocally that perception itself exists only in and through its relational nature: an isolated force free of all relations – in any case an impossible hypothesis, given its essentially functional nature – would be no better than "blind."

Nietzsche's conception of the internal principle of individuality is not to be sought primarily in the notion of *perception* (*Wahrnehmung*) but in that of *perspective* (*Perspektiv*). This distinction is not systematically maintained throughout Nietzsche's work. Nonetheless, it is the only means of grasping another criterion of qualitative differentiation of perceptions employed by Nietzsche, in addition to that already established between organic and inorganic worlds. In fact, to the hierarchy of power-levels of forces there corresponds, he believes, a hierarchy, conceived in terms of extensiveness and accuracy, of the perspectives brought to bear by each force on the totality with which it enters into relation. He writes in 1886, in the preface to the new edition of *Human, All Too Human*: "You shall above all see with your own eyes the problem of *order of rank*, and how power and right and spaciousness of perspective grow into the heights together" (*HH*, preface, 6).

From the viewpoint of the perception of external differences, a greater degree of internal structuring of each force – corresponding to the transition from the inorganic world to the organic – will result in a reduction in the clarity and exactitude of perception. However, Nietzsche counter-argues that an increase in power brings a greater extensiveness and accuracy to the "vision" of each force. Clarity and exactitude of perception vary with the degree of external stability of the differences of power, whereas extensiveness and accuracy of perspective depend on the degree of internal power of each force. The criterion of distinction between degrees of *perception* is, then, extrinsic to the force, while that of degrees of *perspective* is intrinsic to it. Thus, *perception* and *perspective* may be seen as, respectively, the outer and inner faces of the relation between forces. Through perception, each force expresses within itself the viewpoint of the totality of forces and their differences of power; through perspective, each force expresses its own internal degree of power vis-à-vis that same totality.

The concept of perspective indicates the basic principle of the physics of the will to power: an individual is not something primordially functional but something absolutely spontaneous. Any transformation of power occurring within an individual is the result of his perspective, of his internal activity. The global shifts in power within the force field or system in which that individual operates are an expression, or "symptom," of that activity, and not the reverse. As Nietzsche puts it, "the force within is infinitely superior; much that looks like external influence is merely its adaptation from within" (*WP* 70; cf. *GM* III. 12).

The external definition of individuality, as the unique expression of the multiplicity of differential relations of power, thus becomes solely a "symptom" of the internal definition, the degree of power and the quality of perspective. Equally, all movements or events occurring on the plane of representation are "symptoms" of processes of conflict between individuals who are absolutely individualized. The very opposition between the interior and exterior of each individual no longer exists: each individual is pure interiority. If his internal force is infinitely superior to his external influences – given that the latter are now reduced to an expression of the internal force of other individuals – then what exists at each moment is a co-possibility as between a multiplicity of forces, all absolutely spontaneous and individualized, existing within a finite and constant quantity of global energy.

Conclusion

This model of an instantaneous co-possibility among the totality of individual actions in conflict once again confers on individuality the nature of a given and, at the same time, a task. From the internal viewpoint, individuality is the law of the series which already contains the totality of the actions of each individual, grounded in his essential spontaneity. From the external viewpoint, by contrast, if each action results from the relation of co-possibility among individuals who are in conflict in each moment, it has to be conquered through the instantaneous mediation of all other individualities. Co-possibility operates as if it were a natural selection among virtual entities: it actually creates the individuality of each individual. The sphere of individuality is thus not annulled by co-possibility; rather, it is this circumstance that allows its authentic realization. Each instant of universal existence, each event conceived as a co-possibility, thus becomes the expression of each of the individuals in conflict.[3]

The infinite totality of instants of eternal recurrence is the result of a finite totality of individuals. At every moment in the interaction of perspectives and the co-possibility of actions these individuals affirm and realize their individuality. It follows that to say *Yes* to one's own individual existence, to endorse it in its absolute difference and uniqueness, is, according to Nietzsche, also to say *Yes* to the entire universe and to eternity:

> If we affirm one single moment, we thus affirm not only ourselves but all existence. For nothing is self-sufficient, neither in us ourselves nor in things; and if our soul has trembled with happiness and sounded like a harp string just once, all eternity was needed

to produce this one event – and in this single moment of affirmation all eternity was called good, redeemed, justified, and affirmed. (*WP* 1032)

The notion of the *de jure* primacy of individuation and individuality, vis-à-vis the universe of difference and relation, now permits Nietzsche to conceive of an immanent basis for the Dionysian *Yes* to the whole of existence. Within the theory of the will to power the *Yes* to the whole no longer compromises individuation as such. That intuition – as first formulated in *The Birth of Tragedy* – of a purely affirmative existence, of a *Yes* to the world and to all things, can now be conceived within the perspective of the individual. The Dionysian experience no longer has to mean the dissolution of the individual into a delirious merging with the mystical One. Indeed, the contrary now prevails: if each individual's individuality is grounded in the deepest essence of the world – in eternity itself, in that eternity whose existence was required to bring into being every event of one's own existence – then to say yes to that eternity, to say yes to the entire universe, is to say yes to oneself and to one's own character as a unique event.

See also 10 "Identity and Eternal Recurrence"; 12 "Nietzsche on Time and Becoming"; 13 "The Incorporation of Truth: Towards the Overhuman"; 16 "Phenomenology and Science in Nietzsche"; 30 Nietzsche's Theory of the Will to Power"

Notes

1   One of Nietzsche's main sources of inspiration here was Jacob Burckhardt's *The Civilisation of the Renaissance in Italy* (1860), especially its second part on the development of the individual in terms of self-sufficient individuality.
2   Nietzsche accepts the existence of a multidimensional space, considered absolute not as a separate, self-existent substance but as the result of co-localizations of forces: "I believe in absolute space as the substratum of force: the latter limits and forms. Time eternal. But space and time do not exist in themselves" (*WP* 545).
3   It is also the model of co-possibility that enables Nietzsche to conceive the link between the spontaneous nature of each individual and the rule-governed character of each and every one of the events which make up his life-history: "Let us here dismiss the two popular concepts 'necessity' and 'law': the former introduces a false constraint into the world, the latter a false freedom. 'Things' do not behave regularly, according to a rule [. . .] There is no obedience here: for that something is as it is, as strong or as weak , is not the consequence of an obedience to a rule or a compulsion – The degree of resistance and the degree of superior power – this is the question in every event: if, for our day-to-day calculations, we know how to express this in formulas and 'laws', so much the better for us! [. . .] There is no law: every power draws its ultimate consequence at every moment. Calculability exists precisely because things are unable to be other than they are" (*WP* 634).

Editions of Nietzsche Used

The Birth of Tragedy and Other Writings, trans. Ronald Speirs (Cambridge: Cambridge University Press, 1999).

Human, All Too Human, trans. R. J. Hollingdale, 2 vols. (Cambridge: Cambridge University Press, 1986).

Schopenhauer as Educator, in *Untimely Meditations*, trans. R. J. Hollingdale (Cambridge: Cambridge University Press, 1997).

References

Colli, Giorgio (1980). *Scritti su Nietzsche* (Milan: Adelphi).

Fink, Eugen (2003). *Nietzsche's Philosophy*, trans. Goetz Richter (London: Continuum Press).

Kant, Immanuel (1950). *The Critique of Pure Reason*, trans. Norman Kemp Smith (London: Macmillan).

Leibniz, G. W. (1998). *Philosophical Texts*, trans. and ed. R. S. Woolhouse and Richard Francks (Oxford and New York: Oxford University Press).

Schopenhauer, Arthur (1969). *The World as Will and Representation*, trans. E. F. J. Payne, 2 vols. (New York: Dover).

—— (1974). *Parerga and Paralipomena*, trans. E. F. J. Payne, 2 vols. (Oxford: Clarendon Press).

Part II

Nietzsche's Philosophy of the Future

6

Nietzsche's "Gay" Science

BABETTE E. BABICH

Nietzsche's conception of a gay science is alluringly seductive, comic, and light – and accordingly many readers have celebrated it as the art of laughter. And, to be sure, the first edition of *The Gay Science* began with a teasing series of light, joking rhymes.[1] Taking this teasing further, the 1887 title page replaces the 1882 epigraph from Emerson with a gently unserious rhyme, adding a fifth book and finishing it off with an additional cycle of songs – *Songs of Prince Vogelfrei*[2] – invoking at once the knightly as well as the chastely[3] erotic character of the troubadour (and recurring in the arch allusions of Nietzsche's *Ecce Homo*).

Nevertheless, a "gay" science, emphasizing light and laughter, has well-known risks: success in the parodic art of laughter seems to block the seriousness of science. Nietzsche recollected what he mocked as the "vanity" of then contemporary scholars, incensed by his use of the "word 'science,'" – a pique that not has quite played itself out – and their complaint, "'gay' it may be, but it is certainly not 'science'" (*KSA* 12, 2[166]). The objection is a pointed one. Nietzsche had hoped to articulate a profoundly "serious" science (*GS* 382), gay only out of profundity – just as the ancient Greeks had discovered the art of drawing his delight in the surfaces of things, his gay "superficiality," from the depths of tragic wisdom (*GS*, preface, 4).

From the start, Nietzsche's joyful science goes beyond the fun of mockery and "light feet." Alluding to the song art of the troubadours, the book itself might be regarded as a handbook to the art of poetry, as Nietzsche suggests, playing on the notion of *vademecum* in the series of short poems that made up his "'Joke, Cunning, and Revenge': Prelude in German Rhymes," a title which alludes to Goethe's *Scherz, List, und Rache*, via a musical setting.[4] *The Gay Science* thus explicates the science of philology as much as it exemplifies the art of composition. In this sense, one might literally say that *The Gay Science* is Nietzsche's most scientific book.

The dimension of song, the "gay" dimension, complicates this perspective. As we know from the quotation marks in the subtitle Nietzsche added to the second edition of *Die fröhliche Wissenschaft*, the language of *la gaya scienza* is not Nietzsche's coin. Indeed, in his notes, Nietzsche decries the blindness of his academic readers apart from their "misunderstanding of cheerfulness [*Heiterkeit*]," but beginning with the title itself, Nietzsche sniffed, "most scholars forgot its Provençal meaning" (see *BGE* 260; *KSA* 11, 35[84], 36[6]).

From Provence to the Occitan, one of Nietzsche's *Nachlass* drafts, *Gai Saber*, intro-duces an address to "the mistral" (*KSA* 11, 35[84]; cf. *GS Songs of Prince Vogelfrei*; *EH*, "*GS*"). This is the troubadour's art (or technic) of poetic song, an art at once secret (cf. the discussion of *trobar clos* in Aubrey et al. 1999: 263), anonymous and thus non-subjective (Aubrey et al. 1999: 259),[5] but also including disputation[6] and comprising, perhaps above all, the important ideal of action (and *pathos*) at a distance: *l'amour lointain*. Nietzsche's exploration of the noble art of poetic song is intriguing enough to compel attention. As he details these song forms in his notes,[7] Nietzsche also seems to have modeled some of his own poetic forms on this tradition. In one obvious instance, the 1887 appendix of songs to *The Gay Science* includes a dance song entitled "To the Mistral," to be heard together with Nietzsche's praise of the south and affirming Nietzsche's love of Dame Truth herself (*Songs of Prince Vogelfrei*, "In the South"). Even more, as Roger Dragonetti reminds us at the start of his reflections on the origins of the *gay saber*, the playful context of laughter – "hilarity" – and the joy of play are as central to Nietzsche's *The Gay Science* as they are to this same medieval tradition of vernacular song. *The Gay Science* begins with just such a reference to gaiety as such, while recollecting the focus of Nietzsche's first book on musical poetry, *The Birth of Tragedy*, "Not only laughter and gay wisdom but the tragic too, with all its sublime unreason, belongs among the means and necessities of the preservation of the species" (*GS* 1).

Nevertheless a focus on the art of the troubadour as key to Nietzsche's "gay" science inevitably takes the interpreter in only one direction. As the art of contest in poetic song, and given Nietzsche's courtly allusions to Goethe as noted above, or else – and more patently – to Wagner, it is important to explore the tradition of the troubadour. One might go still further afield to an unattested (but rather likely) connection with Frédéric Mistral, the Occitan poet who popularized the inventive Provençal tradition of poetry, and who was a contemporary of Nietzsche.[8] But we should also move slowly here, and not just for reasons of philological care (Nietzsche's *lento*). Thus, just as one might restrain the assumption that the clear erotic undercurrent along with the recurrent focus on shame in *The Gay Science* (Nietzsche concludes both Books II and III on the note of shame: "as long as you are in any way *ashamed* of yourselves, you do not yet belong to us" [*GS* 107] and, again, "*What is the seal of liberation?* No longer to be ashamed before oneself" [*GS* 275, see also *GS* 273 and 274]) entails Nietzsche's homosexuality,[9] a similar restraint is in order in this case as well. If Nietzsche himself claims the reference to the troubadours for his own part (and to this extent, the current reading is not speculation), the riddle of *The Gay Science* hardly reduces to this.

We need more than a recollection of the Provençal character and atmosphere of the troubadour in order to understand Nietzsche's conception of a joyful science, even if, given the element of a complex and "involuntary parody" (*GS* 382), the spirit of the Occitan certainly helps, especially where Nietzsche adverts to dissonance throughout (betraying the disquiet of the mistral wind as well as its seasonal relief). For nothing less than a critique of science understood as the collective ideal of scholarship, and including classical philology as much as logic, mathematics, and physics (Babich 2003, 1994), is essential for an understanding of the ideal of Nietzsche's gay science. A philological reflection on the origins of ancient Greek music drama had occupied

Nietzsche's first concerns with this general question as what he subsequently summarized as the "problem of science" in his 1886 reflections on his first book, *The Birth of Tragedy*. This was Nietzsche's declared discovery of the birth – in music and words – of tragedy in the folk song, in lyric poetry (*BT* 5, 17).

Seen from this perspective, *The Gay Science* articulates Nietzsche's life's work in terms of his scholarly achievements as well as his own deployment of the same: putting this "science" to work on his own behalf and taking this as far as the consummate promise of his troubadour's (and even Catharist) ideal of self-overcoming. This is the context of impossible love, the condemnation "never to love," as that intimate disappointment in which David B. Allison quotes Nietzsche's resolution to effect his own healing transfiguration (Allison 2001: 154). If the gay science is a handbook of song, it prefigures what Allison has delicately analyzed as what will become Nietzsche's recipe for inventing "the alchemical trick for transforming this – muck into gold" (Allison 2001: 115, cited from Nietzsche's letter to Franz Overbeck, December 25, 1882). If Nietzsche's self-therapy works for the love of a woman, for Lou Salomé, as Allison argues, it is because the alchemical transformation consummates *amor fati* – loving life, real life, not just "warts and all," but as intimately necessary to life, the whole gamut of illness and suffering, mis-recognition and disappointment, as well as death.

Nietzsche's gay science is a passionate, fully joyful science. But to say this is also to say that a gay science is a *dedicated science*: scientific "all the way down." This is a science including the most painful and troubling insights, daring, to use Nietzsche's language here, every ultimate or "last consequence" (*BGE* 22; *KSA* 13, 14[79]). Doubting just as well as Montaigne, doubting in a more radical fashion than Descartes, and still more critical than Kant or Schopenhauer, dispensing with Spinoza's and with Hegel's (but also with Darwin's and even Newton's) faith, Nietzsche's joyful, *newly* joyful, scientist carries "the *will* henceforth to question further, more deeply, stringently, harshly, cruelly, and quietly than one had questioned heretofore" (*GS*, preface, 3). Even confidence in life itself, as a value, of course, but also as such, now "becomes a *problem*." The result is a new kind of love and a new kind of joy, a new passion, a "new happiness."

The commitment of a joyful science includes body and mind (Descartes). Nietzsche does not distinguish these any more than he distinguishes between soul and spirit (Kant and Hegel). The reference to the body derives from Nietzsche's experience of suffering as an adventure in transmutation. This transfigured suffering or pain he calls "convalescence," reminding us of the influence of the body and its milieu – interior and exterior, physiological and ecological – in the purest aspirations of reason. Like Montaigne, again, if also playing off Spinoza and Leibniz, Nietzsche invokes the need for self-questioning and for self-experimentation precisely with an eye to the importance of physiological influences as these may be found on every level of thought, finally pronouncing philosophy nothing but an "interpretation" and "misunderstanding" of the body (*GS*, preface, 2).

As a philosopher in the fashion of the gay science, you can play or experiment with yourself in your own thinking, you can be the phenomenologist of yourself, varying the effects of health, illness, convalescence or the persistence of illness and pain on thought itself. For neither science, nor scholarship, nor philosophy, Nietzsche tells us, has ever been "about 'truth'" (*GS*, preface, 2). Each of these occupations, as Nietzsche tells us, has always had some other motivation or aim in mind, e.g., "health, future, growth, power, life" (*GS*, preface, 2). Acknowledging the passions of knowledge heretofore, Nietzsche is at pains to argue that the ideal of objectivity is either a delusion of self-deceiving idealism or a calculated mendacity. Belief in such an ideal is the default of science altogether. In its place, Nietzsche argues against both the idea and the ideal of pure science, dedicated to sheer knowledge as if knowing should be its own end (*GS* 123), as he also argues against knowledge for gain and profit. In every case, his reference-point is the *noble* ideal of *la gaya scienza* (cf. *D* 308 and *BGE* 212). Contra the idealistic convictions of the "will to truth," and "truth at any price," Nietzsche dares the proposition that truth, once "laid bare," no longer remains true (*GS*, preface, 4). A gay science will *need* to know itself as art.

Reflecting on the title of Nietzsche's *Die fröhliche Wissenschaft*, Martin Heidegger has emphasized that metonymically tuned as it is in conjunction with science (*Wissenschaft*), the word *fröhliche*, happy or gay, light or joyful, evokes *Leidenschaft*, passion (Heidegger 1982: 20). In this way, Heidegger argues, Nietzsche's passionate, joyful science can be opposed to the dusty scholarship, let us call it the "grey science,"[10] of his peers. This same claim supports the surmise that, like *Beyond Good and Evil* and *Twilight of the Idols*, Nietzsche's joyful science was intended as a challenge to Wilamowitz (and thence contra philology as the discipline that had excluded Nietzsche's contributions).

The test of Nietzsche's joyful science, *amor fati*, finds its planned and executed exemplification in *Thus Spoke Zarathustra*, as well as in the retrospective song cycle appended to the later written fifth book of *The Gay Science*.[11] In this experimental fashion the promise articulated on behalf of music in *The Birth of Tragedy* might finally be fulfilled, as his reflections in *Beyond Good and Evil* and *Ecce Homo* suggest. If the "spirit of science" and techno-mechanical progress could be shown to have the power to vanquish myth (even if only with a myth of its own) and poetry (even if only with poetry of its own), the "spirit of music" might be thought – this remains Nietzsche's finest hope, it is his philosophical music of the future – to have retained the power to give birth once again to tragedy. Such a rebirth compels us to seek out the spirit of science precisely in terms of its antagonistic opposition to music's power of mythical creativity.

As preserved in written form, like Homer's epic song, like Greek musical tragedy, *la gaya scienza* corresponds to the textual fusion of oral traditions – composition, transmission, performance – in the now frozen poems of the troubadours. It is important, as with the ancient tradition of epic poetry, that the knightly art of poetry, the gay science as recorded in the fourteenth century,[12] presumed a much older tradition dating back to the twelfth or eleventh centuries earlier still.[13] This older legacy was the historical meaning of the *gai saber*. In parallel fashion, Nietzsche's discovery had been that the musical tradition of the folk song gave birth to the archetypical Greek tragic art form, a genealogy which was for Nietzsche to be descried in the rhythmic structures which he called the music of lyric poetry.

The spirit of music gives birth to tragedy, the tragic art and knowledge that are ultimately the metaphysical comfort of the artist (*BT* 25). In *The Gay Science*, Nietzsche articulates this "metaphysical comfort" as the distance and light of art (*GS* 339). By contrast with such a metaphysical or musical comfort, the comfort of the spirit of science is a physical one: "eine irdische Consonanz" (*BT* 17). In *The Gay Science*,

Nietzsche will analyze this saving grace, this working functionality as the reason that we, too, remain "still pious" (*GS* 344). Astonishing in its patent, empirical but insuperably contingent success, what "holds up" (*GS* 46) in science as the (technological) scientific solution to life is the gift of a *deus ex machina*, as Nietzsche clarifies the vision of Prometheus for us (*GS* 300), the "God of the machines and the foundries" (*BT* 17), put to work on behalf of a "higher" egoism, confident in the "world's correction through knowing", and of the viability of a "life guided by science" (*BT* 17) but above all, capable of concentrating the individual within the most restrictive sphere of problem-solving (the scientific method).

To illuminate the point of Nietzsche's allusion here, if Goethe's own Faust had been fixed together with the spirit of the Earth so densely summoned forth at the start and compelled to turn within the same circle, he might well have declared, in advance of the whole tragedy, I and II, "Ich will dich: du bist werth erkannt zu werden" (*BT* 17, cf. *GS* 1). For Nietzsche, as for the rest of us, the method at work – stipulation, mechanism, and above all delimitation, i.e., method *as such* – is the key to the modern scientific age. The same methodification is also the means whereby science becomes art, but to say this is also to say that science departs from theory alone, from its metaphysical heaven or perfection, to become practicable and livable, viable, as such.

However effective they are (and they are very effective as Nietzsche underscores), the expression of natural laws in human relations or numerical formulae (*GS* 246) remains a metaphorical convention: a Protagorean conventionalism Nietzsche famously compares to a deaf person's visually metaphorical judgment of the acoustic quality of music on the basis of Chladni sand/sound figures (*GS* 373), just as we today might reimagine the metaphor as the "music" of a digital music file deliberately downloaded as a text file or a CD hung as a lightcatcher.[14] In this way, when Nietzsche first sets up the opposition between art and science in terms of music and myth – in distinction to logic and calculative advantage – what is at issue is a proportionate achievement. As Nietzsche had argued in his first book, both art *and* science are ordered to life. Art seeks to harmonize dissonance, resolving it by transfiguration: not by elimination but rather by way of musical incorporation: "a becoming-human of dissonance" (*BT* 25). By contrast, especially in the guise of the technological science of modernity, as it begins with Socrates and the promise of logic and truth, mechanical or physical science effectively corrects or improves the world. Science thus substitutes an earthly consonance in place of the elusive promise of the tragic art, or music, which for its part offers no solutions to mortal problems (this is tragedy), only beautiful concinnities or harmonies (this is the art of music).

Nietzsche opposes, first, the failure of music in such a scientifically improved world; second, the self-deceiving truth of earthly consonance with respect to its own illusions (this would be a "lack" of science, beyond the praise for the probity of the thinker that compels him to turn to science [*GS* 335]; this would be "the good, stupid will to 'believe'" which Nietzsche challenges as a "lack of philology," that is, "the lack of suspicion and patience" [*BGE* 192]).

When modern scientific rationality (*GS* 358) turns its eye on suffering, it conceives and so reduces suffering to a problem to be solved (*UM III*, 6). There is a whole skein of difficulties here for Nietzsche, beginning with the question of the nature and extent of suffering (psychic or physical, cultural or historical) and including the quality and character of comfort and relief. The compassionate and tragic element will always be important for Nietzsche, a sensitive pathos he shared with Schopenhauer. But beyond Schopenhauer, Nietzsche would also argue that the problem of suffering eludes ameliorating reduction for the very reason that a solution to the problem of suffering also and inevitably elides the whole fateful range of what belongs to suffering (*GS* 338). This is a complex point and it does not mean that Nietzsche was in favor of passively enduring suffering, much less inflicting it. But to strip off the multilayered, complex covering of truth is also to dissolve what is true (*GS*, preface, 4), in the same way that Rome as an empire came to dominate its world, to use Nietzsche's example of cultural supremacy (for a contemporary example, we can think of what we call "globalism"). Imperial Rome blithely obliterated the traces of its past (or, better, the past of its predecessors) without the slightest inkling of bad conscience (if also with baneful consequences for the science of history): "brushing off the dust on the wings of the moment of the historical butterfly" (*GS* 83). In one's own life this is the inscrutability of suffering (and is that which gives suffering its *meaning*) (*GS* 318). More critically, it is the problem of the meaning and significance of suffering for another (this is the problem of other pains, as it were) (*GS* 338). In this reflection, key to the notion of the eternal return, Nietzsche touches upon the deep relation of suffering to happiness as well as everything that suffering necessitates and makes possible. Nietzsche's appeal to the "higher ethic of friendship" (*KSA* 8, 19[9]) presents a challenge to contemporary expressions of the ethics of care and of compassion: "I want to teach [. . .] what is understood by so few today, least of all by the preachers of pity [*Mitleid*]: *to share not suffering but joy* [*Mitfreude*]" (*GS* 338).

Nietzsche's gay science of morality is complicated precisely because he is interested less in promulgating a moral theory than in questioning the presumptions of the same. For Nietzsche, questioning is the most important element in science. Nietzsche confesses as his personal "injustice" his very scientific conviction that everyone must somehow, ultimately *have to have* this "Lust des Fragen" (*GS* 2). In other words, Nietzsche permitted himself to believe that everyone was in some measure possessed by a desire for questioning, indeed a passion for questioning "at any price" (*GS* 344).

Science and *Leidenschaft*

Reviewing the motivations of established scholarship, i.e., a job, a career, dusty and bored with itself ("lacking anything better to do"), the "scientific drive" of traditional, grey scientists turns out to be nothing but "their boredom" (*GS* 123). By contrast what Nietzsche calls "the passion of the knowledge seeker" is a very erotic drive: a drive for possession. This is acquisitive to the point of abandon, "yearning for undiscovered worlds and seas" (*GS* 302), completely lacking selflessness, lacking disinterest, and in place of the ideal of scholarly detachment, "an all-desiring self that would like, as it were, to see with the eyes and seize with the hands of many individuals – a self that would like to bring back the entire past, that wants to lose nothing it could possibly possess!" (*GS* 249). So far from science's celebrated objectivity and neutrality (*GS* 351), "the great *passion* of the knowledge seeker" is a matter of intimate and absolute or utter cupidity (*GS* 249, 345). As Nietzsche regarded this passionate drive from the perspective of nobility (*GS* 3), the archaic quality of Nietzsche's joyful passion is ineluctably alien to modern sensibilities – if simply and fundamentally because (and this is what Nietzsche always understood by the ideal of nobility) the cupidity or desire of gay science is a non-venal one (*GS* 330). Nietzsche explains this passion as the passion of one "who steadfastly lives, must live, in the thundercloud of the highest problems and the weightiest responsibilities (and thus in no way an observer, outside, indifferent, secure, objective [. . .])" (*GS* 351). The passion of this quite Nietzschean vocational ideal influenced not only Max Weber, who is usually associated with it, but Martin Heidegger as well.

Both science and art draw upon the same creative powers, both are directed to the purpose of life, and, most importantly for Nietzsche, both are illusions. Denying a Platonic world of noumenal truth, there is for Nietzsche only nominal truth (*GS* 58) – sheer illusion – but no noumenon. Indeed what is key to Nietzsche's inversion of Plato/Kant (i.e., Christianity), is that without the noumenal, there is no phenomenal world; without metaphysics, no physics. The world is mere will to power, chaos, and nothing besides (*GS* 109). The only truth is illusion, and there is no truth beyond illusion. But this is Schopenhauer's world, not Kant's. To make any headway with this, one needs a non-Western logic, the logic of the veil of Maya. But to say this, for the Nietzsche who always remains a scientist, ultimately means that one is grateful to art.[15]

But what is science? Science is routinely presumed to be a matter of method (and quantifying analysis) and it was exactly the character of science as method that Nietzsche had in mind. Hence in the context of his early (and later) reflections, when Nietzsche proposed to examine "the problem of science" what he meant by science presupposed its broadest sense (*Wissenschaft*) because what he wanted to address was nothing less than the specifically *scientific* character of science. For this reason too, Nietzsche's talk of science with regard to aesthetics and philology (i.e., in his book on tragedy) inevitably exceeded aesthetic philology (or literary classical theory) in its scope and works and brought Nietzsche to speak of logic, rationality, and even of the mechanized way of life of modernity, in order to speak, in the classical mode, of the contemporary possibilities of Western culture.

It is the meaning of science that remains problematic here. Very few scholars have adverted to the problems of the compound construction of a "gay science." Among the few who have, Heidegger, in asking "What does *gay science* mean?," reminds us that Nietzsche's "science [*Wissenschaft*] is not a collective noun for the sciences as we find them today, with all their paraphernalia in the shape they assumed during the course of the last century" (Heidegger 1982: 20). Nietzsche's conception of a gay science is thus opposed to the nineteenth-century ideal of the positive, measuring, or technologically defined sciences. By contrast with modern science and its calculative technologies (where physics is *the* paradigmatic science), the passion of Nietzsche's *fröhliche Wissenschaft* "resounds" like "the passion of a well grounded mastery over the things that confront us and over our own way of responding to what confronts us, positing all these things in magnificent and essential goals" (Heidegger 1982: 20). As we have already suggested, in order to make some headway with the question of this passion for knowledge, a gay science requires the art of love. And the erotic art must be learned, so Nietzsche argues, exactly as we learn to love anything at all.

Nietzsche's example for such learning is music itself: the cultivated love of which is, like every other art of love, an acquired passion (*GS* 334). Indeed, for Nietzsche, only such a cultivated passion for knowledge has a justifiable claim to the title of science. In this sense, a supposed science of music apart from the art of music, apart from "what is music in it" (*GS* 373), would not be merely abstract. Blind and empty, a tone-deaf musical science would not be a science worthy of the name (*GS* 374).

The Music of the Gay Science and the Meaning of *Wissenschaft*

Regarded as a symptom of life, science, Nietzsche argued, could well constitute a "subtle form of self-defense against the truth" (*BT*, "Self-Criticism," 1). Suggesting that truth (and the will to truth) might be less than salutary, Nietzsche opposes both Socratic rationality (better living through science) and Christianity (truth saves). For the same reason, the task of presenting "*the problem of science itself*, science considered for the first time as problematic, as questionable" exposes the thinker to the danger of truth (*BT*, "Self-Criticism," 2). We recall Nietzsche's description of his own first book's grappling with what he called a "problem with horns." Ignoring the focus on science as problematic, scholars have routinely argued that Nietzsche's attempt "to view science through the lens of the artist and art through that of life" was not addressed to what we take to be science today, not natural science, not *real* science.

Walter Kaufmann sought to assure us that the science in Nietzsche's *The Gay Science* has nothing to do with *science* per se but rather and only refers to the troubadour's art, just as noted above. And it is quite clear that Kaufmann is not uncovering an obscure detail but one Nietzsche himself emphasizes, not only indirectly but on the title page to the second edition as well as in his later writings and throughout his *Nachlass* notes (complete, as we have already seen, with schematizations of the song forms). Indeed, if anything Kaufmann's gloss tells us *less* than Nietzsche does. For *The Gay Science* manifestly refers to the troubadour's art. But what art of song was that to be for Nietzsche? Was that the art of the famous Jaufré Raudel (ca. 1125–8) or Guiraut Riquier, the so-called "last" of the troubadours?[16] Or was it the lyre song of Homer's Achilles? Or Pindar's "crown"[17] of song? Or Machiavelli's musical art? Or are we merely speaking of Orpheus? Or Wagner? Or, and this solution is still the favorite amongst most readers, are we speaking of Nietzsche himself, when he claimed that one *should* range his Zarathustra under the rubric of music, and given the portents of his concluding incipit in *The Gay Science?* At the very least, it would seem that Nietzsche aligns the gay science, as the art of the troubadour, with the ancient musical art of tragedy, as Nietzsche sings himself the song of his songs – and including the troubadour's *serenas* or evensong, or, given the context of music and Venice, his planctus (*planh*) – in his *Ecce Homo*.[18]

For Nietzsche, as for any German, both in his day and our own, the term *Wissenschaft* or science applies as much to historical studies of ancient philology as to the natural sciences.[19] Where the problem of science *qua* science, i.e., the problem of the scientificity of science, also corresponds to the logical problem of reflexivity, the general problem of science as such – both natural (and phenomenological) and philological (and hermeneutical) – calls for critical reflection. Nietzsche had argued that science as such (including the natural, physical sciences, as well as mathematics and logic) cannot be critically conceived (or founded) on its own ground; nor indeed (and this was Nietzsche's most esoteric point as a hermeneutic of hermeneutics) can philology be so founded. It was because he wrote as a philological scholar, as a *scientist*, by his own rigorous definition of the term, that Nietzsche could regard his methodological considerations as directly relevant to the "problem of science."

We may note that, in distinction to the narrow focus of the English *science*, the inclusiveness of the German *Wissenschaft* illuminates the parallels between Nietzsche's self-critique and Kant's expression of metaphysics in terms of a science of the future (as a future metaphysics). Thus it is important to affirm that the present author is well able, as others seemingly are not, to assume that Nietzsche had "read" Kant. We betray our own prejudices when we assert that Nietzsche *could not* have read Kant or argue that he could only have gotten his Kant second-hand, via Schopenhauer or Lange. For Nietzsche, the achievement of Kant's critical philosophy was to engage the logical contradictions of the logical optimism of modern science. For Nietzsche, Kant's critical philosophy, which conceives "space, time and causality as entirely uncondi-tioned laws of the most universal validity," demonstrated that these same concepts "really served only to elevate the mere phenomenon [. . .] to the position of the sole and highest reality, as if it were the true essence of things" (*BT* 18). Logical optimism is the positivist confidence that knowledge is both possible (in theory) and attainable (in practice). We still subscribe to the same optimism in our ongoing conviction that "all the riddles of the universe can be known and fathomed" (*BT* 18) and thus we faithfully denounce anyone who criticizes this conviction in the slightest as anti-scientific and willfully obscure.

Yet here the question of the meaning of *Wissenschaft* for Nietzsche (as for Kant, Hegel, and even Goethe but also Marx, Freud, Weber, Husserl, Heidegger, etc.) remains elusive. For if the *fröhlich* in the title of *Die fröhliche Wissenschaft* has required our attention, taking us to passion (with Heidegger) but also taking us to a willingness to dance over the abyss of unreciprocated or failed love or the dark neediness of the soul (with Allison), and ultimately to Nietzsche's own concerns as he summarizes these for us, daring the dangerous play of experimental questioning (*GS* 374), the meaning of *Wissenschaft* turns out to be similarly complicated. It is worth asking, again, what Nietzsche really means by science, be it gay or otherwise.

Intriguingly, although it is routinely observed that the German term *Wissenschaft* and the English word *science* ought to be distinguished, commentators tend not to explicate the difference in question. Each word carries its own penumbra of mean-ing and substitutions, articulating on each side a divergent range of associations, both metonymic and metaphorical. Dating from the fourteenth century, the term *Wissenschaft* was coined in German for the needs of a theological and mystical context in order to translate the Latin *sciens*, *scientia*, terms given as *science* in English, and related to *scire*, to know, *scindere*, to cut or divide. Key here in understanding *Wissenschaft* is the set of associations of the root terms, in particular the powerful etymological array via *wissen* linked to the Old High German *wizzan* and Old Saxon *wita* but also the English *wit* and *wot* and thence to the Sanskrit *vēda* and the ancient Greek οἶδα as well as the Latin *videre*.[20]

However, it is only from the eighteenth century that the current meaning of the sciences can be dated (that is, as distinct from the arts in the characteristically Anglo-American contrast between *the arts* and *the sciences*). If it can be argued that the meanings of *Wissenschaft* and *science* now and increasingly tend to coincide, *Wissenschaft* yet remains unquestionably broader, as it corresponds to the collective pursuit of knowledge kinds. This collectivity is the meaning of *-schaft*, analogous to the suffix *-ship*, as in scholarship (a term that only partially renders *Wissenschaft*). As the noun corresponding to *wissen*, *Wissenschaft* also retains connotations of the "ways" or conduits of knowing, ways that can still be heard in English with the archaic *wis* (to show the way, to instruct) or *wist* (know).

At a minimum, the above reflections remind us that, although Nietzsche's identification of himself as a "scientific" practitioner strikes a contemporary English speaker as eccentric, routinely calling forth at least a footnote (if not whole books on source criticism) designed to explain the problem away, remanding it to the conventionality of the history of ideas and influences, his identification of his research interests as "scientific" would still be accurate in contemporary German usage. But this is exactly not to say that all Nietzsche was talking about was his own disciplinary field. For Nietzsche, as should now be clear, what made his own discipline scientific was what made any discipline scientific.

The problem is not at issue in German readings of Nietzsche (although a parallel remains in German contributions to epistemology and the philosophy of science to just the degree that these fields continue to be received as Anglo-Saxon disciplines). The problem is in understanding Nietzsche's references. And the problem is the problem of equivocation. For in spite of all the well-known rigor of the study of classics, we are hard pressed to see classics as a "science" per se. For this reason, when Nietzsche, a classicist, speaks of himself as advancing science, we do not quite take his reference except by putatively broadening his claim to an assertion about "scholarship" in general, but by which we mean literature, and particularly classical philology and then, following Wilamowitz's academically devastating critique of Nietzsche's supposed innovations, not even that (see Wilamowitz-Möllendorff 2000, and, further, Porter 2000).

Nietzsche poses the question of science not as a resoluble but much rather as a critical problem. As a critical project, Nietzsche adverts to the stubborn difficulty of putting science in question – the difficulty of questioning what is ordinarily unquestionable. Science, indeed, as presumptive authority and as "method," is ordinarily the ground or foundation for critical questioning. For this same critical reason, Nietzsche holds that the project of raising "the problem of science itself [. . .] as a problem, as questionable" (*BT*, "Self-Criticism," 2) was a task to be accomplished over time, not merely a point to be made, or a problem to be remedied.

If he liked to assert that he aspired to a more radical doubt than Descartes, and if he was more critical than Kant in calling for the reflexivity of the critical project to be turned against itself, Nietzsche nonetheless differs from the Enlightenment project of philosophical modernity in general. Thus Nietzsche *does not* exclude his own deliberately provocative solution as a problem at the limit of critical reflection. Instead, Nietzsche presupposes an unrelenting self-critique, precisely for the sake of science.

106

Self-criticism, critique of one's tacit assumptions, has to be a constant attendant to philosophical critique but – and Nietzsche is just as quick to remind us of this – where are we to position ourselves for the sake of such self-critique? Raising the question of the subject, challenging that there is nothing that thinks, the Archimedean standpoint provided by the Cartesian thinking subject is suspended where it emerges – in the middle of nowhere – and this is, if it is nothing else, a questionable foundation. The result is the giddiness Nietzsche claims as endemic to the modern era, an era without definable up and down (and the orienting disposition of the same to above and below), without belief in God, and increasingly lacking even the firm foundation of the ultimacy of the human subject.

Gay Science: Passion, Vocation, Music

As a *Leidenschaft* in Heidegger's sense, Nietzsche's science opposes the usual conception of either science or scholarship, even and perhaps especially philosophy (even if, as Nietzsche remarks, philosophy is the discipline named for love or passion). Nietzsche's gay science is not just relevant to science in general but is exactly to be understood in opposition to the nineteenth-century ideal of the positive, measuring, or technologically defined sciences.

If this were an armchair problem of the classically metaphysical kind we could let it go at that: as a puzzle of the ordinary Kuhnian kind; science as Popperian problem-solving. But because the problem is the problem of science as the "theory of the real" (see *GS* 57), we have been attempting to take it by its figurative horns, in the very spirit of Nietzsche's own metaphorical invocation of the Cretan art of bull dancing (*BT*, "Self-Criticism," 2). The horns of this dilemma may also remind us of Nietzsche's polemical language in his preface to *Beyond Good and Evil*, whereby all of us, as philosophers and as scientists/philologists, conceived as impotent, or at least as inconsequential, suitors of the truth, are also crowned with all the allusions to the liar that are inevitable with reference to Nietzsche or even, thinking of Ariadne, to Theseus himself. But here, our ambition is more sober than trivial matters of scholarly pride, or what Nietzsche called "scientific pedantry." An unquestioning inattention to modern science and technology continues to rule in modern confidence, that is, in what Nietzsche called our "convictions."

For Nietzsche, we explain (or as he takes care to specify, we "describe") everything with reference to ourselves and our own motivational intentionality; consequently and inevitably (here Nietzsche goes beyond *both* Kant and Schopenhauer), we fashion (or invent) the very concept of a cause, and thereby misconstrue both the world *and* ourselves in a single blow (*GS* 112). Nietzsche argues that "The sole causality of which we are conscious is that between willing and doing – we transfer this to all things and signify for ourselves the relationship of two alterations that always happen simultaneously. The *noun* is the resultant of the intention or will, the *verb* of the doing. The animal as the creature that wills – that is its essence" (*KSA* 7, 19[209]). Like the sand patterns of the Chladni sound figures that so captivated Nietzsche's imagination, the question of science can be raised in terms of music, not only in terms of the troubadour's musical art but also in terms of its remainder. This is its ineffable residue, sedimented in the words that still remain to be sung.[21]

In *The Gay Science*, Nietzsche outlines a critical revision of the standard genealogy of science out of the spirit of myth and magic and alchemy, as he also finds science modeled on the occluded paradigm of religion (*GS* 300; *GM* III. 25). Nietzsche does not merely parallel science and religion in terms of both faith and ultimate goals, that is, piety and metaphysics (*GS* 344) but in Book II, in a rarely remarked upon aphoristic tour de force, Nietzsche plays between science and religion and the prejudices proper to both. Thus Nietzsche tells a parable to explain (and not quite to denounce) an earlier era's wholly scientific (one thinks of the Jesuit scholar Robert Bellarmine) resistance to Galileo and to Copernicus and so on. In the very way that the noble passion of love and the purity of the lover – the same purity that forgives even the visceral vigor of lust itself, as Nietzsche notes (*GS* 62) – would be disinclined to wish or to be asked to imagine the inner guts of the beloved, the whole network of tissue and blood and nerves in all their glistening truth, so the believer had, in times gone by, a similar lover's horror with respect to the divine sensorium. In earlier, more religiously (as opposed to more scientifically) pious times, one recoiled from the viewpoint that would reveal the beloved: the cosmos and thus God himself, laid bare by the incursions of telescopes and astronomical theory: "In everything that was said about nature by astronomers, geologists, physiologists, and doctors, he saw an intrusion on his choicest property and thus an assault – and a shameless one on the part of the attacker" (*GS* 59). We see here the sensitivity of Nietzsche's rhetorical style at work: beginning where "all the world" knows its way around and knows all about (love and love affairs), Nietzsche's parable carries the reader to a more esoteric insight (into scientific cosmology and the trajectories of its historical contextuality and thence to philosophy).

For the sake of the philosophical question of truth and logical rationality, Nietzsche raises the question of science as the question of the measure of the world of real and not ideal things. For Nietzsche, just as one cuts away the metaphysical domain of the noumenal, real/ideal world and loses the phenomenal world in the same process, the clarification of the human being in modern scientific, evolutionary, and physiological terms also works to eliminate the pure possibility of knowledge as such. If what works in us are tissues and cells, genes and evolutionary history, associations and habits, then we cannot speak of knowledge, and certainly not "reality." The problem is worse than a Kantian conceptual scheme, space-time, causality, etc.; the problem is the inmixture of ecology, physiology, and electro-chemical processes. Thus Nietzsche can conclude: "There is for us no 'reality'" (*GS* 57). When, in the following section, Nietzsche goes on to detail his radical nominalism he is not merely invoking the sovereignty of human invention but its impotence. Thus he declares his conviction "that unspeakably more lies in what things are called than in what they are" (*GS* 58). Moreover: "appearance from the very start almost becomes essence and works as such." But cutting through all of this is itself a proof of its efficacy and origin and, above all, "it is, we should not forget, enough to create new names and estimates and probabilities in order to create new 'things' in the long run" (*GS* 58). This poetic creativity is the ultimate meaning of the troubadour's art (*trobar*, an etymologically disputed term, meaning invention but also related to tropes and their variations) as a science: it is the heart of what Nietzsche called *la gai saber*.

For Nietzsche, "all of life is based on semblance, art, deception, points of view, and the necessity of perspectives and error" (*BT*, "Self-Criticism," 5). Nietzsche saw that the critical self-immolation of knowledge ("the truth that one is eternally condemned to untruth," *KSA* 1[760]; "On the Pathos of Truth," 65) that stands at the limit of the critical philosophic enterprise is to be combined with the sober notion that insight into illusion does not abrogate it and, above all, such insight does not mean that illusion lacks effective or operative power. To the contrary, "from every point of view," Nietzsche argued, "the *erroneousness* of the world in which we live is the surest and the firmest thing we can get our eyes on" (*BGE* 34). Nor, as we have traced the etymology of *Wissenschaft*, is this visual metaphor an incidental one here. For Nietzsche, to regard the body as a complex knowing instrumentarium, widely keyed to all its senses and not restricted to sight alone, offers an understanding of the body itself as mind, that is, not opposed to the mind, and not imagined as a Cartesian or Lockean adjunct to the mind, but, writ large and veritably Hobbesian (if beyond Hobbes), a "great reason, a plurality with one sensibility, a war and a peace" (Z I, "On the Despisers of the Body"). Nietzsche continues: "The tool of your body is also your little reason, my brother, which you call 'spirit,' a little tool and plaything of your great reason." With even more Kantian clarity, we hear: "There is more reason in your body than in your reason" (*KSA* 10, 4[240]). Nietzsche thus sets the body in contrast to the intellect, our "four-square little human reason" in the materialist context of empirical science (*GS* 373).

As a physician of culture, the philosopher is to be an artist of science, a composer of reflective thought, refusing the calculations of science as the thickness deadly to the "music" of life (*GS* 372, 373). Refusing such calculations, the gay science promotes a more musical, more passionate science. In this way, the "only" help for science turns out to be not more science or better scientific understanding but the therapeutic resources and risks of art. The goal is not a more charming, comic or "light" science but a science worthy of the name: a gay science with the courage truly to question, resisting what Nietzsche analyzes as the always latent tendency of degraded and ordinary science, grey science as I have been calling it, to rigidify into either dogma – "You must be mistaken! Where have you left your senses! This cannot be true!" (*GS* 25) – or empty and mindless problem-solving, "an exercise in arithmetic and an in-door diversion for mathematicians" (*GS* 373). What Nietzsche means by thinking in the critical service of science (as the artful "mastery" of this newly won gay science) can only be expressed in its contextual connections to topics in other kinds of philo-sophic reflection traditionally regarded as distinct. One allies laughter and wisdom, rejoining art and science because, for Nietzsche, the problem of science corresponds to the problem of art and life.

It is for this reason that one always misses the point when one maintains that Nietzsche is either "for" or "against" science. Instead, Nietzsche's interpretive touch-stone contrasts what affirms mortal life on this earth with what denies that life. But because mortal life includes sickness, decay, and death, this tragic perspective opposes the nihilism (be it mystico-religious or rational-scientific) which would seek, as does religion, to redeem or else, as does science, to improve life because *both* perspectives turn out to *deny* mortality (suffering, frustration, death – an emphasis common to the troubadours as well as ancient Greek music drama or tragedy and, indeed, opera).

Nietzsche's philosophy of science addresses the problem of mortal life without seeking to solve it. For Nietzsche, "knowledge and becoming" (truth and life) mutually and incorrigibly exclude each other (*KSA* 12, 9[89]). Thus, to say that "our art is the reflection of *desperate knowledge*" (*KSA* 7, 19[181]) is to set art and knowledge on the same level and for this same reason: both art and knowledge can be used either against life or in the service of life (and we recall that "life" is the "woman" of Nietzsche's troubadour song in *Thus Spoke Zarathustra* (see too *GS* 229). But when Nietzsche writes in *The Gay Science* that "*science* can serve either goal" (*GS* 12), he cannot be articulating a traditionally naive expression of science's celebrated neutrality, as we have seen. Instead, and precisely as a logical or theoretical project, science is the kind of art or illusion (or convention) that remains inherently nihilistic. Because science (as such) is not objectively neutral, science must *always* be critically reviewed not on its own basis (this cannot be done) but rather on the ground of what makes science possible, and that is what Nietzsche originally named the "light" of art.

Only art gives us perspective on things, only art permits us to see things from the proper distance. This is the knowledge proper to the art or science of rhetoric. That same optic – or perspective prism, to allude to a Goethean metaphor for Nietzsche's own approach to science – focuses on life regarded in such a way that it can be seen in all its shifting complexity: "At times we need to have a rest from ourselves by looking at and down at ourselves and from an artistic distance, laughing *at* ourselves or crying *at* ourselves; we have to discover the hero no less than the fool in our passion for knowledge; we must now and then be pleased about our folly in order to be able to stay pleased about our wisdom" (*GS* 107).

This joyfulness (or gaiety) is what Nietzsche encourages us to learn from "the artists," and in the same manner as we learn from physicians how best to down a bitter drink: by thinning it, to diffuse or veil it, or by mixing sugar and wine into the potion (*GS* 299). Art has at its disposal a variety of means for *making* things beautiful, alluring, and desirable, precisely when they aren't – for "in themselves, they never are" (*GS* 299) Here Nietzsche calls upon us to be wiser than, to go further than, the artist who forgets his magic at the point where his art leaves off: "We however want to be the poets of our lives, and first of all in the smallest and most everyday way" (*GS* 299).

As "the actual poets and authors of life", this poetizing would extend to a benediction of life, as it is, *amor fati*. Promising to bless life, Nietzsche made this his own St. January resolution of the great year of eternity, "I want to learn more and more how to see what is necessary in things as what is beautiful in them – thus I will be one of those who make things beautiful" (*GS* 276). This alliance of science (necessity) and art (creativity) is the art of living, the achievement of Nietzsche's gay science.

See also 3 "The Aesthetic Justification of Existence"; 13 "The Incorporation of Truth: Towards the Overhuman"; 15 "The Body, the Self, and the Ego"; 17 "Naturalism and Nietzsche's Moral Psychology"

Notes

1   Translations are my own, modified to accord, as much as possible, with the usage of Josefine Nauckhoff's translation of *The Gay Science*.

2   The title plays off many things, particularly Wagner's *Meistersinger*, but it also alludes to
    Walther von der Vogelweide, especially as Nietzsche had heard a course on his poetry
    during his time at the University of Bonn.

3   That one should take this "chaste" character lightly seems advisable. See Bec (2003) and
    de la Croix (1999). Nietzsche himself corroborates this erotic dimensionality in a note
    where he affirms the *"Provençale"* as a "highpoint" in European culture just because they
    were "not ashamed of their drives" (*KSA* 10, 7[44]). Despite the appeal of identifying
    Nietzsche's "immortal beloved" with Lou Salomé or tracing his passions for the boys of
    southern Italy, as some have speculated, it is more likely that the addressee of the love
    songs of Nietzsche's "gay science" would have been Cosima Wagner. I say this not because
    I am personally especially persuaded of Cosima's charms but because of the very nature of
    the gay science. The ambiguous coding of the troubadour's message was for public display:
    a love song in the direct presence of the beloved's husband, who, for good measure, would
    also be one's own patron. For a study of this coding see Zumthor (1975).

4   Number 7 of these rhymes is entitled *"Vademecum – Vadetecum,"* literally "go with me" and
    "go with yourself." For the collective title of rhymes taken as a whole, the reference is
    Goethe's *Singspiel* from 1784, originally set to music in 1785 by Goethe in collaboration
    with the composer Philipp Christoph Kayser. In 1799 E. T. A. Hoffman wrote stage music
    for Goethe's lyric play, but in connection with Nietzsche it is especially significant to note
    that among Max Bruch's first compositions included the music for Ludwig Bischoff's 1858
    adaptation of Goethe.

5   Due to its non-modern quality, this anti-lyrical (i.e., a-personal) lyricism absorbed Nietzsche's
    interest in *The Birth of Tragedy*. See *BT* 5.

6   The *tenso* is regarded as the model for scholastic reasoning. See Aubrey et al. (1999: 335).
    Some part of the justification for this association is found in Peter Abelard's compositions,
    compositions which Héloïse recalls to him as seductively enchanting and which, as he tells
    us in his own reflections on his "calamities," he directed into philosophy. Although apart
    from Héloïse's recollection of them to us and his own allusions, Abelard's secular songs
    have been lost, his sacred songs have been transmitted.

7   "*Albas* – Morningsongs; *Serenas* – Evensong; *Tenzoni* – Battlesongs; *Sirventes* – Songs of
    Praise and Rebuke; *Sontas* – Songs of Joy; *Laïs* – Songs of Sorrow" (*KSA* 9, 11[337]).

8   Marcel Decremps (1974) has traced this connection from Herder onwards.

9   Joachim Köhler, among others, has made the case for this claim, but it is complicated
    because, as David B. Allison and Marc Weiner have also shown, another argument for a
    similarly shameful eroticism, namely autoeroticism, can also be made. See Köhler (2002),
    Allison (2001), and Weiner (1995: 335–47).

10 I use the term "grey science" for reasons of assonance and contrast. Nietzsche character-
    izes Platonism in terms of its "grey concept nets" (*BGE* 14), yet he also invokes the color
    grey, especially silver grey among his many declared "favorite" colors. Yet Nietzsche's grey
    is not the grey of Hegel's night of obscurity but of distinctions. The grey of context and
    differentiation, Nietzsche's hermeneutic grey, as he remarks in an arch reference to Paul
    Rée in his preface to *On the Genealogy of Morals*, serves to outline "the whole, long hiero-
    glyphic text, so difficult to decipher of humanity's moral past!". This grey of shades and
    differentiations makes a pencil sketch or pen-and-ink drawing more precise than even the
    most colorful photograph for scientists concerned with pragmatic details, as in a medical
    handbook.

11 Nietzsche's *Thus Spoke Zarathustra* begins with a dawn song (*Albas*) exemplifying another
    of Nietzsche's master song cycles, in addition to the instantiation of, and ironic variation
    upon, the more typical troubadour's dawn song (which was traditionally more a song
    sung less to greet the new day than to mourn the close of the alliances of the night, as the

hours steal into the claims of the day) in the *Songs of Prince Vogelfrei*, "Song of a Theocritical Goatherd."

12 This refers to the *Leys d'Amor* – laws of love – a work compiled in Toulouse by seven troubadours who established the Académie littéraire de Toulouse ou Consistoire du Gai Savoir, a group that transmitted the poetic code of the *gay saber*. On the relation to law see Goodrich (2001: 95–125).

13 Regarding the troubadours see Treitler (2003) and Aubrey (1996). For a discussion of the distinction between vocal and unaccompanied song in the context of the tradition of musical accompaniment, see Page (1976) and Zumthor (1975).

14 The full context here is as follows "The *human being* as the measure of things is similarly the basic concept of science. Every law of nature is ultimately a sum of anthropological relations. Especially number: the quantitative reduction of every law, their expression in numerical formulas is a μεταφτρά as someone one who lacks the ability to hear judges music and tonality according to the Chladni sound patterns" (*KSA* 7, 19[237]).

15 The critical distance Nietzsche maintains with respect to Buddhism may thus be understood with respect to his own rigorously "scientific" temperament. See *GS* 78, 299, 301, 339.

16 See Aubrey et al. (1999: 277–9), "Les Troubadours."

17 For a discussion of this particular metaphor see Steiner (1986).

18 The *planh* is the troubadour song sung to lament the death of the singer's "master" or protector. Although the setting of Nietzsche's Venice poem in his *Ecce Homo*, "On the Bridge . . ." is twilight and thus would seem to be a plain evening song, it may also be regarded as a lament for Wagner, who died in 1883. The 1886 poem, "My Happiness" ("Mein Gluck!"), included in the *Songs of Prince Vogelfrei* would also seem to make reference to this death. For further discussion of Nietzsche's Venice poem, including its association with Wagner, and in the context of Nietzsche's recollection of Hölderlin, see Babich (2000: 267–301).

19 For a longer consideration of Nietzsche and "science" see Babich 1994 and 2003.

20 As a philologist, Nietzsche was characteristically conscious of this root connection between vision and scientific knowledge – hence his focus on the ocular tendency of science in general – but especially natural science. See the following note: "Science aims *to interpret the same phenomenon through different senses* and to reduce everything to the most *exact* sense: the optical. Thus do we learn to understand the senses – the darker are illuminated by the lighter" (*KSA* 11, 25[389]). And it might be worth investigating the degree to which this ocular conception inspired both his focus on what he called the "science of aesthetics" in his first book, his emphasis upon the importance of the haptic sense in the physical sciences (cf. *TI*, " 'Reason' in Philosophy," 3), and his special attention to the sense of "taste," a focus he earlier played back to its etymological association with wisdom as such. The Greek word which signifies "wise" etymologically belongs to *sapio*, I taste, *sapiens*, the one who tastes, *sisyphos*, the man of the keenest taste; a keen ability to distinguish and to recognize thus constitutes for folk consciousness, the authentic philosophical art. Be it deliberate or not, Nietzsche's example remarkably parallels David Hume's reflections on aesthetic taste. I discuss this further in Babich 2003.

21 Like the problem of the "music" of ancient tragedy, the problem of the "gay science" turns out to be the problem of the "music" of the troubadours' songs. The performative parallel to the Homeric problem is clear: there are thousands of preserved songs – and this is only part of the originally greater song tradition, recorded centuries after its heyday – and only a fraction of these preserved songs have written indications of musical melodies. An intriguing application of digital analysis offers some support for Nietzsche's own conviction that the words themselves constitute the music. See Hardy and Brodovitch

(2003: 199–211). The authors use the computer's capacity for phonetic analysis not by relying on transcription into modern linguistic phonetic conventions but by invoking instead Robert Taylor's observation that "Old Occitan is largely phonetic; that is, in most cases, the spelling reflects the actual pronunciation" (in McGee et al. 1996: 105). The literally phonetic quality of Provençal (as opposed to modern French) makes it possible to teach (shades of Nietzsche's own usage) computers "to 'hear'." See *Zarathustra*, prologue, 5. Nietzsche here is inverting Aristotle's reference to the use of proportional metaphor in his *Rhetoric* (bk. III, 10 and 11) for helping one's hearers "see."

Editions of Nietzsche Used

Beyond Good and Evil, trans. Walter Kaufmann (New York: Vintage Books, 1966).
The Birth of Tragedy, trans. Walter Kaufmann (New York: Vintage Books, 1967).
The Gay Science, trans. Walter Kaufmann (New York: Vintage Books, 1974).
The Gay Science, trans. Josefine Nauckhoff (Cambridge: Cambridge University Press, 2001).
"On the Pathos of Truth" (1872), in *Philosophy and Truth: Selections from Nietzsche's Notebooks of the Early 1870s*, ed. and trans. Daniel Breazeale (Atlantic Highlands, NJ: Humanities Press, 1979), pp. 61–9.
Thus Spoke Zarathustra, trans. R. J. Hollingdale, 2nd edn. (Harmondsworth: Penguin, 1969).

References

Allison, David B. (2001). *Reading the New Nietzsche* (Lanham, MD: Rowman & Littlefield).
Aubrey, Elizabeth (1996). *The Music of the Troubadours* (Indianapolis: Indiana University Press).
—— et al. (1999). "Les Troubadours," in Françoise Ferrand (dir.), *Guide de la musique du moyen âge* (Paris: Fayard).
Babich, Babette E. (1994). *Nietzsche's Philosophy of Science: Reflecting Science on the Ground of Art and Life* (Albany: State University of New York Press).
—— (2000). "Between Hölderlin and Heidegger: Nietzsche's Transfiguration of Philosophy," *Nietzsche-Studien*, 29, pp. 267–301.
—— (2003). "Nietzsche's Critique of Scientific Reason and Scientific Culture: On 'Science as a Problem' and 'Nature as Chaos'," in Gregory Moore and Thomas Brobjer (eds.), *Nietzsche and Science* (Aldershot: Ashgate), pp. 133–53.
Bec, Pierre (2003). *Le Comte de Poitiers, premier troubadour, à l'aube d'un verbe et d'une érotique* (Montpellier: Université Paul Valery "Collection lo gatros").
de la Croix, Arnaud (1999). *L'Éroticisme au moyen âge: Le Corps, le désir, l'amour* (Paris: Tallandier).
Decremps, Marcel (1974). *De Herder et de Nietzsche à Mistral* (Toulon: L'Astrado).
Goodrich, Peter (2001). "Gay Science and Law," in V. Kahn and L. Hutson (eds.), *Rhetoric and Law in Early Modern Europe* (New Haven: Yale University Press), pp. 95–125.
Hardy, Ineke, and Brodovitch, Elizabeth (2003). "Tracking the Anagram: Preparing a Phonetic Blueprint of Troubadour Poetry," in Barbara A. Altman and Carleton W. Carroll (eds.), *The Court Reconvenes: Courtly Literature Across the Disciplines* (Cambridge: D. S. Brewer), pp. 199–211.
Heidegger, Martin (1982). *Nietzsche*, vol. 2: *Eternal Recurrence of the Same*, trans. David Farrell Krell (San Francisco: Harper & Row).
Köhler, Joachim (2002). *Zarathustra's Secret: The Interior Life of Friedrich Nietzsche*, trans. Ronald Taylor (New Haven: Yale University Press).

McGee, T. J. et al. (eds.) (1996). *Singing Early Music: The Pronunciation of European Languages in the Late Middle Ages and Renaissance* (Bloomington: Indiana University Press).

Page, Christopher (1976). *Voices and Instruments of the Middle Ages* (Berkeley: University of California Press).

Porter, James I. (2000), *Nietzsche and the Philology of the Future* (Stanford: Stanford University Press).

Small, Robin (2001). *Nietzsche in Context* (Aldershot: Ashgate).

Steiner, Deborah (1986). *The Crown of Song: Metaphor in Pindar* (Oxford: Oxford University Press).

Treitler, Leo (2003). *With Voice and Pen: Coming to Know Medieval Song and How It Was Made* (Oxford: Oxford University Press).

Weiner, Marc A. (1995). "The Eyes of the Onanist or the Philosopher Who Masturbated," in id., *Wagner and the Anti-Semitic Imagination* (Lincoln: University of Nebraska Press).

Wilamowitz-Möllendorff, Ulrich (2000). "Future Philology," trans. Gertrude Pöstl, Babette E. Babich, and Holger Schmid, *New Nietzsche Studies*, 4(1/2), pp. 1–32.

Zumthor, Paul (1975). *Langue, texte, énigme* (Paris: Éditions du Seuil, 1975).

7

Nietzsche and Philosophical Anthropology

RICHARD SCHACHT

> To translate man back into nature [. . .] to see to it that man henceforth stands
> before man as even today, hardened in the discipline of science, he stands before
> the rest of nature [. . .] – that may be a strange and crazy task, but it is a *task* –
> who would deny that?
>
> (*BGE* 230)

Nietzsche calls for "new philosophers," who are to follow his lead and prelude to a "philosophy of the future." But what are his "new philosophers" to do, and how are they to go about doing it? As their herald and trailblazer, what does *he* do, and how does *he* go about it? In a general way, the answers to these questions are quite evident. The twin main tasks of Nietzsche the philosopher, and of the "new philosophers" he envisions, are *interpretation* and *evaluation* – which, more often than not, means *re*interpretation and *re*valuation.

Nietzsche's "revaluation of values" involves reassessing various things that have come to be valued in one way or another and also prevailing values themselves. But what did he propose and undertake to interpret (or reinterpret)? The list includes religion, morality, art, science, and various types of social and political institutions. It also includes truth and knowledge. It further includes a variety of psychological phenomena – and something related but more comprehensive as well, to which he devotes a great deal of attention: *ourselves*. And for him this means first and foremost: what we are *as human beings* – as *Menschen*, or (as he likes to put it), as "the type *Mensch*," and as human (*menschlich*) types.

In this respect Nietzsche makes common cause, in a general but nonetheless significant way, with a number of his philosophical predecessors and contemporaries. He found in Spinoza a kindred thinker, and with good reason; for the reinterpretation of human nature was of no less concern to Spinoza than was the reinterpretation of the natures of divine and mundane reality, and he was much closer to Nietzsche in both the spirit and the substance of his understanding of human reality than their very different idioms might lead one to suppose. Hume, an even closer philosophical cousin, wrote *A Treatise of Human Nature*, proclaiming in his introduction to it that "there is no question of importance, whose decision is not compriz'd in the science of man," understood as inquiry into "the principles of human nature," by way of "a cautious observation of human life"; and Nietzsche may well be conceived as undertaking to follow his lead, both in principle and in practice. Enlightenment French *philosophes* like LaMettrie, in his *Man a Machine*, took up the idea of "man" as part and parcel of the material world with Gallic zest; and as Nietzsche's dedication of *Human, All Too Human* to Voltaire shows, he came early on to see himself as their heir – in his focus upon and naturalistic approach to things "human" in particular.

While Hegel made what he called *Geist* the centerpiece of his reinterpretation of ourselves (and of God and the world along with us), he did – as had Kant – make provision for a philosophical "anthropology" as part of his comprehensive account of what we are and have it in us to become. Feuerbach seized upon this idea and amplified it, rallying post-Hegelians to the banner of a completely naturalistic "anthropology" to which the whole of human "spirituality" was to be "reduced," with "der Mensch" as its proper object; and Marx followed suit. Schopenhauer advocated yet another radical reinterpretation of ourselves as (irremediably and all too) human, and of human reality as a part of a world that is anything but divine or divinely rational in its nature and course. Kierkegaard too made "what it means to exist as a human being" his central concern, but sought to draw its comprehension in a radically different direction, as remote from all naturalism as from any Kantian or Hegelian idealism. While Nietzsche might thus seem to have plenty of philosophical company in his interest in the question of how our human reality is to be understood, however, he pursues that interest very differently, and is highly critical of his precursors on the entire matter.

Foucault would have it that Nietzsche heralds the demise not only of God but also of "man" – that is, not only of the very idea of "God" or of some other such divine transcendent reality, but also of the very idea of "man," as a type of creature with a "human" nature about which there is anything significant (other than of a merely biological sort) to be said (Foucault 1992: 322, 342). For Foucault as for the existentialists, the ideas of "man" and "human nature" stand or fall – and so they fall, and go over the side – with the idea that there is some kind of (metaphysical) human "essence." He and they seem to think that Nietzsche takes the same view of the matter. But does he? Nietzsche does indeed reject the idea of an immutable, ahistorical human essence, as will be seen; but that, for him, is by no means the end of the matter. On the contrary: it is only the beginning. Or so I shall be arguing.

1

As I read him, Nietzsche would have us reconsider rather than abandon the idea of "der Mensch," recast our conception of human reality and the sort of human nature of which it is meaningful and philosophically perspicacious to speak, and then get on with their reinterpretation, in a radical but also robust naturalistic manner appropriate to the kind of thing human reality fundamentally is and also has come to be.

Nietzsche is quite explicit about this, both before and after the three-year *Thus Spoke Zarathustra* (1883–5) period, making clear his continuing commitment to this project to the end of his philosophical life. In the 1882 edition of *The Gay Science*, in conjunction with his announcement (for the first time) of the "death of God" (*GS* 108), he goes on to ask: "When will all these shadows of God cease to darken our minds? When will we complete our de-deification of nature?" And then he gets to the point to which these questions are leading: "When may we human beings begin to *naturalize* ourselves in terms of a pure, newly discovered, newly redeemed nature?" ("Wann werden wir anfangen dürfen, uns Menschen mit der reinen, neu gefunden, neu erlösten Natur zu *vernatürlichen!*," *GS* 109). That is precisely what he takes himself to be attempting to do in *Gay Science*, by means of the very sorts of inquiries on display in it. In the aftermath of the demise of the idea of any sort of transcendent reality in terms of which this life and this world are to be understood, the reinterpretation of human reality in this manner becomes as urgent for him as does the revaluation of values.

As Nietzsche reiterates in 1886, in the passage from *Beyond Good and Evil* cited at the outset, this project involves the "task" of "translating man back into nature" ("den Menschen zurückübersetzen in die Natur", *BGE* 230) – that is, achieving an understanding of human reality purged of religious, metaphysical, and moralistic baggage, as a piece of "de-deified" nature through and through. "We have learned better," he writes two years later, in 1888, in *The Anti-Christian* (as the title of *Der Antichrist* is best translated). "We no longer trace the origin of man in the 'spirit', in the 'divinity', we have placed him back among the animals." Our spirituality is inseparable from our animality: "'Pure spirit' is pure stupidity: if we deduct the nervous system and the senses, the 'mortal frame', *we miscalculate* – that's all!" (*A* 14). But as Nietzsche also makes clear both elsewhere in *Beyond Good and Evil* and subsequently (in the 1887 edition of *Gay Science* and in *On the Genealogy of Morals* [1887] in particular), the reinterpretation of ourselves that he advocates and undertakes further involves going on to elaborate this naturalizing "translation" of our human reality in whatever ways turn out to be required in order to do justice to the respects in which it has come to be something that is no longer merely biological, in consequence of developments in the course of humankind's history that have profoundly transformed it.

Nietzsche pursues this project by examining a wide variety of human phenomena from as many different perspectives – physiological, evolutionary-biological, psychological, sociological, cultural, historical, linguistic – as he suspects may turn out to be illuminating, and by seeking to develop a comprehensive understanding of human reality and possibility that takes account of and makes sense of what thereby comes to light. He reflects upon basic and general human traits, upon their rudimentary and commonplace manifestations, and also upon their more uncommon and exceptional transformations and developments, pathological as well as admirable. And he attempts to do so with human-scientific sophistication – both biological and social.

To be sure, Nietzsche's fundamental and most pressing concern is more than merely interpretive: it is with how we might "become *those we are* – human beings who are new, unique, incomparable, who give themselves laws, who create themselves" (*GS* 335), and, more generally, with "what, given a favorable accumulation and increase of forces and tasks, might yet *be made of man*," who "is still unexhausted for the greatest possibilities" (*BGE* 203) – in short, with what he calls "the enhancement of life." Yet he believes it to be imperative in this very connection to achieve the best possible understanding of how "the type *Mensch*" became other than our protohuman ancestors when they were little more than just another species of animal, and of how we came to be the sort of creature about which and for whom these questions can meaningfully be posed. As he so vividly puts the point: "To that end we must become the best learners and discoverers of everything that is lawful and necessary in the world: we must become *physicists* in order to be able to be *creators* in this sense"

117

(*GS* 335). And "becoming physicists" here is only shorthand for becoming as well informed as possible in all of the cognitive disciplines that have any bearing upon our human constitution and its development.

An interpretive project of this sort cannot possibly ever be completed once and for all, and must remain a "work in progress" – as is the human reality that is its topic (and in part owing to that very fact). Yet Nietzsche is convinced that it is possible to make real gains in the soundness, depth, and justice of our self-understanding. And he further considers it to be of the greatest importance, both philosophically and humanly, that we make every effort to do so, with all of the intellectual honesty, integrity, sophistication, and skill we can muster, and availing ourselves of all we can learn from the various disciplines – natural-scientific as well as social, historical, and cultural – that have any bearing upon such inquiry. My aim in this essay is to consider more fully how he conceives of and pursues this project, and to suggest what (to my way of thinking) is to be made of it.

2

One of the basic questions requiring to be considered, for Nietzsche, is that of how our ancestors' pre- or proto-human animality could have been transformed into our own basic garden-variety humanity – under what conditions, by what sorts of developments, and with what consequences and prospects. This is a question, with an expanding set of subsequent questions, with which Nietzsche was concerned throughout his productive life. In *Thus Spoke Zarathustra* he has Zarathustra proclaim: "body am I entirely, and nothing else; and soul is only a word for something about the body" (Z I, "On the Despisers of the Body"). Yet he also stresses that human life has been more than a merely biological affair for a very long time; that the kinds of transformations involved have not all come about for merely or entirely biological reasons, or in merely biological ways; and that, instead, they have occurred under certain sorts of social and cultural circumstances that are also among the conditions of their possibility.

So, for example, in *The Birth of Tragedy* Nietzsche makes much of the relation of the artistic impulses he calls "Apollonian" and "Dionysian" to the more primordial phenomena of dreaming and intoxication – from which they derive by way of a kind of sublimation process, but from which they also are importantly different in both their manner of expression and their significance. He is very much concerned in this early work to try to understand the social and cultural conditions and practices that engendered them and the associated forms of human spirituality, and the birth and death of their "tragic" offspring. In several posthumously published fragments from the same period, "Homer's Contest" (1872) and "On Truth and Lies in a Non-Moral Sense" (1873), his attention is drawn to some highly significant transformations of human life with the advent of certain such conditions and practices: the impact of the Greek institution of the "contest" upon the affective constitutions of its human participants (in the former essay), and the impact of the requirements of social existence upon the development of human consciousness (in the latter).

Similar themes are sounded and explored throughout *Human, All Too Human* (1878). "The tremendous task facing the great spirits of the coming century," Nietzsche announces, is to "attain to a hitherto altogether unprecedented *knowledge of the precon-ditions of culture*" (*HH* 25). And he takes this to require a new kind of philosophical thinking. In the very first section of this work he criticizes "metaphysical philosophy" for its aversion to thinking in terms of origination and development, and lauds "historical philosophy [. . .] which can no longer be separated from natural science, the youngest of all philosophical methods." Such a wedding of historical and human-scientific perspectives and approaches is precisely what is needed, Nietzsche contends, calling for "a *chemistry* of the moral, religious and aesthetic conceptions and sensa-tions, likewise of all the agitations we experience within ourselves in cultural and social intercourse, and indeed even when we are alone" (*HH* 1; cf. *GM* I. 17n.). And in the next section he extends this line of thought to an appeal for a "historical" kind of thinking about ourselves. "Lack of historical sense is the family failing of all philo-sophers," he laments. "They do not want to learn that man has become." But this is something they are going to have to learn for, he asserts, "everything has become." And the conclusion he draws is that "what is needed from now on is *historical philoso-phizing*, and with it the virtue of modesty" (*HH* 2).

Two years later, Nietzsche concluded the final installment of *Human, All Too Human*, *The Wanderer and his Shadow* (1880), very tellingly. "Many chains have been laid upon man so that he should no longer behave like an animal," he writes. The "chains" he has in mind here are "those heavy and pregnant errors contained in the conceptions of morality, religion and metaphysics." Humanity will not have attained a healthy maturity in its hard-won supersession of its erstwhile animality, he suggests, until they are no longer needed, and the toll they have taken is a thing of the past. "Only when this *sickness from one's chains* has also been overcome will the first great goal have truly been attained: the separation of man from the animals" (*WS* 350). This underscores the importance Nietzsche attaches to the transformation of the character of human reality associated with this "separation of man from the animals" – which is here suggested to be at least well on the way to becoming a reality – and of the role that certain sorts of cultural developments have played in it, by engineering the modification of our original dispositions.

This is one of the recurring themes of *The Gay Science*. It is accompanied by Nietzsche's increasing interest in the phenomenon of *sublimation* and other modifications of our affects and their expressions, and in various forms of consciousness and thought as well, in their relation to different sorts of social and cultural conditions by which they are either prompted or hindered. Case studies of such affects as assertiveness, acquisitiveness, sexual craving, and selfishness, and their various possible sublimations, are presented frequently (e.g. *GS* 13, 14, 21), finding collective expression in *Zarathustra* shortly thereafter: "Once you had wild dogs in your cellar, but in the end they turned into birds and lovely singers" (Z I, "Of Joys and Passions"; see also Z III, "Of the Three Evil Things") And the problem of consciousness, which Nietzsche characterizes as "the last and latest development of the organic" in *Gay Science*'s first edition (*GS* 11), receives a strikingly social interpretation (reminiscent of TL) in its second edition published four years later, in which he proposes that "consciousness has developed only under the pressure of the need for communication," and thus – at least in its origins – "does not really belong to man's individual existence, but rather to his social or herd nature" (*GS* 354).

3

In *Beyond Good and Evil* Nietzsche attempts to think through the idea of the "enhance-ment" of human life and the conditions of its possibility, as well as the kinds of obstacles and threats there may be to it. So he speaks of "having opened our eyes and conscience to the question where and how the plant 'man' has so far grown most vigorously to a height," and to the presumably related questions of what "serves the enhancement of the type '*Mensch*'," and in what ways (*BGE* 44). Morals, for example, are here again suggested to have done so, the detrimental consequences of some types of morality notwithstanding: "What is essential and inestimable in every morality is that it con-stitutes a long compulsion," he writes; for "given that, something always develops, and has developed, for whose sake it is worth while to live on earth" (*BGE* 188).

But now Nietzsche advances a further conjecture: "Every enhancement of the type '*Mensch*' so far as been the work of an aristocratic society – and it will be so again and again." Such transformations of the material of our humanity, he contends, require the mediation of the appropriate sorts of social and cultural conditions and institutions, at least to begin with: "Without that *pathos of distance*," he writes, we never could have become capable of "the craving for an ever new widening of distances within the soul itself, the development of ever higher, rarer, more remote, further-stretching, more comprehensive states" (*BGE* 257). Nietzsche's contention that higher spirituality never could have become humanly possible if there had not first been a kind of psycho-social schooling of the human psyche by way of social stratification is certainly debatable; but this is a paradigm case of the sort of conjecture and debate in which his kind of rethinking of human reality is to consist.

It is in this context that Nietzsche first introduces his distinction between "master morality and slave morality" – a distinction that is explicitly associated with "a ruling group" in a position of social dominance over a "ruled group" (*BGE* 260). Both types of morality – and so also the aspects of human reality that they have helped to shape – are thus social phenomena, rooted in group social dynamics and structural relation-ships. Nietzsche even supposes that social relations can have biological ramifications. So, for example, he subscribes to the (now discredited but then reputable) Lamarckian idea of the biological heritability of acquired characteristics, which he also brings into play in the course of this discussion. "One cannot erase from the soul of a human being what his ancestors liked most to do and did most constantly," he writes. "It is simply not possible that a human being should *not* have the qualities and preferences of his parents and ancestors in his body." Nor is this purported to be merely a family affair; for Nietzsche immediately goes on to say: "This is the problem of race" (*BGE* 264).

This passage is informative with respect to Nietzsche's usage and thinking, however problematic and infelicitous it may be in other respects. It shows that "race" for him is a concept that fundamentally maps something like putative national character (e.g., "the English," "the French," "the Germans") or ethnicity (e.g., "the Jews") with a biological twist, and simply means a subset of humankind that shares – and is dis-tinguished from other subsets by – some such configuration of (purportedly typical, inherited and heritable, and so biologically anchored but alterable) dispositional traits. It further shows something significant about Nietzsche's conception of human reality:

that it *has* this kind of diversity, and further has a mutability that is greater in the longer run than it is in the shorter term, in which both biological and social variables are significantly involved. In any event, the basic question at issue – namely, that of what sort of diversity and mutability does in fact characterize human nature – is one of the kinds of questions with which he takes it to be the task of the philosophical reinterpreter of human reality to come to grips. And it is part of the burden of Nietzsche's argument at least from *Beyond Good and Evil* onward that humanity has come to consist of a considerable variety of different types, differently endowed as well as differently disposed, both by nature and by nurture; and that it is moreover a very open question how this or that particular configuration of human qualities and capacities will express itself.

Nietzsche's acceptance of the idea of the heritability of acquired characteristics – as a seemingly well-founded piece of human-scientific knowledge – is an instance of his determination to heed and take seriously in his philosophical thinking what can be learned about ourselves from the sciences. It also is an obvious example of the hazards of doing so, even with the best of intellectual intentions and conscientiousness. The saving grace of this determination, such hazards notwithstanding, is that, like scientific inquiry itself, philosophical inquiry that is so minded is open to the possibility – and indeed the likelihood – of subsequent correction and rethinking when it goes astray. The enterprise of a Nietzschean naturalistic philosophical anthropology, like Nietzsche's kind of philosophy more generally, does not stand or fall with each and every substantive position he himself takes. A fundamental feature of it is its non-dogmatic, always only provisional, and ever experimental character, and its commitment to remain forever open to good reasons to reconsider any hypothesis ventured, interpretation advanced, and assessment proposed.

I would observe, in passing, that Nietzsche's Lamarckianism does render comprehensible certain otherwise rather puzzling aspects of his thinking. In particular, it leads him to suppose that much is at stake in the kinds of social and cultural developments that affect human attitudes, values, and behavior. For in addition to the existence of significant biological differences as well as commonalities among human beings, he supposes that there is a good deal about human beings that is quite plastic in the long run, but that is only marginally so in the shorter term – and further, that the extent to which this is so varies, in an unfortunate way: the dispositions and capacities involved in all enhancements of life can only be developed slowly and with difficulty, but can all too easily be lost – perhaps owing to the dependence of the realization of such developed traits upon related cultural-environmental conditions, in conjunction with some "use it or lose it" principle (as Nietzsche would appear to suppose). Indeed, the fact that these sorts of human traits have appeared at all, for Nietzsche, is owing to an extraordinarily serendipitous configuration of highly contingent circumstances that came about for quite other reasons. The loss of these traits would thus be a very serious matter indeed, for the odds against their re-emergence would be great, with grave consequences for the future of humanity. And Nietzsche may well be right about that.

Moralities are among the devices that have significantly affected the shaping of human reality, both locally and (over the past few millennia) more broadly. Under their influence the constitutions and dispositions of human beings have been configured in ways that make us very different sorts of creatures from the outset of our lives than our remote ancestors were – and they may do so yet again. Indeed, Nietzsche thinks, they may well be doing so even now, with the spreading of the kind of "herd morality" and associated values and ideologies that he fears may be turning human beings into the sort of "perfect herd animal" he dreads and abhors. Once humans are turned into such creatures, he fears that "herd-animal" nature would be the human nature that would then have to be reshaped over long generations by some new serendipitous arrangements coming about, through something like what he calls "the monstrous fortuity that has so far had its way and play regarding the future of man" (*BGE* 203), for humanity ever again to amount to anything more than such an insipid form of life. And the next time, if the transformation of humanity along these lines were nigh unto complete, there would be no "master"-types around to initiate such a historical process, rendering it all too likely that the type of "the Last Man" envisioned with disgust and dismay in *Zarathustra* would be the final inheritor of the earth.

4

These concerns loom large in *Beyond Good and Evil*; and it was thus with them very much in mind that Nietzsche turned his attention to a "genealogical" project in his next book, *On the Genealogy of Morals* (1887). He had long been convinced that morals have played a key role in the "dis-animalization" of humanity, as the passage cited above from *The Wanderer and his Shadow* illustrates. His project of a de-deified, naturalistic, and "historical" reinterpretation of human reality and all things human ("morals" included) thus quite naturally led him to think about the interplay between their genealogies, and about the sorts of human dynamics that must or may have been involved in both cases, with significant consequences for the understanding of both our morals and ourselves – and of human possibility as well. In this book, written in the penultimate year of Nietzsche's productive life, we encounter him at the height of his philosophical powers, and at the climax of his philosophical development. And in its three "Essays" he pursues these issues in ways that are particularly revealing with respect to both the manner and the substance of his thinking with respect to human reality. For these reasons I shall focus primarily upon it in what follows.

Nietzsche tells us at the outset of *GM*, in its preface, that he is concerned with *die Moral* ("morals"), and so with their genealogy, because he suspects that, their significant role in our "dis-animalization" notwithstanding, it could well be that "precisely *die Moral* would be to blame if the intrinsically possible *highest powerfulness and splendor* of the type 'man' [*des Typus 'Mensch'*] were never to be attained." (*GM*, preface, 6) It is with "the type '*Mensch*'" (the kind of creature we are), and with *how it* (*we*) *will turn out*, that he is fundamentally concerned here; and it is Nietzsche's chief preliminary concern to understand humankind as it has come to be, what has contributed to its development (for the better or for the worse – or perhaps for both), and what this can teach us about what we have to work with. His "genealogical" investigations are thus offered as contributions not only to a revaluation of "moral" values, but also to a reinterpretation of our attained human reality, and to a re-envisionment of human possibility informed by that reinterpretation.

GM's First Essay is a study of the origin and development of the phenomenon and associated morality of the especially poisonous form of resentment Nietzsche designates by the French term *ressentiment*, not only in reaction to "master morality" but also under conditions of domination of one group by another. The morality of *ressentiment* is inseparable from the psychology of *ressentiment*, which he believes to have been occasioned in a very understandable sort of way, but to have resulted in the emergence of a new type of human mentality – and therefore of a new type of human reality. "The man of *ressentiment*" is a very different sort of human being from "the noble man"; and the secretive, furtive nature of the former, whose "spirit loves hiding places, secret paths and back doors," contrasts vividly with "the stronger, fuller nature" of the latter, "in whom there is an excess of the power [*Kraft*] to form, to mold, to recuperate and to forget" (*GM* I. 10–11).

Nietzsche evidently believed (on Lamarckian grounds) that what may have begun as a form of behavior and manner of conducting oneself that was forced upon dominated groups, at a certain stage in our genealogy could and did come to be internalized and ingrained sufficiently not only to become "second nature" to its first generation, but moreover to be transmitted to subsequent generations and developed further in them. So he writes: "A race of such men of *ressentiment* is bound to become eventually *cleverer* than any noble race; it will also honor cleverness to a far greater degree: namely, as a condition of existence of the first importance" (*GM* I. 10). It was forced to be clever, then made a virtue of the necessity, and this reinforcement resulted in further development of the trait. In this way, Nietzsche suggests, the seed of cleverness and thus of intellectual acuity was planted and grew in humankind, itself the product of harsh conditions of existence that required it. And so also a piece of human psychology – the disposition to react with *ressentiment* when confronted with superiority in some respect or other, and to seek some alternative within one's reach by means of which to counter that superiority – came to be coupled with it.

But it is not only among the subjugated that Nietzsche discerns this disposition. He also associates it with "the priestly mode of valuation," which he sees not as having begun in a "slave revolt" against the values of their masters, but rather as having "branched off from the knightly-aristocratic [type] and then developed into its opposite" by way of the degeneration of a "priestly-noble mode of valuation" into a hatred born of "impotence" – "the most spiritual and poisonous kind of hatred." And Nietzsche goes so far as to attribute the emergence of another and very significant form of spirituality to this development: "other kinds of spirit hardly come into consideration when compared with the spirit of priestly vengefulness." But this is by no means something he laments: "Human history would be altogether too stupid a thing without the spirit that the impotent have introduced into it" (*GM* I. 7).

And there is more to this part of Nietzsche's story. For "from the trunk of that tree of vengefulness and hatred," he goes on to contend, "there grew something equally incomparable, a *new love*, the profoundest and sublimest kind of love." The capacity for such a love, he suggests, could have first arisen in us in no other way: it grew out of this "profoundest and sublimest kind of hatred" – not as its opposite or negation, but "as its crown [. . .] driven as it were into the domain of light and the heights in pursuit of the goals of that hatred – victory, spoil, and seduction" (*GM* I. 8).

123

This is more than just a tale of values, their sordid origins and their inversions and developments. It is also a sketch of a proposed account of a part of the genealogy of our human psychological reality and humanly attainable spirituality. These developments are conceived not only to be fostered and reflected in the morals, values, and revaluations on which Nietzsche is commenting, but also to have been gradually ingrained in the constitutions of the strands of humankind in which they took hold, with nature and nurture reinforcing each other, in a manner the cumulative result of which was the existence of a very different sort of human being than had walked the earth before it all began.

The initial upshot of this set of developments, Nietzsche suggests, is that, under the influence of the kinds of cultural developments through which these "instincts of reaction and *ressentiment*" were expressed, the greater part of humanity was "domesticated" to the core. Thus he is prepared to suppose that it "really is true" that "the *meaning of all culture*," at least in the first place and with respect to its original function, "is the reduction of the beast of prey 'man' to a tame and civilized animal, a *domestic animal*" – not just a wild animal that has been broken, but a domestic animal as different from a "beast of prey" as a dog is from a wolf, and with psychological attributes that equip us from the outset for forms of life geared to the demands of the cultural reality that has displaced and "reduced" our erstwhile affective constitution (*GM* I. 11).

The purported anthropological reality of these sorts of basic human dispositions and differences is reflected in the account Nietzsche goes on to give of human action, in which he contends that "there is no 'being' behind doing, effecting, becoming; 'the doer' is merely a fiction added to the deed" – and thus that there is no "neutral substratum behind the strong man, free to express strength or not to do so" (*GM* I. 13). It by no means follows, however, that nothing of the kind, *functionally* speaking, could ever *develop*; and in the Second Essay Nietzsche suggests not only that this did indeed happen, but also how it could have come about.

5

The Second Essay of *The Genealogy of Morals* is as rich as the first in its import for an understanding of the genealogy of our humanity as well as of the kind of morality we have come to take for granted in the modern Western world. It opens with a clear indication that Nietzsche believes that *der Mensch* – or at any rate, a subset of humankind – *has become* something our proto-human ancestors were not: "an animal *with the right to make promises*." That this "right" or ability is no mere fiction or illusion for Nietzsche is indicated not only by his reference to this as "the paradoxical task that nature has set itself in the case of man" and "the real problem regarding man" – that is, regarding the shaping of our attained human reality – but also by his following reflection on how "remarkable" it is "that this problem has been solved to a large extent." And he supposes this to have come about through a "breeding" process, in the course of which our prior constitution was altered, in a manner that is to be understood naturalistically (*GM* II. 1). The question of what that process might have been is the central question of this Second Essay.

Nietzsche considers this development to have been so remarkable precisely because it involves overriding or supplementing what he takes to be an even more fundamental trait of our nature: an "apparatus of repression" that has the function of "active forgetfulness, which is like a doorkeeper, a preserver of psychic order," keeping our consciousness from being cluttered up with the detritus of the moment, "to make room for new things," and to make possible such "nobler functions" as "regulation, foresight, pre-meditation." And it is his contention that "this animal, which needs to be forgetful" in this sense and for these reasons, "has bred in itself an opposing faculty, a memory, with the aid of which forgetfulness is abrogated in certain cases." It is no fiction, but rather the capacity for "a real *memory of the will.*" And he then goes on to observe that this re-engineering of our psychic constitution required other changes and developments of profound significance. In particular: "Man himself must first of all have become *calculable, regular, necessary,*" and further, "able to calculate and compute" correspondingly (*GM* II. 1).

And Nietzsche takes this actually to have happened – at least to some significant extent, even if neither completely and perfectly nor irreversibly. This, he contends, is "the tremendous labor [. . .] performed by man upon himself during the greater part of the existence of the human race, his entire *prehistoric* labor." It was done "with the aid of the morality of mores and the social straitjacket," by means of which "man was actually *made* calculable." And while this "long story" might seem to be the genealogy of nothing more admirable than the "herd mentality" of which Nietzsche is so contemptuous, he is quick to observe that it actually and ironically turns out also to have set the stage for a radical supersession of that type of mentality and humanity; for its "ripest fruit" is said to be "the *sovereign individual,* like only to himself, liberated again from the morality of mores, autonomous and supramoral" (*GM* II. 2).

It is only *this* type of higher humanity, and not the obedient "herd-animal" type (and certainly not the "beast-of-prey" type), that may be said to have "the actual *right* to make promises" – and so to have "superiority over all those who lack the right to make promises and stand as their own guarantors." For such a human being alone is truly "master of a *free* will"; and this "power and freedom" that have "at length been achieved and become flesh in him" may even warrant "a sense of mankind come to completion." In such a person "the consciousness of this rare freedom, this profound power over oneself and over fate," becomes "the dominating instinct"; and Nietzsche suggests that this sort of "consciousness of self-mastery" may aptly – and admiringly – be called by the name of "conscience" (*GM* II. 2). It can hardly be imagined to be operative in such a person from birth, or to become so without an education of great rigor; but the capacity for it is a different story. That is conceived by Nietzsche to have come to exist at all only as a consequence of the "tremendous process" he mentions, whose course was as circuitous as it was fortuitous.

That process, as has been observed, is suggested by Nietzsche to have begun with the cultivation in humankind of both *calculability* and the *ability to calculate*, in practical (behavioral) contexts. These capacities have come to be a part of our human psychological constitution; and even though their realization would appear to be a contingent affair, depending upon a variety of factors affecting one's development, the corresponding traits have come to be widespread, albeit to varying degrees. Human beings thus have acquired the capacity to develop the functional equivalents of two of the very things Nietzsche is at pains to deny that we possess by metaphysical birth-right: *unitary selves* and *rational minds*. Metaphysically considered, he insists, both are fictions; but he further contends that, functionally considered, they are real enough, for they have come or are coming to be humanly possible, and even psychologically real, in the course of human events that have come about for reasons of the most all-too-human of sorts. They have "come true" – at least to some extent, here and there, and promisingly enough that Nietzsche is moved to some of his most soaring rhetoric in an attempt to convey what he believes the "tremendous process" to portend, culminating in the panegyric with which the Second Essay concludes (*GM* II. 24).

6

The last ten sections of *Genealogy*'s Second Essay (*GM* II. 16–25) are in many respects the philosophical and rhetorical high point of the entire work. They are concerned with the genealogy of something far more important than the phenomenon of "bad conscience" itself: the *human possibility* associated with our emergent humanity, and thus the higher humanity that human reality now has it in it to attain. "The bad conscience is an illness, there is no doubt about that," he writes – "but an illness as pregnancy is an illness" (*GM* II. 19). It is not self-punishment as the internalization of the institution and practice of punishment Nietzsche associates in the first part of this essay with the creation of memory and reliability. Rather, he argues, it is *self-torment*, in which one does unto oneself an alternate version of the violence one is unable to do unto others. And it is precisely the possibilities this opens up that he finds so fascinat-ing and promising: "the existence on earth of an animal soul turned against itself, taking sides against itself, was something so new, profound, unheard of, enigmatic, contradictory, and *pregnant with a future* that the aspect of the earth was essentially altered" (*GM* II. 16).

The *übermenschlich* higher humanity that Nietzsche has Zarathustra proclaim to be "the meaning of the earth" (*Z*, prologue, 3) is what he undoubtedly has in mind here, to the realization of which this very development – pathological though it may be, and lamentable though it may also be in certain undeniable respects – opens the way. And the point he is making is that it has the phenomenon of "bad conscience" as a condition of its possibility – not only negatively, as a price that must be paid for its realization, but also positively, as a kind of transforming ordeal of the spirit, upon which the very capacity to attain such a humanity depends. This all-important human possibility would surpass even the "sovereign individuality" celebrated early in the Second Essay, in a crucial respect for which again the phenomenon of "bad con-science" has been genealogically indispensable. For it is the key to the very *creativity* of this "creative spirit" that is for Nietzsche the key to what he calls "the *redemption of this reality*," this life and this world, "from the curse that the hitherto reigning ideal has laid upon it," at the conclusion of this essay (*GM* II. 24). The qualities of the "sovereign individual" are a part of the constitution and "great health" of this envisioned form of higher humanity; but they are not enough – for, admirable as they are, they are no recipe for creativity, any more than is the inventive cleverness that Nietzsche considers to be one of the traits we owe to the "slave" mentality.

Nietzsche proposes a "hypothesis" with respect to "the origin of the 'bad conscience' " that traces it to "the stress of the most fundamental change [man] ever experienced – that change which occurred when he found himself finally enclosed within the walls of society and of peace" (*GM* II. 16). It is thus suggested to be a profound psychological consequence of a social development in the basic circumstances of human life. Memory too, and the punishments that were required to create it, together with the associated calculability and ability to calculate, were likewise purported to be consequences of the socialization of humanity. But here a different sort of dynamic is envisioned; and the proto-human type under consideration is by no means one in which a "slave" mentality has been instilled. Rather, it is a type more akin psychologically to that of the "masters" of the First Essay – but confronted with a very different set of circumstances.

"In this new world," Nietzsche writes, "these semi-animals, well adapted to the wilderness, to war, to prowling, to adventure," could no longer give free rein to "their former guides, their regulating, unconscious and reliable drives" that had served their kind so well prior to the advent of "society and peace." The conditions of social life required that they check these drives, and rely instead on "thinking, inferring, reckoning, coordinating cause and effect [. . .] they were reduced to their 'consciousness,' their weakest and most fallible organ." The development of these capacities thereby received a tremendous impetus. The problem that resulted in the pathology of "bad conscience" was not the relative weakness of their new "conscious" abilities, however, but rather the undiminished strength of their old impulses: "at the same time the old instincts [*Instinkte*] had not suddenly ceased to make their usual demands! Only it was hardly or rarely possible to humor them."

What were these "old instincts"? "Hostility, cruelty, joy in persecuting, in attacking, in change, in destruction" are those that Nietzsche mentions. They were blocked by "fearful bulwarks" so formidable that even these aggressive "semi-animals" were deterred from expressing them in the old direct ways. Severe and gruesome "punishments," he writes, "belong among these bulwarks." And now Nietzsche introduces a theory of drive or instinct inhibition, internalization, and sublimation that is one of the hallmarks and central features of his philosophical psychology and anthropology. His general thesis is that "All instincts that do not discharge themselves outwardly *turn inward* – this is what I call the *internalization* [*Verinnerlichung*] of man." This, he contends, is how our "entire inner world" originated: it "expanded and extended itself, acquired depth, breadth, and height, in the same measure as outward discharge was *inhibited*." Human reality was thereby transformed, but in a manner that is comprehensible in purely naturalistic terms. And, he suggests, "thus it was that man first developed what was later called his 'soul' " (*GM* II. 16).

What made this possible, Nietzsche surmises, was that the inhibited or repressed drives were both obliged and enabled "to seek new and, as it were, subterranean gratifications." It is important to observe here that, while he thus supposes the drives or instincts in question to have been amenable to *redirection*, and even to a degree of *alteration* in their manner of expression, they are not – at least at this stage – supposed to be capable of a more fundamental and thoroughgoing *decomposition* or structural reduction to a mere pool of affective energy, or even of a major *transformation* that would alter their character quite dramatically. They may disguise and redirect themselves; but at this juncture they are purported to have retained their original basic character.

Thus it was, Nietzsche suggests, that these aggressive drives, without losing their basic character, came to be turned upon the only available target: "all this turned against the possessors of such instincts." And, he continues, "*that* is the origin of the 'bad conscience'." Indeed, there is even a further twist to the story; for the target of these drives more specifically was not just "the possessors of such instincts," but rather *these instincts themselves*, in their more overt and undisguised forms. The "bad conscience" thus amounts to "a declaration of war against the old instincts upon which [man's] strength, joy, and terribleness had rested hitherto," using "subterranean" forms of these very "instincts" to combat them. And so it was that there came to be "the existence on earth of an animal soul turned against itself, taking sides against itself" (*GM* II. 16).

Nietzsche's analysis of "bad conscience" is thus that it is the experience of a torment that is the expression of a kind of violence being done to ourselves, akin to the "mortification of the flesh" that ascetics practiced in an attempt to still the promptings of desire, compounding frustration of the desire through its non-fulfillment by measures designed to make one suffer for having had the desire at all. But there is more to the story. Nietzsche is fascinated by the strange pleasure that not only accompanies the phenomenon of "bad conscience" but is a part of it.

Here Nietzsche fastens upon the idea of cruelty and the pleasure that can be taken in it, repugnant though this may seem to our modern sensibility. For if the causing of suffering, as a crude but obvious and commonplace expression of the disposition he calls "will to power," is deeply gratifying (as Nietzsche presumes all expressions of primordial dispositions must be to creatures constitutionally so disposed), rendering us all the more ready to assert ourselves in ways that have – or at any rate are taken to have – that effect, then that very tendency will carry over when one's innate aggressiveness is turned against oneself, and the result is "this uncanny, dreadfully joyous labor of a soul voluntarily at odds with itself that makes itself suffer out of joy in making suffer" (*GM* II. 18).

This is the key to understanding Nietzsche's reason for making so much of the *promise* of this phenomenon – of cruelty as something in which pleasure is taken – its all-too-human origins and pathology notwithstanding. The sentence from which the passage just cited was taken reads more fully as follows: "This secret self-ravishment, this artists' cruelty, this delight in imposing a form upon oneself as a hard, recalcitrant, suffering material," is nothing less than "the womb of all ideal and imaginative phenomena, [which] also brought to light an abundance of strange new beauty and affirmation, and perhaps beauty itself" (*GM* II. 18).

Nietzsche thus is suggesting something profoundly important with respect to the genealogy of humanity here: it was the addition of the phenomenon of the "bad conscience" to the psychological makeup of humanity as it had previously been constituted that made possible the kind of sublimation process that opened the way to all subsequent enhancements of human life, to date and to come. His very image in this passage is highly suggestive of how he conceives of this development: the "bad conscience" was not merely the *impetus* to it, or even merely its *catalyst*; it was its "*womb* [*Mutterschoss*]," providing the nourishment required for it ever to see the light of day.

So it is that we find Nietzsche contending that all of "higher culture," "higher spirituality," artistic creativity, and even intellectual integrity has its roots in cruelty. But this is only his tough-minded, iconoclastic way of making the point that all such higher-human phenomena could neither have originated nor be sustained without a self-dissatisfaction that would be of little consequence (and perhaps would not even be possible) were it not for the happenstance of our having a fundamental zest for doing things that cause suffering. And it explains Nietzsche's worry that, were that zest to be bred out of us, the dissatisfaction with ourselves as we are in the first place (whether we are "blond beasts" or creatures of a more domesticated sort), which is the key to our "self-overcoming" and any "life-enhancing" creative activity in which we might self-transfiguringly involve ourselves, would be lost.

7

This is by no means the whole of Nietzsche's account and reinterpretation of the genealogy and attained character of human reality and possibility; nor is this his last word on the matter. He continues to address it in the flurry of books written in the next (and final) year of his productive life (1888), in a variety of similar and different ways, even if never again with as much sustained reflection upon specific points as we find in *The Genealogy of Morals*. His time was too short, and his polemical agenda in that last year was too long. He left nothing even approaching a comprehensive treatise on the subject (like Hume's *Treatise*, or Kant's *Anthropology*); nor is it at all likely that he ever would have done so, however long a productive life he might have had. But he made a start on the project of the kind of treatment of human reality he believed to be appropriate to its subject, and to be both viable and a high priority for the "philosophy of the future" he envisions and attempts to inaugurate. And the passages discussed above are paradigmatically indicative of what he has in mind, calls for, and tries to do along these lines.

One may well ask: what is the status of the kinds of claims that he makes in them, and that I have been considering? What Nietzsche is doing, I suggest, is neither dogmatizing nor purporting to be relating the straight facts, either historically or as matters now stand with respect to morality and humanity. Rather, I take him to be speculating, in a manner inspired by his sense of recent developments in evolutionary and biological thinking, in an attempt to come up with a plausible naturalistic account of certain phenomena and developments that he believes to have been of crucial importance for the genealogy of both morals and the version and varieties of humanity that have come to exist and to be humanly possible. His aim is to convince his readers that it probably was nothing grander than developments *of the sort* he relates in his "Just So" stories that resulted in the emergence of morals and *Menschen* as we know them; even though it is a further part of his intention to make a case for a particular "hypothesis" with respect to the unfolding of this genealogy. He also draws upon and imports into his story certain biological and psychological ideas that he believed to be sound scientifically, independently of the account he offers, which influence his elaboration of it.

Nietzsche does not hesitate to go out on a limb in both respects. That is not – or at any rate, is not simply – because he is foolishly rash. Rather, it is because he thinks that this is the way to conduct one's philosophical experiments: taking certain ideas that seem plausible, well-warranted, and promising, and running with them interpretively – mindful, however, that these are only hypotheses and interpretations, and that it may turn out there are good reasons to reconsider and revise them. And in the end, it is the spirit rather than the letter of this enterprise that matters most.

Nietzsche professes, in his preface to GM, to aspire to contribute in it to "a knowledge of a kind that has never yet existed or even been desired" – namely, "a knowledge of the conditions and circumstances in which [moral values] grew, under which they evolved and changed" (GM, preface, 6). It goes beyond the "Prelude to a Philosophy of the Future" that preceded it: it is intended to be a contribution to such a philosophy. And Nietzsche is bold enough – bolstered by the sense that his ideas on these matters are the issue of a "*fundamental* will of knowledge [*Grundwillen* der Erkenntniss]" (GM, preface, 2) – to suppose that the contribution it makes is to the attainment of that new kind of knowledge of our morals and ourselves.

Nietzsche's most important actual contribution here (and perhaps elsewhere as well), however, may be to something that is both less and more than that: to their reconception and general comprehension. It is entirely in the spirit of his endeavor to take his most fundamental commitment to be to no particular hypothesis or interpretation, but rather to the quest for the best naturalistic, evolutionarily and historically sophisticated interpretation and understanding we can achieve of our human reality as it has come to be – with the genealogy of morals a part of the story, both affecting it and being affected by the rest of it. He ventures his best guesses, and thereby challenges us and anyone else who might be interested to enter the fray and attempt not only to fault him but to improve upon his attempts and experiments. He would be no Lamarckian today, for example; nor would he have us be Larmarckians if we would be Nietzscheans. Rather, he would have us be the best genealogists and interpreters of morals and of ourselves that we can be. That is how we can best be true to what is best in him, as philosopher and as philosophical mentor and educator. We can learn as much from thinking about where and why and how he goes astray as we can from any of his insights. And we can learn even more from paying attention to what he is trying to do, and how he is trying to do it.

8

In the early decades of the twentieth century, before he was appropriated by *Existenz*-philosophers like Heidegger and Jaspers, Nietzsche was commonly associated with the naturalistic movement known as *Lebensphilosophie*, or the "philosophy of [biological and human] life." A movement known as *philosophische Anthropologie* grew out of *Lebensphilosophie* in the late 1920s, in competition with Husserlian phenomenology and other philosophical fashions of the day. It was initially led by Max Scheler and Helmuth Plessner, whose books *Die Stellung des Menschen im Kosmos* (Man's Place in Nature) and *Die Stufen des Organischen und der Mensch* (The Levels of the Organic and Man) appeared almost simultaneously with Heidegger's *Sein und Zeit* (Being and Time) in the late 1920s.

The *Existenzphilosophie* of Heidegger and Jaspers and its post-World War II French "existentialist" offshoot overshadowed this movement, however, both in Europe and in the English-speaking world. "Existential" philosophers – that is, philosophers focusing first and foremost (in the spirit of Kierkegaard) on first-person-singular human "existing," and approaching it in a manner attuned to its purportedly ineluctable "subjectivity" – often embraced Nietzsche avidly; but they also embraced him selectively, to suit their own philosophical purposes, which were generally hostile to any and all forms of naturalistic interpretation of human reality. That hostility has been shared by many of Nietzsche's more recent admirers and appropriators (such as Foucault and the post-structuralists) as well.[1] Foucault may be seen as heeding Nietzsche's call for a kind of "historical philosophizing" in thinking about human reality, but as utterly rejecting his attempt to integrate it with a naturalistic construal of its fundamental nature and constitution, placing his emphasis instead upon discursive formations. For Foucault there is only the anonymous play of forces and strategies, with history shaped by haphazard conflicts and marked by the dispersion of discontinuous events (Foucault 1977: 146, 154). His structuralist approach ushered in some innovative developments with regard to the assessment of the sciences of "man"; but it loses sight of the specific set of questions and issues that guided Nietzsche in his genealogical inquiry into human reality and possibility.

Nietzsche's philosophical-anthropological interest and efforts thus are among the most neglected (or else misunderstood) parts of his philosophical legacy. The ground for their appreciation may perhaps have been best prepared by developments in Anglo-American philosophy during the last decades of the twentieth century, as "philosophers of mind" – and of action and of cognition – have become more interested in taking account of developments in the various human sciences that have bearing upon our understanding of ourselves, and have become more comfortable with an approach to human reality that is in basic accord with Nietzsche's naturalism. Nietzsche would have much to learn from them, and from our contemporary human sciences as well – and he would be eager to do so. But they also would have much to learn from him – as we all would, and still do, with respect to how to think and what to say about human reality.

See also 17 "Naturalism and Nietzsche's Moral Psychology"; 18 "Naturalism and Genealogy"; 19 "The Philosophical Function of Genealogy"; 20 "Agent and Deed in Nietzsche's *Genealogy of Morals*"; 21 "Nietzsche and Ethics"

Editor's Note

1   A notable exception is Gilles Deleuze (1925–95). In his classic book on Nietzsche, first published in France in 1962, Deleuze interprets Nietzsche as a radical pluralist and empiricist and places him alongside naturalists such as Spinoza and Hume (see Deleuze 1983).

Editions of Nietzsche Used

Beyond Good and Evil, trans. Walter Kaufmann (New York: Vintage Books, 1966).

131

The Birth of Tragedy, trans. Walter Kaufmann (New York: Vintage Books, 1967).

The Gay Science, trans. Walter Kaufmann (New York: Vintage Books, 1974).

On the Genealogy of Morals, trans. Walter Kaufmann and R. J. Hollingdale (with *Ecce Homo*) (New York: Vintage Books, 1967).

"Homer's Contest," in *The Portable Nietzsche*, ed. Walter Kaufmann (New York: Viking Penguin, 1954; pbk edn. 1959).

Human, All Too Human, trans. R. J. Hollingdale, 2 vols. (Cambridge: Cambridge University Press, 1986).

Thus Spoke Zarathustra, in *The Portable Nietzsche*, ed. Walter Kaufmann (New York: Viking Penguin, 1954; pbk edn. 1959).

"On Truth and Lies in a Non-Moral Sense," in *Philosophy and Truth: Selections from Nietzsche's Notebooks of the Early 1870s*, ed. and trans. Daniel Breazeale (Atlantic Highlands, NJ: Humanities Press, 1979).

Twilight of the Idols, in *The Portable Nietzsche*, ed. Walter Kaufmann (New York: Viking Penguin, 1954; pbk edn. 1959).

On the Uses and Disadvantages of History for Life, trans. R. J. Hollingdale, in *Untimely Meditations* (Cambridge: Cambridge University Press, 1983).

Further Reading

Deleuze, Gilles (1983). *Nietzsche and Philosophy*, trans. Hugh Tomlinson (London: Athlone Press).

Foucault, Michel (1989). *The Archaeology of Knowledge*, trans. A. M. Sheridan Smith (London: Routledge).

—— (1977). "Nietzsche, Genealogy, and History," in id., *Language, Counter-Memory, Practice: Selected Essays and Interviews*, trans. Donald F. Bouchard and Sherry Simon (Oxford: Basil Blackwell), pp. 139–65.

—— (1992). *The Order of Things: An Archaeology of the Human Sciences*, trans. A. Sheridan (London: Routledge).

Kant, Immanuel (1798). *Anthropology from a Pragmatic Point of View*, trans. Victor Lyle Dowdell (Carbondale and Edwardsville: Southern Illinois University Press).

By Richard Schacht, on Nietzsche and on philosophical anthropology, with bibliographies:

1975. *Hegel and After* (Pittsburgh: University of Pittsburgh Press), ch. 10, "Existentialism, *Existenz*-Philosophy, and Philosophical Anthropology."

1983. *Nietzsche* (New York and London: Routledge & Kegan Paul), esp. ch. 5, "Man and Men."

1990. "Philosophical Anthropology: What, Why and How," *Philosophy and Phenomenological Research*, 50, supplement (Fall), pp. 155–76.

1995. *Making Sense of Nietzsche* (Urbana and Chicago: University of Illinois Press).

Nietzsche's Philosophy and True Religion

LAURENCE LAMPERT

Was Nietzsche an atheist? He is famous for the words "God is dead," but he put those words in the mouth of "the Madman" (GS 125). He also had Zarathustra speak those words but at the very beginning of his career (Z, prologue, 2) whereas at the end of *Thus Spoke Zarathustra*, as at the end of *Beyond Good and Evil*, gods reappear, a god and a goddess, Dionysus and Ariadne (Z 3, "On the Great Longing"; BGE 295). Who are these two gods and why would they reappear in the writings of the philosopher famous for the phrase "God is dead"? I will argue that Nietzsche's books show that Dionysus and Ariadne reappear for one reason alone: they are the true gods of genuine philosophy, the logic of their reappearance lies in philosophy itself. What must *philosophy* be for Nietzsche if it makes the reappearance of Dionysus and Ariadne possible and desirable? My theme, therefore, is Nietzsche's philosophy and one of its upshots, its non-atheistic, religious upshot. My argument is based on an interpretation of *Beyond Good and Evil* (1886).

Beyond Good and Evil is a beautifully structured book with a carefully organized movement from beginning to end. Its opening preface and closing Aftersong enclose nine chapters, one of which, "Epigrams and Interludes," is itself an interlude dividing the book into two main divisions: the first three chapters deal with philosophy and religion, the last five with morals and politics. Philosophy and religion belong together as connected themes; they are the two greatest themes and they prepare themes that are great but subsidiary, morals and politics, which must now be altered by the new philosophy and religion.

The first chapter is a critique of philosophy – "On the Prejudices of Philosophers." The critique, however, contains something unexpected: unargued assertions of a new basis for philosophy. Four times one hears the words *will to power*. They name first the fundamental process present in philosophy, "the most spiritual will to power" (aphorism 9); they then appear as assertions about what is fundamental in the three basic sciences, biology, the science of the organic (13), physics, the science of nature as a whole (22), and psychology, the science of the human soul (23). Cumulatively, these assertions about philosophy, biology, physics, and psychology point to the comprehensive ontological claim that reality is ultimately will to power. But how, in a critique of philosophy as always perspectival and always driven by passion, can a philosopher have a right to true ontological claims? The second chapter of the book shows how a philosopher wins that right by showing what a philosopher is.

The Philosopher

Nietzsche displays what a philosopher is to a select audience only, the one selected out by the first chapter which ends on an invitation to lay the book aside if the dangerous voyage on which it now embarks appears too unsettling. The title of the second chapter names the select audience, "The Free Mind." (*Der freie Geist* is customarily translated "free spirit." As important as the connotations of free-spiritedness are, it seems more important to capture, as the first impression of Nietzsche's meaning, free-mindedness. *GM* I. 9 presents one way in which "free spirits" differ from Nietzsche's free mind.) The free minds who need to be told what a philosopher is are modern minds produced by the democratic Enlightenment, contemporary, intellectually enlightened minds. We are told first (24) that the philosopher is someone who "can never cease wondering" about one specific wonder: "In what strange simplification and falsification man lives!" Different from others as a spectator on the great play of simplification and falsification, the philosopher must avoid the temptation of acting too soon and becoming a martyr by insisting that others see the truth about their simplifications and falsifications (25). He must not follow Socrates, that supposed model of the philosopher whose public defense of himself showed how he insisted on proving the falsity of authoritative opinion while others looked on. The philosopher, Nietzsche goes on, is like all exceptions: all "strive instinctively for their citadel and secrecy where they are permitted to forget the 'rule' among men, as its exception" (26). But the philosopher is an *exception among exceptions*: "as a seeker after knowledge in the great and exceptional sense," he will be "pushed straight back to these men of the rule" (26). Abandoning his citadel of solitude, he turns – like Socrates – to a study of the Many and the opinions that rule us, a study of how he differs from us.

Such study teaches the philosopher that "it's difficult" to understand him "because he thinks and lives gangastrotagati among men who think and live differently, namely, kurmagati or in the best case, 'the way frogs walk,' mandukagati" (27). Nietzsche knew his readers would not know these Sanskrit words – he himself didn't know them and he copied them out in his notebook with reminders of what each meant (*KSA* 12, 3[18]). As foreign words they express beautifully the communication problem faced by the exception among exceptions, for Nietzsche ends his little play with Sanskrit words saying: "– I myself do everything I can to be hard to understand?" No, he just showed that he does what he can to make his foreign way of living and thinking understandable – he translated one of the foreign words. Leaving two *untranslated* is part of the communication: to understand him we'll have to work at translating the foreign into our own very different way of living and thinking. A philosopher thinks and lives gangastrotagati – as the sacred Ganges flows – swift, steady, relentless. Such a thinker must communicate across ineradicable difference to those who think and live as the tortoise creeps or the frog hops. As this example shows, it is offensive to claim to be exceptional. Therefore, wanting to communicate what his exceptional experience gained him, the philosopher must be playful and gracious:

he must seduce and enchant the potentially offended into exercising the necessary subtlety that will be our sole means of translating his foreign experience into our own – and into exercising the necessary hardness with ourselves that is our sole means of bearing the offense.

To confirm that a philosopher cannot avoid offense, Nietzsche opens a closed chapter in the history of philosophy: esotericism. "Our highest insights [the insights of the exception among exceptions] must – and should! – sound like follies and sometimes like crimes when they come without permission to the ears of those who are not the kind for them" (30). Having turned to the Many to study their ways, and wanting to communicate their conclusions, philosophers always learned they would be ridiculed as mad or persecuted as criminal. (As Plato learned: when Socrates claims that the philosopher has a right to rule, Adeimantus objects, saying that people commonly judge the philosopher either useless or vicious; Socrates responds: "it looks to me as if they are speaking the truth" [*Republic* 6.487d].) Consequently, philosophers invented a practice that the modern Enlightenment forgot but which Nietzsche rediscovered: "the exoteric and the esoteric as one formerly among philosophers distinguished them." All philosophers before modern times distinguished exoteric and esoteric and did so because they knew their highest insights would – *and should* – be judged mad or criminal. (On the universality of the practice of esotericism among philosophers, see the account by its twentieth-century rediscoverer, Leo Strauss [1952]). Nietzsche treats this rediscovered old distinction as itself esoteric; it

> does not so much consist in this, that the exoteric stands outside and from outside, not from inside, views, evaluates, measures, judges; the more essential is that he sees things from below – the esoteric, however, *down from above!*

The outer–inner distinction could suggest that entering the esoteric requires only permission or instruction. The more essential distinction suggests that the esoteric can be achieved only by ascent, making it inaccessible to anyone who is not the kind for it, which means almost all. This esoteric insight into the esoteric is itself mad or criminal, radically anti-democratic, but Nietzsche speaks it openly to democratically disposed readers who cannot help but feel its offense while also feeling predisposed to disbelieve it.

Nietzsche's criminal insight into the esoteric is a prelude to the criminal insight he now announces: what the philosopher sees from above. "There are heights of the soul where, looking out from them, tragedy itself ceases to have a tragic effect." The view down from above does not abolish tragedy but liberates from its *effects*, pity and fear. Nietzsche puts the crucial claim as a question: "and taking all the woe of the world together, who may dare decide whether its sight would *necessarily* seduce and compel precisely to pity and thus to doubling the woe?" The exception among exceptions, whose view on the woe of the world sounds mad or criminal, must dare to share his esoteric, privileged view with those who can never fully look down from the height (a beautiful elaboration of this thought ends *TI*, "What I Owe the Ancients," 5). Can all the woe of the world be lived communally without the fear and pity that the view from above transcends? This is an initial glimpse into the problem of the philosopher's insight and communication: can the view from above be translated into simplifications

135

and falsifications within which humans inescapably live? The only solution is the one Nietzsche in fact attempted: the esoteric man of insight must become a man of action whose actions are persuasive words.

The next two aphorisms treat the philosopher's problem of communication as a problem of the maturity of his audience, individual maturity (31), and the maturity of our whole species (32). The free minds have matured out of youthful dogmatism into skepticism, but Nietzsche suggests that a maturity beyond skepticism could attain true judgments on the deepest problems: philosophy is possible. Is a corresponding growth in the maturity of the whole species possible? The species too has passed through a maturation process, one that may have placed it on the threshold of a new maturity regarding truth, a new experiment with self-knowledge that could move humanity into a "post-moral" period, beyond the belief basic to the punitive or moral view that intention directs our actions and renders us deserving of reward or punishment. This possibility of experiments with the truth that affect the whole species prepares the central aphorisms of this chapter. The first issue the experimenter faces is attaining truth, the second is communicating it.

Philosophy

In the central aphorism of this chapter (34) Nietzsche acknowledges that the "epistemo-logical skepticism" of the free minds rightly dominates modern intellectual life. The philosopher, however, must now extend skepticism from the object of thought to thinking itself, despite the fact that this expansion of skepticism puts the philosopher at risk again, because "in civil life ever-present skepticism may be considered a sign of 'bad character' and hence belong among the imprudencies." But,

> among ourselves, beyond the civil world and its Yeses and Nos, – what prevents us from being imprudent and saying: the philosopher has nothing less than a *right* to "bad character" as that being on the earth which till now has always been most made a fool of?

"Among ourselves" – in the relative privacy of a philosopher's book addressed to his now prepared and genuine audience – his "bad character" can give itself the right to pursue relentlessly the mistrust natural to it, justified by his knowledge that the civil world always gives itself the right to judge the philosopher mad or criminal. The philosopher-criminal has "the *duty* to mistrust, to the most malicious cross-eyed squinting up out of every abyss of suspicion." With "the little joke of this dismal grotesque" Nietzsche interrupts his defense of dutiful mistrust. Is the philosopher only a fool of extreme skepticism, some frog peering up out of a swamp of suspicion? No, but Nietzsche's grotesque proves that he is not above making the philosopher seem a fool for he always keeps "at least a few pokes to the ribs for the blind rage with which philosophers resist being deceived" – a blind rage that now puts them at risk of falling prey to epistemological skepticism. This first poke to the ribs leads to the next: philosophers, tricked by grammar, find a fixed thinking subject where there is only process and activity:

Shouldn't philosophers be permitted to rise above faith in grammar? All due respect to nannies, but hasn't the time come for philosophy to renounce the faith of our nannies? –

A dash ends this long central aphorism on its demand to break faith with modern trust in skepticism and binds it to the next, tiny aphorism where Nietzsche quotes one of our Enlightenment nannies and directs a poke to the ribs against the most important of all nanny-beliefs:

O Voltaire! O Humanity! O Nonsense! There's something about the "truth," and the *search* for truth; and when a human being goes about it too humanly – "il ne cherche le vrai que pour faire le bien" – I bet he finds nothing!

Here is the chief theme of philosophy: *le vrai* – truth, the search for the truth that has moved philosophy from its beginnings. Here it faces its chief rival: *le bien* – the good, what counts as the good in itself. These are the classical terms, the True and the Good. And Nietzsche states openly (though in a foreign language) the classic, esoteric, criminal insight: belief in the Good blinds one to the True. Blinded by today's Good, "Humanity," the Good of the Enlightenment, today's searcher for the True – finds nothing. But Nietzsche's point is: he *wants* to find nothing, he needs his skepticism as a last resort allowing him to cling to his belief in the Good. Epistemological skepticism is justified by faith alone – no wonder that "when a philosopher these days lets it be known that he is not a skeptic [. . .] everyone is annoyed" (208).

Free-minded skepticism is not skeptical enough, it is dogmatic about its Good. Axiological dogmatism is sheltered by epistemological skepticism which entails ontological skepticism. Principled ignorance about the ultimate character of the world allows enlightened moderns to hold on to our Good. Reasonable ontological insight, were it only possible, could threaten the Good. Could a philosopher free of the Good, with a criminal mistrust of thinking itself, discover the True? And if he could, what would the True imply about the Good? These questions, provoked by the central aphorism and its little follow-up, prepare the next two aphorisms, the most important in the book for here a philosopher's mistrust of thinking leads to a new conclusion about the True and to the possibility of a new Good.

Can the search for the True free itself from convictions about the Good? Aphorism 36 conducts an experiment suggesting the answer is Yes – if the search obeys another human characteristic, conscience, the intellectual conscience produced by two millennia of Christianity and now "grown hard in the discipline of science" (230). This "conscience of method" or "moral of method" (36) conducts an experiment with thinking that puts in play the mistrust of thinking called for in the central aphorism: "Granted that nothing else is 'given' as real except our world of desires and passions [. . .] – for thinking is only a relation of these drives to each other –" one could still, experimentally, draw a true conclusion about what is *not* given, the world as a whole, if the intellectual conscience dictates the rational principle of simplicity, that reality is of one kind. "Granted" as well that one succeeded in explaining our entire life-drive as will to power, "as is *my* principle," Nietzsche says, "one would have gained the right" to draw the most general of all possible conclusions, a reasonable, potentially testable ontological inference about the world as a whole. "The world seen from within, the world defined and described according to its 'intelligible character' – it would be precisely 'will to power' and nothing besides. –"

This ontology of will to power is, Nietzsche says later, "as theory an innovation, – as reality it is the *Ur-fact* of all history" (259); Nietzsche, therefore, is the first to assign the fitting name to the force at work in all events. He had indicated that will to power is the "fundamental fact" of all phenomena (*KSA* 13, 14[79]) by the way he introduced the topic in the bare assertions of the chapter criticizing the prejudice of philosophers: it is the Ur-fact of the highest phenomenon, philosophy (9), of organic phenomena (13), of the totality of nature (22), of human nature (23). Is this just the prejudice of the new philosopher who flaunts the prejudices of past philosophers? What initially seemed mere prejudice has now been outfitted with its most basic possible argument: a reasonable account of the fundamental causality at work in the most knowable phenomenon – Know thyself! – gives one the right to an inference about what is knowable only indirectly, "the world." What remains is the massive project of all the scientific faculties: does this inference satisfactorily save the phenomena investigated by the sciences? Nietzsche issued an invitation to undertake this shared investigation after his first ever public account of will to power as "the way of all beings." Zarathustra has just made his discovery that Life is fathomable as will to power in the privacy of the songs in *Zarathustra* Part II; he breaks his privacy to offer an argument on behalf of his discovery of will to power to one audience alone, "you wisest." He ends his argument invitingly: let us reason about this (Z II, "On Self-Overcoming"). The central section of the central treatise of the book added to *BGE* as its "supplement and clarification" likewise addresses the fundamental theme of will to power, moving from the ultimate explanation of the origin and purpose of punishment to a general point about all "historical method," the "theory of a *power-will* playing itself out in all phenomena." Despite its explanatory power, this theory goes against "the ruling instincts and taste of the times" which have insinuated themselves into the most sophisticated science at high cost: one thereby "mistakes the essence of life, its *will to power*" (*GM* II. 12).

The economy or brevity with which Nietzsche chose to express his fundamental thought must not be allowed to detract from its centrality: this is the fundamental matter the presentation of which requires preparation and tact because the times dictate that this theoretical innovation be poorly heard and vehemently opposed. Nietzsche's economical presentations of the will to power in the books he published are illuminated by an important fact about Nietzsche's authorship: while writing *Beyond Good and Evil* and the books that followed, Nietzsche was composing elaborate notes on a general ontology of will to power, intending to publish their finished versions in the book announced on the back cover of *Beyond Good and Evil*: *The Will to Power: An Experiment in the Revaluation of All Values*, the major work Nietzsche did not get to complete. The notes confirm what the books should have made clear: Nietzsche's highest thought is an ontology, an account of the way of all beings. To be is to be energy; packets or quanta of energy are the ultimate constituents of everything that can be said to be. Energy quanta have describable qualities: inherent in them is the drive to express themselves, to expand, discharge, multiply, articulate their strength. Because such quanta of energy are always present only in a field of such quanta, expression-expansion always confronts expression-expansion: it always encounters resistance; it always submits to force superior to itself or subjects force inferior to itself.

138

Beyond Good and Evil is "a critique of modernity" (*EH*, "BGE"); it is also a "fish hook" aimed at luring a few readers into what Zarathustra had already entered and what Nietzsche intended to elaborate in the promised major work. *Beyond Good and Evil* indicates the direction Nietzsche had begun to take and invited his readers to take: consider the compatibility of the inferred ontological conclusion with contemporary gains in physics, biology, and physio-psychology, the three basic sciences – along with philosophy – that must learn to trace their subject-matter to what is ultimate: will to power. *Beyond Good and Evil* itself had no intention of pursuing that question. It pursues a more pressing, completely unavoidable question: just how will this rational reductionism be heard by contemporaries who get wind of it? Nietzsche had already said how we would hear it: in the way that every high insight of philosophy must – and should! – be heard: as folly or crime. Therefore, immediately after experimentally drawing his fundamental ontological conclusion, Nietzsche allows his desired audience, his "friends" the free minds, to express their reaction. They denounce him for the highest crime.

Aphorism 37, linked by a dash to the words " 'will to power' and nothing besides," is a dialog of the greatest brevity on the fundamental issue of the true and the good. At the peak of his book Nietzsche's friends speak their denunciation: "What? Doesn't that mean, to speak in the common language, 'God is refuted, but the Devil is not?'" The "free" minds are bound minds, bound to the old good. Your will to power ontology, they say, commits the highest crime, making everything sacred demonic and everything demonic sacred. The free minds employ the "common language," the religious language of God and Devil, because the more sophisticated language proper to these offspring of the Enlightenment lacks extremes vehement and absolute enough to express their horror at his teaching. They don't believe in God or Devil, but only this old language of extremes can express their revulsion at Nietzsche's ontological crime against humanity. They are still victims of "old metaphysical bird-catchers" who say "you are more, you are higher, you are of a different origin" (230). Nietzsche knew how his natural audience would react to his deepest teaching; he had no illusions about the immediate future of his philosophy. Nevertheless, his task was clear to him: "the terrible basic text of *homo natura* must again be recognized." Already "hardened in the discipline of science" to stand before the rest of nature as nature is, humanity must now, "with intrepid Oedipus eyes and sealed Odysseus ears," stand before itself as the piece of nature that it is (230). Can humanity as a whole learn to do what even Oedipus and Odysseus could not? For Oedipus plucked out his eyes when they beheld the awful truth and Odysseus opened his ears to the metaphysical bird-catchers no longer worthy of even being heard. Nietzsche's response to his friends at the peak of his book suggests how humanity can do what even old heroes of knowledge could not.

Nietzsche's reply to his friends' use of the old theology against the new ontology legitimates their turn from all beings to the highest beings. Speaking theologically, he says, "On the contrary! On the contrary! My friends!" The exact contrary is: the Devil is refuted but God is not. Your feeling is right, he says in effect, the will to power teaching does refute God, the God of our tradition, but is that god God? On the contrary, that supernatural God must be seen as the Devil, an all-powerful tyrant who set the world under a curse, assigning it to the Prince of this World, the so-called Devil. Nietzsche tempts his friends to think the most extreme blasphemy about our God;

139

going far beyond the historical judgment that God is merely dead, we are to judge our supernatural God to have been a crime against nature. The will to power teaching refutes that God and – you're right again – it does not refute the Devil, or what that God assigned to the Devil, our world of incessant change. But is the world the Devil's? On the contrary, what was once seen as the Devil's is vindicated as divine. With that suggestion, Nietzsche's dialog with his friends opens a whole new dimension for theological thought – can the divine be thought within a view that understands the world to be will to power and nothing besides? If it can be, one immediate correction to the old theology is indicated: "And as to the Devil, goddamn it, who compels *you* to speak in the common language!" Who but that old Devil himself, God, dead but not gone, lingering on for centuries as a powerful shadow on the wall of our cave dictating the language of divinity even to modern free minds (*GS* 108). The new theology accepts no Devil except, for now, the Devil-creating dead God, but this little exchange suggests that the new theology may well have gods, as yet unnamed.

In moving from 36 to 37 the account of all beings moves to the highest beings at the outcry of the offended being. The new philosophy clashes with the old religion; but what matters more for its communication is its clash with the relics of the old religion still ruling the minds of the supposedly liberated. In a book for modern free minds, this is the indispensable dialog; here, the new philosopher communicates the view down from above, the ontological conclusion about beings as a whole, and shows how it will be measured by the good that rules modern minds. This little dialog shows why the chapters on philosophy must be followed by a chapter on religion. The negative reason is that philosophical insight from above is bound to be *mis*measured by Voltaire's children; the positive reason is that the antitheological ire of post-Christian atheists can and must be replaced by an understanding of how religion can be true.

The future of the new philosophy hinges on a private dialog between the new philosopher and his only possible friends, modern free minds. Initially, even progressive minds react with fear and hate to the new ontology; but, invited to reflect on the possibility that that very reaction is merely a reflex dictated by the reigning good, Nietzsche's natural friends may learn to free themselves from their natural fear. Then what? Then they may want to work at hearing what the new philosopher indicates is the *fitting* response to the new ontology. Will the chapter on religion show how the true leads to a new good?

Religion

The chapter on religion indicates in its first aphorism that it is a philosopher's view of religion, a view onto high spirituality down from above, from the highest spirituality (45). The chapter deals first with Christianity, our primary religious *past*. The religious *present*, the two central aphorisms report, is a religious crisis of atheism and the assassination of the old soul concept (53–4). Next comes our religious *future*, our dawning nihilism – "To sacrifice God for the nothing: we all already know something of that" (55). Then Nietzsche touches what he alone already knows something about, a possible further future, the teaching of eternal return in its one appearance in the book (56), the teaching with which Nietzsche wanted to be identified: "I, the teacher of eternal return" – he says to end the *Twilight of the Idols*. After reaching this high point, the chapter on religion advances a claim: because the enlightened "no longer even know what religions are good for" (58), the philosopher of the future must take responsibility for the religion of the future. The sweep of the whole chapter thus suggests that a philosopher sees a new possibility for religion arising out of the crisis caused by the Enlightenment's successful fight against our religion; eternal return appears to be the essential item in a possible religion of the future.

The one aphorism on eternal return shows the new religion arising naturally out of the new philosophy. The aphorism follows the thought of some "Whoever" – "like me" Nietzsche says. It *is* him and at first it's only him. What this *whoever* thinks, Nietzsche had already described in detail, for this *whoever* looks down into things "with an Asiatic and supra-Asiatic eye" – Zarathustra's eye. This is the key to the extreme shorthand of aphorism 56: it describes in a single sentence the experience the whole of *Zarathustra* exists to exhibit. Its most important point is this: The supra-Asiatic eye has "looked into, down into the most world-denying of all possible ways of thinking." *Zarathustra* shows that this way of thinking is the way that thinks to be is to be will to power, the way of thinking that just caused the free minds to conclude that it refutes God but not the Devil. (The drama of *Zarathustra* follows a sequence similar to the path of thought in *Beyond Good and Evil*: it reaches its turning point in Part II when Zarathustra discovers that his former skepticism must be suspended because inquiry leads necessarily to the conclusion that "life" is fathomable as will to power ["The Dance Song"]; he reports this discovery only to "you wisest" ["On Self-Overcoming"] and then, alone, sees that the implication of this discovery is eternal return ["On Redemption"].)

Whoever looks down into this way of thinking with a supra-Asiatic eye "may just thereby, without really meaning to do so, have opened his eyes to the opposite ideal." Without really meaning to do so – this little aside asserts that the *whoever* is essentially an inquirer, not a teacher; he aims to understand, not to edify – the edifying, a new ideal, is the fruit of Nietzsche's inquiry without ever having been its goal. Driven by the dictates of truth alone to conclude that the world is will to power and nothing besides, he glimpses the ideal *opposite* to the ideal of world-denial – the most world-affirming ideal. The core of the new religion seems to be a new *ideal*, a new Good.

The new ideal is *ideal* for one kind of person only: "the most high-spirited, most alive, most world-affirming human being." *His* ideal has two aspects already set out in *Zarathustra*: first, it has "come to terms and learned to get along with whatever was and is." *Reconciliation* is Zarathustra's word for this, and as Zarathustra showed in one of his most important speeches, reconciliation is a rare and high achievement that overcomes what has prevailed till now, *revenge* against world and man for being what they are (Z II, "On Redemption"). Reconciliation liberates from the historic teachings that have housed humanity in the fantasy that we are essentially different from the world, but something "higher than all reconciliation" must be learned next – what Zarathustra himself enters at the highest point of *Zarathustra*, the end of Part III. The world-affirming human being of aphorism 56 glimpses that ultimate step as the new ideal: he "wants to have [what was and is] exactly as it *was and is* repeated out into all eternity."

Wanting the eternal return of everything that was and is, this world-affirming human being expresses his want in the most extreme way possible, "shouting insatiably da

LAURENCE LAMPERT

capo" – the musical instruction "Once more," the title of the song Zarathustra taught the higher men (Z IV, "The Night-Wanderer's Song," 12). The shouter shouts da capo "not only to himself, but to the whole play and spectacle" (*BGE* 56). Nietzsche then reverses the order of the "not only" and "but," giving primacy to one of the two items affirmed: "and not only to a spectacle but fundamentally to him who needs this spectacle – and makes it necessary." Nietzsche then adds a decisive "because," confirming that the affirmation has an originating source. The shouter needs this spectacle and makes it necessary: "*because* again and again he needs himself – and makes himself necessary." The unbounded affirmation of everything that was and is grounded in the self-affirmation of *this* self, *this* spectator. Viewing the world as will to power and nothing besides, he glimpses the new ideal, the affirmation of everything that was and is because it generated *him*.

Is this narcissism? No. The inquirer, the philosopher, affirms the whole play and spectacle because inquiry leads to the "intelligible character" of the whole as will to power. This inquirer affirms the *world* because *philosophy* is possible, because the world generates the possibility of its being thought. The most affirmative of all possible ways of thinking arises from one source alone: the thinker's recognition that in himself the world becomes, to a degree, transparent to itself. The ungoverned surge and pulse of mere energy generates the thinker who can think it – and must celebrate it because of what his thinking discloses.

The philosophical spectator of the ultimate spectacle, Nietzsche reports, makes the spectacle necessary because again and again he makes himself necessary. Necessary in what sense? It cannot be physical necessity: the spectator has not *made* the whole he views nor does he imagine he *made* himself. It cannot be teleological necessity: the spectator is not the purpose of the purposeless. The spectator who speaks here is the Zarathustra of "Before Sunrise" (Z III); gazing up into the open sky before dawn, he celebrates the *absence* of law-giving necessity, whether transcendent, mechanical, or teleological; he finds instead the *presence* of a totality of mere power relations and claims, "over all things stands the heaven Accident, the heaven Innocence, the heaven Chance." Seeing this, he necessarily blesses the world: the necessity is a lover's necessity, erotic necessity. Seen as will to power and nothing besides, the world becomes, to a degree, transparent as excess, overflow, gift-giving in the purposeless surge and excess of its energy. The world as will to power is lovable for the gift-giving it is *and* for the gift it is capable of receiving, its openness to interpretation, including the lover's ideal of wanting the eternal return of the beloved.

The argument of *Beyond Good and Evil* displays the connection between will to power and eternal return as a connection of fact and value. In the classical language Nietzsche restores, the true is related to the good, but in Nietzsche's version the true *generates* the good. Eternal return is not itself an ontological claim but the ideal arising out of the fundamental ontological discovery. Finding (*finden*) leads to inventing (*erfinden*) where the invented (*erfundene*) is the ideal of the inventive nature, the poetic, religious nature. The gift-giving philosopher becomes the central node of the whole economy of being and value; he, a product of the world's superfluity, gives back the gift in an ideal that blesses the world.

Will to power stands to eternal return as philosophy stands to religion. As understood by philosophy, religion elevates an ideal out of roots in the passions, particular

142

passions among rival passions. The new ideal is rooted in the passion of love and gratitude for life and world as they are. Nietzsche had interrupted his critique of Christianity to say that gratitude lay at the heart of Homeric religion (49), the religion supplanted in Greece by a religion based on the rival passion of fear – the otherworldly religion that the philosopher Plato put to use for his own ends, thereby establishing in our civilization a religion of immortal souls taught to fear the judgment of punitive gods. The religion whose ideal is eternal return recovers the passions foundational to the Homeric, the religion that generated the greatest cultural achievements of our species till now, the religion supplanted by Platonic religion, the still reigning religion whose God is dead.

The end of aphorism 56 acknowledges that a new ideal is not enough for a new religion. It echoes aphorism 37, for here too its audience raises a theological objection: "What? And this wouldn't be – circulus vitiosus deus?" Is the new ideal just a vicious circle made god? This time *we* have to add "On the contrary! On the contrary!" where the contrary is the *virtuous* circle, the circle of *life*, made god. The peak of the chapter on religion, like the peak of the chapters on philosophy, suggests again that new gods are necessary.

Gods don't return in the chapter on religion. Instead, the theoretical preparation for their return is made in the two chief claims of the rest of the chapter. The first concerns what religion is good for: religion cultivates and educates; its beliefs and practices establish the climate of opinion within which humans are raised to maturity and dwell; that climate of opinion is inescapably a system of simplification and falsification that encourages and enhances some characteristics of our species while discouraging and diminishing others (61). The second chief claim argues that religion serves humanity only when it is an instrument of the trans-religious (62). Religion must once again pass into the care of philosophy. Wisdom, the highest theoretical understanding of the world, must generate comprehensive opinions that are ministerial to the human species and that enhance the species by enhancing the true view of things. But how can a theoretical understanding, once arrived at, be translated into effective, persuasive opinion? How can true philosophy generate true religion? Mahdi quotes *BGE* 61–2 to show that, while Nietzsche's claims "seem somewhat bold," they are not "revolutionary," nor "do they represent an innovation, but only a renovation, restoration, or revival of a strain in the philosophic tradition" (2001: 229–30). The tradition they restore was shared by Alfarabi, the first to establish philosophy within Islam. Alfarabi taught that a rational understanding of the world must take responsibility for a public teaching that is inescapably pictorial or metaphoric, employing images and similitudes for the worthwhile, the noble, the holy. Nietzsche is "the last philosopher to reflect seriously on this topic" (2001: 237–40). Mahdi shows that Alfarabi's essential teacher was Plato, confirming Nietzsche's view that Plato shared his understanding of philosophy's responsibility for religion.

Gods

At the end of *On the Genealogy of Morality* (GM III. 27) Nietzsche speaks of "unconditioned honest atheism," adding: "(– and *it* is the only air we breathe, we more spiritual men of this age!)." Spiritual atheism is the natural product of "the awe-inspiring *catastrophe* of two thousand years of training in truthfulness that finally forbids itself *the lie of belief in God.*" Can honest, post-Christian atheists believe in gods? The answer is surely No, but Nietzsche adds a remark that puts a different perspective on the problem: regarding our 2,000-year training in truthfulness, he says,

> The same evolutionary course in India, in complete independence, and therefore proving something; the same ideal [truth] leads to the same conclusion; the decisive point is reached five centuries before the beginning of the European calendar, with Buddha; more exactly, with the Sankhya philosophy, subsequently popularized by Buddha and made into a religion.

What does *that* prove? Presumably that our atheistic philosophy, arrived at after centuries of discipline in the truth, ultimately seeing the world as will to power and nothing besides and glimpsing the ideal of unconditioned affirmation of that world, could likewise be popularized and made into a powerful world religion.

But why are gods necessary? Nietzsche's answer may lie in what is arguably the central aphorism of *Beyond Good and Evil* (*BGE* 150) (Its literal "centrality" depends on counting twice the three aphorisms which repeat numbers [65, 73, 237], making 299 in all, and ignoring the fact that "150" is then 152.): "Around the hero everything turns to tragedy, around the demigod everything turns to satyr play: and around god everything turns to – what? perhaps to 'world' –?" Yes, Nietzsche invites us to say, to world. A mere everything worlds, forms a world, only around a god – and it worlds not as tragedy or satyr play but as *comedy*, for in classical Athens on the great days of theatre at the Dionysia festival, first came the tragedies, then the satyr play, and last the comedy. "Everything" turns to world only around a god – and turns to comedy. The *true* everything then, the whole as will to power and nothing besides, can world only around a god or gods who themselves embody or simulate the true and live the new ideal, the unbounded Yes to everything that was and is. Modeling the true and the good, such gods make a world out of the philosopher's view from above that tragedy, the whole of human suffering, plays out within the eternal comedy of existence (*GS* 1).

But if gods alone create a world, what creates a god? The religious instinct, Nietzsche suggests, is ultimately a god-creating instinct (*gottbildende Instinkt*, *KSA* 13, 17[4 no. 5]); humans by nature raise what they passionately desire to the highest plane, to divinity. All gods are divinizations of human passions or of the objects of passion. Because passions range from healthy to unhealthy, from love and gratitude to fear and vengeance, gods range from healthy to unhealthy. The unhealthiest of gods, Nietzsche charges, are the gods of Platonism, punitive gods serving fear and vengeance by reinforcing the fiction of a cosmic moral order. Nietzsche prefaced *Beyond Good and Evil* with an indictment of Platonism, "the worst, most durable, most dangerous of all errors so far" – an extreme but historical judgment based on what actually happened to "Plato's invention of the pure mind and the good in itself." What happened (to use an available shorthand) was that Platonism made it possible for Athens, home of the rational, to fall victim to Jerusalem, home of a punitive monotheism. Nietzsche's history of our civilization argues that Platonic philosophy paved the way for the religion of the

144

God who still defines religion for us. That God is now dead thanks to the long modern fight against him, the spiritual warfare between science and religion purposely set in motion by modern philosophers like Bacon and Descartes. The preface to *Beyond Good and Evil* ends suggesting that the goal now is a new philosophy plus *its* popularization as the next great event in our history. Beginning this way, the book ends with the return of Dionysus and Ariadne, gods around whom – we have to suppose – the true everything turns to world. The healthy atheism that destroyed unhealthy Platonism can give rise to gods of healthy affirmation.

Why Dionysus and Ariadne? Nietzsche's answer seems to be that these two gods represent *true* religion as divinizations of the true. When Dionysus actually steps forth in the penultimate aphorism, he permits his latest disciple and initiate to say, "in a whisper," that Dionysus is a philosopher. "And that gods too philosophize," the disciple adds, "seems to me to be a novelty that is not harmless." Philosophizing gods fatally harm what Platonism divinized: the permanent and transcendent. "We're proud not to have to be liars any more, not slanderers, not accusers of life," Nietzsche says (*KSA* 13, 15[44]). Philosophizing gods free philosophy from the need to slander life with the lie of transcendence. They do good in a positive way as well, for god-making seems to be what Xenophanes said it was – the gods of horses and lions would resemble horses and lions. Philosophizing gods resemble truth-seeking philosophers and that resemblance is the privileged resemblance raising highest what *is* highest: philosophizing gods divinize the divine in humanity, the passion to understand.

There's more to Dionysus and Ariadne than philosophizing: they *celebrate* the understood, the world as it is. This god and goddess preserve in their twoness what the whole of the Hellenic represented:

> What was it that the Hellene guaranteed himself with [the Dionysian] mysteries? [. . .] the eternal return of life [. . .] *true* life as the over-all continuation of life through pro-creation, through the mysteries of sexuality [. . .] I know no higher symbolism than this *Greek* symbolism of the Dionysian festivals. Here the most profound instinct of life, the eternity of life, is experienced religiously. (*TI*, "Ancients," 4)

By having this pair, and only this pair, return at the end of *Beyond Good and Evil* (and at the end of *Zarathustra*) Nietzsche points to the welling up again of that Hellenic instinct of life to celebrate and elevate what we are and what we are part of. As the divine male and female who dance, court, make love and war, marry, have progeny, Dionysus and Ariadne divinize human eros as part of eros as a whole, nature's process as a whole. They are gender divinized, a duality of mutual desiring who symbolize the fundamental eros resident in all things. As divine manliness and divine womanliness they celebrate the natural fecundity of the world. Nietzsche's philosophy expressed religiously divinizes nature, from the most general to the most high, from the character of all beings to the natural peak of beings, philosophy, the most spiritual eros. Dionysus and Ariadne re-establish the natural order of rank suppressed by the modern doctrine of equality with its "second atheism," the atheism of hatred of the high (*BGE* 22). The possibility of philosophy, that highest attainment of nature, seems to be tied to the idea of gods.

Dionysus and Ariadne are gods who gather into personhood the true character of the whole and of the highest. Dionysus divinizes philosophy, impassioned pursuit of the elusive, the always veiled, always withdrawing. The object of that passion, Truth, the elusive, veiled, fleeing quarry in the great hunt, is itself worthy of a divine name: Ariadne. "Assuming truth is a woman –" *Beyond Good and Evil* opens with these words, taunting philosophers as unworthy lovers who do violence to this greatest beloved with their dogmatism. The book ends with the philosopher god avowing love for Ariadne, reciprocated love. Love of the truth becomes love of the true.

By ending on Dionysus and Ariadne, Nietzsche invites his genuine audience, modern free minds, to think the possibility of true religion, beliefs, and practices true to what is and seeking celebration in festival and song. A religion of Dionysus and Ariadne would do what religions do: cultivate and educate in correct opinion and salutary practice from childhood on up, training in love of the true and the good through similitudes of the true and the good. Dionysus and Ariadne are exemplars who are already what the best of humans would most dearly love to be like – not permanent and fixed but dying and rising, not all-powerful but striving and vying, not all-knowing but philosophizing, not needing worship or groveling but modeling what is most worthy of imitation and emulation.

Philosophers and Gods

The Nietzsche who argued that the philosopher had a responsibility for religion and who showed the way to a religion true to the earth also said: "There is nothing in me of the founder of religion, I want no believers. I never speak to the multitude" (*EH*, "Why I Am a Destiny," 1). Religion, however, *is* belief and religion alone moves the multitude. So how can Nietzschean philosophy lead to Nietzschean religion?

If we consider only the *truth* of philosophy and religion, it seems to me that we can grant the rationale of Nietzsche's argument. Dwelling ever more fully within a successful science of nature – "Hooray for physics!" (*GS* 335) – we can grant that philosophy as the passion to understand the whole leads reasonably to the fundamental fact that to be is to be energy that by nature structures and decays. Recognizing this fact leads reasonably to its affirmation in a new ideal or highest value. Fact and value so construed provide a rational view of the universe and a rational response to the universe by that fragment of the universe graced by openness to it.

But is there a reasonable possibility that this rational view could unfold into true religion? Spectators considering this great matter may be kept from simply saying No by one fact: the history of philosophy understood in a Nietzschean manner. Nietzsche intimates in *Beyond Good and Evil* that he had a predecessor, and what a predecessor: Plato. Plato's dialogs show that his situation was analogous to Nietzsche's: Plato knew (as shown for instance in Glaucon's and Adeimantus' speeches in *Republic* Book 2) that he occupied a time of the death of gods, the Homeric gods ultimately responsible for Greek civilization. Plato responded Homerically to that religious catastrophe – he poetized new gods into existence, not simply the pale gods of the ideas but moral or punitive gods akin to the dying gods but more moral, more punitive. And Plato recast the soul, poetizing it as immortal and subjecting it to rewards and punishments in a newly moralized Hades. Plato allows us to view this spectacular, culture-creating enterprise at its beginnings and to understand it as the work of a supremely rational

146

man who judged it necessary to lie morally. Plato claimed that noble lies were basic to civil order (*Republic* 414b; see *TI*, "The 'Improvers' of Humanity," 5) and his moral gods, immortal souls, and revamped Hades served that end. Students of Nietzsche, who knew that every philosopher before the Enlightenment knew the difference between exoteric and esoteric, need not believe that Plato believed these once edifying tales. The greatest philosophers after Plato were taught by Plato on philosophy's responsibility for religion; Alfarabi, Maimonides, Montaigne, Bacon, Descartes, and other great philosophers saw it as their responsibility to preserve philosophy by preserving the civil order within which alone it could survive. The history of philosophy understood from this perspective was greatly advanced by Strauss (1952 and other writings); Mahdi (2001) presents Alfarabi from this perspective; Adler (2003) shows the responsibility the philosopher-poet Virgil consciously assumed in founding the Roman empire; Benardete (1997) carries the argument back to the founding poet of the West, Homer.

When the role philosophy played in Western religion is granted, there is reason to think that Nietzsche's rational view of what philosophy can do now for religion may, over the long term, have a future. Because the religious issue as framed by both Plato and Nietzsche recognizes the need to serve the instincts or fundamental passions, the Nietzschean possibility for religion can be framed this way: the history of our species may bring us to a point where love and gratitude could serve as the basis for the god-creating instinct, replacing the fear and vengeance tapped by Platonism. Nietzsche's thought on philosophy and religion leaves us with this question. Given that humanity always lives a divinization of what it takes to be true, can what has always been true for the few philosophers be made livable in mature simulations that allow humanity to live a divinization of the actually true?

See also 13 "The Incorporation of Truth: Towards the Overhuman"; 27 "Nietzsche, Dionysus, and the Ontology of Music"; 29 "Life and Self-Overcoming"; 30 "Nietzsche's Theory of the Will to Power"

References

Adler, Eve (2003). *Vergil's Empire: Political Thought in the Aeneid* (Lanham: Rowman & Littlefield).

Benardete, Seth (1997). *The Bow and the Lyre: A Platonic Reading of the Odyssey* (Lanham: Rowman & Littlefield).

Mahdi, Muhsin S. (2001). *Alfarabi and the Foundation of Islamic Political Philosophy* (Chicago: University of Chicago Press).

Strauss, Leo (1952). *Persecution and the Art of Writing* (Chicago: University of Chicago Press).

9

The Naturalisms of *Beyond Good and Evil*

MAUDEMARIE CLARK AND DAVID DUDRICK

One of the most important recent trends in the literature on Nietzsche is to interpret him as a naturalist (e.g., Richardson, 2004; Leiter, 2002; Cox, 1999; Clark, 1998; Schacht, 1998). Although we take this to be correct and important, we will argue here that there is also an important sense in which Nietzsche is not a naturalist. We were led to this view by problems we encountered when we attempted to interpret *Beyond Good and Evil* as endorsing naturalism. Although it does endorse naturalism, and is arguably the most important book for understanding why Nietzsche endorses it, it also presents a problem for interpreting him as a naturalist. In section 1 we explain why we take *BGE* to endorse naturalism and why this interpretation is nevertheless problematic. In section 2, this problem leads us to attribute to Nietzsche a position that sounds similar to a puzzling claim about truth he himself makes in the new preface to the second edition of *The Gay Science*, the book he published immediately after *BGE*.[1] We then argue (in sections 3–6) that the problem we have discovered for interpreting Nietzsche as a naturalist helps us to illuminate other material that he added to the second edition of *GS*, and that our analysis of this material helps to explain the puzzling claim about truth from the preface to the same book. We conclude (section 7) that our analysis of these passages helps to clarify the distinction between the type of naturalism Nietzsche embraces in *BGE* and the type he rejects.

1 *Beyond Good and Evil* and the "Magnificent Tension of the Spirit"

Beyond Good and Evil is usually treated as little more than a collection of aphorisms.[2] We contend, as does Lampert (2001), that it is a much more unified work than it first appears to be, that, in fact, the whole work is an attempt to clarify and expand on the themes laid out in its two-page preface. This preface portrays the history of philosophy as a story of dogmatism and the struggle against dogmatism, which we interpret according to the Kantian terminology that was familiar when Nietzsche was writing. That the Kantian sense of the term is the one with which Nietzsche was familiar is clear from the opening lines of Afrikan Spir's *Denken und Wirklichkeit* (Spir 1877: vol. 1, p. 1), a work Nietzsche was rereading and taking notes on during the time he was composing *BGE*. Dogmatism, in this Kantian sense, commits one to the assumption that reality can be known by a priori means. The fight against dogmatism that Nietzsche sees in the history of philosophy is directed precisely against this assumption. He thinks that fight has largely been won; dogmatism is in its last throes and its most important dogmas have been overcome, in particular "Plato's invention of the pure spirit and the good in itself." This process has resulted in "a magnificent tension of the spirit," which is embodied in the "tense bow" of "we good Europeans and free, very free spirits" and makes it possible "to shoot for the most distant goals" (*BGE*, preface). In his preface, Nietzsche criticizes two attempts to "unbend the bow" – to slacken the tension so that the arrow cannot be shot – that of the Jesuits and the democratic Enlightenment. Nietzsche's own goal, in contrast, is clearly not only to maintain the tension, but to heighten it so that the arrow can be shot, i.e., so that a new philosophy can come into being.

This new philosophy is presumably the philosophy of Nietzsche's later works, perhaps including *BGE* itself. Nietzsche claims that all his works, with one exception – probably *Zarathustra*, articulate (and exploit) positions he was already beyond (*HH*, preface, 1). *BGE* is plausibly interpreted as designed to set out the "tension of the spirit" that Nietzsche takes to be the culmination of the previous history of philosophy and that which has made his later philosophy possible. But what exactly is this "magnificent tension"? No answer to this question can be found in the literature on *BGE*. Although Laurence Lampert makes clear its importance for understanding *BGE* and repeatedly appeals to the metaphor of the "tense bow" in his account of the book (Lampert 2001), he does little to illuminate the nature of the tension or to analyze the metaphor of the bow. This is perhaps because he misses the most helpful source for the bow imagery, which is Plato's *Republic*, where Socrates uses it in a crucial argument to establish that there are different parts of the soul.[3] Plato's theory of the soul is in fact central to what Nietzsche is doing in *BGE*.[4] For present purposes, however, the most important point is Socrates' observation that "it is wrong to say of the archer that his hands at the same time push the bow away and draw it towards him. We ought to say that one hand pushes it away and the other draws it towards him" (438b–c). This suggests that we think of Nietzsche's "magnificent tension of the spirit" as likewise the product of opposing tendencies of different parts or aspects of the philosopher's soul, the part that pushes dogmatism away and the part that draws it back towards the philosopher.[5] This does not get us very far towards understanding it, of course, because we do not yet know anything about the two opposing forces that produce it. What is it in the philosopher that pushes dogmatism away? And what is it that pulls it back? The preface to *BGE* doesn't tell us. Its job is to alert us to what we should be looking for in the body of the work.

And if, knowing what we are looking for, we ask the right question, we will find that the first two sections of *BGE* already offer us answers. The first section introduces the will to truth, raising questions about its origin and value that will not be answered until much later in the book (*BGE* 229–30). It is reasonable to suppose that its function is precisely to introduce one side of the "magnificent tension of the spirit," the side that struggles against dogmatism. After all, the preface tells us that Plato's dogmatic doctrines "stood truth on her head." Nietzsche thus denies that a will to truth rules in Plato's philosophy, and such a will or commitment to truth is precisely what would seem necessary to put truth back on her feet. Accordingly, when *BGE* 2 denies that the will to truth is the deepest drive behind metaphysical or dogmatic philosophy,[6] it begins to introduce the drive that forms the other side of the "magnificent tension of the spirit." Nietzsche's initial claim about this other drive is that metaphysicians care about what they call "knowledge" and "truth" – that is, a priori knowledge and the truth about a metaphysical world – only because of their commitment to a certain "valuation" of the natural world, an assumption that things of the highest value, like knowledge and truth, cannot be "derived from this transitory, seductive, deceptive, paltry world, from this turmoil of delusion and lust."[7] This assumption is clearly a philosophical expression of the ascetic ideal, which Nietzsche analyzes at length in the Third Treatise of *On the Genealogy of Morality.*

Now Nietzsche does not think that all philosophy is committed to the ascetic devaluation of nature that he claims to find behind metaphysics, for his own philosophy is not. But he does think that all philosophy shares with metaphysical philosophy the fact that a "valuation" lies behind it. After claiming that philosophers are "one and all advocates who resist the name, and cunning spokesmen for their prejudices, which they baptize 'truths'" (*BGE* 5), he lets us know that the "prejudices" in question are moral or ethical prejudices, more literally, "prejudgments" (*BGE* 6). He makes this point even clearer when he claims that "the moral (or immoral) intentions in a philosophy" are "the real germ of life out of which the whole plant has grown," and that a philosopher's morality bears witness to "who" he is. Finally, he tells us that what happened in the case of the Stoics – who, Nietzsche claims, arrived at their view of nature as following rational laws by reading their own ethical ideal into nature – "is an ancient, eternal story." Philosophy "always creates the world in its own image," that is, in the image of who the philosopher is, the philosopher's values (*BGE* 9).[8]

Accordingly, the two sides of Nietzsche's "magnificent tension of the spirit" are the drive or will to truth and what we can call the "drive to value." Whereas the truth drive aims to capture the truth about the world, the value drive doesn't care about truth. It aims to represent the world in terms of the philosopher's values, to construct it in such a way that she can recognize in it her own image – in Zarathustra's words, to "create a world before which [she] can kneel" (Z II, "Self-Overcoming"). If philosophers care about truth, it is due to the truth drive, not the value drive. Nietzsche's view is clearly that the value drive dominated the truth drive in dogmatic philosophy – that dogmatists did not care about truth as much as they claimed to. What they called "truth" was what satisfied their value drive. Some readers think that this is Nietzsche's view of all philosophers, that no real commitment to truth is found among them. We disagree. Nietzsche clearly believes that the doctrines or dogmas of pre-Kantian metaphysical philosophy are a product of the rule of the value drive over the truth drive. But he takes our current situation to reflect a strengthening of the truth drive, which has expressed itself in the struggle against dogmatism that eventually overthrew those metaphysical doctrines that satisfied the value drive.

What philosophical doctrines does Nietzsche think emerge from this struggle, that is, from the strengthening of the truth drive relative to the value drive? In epistemology, empiricism is the obvious answer. Dogmatism assumes that we can arrive at the truth about reality in a completely a priori manner, without dependence on anything empirical. Now if that assumption is overthrown by the will to truth, it should lead to empiricism, to the claim that there is no a priori knowledge to be had, that all we have to go on is experience and its refinement within the various sciences. But isn't empiricism itself dogmatic? Not on Nietzsche's reading of it. In *BGE* 15, he approaches "sensualism, at least as a regulative hypothesis, if not as a heuristic principle." "Sensualism" is just another name for empiricism (according to Spir, for example), and the qualification Nietzsche puts on it indicates that he understands the empiricism he endorses as an empirical hypothesis concerning the role of the senses in knowledge. The same passage suggests that this hypothesis is that the senses are causal conditions of knowledge (Clark and Dudrick 2004). But although it is an empirical and therefore descriptive hypothesis, it can imply a heuristic principle that has regulatory importance for our behavior. It tells us how to proceed in attempting to acquire knowledge without having to claim that a priori knowledge is logically impossible. The point is that, given our best theory of how we in fact acquire the knowledge we take ourselves to have, we should turn our backs on the quest for a priori knowledge and pursue empirical inquiry.

But this evidently amounts to naturalism. On Brian Leiter's recent account of it, Nietzsche's naturalism is methodological naturalism, the doctrine that philosophy should follow the methods of the sciences, the empirical sciences (Leiter 2002). Why should philosophy follow these methods? Leiter's answer is basically that these methods have "delivered the goods," i.e., allowed us to find whatever truth we have been able to find beyond that accessible to ordinary perception and common sense. If this is all there is to naturalism, it seems equivalent to the claim that philosophy should accept empiricism, "at least as a regulative hypothesis." In that case, we should take *BGE* to show that its author is a naturalist. Indeed the book contains what is probably the most striking and frequently quoted expression of Nietzsche's commitment to naturalism, his description of his "task" as that of "translat[ing] human beings back into nature," of "becom[ing] master over the many vain and overly enthusiastic interpretations and connotations that have so far been scrawled and painted over that eternal basic text of *homo natura*" (*BGE* 230).

The problem with attributing this view to the author of *BGE* is that the book seems intent on showing us that truth is only one of the important and indispensable aims of philosophy and only one of two main drives that Nietzsche's own philosophy seeks to satisfy. The other major drive, as we have indicated, is the value drive, which aims to create or construct the world in accordance with the philosopher's values. Nietzsche clearly believes that this drive has led previous philosophers astray, into illusion, that what they claimed to find in the world – e.g., Plato's forms, rational laws, necessary connections – appeared to be there only as a projection of their way of looking at the world, and ultimately of their values. So they have found only an image of themselves in the world rather than what was really there. Since Nietzsche portrays naturalism as coming to the fore in philosophy due to the strengthening of one side of the "magnificent tension of the spirit," the truth drive, evidently at the expense of the other side, the value drive, he suggests that naturalism satisfies only one side of the philosophical soul. But if Nietzsche's later philosophy is designed to satisfy both sides, it would follow that the naturalism we have so far attributed to Nietzsche cannot be his doctrine. And indeed Nietzsche seems to show a negative attitude towards naturalism early in *BGE* when he refers dismissively to "clumsy naturalists" (*BGE* 12) and to "whoever, like [natural scientists] now 'naturalizes' in his thinking" (*BGE* 21). So this suggests the need for a distinction between two versions of naturalism, the one Nietzsche accepts and the one he rejects.

2 The Unveiled Truth: Preface to *The Gay Science*

Our suspicion, then, is that methodological naturalism can't be Nietzsche's doctrine because it only satisfies the will to truth and not the will to value. But this seems to put us in the difficult if not impossible position of claiming that Nietzsche rejects naturalism even though he holds it to be true, on the grounds that this truth does not satisfy our need for value. *This is not what we want to say.* But the only way to avoid it, given our claims that Nietzsche's mature philosophy is designed to satisfy both the will to truth and the will to value, and that naturalism satisfies the former but not the latter, is to say that the form of naturalism in question satisfies the will to truth but is nevertheless not true. Can this make sense?

Nietzsche seems to think so. Consider the following from the preface to *GS*:

> One will hardly find us again on the paths of those Egyptian youths who make temples unsafe at night, embrace statues, and want by all means to unveil, uncover, and put into a bright light whatever is kept concealed for good reasons, No, we have grown sick of this bad taste, this will to truth, to "truth at any price," this youthful madness in the love of truth: we are too experienced, too serious, too jovial, too burned, too deep for that. [. . .] We no longer believe that truth remains truth when one pulls off the veil; we have lived too much to believe that. Today we consider it a matter of decency not to wish to see everything naked, to be present everywhere, to understand and "know" everything. "Is it true that God is everywhere?" a little girl asked her mother; "I find that indecent!" – a hint for philosophers!

Consider the paradoxical-sounding suggestion that truth is no longer truth when it is exposed or presented naked. This is plausibly connected to the naturalism at issue in *BGE*. First, it was added to the second edition of *GS*, which was written right after Nietzsche finished *BGE*. Second, its opening claim is that we will not be found *again* acting like those youths in Schiller's poem who wanted to unveil the truth or see her naked, implies that we once could have been found doing exactly that. When? No doubt, when we were writing *Human, All Too Human* – remembering here that Nietzsche uses "we" for the sake of politeness. (*TI*, "Reason," 5). And in *HH* we do clearly find Nietzsche committed to naturalism, which means, to exposing human beings in a completely naturalistic light. It is really human beings and their "higher activities," the ones that seem to make us more than animals, that are stripped naked in *HH*. That is, they are reduced to no more than can be seen from the viewpoint of the methodological naturalist, which is constituted by a commitment to using only the methods of the sciences in the pursuit of knowledge. In the preface to *GS*, then, Nietzsche is saying that we will not find him again on that path, committed to exposing human beings and their behavior in completely naturalistic terms. Now, this might be taken to mean simply that *in addition* to exposing naturalistic truths about human beings, he will also do something else: e.g., point to what we can become, as Richard Schacht (1998) suggests, or try to free potential "higher men" from their bad conscience, as Brian Leiter (2002) suggests, or use the naturalistic truth to diagnose our own value commitments and get control over them, as John Richardson (2004) suggests. But something more seems to be going on. Nietzsche is claiming that he will no longer write as he did in *HH*, that he will no longer attempt to rip the veil off human beings to expose the naturalistic truth about them – either that he will veil this truth instead of trying to expose it, or that he will show us this truth only (or perhaps largely) in veiled form. And he will do this, at least in part, because in its unveiled or naked form, naturalism actually distorts the truth. So the philosopher's full-out pursuit of truth – the attempt to satisfy the will to truth without at the same time satisfying the value drive – does not in fact yield truth. Although it is what the preface to *GS* suggests, it is difficult to understand why Nietzsche would take it to be the case.

We believe that an explanation can be found in sections 371–4 of *GS*, which belong to the material added to the work shortly after he finished *BGE*. We will argue that, when read together and in the light of our analysis of *BGE*'s "magnificent tension of the spirit," these four sections provide Nietzsche's account as to (a) how the will to truth can lead one to a view that is false, and (b) how the falsity of this view is deeply connected to its failure to satisfy the will to value.

3 *Beyond Good and Evil*'s "Tension of the Spirit" as it Appears in *Gay Science* 371 and 372

In *GS* 371, Nietzsche claims that he is misunderstood – not just as a matter of fact but, given the circumstances of his age, as a matter of necessity. For now, he says, he is "incomprehensible." He does offer us the reasons for this incomprehensibility, but only in highly metaphorical language. He says, first, that "we"

> are misidentified – for we ourselves keep growing, changing, shedding old hides; we still shed our skins every spring; we become increasingly younger, more future-oriented, taller, stronger; we drive our roots ever more powerfully into the depths – into evil – while at the same time embracing the heavens ever more lovingly and broadly, and absorbing their light ever more thirstily with all our sprigs and leaves.

One point is clear from these lines: Nietzsche is admitting that his views have changed or grown, that he has now rejected crucial components of his earlier works. But this is clearly insufficient to explain his incomprehensibility, which Nietzsche presents as due to his being like a tree that drives its roots "into the depths [. . .] while at the same time embracing the heavens ever more lovingly and broadly." We suggest that these two aspects of the tree stand for the will to truth and the will to value. The will to truth leads us to "the earth," to what is known through the senses. And it leads us to acknowledge and pursue the "rootedness" in "the earth" – in our affective, and decidedly "earthly" nature – of those things that seem to tower above it, the values that appear as if in "the heavens," to which we are driven by our will to value. That is, Nietzsche's will to truth leads him to be rooted in the earth while his will to value leads him to embrace the heavens.

The relationship between these wills leads to those aspects of his thought that make him incomprehensible.

> Like trees we grow – it's hard to understand, like all life! – not in one place, but every-where; not in one direction, but upwards and outwards and downwards equally; our energy drives trunk, branches, and roots all at once; we are no longer free to do anything singly, to *be something single.*[9]

This makes explicit that what makes Nietzsche incomprehensible is not simply his growth, but the manner of that growth – that, like all life, he grows in more than one direction at once. Although he doesn't take his "rootedness" to be an objection to "embracing the heavens ever more lovingly and broadly," he thinks that these two aspects of his being will seem incompatible to others. How can a thing grow up and down at once? Mustn't it grow from some stationary point, a foundation? In the case of the tree, in fact, these two different directions of growth are not just compatible but necessary. If a tree were not rooted, it would not surge into the heavens; if didn't grow toward the heavens, its roots would perish. This suggests that Nietzsche is like a tree in that the growth of his will to truth depends on the growth of his will to value, and the growth of his will to value depends on that of the will to truth. The product of this growth is the fruits he warns may not "taste good to [us]" (*GM*, preface, 2), the fruits being the views expressed in his writings. Nietzsche is concerned that he will seem incomprehensible in that his views will seem this way precisely because they cannot be seen simply as an attempt to state the truth (as natural scientists do) or simply as an attempt to show the world in terms of values (as he thinks previous philosophers have done). It is, thus, insofar as he is doing *both* these things – not "singly," but "all at once" – that he is incomprehensible.[10]

GS 372 continues Nietzsche's reflections on the relationship between the will to truth and the will to value. Because this section is titled "Why We Are Not Idealists," we expect it to criticize idealism and to endorse those who reject it. And these expecta-tions are met – Nietzsche calls idealistic philosophizing "vampirism" and says that "today we are all sensualists, we philosophers of the present and future, *not* in theory but in *praxis*, in practice." The point here is that those who embody the "magnificent tension of the spirit," the "philosophers of the present," as well as the future philo-sophers to whom Nietzsche hopes that this tension gives rise, will be empiricists who reject the search for a priori knowledge and therefore reject idealism. The qualification that they will be sensualists "*not* in theory but in *praxis*, in practice" may seem to make it implausible that Nietzsche is talking about something as straightforward and unexciting as an epistemological theory here. But we should remember that he presents the sensualism to which he commits himself in *BGE* 15 as a "regulative hypothesis, if not a heuristic principle" – thus as a practical maxim as to how to conduct an inquiry or the search for truth. This is plausibly seen as simply a different formulation of the claim that we are sensualists or empiricists "in practice" – methodological empiricists rather than dogmatic ones. Further, the connection we are drawing between *BGE* 15 and *GS* 372 fits the context of both passages, namely, a concern with idealism. In *BGE* 15, Nietzsche puts forward sensualism precisely as a premise in an argument against a particular version of idealism, namely, phenomenalism (Clark and Dudrick 2004).

But if *GS* 372 meets the expectations aroused by its title, it also unsettles them, beginning with its first sentence: "Formerly, philosophers feared the senses: is it possible that we have unlearned this fear all too much?" The suggestion is that we philosophers should fear the senses more than we in fact do. But if the senses are the road to truth, what is there to fear? Nietzsche concludes *GS* 372 by saying that

> all philosophical idealism until now was something like an illness, except where, as in Plato's case, it was the caution of an overabundant and dangerous health; the fear of *overpowerful* senses; the shrewdness of a shrewd Socratic. – Maybe we moderns are not healthy enough *to need* Plato's idealism? And we don't fear the senses because –

Nietzsche thus leaves it to us to figure out why we don't fear the senses. The first point to make is similar to the one made about Nietzsche's reference to "sensualists [. . .] in *praxis*" earlier. Although Nietzsche's rhetoric about "*overpowerful* senses" may suggest that he is talking about something more exciting than epistemological matters, when considered in the context of the whole passage, such matters are plausibly considered the source of the danger to which he refers. To say that we don't fear the senses is to say that we don't fear the all-out pursuit of empirical knowledge. To see what it means that we lack this fear, consider what the passage suggests about why Plato feared the senses. It portrays Plato as unlike other philosophers of the past, behind whose philosophizing Nietzsche senses "some long-concealed bloodsucker who starts with the senses and finally leaves behind and spares only bones and rattling," that is, "categories, formulas, words." So these philosophers were left unable to recognize the truth about the natural world. To say that Plato, by contrast, never lost the power of his senses is to suggest that he recognized the basic character of the natural world and saw that it did not satisfy the will to value. This is why he feared the senses. We do not fear them not because of our greater health, but because we lack Plato's insight into the conflict between the will to truth and the will to value.

4 *Gay Science* 373 and 374: Values and Intentionality

According to our analysis, then, whereas *GS* 371 presents the growth of the will to value and the will to truth as interdependent, *GS* 372 portrays the two wills as in conflict. Plato recognized this conflict, and idealism was his solution, the placement of the standards of value in a world higher than the natural world, a worth accessible only to reason, to "pure spirit" in Nietzsche's terminology (*BGE*, preface). Plato was thus willing to sacrifice the will to truth to the will to value, whereas Nietzsche's philosophers of the present and future are not. *GS* 373 attempts to help philosophers of the present become philosophers of the future by helping them to recognize the conflict between the will to truth and the will to value as a problem.

If Nietzsche refuses to sacrifice the will to truth, which has led to our current scientific or naturalistic outlook, the title of *GS* 373 seems misleading. "'Science' as prejudice" suggests that he rejects science. The quote marks around "science" already warn us, however, that Nietzsche's concern here is not science, but a certain conception or image of science. The passage opens with the cutting remark that scholars (those who pursue knowledge, including scientists) "are not even allowed to catch sight of the

155

truly *great* problems and question marks" because "the need that makes them scholars, their inner expectations and wish that things might be *such and such*, their fear and hope, too soon find rest and satisfaction." The clear implication is that scholars are led to what they take to be true by the will to value. When that will is satisfied, they take themselves to have the truth. It therefore makes sense to suppose that a "great problem" to which scholars are particularly blind is the one constituted by the conflict between the will to truth and the will to value. In the rest of the passage, Nietzsche gives examples of two ways in which scholars can become blinded to this problem.

The first is that of "the pedantic Englishman Herbert Spencer," who "raves" and "spins fables" about the "definitive reconciliation of egoism and altruism." Spencer, the father of Social Darwinism and the coiner of the phrase "survival of the fittest," holds that the altruistic are more fit than the merely egoistic, thus that the reconciliation of egoism and altruism is a necessary outcome of the evolutionary process. Nietzsche clearly has two objections to Spencer's view, first to its truth and then to the values that lie behind it. It is false, he claims – a "fable" – that such reconciliation is a necessary outcome of the evolutionary process, in more general terms, that evolution favors those Spencer considers morally "fit." Spencer only thinks so because he looks at the evidence through the lens of his will to value – his desire that the world be in accord with what he considers desirable. Further, the values that constitute Spencer's lens "almost nauseate" Nietzsche. But his ultimate point about Spencer, which follows out his opening charge against scholars, is that Spencer is blind to the "question mark" constituted by the fact "*that* he had to view as his highest hope what to others counts and should count only as a disgusting possibility." This blindness is plausibly seen as due to his failure to see that he is looking at the empirical evidence through a lens constituted by his values. He thinks he is just seeing things as they are – that the people who belong to the group he considers morally desirable just *do* as a matter of fact have an evolutionary advantage. He doesn't see that the values that constitute his viewpoint may strike others as nauseating because he doesn't recognize that his viewpoint is constituted by values at all: he thinks he is simply using empirical methods to read the facts off from the natural world. Spencer is, therefore, necessarily blind to the problem of the conflict between the will to truth and the will to value.

Nietzsche's second example of a scholar who has been blinded to this great problem is "Mr. Mechanic," who "nowadays likes to pass as a philosopher and insists that mechanics is the doctrine of the first and last laws on which all existence must be based as on a ground floor." He is among the "many materialistic natural scientists" who "rest content" with "faith in a world [. . .] that can be grasped entirely with the help of our four-cornered little human reason," that is, using the methods of the natural sciences. Nietzsche objects to this faith in the following:

> that the only rightful interpretation of the world should be the one to which *you* have a right; one by which one can do research and go on scientifically in *your* sense of the term (you really mean *mechanistically?*) – one that permits counting, calculating, weighing, seeing, grasping, and nothing else – that is a crudity and naiveté, assuming it is not a mental illness, an idiocy [. . .] a "scientific" interpretation of the world, as you understand it, might still be one of the *stupidest*, i.e., poorest in meaning [*sinnärmsten*], of all possible interpretations of the world. (*GS* 373)

156

Here, again, it may seem that Nietzsche is expressing a negative attitude towards science, or is at least opening the door to all sorts of interpretations and explanations as on a par with scientific ones, which seems incompatible with any form of naturalism. But he is actually not denying that the "the world can be grasped" using the methods of the natural sciences. He objects only to Mr. Mechanic's "faith" that the world can be grasped "entirely" using these methods, which is precisely the point at which his will to value – to have the world correspond to what he considers desirable – blinds him to the problem of the conflict between the will to truth and the will to value. This faith is what makes Mr. Mechanic a philosopher rather than merely a natural scientist. A natural scientist puts forwards scientific explanations of phenomena as true. He turns into a philosopher when he claims that his methods are the only path to truth, and thus that philosophy should admit only those views that are arrived at using those methods.

Now, this is exactly how Leiter understands Nietzsche's naturalism and how we provisionally interpreted it earlier: that philosophy should follow (only) the methods of the sciences. But even Leiter must admit that GS 373 denies that everything real can be seen from the perspective constituted by these methods. The passage clearly implies that something important lies beyond the "horizon" of science. The question that divides our reading of the passage from Leiter's concerns what this is. We agree with Leiter that Nietzsche's opponent in this passage is not the naturalist per se, but the reductive materialist who insists that "all facts – psychological, aesthetic, ethical, etc. – must be reducible to physical facts" (Leiter 2002: 25). Using Nietzsche's terms, this means that they must be reducible to what can be "counted, calculated, and expressed in formulas," i.e., to precisely the kinds of facts to which the methods of the natural sciences allow access. We also agree with Leiter's suggestion concerning the kind of facts to which these methods do not give access, namely, "psychological, aesthetic, [and] ethical" facts. But Leiter seems to ignore this point in the remainder of his account of Nietzsche's naturalism. For if the methods of the sciences do not give access to "psychological, aesthetic, [and] ethical" facts – arguably the facts about which philosophers are most concerned – why should philosophy restrict itself to following these methods? Leiter avoids this question by offering an example of what Nietzsche could have thought science leaves out that is more innocuous from his point of view, namely, the "qualitative or phenomenological aspect of experience, e.g., what it is like to experience a piece of music as beautiful." If it is only phenomenological properties that Nietzsche takes to lie beyond the horizon of science, this would not be any threat to his naturalism, as Leiter understands it. The methods of the sciences would still govern the pursuit of knowledge and therefore philosophy, but there would be an additional aspect of reality that could only be experienced. Our objection to this suggestion is twofold. On the one hand, there is no textual evidence that Nietzsche's concern in this passage is that phenomenological properties, such as what it is like to *experience* music as beautiful, lie beyond the horizon of science. On the other hand, there *is* clear evidence that he is concerned to indicate that values lie beyond that horizon.

The evidence for the latter point is that Nietzsche objects to Mr. Mechanic on the grounds that "an essentially mechanistic world would be an essentially *meaningless* [*sinnlose*] world!" adding that Mr. Mechanic's position is therefore comparable to judging "the *value* of a piece of music according to how much of it could be counted, calculated, and expressed in formulas." It is not the experience of a piece of music – the phenomenological properties that belong to that experience – but the *value* of the music – its beauty or greatness or sentimentality, for instance – to which Nietzsche is here calling our attention as something that lies behind the "horizon" of science. In rejecting Mr. Mechanic's position, Nietzsche denies that the fact that the value of a piece of music cannot be recognized from the "scientific" perspective implies that it deserves no recognition or is not real. The implication of the analogy he sets up is that, likewise, the fact that, say, the ethical qualities of a piece of behavior cannot be recognized from a scientific of naturalistic perspective do not show that they deserve no recognition or are not real. What it shows instead is the need for the mechanist to have "what *good* taste demands – above all, the taste of reverence for everything that lies beyond your horizon!" What lies beyond the horizon of science and demands reverence, according to this passage, is not phenomenal properties, but value properties.

If we put together what *GS* 373 says about Spencer with what it says about Mr. Mechanic, we can take its point to be that we must look at the world from a viewpoint that involves value commitments if we are to see it as embodying our values, and thus in a way that satisfies the will to value. We have argued that Nietzsche's discussion of "the Spencerian perspective" makes it clear that precisely such a viewpoint keeps Spencer from seeing that his will to value interferes with his recognition of truth. Mr. Mechanic evidently does not have the same problem. The methods of the sciences that he follows have been set up specifically to keep the will to value under control – precisely this blinds him to the "great problem" constituted by the conflict between the will to truth and the will to value. As a scientist, the will to value does not interfere with his pursuit of truth: the truth often turns out to be something that he does not consider desirable. Mr. Mechanic is therefore unlikely to think that he has any concerns that embody a will to value. Yet, this is clearly false, on Nietzsche's view. Mr. Mechanic's value-driven or philosophical instincts come to the fore not in his science but in his claim that science provides the only methods for getting truth; this claim is one he makes not as a scientist, but as a philosopher. Nietzsche thinks this claim clearly reflects Mr. Mechanic's desire to make the world *his*; it is an expression of Mr. Mechanic's conviction that, as Nietzsche describes it, "the only rightful interpretation of the world should be the one to which *you* have a right."

Thus, both Spencer and Mr. Mechanic are guilty of mistaking an exercise of the will to value for the simple pursuit of the truth. Spencer claims, in effect, to find that the values he favors are also favored by natural selection, without realizing that this claim is an expression of his will to value. Mr. Mechanic sees no values in the world – no beauty or ugliness, no greatness or baseness, no justice or one-sidedness, etc. – and therefore declares that there simply are none. But this latter claim is an expression of his will to value. We therefore take the central thought of *GS* 373 to be, on the one hand, that one must not confuse what satisfies one's will to value with the truth, but on the other, that one should not deny the existence of values simply because they do not show up from the particular perspective offered by the sciences.

We must pause here to consider a response open to Mr. Mechanic concerning this latter half of this claim. For he may grant the point that values cannot be seen from his empirical perspective, and that they show up only from a perspective that involves value commitments. He may take this to show that, simply put, there are no values (or, as Leiter seems to hold, that values are not "objective"). "You appear to be claiming that values are real, though visible only from a perspective that expresses value commitments," says Mr. Mechanic. "But consider this analogy: 'the fairies in the grass are real, though no scientific perspective makes them visible. Rather they can be seen only by those who are open to their magic – only by those who take up a perspective that expresses fairy-commitments.' If it's fairies – or values – you want," Mr. Mechanic concludes, "the empirical perspective is useless, it's true; but if you want knowledge then it is, alas, the only perspective for you." Nietzsche offers two responses to such a claim In the concluding lines of *GS* 373, he suggests that one would have "comprehended, understood, cognized" nothing of a piece of music – "nothing of what is 'music' in it" – if one considers in it only what can be "counted, calculated, expressed in formulas." Music can be comprehended *as music*, we take Nietzsche to be saying, only from a perspective constituted by affective dispositions that give rise to value judgments. In its simplest terms, the claim is that the understanding or comprehension of music is dependent on the ability to distinguish good from bad music. But this might only require Mr. Mechanic to back down as far as Leiter's position: namely, to the point of admitting that science does leave out phenomenological properties that belong to our affective responses to music (and, analogously, to behavior): what it is like to experience a piece of music as beautiful, for instance, or a human action as vicious. We will argue that *GS* 374 contains the resources for a second and more powerful response to Mr. Mechanic. But to see it this way, it is helpful to understand the impact of African Spir's work on Nietzsche, and so we turn briefly to that now. What Nietzsche learned from Spir, we argue, is what many later philosophers learned from the work of Wilfrid Sellars: the distinction between the space of causes and the space of reasons.

5 Spir's Relevance to *Gay Science* 373 and 374

As Michael Green has made clear in *Nietzsche and the Transcendental Tradition*, Spir functioned for Nietzsche as an important source of insight into the achievements of the critical or transcendental tradition and of what was wrong with the alternative empiricist/naturalist tradition. He was also, however, *at least* equally important as a resource for Nietzsche's knowledge of the British empiricist tradition and its virtues, and he might well be considered the "missing link" between Nietzsche and that tradition. Nietzsche could have been referring to Spir rather than to Schopenhauer when he cites the latter's "sense for hard facts, his good will for clarity and reason, which so often makes him appear so English and un-German" (*GS* 99). Anyone who thinks that Nietzsche did not value highly rigorous argument and clarity of expression in the discussion of philosophical issues, or did not appreciate the virtues of British ("English" in Nietzsche's vocabulary) philosophy, should read Spir's work and ponder the great amount of time Nietzsche spent on it.

Although Spir's work is a very sympathetic and illuminating thinking through of the empiricist/naturalist tradition, above all, of Locke, Hume, Darwin, and Mill, he denies that this tradition has the resources to explain the possibility of objective validity.

159

MAUDEMARIE CLARK AND DAVID DUDRICK

Green seems right to take what Spir calls "objective validity" to be a matter of having a truth value. Every genuine judgment has objective validity in the sense that it has an object, which means that it makes a claim that can be true or false. So the problem of objective validity is the problem of intentionality, of understanding how the mind or its states can have a content, how they can be *about* something. A judgment, Spir makes clear, just is a claim about reality and therefore all judgments are objectively valid, even if they are false. Spir argues repeatedly and convincingly that because empiricists like Hume attempt to explain everything in terms of natural or physical processes, they cannot explain the possibility of judgment. Physical processes do not make claims; they just are. So what one needs to understand the possibility of judgment is not physics but logic. This is, we contend, what Nietzsche learned from Spir, namely, that if we view an utterance simply from a naturalistic perspective – i.e., in terms of its causes and effects – we do not yet have the resources for thinking of it as making a judgment or expressing a thought, i.e., of being "objectively valid." To take a series of sounds to express a thought or judgment, one must interpret them as placing the being who makes the sounds in a space of reasons rather than causes, i.e., in a web of connections that are not simply natural or causal but rational or normative. Spir articulates the distinction between the space of reasons and the space of causes over and over in his two-volume work, but two footnotes are of particular relevance. In the first, which occurs very early in volume 1, Spir rejects the "increasingly wide-spread view first put forward by Herbert Spencer" that there are a priori elements of knowledge, such as Kant's categories, "but that these have their origin in the experience of our ancestors, from whom we have inherited them along with our bodily organization." Spir objects that it involves "a complete misunderstanding" to take the a priori elements of knowledge to be "a consequence of our bodily, or more accurately, cerebral, organization."

> For our bodily organization can certainly contain the physical antecedents or causes of our judgments, but not the logical antecedents (the principles) of cognition. A principle or law of cognition is the inner disposition to believe something of objects, and as such it can never be a product of physical causes, with which by its very nature it has nothing in common. I will attempt to illuminate the radical difference between the logical and the physical in detail below. (Spir 1877: vol. 1, pp. 8–9)

When we get to his more detailed account of the distinction between the physical and the logical, we find this footnote:

> A physical law is an unchangeable kind and manner of the conjunction or succession of appearances or real processes. A logical law in contrast is the inner disposition to believe something about objects. Physical laws govern the real succession of goings-on [*Begehenheiten*] in the order of time; logical laws govern logical succession of thoughts in the order of reasons [*Begründens*]. It is clear that the two are of a completely different nature. (Spir 1877: vol. 1, p. 79)

This makes explicit the distinction between the physical order of causes and the normative order of reasons. Given the careful study Nietzsche made of Spir, it seems unlikely that he could have missed this distinction or the force of the arguments in the surrounding pages. *BGE* responds to Spir on a number of points, rejecting several of his central doctrines – on immediate certainty (*BGE* 16), atomism (*BGE* 12), and the common good (*BGE* 43), to name a few. But there is nothing in *BGE* that looks like a rejection of Spir's central distinction between the sphere of causes and that of reasons. In fact, *BGE*'s first section seems to affirm this distinction when it formulates two different questions concerning the will to truth: (1) the question of its cause, meaning how it came to be, and (2) the question of its value. "We want truth? Why not rather untruth?" In other words, what is the reason or justification behind the value we place on truth? It therefore seems extremely likely that Nietzsche took over from Spir the distinction between the space of reasons and that of causes that we have been discussing.

6 *Gay Science* 374, in Light of Spir

We argue in this section that Spir's influence on Nietzsche helps us to see that *GS* 374 completes the argument of 373 against Mr. Mechanic. We begin by noting that, as happens so frequently in *BGE* and *GS* V, this passage (*GS* 374) is written so as to make it appear disconnected from the previous section (*GS* 373). It appears to introduce big ideas about a "new infinite," which culminate in its claim that "today we are at least far away from the ridiculous immodesty of decreeing from our angle that perspectives are *permitted* only from this angle. Rather the world has once again become infinite to us insofar as we cannot reject the possibility *that it includes infinite interpretations*." This seems incompatible with the priority a naturalist accords to science. Nietzsche again seems to be opening the door to many other interpretations of the world as on a par with scientific ones.

But we should ask why these other interpretations matter. Why does it matter that we can't rule out the mere possibility that the world contains infinite interpretations? What are these other interpretations to us? – especially since they may not be very good interpretations, as Nietzsche goes on to indicate. We suggest that careful reading allows one to see through Nietzsche's rhetoric about the exciting possibility of all these other interpretations to his point, but that the rhetoric does tend to distract readers from that point by obscuring the connection between this passage and the previous one. This connection is suggested by its opening lines:

> How far the perspectival character of existence extends, or indeed whether it has any other character, whether an existence without interpretation, without "sense" [*Sinn*] doesn't become nonsense; whether, on the other hand, all existence isn't essentially an *interpreting* existence – that cannot, as would be fair, be decided by even the most industrious and extremely conscientious analysis and self-examination of the intellect; for in the course of this analysis, the human intellect cannot avoid seeing itself under its perspectival forms, and only in these. We cannot look around our own corner. (*GS* 374)[11]

GS 373 has argued, in effect, that value is recognizable in the world only from a *perspective* constituted by value commitments, one that brings value assumptions to bear on conclusions to be drawn about objects in the world. When Nietzsche opens *GS*

374 by wondering "how far the perspectival character of existence extends," he is asking what else is such that it is visible or knowable only from such a perspective (i.e., one constituted by value commitments). Nietzsche tells us that neither this question nor several other exciting-sounding questions can be answered by "examination of the intellect" – i.e., by looking at how inquiry into different areas proceeds, to see whether those areas are "perspectival in character" (knowable only from a perspective constituted by value commitments). Here Nietzsche stops short. With the mention of this "examination of the intellect," the focus of the passage turns, without further notice, to reflection on it. Nietzsche does not proceed, as one might have expected initially, to classify different areas of inquiry (as "perspectival" or not); instead, he reflects on the "examination of the intellect" by which such a classification would proceed. It is with respect to this "examination" that Nietzsche makes the key claim of the passage.

This claim comes when Nietzsche suggests that the "examination of the intellect" must *itself* proceed "perspectivally": "The intellect cannot avoid seeing itself under its perspectival forms, and *solely* in these." Nietzsche thus makes a point about the intellect similar to the one made in GS 373 about value: both are "perspectival" in character. That is, it seems that the intellect, like value, can be seen only from a perspective that embodies value commitments. Just as the virtuous character of a piece of behavior or the beauty of a piece of music is only accessible to someone who is equipped to make value judgments about actions or music, Nietzsche is suggesting, intellectual activity – the activity of making claims, of considering reasons, of drawing conclusions, etc. – can be understood only by someone who is equipped to make value judgments concerning these activities.

Why should this be so? The answer, which we think Nietzsche got from Spir, is that to describe human beings as intellectual beings (e.g., as acting, believing, knowing, etc.) is to see them in a network that is not merely causal but normative. To examine the intellect *as intellect* (or, e.g., an event as an action) is to try to *make sense* of it. This helps us to understand what Nietzsche means when he says.

> We cannot look around our own corner. It is hopeless curiosity to want to know what other kinds of intellects and perspectives there *might* be; e.g., whether other beings might be able to experience time backwards, or alternately forwards and backwards (which would involve another direction of life and a different conception of cause and effect).

Now Nietzsche goes on to insist that it is "ridiculously immodest" to rule out the possibility of the kinds of beings he describes here. He nevertheless denies, in what we have just quoted, that it would possible to have knowledge of such beings. We can understand his reasoning by interpreting what he says in light of Spir's position. As a Kantian, Spir holds that the basic unit of experience is the judgment. Thus, to understand a being as having experiences is to see it as making judgments; it is to place the being not just in the space of causes but in the space of reasons. So placing the being is a matter of *making sense* of it. To see a being as a subject of experiences, then, is to try to make sense of its behavior in terms of beliefs and desires. If that's so, however, we never have grounds to justify the claim that a being experiences time alternately backwards and forwards. Why? Because we can make *no sense* of such experience. If to see a being as having experiences is to see it as making sense, it will never be the case that a being is *best* interpreted as experiencing time backwards, and not, e.g., as being mistaken in certain of its beliefs.

GS 374 thus completes the argument against Mr. Mechanic of GS 373. It shows that Mr. Mechanic's view is not only a "crudity and naiveté," but that it is also "a mental illness, an idiocy." That the mechanistic picture of the world is the only admissible picture is a "crudity" because it denies the values of ethics and aesthetics, but it is sheer "idiocy" when it denies the values of rationality. For when it does the latter, it makes nonsense of *itself*. Mr. Mechanic's interpretation is *"one of the stupidest* of all possible interpretations of the world" precisely because it renders inquiry – and any other form of agency – incomprehensible. Mr. Mechanic's claims to knowledge are themselves among the things that cannot be understood from an empirical perspective. To make sense of those claims – even to encounter them *as claims* – is to take up a perspective constituted by value commitments. Mr. Mechanic might well claim to do without ethical values no less than fairies; he would undoubtedly, though, find it awkward to claim to do without inquiry – much less without claims.

7 The Unveiled Truth, Revisited

We can now distinguish the type of naturalism Nietzsche rejects from the type he affirms in *BGE*. And we can do so in such a way as to explain (a) how the will to truth may be satisfied by a view that is false, and (b) how the falsity of the view is due to its failure to satisfy the will to value. We do so by distinguishing the following two claims:

1   If an empirical explanation of a phenomenon is possible, that explanation is to be preferred to an explanation of another kind (e.g., one that claims a basis in rational intuition).
2   Empirical explanation of any phenomenon whatsoever is possible; i.e., X is real if and only if X is subject to (or figures in) empirical explanation.

Nietzsche accepts (1); he thinks that one should prefer, in every case, empirical explanation to any alternative explanation of the same phenomenon. He is led to this conclusion by the will to truth and not by the will to value since the world revealed by empirical methods is not the world as the will to value would have it. Understood as the acceptance of (1), Nietzsche's naturalism is methodological, in the sense that he thinks that whenever a scientific explanation is available, one should accept that explanation. And this naturalism has ontological consequences: it refuses to posit entities invoked by explanations that compete with empirical explanations. If X can be explained empirically without positing A, then X provides no basis for positing A. Because Nietzsche thinks that many entities are rendered superfluous by empirical explanations (e.g., Platonic forms, immaterial souls, God), his naturalism leads him to deny the existence of those entities.

Nietzsche does not, however, accept (2). While he is certainly committed by (1) to *attempting* to give an empirical explanation of any phenomenon whatsoever, he doesn't hold that to be real *just is* to be subject to empirical explanation. As we saw above, he

MAUDEMARIE CLARK AND DAVID DUDRICK

thinks that such a claim rules out perspectives from which the value properties of things (their beauty or baseness, for example) show up. Nietzsche objects to this implication not on the grounds that it renders one unable to account for the truth of ethical and aesthetic claims, but on the grounds that it renders one unable to account for how it is that anything can be *a claim at all*. Yet, the acceptance of (2) is not a simple mistake. Nietzsche holds that its acceptance is initially the result of the will to truth's putting the will to value into abeyance: one accepts (2) precisely when one has become strong enough to deny satisfaction to the urge to "create a world before which [one] can kneel." And yet Nietzsche holds that (2) *is false*. And it is thus that (a) is explicable: the will to truth may be satisfied by a view that is false.

Now, the will to value is satisfied when one sees one's image reflected in the world, when the world is seen as it *ought* to be, whether or not it *is* so. Our discussion of *GS* 374 helps us to see that Nietzsche's naturalism allows the will to value to be satisfied in a way that not only avoids conflict with, but actually serves, the will to truth. We saw that to describe human beings using the language of agency (as acting, believing, knowing, etc.) is to see them in a network that is not merely causal but normative. This means that to so describe them is to "rationalize" them: it is to see them as making sense. So, insofar as a being can be seen as an agent, as a rational being, the being must, for the most part, behave in accordance with our standards for rational behavior. When it comes to agency, then, things *are*, by definition, as they *ought* to be (at least in general) – if they weren't, it wouldn't be agency. But if this is so, then truths about agents can be had only from a perspective constituted by values, by our understanding of how one ought to act or think – only, that is, when the will to value is satisfied. When the will to value operates with respect to agency, what it sees *is* the truth; it is *only* through such operation that these truths can be seen. That being so, we can see (b): how the falsity of the view that satisfies the will to truth is due to a failure to satisfy properly the will to value.

We can therefore take the paradoxical-sounding statement from the preface to *GS* – "we no longer believe that truth remains truth when the veils are withdrawn" – to express Nietzsche's rejection of (2) above. This means: scientific explanations at their best are true, but truth is lost when these explanations are combined with an insistence that everything can be explained scientifically. As we have interpreted this claim, however, it does not leave the door open to all sorts of non-scientific or unscientific ways of explaining things. The only things that stand outside the range of scientific explanation, on our account of Nietzsche's naturalism, are the thoughts and behavior of human beings. While Nietzsche may well hold that the phenomenal properties of experience cannot be given empirical explanation, his primary objection is more basic. To hold that everything is explicable using the methods of the natural sciences is to hold that from the empirical perspective nothing is "veiled," to use the imagery of the preface to *GS*. But this is to deny that there is anything that scientific explanation leaves out. To say, then, that truth no longer remains truth when the veils are withdrawn is to say that when true scientific explanations of human cognitive processes and behavior are coupled with a denial that there is anything about human beings that cannot be seen from the empirical perspective, the resulting, conjunctive claim is not true. When coupled with a such denial, scientific explanations offer us a false picture of what human beings are like.

164

What remains veiled when one adopts the perspective of the natural sciences is, as we have seen, activities that take place in the space of reasons, the activities of rational interpreters and agents. To claim that all phenomena admit of empirical explanation, then, is to deny the existence of such activities, which is to say that if such activity *is* to be understood, it will be from a perspective other than that of the natural sciences. We take this to be Nietzsche's point in two passages in which he refers to certain sciences as "unnatural" – namely, "psychology and the critique of the elements of consciousness" (*GS* 355; cf. *GM* III. 25). The suggestion is that the nature of rational or sense-making activity shows that its examination must be conducted from a perspective that differs from that of the natural sciences. The natural sciences employ norms, of course, and that is certainly something to which Nietzsche calls our attention in *BGE*. But these norms are not such as to insist that the phenomena in question must "make sense," that they must accord with how a rational agent would arrange them. The success of the natural sciences, Nietzsche tells us in the same passage in which he designates psychology an "unnatural science," lies in their making visible their objects "as strange, as distant, as 'outside us'." Psychology is an unnatural science precisely in its inability to make its objects visible in this way – its objects are visible only insofar as they are seen as making sense.

We have, as should be clear, interpreted Nietzsche's naturalism as claiming that the best explanation for everything that is not rational or sense-making activity is the kind of causal or mechanistic explanation that natural science provides. Of course, beings that engage in sense-making activities are part of nature, according to Nietzsche, and therefore much about them is explicable in scientific terms. But although human beings are part of nature, Nietzsche's version of naturalism insists that science doesn't tell us all there is to know about their doings. Nietzsche's view doesn't have us postulating any extra *things* (e.g., immaterial, immortal souls); rather, it says that fully natural beings have developed in such a way as to admit of true descriptions that cannot be had from an empirical perspective.

See also 16 "Phenomenology and Science in Nietzsche"; 17 "Naturalism and Nietzsche's Moral Psychology"; 18 "Naturalism and Genealogy"; 27 "Nietzsche, Dionysus, and the Ontology of Music"

Notes

1   This is technically inaccurate since Nietzsche published new editions of *BT, HH*, and *D* in 1886, after finishing *BGE* but before publishing the second edition of *GS*. Nothing was added to these new editions of 1886, however, except new prefaces. None is really a new work, but the same work with a new preface. In the case of *GS*, in contrast, the new edition added a whole fifth part, which establishes it as a different book than the first edition.

2   One extreme exception to this rule is Laurence Lampert (2001), who argues that *BGE* as a whole is "a coherent argument that never lets up" and that each of its nine parts, with the possible exception of part 4, is a coherent argument and that the placement of each section is determined by what it contributes the argument of that part.

3   Bow imagery is also used by Nietzsche himself in *HH* 265 and *BGE* 262, two important passages for understanding it, and, as Lampert (2001) mentions, in *Zarathustra* ("One Thousand and One Goals").

4 In the preface, he tells us that "Plato's invention of the pure spirit and the good as such" was a "dogmatist's error" and the "worst, most durable, and most dangerous of all errors." He also identifies the fight against dogmatism with the fight against Platonism, thus with the fight against these errors. One of the Platonic errors he is denouncing here (and the most important one, because the other one depends on it) is precisely the theory of the soul that gives reason an independent and ruling role in it. Nietzsche begins to offer an alternative vision of the parts of the soul in *BGE* 12, the middle section of the book's first part.

5 Perhaps the preface is designed to suggest something of this tension precisely by repeatedly pushing dogmatism away as, for instance, a "monstrous and frightening caricature" or as involving "the worst, most durable, and most dangerous of all errors," and then pulling it back as having inscribed itself "in the hearts of humanity with eternal demands," and as something to which we should not be "ungrateful."

6 These two terms do have different senses. Dogmatism is an epistemological position, an insistence on the possibility of substantive a priori knowledge, whereas one is a metaphysician by virtue of an ontological position, a commitment to the existence of objects that can be known (if at all) only by a priori means. But the terms tend to pick out the same group of philosophers.

7 The passage identifies this "valuation" as "the faith in opposite values," which would be more accurately (if much more clumsily) translated as "the faith in the oppositeness of things valued," i.e., the faith that things of high and low value are related to each other as opposites. If they are so related, they are related in such a way that the lower things could never be refined into things of high value, and the value of the highly valued things could certainly not depend on the lowly valued things. The implication, which Nietzsche does not make clear here, is that the insistence on a priori (i.e., dogmatic) procedures in philosophy is due to the influence of this valuation, which insists that things of the highest value, such as knowledge, truth, and virtue, cannot be connected to things of the lowest value, like the senses, the world knowable through the senses, and desire. The way in which the passage fills in the "opposites" makes clear that this is the valuation Nietzsche claims to find behind metaphysics.

8 We leave out of consideration here the fact that this same passage also claims that philosophy is an expression of the will to power. Some will wonder why we do not take the will to power to be the drive that opposes the will to truth in the "magnificent tension of the spirit to be the will to power." Although we cannot argue this in any detail here, our answer is that Nietzsche makes clear that the will to power (to mastery) is not a particular drive, but a property of all drives (*BGE* 6). It is only after one understands philosophy as a product of different drives in the philosopher's soul that one can begin to understand it as an expression of the will to power.

9 We have changed Nauckhoff's translation of *einzeln* and *Einseln* from "individually" and "individual" to the more literal "singly" and "single" because it both fits the passage better and matches the Clark–Swenson translation of the similar passage of *GM* cited in the following note.

10 Nietzsche makes similar use of organic imagery in *GM*, preface, 2.

11 Some may take this passage to point to Nietzsche's alleged pan-psychism. To do so, however, is to fail to follow Nietzsche's own instructions for reading him well, which include "looking cautiously, before and aft" (*D*, preface, 6), i.e., trying to see the connections to surrounding passages. We can reasonably take the passage's question as to whether "all existence isn't an *interpreting* existence" to concern only *human* existence – and not e.g. the existence of tables, rocks, and chairs – if we can see that there is an important question about human existence that can plausibly be seen as a continuation of the reflection carried out in the

166

previous passage. That question, we shall argue, concerns how far the perspectival character of existence extends.

Editions of Nietzsche Used

Beyond Good and Evil (1886). All translations are Clark's, and are indebted to both Kaufmann's and Hollingdale's translations of the book.

Daybreak, trans. R. J. Hollingdale, 2nd edn., ed. Maudemarie Clark and Brian Leiter (Cambridge: Cambridge University Press, 1997).

The Gay Science, trans. Josefine Nauckhoff, 2nd edn., ed. Bernard Williams (Cambridge: Cambridge University Press, 2001).

On the Genealogy of Morality, trans. Maudemarie Clark and Alan Swenson (Indianapolis: Hackett, 1998).

Human, All Too Human, trans. R. J. Hollingdale (Cambridge: Cambridge University Press, 1986).

Thus Spoke Zarathustra, in *The Portable Nietzsche*, ed. Walter Kaufmann (New York: Viking Penguin, 1954; pbk. edn. 1959; repr. 1982).

Twilight of the Idols, in *The Portable Nietzsche*, ed. Walter Kaufmann (New York: Viking Penguin, 1954; pbk. edn. 1959; repr. 1982).

References

Clark, M. (1990). *Nietzsche on Truth and Philosophy* (Cambridge: Cambridge University Press).

—— (1998). "On Knowledge, Truth and Value: Nietzsche's Debt to Schopenhauer and the Development of Empiricism," in C. Janaway (ed.), *Willing and Nothingness: Schopenhauer as Nietzsche's Educator* (Oxford: Clarendon Press), pp. 37–79.

—— (2005). "Nietzsche and Green on the Transcendental Tradition," *International Studies in Philosophy*, 37(3).

Clark, M. and Dudrick, D. (2004), "Nietzsche's Post-Positivism," *European Journal of Philosophy*, 12(3), pp. 369–86.

Cox, C. (1999). *Nietzsche: Naturalism and Interpretation* (Berkeley: University of California Press).

Green, M. S. (2002). *Nietzsche and the Transcendental Tradition* (Urbana: University of Illinois Press).

Horstmann, R.-P. (2002). Introduction to Nietzsche's *Beyond Good and Evil* (Cambridge: Cambridge University Press).

Lampert, L. (2001). *Nietzsche's Task* (New Haven: Yale University Press).

Leiter, B. (2002). *Nietzsche on Morality* (London and New York: Routledge).

Nehamas, A. (1987). *Nietzsche: Life as Literature* (Cambridge, MA: Harvard University Press).

Plato (1992). *Republic*, trans. G. M. A. Grube, revised C. D. C. Reeve (Indianapolis: Hackett).

Richardson, J. (2004). *Nietzsche's New Darwinism* (Oxford: Oxford University Press).

Schacht, R. (1998). "Nietzsche's *Gay Science*, Or, How to Naturalize Cheerfully," in R. Solomon and K. Higgins (eds.), *Reading Nietzsche* (Oxford: Oxford University Press).

Spir, A. (1877). *Denken und Wirklichkeit. Versuch einer Ereuerung der kritischen Philosophie*, 2 vols., 2nd edn. (Leipzig). All translations are Clark's.

Stegmaier, W. (2004). " 'Philosophischer Idealismus' und die 'Musik des Lebens'. Zu Nietzsches Umgang mit Paradoxien. Eine kontextuelle Interpretation des Aphorismus Nr. 372 der *Fröhlichen Wissenschaft*," *Nietzsche-Studien*, 33, pp. 90–129.

Part III

Eternal Recurrence, the Overhuman, and Nihilism

10

Identity and Eternal Recurrence

PAUL S. LOEB

To paraphrase Kant, it remains a scandal to Nietzsche scholarship that we are obliged to assume the centrality of his doctrine of eternal recurrence but we are not able to give a satisfactory reply to anyone who may claim to refute this doctrine. Because Nietzsche has proven so insightful in so many areas of inquiry, we want to believe him when he tells us that eternal recurrence was his most important discovery ever. But in truth, since Georg Simmel's summary dismissal in 1907 merely 26 years after this discovery, even Nietzsche's admirers have conceded that his emphasis on the complete qualitative identity of eternal recurrence renders his idea insupportable, insignificant, and incoherent.

Simmel begins with Nietzsche's insistence on the reality of eternal recurrence and with Nietzsche's conviction that he had discovered a fundamental truth about the nature of the cosmos that would change his life and the history of humankind. In his last work, *Ecce Homo*, Nietzsche describes eternal recurrence as a cosmological theory comparable to those proposed by the ancient Greeks:

> The doctrine of "eternal recurrence," that is to say, of the unconditional and endlessly repeated circular course of all things – this doctrine of Zarathustra could possibly already have been taught by Heraclitus. At least the Stoa, which inherited almost all its fundamental ideas from Heraclitus, shows traces of it. (*EH*, "BT," 3)

Upon making his discovery in August 1881, Nietzsche wrote about the impact on his own life: "What do we do with the *rest* of our lives – we who have spent the greatest part of them in the most essential ignorance? We *teach the doctrine* – it is the strongest means of *incorporating* it into ourselves. Our kind of bliss, as teacher of the greatest doctrine" (*KSA* 9, 11[141]). And a little later, in a remark that anticipated the skepticism of his later commentators, Nietzsche wrote about the impact his discovery would have on humankind:

> Let us guard against teaching such a doctrine as an upstart religion! It must sink in slowly; entire generations must cultivate it and become fruitful on it – in order that it may become a great tree overshadowing all humankind still to come. What are the two millennia during which Christianity has survived! For the mightiest thought many millennia are needed – *long, long* must it be small and powerless! (*KSA* 9, 11[158])

Here now is Simmel's influential early verdict regarding these assorted claims: "The deep emotion and devotion with which Nietzsche speaks of his doctrine can be explained, it seems to me, only in terms of a certain imprecision in its logical conceptualization" (1986: 170–8; 1920: 246–59, emended translation in favor of greater literalness here and throughout this essay). In the first place, he argues, suppose a phenomenon appears that is absolutely identical with me in all of its traits and experiences. It follows that this qualitatively identical recurrence of me cannot *recognize* or *acknowledge* itself as such. For "if there were something qualitatively real in the second instance whereby it pointed back to the earlier instance and thereby acknowledged itself to be the later instance, then it would not be the exact repetition of the first, but rather would be differentiated from it just by the virtue of that acknowledgement." Thus, there can never be any human awareness of recurrence that could count as evidence in support of the truth of Nietzsche's doctrine, and we are forced to rely instead on his weak and unscientific proofs.

Second, Simmel writes: "If an experience is repeated within my existence, this repetition as such can be of the most enormous importance for me; but only because I am reminded by it of the first instance." But, as we have just seen, our supposition that the repetition of my experience is qualitatively identical entails that I cannot be reminded of the first instance of this experience. Besides, as most later commentators have agreed, the exact repetition of my experience means that all my choices and actions are predetermined. So eternal recurrence cannot be of any importance to those who recur, and Nietzsche's thought is psychologically and ethically insignificant.

Finally, Simmel suggests, even if we were to grant the possibility of recurrence-awareness, the importance of repetition "requires rather that an ego persists." But "in reality it is in no way *I who* recurs, but only a phenomenon appears that absolutely agrees with me in all of its traits and experiences." So Nietzsche needs to postulate the *numerical* identity of eternal recurrence. And, indeed, as several commentators have since elaborated, if the repetitions of my experience are to be *qualitatively* identical in every respect, then they must also be *temporally* identical. But since time was our only means of differentiating these repetitions (as "first" and "second," or "earlier" and "later"), this means that they are in fact *numerically* identical. So what were supposed to be infinitely many *recurrences* or *repetitions* turn out to be only a single *occurrence*. Nietzsche's doctrine thus proves to be conceptually incoherent.

Anticipating Heidegger (1977), Simmel concludes his evaluation with a psychological diagnosis: "And we also find here a hidden and profound reason, which is not otherwise easily detected, why Nietzsche felt that recurrence was an absolutely essential and central element in all of his thinking." Having abandoned the idea of any final and absolute goal of being, Nietzsche found it "comforting and beneficial" that "endless becoming achieves form and secure boundaries" through the eternal recurrence of the same: "The infinite drifting that results from the restlessness of his nature and his negation of a cosmic goal are placed within the limits of the circumference of the 'ring'."

1 Recurrence-Awareness

As this review indicates, the key premise in Simmel's classic analysis is that the complete qualitative identity of eternal recurrence logically precludes any awareness or recognition of that recurrence. From the impossibility of such recognition, it does seem to follow that Nietzsche's doctrine is insupportable, insignificant, and incoherent. But is Simmel's premise obviously true? A survey of the literature from the last 40 years shows a wide range of influential scholars who think it is: Arthur Danto (1965: 204–5), Ivan Soll (1973: 335, 339–41), Bernd Magnus (1978: 156–7), Alexander Nehamas (1985: 152), Kathleen Higgins (1987: 163–4, 2000: 128), Erich Heller (1988: 183), David Wood (1988: 37, 46), Gary Shapiro (1989: 84), Alan White (1990: 64–8), Maudemarie Clark (1990: 266–70), Michael Tanner (1994: 54), Aaron Ridley (1997: 20), Robin Small (2002: 12), Robert C. Solomon (2003: 14, 202), and most recently Lawrence J. Hatab (2005: 64, 115–16). Even those who have successfully criticized Simmel's famous refutation of Nietzsche's proofs of eternal recurrence, such as Alistair Moles (1990: 285, 295, 412–13) and Günther Abel (1998: 217–46), accept this premise.

In fact, as far as I know, there has been only one challenge of this premise in the literature, by Philip J. Kain, in a paper entitled "Nietzsche, Skepticism and Eternal Recurrence." However, Kain's argument has not been noticed, perhaps because he includes it only as a brief aside:

> But Nietzsche's view, I think, is that one can in fact have an opinion concerning another cycle. Eternal recurrence is revealed by a demon within each cycle who conveys a message about other cycles. [. . .] Furthermore, it would certainly seem possible, if not exactly to remember, at least to be aware of (in the sense of believe in) earlier recurrences and thus for the demon's message to cause us to react to events in the present cycle negatively. This would be the case as long as the very same awareness and reaction were to recur in each and every cycle at the same point. To assume that such feelings would make the cycles different would be to assume that the awareness and thus the reaction would be absent in one cycle, the first. But Nietzsche is quite clear that time is infinite; there is no first cycle. These feelings could occur in all cycles at exactly the same point in the sequence. (1983: 376–7)

Kain's mention of the "demon's message" refers, of course, to Nietzsche's presentation of eternal recurrence in *Gay Science* 341. Because this presentation is so compact, and because Nietzsche himself drew attention to it as the first and carefully planned public appearance of his doctrine (*EH*, "Z," 1), Simmel and other scholars have concentrated on it as the place where they find the flaws in Nietzsche's doctrine. As they observe, the demon's message insists on a complete qualitative identity among my innumerable recurring lives:

> This life, as you now live it and have lived it, you will have to live once more and innumerable times more; and there will be nothing new in it, but every pain and every joy and every thought and sigh and everything unspeakably small and great in your life must return to you, and all in the same succession and sequence – and even this spider and this moonlight between the trees, and even this moment and I myself. The eternal hourglass of being is turned over again and again – and you with it, speck of dust!

However, as Kain notes, I may be said to possess an awareness of my eternally recurring lives as soon I hear the demon's message. Moreover, as Kain also points out, this awareness introduces no qualitative difference as long as the very same awareness recurs in each and every one of my recurring lives at the very same moment. And, indeed, if we look more closely at the demon's message, we see that it is recursive in the sense that he explicitly insists on his own return, and thus on his same insistence within that return, and so on innumerable times more. Nietzsche's long dash thus indicates the demon's deduction: from his general claim of complete qualitative identity among my recurring lives to his specific claim that his own message, and presumably my reaction to it (whether pain or joy), must return in each and every recurring life at exactly the same moment. Since the aphorism later instructs me to count the demon's message as a kind of thought that overpowers me, the demon is implying that his message must itself be included among all the thoughts that he says must return to me in the same succession and sequence. Nietzsche makes this recursive point fully explicit when he writes in an 1881 preparatory note: "Everything comes again: Sirius and the spider and your thoughts in this hour and this thought of yours that everything comes again" (*KSA* 9, 11[206]).

It would seem, then, that Nietzsche's *Gay Science* presentation of his doctrine is designed to emphasize precisely, and especially, the awareness of recurrence that students of this aphorism argue is logically prohibited. In addition, Nietzsche's presentation seems designed to call our attention to the demon's deduction of the *recurrence* of this very same awareness – thereby avoiding the charge that this awareness would introduce some qualitative difference. The demon says that his qualitatively identical self must deliver his qualitatively identical message in the life I must live once more. In Simmel's terms, the first instance of the demon refers to the second instance of the demon and thereby acknowledges itself to be first *while still remaining qualitatively identical with the second*. Since there is no logical contradiction whatsoever in this scenario, why have so many careful students of Nietzsche's aphorism thought it obvious that there is?

I think Kain is right to suppose that Simmel, and those scholars who have followed his lead, are inadvertently assuming that the interlocutor in *Gay Science* 341 is living some "initial" or "original" life that he has never lived before and that hence could not include any recognition of having been already lived. This assumption is expressed, for example, in Kathleen Higgins' recent summary of the consensus: "[T]he recurrence would not be a repetition of the *original* with the addition of a recognition that it is a recurrence. This recognition, or any memory of a previous iteration, would be ruled out as deviations from the *original* life" (2000: 128, my italics). Moreover, this assumption would seem to be supported by the demon's tense-asymmetrical claim that I *will* have to live again the identical life I am now living and have lived so far. The demon does not say that I must *have already* lived this identical life once before and innumerable times before. So it might seem that my recurring lives will not be qualitatively identical to my present life precisely because they will include within them an additional recognition of having been lived before.

Nevertheless, Nietzsche is quite clear elsewhere (most importantly, in *Thus Spoke Zarathustra*) that eternal recurrence extends backward as well as forward: there is no initial or original life that I have not already lived, and there is no final or concluding life that I will not live again. Applying this point to the *Gay Science* aphorism, it is simply not plausible that Nietzsche meant the demon to inform me of the innumerable qualitatively identical lives to come after this *very first non-recurring* life that I am now living. The demon's message implicitly instructs me to extrapolate backward so that I recognize this message as an exact repetition of the message that was delivered in a previous identical life, and so on. Indeed, Nietzsche's unpublished first draft of the demon's message does include the broader claim that the moment of this message "was already there once and many times" ("So diesen Augenblick: er war schon einmal da und viele Male und wird ebenso wiederkehren"; *KSA* 9, 11[148]). But this means that the demon's message does provide me with a *non-differentiating* awareness that I have already lived the life I am now living.

2 Recurrence-Evidence

Having set aside Simmel's premise by showing that Nietzsche emphasized the exact repetition of any recurrence-awareness, I turn now to the objection that this recognition cannot count as *evidence* of the reality of recurrence precisely because it *is* exactly repeated. Arthur Danto, for example, argues that any evidence of the reality of eternal recurrence would have to differentiate what is identical. But exactly repeated recurrence-awareness cannot provide any differentiation at all:

> There can hardly be anything like *evidence* for the doctrine in any simple sense of "evidence." We could not, for example, find in the world as it is now any *traces* of another and exactly resemblant world or world state. If they do *exactly* resemble each other, there would be no traces or scars left by one upon the other to differentiate them: any traces in the one would have identical counterparts in the other. [. . .] When two things are so exactly alike that they cannot in principle be told apart, nothing is to count as evidence that there are two things to be told apart. If they could be told apart, they would differ just at the point of differentiation, and this is ruled out by the hypothesis. (1965: 204; see also Magnus 1978: 66–7)

Notice, however, Danto's imprecise use of the concepts of identity and difference. Certainly, as we have seen, the demon's message cannot in any way help me *qualitatively* distinguish among my recurring lives. But this does not mean, as Danto further suggests, that the message cannot help me *numerically* differentiate among them. In fact, the language Nietzsche uses to describe his doctrine – *Wiederkehrung, Wiederkunft, Wiederholung* – clearly implies numerical difference. Also, as we have seen, Nietzsche's presentation in *Gay Science* 341 emphasizes the numerical distinctness of my qualitatively identical recurring lives. Both the demon and the narrator say to me that I will have to live my qualitatively identical life "once more and innumerable times more" ("noch einmal und noch unzählige Male"). To be precise, then, any evidence of the reality of eternal recurrence would have to numerically differentiate what is qualitatively indiscernible. But there is no contradiction in thinking there can be such evidence (Black 1952), and in fact the immanent awareness conveyed by the demon's message would seem to be an ideal candidate for this role.

Leaving behind this logical objection, we still need to address the scholarly consensus that Nietzsche's aphorism shows no interest in any epistemic questions regarding his doctrine. The chief reasons for this consensus are as follows: the aphorism is introduced as a hypothetical thought-experiment; it does not include any proof or demonstration; it seems to emphasize the interlocutor's epistemically uncritical state; and it describes the demon's message as an overpowering thought rather than as a well-founded true belief. What really matters in this aphorism, commentators agree, are the psychological effects of the merely hypothetical thought of recurrence and the non-epistemic role of this thought as a kind of test or ideal of life-affirmation (Soll 1973: 322–6; Magnus 1978: 111–54).

But there are problems with each of the reasons behind this consensus. In the first place, when Nietzsche writes, "What if some day or night a demon were to steal into your most solitary solitude and say to you: 'This life [. . .] '" skeptical scholars usually import Nietzsche's initial phrase, "What if" (*Wie, wenn*), into the demon's message itself and interpret it as a conditional phrase. As Bernd Magnus writes: "Recall that the demon presents us with a hypothetical state-of-affairs. '*What if*' . . . recurrence were true" (1978: 40, see also 74–5). This phrase, they then argue, is Nietzsche's device for suspending the question whether eternal recurrence is true or whether we have good evidence for its truth (Clark 1990: 248, 254; Tanner 1994: 53; Allison 2001: 123–4).

In fact, however, the demon's message is flatly categorical and concludes with the broader cosmological assertion that is supposed to entail my eternally recurring life: "The eternal hourglass of being is turned over again and again – and you with it, speck of dust!" Properly read, then, Nietzsche's "What if" is an interrogative phrase that anticipates the string of interrogative sentences that follow the demon's assertion. These sentences do not in any way hypothesize the demon's assertion, but only the interlocutor's response to this assertion:

> Would you not throw yourself down and gnash your teeth and curse the demon who spoke thus? Or have you once experienced a tremendous moment when you would have answered him: "you are a god and never have I heard anything more divine!" If this thought gained power over you, it would transform and perhaps crush you, as you are; the question in each and every thing, "do you want this once more and innumerable times more?" would lie on your actions as the greatest heavy weight! Or how well disposed would you have to become to yourself and to life to *long for nothing more fervently* than for this last eternal confirmation and seal? (GS 341)

It is certainly true that this set of concluding questions focuses our attention upon the possible psychological consequences of accepting the demon's message. But why should we suppose that this acceptance and these consequences are unrelated to the *evidentiary* power of the demon's message? One reason, scholars claim, is that only a *rational proof* or *demonstration* of the eternal recurrence cosmology could bring about the kind of reactions described in *Gay Science* 341. As Maudemarie Clark writes: "If Nietzsche is concerned to produce such effects, he must convince us to accept the cosmology. If we are rational, we will ask what reason exists for accepting this cosmology" (1990: 251; see also Soll 1973: 326). Yet even though Nietzsche had worked out such proofs in his unpublished notebooks, he did not include any of them in his first published presentation of his doctrine. It must be the case, Clark concludes, that Nietzsche is not interested in our *warranted* acceptance of his doctrine or in showing how such warranted acceptance would lead to its transformational effects. In support of this conclusion, she notes especially the aphorism's emphasis on the interlocutor's loneliest of loneliness, "a situation of vulnerability to suggestions one would otherwise dismiss, a situation in which one's critical powers are at a minimum" (1990: 251).

Although ingenious, this account relies upon an understanding of evidence that is not Nietzsche's. At the start of *Beyond Good and Evil*, and in a direct allusion back to the demon of *Gay Science* 341, Nietzsche indicates that, unlike other philosophers who *pretend* to have discovered their insights through pure reason, he courageously and honestly shows us the inspiring spirits or demons (*inspirirende Genien oder Dämonen*) that *actually* led him to his discoveries. He does not defend his doctrines – not even his abstrusest metaphysical claims – with proofs that he sought after the fact of his discoveries and that were themselves produced at the behest of his inspiring demons (*BGE* 5–6). This point is supported by Nietzsche's reference in *Gay Science* 341 to Socrates' *daimonic* inner voice and to his claim that this voice expressed Socrates' instinctive wisdom (*GS* 340; *BT* 13). To be sure, Clark's translation of "loneliness" for *Einsamkeit* is certainly suggestive of vulnerability and diminution of critical power. But the more usual translation of "solitude" better captures Nietzsche's typical praise of *Einsamkeit* as the supreme condition for maximizing one's critical powers – that is, for isolating oneself from the common opinion in order to discover and bring to the surface one's own deepest instinctive wisdom (*D* 440; *Z* III, "Homecoming"; *BGE* 44, 231, 284; see also Higgins 1987: 114–16; Salaquarda 1989: 323–5; Oger 1997: 10). So it is open to Nietzsche, in his public introduction of eternal recurrence, to completely omit his rationalistic proofs while still presenting what he regards as the most critically powerful grounds for believing in the truth of his doctrine.

Finally, it is true, as some commentators point out, that the narrator of Nietzsche's aphorism describes the demon as conveying to me an overpowering thought rather than as providing me with evidence for believing in the truth of this thought (Soll 1973: 324–5). And certainly my mere contemplation of this thought, or even the psychological force of this thought, cannot count as evidence for this thought. But this observation overlooks two crucial aspects of Nietzsche's presentation. In the first place, his poetic devices indicate that I am also being overpowered by a *sensory experience*: some sunny day perhaps, I find myself suddenly plunged into an intensely solitary moment in which I literally *see* moonlight streaming between the trees and a spider crawling nearby; I literally *feel* a demon creeping next to me; and I literally *hear* the demon whispering to me in the most personal terms about even the smallest and most intimate details of my life. In keeping with his remark that mystics of every rank are more honest in showing their inspiring spirits and demons (*BGE* 5–6), Nietzsche's religious imagery in this aphorism suggests that he is concerned honestly to communicate the quasi-mystical sensory experience that he says inspired his thought of eternal recurrence. This is how he describes this experience in *Ecce Homo*:

> The concept of revelation, in the sense that something suddenly, with unspeakable certainty and subtlety, becomes *visible*, audible, something that shakes and overturns one

to the depths, simply describes the fact. One hears, one does not seek; one takes, one does not ask who gives; a thought flashes up like lightning, with necessity, unfalteringly formed – I never had any choice. (*EH*, "Z," 3; see also Salaquarda 1989: 334–7)

In the second place, Nietzsche's presentation of the demon's message also includes a *performative* aspect that is directly tied to the message's focus on time. Besides conveying to me the abstract thought of eternal recurrence, the demon *prophesies* to me that I will have to relive my identical life. So in experiencing the demon's message, I may be said to have a precognition or prevision of a future that includes and extends beyond the moment of my death. This prevision is extremely concrete, since this future consists of everything small and great in the life I have already lived. Moreover, since the demon implicitly instructs me to extrapolate backward, he also *reminds* me that I have already lived this identical life. So I also may be said to have an extremely concrete memory or recollection of a past that includes and extends beyond the moment of my first conscious awareness.

3 Recurrence-Significance

On this reading of Nietzsche's aphorism, we do not need to follow recent commentaries that struggle to find some means of divorcing Nietzsche's ideal of life-affirmation from questions about the truth or evidence of eternal recurrence (Clark 1990: 247–54). Suppose I am like Socrates in the preceding aphorism, and I have suffered from life-impoverishment (*GS* 340, 370). In that case, the demon's recursive message will give me good reason to anticipate with dread the heavy, crushing weight of innumerable more such livings of my identical suffering life, and to recall with horror the heavy, crushing weight of my innumerable previous livings of this identical suffering life. Indeed, the demon's insistence on his own return lets me know that the very pain I am feeling when hearing this message – the pain that leads me to throw myself down, gnash my teeth, and curse the demon who speaks to me thus – will overwhelm me again innumerable times more and has already overwhelmed me innumerable times before.

On the other hand, suppose I am like Zarathustra in the next aphorism, and I have enjoyed a life overflowing with energy (*GS* 342, 370). In that case, the demon's recursive message will give me good reason to embrace Nietzsche's ideal of life-affirmation: that is, to anticipate with craving innumerable more such livings of my identical joyful life and to recall with gratitude my innumerable previous livings of this identical joyful life. Again, the demon's insistence on his own return lets me know that the very bliss I feel when hearing this message – the bliss that leads me to bless the demon as a god and the demon's message as divine – will overwhelm me again innumerable times more and has already overwhelmed me innumerable times before.

Either way, Nietzsche's title for his aphorism – "The Greatest Heavy Weight" – emphasizes his belief that the thought of my life's eternal recurrence could, and, indeed, should, have a life-changing impact: "If this thought gained power over you, it would transform and perhaps crush you, as you are; the question in each and every thing, 'do you want this once more and innumerable times more?' would lie on your actions as the greatest heavy weight!" This belief is best captured in a famous 1881 note in which Nietzsche ridicules secularization as a contemporary political madness whose goal is the well-being of the *fleeting* individual. By contrast, he writes:

> My doctrine says: the task is to live in such a way that you *must* wish to live again – you will *anyway*! To whom striving gives the highest feeling, let him strive; to whom rest gives the highest feeling, let him rest; to whom ordering, following, obedience give the highest feeling, let him obey. **May** he only *become aware of* **what** *gives him the highest feeling* and spare *no means! Eternity is at stake!* (*KSA* 9, 11[165])

Given our refutation of Simmel's argument against the possibility of recurrence-awareness, there would seem to be no contradiction in Nietzsche's supposition that his thought could have this kind of tremendous personal significance and transformational power. Unfortunately, the point on which this refutation depends – that the qualitative identity of eternal recurrence extends *backward* as well as forward – would itself seem to nullify this significance and power. For, as Karl Löwith first observed in 1935, this backward extension would seem to entail that all my choices and actions are fated (Löwith 1997: 87). Applying this point to Nietzsche's aphorism, Aaron Ridley comments:

> And if the demon is coming to me *now*, he has presumably also been to me at precisely the same point of my life innumerable times before – and what difference has *that* made? If I passed the test I passed, if I failed I failed, and I'll go on doing whichever I did infinitely many more times, without it changing a thing. The thought of eternal recurrence, then, should be a matter of the deepest indifference. Why *care*? (1997: 20)

Indeed, Magnus argues, the backward extension of eternal recurrence obviously defeats the imperative force of Nietzsche's exhortation that I live in such a way that I must wish to live again: "Then how I now live must be how I lived an infinite number of previous occasions. But I can only live in such a way that I must wish to live again if, in previous recurrences, I lived in such a way that I must live again" (1979: 364). Worse, he suggests, this recurrence fatalism would seem to undermine even my choice of how to react to Nietzsche's thought and thus the significance of this reaction as a test or diagnosis of my life-affirmation (1978: 141, 1979: 363–8, 1999: 101).

It seems to me, however, that this widely accepted charge of recurrence fatalism still relies upon the same kind of reasoning that motivates Simmel's influential premise. It is argued that the demon's message cannot change the life I am living *now* without negating its qualitative identity with the life I have *already* lived. But this is to assume that I have lived some *initial* or *original* life in which I did not hear the same demon's message, or in which that same message did not change my life in just the same way. In fact, the qualitative identity among my recurring lives is preserved as long as the identical message-inspired change or difference takes place in *all* of my recurring lives. So there is no contradiction in Nietzsche supposing that the revelation of my life's eternal recurrence could lead me to overturn my life now so as to spare no means in searching out and doing whatever gives me the highest feeling. "Fated" change – or change that must agree exactly with innumerable corresponding changes in the past – is still change.

Granting, then, that Nietzsche's doctrine does indeed allow personal transformation and change, we still may wonder whether the backward extension of eternal recurrence does not render any such change *meaningless*. This is because, as Joe Krueger writes, "our decisions would not truly be our own; our choices and actions will have been determined for us since the infinite past and into the infinite future" (1978: 442). Or, as Magnus asks, "given recurrence fatalism, what sense can be made of 'my' voluntary behavior?" (1979: 366).

However, these very abstract formulations obscure the more precise sense in which it is of course always *me* who has made the choice in the innumerable previous recurrences of my life. Magnus himself admits this when he imagines a respondent saying "that whatever causes me to behave as I do, it could only be 'me.' That is, if this moment repeats a past recurrence, 'necessarily,' then 'my' present choices are a repetition of 'my' past choices. The choices are no less 'mine' for having been past, it might be argued" (1979: 367). Although Magnus does not accept it, I think this is indeed the right response. Given this more precise formulation, the fatalism objection envisages a spurious sense of freedom according to which I can make a choice that is not my choice. Although we are accustomed to think that my choice cannot be truly determining unless I am making it for the *first* and *only* time, this conviction assumes again the original non-repeated life that Nietzsche's doctrine denies.

4 Recurrence-Time

Against this defense of Nietzsche's thought from the charge of fatalism, Simmel and his followers would most likely point to the different tenses in the demon's message: "This life, as you *now* live it and *have* lived it, you *will* have to live once more and innumerable times more; and there *will* be nothing new in it" ("Dieses Leben, wie du es jetzt lebst und gelebt hast, wirst du noch einmal und noch unzählige Male leben müssen; und es wird nichts Neues daran sein"). It might seem, that is, that my recurring lives are not qualitatively identical in *every* respect since they take place at different times (Čapek 1960: 295; Magnus 1978: 67–8, 104–10). But this means that the enormous *temporal gap* between successive iterations of my life makes it impossible for me to experience any of the psychological reactions described in Nietzsche's aphorism. When an experience is repeated *within* my existence, Simmel writes, we can understand how a synthesis is possible of this repetition and how the repetition is therefore of importance to me. But when it is the *whole* of existence that returns, no synthesis is possible of successive repetitions: no one can watch, reflect on, and unite the many returns in his consciousness. Or, as Clark puts it more recently:

> So I live and die, and eons later someone is born whose life has exactly the same characteristics as mine, including temporal/spatial relation to everything else in its cycle. No connection exists between the two lives, nothing carries over from my death to the birth of my double in the later cycle. A clear conception of this lack of connection should reduce a person's concern for her double in the next cycle to the level of concern one would have for any human being. (1990: 267)

Indeed, Simmel writes, Nietzsche's idea is comparable to that of absolutely identical worlds existing *in infinite space* but with absolutely no knowledge of each other: "And it is obvious that these absolutely identical persons existing *alongside* one another would relate in exactly the same way as those living *after* one another that are spoken of by the eternal recurrence of the same."

If Simmel's spatial analogy is right, then the fatalism objection does not involve a spurious sense of freedom after all. For my choices and actions would no longer seem to belong to my *present* self, and the question arises whether I can now decide to live differently than my *unconnected* double(s) decided to live eons earlier (or, by analogy, on some other world in infinite space). This question is especially important in light of Nietzsche's claim that my belief in the eternal *future* repetition of my *present* choices should place a special psychological weight on these present choices. For this weight would seem to disappear altogether once I recognize that my present choices have themselves already been chosen eternally *in the past* (Magnus 1979: 367; Magnus, Stewart, and Mileur 1993: 27). As Soll rightly comments, this "undermining of the significance of the concepts of choice and action is particularly problematic for a theory one of whose purposes is to increase our sense of the significance of the choices we make" (1973: 332–3).

However, I think that a closer look at the demon's message shows this follow-up objection to be unfounded as well. For the demon explicitly says that *the very moment* (*Augenblick*) in which he is speaking must return to me. So it is a consequence of the demon's thought that *time itself* recurs – "the eternal *hourglass* of being is turned over again and again" – and that the temporal moments of events recur along with those events. This means that the demon denies the existence of any absolute or universal time independent of, and outside, the recurrences wherein they can be successively ordered and differentiated (Moles 1989: 30, 1990: 233–4, 285–6, 295, 310ff.; Abel 1998: 236ff., 420ff.). Still, this denial does not prohibit the demon from continuing to use tense language (any more than the denial of absolute space prohibits our use of terms like "up" and "down" or "east" and "west"). Instead, the demon implies, my next living of my temporally identical life is "future" only in a *relative* and *perspectival* sense – that is, relative to, and from the perspective of, the moment in which I am hearing his message. But since this moment must itself return, my next living of my life may also correctly be described as "present" and "past" relative to, and from the perspective of, this moment. Unless one holds a conception of absolute and universal time that entails absolute and universal distinctions among past, present, and future (Magnus 1978: 107–8; Gooding-Williams 2001: 218), there is no contradiction in this idea of recurring moments that are at once past, present, and future.

Time, therefore, cannot be said to introduce any qualitative difference among recurrences, and eternal recurrence is not be imagined as an infinite number of cosmic cycles (or spirals) succeeding each other in some absolute linear time. Instead, Nietzsche encourages us to imagine just a single finite (though unbounded) circular course (*Kreislauf*) in which is represented, not just the recurrence of all things, but also of all those moments of time that cannot exist independently of those things. Since for Nietzsche time just is a series of those moments, it follows that time itself is destroyed, re-created, and repeated along with everything else. Thus, when I am re-created so as to relive my identical life, the time at which I am re-created and live my life is always exactly the same.

Contrary to Clark, then, there are no eons of elapsed time for me to traverse in order to make a connection with my re-created self in some temporally *subsequent* or *later* cycle of cosmic history. Of course, such a connection might still seem impossible because, even *within* the single circular course of the cosmos, much time elapses after the moment of my death and before the moment of my re-creation. But a corollary of Nietzsche's denial of universal time is his claim that any observation of time's passing depends upon some particular perspective or frame of reference. Hence, although the perspective of other living beings will show time passing both before and after the span of my existence, my own perspective cannot show any such elapsed time. Nietzsche explains why in a note he wrote shortly after formulating his doctrine for the first time:

> You think you will have a long rest until rebirth – but do not deceive yourselves! Between the last moment of consciousness [*dem letzten Augenblick des Bewusstseins*] and the first appearance of new life there lies "no time" – it passes by as quickly as a flash of lightning, even if living creatures were to measure it in terms of billions of years, or could not even begin to measure it. Timelessness and succession accommodate themselves to one another as soon as the intellect is gone. (*KSA* 9, 11[318])

Applying this important point to *Gay Science* 341, the demon's insistence on the recurrence of time itself lets me know that the moment in which I begin to relive my life is only as far away as the last moment of the life I am now living. From my perspective, that is, there can never be any end or any sort of break in my life, and my dying consciousness is immediately succeeded by my returned awakening consciousness. So whatever (presumably substantial) concern I might now have for my dying self is precisely the same concern I should have for myself as I begin to relive my life.

Given Nietzsche's conception of time, then, there are substantial psychological relations among my numerically distinct selves. In addition, as the performative aspect of the demon's message suggests, there are interesting epistemic relations among these selves. Since my life is for me a ceaselessly forward-flowing ring in which the endpoint eternally turns back to become the starting point, I may remember events that still lie ahead in my current living of that life. In particular, I may suddenly remember – in some solitary moment that could come at any day or night – the key future moment in which I will die and, as the demon whispers, immediately begin reliving my life. This is why, I would argue, Nietzsche has the demon allude back to the last moment (*letzte Augenblick*) of Socrates' life (*GS* 340) and why he includes death-related imagery of midnight-moonlight, spider-cobwebs, and tomb-dust (Loeb 1998). Thus, the source of my precognitive certainty is my mnemonic certainty: it is precisely because I suddenly and overwhelmingly *recall* having died and recurred innumerable times that I am able to *foresee* that I will do so innumerable times more. Indeed, since my life is eternally recurring, I am able to impress into my memory messages that will be buried in my younger self's subconscious and that will manifest themselves in the form of precognitive dreams, visions, omens, and voices. The voice I hear is thus my *own future voice* reminding me of my eternally recurring life (Loeb 2001, 2005). Accordingly, as the narrator suggests, my response to that voice is evidence of how well disposed I am towards *myself*: cursing the "demon" who speaks thus shows my self-hatred; blessing the "god" who speaks thus shows my self-love.

Let us return now to the fatalism objection. In the first place, Nietzsche's claim of the temporal identity of my recurring selves means that my choices and actions can always correctly be described as belonging to my *present* self. So the question simply does not arise as to whether my present self can decide differently than my self in some earlier eon. Secondly, Simmel's spatial analogy fails because, although my temporally identical selves are indeed numerically distinct, Nietzsche's denial of absolute and universal time allows him to posit substantial connections among them.

Finally, and perhaps most importantly, in suggesting that the choices I make in the life I am now living are predetermined by my identical choices in all the innumerable lives I have already lived, the fatalism objection assumes precisely the conception of linear absolute time that Nietzsche rejects. On this conception, that is, there is an absolute distinction between the past and the present such that the past always precedes and determines the present. Since this past is gone forever and is outside of my reach when I am making my present choices, there is no reason for me to feel any special weight on these present choices as determining the eternally repeating future.

By contrast, I have argued, Nietzsche's doctrine proposes a circular relational time according to which my past can also correctly be described as my future and therefore as *following* and being *determined by* my present. On this view of time, the past is never gone forever and outside my reach when I am making my present choices. So whereas the fatalism objection imagines that the weight of my present choices can concern only their eternal *future* repetition, Nietzsche actually means that this weight also concerns their eternal *past* repetition. When the aphorism's narrator exclaims that the question in each and every thing, "do you want this once more and innumerable times more?" would lie on my actions as the greatest heavy weight, he means that my actions now determine *both* the forward *and* the backward extension of my eternally recurring life. And when Nietzsche himself exclaims, "Eternity is at stake!" he means that my decisions now determine all at once the *entire* circular course of my eternally recurring life.

5 Recurrence-Coherence

To this last reply, I can imagine two final objections. On the one hand, supposing that Nietzsche's doctrine actually entails the *temporal* identity of recurrences, we might wonder why it does not likewise entail their *numerical* identity and hence its own incoherence. As Milič Čapek observes in the *Encyclopedia of Philosophy*, "either the successive identical cycles are distinguished by their positions in time – which means that we surreptitiously introduce an irreversible time as their container – or we insist on the numerical identity of the cycles. But we then have only one cosmic cycle, and it clearly becomes meaningless to speak of a 'succession of cycles' or of their 'repetition'" (1967: 63). Or, as Magnus notes: "If time is not the basis for distinguishing between events and recurrences, the evidence seems overwhelming that we are giving a single event two or more names. On this view, there is no cosmic recurrence of the same at all, only a systematically misleading expression wantonly misapplied" (1978: 109).

On the other hand, Simmel insists, no matter how much *qualitative* identity might obtain between my recurring selves, including even their *temporal* identity, these cannot be *numerically* identical selves. But this means that they cannot be of any significance to each other: "I think that Nietzsche has been tempted by an imprecise formulation of the I-concept to see a resurrection of the I where there is only a recapitulation of the same phenomenon. Therefore, he grants significance to the successive egos, none of which is the first ego and each of which is merely qualitatively of the same type as the others."

Thus, either the temporal identity of recurrences entails their numerical identity, in which case the doctrine is conceptually incoherent; or it does not, in which case the doctrine is psychologically insignificant. Although these two final objections attack Nietzsche's doctrine from opposite standpoints, they both presuppose the impossibility of any recurrence-awareness. But I have argued that such awareness is indeed possible, and that it would serve to numerically differentiate temporally identical recurrences as well as to establish some kind of substantial concern and communication among numerically distinct recurring selves.

Should we follow Simmel in demoting this concern and communication by comparison to the kind we usually posit among the *temporally* distinct stages of my numerically identical self? Perhaps, but only if we assume what philosophers since Locke have questioned – namely, the numerical identity of the self over time. If we do not assume this, and Nietzsche certainly does not (*BGE* 16; *GM* I. 13), then we should rather *promote* recurrence-concern and recurrence-communication as obtaining among selves who are at least *temporally* identical. If, for example, we follow Derek Parfit (1975: 218–20) and use the word "I" to imply the greatest degree of psychological connectedness, which in turn depends upon temporal proximity, then there is *more* reason to use this word with respect to my eternally recurring self-*iterations* than with respect to my temporally successive self-*stages*. Indeed, on the account of mnemonic relations suggested by Nietzsche's aphorism, my "future" self-stages can actually communicate with, and care for, my "past" self-stages. So we might want to conclude that eternal recurrence allows for a much richer and thicker concept of personal identity than the usual one that emphasizes only the unidirectional relations from my past self-stages to my future self-stages.

Conclusion

In this essay I have aimed to counter a dismissal of Nietzsche's doctrine of eternal recurrence that is nearly a century old now and still dominant. I have looked carefully at Nietzsche's presentation in *Gay Science* 341, because this is his best-known and briefest discussion where critics since Simmel have concentrated their attacks. Having argued that their chief objections all presuppose the denial of Nietzsche's doctrine,

I have suggested further that we may now be able to make new progress in understanding why Nietzsche insisted that eternal recurrence was his most consequential thought – "that splits the history of humankind in two halves" (*KSB* 6, 485). The reason is that he thinks each one of us holds a memory of our life's eternal recurrence that can grant us a precognitive knowledge extending even to the moment in which we die and begin reliving our life. Since our younger immature selves can carry our adult memories, our adult selves may deliberately choose to remember "divine" messages that will grant us prophetic powers and help us grow into our perfected selves (a feat we achieve identically in all our recurring lives). In this way, our knowledge of the truth of eternal recurrence may grant us a power over time that will allow us finally to affirm our selves and our lives completely and without reservation (Loeb 2001, 2005).

Of course, *Gay Science* 341 is a slender reed on which to hang such weighty interpretive conclusions. In following this aphorism with the beginning of his next book, Nietzsche lets us know that any serious investigation of his doctrine must turn next to *Thus Spoke Zarathustra*. And, indeed, even a cursory reading of this book shows that its discourses and narrative are shaped by the above themes of death, prophecy, and power over time. But because Nietzsche's thought of eternal recurrence has so far not been taken seriously, neither have these major themes. Over a century after its publication, Nietzsche's *magnum opus* remains shrouded in obscurity (Pippin 1988: 45). A newly revived doctrine of eternal recurrence should therefore help to revive as well the artistic work that Nietzsche said was founded upon this doctrine.

But this is a task I must leave for another time (Loeb, forthcoming). If I may appeal to the poetic language of Nietzsche's *Gay Science* 339, here I hope merely to have dispersed some of the clouds that have so far kept the highest peak of Nietzsche's thought concealed and veiled from his many admirers. It may be asked, however, as one admirer has recently asked about his own exegesis (Leiter 2001: 319), whether I have done Nietzsche any favor by showing him to hold views that appear beyond the pale of "reasonable" opinion. My answer is equivocally Yes. Speaking as the last disciple of the god Dionysus, as the teacher of eternal recurrence, Nietzsche concludes *Beyond Good and Evil* with an offer finally to begin providing a few tastes of this god's philosophy: "In a hushed voice, as is only proper: for it concerns much that is secret, new, strange, odd, uncanny." Nietzsche predicts that his audience of philosopher-friends will become suspicious and that he may have to carry his frankness further than will always be agreeable to the strict habit of their ears (*BGE* 295; *TI*, "What I Owe the Ancients," 5). But this is as it should be, since, as he anticipated in 1881, he himself had trained these ears to be prepared for his thought of thoughts:

> Are you *prepared* then? You must have lived through every degree of skepticism and bathed voluptuously in ice-cold streams – otherwise you have no right to this thought; I want to guard myself well against the credulous and enthusiasts! I want to *defend* my thought in advance! It should be the religion of the freest, cheeriest and loftiest souls – a lovely meadow in between gilded ice and pure sky! (*KSA* 9, 11[339])

See also 5 "The Individual and Individuality in Nietzsche"; 29 "Life and Self-Overcoming"

Acknowledgments

I wish to thank Keith Ansell Pearson for his valuable suggestions regarding this essay. I am also grateful to Greg Oakes, Dugald Owen, and Lawrence Stern for their very helpful comments on earlier versions of this essay.

References

Abel, Günter (1998). *Nietzsche. Die Dynamik der Willen zur Macht und die ewige Wiederkehr*, 2nd edn. (Berlin: Walter de Gruyter).

Allison, David B. (2001). *Reading the New Nietzsche* (Lanham: Rowman & Littlefield).

Black, Max (1952). "The Identity of Indiscernibles," *Mind*, 61, pp. 153–64.

Čapek, Milič (1967). "Eternal Return," in P. Edwards (ed.), *The Encyclopedia of Philosophy*, vol. 3 (New York: Macmillan), pp. 61–3.

Clark, Maudemarie (1990). *Nietzsche on Truth and Philosophy* (New York: Cambridge University Press).

Danto, Arthur C. (1965). *Nietzsche as Philosopher* (New York: Macmillan).

Gooding-Williams, Robert (2001). *Zarathustra's Dionysian Modernism* (Stanford: Stanford University Press).

Hatab, Lawrence J. (2005). *Nietzsche's Life Sentence: Coming to Terms with Eternal Recurrence* (New York: Routledge).

Heidegger, Martin (1977). "Who Is Nietzsche's Zarathustra?," trans B. Magnus, in D. Allison (ed.), *The New Nietzsche: Contemporary Styles of Interpretation* (Cambridge, MA: MIT Press), pp. 64–79.

Heller, Erich (1988). *The Importance of Nietzsche: Ten Essays* (Chicago: University of Chicago Press).

Higgins, Kathleen (1987). *Nietzsche's Zarathustra* (Philadelphia: Temple University Press).

—— (2000). *Comic Relief: Nietzsche's Gay Science* (New York: Oxford University Press).

Kain, Philip J. (1983). "Nietzsche, Skepticism and Eternal Recurrence," *Canadian Journal of Philosophy*, 13, pp. 365–87.

Krueger, Joe (1978). "Nietzschean Recurrence as a Cosmological Hypothesis," *Journal of the History of Philosophy*, 16, pp. 435–44.

Leiter, Brian (2001). "The Paradox of Fatalism and Self-Creation in Nietzsche," in J. Richardson and B. Leiter (eds.), *Nietzsche* (New York: Oxford University Press), pp. 281–321.

Loeb, Paul S. (1998). "The Moment of Tragic Death in Nietzsche's Dionysian Doctrine of Eternal Recurrence: An Exegesis of Aphorism 341 in *The Gay Science*," *International Studies in Philosophy*, 30(3), pp. 131–43.

—— (2001). "Time, Power, and Superhumanity," *Journal of Nietzsche Studies*, 21, pp. 27–47.

—— (2005). "Finding the *Übermensch* in Nietzsche's *Genealogy of Morality*," *Journal of Nietzsche Studies*, 30.

—— (forthcoming). *The Death of Nietzsche's Zarathustra*.

Löwith, Karl (1997). *Nietzsche's Philosophy of the Eternal Recurrence of the Same*, trans. J. H. Lomax (Berkeley: University of California Press).

Magnus, Bernd (1978). *Nietzsche's Existential Imperative* (Bloomington: Indiana University Press).

—— (1979). "Eternal Recurrence," *Nietzsche-Studien*, 8, pp. 362–77.

—— (1999). "Asceticism and Eternal Recurrence: A Bridge Too Far," *The Southern Journal of Philosophy*, 37, supplement, pp. 93–111.

Magnus, Bernd, Stewart, Stanley, and Mileur, Jean-Pierre (1993). *Nietzsche's Case: Philosophy as/and Literature* (New York: Routledge).

186

Moles, Alistair (1989). "Nietzsche's Eternal Recurrence as Riemannian Cosmology," *International Studies in Philosophy*, 21(2), pp. 21–35.

—— (1990). *Nietzsche's Philosophy of Nature and Cosmology* (New York: Peter Lang).

Nehamas, Alexander (1985). *Nietzsche: Life as Literature* (Cambridge, MA: Harvard University Press).

Oger, Eric (1997). "The Eternal Return as a Crucial Test," *Journal of Nietzsche Studies*, 14, pp. 1–18.

Parfit, Derek (1975). "Personal Identity," in J. Perry (ed.), *Personal Identity* (Berkeley: University of California Press), pp. 199–223.

Pippin, Robert (1988). "Irony and Affirmation in Nietzsche's *Thus Spoke Zarathustra*," in M. Gillespie and T. Strong (eds.), *Nietzsche's New Seas: Explorations in Philosophy, Aesthetics, and Politics* (Chicago: University of Chicago Press), pp. 45–71.

Ridley, Aaron (1997). "Nietzsche's Greatest Weight," *Journal of Nietzsche Studies*, 14, pp. 19–25.

Salaquarda, Jörg (1989). "Der ungeheure Augenblick," *Nietzsche-Studien*, 18, pp. 317–37.

Shapiro, Gary (1989). *Nietzschean Narratives* (Bloomington: Indiana University Press).

Simmel, Georg (1986). *Schopenhauer and Nietzsche*, trans. H. Loiskandle, D. Weinstein, and M. Weinstein (Amherst: University of Massachusetts Press).

—— (1920). *Schopenhauer und Nietzsche. Ein Vortragszyklus. Zweite, unveräanderte Auflage* (Munich: Duncker & Humblot).

Small, Robin (2002). *Nietzsche in Context* (London: Palgrave).

Soll, Ivan (1973). "Reflections on Recurrence: A Re-examination of Nietzsche's Doctrine, *Die Ewige Wiederkehr des Gleichen*," in R. C. Solomon (ed.), *Nietzsche: A Collection of Critical Essays* (Garden City, NY: Doubleday), pp. 339–42.

Solomon, Robert C. (2003). *Living with Nietzsche: What the Great "Immoralist" Has To Teach Us* (New York: Oxford University Press).

Tanner, Michael (1994). *Nietzsche* (New York: Oxford University Press).

White, Alan (1990). *Within Nietzsche's Labyrinth* (New York: Routledge).

Wood, David (1988). "Nietzsche's Transvaluation of Time," in D. F. Krell and D. Wood (eds.), *Exceedingly Nietzsche: Aspects of Contemporary Nietzsche Interpretation* (New York: Routledge), pp. 31–62.

Further Reading

Čapek, Milič (1960). "The Theory of Eternal Recurrence in Modern Philosophy of Science, with Special Reference to C. S. Pierce," *Journal of Philosophy*, 57, pp. 289–96.

—— (1983). "Eternal Recurrence – Once More," *Transactions of the Charles S. Pierce Society*, 19, pp. 141–53.

Deleuze, Gilles (1983). *Nietzsche and Philosophy*, trans. H. Tomlinson (New York: Columbia University Press).

—— (1994). *Difference and Repetition*, trans. P. Patton (New York: Columbia University Press).

Derrida, Jacques (1985). "Otobiographies: The Teaching of Nietzsche and the Politics of the Proper Name," trans. A. Ronell, in C. V. McDonald (ed.), *The Ear of the Other: Otobiography, Transference, Translation*, trans. Peggy Kamuf (New York: Schocken Books).

Heidegger, Martin (1984). *Nietzsche*, vol. 2: *The Eternal Recurrence of the Same*, trans. D. F. Krell (San Francisco: Harper & Row).

Irigaray, Luce (1991). *Marine Lover of Friedrich Nietzsche*, trans. G. Gillian (New York: Columbia University Press).

Klossowski, Pierre (1997). *Nietzsche and the Vicious Circle*, trans. D. W. Smith (Chicago: University of Chicago Press).

Loeb, Paul S. (2002). "The Dwarf, the Dragon, and the Ring of Eternal Recurrence: A Wagnerian Key to the Riddle of Nietzsche's *Zarathustra*," *Nietzsche-Studien*, 31, pp. 91–113.

Lukacher, Ned (1998). *Time-Fetishes: The Secret History of Eternal Recurrence* (Durham: Duke University Press).

Reeves, Sandra J. (1986). "Eternal Recurrence and the Principle of the Identity of Indiscernibles," *International Studies in Philosophy*, 18(2), pp. 49–59.

Rogers, Peter (2001). "Simmel's Mistake: The Eternal Recurrence as a Riddle About the Intelligible Form of Time as a Whole," *Journal of Nietzsche Studies*, 21, pp. 77–95.

Stambaugh, Joan (1972). *Nietzsche's Thought of Eternal Return* (Baltimore: Johns Hopkins University Press).

Sterling, M. C. (1977). "Recent Discussions of Eternal Recurrence: Some Critical Comments," *Nietzsche-Studien*, 6, pp. 261–91.

Van Fraasen, Bas C. (1962). "Capek on Eternal Recurrence," *Journal of Philosophy*, 59, pp. 371–5.

Winchester, James J. (1999). "Of Scholarly Readings of Nietzsche: Clark and Magnus on Nietzsche's Eternal Return," *New Nietzsche Studies*, 3(3/4), pp. 77–97.

11

Nietzsche and Cosmology

ROBIN SMALL

Nietzsche's thought seldom fits readily into familiar categories, and his relation to cosmology is a case in point. There are several problems in seeing him as engaging with this branch of philosophy. If cosmology takes the world as a whole as its object, it is open to the question raised by Kant: whether the world can be comprehended – or evaluated, Nietzsche would add – by our minds. In Kant's critical philosophy, rational cosmology shared the fate of its two counterparts, theology and rational psychology: it was condemned for exceeding the bounds of possible knowledge. Given Nietzsche's frequent judgments on the concepts of God and the soul, one might expect an equally dismissive attitude from him. Even without querying a conception of the world, one might recall his critique of familiar concepts in their application to reality. Anyone who questions the categories of substance and causality as Nietzsche does, and suggests they are metaphorical in character, can hardly be one of those thinkers who set out to provide a straightforward characterization of the world as a whole.

A second issue has less to do with Nietzsche than with interpreters who use the label "cosmology" to separate some of his ideas from others, and more often than not to suggest tensions or inconsistencies between the several sides. For most of these writers, Nietzsche's importance lies in what he has to say about human life.[1] Despite repudiating the morality of responsibility and guilt, he is concerned with the task of finding goals and ways of achieving them. A century of positivist influence, however, has accustomed us to separating questions about the conduct of life from the concerns of natural science and its philosophical analysis. This interpretive issue arises with particular force in relation to Nietzsche's thought of eternal return, whose presentations in his writing can be identified with both ethical and cosmological frameworks. Sometimes the tension is present within a single sentence, as when he writes: "My doctrine says: to live *in such a way* that you must *wish* to live again, that is the task – you will do so *in any case*" (KSA 9, 11[163]).

Those favoring an ethical reading tend to dismiss Nietzsche's ventures into natural philosophy as irrelevant to his more important ideas. Common though this view has been, it imposes categories that he would not have accepted. The notion of a factual reality accessible prior to all interpretation was, he thought, a self-deception, covering up processes of knowing that ruled out once and for all any objective grasp of reality. The nature of reality itself made interpretation inevitable, for it consisted in a Heraclitean flow of becoming that could not be negated merely by postulating gaps between successive things or identities between similar things. In this Nietzsche wanted, if anything, to go further than positivism. He endorsed its demythologizing of the notion of force, eliminating associations with everyday experiences of pushing and pressing. He accepted its interpretation of the formulae of physical theory as positing equivalences of matter or energy without attempting to identify the source of the processes corresponding to them. But he also wanted to find some answer to that question of origin. In postulating the will to power and the Dionysian conception to be discussed below, he thought that he had found the source of the activity of interpretation out of which both facts and values arise.

It should not be assumed, though, that the interpretive distinction between cosmology and ethics always has a positivist character. In his acute study of the doctrine of eternal return, first published in 1935, Karl Löwith distinguishes between the "cosmological mode" and the "anthropological mode" of its presentation (Löwith 1999: 92). According to Löwith, Nietzsche is concerned with two historic cultural crises: the removal of human meaning from the natural world (an event epitomized by positivism) and the removal of goals from human life (which Nietzsche identifies as nihilism: the nothingness which human beings would rather will than not will at all). Löwith sees the eternal return as Nietzsche's supreme effort to find an answer to both predicaments. Like any metaphor (*Gleichnis*) its task is to unite. The thought is designed to do this by, on the one hand, regarding the world as a self-willing world of creation and destruction and, on the other, setting human existence a new goal of willing its own self-creation as an indivisible part of this world. For Löwith the attempt is unsuccessful, because the conflict breaks out again within each side of the solution as soon as one tries to give a further account of what the metaphor means: Nietzsche's "physical metaphysics" is incoherent, and his "atheistic religion" contains its own antinomies.

It seems, then, that the relation between Nietzsche's thinking about the nature of the world and other aspects of his thought is a problematical one. Nevertheless, even to identify these issues we need to see what cosmology means for him. For that reason, I shall discuss various aspects of this theme before returning to the tensions mentioned above.

Nietzsche's relation to cosmology is closely linked with his lifelong interest in natural science. It has little to do with the German idealist tradition of *Naturphilosophie*. By his time that had been made irrelevant by advances in positive science, although his contemporary Friedrich Engels made a brave attempt to translate aspects of the Hegelian version of *Naturphilosophie* into a materialist vocabulary. So, where is the philosophical link to be made? In approaching Nietzsche it is often wise to start with the ancient Greek thinkers. Heraclitus's vision of a world of continual conflict ruled by an innate justice appealed to him. His incomplete survey of ancient thought, *Philosophy in the Tragic Age of the Greeks*, treated the philosophical systems as expressions of their inventors' personalities, but it also imported modern scientific ideas. His primary source for these was Friedrich Albert Lange, whose *History of Materialism* provided a well-informed survey of natural science, with particular emphasis on its philosophical dimension (see Salaquarda 1978; Stack 1983). Nietzsche borrowed Lange's comparison between Daltonian atomism and that of Leucippus and Democritus, and repeated Lange's suggestion that the Empedoclean idea of variation and selection of biological organisms resembled Darwin's theory of the evolutionary origin of species. On Nietzsche's account, the tendency of Greek thought is away from mythological conceptions and towards a naturalistic view of the world. For that reason, the atomists figure as the most consistent of ancient thinkers. Nietzsche aspired to repeat their achievement by eliminating anthropomorphism from the modern scientific conception of the world. In his later thinking, even seemingly innocent conceptions of substance and causality are identified as unjustified extrapolations from familiar (though just for that reason, not truly understood) human experiences.

In Nietzsche's intellectual environment, battle lines had been drawn between a mechanistic materialism whose native home was England (as Heinrich Heine put it, "John Bull is a born materialist": Heine 1985: 169) and a more spiritual or at least philosophical philosophy of nature whose main support was found in Germany. Many of his German contemporaries adopted this latter standpoint, often drawing on Leibniz or Kant as a countervailing influence to the empiricism of their English counterparts. Nietzsche read widely in scientific and pseudo-scientific literature, and never more than in the summer and autumn of 1881. During that period of solitude he recorded in his notebook the thought of the eternal return, with a cryptic annotation: "Early August 1881 in Sils-Maria, 6,000 feet above the sea and much higher above all human things!"(*KSA* 9, 11[141]). Despite this suggestion of intuitive insight, it can hardly be a coincidence that Nietzsche was studying intensively contemporary writing on natural philosophy at the time. A collection of critical reviews by the neo-Kantian Otto Caspari led him to several other writers (Caspari 1881). One was the eccentric J. G. Vogt, whose elaborate a priori construction of a physical universe from expanding and contracting "spheres of influence" recalled the physics of the ancient Greeks.

Like Nietzsche, Vogt sought an alternative to materialistic atomism. He argued that materialism failed to explain how atoms could provide a basis for several quite different kinds of force (Vogt 1878: 7–12). Moreover, a plurality of opposing forces raised a cosmological problem: why had no one force attained a permanent dominance over the others during an infinite past time? Nietzsche's friend Heinrich Köselitz recommended the writings of Robert Mayer, a pioneer of modern thermodynamics, but after an initial enthusiasm Nietzsche quickly tired of Mayer's prosaic (and in fact, responsibly scientific) approach to the scientific investigation of energy. He preferred Vogt's imaginative construction of a universe from first principles (see Small 2001: 135–50).

In Basel Nietzsche had been impressed by reading Roger Joseph Boscovich's *Theory of Natural Philosophy*, in which solid atoms were replaced by unextended "points of matter" and their surrounding fields of force. This dynamic physical theory not only inspired later empirical research into electricity and magnetism but was taken up by German philosophers. Many of these supported the Leibnizian idea of an inner aspect of matter, and echoes of their approach can be found in many passages in Nietzsche's writing, although it is unlikely that he ever read Leibniz's own philosophical works.

Cosmology was on the agenda for both natural science and philosophy in the second half of the nineteenth century. Recent scientific developments, especially in the new science of thermodynamics, opened up questions which science seemed unable to solve from its own resources. Prominent amongst these was an issue involving the finitude of the world. An important paper by the British physicist William Thomson (later Lord Kelvin) had been taken up by Hermann von Helmholtz, who in his 1854 lecture "On the Interaction of Natural Forces" spelled out a broader prediction that Thomson had only hinted at when he concluded that, given the continual increase of entropy in any closed system, the earth would not always be capable of supporting human life (Thomson 1882: vol. 1, p. 514). At some future time, Helmholtz said, the entire universe would reach a state of thermal equilibrium (Helmholtz 1962: 90). Then all becoming would necessarily come to a permanent end. This conclusion was not a paradox by itself, except in the sense of challenging common ideas, but it raised a question for humanity. What meaning could be given to human goals if they come to nothing in the long run, even if that might be millions of years away? Another, more purely theoretical, problem concerned the beginning of the world. If the entropy of the world is steadily increasing, must not there be a time at which it had been at its minimum? If so, what came before this? Thus, an old cosmological debate was once again raised, but without reference to religious doctrine.

Time, Space, and Finitude

The issue of the eternity of the world had been dismissed in Kant's *Critique of Pure Reason* as an illusion of reason arising from the misapplication of categories to something lying outside possible experience, namely, the world as a whole. Nevertheless, it made a reappearance in Nietzsche's time as part of a scientific raising of cosmological issues. Nietzsche had a definite view: he firmly rejected a finitude of past time. Moreover, he suggested that any such idea was just the old doctrine of creation in a disguised form. In one sense this is wrong: the contemporary thinkers who supported that idea were by no means believers in a divine creation. It is true that they left the postulated beginning of the universe a mystery – but no more, one might say, than do today's proponents of the "big bang" theory in cosmology.

Nietzsche was suspicious of the motives behind this "fashion," as he called it, but he also considered its arguments to be fallacious (*KSA* 11, 26[383]). His main target here is Eugen Dühring, whose systematic philosophy covered everything from metaphysics to social philosophy and economic theory. He knew Dühring as the author of *Der Werth des Lebens*, in which the idea of *ressentiment*, so important for Nietzsche's later thinking about morality, was advanced as the origin – and justification – of the "sense of justice," that is, the demand that wrongdoers be made to suffer (Dühring 1865: 222–4). In Dühring's comprehensive *Cursus der Philosophie* Nietzsche encountered a doctrine of finite time that he found equally unacceptable.

For Dühring, the first task of philosophy is to eliminate any conception of the infinite as something actual. He holds that infinitude can be conceived only as an endless progression. This principle is formalized in what Dühring calls "the law of definite number." Everything real must have a number or quantity, and for Dühring this means that it must be finite. Thus, the plurality of substances that constitute the real world at any given time must be limited. A more debatable conclusion is that the sequence of events cannot have proceeded from a past eternity. If it had, Dühring argues, then an infinite series would have been completed as an actuality. To avoid this "contradiction" we must suppose that the world came into being at some finite past time. This is a familiar argument in the Christian tradition. Based on an interpretation of Aristotelian philosophy, it goes back to John Philoponus, whose doctrine was transmitted through the Islamic *kalām* school into the Scholastic tradition (Philoponus 1987). Debate continued in the thirteenth century with St. Thomas Aquinas opposing Franciscan thinkers such as St. Bonaventure, who claimed that natural reason alone could show that the world must have a beginning (Aquinas 1954: 103–8).

Early in 1888, Nietzsche set out a general statement of his "new world-conception" in a notebook. He rejected any idea of creation as an indefinable concept, and noted that the latest attempt to think of the world as having a beginning had been made "with the aid of a logical conception," although he thought that had a hidden theological character.

> Lately one has sought several times to find a contradiction in the concept "temporal infinity of the world *behind*": one has even found it, although at the cost of confusing the head with the tail. Nothing can prevent me from reckoning backward from this moment and saying "I shall never reach the end"; just as I can reckon forward from the same moment into the infinite. Only if I made the mistake – I shall guard against it – of equating this correct concept of a *regressus in infinitum* with an *utterly unrealizable* concept of an infinite *progressus* up to the present, only if I suppose the *direction* (forward or backward) to be logically indifferent, would I take the head – this moment – for the tail: I shall leave that to you, my dear Herr Dühring! (*KSA* 13, 14[188])

What is Nietzsche arguing here? Dühring had not denied that one can count backwards from the present moment, and continue indefinitely. What he argued was that this is insufficient for a conception of the infinitude of the past, because it leaves out the *direction* of the temporal process. In this response Nietzsche is asserting the separateness of the counting process from reality, and so rejecting Dühring's assumption that the procedure needs to replicate the actual course of becoming. Nietzsche's argument is thus different from Aquinas's rebuttal of the *kalām* argument. Aquinas accepts the demand for a forward transition, and argues that what is involved is always the transition from a past moment which is located at a *finite* distance from the present, so that there is no question of having to complete an infinite progression.

A related objection to a past infinitude is that it implies some moment or period of time located at an infinite distance from the present, and that either this is an impossibility, or it is impossible to say how there could be a transition from such a moment to the present moment (since "the infinite cannot be traversed"). The claim was made by St. Bonaventure and rebutted by Aquinas, who argued that an infinite past did not involve postulating any such day. As he put it, "A passage is always from one limit to another limit. But whatever day from the past we pick on, between that and the present day there is only a finite number of days, which can be traversed" (Aquinas 1965–81: 1a q. 46 art. 2, vol. 8, 82). Aquinas does not ask why anyone should imagine that an infinite past or future requires days infinitely distant from the present one. Presumably it is the confusion of taking what would nowadays be called a transfinite number as belonging to the set of finite numbers of which it is the number, so that an infinite sequence of days (counting either forwards or backwards) would

193

have to include one corresponding to the infinite number itself. Georg Cantor's new conception of the actual infinite, developed at about the same time as Nietzsche's remarks on Dühring, overtook these controversies, although Cantor seems nevertheless to have accepted some version of the *kalām* argument for a finitude of past time (see Small 1992).

Despite his attack on Dühring's view of time, Nietzsche supports the so-called "law of finite number," at least as regards simultaneous existence. Hence, he accepts the proposition that the elements of the universe at a given time must be finite in number. For Nietzsche these are Boscovichian "centers of force" rather than material atoms. He goes further than Dühring in arguing that their possible combinations must also be finite in number, a crucial proposition in his sketches for a physical theory of eternal recurrence. That argument had been expressed by David Hume in his *Dialogues Concerning Natural Religion* (of which Nietzsche owned a German edition):

> Instead of supposing matter infinite, as Epicurus did, let us suppose it finite. A finite number of particles is only susceptible of finite transpositions: and it must happen, in an eternal duration, that every possible order or position must be tried an infinite number of times. This world, therefore, with all its events, even the most minute, has before been produced and destroyed, and will again be produced and destroyed, without any bounds and limitations. (Hume 1957: pt. VIII, p. 52)

Debates over the finitude of space and matter engaged Nietzsche. He was aware of Olbers' paradox: that in an infinite universe, the night sky would necessarily appear to be infinitely bright, so that its actual darkness is a puzzle in need of solution. A note on the argument appears in a notebook of early 1884: "According to Fr. Secchi space cannot be unbounded, because nothing composed of particular bodies can be infinite, and because an infinite firmament populated by innumerable stars would appear as bright as the sun across its entire extent –" (*KSA* 11, 25[518]).

The Leipzig physicist Friedrich Zöllner, whose 1872 book *Über die Natur der Cometen* was admired by Nietzsche, solved such cosmological problems by invoking Bernhard Riemann's concept of a finite but unbounded three-dimensional space. Zöllner allowed that space must necessarily be regarded as unbounded, but asserted that its other properties were to be determined by empirical research. He noted the recent development of alternatives to the Euclidean axioms and their theorems. These models of space, he insisted, were no more difficult to grasp conceptually than the Euclidean one, and could as readily be brought to bear on physical phenomena. The central cosmological issue for Zöllner concerns the tendency of matter to disperse, a property that would lead to the eventual disappearance of all solid bodies, assuming space to be infinite. In a closed space, the scattered particles would converge and combine again, so that there would be no question of a permanent dissolution of matter (Zöllner 1872: 308–9). This looks like a solution, and yet Zöllner's appeal to the Riemannian concept of closed space remains a token gesture. His treatment uses almost no mathematics and relies far more on epistemological considerations. For this reason alone, Zöllner's contribution to science has remained a marginal one, even if his appeal to a concept of closed space is sometimes cited as a precursor of Einstein's theory of general relativity.

Zöllner's theoretical dilettantism was not necessarily a fault in Nietzsche's eyes. His own ignorance of mathematics was a barrier to any closer engagement with current physical science, and Zöllner's claim that too much weight was being placed on experimental evidence encouraged a reliance on philosophical reasoning to settle cosmological issues. He adopted Zöllner's solution as his own: "Only on the false assumption of an infinite space, in which force so to speak evaporates, is the final state an *unproductive, dead* one" (*KSA* 10, 1[27]). Similarly, "That a state of equilibrium has never been reached proves that it is not possible. But in an indeterminate space it must have been reached. Similarly in a spherical space. The *shape* of space must be the cause of eternal motion, and ultimately of all 'incompleteness'" (*KSA* 11, 35[54]). These comments addressed the shape of space, but said nothing about its nature – that is, about its reality or ideality. Nietzsche's ideas on space were formed by the theory that he had taken up with enthusiasm in his Basel days, the dynamic physics of Boscovich, which replaced the solid atoms of materialism with unextended "points of matter" or, as they were later called, "centers of force" (*KSA* 11 26[384], 26[431], 34[65], 36[34] and 38[12]). The implied corollary, a denial of empty space, became an explicit thesis in the work of Michael Faraday, who raised a problem for the new science of electricity and magnetism: how can substances have different electrical conductivities if they mainly consist of the same empty space? Faraday's answer was that space is occupied – by fields of force (Faraday 1965: 291). The advantage of this is that it eliminates action at a distance, always a disputed notion for the Newtonian tradition. Zöllner had defended the idea, and even attributed it to Newton himself, in defiance of orthodox interpretation. Nietzsche disagreed, and set out to combine a relativist conception of space with the finitude that he thought provided a way of countering the implications of the second law of thermodynamics, as Zöllner had argued.

From a Final State to Eternal Recurrence

The prediction of a final state was much discussed in Germany, where the opportunity to invoke Leibnizian ideas to resolve the quandary of Newtonian science must have seemed irresistible. Otto Caspari believed that the solution lay in the notion of a cosmos as a living being – one that could go into hibernation, so to speak, and later revive of its own accord (Caspari 1874: 48). Nietzsche was strongly opposed to this suggestion: he considered the idea absurd and self-contradictory, expressing himself with some annoyance ("This nauseates me") (*KSA* 13, 11[72]). Yet the impossibility of a final state was extremely important for Nietzsche, not just for the sake of eternal recurrence but because he thought it amounted to a refutation of materialism in its existing form.

> If the world process had a final state, that would have been reached. The sole fundamental fact, however, is that it does *not* have a final state; and every philosophy or scientific hypothesis (e.g. mechanism) which necessitates such a state is *refuted* by this single fact. (*KSA* 13, 11[72])

The "sole fact" was guaranteed by the character of the present state, which could only be one of becoming, as our own thinking made evident:

> If the world had a goal, it must have been reached: if there were some (unintended) end state for it, this must also have been reached. If it were in any way capable of a pausing and becoming fixed, if there were in its course just one moment of "being" in the strict sense, there could be no more becoming, and therefore no more thinking of or observing a becoming either. (*KSA* 9, 11[292], 11, 36[15])

In various notes related to these Nietzsche tries to show how a set of assumptions which are consistent with a mechanistic view lead to the conclusion that the world consists of a set of states which occur again and again, without end or beginning. The overall strategy of his argument for eternal recurrence is worth remarking on. Nietzsche reaches it through a process of elimination. In considering the course of the universe there are three alternatives, as he supposes. One is that change goes on forever without repeating itself. Another is that a state is reached after which no change occurs. The third possibility is that the universe traverses a cycle which is repeated infinitely many times. Nietzsche arrives at an affirmation of this last theory only through eliminating the first two. He cannot accept that the course of becoming might come to an end, since such a standstill would have been reached already, and would have persisted ever since. He also rejects the idea of an endless sequence of new states of affairs which, he argues, requires force to contain within itself a capacity for an infinite number of states. Nietzsche's prejudice against anything infinite (apart from the potential infinity of time) is linked with his conception of science as admitting only those concepts which can be defined in a clear and "usable" way. Like the Greek thinkers he admired, Nietzsche assumed that the concept of the infinite could not pass this test. Thus, an endless succession of new states is ruled out by the finitude of the elements of becoming and their combinations.

The remaining option is eternal recurrence. As we have seen, this is supported in a curiously inglorious way, uncharacteristic of those of whom Zarathustra says, "where you can guess, you hate to deduce" (Z III, "On the Vision and the Riddle"). The doctrine is not a bold hypothesis: it offers no explanations for empirical phenomena and makes no predictions about the further course of experience. Hence, it is not capable of being directly confirmed or falsified. That makes it very different from scientific hypotheses such as those of Copernicus or Darwin, which are tied to observational evidence. As far as any scientific program is concerned, the doctrine of eternal recurrence is a dead end. It leads nowhere within scientific theory: that is, it is not a premise which enables scientific theory to take in a wider range of phenomena. Of course, one might say the same about the prediction of a final state. To that extent, Caspari's title *Die Thomson'sche Hypothese* was wrong. Thomson's claim about the future of the human environment explains nothing; rather, it is a conclusion reached by bringing together a number of already established theories. Helmholtz is right when he speaks of "inferences" and "consequences" here (Helmholtz 1962: 73–4).

There can be no doubt that Nietzsche's renewed interest in scientific cosmology was an important factor in his formulation of the eternal return in 1881. Yet the thought escaped this limited context from the beginning, its earliest notebook appearances being surrounded by reflections on fatalism and the possibility of achieving "indifference" towards the course of events. Nietzsche does have a line of argument for the eternal return: the question is how seriously we are to take his reasoning, or how seriously Nietzsche intended it to be taken. Its presentations occur in notes which cannot be taken as having the same status as Nietzsche's published work. There is one exception, though: the passage in the third part of *Thus Spoke Zarathustra* where the eternal return is introduced, as it had been in *The Gay Science*, as a challenge posed in an imagined personal confrontation. It occurs within a dramatic episode in which Zarathustra meets and quarrels with an adversary designated as "the spirit of gravity." After a contestation over the infinitude of time, the debate turns to the profound possibility of the eternal return.

> "Behold," I continued, "this moment! From this gateway, Moment, a long eternal lane runs *backward*: behind us lies an eternity. Must not whatever *can* run have run on this lane before? Must not whatever *can* happen have happened, have been done, have passed by before? And if everything has been there before – what do you think, dwarf, of this moment? Must not this gateway too have been there before? And are not all things knotted together so firmly that this moment draws after it all coming things? Therefore – itself too?" (Z III, "On the Vision and the Riddle," 2)

This is uncharacteristically argumentative for Zarathustra, for these are not open-ended inquiries but questions that invite a particular response, such that the respondent is led step by step towards an intended conclusion. The passage thus presents a line of thought: it is, in effect, a Socratic dialog with one side left unstated. Since the language ("Must not", "so . . . that", and "Therefore") is clearly that of logical reasoning, it is appropriate to recast the overall argument as a set of premises together with propositions derived from them through logical inference, along the following lines.

1 If past time is infinite, whatever is possible must have occurred before.
2 Past time is infinite.
3 Whatever is possible must have occurred before. (1, 2)
4 This moment is possible.
5 This moment must have occurred before. (3, 4)

At this point, only a single recurrence has been established. To expand the scope of the argument into infinitude by means of a recursive operation, a further premise is needed.

6 The time between any past occurrence and the present is finite.
7 The time before any past occurrence is infinite. (2, 6)
8 The time before the previous occurrence of this moment is infinite. (5, 7)
9 Whatever is possible must have occurred before the previous occurrence of this moment. (1, 8)
10 This moment must have occurred before its previous occurrence. (4, 9)

Now we have a procedure which can be repeated an infinite number of times, enabling the conclusion of the argument as a whole:

11 This moment must have taken place an infinite number of times in the past.

A parallel line of reasoning proves that this moment will take place an infinite number of times in the future. Thus, an eternal return has been established for at least one state of affairs, namely the present one. The same argument applies to any other moment that can be identified as possible. Since whatever is actual is possible, everything that has ever occurred satisfies that description. It follows that everything that has occurred has done so infinitely many times in the past, and will recur infinitely many times in the future.

Only one step now remains for a doctrine of eternal recurrence that applies not just to particular states but to whole sequences such as those that constitute an individual life. Nietzsche assumes the Laplacean notion of a "total state" that determines all future states and, for that matter, all past ones as well. He can therefore adopt the argument of J. S. Mill in his *System of Logic*:

> The state of the whole universe at any instant, insomuch that one who knew all the agents which exist at the present moment, their collocation in space, and their properties, in other words the laws of their agency, could predict the whole subsequent history of the universe, at least until some new volition of a power capable of controlling the universe should supervene. And if any particular state of the entire universe could ever recur a second time, all subsequent states would recur too, and history would, like a circulating decimal of many figures, periodically repeat itself. (Mill 1851: 358–9)

Allowing that this argument is a valid one, how plausible are its premises? Some are not problematical: the assumption that the present moment is possible follows from two other propositions, that whatever is actual is possible, and that the present moment is actual. These simply express the concepts of necessity and possibility that are common ground. The proposition that whatever is possible must occur in an infinite time is another matter altogether. It is highly debatable, and calls for a justification that Nietzsche nowhere attempts. For that reason, we need to look into it more closely.

Possibility and Time

Nietzsche is clearly committed to this principle, even if his earliest reference to it is hostile. A philosopher whom he treated with scorn, Eduard von Hartmann, had argued that "it would be inconsistent with the concept of development to attribute an infinite duration in the *past* to the world-process, since then every thinkable development would have been run through, which after all is not the case" (Von Hartmann 1871: 747; cf. Schopenhauer 1969: vol. 2, p. 489). Nietzsche cites this passage with evident disapproval ("oh rogue!") in his second *Untimely Meditation* (*UM II*, 9). Yet he later invokes the same proposition several times. It is used against the notion of the universe as a kind of single organism: if the world could ever become an organism, it would have done so already (see *KSA* 9, 11[201]). But its main contribution is to the argument concerning the eternal return.

If Nietzsche had any proof of the thesis in mind, the most likely candidate would rest on a principle concerning finite quantities. If only a finite number of states of affairs are possible, and if each of these has a finite duration, there must be a period after which any further states of affairs will be earlier ones. Now, this argument in turn relies on two premises whose validity is far from evident. The first is just the "law of definite number." Nietzsche takes that to imply not only that the things that constitute the world are finite in number, but that their possible arrangements and combinations are also finite in number. Dühring, it should be noted, rejected this last proposition, and for that reason refused to accept a recurrence of the same states of affairs (Dühring 1875: 84–5). He believed that space and time were an inexhaustible source of new possibilities – a view later used as an objection to Nietzsche's model by critics such as Georg Simmel (Simmel 1986: 172–3).

As for the second premise, Nietzsche does remark in one notebook entry that "All struggle – every process [*Geschehen*] is a struggle – takes time. What we call 'cause' and 'effect' leaves out struggle and thus does not express becoming. It is consistent to deny the time in cause and effect" (*KSA* 12, 1[92]). Similarly, an earlier note states that "Forces take definite times to become definite qualities" (*KSA* 9, 12[160]). His idea of reality as consisting of processes rather than things – as a world of becoming rather than being – is never set out in detail, but it clearly involves including duration within the simplest processes and eliminating action at a distance in time between distinct events. As he notes, the notion of causal efficacy allows cause and effect to occur at the *same* time, leaving temporal difference unexplained. Nietzsche is influenced here by the contemporary writer Adolf Fick, who argued that the causal relation could not involve a lapse of time: "It therefore does not join successive occurrences," Fick wrote, "but only the two sides of one and the same occurrence. The reason why one occurrence follows upon another rests on a completely different principle from that of causality" (Fick 1903: 118).

Some Nietzsche commentators have addressed the issue of possibility, actuality, and time using an argument concerning *probability*. Noting that whatever has a finite probability must occur in an infinite sequence of trials, they interpret Nietzsche as suggesting that every possible event fits this pattern, so that over an infinite time the probability of its *not* occurring will be reduced, if not to nothing, then to less than any given magnitude. If that is not straightforward necessity, it amounts to the same in practice. There are problems with this interpretation, however. It is true that Nietzsche uses dice games as a symbol for the character of becoming, but that is not an appeal to the theory of probability pioneered by Laplace and others. Rather, it emphasizes the absence of design or purpose in the world, as well as the uncertainty of prediction. Even so, one might suggest a model based on probability as the best way of constructing a coherent line of thought on his behalf. Crucial here is the assumption that every possible event has a certain finite probability. That claim needs justification. For probability is not a characteristic that can be attributed to a state of things without further inquiry, even given its possibility. The most common way of assigning probabilities to outcomes is to draw upon information about the actual frequencies of different events. This is how records of death rates in given populations are turned into estimates of life expectancy, for example. But how could that procedure be followed for the present state of affairs, taken as a whole? To assume that it recurs would be to beg the whole question. If we do posit an infinite recurrence, then every state that occurs has exactly the same frequency, since their sequence is the same in every cycle. The attribution of a particular probability to any general state of the world presents problems that seem insoluble, and so one suspects that this interpretation arises from a conflation of the concepts of possibility and probability, and fails for the same reason.

Is it true that whatever is possible must also be actual in an infinite time? Consider events that we might consider possible, but which do *not* occur. It is easy enough to say that an event has been prevented from occurring, but this does not rule out its occurrence in other circumstances. We can think of one way in which events are prevented from occurring at any time whatever: in consequence of an eternal recurrence. If a certain sequence of events leads back into itself, then all other events are ruled out, just as (to recall Mill's example) a recurring decimal expansion excludes all digits not belonging to the recurring sequence.[2] With an eternal return it would just be a fact that some events are not among the privileged ones. Even so, their occurrence in the past and future is impossible, even though in other respects (that is, in relation to the laws of nature, although Nietzsche would not take that phrase at face value) they are entirely possible. Nietzsche states this idea in relation to one special case when he writes: "Complete equilibrium must either be an impossibility in itself, or the alterations of force enter into a circular course before the occurrence of that equilibrium, which is possible in itself" (*KSA* 9, 11[265]). On the first alternative, a state of rest is impossible because the "essence" of force involves inner conflict which produces ceaseless change. The second alternative is the one that, as we have noted, presupposes the hypothesis of an eternal recurrence – which would thus have to be established on different grounds.

That a final state is impossible is inferred from the fact that it has never occurred. That in turn is shown by arguing that any state of equilibrium would have persisted to the present moment, which would also be a state of rest. As we can see immediately, that is not the case: our thinking makes the fact self-evident. Nietzsche comments: "This is the sole certainty we have in our hands to serve as a corrective to a great host of world hypotheses possible in themselves" (*KSA* 13, 14[188]). But any resemblance to the Cartesian *cogito* is very limited. Nietzsche denies that this truth can be expanded in the way Descartes imagined to take in a definition either of the "I" or of its activity of thinking. Such inferences, he argues, are hasty and can be seen to build in assumptions taken from elsewhere.

One other way of linking infinite time with the realization of every possibility may be mentioned, given Nietzsche's familiarity with ancient Greek thinkers such as the Stoics who related possibility and necessity to time in a straightforward way: the necessary is just what is actual at every time, while the possible is what is actual at some time. It follows that what never occurs is impossible, a proposition contradicting the commonsense idea that many things which do not happen are nevertheless in some sense possible. Even so, the simplicity of the doctrine that whatever is possible must happen recommends itself. This "Master Argument" was attributed to the Megarian thinker Diodorus Cronus, who according to Cicero maintained that "only what either is true or will be true is a possibility" (Cicero 1940: 13). Cicero gives an apt example: is it true to say that a jewel is breakable, even though it is at the bottom of the sea, and so will certainly never be broken? The premise on which the negative response of Diodorus Cronus depends is: "The impossible does not follow the possible." Modern commentators have puzzled over this proposition, without finding a way to make it seem plausible, given the everyday observation that what is possible at one time may become impossible at a later time, if some event prevents it from occurring from then onward. The Diodorean approach to modality was no doubt known to Nietzsche from his reading of Cicero and Epictetus, but he nowhere cites it, and so his reasons for holding that whatever is possible must occur remain unclear. We are left with several possible interpretations, none of which can be seen as having a strong claim to credibility.

A Dionysian World

The philosophical dispute between "optimism" and "pessimism" was much discussed in Nietzsche's time. Does the world as a whole contain more good than bad? The pessimistic influence of Schopenhauer, reinforced by later contributors such as the quasi-Hegelian Eduard von Hartmann and the extravagantly morbid Philipp Mainländer, dominated the debate. In response, Eugen Dühring defended the claim of life to have its own value and meaning. David Friedrich Strauss argued that pessimism was self-refuting, since anyone believing that the world should not exist should include his or her own speculation in that judgment. Strauss concluded that "every true philosophy is necessarily optimistic, as otherwise it denies its own right to exist" (Strauss 1872: 143). Nietzsche denounced this passage, commenting: "Optimism has here for once made things too easy for itself." Yet he seems to endorse its argument when he writes: "in a reprehended world reprehending would also be reprehensible" (KSA 13, 14[31]).

In fact Nietzsche disliked both optimism and pessimism, especially when the conflict between them was defined using pleasure and pain as standards of value. The world is neither good nor evil, he writes – such concepts are not to be used except in relation to human beings (HH 28). Pessimism is not a genuine problem, then, but a symptom of nihilism. At the theoretical level he thought the question of assessing the value of the world as a whole absurd. By what further standard could it be measured? "The total value of the world cannot be evaluated; consequently philosophical pessimism belongs among comical things" (KSA 13, 11[72]; WP 708). Further, the idea of an awareness of the world as a whole implies a standpoint which is impossible: observers are necessarily limited to their perspectives within reality. Nietzsche's skepticism on this point comes out in his remarks on Hartmann's notion of an overall world-process leading toward a necessary goal. "Even the concept "world" is a limit-concept: with this word we grasp a realm into which we can put all our necessary uncertainties" (KSA 12, 6[10]).

In this formulation Nietzsche places conceptual thinking itself under deep suspicion. More and more he asks: what is its motivation? Are the impulses that find expression there life-promoting ones, or the reactive drives of ressentiment? In Human, All Too Human he argued that the meanings given to things by religion, art, and metaphysics are strategies for achieving illusory solutions to our problems in living. "The more someone inclines towards reinterpretation and rationalization, the less attention he will give to the causes of the ill and to doing away with them" (HH 108). How far does this diagnosis extend, given his later claim that there are no facts but only interpretations? Categories such as substance and accident, cause and effect, subject and object, active and passive are, as he puts it, "projected" into the world by the knower's drives. They constitute a system of ideas which rationalizes the moral worldview, for by interpreting every event as the action of a subject upon an object they extend its preoccupation with assigning responsibility and blame to occurrences in general.

Could it be, then, that there is no innocent reading of reality? Even in his most nihilistic frame of mind, Nietzsche never rules out the prospect of liberation from the spirit of revenge, even if his indications of what this might consist in are expressed in allegorical forms. An active acceptance of reality would require a strong and healthy will to power, capable of acknowledging a world of incessant becoming and conflict, of indiscriminate creation and destruction. This is not a world of meaning in the traditional sense – that is, of meaning (or rather, value) whose source and authority lie in a higher realm of timeless being. Nietzsche's final view, expressed with eloquence in late notes, is that of a *Dionysian world*. At the end of the notebook compilation published as *The Will to Power* his editors placed a long paragraph which begins with the words "And do you know what 'the world' is to me?" (*KSA* 11, 38[12]; *WP* 1067). Nietzsche's answer is a balance between two equally powerfully asserted themes. The world is "a sea of forces flowing and rushing together, eternally changing, eternally flooding back." He postulates a cosmic cycle of organization and disorganization, expressing the will to power in its elemental form.

> Regarded mechanistically, the energy of the totality of becoming remains constant; regarded economically, it rises to a high point and sinks down again in an eternal circle. This "will to power" expresses itself in the interpretation, in the manner in which force is used up: – transformation of energy into life, and "life at its highest potency," thus appears as the goal. The same quantum of energy means different things at different stages of development.
>
> That which constitutes growth in life is an ever more healthy and far-seeing economy, which achieves more and more with less and less force – as an ideal, the principle of the smallest expenditure – (*WP* 1067)

In *Beyond Good and Evil* Nietzsche writes: "Around the hero everything turns into a tragedy; around the demi-god, into a satyr-play, and around God – what? perhaps into 'world'?" (*BGE* 150). Similarly, in a draft note, "God the *highest power* – that suffices! From it follows everything, from it follows – 'the world'!" (*KSA* 12, 10[20]). These formulations are startling condensations of theology and cosmology. Using ancient symbolism, they postulate the correlation of a form of life and its surrounding world. Yet in both texts we see inverted commas around "world." According to Plato, the concept of a *kosmos* implies order and harmony: "And philosophers tell us, Callicles, that communion and friendship and orderliness and temperance and justice bind together heaven and earth and gods and men, and that this universe is therefore called *kosmos* or order, not disorder or misrule, my friend" (Plato 1937: 508). In that sense, Nietzsche rejects the idea of a *kosmos*. So understood, cosmology as a philosophical science is as fictitious as the other two divisions of "special" metaphysics, theology and "rational" psychology, since its supposed object is equally lacking.

What is the alternative? In the end, Nietzsche's cosmology has a poetic quality. One natural philosopher he admired was Lucretius, the first and last materialist to do justice to the poetic character of the doctrine. There is a great poetry about atomism, with its eternal rain of diverse particles, Nietzsche comments. Modern atomists are prosaic spirits who fail to see this side of their own ideas. Nietzsche was fond of an image attributed to Heraclitus, reported by Lucian as answering the question "What is time?" with the words *pais paizon, pesseuon, sumpheromenos, diapheromenos*: "A child playing, moving counters, gathering and scattering" (Lucian 1913–67: 476). This is the playful cosmic process, in which the *Übermensch* participates on attaining the third "metamorphosis of the spirit" described in the first discourse of Zarathustra. Play is defined by its absence of purpose – in contrast with sport, which has both rules and aims, however arbitrary, in terms of which one can speak of winning or losing. The child's activity has no beginning or end of its own. Patterns may emerge from the freedom, as with Nietzsche's picture of a cyclical ebb and flow of forces throughout the universe. We cannot assume that he meant such descriptions of the world to be taken literally, though. They are metaphors for life, and the projection of a form of life on a grand scale.

In a note written in 1881, at the height of his preoccupation with cosmological debates, Nietzsche rejected any view of the universe as an organism and added: "We must think of it precisely as far as possible from the organic!" (*KSA* 9, 11[201]). What conception would fit this prescription? If "the organic" implies an emphasis on *form*, and what constitutes a living organism is the maintenance of its form by means of control over material interaction with the environment, then the opposite would presumably be formlessness, limitlessness, and an economy not of regulated exchange but of arbitrary appropriation and discharge. Here Nietzsche is showing one of his preoccupations: a hostility to all forms of teleology, whether of the traditional religious kind or in some biological version. The aspect of Darwinism that appealed to him most (as it did to his scientific mentor Lange) was its rejection of all purpose in biological explanation. Natural selection provided a far more economical account of those features of organisms for which purpose had been invoked. This attitude also rules out any teleological interpretation of the world as a whole. Moreover, it removes any privileged status for the phenomenon of life which, Nietzsche says, is only a "particular case," not something different in kind from the general phenomena of nature (*KSA* 13, 14[121]).

These reflections enable us to see why, for Nietzsche, the question about the nature of the world is not to be separated from the question about the *value* of the world, and why – to return to our opening discussion – a separation of "cosmology" from "ethics" (whether in relation to the eternal return or in general) misrepresents his intentions. Any idea of *applying* a cosmology to ethics or thinking of its "implications" for ethics must be an equally mistaken interpretation. That is never the direction of Nietzsche's thinking. Rather, he poses the task of finding the common source of the two: an affirmative form of life and a world that can be affirmed, without any trace of the moralistic interpretation that, as he suggests in *Ecce Homo*, originated with the ancient prophet whose namesake is now entrusted with the task of its overcoming. This is what corresponds to his theoretical view of the world as a chaos, for that characterization was always counted as an objection to existence. "An absolute saying Yes to the world – but for the very reasons from which one used to say No to it" (*KSA* 12, 10[21]; *WP* 1019). In the end, a cosmology in any traditional sense is irrelevant to Nietzsche's

Dionysian mode of thought. The philosophers have only interpreted the world in various ways, he might have said, but the point is to *affirm* it.

See also 3 "The Aesthetic Justification of Existence"; 5 "The Individual and Individuality in Nietzsche"; 8 "Nietzsche's Philosophy and True Religion"; 29 "Life and Self-Overcoming"

Notes

1 This is the approach of the first important book on Nietzsche, Lou Andreas-Salomé's *Friedrich Nietzsche in seinen Werken* (1894), and of numerous others throughout the twentieth century.
2 For example, $1/7 = .1428571428571 \ldots$ There will never be a 3 in this sequence, however far it is followed.

References

Aquinas, Thomas (1954). *De Aeternitate Mundi*, in *Opuscula Philosophica*, ed. R. M. Spiazzi (Turin and Rome: Marietti).
—— (1965–81). *Summa Theologiae* (London: Blackfriars).
Caspari, Otto (1874). *Die Thomson'sche Hypothese von der endlichen Temperaturausgleichung im Weltall beleuchtet vom philosophischen Gesichtspunkte* (Stuttgart: August Horster).
—— (1881). *Der Zusammenhang der Dinge. Gesammelte philosophische Aufsätze* (Breslau: Eduard Trewendt).
Cicero (1940). *De Oratore, De Fato, Paradoxa Stoicorum and De Partitione Oratoria*, trans. H. Rackham (London: Heinemann).
Dühring, Eugen (1865). *Der Werth des Lebens. Eine philosophische Betrachtung* (Breslau: Eduard Trewendt).
—— (1875). *Cursus der Philosophie als streng wissenschaftlicher Weltanschauung und Lebensgestaltung* (Leipzig: Erich Koschny).
Faraday, Michael (1965). *Experimental Researches in Electricity*, vol. 2 (New York: Dover).
Fick, Adolf (1903). *Gesammelte Schriften*, vol. 1 (Würzburg: Stahel'sche Verlags-Anstalt).
Heine, Heinrich (1985). *The Romantic School and Other Essays*, ed. Jost Hermand and Robert C. Holub (New York: Continuum).
Helmholtz, Hermann von (1962). *Popular Scientific Lectures* (New York: Dover).
Hume, David (1957). *Dialogues Concerning Natural Religion*, ed. H. D. Aiken (New York: Hafner).
Löwith, Karl (1999). *Nietzsche's Philosophy of the Eternal Recurrence of the Same*, trans. J. Harvey Lomax (Berkeley: University of California Press).
Lucian (1913–67). "Philosophies for Sale," trans. A. M. Harmon, in Lucian, *Works*, vol. 2, Loeb Classical Library (London: Heinemann).
Mill, John Stuart (1851). *A System of Logic, Ratiocinative and Inductive*, 3rd edn. (London: John W. Parker).
Philoponus [John] (1987). *Against Aristotle on the Eternity of the World*, trans. Christian Wildberg (London: Duckworth).
Plato (1937). *Gorgias*, in *Dialogues*, trans. B. Jowett (New York: Random House).
Salaquarda, Jörg (1978). "Nietzsche und Lange," *Nietzsche-Studien*, 7, pp. 236–53.
Schlechta, Karl, and Anders, Anni (1962). *Friedrich Nietzsche. Von den verborgenen Anfängen seines Philosophierens* (Stuttgart-Bad Cannstatt: Friedrich Frommann).
Schopenhauer, Arthur (1969). *The World as Will and Representation*, trans. E. F. J. Payne, 2 vols. (New York: Dover).

Simmel, Georg (1986). *Schopenhauer and Nietzsche*, trans. Helmut Loiskandl, Deena Weinstein and Michael Weinstein (Amherst: The University of Massachusetts Press).

Small, Robin (1992). "Cantor and the Scholastics," *American Catholic Philosophical Quarterly*, 66(4), pp. 407–28.

—— (2001). *Nietzsche in Context* (Aldershot: Ashgate).

Stack, George J. (1983). *Lange and Nietzsche* (Berlin and New York: Walter de Gruyter).

Strauss, David Friedrich (1872). *Der alte und der neue Glaube* (Leipzig: S. Hirzel).

Thomson, William (1882–1911). *Mathematical and Physical Papers*, 6 vols. (Cambridge: Cambridge University Press).

Vogt, Johannes Gustav (1878) *Die Kraft. Eine real-monistische Weltanschauung* (Leipzig: Haupt und Tischler).

Von Hartmann, Eduard (1871). *Philosophie des Unbewussten*, 3rd edn. (Berlin: Carl Dunckers).

Zöllner, Johann Carl Friedrich (1872). *Über die Natur der Cometen. Beiträge zur Geschichte und Theorie der Erkenntnis* (Leipzig: Wilhelm Engelmann).

Further Reading

Abel, Günter (1984). *Nietzsche. Die Dynamik der Willen zur Macht und die ewige Wiederkehr* (Berlin: Walter de Gruyter).

Andler, Charles (1958). *Nietzsche, sa vie et sa pensée*, 3rd edn. (Paris: Librairie Gallimard).

Andreas-Salomé, Lou (1894). *Friedrich Nietzsche in seinen Werken* (Vienna: Carl Konegen).

Babich, Babette E. (1994). *Nietzsche's Philosophy of Science: Reflecting Science on the Ground of Art and Life* (Albany, NY: State University of New York Press).

Babich, Babette E., and Cohen, Robert S. (eds.) (1999a). *Nietzsche, Theories of Knowledge, and Critical Theory: Nietzsche and the Sciences I* (Dordrecht: Kluwer Academic).

—— (eds.) (1999b). *Nietzsche, Epistemology, and Philosophy of Science: Nietzsche and the Sciences II* (Dordrecht: Kluwer Academic).

Batault, Georges (1904). "L'Hypothèse du retour éternel devant la science moderne," *Revue philosophique de la France et de l'étranger*, 57, pp. 158–67.

Bauer, Martin (1984). "Zur Genealogie von Nietzsches Kraftbegriff. Nietzsches Auseinandersetzung mit J. G. Vogt," *Nietzsche-Studien*, 13, pp. 211–27.

Becker, Oskar (1963) *Dasein und Dawesen: Gesammelte philosophische Aufsätze* (Pfullingen: Günther Neske).

Bois, Henri (1913). "Le 'Retour éternel' de Nietzsche," *L'Année philosophique*, 24, pp. 145–84.

Boscovich, Roger Joseph (1966). *A Theory of Natural Philosophy*, trans. J. M. Child (Cambridge, MA: MIT Press) .

Brobjer, Thomas H (1997). "Nietzsche's Reading and Private Library, 1885–1889," *Journal of the History of Ideas*, 58, pp. 663–93.

Brush, Stephen G (1981). "Nietzsche's Recurrence Revisited: The French Connection," *Journal of the History of Philosophy*, 19, pp. 235–8.

Čapek, Milič (1960). "The Theory of Eternal Recurrence in Modern Philosophy of Science, with Special Reference to C. S. Peirce," *Journal of Philosophy*, 57, pp. 289–96.

—— (1961). *The Philosophical Impact of Contemporary Physics* (New York: Van Nostrand Reinhold).

—— (1967). "Eternal Return," in Paul Edwards (ed.), *The Encyclopedia of Philosophy*, vol. 3 (New York: Macmillan and The Free Press), pp. 61–3.

—— (1983). "Eternal Recurrence – Once More," *Transactions of the Charles S. Peirce Society*, 19, pp. 141–53.

205

Couprie, Dirk L. (1998). "'Hätte die Welt ein Ziel, [. . .] so wäre es [. . .] mit allem Werden längst zu Ende.' Ein Beitrag zur Geschichte einer Argumentation," *Nietzsche-Studien*, 27, pp. 107–18.

Danto, Arthur (1965) *Nietzsche as Philosopher* (New York: Macmillan).

Deleuze, Gilles (1983) *Nietzsche and Philosophy*, trans. Hugh Tomlinson (London: Athlone Press).

Delevsky, Jacques (1945). "Note sur la possibilité des répétitions cosmologiques," *Isis*, 36, pp. 1–21.

D'Iorio, Paolo (1995). "Cosmologie de l'éternel retour," *Nietzsche-Studien*, 24, pp. 62–123.

Ewald, Oscar (1903). *Nietzsches Lehre in ihren Grundbegriffen. Die ewige wiederkunft des Gleichen und der Sinn des Übermenschen: Eine kritische Untersuchung* (Berlin: Ernst Hofmann).

Hatab, Lawrence J. (1978). *Nietzsche and Eternal Recurrence: The Redemption of Time and Becoming* (Washington, DC: University Press of America).

Juranville, Alain (1973). *Physique de Nietzsche* (Paris: Denoël/Gonthier).

Klossowski, Pierre (1997). *Nietzsche and the Vicious Circle*, trans. Daniel W. Smith (London: Athlone Press).

Krueger, Jerry (1978). "Nietzschean Recurrence as a Cosmological Hypothesis," *Journal of the History of Philosophy*, 16, pp. 435–44.

Lange, Friedrich Albert (1866). *Geschichte des Materialismus und Kritik seiner Bedeutung in der Gegenwart* (Iserlohn: J. Baedecker).

Magnus, Bernd (1973). "Nietzsche's Eternalistic Counter-Myth," *Review of Metaphysics*, 26, pp. 604–16.

—— (1978). *Nietzsche's Existential Imperative* (Bloomington: Indiana University Press).

—— (1979). "Eternal Recurrence," *Nietzsche-Studien*, 8, pp. 362–77.

Mainländer, Philipp (1876). *Die Philosophie der Erlösung* (Berlin: Theobald Grieben).

Marton, Scarlett (1996). "L'Éternel rétour du même: Thèse cosmologique ou impératif éthique?" *Nietzsche-Studien*, 25, pp. 42–63.

Moles, Alistair (1989). "Nietzsche's Eternal Recurrence as Riemannian Cosmology," *International Studies in Philosophy*, 21(2), pp. 21–35.

—— (1990). *Nietzsche's Philosophy of Nature and Cosmology* (New York: Peter Lang).

Moore, Gregory, and Brobjer, Thomas H. (eds.) (2004). *Nietzsche and Science* (Aldershot: Ashgate).

Müller-Lauter, Wolfgang (1971). *Nietzsche. Seine Philosophie der Gegensätze und die Gegensätze seiner Philosophie* (Berlin and New York: Walter de Gruyter).

Nehamas, Alexander (1980). "The Eternal Recurrence," *The Philosophical Review*, 89, pp. 331–56.

Richardson, John (1996). *Nietzsche's System* (New York: Oxford University Press).

Rogers, Peter (2001). "Simmel's Mistake: The Eternal Recurrence as a Riddle About the Intelligible Form of Time as a Whole," *Journal of Nietzsche Studies*, 21, pp. 77–95.

Soll, Ivan (1973). "Reflections on Recurrence: A Re-examination of Nietzsche's Doctrine, *die Ewige Wiederkehr des Gleichen*," in Robert Solomon (ed.), *Nietzsche: A Collection of Critical Essays* (New York: Doubleday Anchor), pp. 322–42.

Spiekermann, Klaus (1988). "Nietzsches Beweise für die ewige Wiederkehr," *Nietzsche-Studien*, 17, pp. 497–504.

—— (1992). *Naturwissenschaft als subjektlose Macht? Nietzsches Kritik physikalischer Grundkonzepte* (Berlin and New York: Walter de Gruyter).

Stack, George J. (1981). "Nietzsche and Boscovich's Natural Philosophy," *Pacific Philosophical Quarterly*, 62, pp. 69–87.

—— (1984). "Eternal Recurrence Again," *Philosophy Today*, 28, pp. 242–63.

—— (1989). "Riemann's Geometry and Eternal Recurrence as Cosmological Hypothesis: A Reply," *International Studies in Philosophy*, 21, pp. 37–40.

Stambaugh, Joan (1972). *Nietzsche's Thought of Eternal Return* (Baltimore: Johns Hopkins University Press).

—— (1987). *The Problem of Time in Nietzsche*, trans. John F. Humphrey (Lewisburg: Bucknell University Press).

Sterling, M. C. (1977). "Recent Discussions of Eternal Recurrence: Some Critical Comments," *Nietzsche-Studien*, 6, pp. 261–91.

Van Fraassen, Bas C. (1962). "Čapek on Eternal Recurrence," *Journal of Philosophy*, 59, pp. 371–5.

Whitlock, Greg (1996). "Roger Boscovich, Benedict de Spinoza and Friedrich Nietzsche: The Untold Story," *Nietzsche-Studien*, 25, pp. 200–20.

—— (1997). "Examining Nietzsche's 'Time Atom Theory' Fragment from 1873," *Nietzsche-Studien*, 26, pp. 350–60.

12

Nietzsche on Time and Becoming

JOHN RICHARDSON

1 Introduction

In this essay I shall provide a reading of Nietzsche's "theory of time." This theory includes, most obviously, what he says about "becoming": his well-known insistence that the world is "not being but becoming." But the theory also draws in a variety of his other positions, including his critical treatments of concepts such as substance and causation, his teaching of the eternal return, and his complex views about memory, guilt, and responsibility. I want to suggest a way in which these seemingly separate views cohere well enough to amount to a theory of time.

My reading will make use of the neo-Darwinian account of Nietzsche I presented in *Nietzsche's New Darwinism* (Richardson 2004). I want on the one hand to use this to clarify Nietzsche's views about time, but on the other to emphasize and develop the crucial temporal element already in that neo-Darwinian account. Nietzsche takes his underlying sense of becoming from Darwin's new way of "setting things in motion" – evolution. Nietzsche's grasp of the logic of evolution – an evolution that determines the will and meaning he attributes to everything alive – is the crux of his new notion of time and becoming.[1]

First some preliminary points. Let me note but quickly set aside (to the background) one set of questions that arise for just about *any* effort to attribute to Nietzsche anything so pedestrian as a "theory." These doubts will strike many readers just as forcibly on this topic of time as they have on such other topics as truth and politics.

How can Nietzsche have a theory of time, when (1) he says opposite things about time in different places, for example that time is real and that it is not real; and when (2) he never treats the topic at length, or in a focused and methodical way; and when (3) he doesn't explicitly or methodically link his views on those several topics I've mentioned, to show that he thinks of them in relation to one another and under the overall heading of time? Altogether, it may be felt, his writings express spontaneous and shifting views about time, never marshaled into a position or theory.

My answer to this first set of challenges will be simply to describe a way in which these seemingly disparate ideas *do* hang together in a "theory." To be sure, this theory will involve, at a crucial point, a division or bifurcation in Nietzsche's view: he is attracted, at a certain junction in the ideas, to two different routes. So some of those "opposite things" he says about time express a genuine tension in him. But this dividedness can be located within a larger theory where his view is more settled. This theory draws in many points that seem separate; we grasp them better by seeing how they support and explain one another.

There is a second set of grounds for denying that Nietzsche has a "theory of time" which requires more direct attention. It may seem that Nietzsche's real interest is in diagnosing and criticizing our *attitudes* towards time, not in developing a positive theory about it himself. Just as Gemes has argued that Nietzsche has no theory of truth, but rather an interest in how we think about truth (Gemes 1992), so it might be argued for time: that his focus is all on the ways in which we think and feel about time and becoming, and that he makes no metaphysical (or other) claims about these themselves.

This objection might be illustrated in the way Nietzsche thinks of eternal return. For (most interpreters now think) he intends this not as a "cosmological" doctrine – a claim as to how the world or universe really is – but as a way we are challenged to believe and want reality to be, within a certain kind of thought experiment.[2] What matters is whether one is strong enough to "will" eternal return, not whether it is true. And so too, it might be said, for becoming: Nietzsche cares about the psycho-logical implications of believing in either being or becoming – of seeing the world in one of these ways – not in whether these beliefs are true (match reality).

Now I think there's no doubt that Nietzsche's main interest is in our views about time, and not in the nature of time itself. He means to offer a description and critique of these views. And of these views he is less interested in our beliefs about time than in our evaluations of time and becoming, and our feelings about them. What matters especially is not one's theory whether the world is being or becoming, but which of these one values, which of them one *wants* the world to be.[3] Indeed it matters what one wants them to be not consciously but in one's body, one's drives. It is the temporal viewpoint built into our drives that Nietzsche most wants to describe. Moreover – displacing him still more from aiming at "the truth about time" – he examines these evaluations not chiefly to describe them but to judge them, and often by non-epistemic standards. He wants less to understand the different kinds of people who favor becom-ing or being than to assess and "rank" them, in particular by their degrees of strength. He promotes above all, as strongest, the "Dionysian" type that sees and wants a world of becoming. Or, perhaps, he merely shows us that *he* is the kind of person who favors becoming over being – i.e. merely expresses the attitude without asserting it.[4] All of this ranges very far from the goal of a theory of time.

So the second challenge is that whatever "theory of time" Nietzsche has is really a theory of our views about time, and is besides subordinate to evaluating these views. My answer to this challenge will be partly concessive. I agree that he cares about all of these other things more than he does about giving a theory of time (itself). But I claim that a certain theory of time is nevertheless embedded in those diagnoses and evalua-tions of our views about time. Some of those evaluations *are* epistemic – assess views by their truth. And those diagnoses rest upon a considered theory about what "views" – including these views about time – really are, and treats them as temporal.

There is a different way of understanding Nietzsche's preoccupation with our views about time, and this brings me to a principal issue of this essay. Perhaps he dwells on our views about time because he thinks that these somehow "make time what it is." Studying these views would be the proper way of getting at what time is. Perhaps, in other words, he does have a theory of time, but an "idealist" theory: he thinks that time arises only in or by virtue of certain viewpoints or – in his familiar term – *perspectives*. It's clear enough that he thinks perspectives involve a kind of time; perhaps he denies that there is any "real" time independent of them. In addressing the question whether Nietzsche's theory of time is "idealist" or "perspectivist" I mean these labels in very general or adaptable senses. Temporal idealism, for example, must not be understood to require that time be expressed in ideas understood as mental or conscious. And temporal perspectivism must not require that all ideas of time be equally legitimate or true. It is only when we broaden the senses of idealism and perspectivism to fit Nietzsche's distinctive positions that we can face the true issue, whether he thinks there is a real time, a time "in itself" apart from all viewpoint and perspective.

The time he is most interested in is this time that arises by and for perspectives. He tells an elaborate and appealing story about how it arises for different kinds of perspectives. Although his interest is all in the human, it is important to him that perspectivity extends far more widely: everything alive involves will and perspective, and to understand the human we need to grasp it in this context. Within this broad domain he tends to think of three principal kinds (or levels) of perspectives: animal, human, and superhuman. My central sections will look at these main kinds, which involve three distinct ways of experiencing or living through time – "temporalities." As I will try to show, Nietzsche's well-known ideas about will to power, morality, and eternal return respectively concern these three different temporalities.

But as I will also try to show, Nietzsche's story about the way perspectives "make" time has two sides, one of which we tend to miss. First and more obvious is the way time "appears to" perspectives, the way time "seems" to them to be. As I will put it, time arises as a perspectival (or intentional) *content*. Less obvious is the second way Nietzsche thinks there is time through perspectives: they themselves involve a time that is not presented to them. Their very *structure* has a certain temporal character – the structure by which there is a content or meaning for them. So on the one hand there is a time "for" (or to) perspectives, but on the other a time "of" (or about) them. These are the bases for somewhat different kinds of perspectival time. One main task will be to pry them apart in our account of the time Nietzsche treats.

This second kind of perspectival time has implications for the further question, whether he allows (believes in) any time *apart from* the time that arises in and for perspectives. And it is here, I will argue, that we come to that dividedness in Nietzsche's theory of time. For this time-structure to perspectives seems to depend on the reality of a non-perspectival time, against the inclinations of his own thinking. He wants to describe and explain our lived temporality in ways that draw on assumptions about a time logically prior to any lived time. But this collides with his own strong sentiments against an "objective time." In my last section I will look quickly at this tension his thinking brings him into.

2 The World as Becoming

It bears remarking that the theory of becoming is not directly about time, but about a change or process that takes place "within" time. Part of our challenge will be to give Nietzsche's view of the relation between time and becoming. Now perhaps the most striking feature of Nietzsche's "theory of becoming" is the use he puts it to: he frequently insists that it has radically skeptical consequences: "Heraclitus will eternally have it right, that being is an empty fiction. The 'apparent' world is the only one: the 'true' world is merely *lied into it [hinzugelogen]*" (*TI*, "'Reason' in Philosophy," 2).[5] Becoming entails the falsity of both our scientific and commonsense theories of the world. It does this by falsifying (showing to be false or inapplicable) certain concepts that belong to the deep structure of all of our descriptions and explanations. Nietzsche's accounts of the concepts that becoming falsifies are some of our best clues as to what he thinks becoming positively is. In each case we can start with the skeptical consequence – the way it shows our concepts to be false – and extract a certain positive claim – how the world is, so as to falsify our views of it.

(a) Becoming rules out *substances*. Here Nietzsche has foremost in mind the notion of a "substratum" – a logical support for properties, which persists "beneath" the changes in properties. Nietzsche takes "becoming" to rule out such substrata, whose persistence was supposed to ground things' identity through time. Change "goes all the way down." There are no such exemptions from it – nothing that does not change: so *change is pervasive*.

(b) Becoming rules out *rest*. Nietzsche claims there are no true stabilities. Everything that exists is constantly changing: after any interval of time, no matter how short, it has become something different, strictly speaking. *WP* 688: "it is simply a matter of experience that change *does not stop*."[6] There are no interruptions or pauses in change: so *change is constant*.

(c) Becoming rules out *causes*. Since becoming is a continuum, we falsify it when we isolate within it "causes" and "effects." So *GS* 112: "Cause and effect: such a duality probably never exists, – in truth a continuum stands before us, from which we isolate a couple of pieces [. . .] An intellect that saw cause and effect as a continuum, not in our way as an arbitrary division and dismemberment, that saw the flux of happening, – would throw away the concept of cause and effect and deny all conditionality." There are no discontinuities in change: so *change is along a continuum*.

(d) Becoming rules out any *"doer behind the doing."* In part this merely restates the previous denial of causes: no doers in a continuum. But it also makes a stronger, ontological claim: that what is basic is "doing" or becoming *rather than* beings or things. It's not just that "things change" – as (a)–(c) could be heard – but that things are artificially separated or abstracted from a change that is what's "truly there" (see Richardson 1996: ch. 2). We conceive of the world as the set of all things, and of their motions as simply facts about them (ways in which they succeed one another). Nietzsche wants us to reverse this priority: what is basic are those motions, and "things" are merely "slow motions" we misinterpret as stabilities. There are no underlying beings that change is of: so *change is what there (basically) is.*[7]

In each case Nietzsche's skeptical argument involves a certain positive characterization of becoming, as how the world "is." However, this positive account is still unclear to us in a crucial respect: we need to say whether he thinks becoming is ideal or real. What kind of world is it that becomes, and that these concepts like "substance" and "cause" are *false about?* To put it in Nietzschean terms, is it perspectives that become, or a reality independent from perspectives? In Kantian terms, is becoming phenomenal or noumenal, something (transcendentally) ideal or real? I will distinguish four ways of locating Nietzsche's view within a broadly Kantian framework. The first two readings assign him versions of realism, the latter two, versions of idealism.

2.1 Becoming is the noumenon-as-inaccessible

On this first reading Nietzsche uses "becoming" to characterize the world as it is really or "in itself" and apart from all perspectives – but he characterizes it *only* negatively, *as* inaccessible to our knowing. We can never escape our perspectivity so as to reach reality, and all the properties we apply to the world, all the ways we "determine" or specify it in our theories, are false about it. The world, as becoming, is *indeterminable*. Sometimes Nietzsche seems to mean just this negative point: the world's becoming is no more than its unknowability, its unintelligibility. We might call this *negative realism*: becoming is indeed a feature of the world independently of perspectives, but it is precisely and only this world's indeterminableness.[8]

On this reading Nietzsche's characterization of the world as becoming does the same work as Kant's denial that the noumenon is knowable. But whereas Kant thinks the (transcendentally) real is unknowable (in large part) because it is *not* temporal, Nietzsche chooses to pick out its inaccessibility precisely by its temporal character, its "becoming." He thinks that Kant deletes time from the noumenon because he has a deep Christian allegiance to eternity. He thinks that the reality of the world is indeed beyond our comprehension, but by being as it were "too temporal" – or too changing – not by being timeless.

This reading has a cousin, according to which Nietzsche thinks that our efforts to "determine" the world are not just hopeless – since we can never know whether our determinations are true – but incoherent – since the world in itself is radically *indeterminate*. So here the point about becoming is not just epistemic but ontological: the world is "flux" or "chaos" insofar as it has no determinate structure in itself. All properties, including temporal ones, are imposed by perspectives – are not it but us. Our theories are false because their very project is ill formed: they try to match the structure of a structureless world. And this cousin has a cousin of its own, which pushes the point further still: it's not just that the noumenon is indeterminate, but that there is and can be no such thing: the very notion of a noumenon is ill formed or contradictory. On this reading, Nietzsche's insistence on "the world as becoming" is meant to rule out any noumenon – so that "becoming" applies to the phenomenal, and refers just to its non-noumenality, to the non-existence of any real or noumenal world. This carries us out of realism, so that this second cousin properly belongs under 2.3 or 2.4 below.

212

This first reading of becoming – as making a purely negative point – seems to fit well with one striking feature of Nietzsche's use of the term: the huge imbalance between his many skeptical uses of it, and his very scarce efforts to develop a positive content for it. Nevertheless, he does clearly give it *some* content, which (I think) this reading can't do justice to. His pervasive implication that the point has to do with change or time suggests that reality *can* be determined and known *as* temporal in this way. The four claims about change listed above – that it is pervasive, constant, along a continuum, and basic – are in fact ambitious characterizations, and if they apply to the noumenon, Nietzsche thinks he knows quite a bit about it. Moreover these four claims leave open the effort to extend and elaborate our understanding of the world as change – and just how it renders the world *otherwise* indeterminable (or indeterminate). This pushes us towards our second option.

2.2 Becoming is the describable structure of the noumenon

Here becoming is read as a positive characterization of the world as it is "in itself" and independently of perspectives upon it. This world is pervasively and constantly changing along a continuum – indeed this world *is* change. This world is unknowable *because* it has this general character.[9] Perhaps it is also indeterminate, below the level of this general account of it, so that *all* one can say about it is that it thus becomes. We can call this *positive realism*: time is a real feature of the world, as it is independently of perspectives; it is the way the world really is change or flux.

This reading takes up the positive content of becoming that was ignored by 2.1: it lets Nietzsche's point be indeed about change. The reading also accords with a strong realist flavor in his talk about becoming. He mostly stresses ways in which we *miss* becoming – i.e. ways it *does not* "appear" to us – so that it is difficult to see how he could treat it as an appearance or phenomenon. Becoming seems rather the way the world really is, which our beliefs and perspectives are inadequate to.[10]

However this reading seems to be quite ruled out by Nietzsche's many attacks on the very notion of a noumenon – arguments we have already noticed, that the concept is contradictory or incoherent. To make becoming how the world is "in itself" would be inconsistent with Nietzsche's perspectivism, it seems.[11] He often wields this against realist notions of the world.[12] I will return near the end to reconsider this quick dismissal. But for now we should move to more promising alternatives, the ways in which becoming could be something about perspectives, something "ideal."

2.3 Becoming is the structure of the phenomenal world

A first way in which becoming could be ideal is by being a basic structure to the *content* of perspectives, what they are "of." Becoming and time would be fundamental ways the phenomenal or empirical world does – and must – appear to us. Becoming would be an "appearance," or rather a general structure of all appearances. Nietzsche's theory would be an analog to Kant's account of time as a "form of intuition," i.e. as a formal structure imposed on all appearances. I will call this *content idealism*: time is a content of perspectives.

213

This reading faces the objection mentioned before: how can becoming be phenomenal – the way the world appears – when Nietzsche insists that it falsifies all our commonsense and scientific views? He seems to accept Kant's claim that we structure our world by concepts such as substance and cause – so it seems it is these that play the role of phenomena, and not the becoming that shows them false. However, there may be a way around this problem: Nietzsche can distinguish *levels* of phenomenality. He can hold that becoming is a deeper layer of structuring of phenomena than that provided by the concepts of substance and cause. Now becoming might "lie deeper" in either of two ways: (a) it could be a structure that we ourselves impose on experience prior to structuring by the categories, or (b) it could be a structure in the original input of experience prior to the structuring we impose.

In the first case becoming would falsify substance and cause by showing them inconsistent with a more basic way we *must* view change and time: we have to experience the world as becoming more pervasively or indispensably than we need to order it into substances and causes. In the second case becoming would falsify substance and cause by showing them inconsistent with the given or raw material of our experience: this is chaotic in a way that makes any ordering false.

Each of these ways of making becoming phenomenal faces problems. The claim that becoming is our deeper way of ordering experience faces the obvious challenge of saying why this should be so. What could be the need or advantage in this ordering – and what kind of ordering is it, to experience the world as becoming? The claim that becoming is the character of our experiential input or given faces problems of consistency with Nietzsche's general denial of any such "given." Instead of tackling these problems here, let's turn to a last option for locating becoming within our (broadly) Kantian framework.

2.4 Becoming is the form of perspectives

Here becoming is not a phenomenon, in the sense of a perspectival content, but a real feature of perspectives themselves. Becoming isn't what these perspectives are "of" or "about" – instead the perspectives themselves "become." Perspectives have a temporal structure that needn't occur as what they are perspectives of.[13] Potentially this opens up a gap between how time appears to be, and how it is – opens it up within a perspectival idealism. So it's important to distinguish this option from 2.3 – and to determine the share of each in Nietzsche's views about becoming. I will call this *formal idealism*: time is the form or structure *of perspectives*, by which a content appears to them. (It is important *not* to include here the view of time as the form *of appearances*; this belongs under 2.3.)

A strength of this reading is that it offers a kind of middle ground between the extremes of realism and idealism: it allows becoming a kind of reality it lacks in 2.3, while treating it still as a fact about perspectives. It is a fact not about what perspectives are of, but about their own structure – their "real" structure insofar as it is not determined by how the perspectives view their own structure. So the truth we can say is not just what perspectival contents there are – the ways things seem to different viewpoints – but the structure of those perspectives themselves, by which they have those contents.

214

But the problem is that this degree of realism threatens to burst the bounds of Nietzsche's perspectivism: can he allow *non*-perspectival truths *about perspectives?* It would be one thing for there to be truths and facts about what perspectives see, their contents. There is a way things seem and matter to each perspective, which Nietzsche aspires to describe accurately; he wants to get right how Christians see and value, for example. Here the facts are precisely the seemings, and Nietzsche thinks he grasps these facts by inhabiting the viewpoints and describing them "from within." Such "facts" might not threaten perspectivism. But if there are facts about perspectives that go beyond their content, would Nietzsche still have a "perspectivism" – would he still hold that "truth is perspectival"?

I will come back in my last section to these questions about the overall logic of Nietzsche's position. But first – in the next three sections – I will recount his story of how perspectives in and about time evolve. That is, I will try to state Nietzsche's *genealogy of time* (i.e. of time-perspectives or "temporalities"). Here he operates with the same three-part dialectic he employs much more generally: animal, human, superhuman. Each of these involves, I will try to show, a distinctive temporality. Our human way of being in time evolves as a kind of negation of an animal temporality, a rift that is healed in the superhuman. When we sort Nietzsche's remarks on time in relation to these three ways of being in time, we see how they hang together into a complex overall theory.

3 How Time Arises for Organisms

So we turn to the start of Nietzsche's positive theory of time: his account of how time arises by and for life. Time arises by life's "perspectivity." By the latter Nietzsche means, I will claim, a minimal kind of "intentionality," one that need not be conscious or mental, and in fact typically is not. As intentionality it involves a certain content – what the perspective is "about," what it "intends"; Nietzsche often speaks of this content as a *meaning*. He attributes this intentionality to all of life: everything organic has or involves perspectives and meanings. When we describe and explain organisms we need to do so in terms of these intendings. Nietzsche offers an analysis of this basic and general perspectivity. It involves, crucially, certain temporal features – relationships among present, future, and past. And it's just here, I claim, that he principally locates becoming.

But as I have said, I think we need to distinguish between two ways in which time arises by perspectivity. More obvious is the time "for" perspectives, the time that appears to them. Less obvious is the time involved in perspectivity itself, the time "of" those perspectives, as they generate that content. For the most part the latter time does not appear to life. The difference between these two kinds of phenomenal time is at the root of Nietzsche's emphatic skepticism against the ways in which we humans view and experience time. Life itself (the organism) views time differently than it lives it. Since becoming lies in the temporal structure of perspectives, and not in how they view time, life tends to miss its own becoming.

Nietzsche claims that life's basic intentionality occurs as a *willing* or striving – to be heard non-mentally as well. This willing operates in the *drives* that are his principal explainers of human and other organisms. A meaning or content first arises within life's arc towards what it wills: meaning arises *as* the object – and target – of a willing. We need to see how this organic willing – which Nietzsche famously insists is chiefly a "will to power" – possesses a certain temporal structure, by virtue of which it has an intentional content, which itself has a (somewhat different) temporal character. He thinks both of these times lie at the bottom of us – are built into us just "as alive."

This account of life's time bears interesting comparison with the time Kant treats as a "form of intuition" for us. Nietzsche claims to describe a far more widespread phenomenality: how "time is" not just for human experience, but in and for the will occurring in all organisms. It depends not on consciousness, but on directedness, effort, will. And Nietzsche makes this time a condition not chiefly for experience (life's epistemic relation to the world), but for action (life's practical relation).[14] Ultimately, it is so that the organism can survive and compete that it has the temporal structure and content it does.

We must think of this will in some special ways in order to think it consistently with Nietzsche's attacks on "will," and on other notions involved in our usual idea of will. The latter include the concepts we have just seen are ruled out by becoming: substance, cause, being, the "doer behind the doing." We need to apply these negative lessons in interpreting his positive notion of will. So, first, we must think of Nietzschean will not as a persisting thing, but as a feature of doing or activity: will occurs as a willing, which lies in the way a process occurs "for the sake of" some outcome and goal. This is the basic "intending" by which meaning comes into the world.

We must also make sure not to think of this will as a single "faculty" possessed and governed by a person. Willing is not centralized in a consciousness or ego, but is dispersed in a mix of efforts, by what Nietzsche calls "drives," abilities of our bodies. An organism is a system of drives – a complex of plastic tendencies (efforts) towards various outcomes. So each drive has its own intentional arc towards a goal, that identifies *which* drive it is. Putting this point together with the first: a drive is a pattern or strand in the directed activity of the organism; the organism, and its "will," is really no more than the web of these strands.

3.1 Life's true temporal structure

Life gets its original time from this logic of drives or wills. This basic time lies in the way the meaning or reason for what the drive does is dispersed into both the future and the past of the present doing. It is dispersed there partly *within* the drive's own perspective, but primarily as an external fact *about* that perspective. It is a fact about the logic by which the drive "projects" its meaning or content; it belongs to the temporal structure of perspectivity or intentionality itself. Meaning depends – depends logically – on past and future. Let's begin by looking at this "formal temporality," the time involved in the way perspectival meanings or contents arise.

3.1.1

So how does life, as will or drive, get its meaning or content? It gets it, first, by being a directedness, a striving. Willing involves a reach towards some goal or end, so that the

216

goal explains what the willing now does. What an organism does has meaning – a meaning inorganic activity lacks – because there is something it is "trying to do."[15] And Nietzsche treats this relation to a goal as a relation to the future, a certain feasible future. So when he explains by a will, he explains (in part) by an aimed-at future. This future (partly) determines the meaning of what the organism does. Nietzsche wants to know "which drive" is active in a doing, as a step to identifying the aim for which the doing was done. This arc towards a future is a first side of the will's temporality. Nietzsche's commonest way of referring to these goals is as "*values*"; all life and all willing involve valuing.[16]

Nietzsche characterizes this reach to the future further by calling it will to power. The drive's effort towards its distinctive goal is, as well, an effort at "power" – so that power is another kind of end, which the drive is supposed to share with all other drives. I won't elaborate on this notion here, but simply say that power is a kind of growth – a growth that depends both on mastering other forces, and on "overcoming" the will as it has been. For our purposes, what matters especially is the way this point heightens how the will is bent on the future, according to Nietzsche. In willing power a drive wills to replace its present state with a new one – it tries to kill its present to make a stronger future. It wills, in this sense, becoming or change, which Nietzsche thus claims is a deep value in life itself. And we should hear this too as a temporal point, part of how a drive is "in time."

In willing its goal, and willing power, a drive also stands in relation to the possible failures in these projects – the possible futures in which it is thwarted from its goal, and declines in power. So its future more fully consists not just of those goals, but of a "way up" and a "way down," as both feasible for it. The drive's intentionality takes in these routes of ascent and decline, the latter as to be avoided, the former attained. So the future is intended as a nexus of values, positive and negative, accruing to possibilities previewed in the will's anticipation.

It is important to remember that this "preview" of future aims and obstacles is not to be understood as mental or conscious. Nietzsche means it to extend, I think, to all biological processes we interpret as directed or functional. It applies to the amoeba's reach towards its prey, and to the organic functionings that support and constitute the organism's life. These processes are plastically responsive to conditions – including adverse conditions – in such a way as to arrive regularly at certain outcomes. Nietzsche views organisms as systems of such processes, each "intending" and "valuing" the outcome it tends thus plastically towards.

So far the point is that a possible future, an aimed-at future, determines the meaning of what the living thing does. But Nietzsche carries this an important step further: a will's meaning lies not just in what its goal is – which is set by its willing – but also in whether it *will* be achieved. A will is essentially a striving, and its meaning lies not just in what it strives for, but in whether it will (whether in the future it does) reach its goal. So what does happen in the future – whether the drive in fact goes on to take an upward or a downward course – gives retroactive meaning to what the drive is doing now. Thus Nietzsche insists that we only understand a drive when we know whether it *will* overcome itself and make something stronger. He applies this especially to himself: he only grasps the significance of his earlier work by seeing later the mature achievements they issued in.

217

3.1.2

But it is vital to Nietzsche that this first temporal aspect of willing – its arc towards a goal – is not sufficient to determine meaning. Our deep belief in this sufficiency is reflected in our faith in our own free will: we suppose that will sets goals for itself by its own free acts, so that it *aims itself* at its goals. But in fact every will and drive *has been* aimed towards its goal by a process in the past, the process that "selected" this drive. And this is not, for Nietzsche, merely a causal point – nor his point against free will merely the lesson of a universal causal determinism. For the past process doesn't (as it were) release the drive to its own authority – the authority to have these meanings simply by the drive's own act of intending them. The selecting process doesn't merely cause the drive to have the end it does; it helps determine – logically – what that end is. It joins in settling the meaning of the drive, what it is for. It reaches into the drive's intentionality – helps to fix its content.

This idea belongs to Nietzsche's broad attack on our mental (or Cartesian) model of ourselves. That model, by which we ordinarily and automatically interpret our own agency, makes us miss the role of the past. We think the present is sufficient to settle our ends, because we think that our aiming consists (entirely) in a present representation or image of the outcome, plus a present desire that guides action towards it. But Nietzsche denies that this is how drives aim. They don't, as this model presumes, "aim themselves," by their own representation and desire. They *have been* aimed, by a process behind them, a selective process that assigns their aims for the sake of further ends of its own.

Nietzsche thinks that the past process helps to set meaning because he thinks of it too as intentional, as a kind of willing. The process that formed the drive gave it its goal for the sake of its own goal, its "selective criterion." It is part of the meaning and identity of the drive that it has been aimed in this way. Every drive has been "thrown" at its goal (to use a Heideggerian term), and as a means to some further goal. So it is never enough to say how it aims; we must add how (and for what) it was aimed.[17] This further element of meaning is usually not available to the drive itself.

To understand my own aims I must uncover the processes that shaped the drives working in me. I must grasp what *function* the drive plays in me, by seeing why I have it. Indeed the problem is harder. For typically a drive has been made not by a single directed process, but by a series of them, which have layered into it a series of functions still active in it, still part of the meaning of what it does. To understand such a drive I must identify these factors that made it, and untangle the layered functions it has been made to serve.[18] I must see how the drive is still playing these several roles in me.

So Nietzsche rejects our standard assumption that intentionality occurs in a present that all by itself has a content and aim. It is not only the present intention of the doing, but how it has been aimed, that fixes what it is genuinely "for." This shows that inhabiting perspectives is not enough to understand them: one needs also to step back from them to the viewpoints that made them. This point about the determination of meaning is at the root, I think, of the importance Nietzsche gives to *genealogy*. It is because meaning is received from the past that genealogy is necessary to uncover it. A drive has some of its meaning from its past. And since (we've seen) its meaning is also its effort at a future, we can really only specify its meaning when we see whether the effort will succeed. So meaning accrues to a willing from both its past and its future. Since meaning is dispersed into past and future in these ways, an organic process can't be understood as a succession of self-sufficient moments.[19] This temporal account of will is at the root, I think, of Nietzsche's insistence on a world of becoming not being: what is basic are processes, because what is basic are these wills, these perspective-meanings stretched from a past towards a future.[20]

3.2 The error in life's time

Let's turn from this temporal structure by which life makes meanings or contents to the way in which time shows up within these contents, i.e. to the time a will's perspective is "of." The time that shows up for life's perspective is different from the time that structures this perspective. Nietzsche treats this discrepancy as an *error* in life's view: the time it sees is different from the time it lives. Although life makes time by the temporal structure of its willing or striving, it has an equally deep-rooted tendency to mistake or distort this time whenever it brings it into view. Indeed it "serves life" (is of selective value) for life to misunderstand its own time.

Above all this error has to do with will's relation to its past. Will tends not to notice the past at all, and when it does it tends to mistake it. And these epistemological failures are connected with an affective misrelation to the past: life experiences "ill will" towards the past, due to its own inability to operate on the past. As we shall see, Nietzsche thinks this error over the past is compounded in the human case – and of course that's where his main interest lies. But he thinks our human error has its roots in an error built deeply into our bodies and drives. *HH* 18 says that all organisms miss the meaning of their experiences:

> when the sentient individuum observes itself, it regards every sensation [. . .] as something *isolated*, that is to say unconditioned, relationless; it emerges out of us without connection to the earlier or later. We are hungry, but originally we do not think that the organism wills to preserve itself, but that feeling seems to assert itself *without ground and purpose*, it isolates itself and considers itself *willful*. Thus: belief in freedom of the will is an original error of everything organic.

The beginning of the error is the obvious futural thrust of will. Its attention is primarily focused ahead at what is doable, and even the present is experienced secondarily in relation to this future. It is the nature of a will or drive to refer first to its goal, and to consider present conditions as (mere) means. And the past it need not refer to at all – the past needn't be a content in its perspective, and is probably not for most wills. And where a will does bring the past "into view" – where the drive orients its pursuit of its goal by some kind of reference to the past – it treats the past merely as a more removed kind of means, as a help in orienting its use of the present. To be helpful in this way, only small bits of the past can be noticed; most of it needs to be "forgotten" and suppressed. The organism's past experience is far too rich and complex to be a useful guide; it needs to forget nearly all of this experience.[21] It needs, in particular, to forget or overlook the role of the past in shaping its aims. To pursue wholeheartedly what it wants, it needs to suppress how its meanings have been set in the past. An organism that could not forget its own becoming this way could not succeed.[22]

Life's practical thrust as will or drive induces other temporal errors besides this mistake towards the past. Effective action depends, Nietzsche thinks, on the organism dividing up its environment into proto-substances persisting under change of properties, and interacting as proto-causes and effects. Organisms generally, in their plastic and responsive dispositions, sort their surroundings in this way, a deep root to our human faith in substances and causes. WP 552: "Life is founded on the presupposition of a belief in the enduring and regularly-recurring."[23]

Beyond these practical incentives for error Nietzsche also finds what we might call "existential" motives for *avoiding* seeing or acknowledging becoming. Becoming is disturbing to organisms in such a way that it is unpleasant to recognize it.[24] We can sum this up in the "ill will" Nietzsche says life feels towards time. This includes not only an aversion to the mutability of everything, but more particularly a dissatisfaction with the past, as beyond its effort. So, famously, in "Of Redemption" in *Thus Spoke Zarathustra*: "'It was': so is named the will's gnashing of teeth and most lonely misery. Powerless against what has been done – he is an angry spectator of all that is past." I will develop this point in the human case, where indeed it seems more plausible.

4 Human Time

A new kind of time develops in humans, by the evolution of memory, promising, and other capacities. As usual Nietzsche is largely critical of what others have generally seen as a pure progress our species has made. He offers ways in which human time is peculiarly "sick." He presents it as a distortion of the original time – uglier and less true (in key respects) than the time of will, which itself already tends to error, as we have seen.

For us the most obvious feature of human time is that it "reaches up into" consciousness: we take ourselves to be aware of time in a way that other organisms are not. But Nietzsche generally downgrades the importance of consciousness, and here too. That our time is conscious is only the tip of our difference from other organisms. A much more basic distinction is the special way in which we have become a "social animal." The key change in our temporality is the way this alters our relation to the past. I take Nietzsche to mean a point that has recently become popular: that humans are distinguished by their capacity to "learn habits" in social groups. As this capacity develops, a new kind of behavioral disposition comes onto the scene – one that replicates not by genetic inheritance, but by imitation or copying within a social group. Nietzsche often still calls these dispositions "drives," but I will call them "habits" or "practices." They are what Richard Dawkins has dubbed "memes." A new selection works on these new replicators, as they "compete" to disseminate through the population: habits are "judged" by their success at social transmission, at getting themselves copied (this is their fitness) (see Richardson 2004: ch. 2).

This doesn't really change the overall temporal logic by which our meanings are generated. What we do still has its meaning both in the way we reach towards goals, and in the way these goals have been embedded into us by selective processes (and aims) reaching well behind us. It's just that now the selective processes are social or cultural ones, designing habits or practices for social success. But the change does introduce a new selective criterion – success at social dissemination. Our learned habits have been designed for this end, and not to help us survive and grow. I think the root of Nietzsche's critique of "the human" is his diagnosis of how this new selective criterion works: in designing our habits/practices to be socially transmissible, this selection also designs *us* to be more effective instruments for such transmission. So it strongly designs us to be copiers, building into us an inclination to do as others do, and especially what "everyone" does. As Nietzsche succinctly puts it, it builds into us a "herd instinct." More generally, it designs individual humans "for the sake of" the social group – for the latter's cohesion and efficiency.

Our distinctive human time – the time that "appears" to us – is principally designed to further this socialization – to render us more viable social members, with a deep need to do and value the same as others. This socialization is chiefly served by developing – by overdeveloping – a relationship to the past, which aggravates both the epistemic and affective failings we have seen arise with life itself. It is this aggravated relation to the past that most distinguishes our human temporality – and that is most at fault in Nietzsche's critique of it. Our temporality is spoiled by the way we dwell on the past, and subject ourselves to it.

Humans' new kind of disposition – the socially transmitted habit – is only possible by individuals becoming able to remember, first and most importantly, the social practice, "what one does." This is why, as *GM* II. 1 famously says, a memory has been bred into humans. Members need to remember the rules – and need to remember them especially when their bred-in bodily drives incline and impel them differently. The hungry person has to remember not to take another's food. Something needs to be interposed between the instinctive desire and its impulsive execution, and what is interposed is this newly explicit memory. Our human intentionality is stretched back into our past, as a way to herd (socialize) us.

At an early stage of this social evolution – the long phase Nietzsche calls the "ethic of custom" (*Sittlichkeit der Sitte*) – this memory was especially a memory of the grotesquely harsh punishments inflicted on rule-breakers. So memory reminded of a threatened pain, of a pain one had seen inflicted on others, or felt oneself. Nietzsche emphasizes the bloodiness of those punishments, and hence of the memory that kept them in mind. *GM* II. 3: "With the help of such images and procedures one finally holds in memory five or six 'I will nots', in regard to which one had given one's *promise*, in order to live under the benefits of society, – and really! with the help of this kind of memory one came finally 'to reason'!" Memory short-circuits some insistent bodily drive, by recalling the pain linked with the drive's satisfaction.

Nietzsche distinguishes a second phase in social evolution, "morality" (*Moral*). Here memory serves the same function, but in a different way. Memory is "moralized," by becoming an awareness not of punishment, but of guilt. Society's members now copy the practice of feeling bad conscience for past noncompliance with "what's done"; this is magnified by treating this guilt as "before god," and a god that is rendered all-present and all-knowing. Now memory intrudes on drives and desires not by inter-posing fear of punishment, but with a chronic and gloomy guilt over our bodily drives, and the past misdeeds they've led us to. And this worsens our already unhappy relation to the past.[25]

So our time-consciousness is originally an awareness of the past, used to stall and inhibit action by the drives. Secondarily it also extends forwards: we remember the rules in order to set our sights on new goals different from the objects of our drives. This awareness likewise functions to align us with our duties. Humans first learned to fix consciously on goals, as animals cannot, for the herding purpose of conforming them to social rules. Once this consciousness of future and past is developed, it can of course be given other functions and applications – we can remember more than our duties, and foresee more than our commitments. But Nietzsche thinks our temporality's long design for the latter purposes has not and cannot be left behind altogether. Our awareness of time still bears marks of this initial (and ongoing) function.

Our unhealthy relation to our past is Nietzsche's favorite point about our human temporality – and his commonest criticism of it. But beyond this he tells a much richer story, detailing many other aspects, and to support other criticisms. I will quickly mention two of these further points. Each is a way in which he thinks humans worsen defects we have seen are already present in the "time of will." First, our consciousness of time aggravates a fear of becoming. We invent being as an effort to forget or avoid change – in particular the inevitability of decline and death. We are particularly disturbed by any thought of flux in values. Our faiths in absolute and permanent values, and in our own deathless essences, are ideologies selected as responses to that fear. Second, our consciousness also worsens mistakes about time that arose with animality. We develop as conscious theory the view animals already take, of the world as carved up into persisting things – discrete causes working on one another and on us. We embed in our language and common sense a "metaphysics" already at work in organisms' experience generally, so that it permeates all our thoughts and theories. These mistakes are the channels through which we are able to speak and think.

5 Eternal Return

Nietzsche aspires to show us a way we can overcome this human predicament – our unhappy relation to time. He preaches, of course, the overman, who is distinguished, I will suggest, by a new temporality. Nietzsche's ideal is a new way of "being in time," consisting especially in a new practical orientation – a new way of aiming (and of acting with aims). In its full or strict form, Nietzsche thinks no one has achieved this: it lies as far above us as we lie above animals. He often depicts the overman as a solitary, world-historical individual, which (post-adolescent) readers see they have no chance to become. Still, he also offers *parts* of this ideal to us to pursue: we should try to have whatever and as much as we can of it. By achieving the parts in ourselves, we prepare for our human achievement (in another individual) of *all* these parts. Programmatically put: this new way of "being in time" heals the unhealthy obsession with the past that characterizes our moral stance. It cures our species-typical ill will towards time, and overcomes our fear of becoming. Indeed it resolves a more basic discrepancy that (we've seen) typifies life and drives generally: between the time "in" them and the time "for" them; it aligns or harmonizes these, so that one views time just as one lives it. Nietzsche often calls this new temporality "Dionysian," and developing this concept would be one way to specify the point about time I think he has in mind. But I will focus instead on his thought of eternal return, his densest clarification of the new temporality.

Nietzsche regarded his thought of eternal return as his most important idea about time. It is the capstone of the book (*Thus Spoke Zarathustra*) he never ceased to think was his deepest and most telling. As is now familiar, he mainly means this idea not as a "cosmological" thesis about the real structure of the world-process, but as a psychological challenge or test. He calls on us to "will" the eternal return of everything – everything about our own lives, and about the world's whole course. This would be a Dionysian willing, and the way an overman wills. We are to live so that we *can will* eternal return. So his point is to offer us not primarily a theory, but a certain project or effort (see *GS* 341).

It is a project whose role is to control other projects – so that it is a kind of meta-project. It is to be, indeed, one's ruling project, or archi-project. A first way Nietzsche puts this is that eternal return is a test one makes other projects pass, before pursuing them: you need to ask yourself in each act whether you want it always again. So it plays the same role as Kant's categorical imperative – it looks very much like Nietzsche's revision of Kant's criterion. In this role the project rules by standing back and waiting for action plans to be offered by other sources; it then exercises a veto power over some of them, authorizing others to proceed.

But I think Nietzsche wants the idea of return to do more than this. It's not just a prior test, external to the projects it approves – a mere gatekeeper. It plays too a more active part in generating and shaping those action plans.[26] One shapes them so as to be better able to will their return, and one tries so to will them while pursuing them. So the idea reaches into those projects themselves, is a new way of aiming within those projects. This is what it is to "incorporate" that idea: one needs to work it into one's practical, "bodily" efforts. You pursue your projects *as* embedded in a world that eternally returns. Nietzsche is convinced that this works a major transformation in your practical stance: it gives you a new way of going towards goals, and a new way of being in time.

What most distinguishes and favors this new project, I think, is an epistemic virtue, together with the health and strength it both manifests and furthers. This temporal stance overcomes the errors ("lies") about time that have typified humans. And in doing so it removes – or shows that one no longer suffers from – the needs and motives that had driven us into these lies. Up to now we have needed to *view* time differently from how we *are* in time, by the logic of our drives' perspectivity. We have needed to view acts and goals as set in a temporal context quite unlike the one in which they really occur. Willing eternal return proves one strong enough to master this need for lies, and to view goals with the temporality they really do have.

There is a problem here. If Nietzsche doesn't mean to claim ("cosmologically") that the world cycles eternally through the same overall process – if he allows that this is or may be false – how could he think that believing or willing eternal return overcomes errors? If becoming doesn't (or even can't) have this circular character, how could believing or willing it bring us into any truth about time?[27] I think the answer must be that eternal return is a kind of metaphor or stand-in for other things that Nietzsche claims *are* true. We make ourselves strong enough for those other truths, by willing eternal return. The challenge is then to specify these truths that stand behind the idea of eternal return.[28]

I think the most important such truth is the one treated above: the temporal structure of will and perspectivity. Eternal return is a metaphor for how meaning is not determined in any present by itself, but only in this present's relation to a future goal, and a past "aimedness." Meaning lies in what the present is trying to do, and in what the past was trying to do by making the present try to do it. And it lies in whether these projects will succeed – in what will come from them. So meaning lies not in self-contained Nows, but in the nexus of each Now with its distinctive future and past. This idea, if we can incorporate it, will work a major change in how we think of and enact our agency. It is this idea that lies behind Nietzsche's favorite model for eternal return, the *circle*. In willing eternal return we think of becoming as a circle, or even time as a circle. This model stresses to us how times are knotted together: how the present never leaves behind its past, and how it is also tied to a fated future. In thinking time as a circle, we imagine that the future has already been, and that the past will be again, which conveys the relevance they really do have to meaning now. We imagine them all "present" together in the ring, which reminds us how meaning lies in temporal relations.[29]

In the metaphor of eternal return what binds the circle together is an inexorable causal determinism, which leads the world-process eternally back through the same sequence. So future events are causes of past events, the next time the latter come around, and "determine" them in this sense. This metaphor stands in, I suggest, for the different way in which the future determines the meaning of the past, sketched above: the future specifies what the past was on the way to.[30] So time is bound together not by a back-looping causality, but by the logic of the meaning of intentional wills.

Of course the challenge is not just to imagine becoming as a circle in this way, but to will it so, and to do so within one's particular projects. I must try to will my goals as carrying around the circle to my past – the past that made me such as to will those goals. Again the point is not the literal one: there are no concrete things I can do to make it more likely that the whole world-course will repeat. So I can't try to cause the past by my choice of future goals.[31] The circle is not a causal one, but a meaning-giving one: I choose my goals (partly) for the sake of the past – for the sake of making that past issue in as fine a future as I can achieve. So, again, we can cash out the metaphor in "willing the eternal return of the same." I want my goals for the sake of my past, and for my past just as it was. But with these goals I try to change the meaning of that past – making it turn out to issue in an upshot that honors and ennobles it. So I aspire to "redeem" the past, in a favorite expression of Nietzsche's.[32] By willing in this spirit I affirm my past, rather than resenting it (as beyond my control) or feeling guilty over it (as poorly done by me). This proves that I have overcome the "ill will" towards the past that Nietzsche thinks typifies humanity. This meta-project of willing return also changes my relation to the present. I see that it too will be magnified and glorified by "becoming" something different and finer. So I give up clinging to present conditions, and take on that delight in destroying which Nietzsche associates with Dionysus. I see that even my allegiance to who and what I am, is best served by overcoming this present for the sake of a future that reflects well on

224

its capacity. The overman instantiates this stance at the broad cultural level: in the overman, who makes new values by destroying the old, the culture redeems itself by destroying itself (its present condition).

In these ways willing eternal return expresses a "good will" towards the past and becoming that Nietzsche thinks humans have deeply lacked. So he thinks it is the healthiest way of willing – and the healthiest way of living with time. It overcomes guilt and resentment at becoming and the past. So it re-achieves an "innocence of becoming" that has always characterized non-human life. This new temporality is also the hardest way of willing, which commends it still more to Nietzsche. As he early interprets Heraclitus: "The everlasting and exclusive becoming, the complete imper-manence of everything actual, which constantly acts and becomes but is not, as Heraclitus teaches, is a terrible and paralyzing idea [. . .] It takes astonishing strength to transform this reaction into its opposite, into sublimity and delighted astonishment" (PTAG 5).

6 Conclusion on Realism and Idealism

Now that we have Nietzsche's story about our temporality, let's return briefly to our framing question whether his theory of becoming is ultimately realist or idealist. In order to say what he does in this story, what are his commitments?

The story describes how a phenomenal or intentional time – a temporality – arises and evolves in animals, humans, and (potentially) superhumans. This phenomenal time has two aspects that are separated already among animals, forced further apart in humans, but then (potentially) reconciled and resolved in the overman's willing of eternal return. There is, on the one hand, the background temporality by which perspectivity and meaning arise and evolve, and on the other the way time appears for (or to) the perspectives that so arise. Temporality occurs both as the form and the content of perspectives. Only by willing eternal return can we hope to align these with one another. These two aspects of perspectivity already give Nietzsche a kind of appearance–reality distinction, even while he talks only about perspectives. We have seen that he indeed treats our conception of time as *false about* the time that constitutes our meanings and values. This responds to the puzzle we saw is posed to an idealist or perspectivist reading of him: how to interpret his strong skepticism against most perspectives – his insistence they are *false* – if there is no non-perspectival reality to judge them against. The time by or in which perspectives with meanings arise can serve as such a standard, and the time that appears to or for perspectives can be plausibly judged against it – and all while talking only about perspectives.

Yet I don't think we should conclude that Nietzsche's theory of time is therefore idealist rather than realist. Indeed, even that notion of a time that is "of" but not "for" perspectives – that belongs to them without appearing to them – introduces a kind of non-perspectival truth about time. Wills and their meanings are "stretched" through time, at future ends and by a past design; this time belongs to these wills even though it doesn't appear to them. So wills have a time not constituted by any perspectives on it – which already makes the "perspectivism" less radical than we might have thought. That is, we might take perspectivism to claim not just that all truths "have to do with" perspectives, but that all truths must be "for" perspectives, i.e. contents for them. This realist tendency is even stronger because of how Nietzsche determines this temporal logic of wills. He does so in the light of the most recent biology, and especially its evolutionary theory. He interprets these wills as drives in organisms – as powers of complex physical bodies. He takes that theory to show how these drives have their aims and meanings through selective processes that worked on prior generations of such bodies. Bodies are selected for their powers to grow and replicate themselves, within environments consisting not just in other organisms, but in inorganic stuffs and conditions as well. So Nietzsche's account of the temporality of wills rests back on his naturalist allegiance to a physical reality, within which these wills have evolved.

Given this naturalistic way in which Nietzsche means to explain wills and perspectives, I don't think he can avoid supposing a time that is independent of those wills – a time in which not just organisms' bodies but all matter interacts, including inorganic matter that does not support perspectival wills. Although Nietzsche is of course mainly or even purely interested in understanding these wills and their temporalities, this understanding locates them in a natural world to which I think he can't help but assign a prior, non-perspectival time of its own. So despite his strong sentiments in favor of a temporal idealism or perspectivism, I think Nietzsche's naturalistic account of perspectives, including of the temporalities I have surveyed, draws him back towards a temporal realism after all.

See also 3 "The Aesthetic Justification of Existence"; 5 "The Individual and Individuality in Nietzsche"; 16 "Phenomenology and Science in Nietzsche"; 28 "Nietzsche and Evolutionary Theory"

Notes

1 On my reading Nietzsche's treatment of time has many points of contact with that of Henri Bergson. I will point out some of these connections in notes. An analysis of the intimate connections between Nietzsche and Bergson as philosophers who think notions of time and life in the wake of the Darwinian revolution merits the future attention of Nietzsche research.

2 See Clark 1990 on different versions of this reading of eternal return.

3 See e.g. *GS* 370 on different motives for these preferences. *TI*, "'Reason' in Philosophy," 1, associates philosophers' "lack of historical sense" with a hatred of becoming.

4 In *HH* 638 he describes himself as a "wanderer" who finds pleasure in "change and transitoriness."

5 This is in strong contrast, we should note, with Kant's *justificatory* use of his own theory of time. Positive and negative verdicts about appearance are both ingredients in Kantianism, as beliefs are judged by either empirical or transcendental standards. But Kant stresses appearance's truth, Nietzsche its falsity.

6 *WP* 1064 makes the point about "force": "That 'force' and 'rest' 'remaining the same' contradict one another. The measure of force as magnitude as fixed, but its essence fluid, stretching, forcing, – / 'Timelessness' to be rejected. In a determinate moment of the force the absolute conditionality of a new distribution of all its forces is given: it cannot stand still."

7   Bergson concurs in (a), (b), (c), and (d), in application to our experience: "this substratum [the ego persisting beneath changing psychic states] has no reality" (Bergson 1983: 4); "[t]he truth is that we change without ceasing, and that the state itself is nothing but change" (1983: 2); "states thus defined cannot be regarded as distinct elements. They continue each other in an endless flow" (1983: 3). See also "The Perception of Change" (Bergson 1946), page 147: "*There are changes, but there are underneath the change no things which change; change has no need of a support.*"

8   So Green (2002: 51–2): "Thus Nietzsche's rejection of a real world of 'being' in favor of a contingent world of 'becoming' is less a claim about what the world is like than a claim about our cognitive relation to the world. It means questioning our ability to make objectively valid judgments about the world at all."

9   For an analog in Kant we would need to find suggestions that the noumenon is not just non-temporal, but positively eternal etc.

10 We'll see that reading 2.4 will show another way to accommodate this point: becoming is really true of perspectives, even though it is not what appear to perspectives, not what they are "of."

11 See the argument to this effect in Cox (1999: 176–84). He goes on to argue for what I read as a version of my 2.3 following.

12 *WP* 567: "As if a world would still remain over when one deducted the perspective!"

13 For an analog in Kant we would need to find ways he characterizes the time in which the self or mind "makes phenomena" by imposing time, space, and the categories on raw sensation.

14 In both respects Nietzsche has more affinity with Bergson, who says, "Each being cuts up the material world according to the lines that its action must follow: it is these lines of *possible action* that, by intercrossing, mark out the net of experience of which each mesh is a fact" (1983: 367).

15 *WP* 260: "But willing: = willing an end. End includes an evaluation." *WP* 668: "there is no 'willing,' but only a *willing-something*: one must not remove the aim from the situation." In many cases, I think, we should think of this aiming as towards not just a single goal, but a nested network of goals, including means and submeans. The will's effort at the goal includes an ability to navigate towards it; it perceives signs of helps or avenues, and aims for these as well.

16 *KSA* 11, 25[433]: " 'Alive:' that means already *valuing* – / In all willing is *valuing* – and will is there in the organic."

17 In *Nietzsche's New Darwinism* (Richardson 2004) I argue that it is only by an "etiological" sense for ends that Nietzsche is able, as he so wants, to dispense with the mental model for directedness and meaning. For the drive's present plastic disposition is insufficient to make its outcomes "goals" at all. It is only because the disposition was "selected" for this outcome that the outcome can explain the disposition in the way it must if it is to be a goal.

18 Nietzsche sometimes suggests that the whole evolutionary history of the organism's line, all its ancestors, contribute to its meaning or identity; see e.g. *WP* 687, 785. Compare Bergson: in order to explain it, "*all* the past of the organism must be added to that moment [immediately before], its heredity – in fact, the whole of a very long history" (1983: 20; also 43).

19 Bergson likewise denies that this "mathematical" conception of "a world that dies and is reborn in every instant" is valid for life (1983: 22).

20 See how *WP* 556 calls wills to power becomings: "One should not ask: 'so *who* interprets?' but rather the interpreting, as a form of will to power, itself has existence (but not as a 'being,' but as a *process*, a *becoming*) as an affect."

21 Compare Bergson: "Our past [...] is necessarily automatically preserved. It survives complete. But our practical interest is to thrust it aside" (1946: 137). And later: "Nature has invented a mechanism for canalizing our attention in the direction of the future, in order to turn it away from the past – I mean of that part of our history which does not concern our present actions" (1946: 153).

22 See *UM II*, 1: "Imagine [...] a human who does not possess the power to forget, who is condemned to see a becoming everywhere: such a one no longer believes in his own being, no longer believes in himself, sees everything flowing apart in moving points and loses himself in this stream of becoming: like the true student of Heraclitus he will finally scarcely dare to lift a finger."

23 *WP* 517: "a kind of becoming must itself create the *deception* of *beings*." *WP* 480: "In order for a determinate kind to preserve itself – and grow in its power – , it must grasp in its conception of reality enough that is calculable and constant, that it can construct a scheme of behavior on it."

24 *KSA* 10, 2[110]: " 'Being' as an invention by one suffering from becoming."

25 This guilt is designed not just to herd us, but also to vent the aggressive and cruel drives that have been suppressed by the first stage's "civilizing" work. *GM* II gives Nietzsche's elaborate account of this development.

26 See how Clark argues (1990: 252) that it is not a decision-procedure but an ideal – to be the kind of person who would affirm eternal return (under conditions Clark specifies).

27 It may be less of a problem why believing a (possible) falsehood should *benefit* us: Nietzsche gives many examples how errors can be selected. But I claim that this benefit comes in grasping certain truths.

28 Other interpreters who deny that Nietzsche means the cosmological point have likewise tried to find some other truth behind it. Compare the "weaker view" that Nehamas argues (2001: 123) Nietzsche really means: "in this, and in every moment, is implicit everything that has occurred in the past and everything that will occur in the future." Nehamas later describes the core idea: "if we were to have another life it would have to be, if it were to be *our* life at all, the very same life that we have already had" (2001: 129).

29 Bergson likewise advocates a grasp of the interconnections of present with past and future: "Through philosophy we can accustom ourselves never to isolate the present from the past which it pulls along with it [...] [permitting] anterior perceptions to remain bound up with present perceptions, and the immediate future itself to become partly outlined in the present" (1946: 157).

30 Again compare Nehamas (2001: 133), on "the realization that the significance of the past depends on its importance to the future."

31 Clark (1990: 259) points out that it is a feature of eternal return that when the past repeats it does so exactly, so that we can't change the past; she thinks Nietzsche's point can only be, then, that we change our attitude towards it, by affirming eternal return. But this leaves out a way in which I *can* "change the past," i.e. by giving it different significance by the future I make for it now.

32 Z, "Of Redemption": "To redeem the past of humans and to recreate all 'It was,' until the will says 'But so I willed it! So shall I will it –.' " On redemption see especially Anderson (forthcoming), and his development of the idea in the example of Jimmy Carter.

References

Anderson, R. L. (2005). "Nietzsche on Truth, Illusion, and Redemption," *European Journal of Philosophy*, 13(2), pp. 185–226.

Bergson, Henri (1946). "The Perception of Change," trans. M. Andison, in *The Creative Mind: An Introduction to Metaphysics* (New York: Philosophical Library).

—— (1983). *Creative Evolution*, trans. A. Mitchell (Lanham, MD: University Press of America).

Clark, Maudemarie (1990). *Nietzsche on Truth and Philosophy* (Cambridge: Cambridge University Press).

Cox, Christoph (1999). *Nietzsche: Naturalism and Interpretation* (Berkeley: University of California Press).

Gemes, Ken (1992). "Nietzsche's Critique of Truth," *Philosophy and Phenomenological Research* 52(1), pp. 47–65.

Green, Michael S. (2002). *Nietzsche and the Transcendental Tradition* (Urbana and Chicago: University of Illinois Press).

Nehamas, Alexander (2001). "The Eternal Recurrence," in John Richardson and Brian Leiter (eds.), *Nietzsche* (Oxford: Oxford University Press), pp. 118–39; first published in *The Philosophical Review*, 89 (1980), pp. 331–56.

Richardson, John (1996). *Nietzsche's System* (New York: Oxford University Press).

—— (2004). *Nietzsche's New Darwinism* (New York: Oxford University Press).

Soll, Ivan (1973). "Reflections on Recurrence: A Re-examination of Nietzsche's Doctrine, *die ewige Wiederkehr des Gleichen*," in Robert Solomon (ed.), *Nietzsche: A Collection of Critical Essays* (Garden City, NY: Doubleday).

13

The Incorporation of Truth: Towards the Overhuman

KEITH ANSELL PEARSON

Has not the philosophy that aims primarily for *certainty* already passed over *all fundamental truths*, and opened out into the inconsequentiality of a "wholly secure" knowledge? To put the question still more radically: is not regress to secure and apodictically certain truths an *avoidance* of the real problems, a *flight* from the insecurity and *eeriness* of unsettled human existence?

(Fink 1995: 46)

We, however, *want to become those who we are* – the ones who are new, unique, incomparable, self-legislating, self-creating.

(*GS* 335)

In this essay I provide a treatment of unfamiliar (and remarkable) material from Nietzsche's unpublished writings, alongside published material that is often not given the attention it merits, in an effort to secure some new and fresh insights into his figuration of the overhuman (*Übermensch*). The overhuman is often taken to be a projection of Nietzsche's personal ideal of human excellence and flourishing. For many readers and commentators it is an utterly fantastical one. I would argue, however, that this "projection" is, in fact, intimately bound up with the tasks and experiments Nietzsche outlines in his "free-spirit trilogy" of 1878–82 (the books *Human, All Too Human, Daybreak, and The Gay Science*). We find them outlined as a set in his very first sketch of the thought of the eternal return from August 1881 in which Nietzsche presents himself as the teacher of "the weightiest knowledge." If Nietzsche has a conception of the perfectibility of the human this cannot be thought independently of our recognizing the complexity and difficulty of our now being human. The declaration made in the prologue to *Thus Spoke Zarathustra* that the overhuman "shall now be the meaning [*Sinn*] of the earth" should not be understood in abstraction from the tasks of the free spirit. This is not to say that the notion is *not* a fantastical projection on Nietzsche's part. The task is to understand the nature of the so-called fantasy at work in Nietzsche's thinking.

Operative throughout Nietzsche's writings, from his early reflections on the pathos of truth (1872) to his later call for a critique of the will to truth (1887), is what we might call a certain "care" of truth, even where this involves posing strange and novel questions of it and calling our will to it into question. In 1881/2 Nietzsche's specific question about truth concerns its incorporation. My claim is that when Nietzsche inquires after the incorporation of truth, he is in essence asking after the possibility of our becoming overhuman (conceived as a condition of maturity), and showing that this denotes a site of difficulty and complexity.[1]

The essay is divided into three parts. In the first section I discuss Nietzsche's first sketch of the eternal return. This sketch is of great interest on account of Nietzsche's stress on the "incorporation of truth and knowledge" as a principal task now confronting human beings. In the second section I turn my attention to the presentation of the incorporation of truth we encounter in *GS* 110 and explore the kind of truth Nietzsche has in mind. In the third and final section I highlight some of the core aspects of Nietzsche's thinking on knowledge and self-knowledge. My overriding aim in the essay is to cast some light on the deeply enigmatic character of Nietzsche's thinking and to begin the task of opening up the riddles he presents his readers with.

The Weightiest Knowledge

In Nietzsche's first sketch of the doctrine of the eternal return of the same the thought is invoked in the context of his attempt to highlight the fundamental issues that concern the fate of the human being.[2] The sketch takes the form of a plan for a book in five parts and appears in the notebook "M III, 1." Part 1 will be on the incorporation of the fundamental errors; part 2 will be on the incorporation of the passions; part 3 will cover the incorporation of knowledge and of renunciatory knowledge (Nietzsche calls this the "passion of knowledge"); part 4 will be on "the innocent one" and "the individual as experiment" (Nietzsche refers to "the alleviation of life, abasement, enfeeblement," and speaks of a point of transition (*Übergang*)); part 5 will be on "the heavy new *burden* [*Schwergewicht*]: *the eternal return of the same.*" The task, Nietzsche says, is to demonstrate the "infinite importance of our knowing, erring, habits, ways of living for all that is to come." The question is then asked: "What shall we do with the *rest* of our lives – we who have spent the majority of our lives in the most profound ignorance? We shall *teach the teaching* – it is the most powerful means of *incorporating* [*einzuverleiben*] it in ourselves. Our kind of blessedness [*Seligkeit*], as teachers of the greatest teaching." There then follows the sublime signature, "Early August 1881 in Sils-Maria, 6,000 feet above sea level and much higher above all human things!"

In the sketch only part 4 of the projected book is given an extended treatment by Nietzsche, and this forms the bulk of the rest of the sketch. It is worth citing in full:

> On 4) Philosophy of Indifference [*Gleichgültigkeit*]. What used to be the strongest stimulus now has a quite different effect: it is seen as just a *game* and accepted (the passions and labors), rejected on principle as a life of untruth, but aesthetically enjoyed and cultivated as form and stimulus; we adopt a child's attitude towards what used to constitute the *seriousness of existence*. The seriousness of our striving, though, is to understand everything as becoming, to deny ourselves as individuals, to look into the world through as *many* eyes as possible, to *live in* drives and activities **so as** to create eyes for ourselves, *temporarily* abandoning ourselves to life so as to rest our eye on it temporarily afterwards: to *maintain* the drives as the foundation of all knowing, but to know at what point they

become the enemies of knowing: in sum, to **wait and see** how far *knowledge* [*Wissen*] and *truth* can be **incorporated** – and to what extent a transformation of man occurs when he finally lives only *so as to know* [*erkennen*]. – This is a consequence of the passion of knowledge [*Erkenntniss*]: there is *no way of ensuring its existence* except by preserving as well the sources and powers of knowledge, the errors and passions; from the *conflict* between them it draws its sustaining strength. – What will this life look like from the point of view of its sum total of well-being? *A children's game* under the gaze of the wise man, with power over *the latter and the former* conditions – and over death, if such a thing is not possible. – But now comes the weightiest knowledge [*Erkenntniss*], one which prompts the terrible reconsideration of all forms of life: an absolute surplus of pleasure **must** be demonstrable, or else we must choose to destroy ourselves with regard to humanity as a means of destroying humanity. Just this: we have to put the past – our past and that of all humanity – on the scales and *also* outweigh it – no! this piece of human history *will* and must repeat [*wiederholen*] itself eternally; we can leave *that* out of account, we have no influence over it: even if it afflicts our fellow-feeling and biases us against life in general. If we are not to be overwhelmed by it, our compassion must not be great. Indifference needs to have worked away deep inside us, and enjoyment in contemplation, too. Even the misery of future humanity must *not* concern us. But the question is whether *we* still *want to live*: and how![3]

Incorporation is clearly the key word at work in the first sketch, and it is the incorporation of truth and knowledge that I want to focus on in my interpretation. First, however, let me attempt to open up some of the other intriguing motifs at work in the sketch, including the passion of knowledge, the principle of indifference, and the thought of innocence (*Unschuld*).

In a note from 1881 Nietzsche writes on Spinoza and his own project as follows: "Spinoza says: We are only determined in our actions by desires and affects. Knowledge must be affect in order to be a motive. I say: it must be a *passion* to be a motive" (*KSA* 9, 11[193]). Nietzsche first writes of the "passion of knowledge" (*Leidenschaft der Erkenntniss*) in *Daybreak* (1881) and it is referred to earlier in the notebook prior to its appearance in the sketch on the eternal return (see *KSA* 9 11[69]). In *D* 429 Nietzsche notes that the drive to knowledge has become so strongly rooted in us that we cannot now want happiness without knowledge. Knowledge has become a deep-rooted passion that shrinks at no sacrifice. Indeed, such is now our passion for knowledge that even the prospect of humanity perishing from this passion does not exert any real influence on us.

Part 4 of the planned book on "the philosophy of indifference," and the appeal to a principle of "indifference" as that which must have worked its way deeply into us, refer us back to the decision Nietzsche had made in the opening chapter of *Human, All Too Human* with respect to the first and last things. Nietzsche provides the clearest account of his post-metaphysical position in aphorism 16 of *The Wanderer and his Shadow* entitled "where indifference is needed" (*Worin Gleichgültigkeit noth thut*). Here he states that the impulse to want certainties in the domain of the first and last things is a "*religious* after-shoot" and is to be approached as "a hidden and only apparently skeptical species of the 'metaphysical need'." He insists that a "full and excellent human life" can be led without these certainties. What is needed is knowledge of the origin of the "calamitous weightiness" mankind has for so long accorded to these things. A history of ethical and religious sensations and concepts, such as guilt and punishment, will provide us with the knowledge we now require. The new "lovers of knowledge" will practice indifference against the claims of both faith and knowledge in the domain of the last things (what is the purpose of man? What is his fate after death? how can he be reconciled with God?, and so on). In a note in M III, 1 that is prior to the sketch on eternal return, Nietzsche presents indifference as a specifically modern phenomenon and proposes that it can serve as a basis for the scientific spirit. He argues that the quantity of things that do not concern us and that we can think what we like about is increasing: "the world has become ever more indifferent to us, therefore this neutral knowledge is also on the increase. It gradually becomes a *taste* and finally a passion" (11[110]).

In the 1881 sketch Nietzsche is making use of indifference as a means of enabling the decision that is required of our singularity: what is it now that we are to be indifferent towards and what is to be our utmost concern? Eternal return is the thought that seeks to establish a center of gravity with respect to this unique task. In number 220 of this notebook from 1881 Nietzsche writes that "the most powerful thought" uses the energy that has hitherto been at the command of other goals (*Zielen*). It thus has a "transforming effect" not through the creation of any new energy but simply by creating "new laws of movement for energy." It is in this sense that it holds "the possibility of determining and ordering individual human beings and their affects differently."

Part 4 of the plan contains a cryptic reference to the innocent man. We know that the thought of innocence runs deep in Nietzsche; his most fundamental anti-metaphysical doctrine is that of the "innocence of becoming." As Heidegger notes, with the death of the moral God notions of sin and guilt "vanish from being as a whole" (Heidegger 1961: 333, 1984: 77). Nietzsche posits himself as a "halcyonian" who will work with all his might, and utilize the energy of knowledge, to purify psychology, the study of history, social institutions, and sanctions of the concepts of guilt and punishment, that is, of the entire metaphysics of morality (*KSA* 13, 15[30]; *WP* 765), including the "cloddish simplicity" of the notion of free will which involves the self yearning to construe itself as a metaphysical *causa sui* (a miraculous self-causing substance) (*BGE* 22; see also *TI*, "The Four Great Errors," 8).[4] There will necessarily be different psychological reactions to the new conditions of human existence. Some will experience a sense of liberation, some a sense of abasement, and others will feel enfeebled. The situation is similar to how Nietzsche will portray the advent of nihilism in later notebooks of the 1880s, where he construes nihilism as the "ultimate logical conclusion of our great values and ideals" (*WP*, preface, 4), and speaks of active and passive modes of nihilism that reflect either an increased power or a diminished power of the spirit (*WP* 22). Part 5 of the sketch follows the point of transition (*Übergang*) with the new teaching presented as the new burden: the eternal return of the same. Contained in the thoughts for part 5 is what we might call Nietzsche's unique Spinozism. We know that the thought of eternal return comes to Nietzsche only a few days after his discovery of Spinoza. In a letter to his friend Franz Overbeck postmarked July 30, 1881, Nietzsche enumerates the points of doctrine he shares with Spinoza, such as the denial of free will, of a moral world order, and of evil, and also mentions the task of "making knowledge the most *powerful passion*" (Middleton 1996: 177). In the sketch of 1881 Nietzsche conceives the movement beyond previous ignorance in terms of a new practice of knowledge and suggests that the new knowers will find their blessedness or beatitude in being the teachers of the doctrine of eternal return.[5] This can be understood as a kind of ultimate or decisive knowledge with respect to our looking at life from out of a concern with, and an awareness of, its overall well-being. Let's suppose we discover that we do indeed wish to live; we then face the difficult question of *how* we will live.

In the final part of the passage concerning the "weightiest knowledge" the essential movement of thought at work in the sketch discloses itself. It appears to be twofold: a stress is placed on the incorporation of truth and knowledge as the distinctive task of modern humanity, as that which will mark it out, and the disclosure that this singular experiment will repeat itself and do so eternally. The disclosure of the eternal return of the same places a specific burden on us: we are to experience the "infinite importance" of our knowing, erring, habits and ways of life for all that is now to come (the thought seems to concern our futural present and to do so at its deepest level), *and* we are not to feel overwhelmed by this insight. Modern human beings can learn to practice indifference with respect to the first and last things of traditional metaphysics. In the 1881 sketch indifference is aimed not at these first and last things but at the eternal repetition of the different ages or epochs of human history, including our own. The possible future misery of humanity – that it may regress, that it may be wiped out or suffer in some way we cannot foretell – is not our concern. Our concern is with ourselves (we idealists of knowledge and godless anti-metaphysicians, as Nietzsche defines us in the *Genealogy*), and with whether we godless moderns, who exist largely in order to know, wish to live, and how.

In number 144 of the notebook Nietzsche stresses the innocent character of his thought; it is one that neither apportions blame to those who are overwhelmed by it nor merit to those who are not. He advises that whilst we can lament the incorporated errors of previous humankind we cannot attribute any "evil." We find ourselves being milder towards our ancestors than they could be to themselves. He then speaks of "the most powerful knowledge" and acknowledges the transformative character of incorporated errors (they provide us with new drives), and concludes with an appeal to "the play of life." This is in accord with what we encounter in the long sketch 141: we are to adopt an attitude of play and innocence with respect to the past. Nietzsche envisages the project of the gay or joyful science being practiced in this manner. It refers to the "ideal of a spirit who plays naively – that is, not deliberately, but from overflowing powers and abundance – with all that has hitherto been called good, untouchable, divine . . . the ideal of a human, superhuman well-being and bene-volence that will often appear *inhuman* – for example, when it confronts all earthly seriousness so far" (GS 382). Nietzsche stresses that although an incarnate and in-voluntary parody is operative in such a well-being and generosity of life, "the real question mark is posed for the first time," "the destiny of the soul changes," and "the tragedy *begins*."

The first sketch shows that at the center of Nietzsche's thinking is the issue of the incorporation of truth and knowledge. But how does Nietzsche conceive incorporation? And what exactly does he have in mind when he speaks of the incorporation of truth? What is the "truth" he is appealing to and naming? To these topics I now turn.

Truth and its Incorporation

Although incorporation is a crucial term in Nietzsche's philosophical vocabulary, it is rarely subjected to investigation.[6] David Farrell Krell has argued that the emergence of incorporation in Nietzsche's thinking in 1881 is the direct result of his reading work in the natural sciences, notably physiology, and especially Wilhelm Roux's text of 1881 *The Struggle of Parts in the Organism*.[7] However, while Nietzsche did indeed read Roux at this time, and then several times again in the 1880s, the notion of incorporation is one that figures in Nietzsche from his earliest published writings. It plays an important role, for example, in his thinking on the uses and disadvantages of history for life. In the opening section of this meditation Nietzsche situates incorporation in the same context of problems that come to inform his first sketch of eternal return in 1881, including the regulation of knowledge, the importance of forgetting, and determining the time of memory and of forgetting within the economy of the living (Nietzsche speaks of being able to forget and to remember at the right time). He writes: "this is a universal law: a living thing can be healthy, strong and fruitful only when bounded by a horizon" (*UM II*, 1). The living power of a human being, a people, and a culture is a plastic power, which is a power formed through processes of assimilation and incorporation. Nietzsche writes: "I mean by plastic power [*die plastische Kraft*] the capacity to develop out of oneself in one's one way, to transform [*umzubilden*] and incorporate [*einzuverleiben*] into oneself what is past and foreign, to heal wounds, to replace what has been lost, to recreate broken moulds" (*UM II*, 1).

Like the English word incorporation, *Einverleibung* means literally a taking into the body, and on the level of human existence it denotes a complex practice of spiritual ingestion. The complexity of "spirit" is perhaps most fully addressed by Nietzsche in his meditation on its "fundamental will" (*Grundwillen*) in *BGE* 230. Here Nietzsche calls for the human to be translated (*übersetzen*) back into nature and for a skillful mastery over the numerous vain and fanciful interpretations and secondary meanings that have been scrawled over "the eternal basic text, *homo natura*." In this way man will stand before himself as he now stands, "hardened by the discipline of *Wissenschaft* [science]," before the rest of nature, "deaf to the siren songs of old metaphysical bird-catchers" who for aeons have piped to him that he is something higher and of a different origin. The spirit of the human being is a complicated one, expressing, on the one hand, a will to appearance, to semblance, to simplification, and to the mask, and, on the other, a will to knowledge that assumes a profound and many-sided view of things, practicing a "cruelty of the intellectual conscience." What Nietzsche calls "spirit" denotes a will to mastery; it is a "will to go from multiplicity to simplicity, a will that binds together, subdues, a tyrannical and truly masterful will" (*BGE* 230). Nietzsche then states that the needs and capacities of spirit can be likened to the same ones that physiology claims for that which lives, grows, and reproduces. The energy of spirit consists in appropriating the foreign, and its fundamental tendency is to make the new resemble the old and to simplify the multiplicity it encounters.[8] In short, incorporation proceeds in terms of a logic of identity and similitude. For Nietzsche the highest functions of spirit are to be understood as sublimated organic functions, such as assimilation, discrimination, and secretion. Modern human beings are the inheritors and practitioners of these various tendencies of the spirit.

In *The Gay Science* Nietzsche makes significant usage of incorporation in a long aphorism devoted to truth and knowledge (*GS* 110, entitled "Ursprung der Erkenntniss"). This aphorism helps to clarify what Nietzsche has in mind with regard to the incorporation of truth and knowledge (see also *GS* 11). However, as we shall see, Nietzsche leaves it to his readers to work out his meaning and to negotiate the most difficult questions.

Although we exist today in a situation where knowledge itself has now become a part of life, a preoccupation with truth actually appeared late in the evolution of human life and was for a long time held to be "the weakest form of knowledge" on account of the fact that humans found it hard to endure it as a practice of living. In the story Nietzsche is telling in this aphorism, this was owing to the fact that for the greater part of its evolutionary history the human animal has survived, prospered even, by incorporating a set of "basic errors" which became for it a set of "erroneous articles of faith," such as that there are equal things, enduring things, indeed that there are things such as substances and bodies, that things are what we immediately take them to be, that the will is free, and so on. All the higher functions of our organism, including sense perception, have worked with these basic errors and incorporated them. Moreover, these propositions concerning self and world established themselves as the norm according to which "true" and "untrue" could be determined. Truth, then, at least initially and during this highly formative period of human evolution, operates in the context of the incorporated errors. In the section that immediately comes after *GS* 110 he presents a quasi-Darwinian account of the origins and development of our basic ways of thinking. For example, to be able to think all the time in terms of identity proves helpful in the struggle for survival since it means things in the environment can be recognized and acted upon with speed and quickness. To see only a perpetual becoming everywhere would be disastrous for the evolution of a species of animal. As Nietzsche points out, "the beings who did not see exactly had a head start over those who saw everything 'in a flux'" (*GS* 111). What has so far determined the strength or power of knowledge is not its degree of truth, as we might suppose, but rather its "character as a condition of life" (the conditions of life include error). Wherever life and knowledge came into conflict, denial and doubt were taken to be expressions of madness. Where a more truthful humanity has sought to come into being – Nietzsche mentions the school of the Eleatics (Parmenides and his disciples, such as Zeno) – it has arrived at "truth" only by deceiving itself about its own states, for example positing a fictitious impersonality and an unchanging duration. In the process it misunderstood the nature of the knower and lived in denial of the impulses that inform knowledge. Although these human beings cultivated honesty and skepticism, it was these which led to their downfall since their ways of living and judging were seen to be also dependent on the primeval impulses and basic errors of sentient existence.

A subtle kind of skepticism comes into being when two opposing propositions about the world appeared to be applicable to life, simply because both proved compatible with the basic errors and an argument could be put forward about the degrees of utility for life. The same was true, Nietzsche notes, where new propositions came into being that were neither useful nor harmful to life. Such a situation creates room for the expression of an intellectual play impulse. Gradually the human brain becomes full of antinomical judgments and convictions – contradictory propositions that have a rightful claim to validity – to the point where a "lust for power" manifests itself in this tangle of knowledge. It is in this context that knowledge and a striving for truth come to inform what we take to be our innermost needs and desires: "all 'evil' instincts were subordinated to knowledge, employed in her service, and acquired the splendor of what is permitted, honored, and useful" (*GS* 110). With this stage in our evolution we find ourselves in a new situation in which the quest for knowledge and the striving for the true have taken their rightful place among others as being considered among the most fundamental needs, to the point where we now have techniques and disciplines of scrutiny, of denial, and of suspicion. Nietzsche brings the aphorism to a close by saying that the thinker today is "the being in whom the drive to truth and those life-preserving errors are fighting their first battle." Such a battle is now taking place because the striving for the true has also shown itself to be a life-preserving and life-enhancing power. In order to make further progress with truth it is necessary to conduct an experiment. Nietzsche's question is: "to what extent can truth stand [*verträgt*] incorporation?"

The precise meaning of Nietzsche's questioning is not self-evident. He appears to leave open the result of the experiment that is to be conducted, as well as the precise nature of the fundamental question he has posed. As Heidegger (2004: 28) asked, what kind of "truth" is it that stands outside incorporation and that now challenges us in the manner of incorporation? What is the precise nature and status of this "truth"? Although we can say that the truth Nietzsche has in mind is neither the articles of faith of primeval humanity nor the knowledge sought by refined truth-seekers such as the Eleatics, it is very difficult to determine exactly what he does have in mind. We could suggest that what Nietzsche has in mind is truth conceived as a set of *practices* of truthfulness that is now part and parcel of our passion of knowledge, such as doubt, suspicion, critical distance, subjecting all things to scrutiny, and so on. Here we might want to phrase the question of incorporation in the following terms: can there be a diet of knowledge? How will our commitment to truth work itself out in the context of an appreciation of the general economy of life, including our recognition of the need to will illusion, appearance, and semblance?

In number 162 of the 1881 notebook (M III, 1) Nietzsche states that the organs of a living system work in favor of error, and therefore the "ultimate truth" (*die letzte Wahrheit*) of the flux of things cannot stand incorporation. Is this then perhaps the sort of truth Nietzsche is inviting us to conduct an experiment over in *GS* 110? If it is, we could construe Nietzsche as asking whether humanity is now able to incorporate something it has hitherto been unable to. (Nietzsche is claiming that the human animal's inability to incorporate a reality of continuing change and perpetual becoming has facilitated its evolution; see *GS* 111.) What is the nature and status of the "ultimate truth" Nietzsche invokes? Surely he cannot be appealing to a metaphysical reality that we can have no relation to and cannot care about? Does he not state (*HH* 16) that the idea of a thing-in-itself is worthy of Homeric laughter? A number of commentators have read Nietzsche's positing of a reality characterized by becoming and perpetual flux as resulting in a reformulated thing-in-itself, conceived as an unconceptualizable otherness. However, Nietzsche himself points out that the positing of a metaphysical world – conceived as that which lies beyond what is knowable as a kind of "inaccessible and incomprehensible being-other" – can only be done in terms of a negative ontology, which would be fruitless (*HH* 9). Admittedly, Nietzsche does say that knowledge and becoming exclude one another (*WP* 517), and that a world in a state of becoming could not, strictly speaking, be comprehended or known (*WP* 520). However, he has to be read carefully on this issue. As one commentator has noted, if we assume that our existence and activity are a piece with life and the world – and what else ultimately could they be part of? – "this means that we are not in principle debarred from ever achieving any comprehension of the character of the reality they and we comprise" (Schacht 1983: 105). However, we need to grasp the precise manner in which Nietzsche ascribes positive tasks to knowledge and the expectations he has of it. Nietzsche could be arguing that knowledge of becoming is not possible owing to the "errors" contained in our evolved habits of representation and modes of knowing, to say nothing of the moral prejudices that have hitherto constituted the horizon of truth and knowledge. But it is the "old morality," including the morality of knowledge, which Nietzsche holds we are now moving beyond: "What was formerly despised as unholy, forbidden, contemptible, fateful – all these flowers grow today along the lovely paths of truth" (*WP* 459). Much, if not everything, depends on how we understand Nietzsche's figuration of the *incorporation* of truth and knowledge.

It is clear, I think, that for Nietzsche a *new* mode of incorporation is now to take place. We would be mistaken, however, if we supposed that this entailed a direct and immediate incorporation of the "ultimate truth." Rather, his idea is that we, along with everything else that lives, are implicated in the perpetual flux, and the challenge we are now confronted with is one of developing a more refined knowledge of ourselves and the world in the light of this truth. This is not a truth we can possess, neither is it a truth that is simply to be "found" by us. Nietzsche rejects this kind of conception of what truth is "because it cuts off the forces that work toward enlightenment and knowledge," and is thus "more fateful than error and ignorance" (*WP* 452). He insists that "truth" is not simply "something there, that might be found or discovered." Rather, we do better when we approach it as something "that gives a name to a process," as "a will to overcome that has itself no end," and as an "active determining" and not "a becoming-conscious of something that is in itself firm and determined" (*WP* 552). His "ultimate" truth is such in perhaps more than the one sense: first, as that which exceeds the measuring capacities of the human being, and so puts the measure of man to the test, and, second, as that which will provide human beings with new and decisive knowledge about their future "evolution." To date, human beings have incorporated the basic or fundamental errors, and this has aided their evolution. There was a clear incentive informing this incorporation, that of evolutionary advantage. Now, however, the new incorporation of truth and knowledge demands that we go beyond what is prescribed within evolution, and it is on these grounds, at least in part, that Nietzsche is compelled to appeal to our becoming *overhuman*. As he puts it in the 1881 sketch on the eternal return, we must now wait and see "how far" truth and knowledge can be incorporated. The experiment is by definition an open-ended and ongoing one, bound up with the kind of creatures we are, and are in the process of becoming. We moderns, understood as those who are caught up in the "passion" of knowledge, are in the process of complicating our evolutionary conditions of existence. In one sense we are becoming "more" human; in another sense we are becoming "more than" human. The *Sinn* (sense, meaning, direction) of our newfound conditions of existence is necessarily unclear, but it is this lack of clearness that Nietzsche is inviting us to affirm as a constitutive feature of our practice of knowledge and incorporation of truth. Let's now see how he finesses the idea of a new incorporation.

Humanity has cultivated itself on the basis of a set of fundamental errors, and this has involved the development of certain kinds of sensation and perception in which the changes in things go unperceived and all kinds of influences are not felt. In addition, a certain mode of judging and valuing has been cultivated, one that affirms rather than suspends judgment, that errs and fabricates things rather than *waits*, and that passes judgment rather than strives to be just (*GS* 111). Nietzsche argues that our knowledge amounts to a humanization of things; we perfect an image of becoming for ourselves but do not see beyond or behind this image. We have done this, for example, by diagramming reality in a specific manner, such as through "lines, planes, bodies, atoms, divisible time spans, divisible spaces" (*GS* 112). In *GS* 121 he writes: "We have arranged for ourselves a world in which we are able to live – by positing bodies, lines, planes, causes and effects, motion and rest, form and content; without these articles of faith no one could endure living! But that does not prove them." Our fundamental schemas of thought and habits of representation are imprecise and make us reliant on perceptions that are too coarse. For example, we have developed the habit of positing identical facts and isolated facts, which shows that we are committed to a fundamental atomism in the domain of our willing and knowing (*WS* 11).

In his first sketch of the eternal return Nietzsche speaks of "the seriousness of our striving" as one of understanding everything as implicated in becoming and denying ourselves as individuals. The challenge he presents is that of learning "to live in drives," as that through which we come to see, and to uphold this mode of living as a foundation of all our knowing; but then to cultivate at the same time the superior knowledge that will enable us to discern at what point the drives become the enemies of knowing. Our drive to knowledge has its presuppositions in the conditions of life and these conditions include error (*KSA* 9, 11[162]). The fundamental errors of humanity – the error of the judgment that there are identical things, enduring and unconditioned substances, a free will, and so on – have their basis in organic life (see *HH* 18). Nietzsche writes: "There would be no suffering [*Leiden*] if there were nothing organic; that is, without belief in *the same* [*Gleiches*], that is, without *this error, there would be no pain* in the world!" (*KSA* 9, 11[254]). Where does all this leave truth, however?

Several notes from the M III, 1 notebook provide insight into the kind of things that are at stake for Nietzsche. In 156, for example, he indicates that a fundamental rethinking of the individual is required, and away from the coarse "error" of the species; the individual struggles for its existence, for its new taste, and for its relative singular position in relation to all things. It despises the general taste and wants to rule supreme. But the notion of the individual also has its error, a more refined one to be sure, and its nature must be intensified: it discovers that it itself is something wandering and has a taste that changes; in the smallest moment it is something other than in the next and its conditions of existence are that of a host of individuals. Nietzsche declares: "the *infinitely small moment* is the highest reality and truth, a lightning-image that emerges from the eternal river [*ein Blitzbild aus dem ewigen Flusse*]" (*KSA* 9, 11[156]). Nietzsche concludes this note by reflecting on what we learn from this and argues that all pleasure-taking knowledge (*geniessende Erkenntniss*) rests on the coarse error of the species, the finer error of the individual, and the finest error of the creative moment. In 162 Nietzsche argues that "life is the condition of knowing" and "error is the condition of the living" at its deepest level. It is thus necessary to love and cultivate error as it is the womb (*Mutterschoss*) of our knowing. It is for this reason that art can be prized as the activity that cultivates illusions (compare *GS* 107 on our ultimate gratitude to art). We are to advance life for the sake of knowledge and promote illusion for the sake of life (compare Kofman 1993: 130–2). Nietzsche then states that the "fundamental condition" of the whole passion of knowledge is to grant existence an "aesthetic meaning," that is, to "increase our taste for it." What we discover in this play of life is a night and a day, the ebb and flow of our desiring knowledge and our desiring error. Ruled absolutely by one of these desires, the human and its capacities would perish. In note number 229 Nietzsche states that only by adapting to the living errors can the "*initially **dead** truth*" be brought to life. This adaptation (*Anpassung*) is necessarily an essential ingredient in our incorporation of truth and knowledge. In note 325 he spells out what is to be the task of science (*Wissenschaft*): "Not to ask the question how error is possible, but how a kind of truth is at all possible in spite of the fundamental untruth in knowing."

With a few exceptions Nietzsche's question about the incorporation of truth has not been considered by his commentators (see Schacht 1983: 97; Kofman 1993: 130ff.; Williams 2004: 15ff.; in an instructive essay on Nietzsche and truth Gemes [2001] does not even consider it and makes no reference to *GS* 110). Although Bernard Williams rightly stresses that Nietzsche's criticisms and exposures of the idols and self-deceptions of his age are motivated by a spirit of truthfulness, he lacks a genuine knowledge of the actual details and character of Nietzsche's thinking, with the result that his claims about Nietzsche's commitment to truth and truthfulness do not adequately center on the issues that occupy Nietzsche's attention, such as the ones that I have sought to highlight. Kofman insists that although truth is put into operation by Nietzsche it is never construed by him as functioning outside of the interpretation and evaluation that are the constitutive elements of "life" (there is no text-in-itself, she insists, that is, no "absolute text" to which we can refer our interpretations in order to judge their truth: "A text without interpretation is no longer a text": Kofman 1993: 140). This means, she argues, that for Nietzsche it is never a question of unveiling Being in its truth or of rendering existence naked and bare, simply because we can never remove ourselves from a horizon of interpretation and evaluation. To do so would mean we step outside life and its conditions, but this is impossible. If these conditions include error, as Nietzsche claims, then truth is of necessity always bound up with error, which, in fact, constitutes its basis. For Kofman the virtue of truthfulness operates in Nietzsche as a commitment to multiplying perspectives and hierarchizing drives (for her this is what it means to employ "life as a means to knowledge"), and enables us to see a spirit of justice at work in Nietzsche's new philology of interpretation (see also Schacht 1983: 99). I differ from Kofman in holding to the view that Nietzsche does think that a transformation in our knowledge is taking place and that this new mode and practice of knowledge will inform our interpretations and evaluations and provide us with a new spirit of truth and truthfulness. The passion of knowledge has taken hold of us, according to Nietzsche, and his critical question is focused on our incorporation of it.

Knowledge and Self-Knowledge

Nietzsche's "gay science" makes certain demands upon knowledge and its future development. In *GS* 354 he writes of "phenomenalism" and "perspectivism" as he understands them, arguing that the world of which we become conscious is only a "surface- and sign-world" that, strictly speaking, belongs to our herd-animal existence and the species, and in which "becoming conscious" rests on a falsification, generalization, and reduction to superficiality. He then notes that what concerns him in advancing this critique are not the distinctions made by epistemologists between subject and object and between the thing-in-itself and appearance – he states, with more than a touch of wit and irony, that we don't "know" enough to be entitled to this latter distinction – but rather the fact that we "lack any organ for knowledge, for 'truth'"; rather, we "know" what proves to be useful for our interests as a species and this knowledge may simply be belief or imagination, and we then confuse "truth" with them. In the next aphorism, Nietzsche makes it clear that he is taking "knowledge" (*Erkenntniss*) in this context to be an evolved social practice that aims to reduce something strange to the familiar. The knowledge that philosophy hitherto has sought is the kind that will provide the species with a sense of security and make it feel at home in the world. We approach the entire riddle of the world with some rule in which we are stuck and in terms of *accustomed* perspectives. This explains philosophy's preference for starting with the "inner world," with so-called "facts of consciousness." Nietzsche pronounces this to be the "Error of errors!" (*GS* 355). He then argues that that which we are used to is what is most difficult to know, simply because we lack the distance that would enable us to see it as a problem and as something strange. He concludes by noting, first, that the natural sciences acquire their certainty (*Sicherheit*) by taking as the object of their inquiries what is strange and unfamiliar and, second, that for common sense it is contradictory to want to take the non-strange as an object of inquiry. The "gay science" has a major investment in the development of new techniques and sciences of knowing and inquiry: "We ourselves wish to be our experiments and guinea pigs" (*GS* 319). Proving equal to the task of "incorporating" truth and knowledge constitutes an essential dimension of what it means for us to become the overhuman ones that we, paradoxically, are.

For Nietzsche the incorporation of truth and knowledge will also now inform the art of living well, which for him takes the form of self-creation and self-legislation. In *GS* 335 Nietzsche declares that "we want to become the ones that we are," conceived as the new, the unique, and the incomparable. He also speaks of new human beings "who are bent on seeking in all things for what in them must be *overcome*" (GS 283). At the very end of this aphorism he makes the following appeal to knowledge: "At long last the search for knowledge [*Erkenntniss*] will reach out for its due; it will want to *rule* and *possess*, and you with it!" In another aphorism from this part of *The Gay Science* Nietzsche writes of the need to make "conscience [*Gewissen*] an object of science

[*Wissen*]" (*GS* 309). It is this kind of thinking about the self that informs his presentation of the demonically inspired thought of the eternal return in *GS* 341 with its question "in each and every thing": "Do you desire this once more and innumerable times more?" How are we to go about answering this question? Nietzsche's response is to offer a new center of gravity that will enable us to discover the "law" and power of our desire.

In *GS* 335, entitled "Long Live Physics!," Nietzsche addresses the issue of self-knowledge and writes of our now learning to impose a new limit upon ourselves, namely, limiting ourselves to the "purification" (*Reinigung*) of our values and to "*the creation of our new tables of what is good.*" We need to appreciate that every action in the past has been done, and every action in the future will be done, "in an altogether unique and irretrievable way." Nietzsche's hope is that if we take proper cognizance of this insight then we will stop brooding over the moral value of our actions and regard the moral chatter of some about others as something distasteful. Nietzsche writes in praise of "physics" by appealing to the supra-moral virtue that compels (*zwingt*) us to it, namely, probity (*Redlichkeit*), and which gains its voice from the superior form of conscience that he names the "intellectual conscience." It is superior to the moral conscience simply because it acknowledges that we do not have an adequate knowledge of our actions and valuations; rather, "all regulations about actions relate only to their coarse exterior." The "physics" Nietzsche has in mind concerns the experimental knowledge that will reveal to us what is "lawful and necessary" in the world and as it affects the task of our becoming the ones that we are. At the same time, however, he stresses that in any particular case the law of the mechanism of our actions cannot, in fact, be demonstrated. This means that "law" and "necessity" are not simply discoverable by us as brute facts, but rather will disclose themselves through testing and experimentation, for which we will need to draw on the resources of refined self-observation. When Nietzsche conceives the eternal return itself working as an incorporating thought, and on the level of the care of the self, he does so precisely in terms of an experimental self-knowledge and testing: "Thought and belief are a weight pressing down on me as much as and even more than any other weight. You say that food, a location, air, society transform and condition you: well your opinions do so even more, since it is they that determine your choice of food, dwelling, air, society. If you incorporate this thought within you, amongst your other thoughts, it will transform you. The question in everything that you will: 'am I certain I want to do to an infinite number of times?' will become for you the heaviest weight" (*KSA* 9, 11[143]).

On my interpretation the truth that Nietzsche is inviting us to subject to an experiment is the kind that is bound up with the new knowledge sought by the gay science, the goal of which is to develop a more refined appreciation of our actions and identities. In *The Gay Science* itself Nietzsche writes of our now seeking to become better known to ourselves with the aid of better descriptions (*GS* 112). We also need to come up with new evaluations based on new modes of perception and judgment. We will do this, for example, by cultivating the new tools (organs) and norms offered by the developing sciences of physiology and psychology, constantly refining their insights, and by the "spiritual perception" that is unique to philosophy (*BGE* 252). These norms concern our conceptions of life and the living, revolving around questions of health and sickness (decadence), the natural and anti-natural, growth and decay, preservation and enhancement, and so on. Running throughout Nietzsche we find ongoing treatments of human pathologies, including the "bold insanities of metaphysics" (*GS*, preface, 2), ascetic ideals (*GM* III as a whole), and nihilism (said by him to be a "pathological transitional stage"; what is pathological is the inference that there is no "meaning" [*Sinn*] *at all*, *WP* 13). Nietzsche follows the French physiologist Claude Bernard (1813–78) in regarding the normal and the pathological to be different degrees of the same condition and not distinct entities (see *KSA* 13, 14[65]; for further insight see Canguilhem 1991 and Moore 2002). Nietzsche's concern is with how much of the pathological we are able to take on and render healthy.

In the *Genealogy of Morality* he writes of a new discipline of the intellect that will prepare it for its future "objectivity," in which the intellect will make use of the difference in perspectives and affective interpretations for the sake of knowledge: "the more affects we allow to speak about a thing, the *more* eyes, various eyes we are able to use for the same thing, the more complete will be our 'concept' of the thing" (*GM* III, 12). Nietzsche ridicules the positing of what he regards as contradictory notions, such as "pure reason," disinterested knowledge, and a "pure, will-less, painless, timeless subject of knowledge" (Schopenhauer, *WWR*, vol. 1, sect. 34), and insists that to "see" is to see something come into existence and under some point of view. In short, an "eye" has a direction and involves active and interpretive forces or powers. However, although we are at liberty to practice and experiment with them, Nietzsche's celebrated "perspectivism" does not invite us to grant equal value and validity to any and all perspectives; rather, we are to employ the difference in perspectives and interpretations on the basis of the new incorporation of truth and knowledge now called for (the stress that we find placed on new ways of seeing and looking into the world in the 1881 sketch clearly anticipates the perspectivism that is put to work in the Third Essay of the *Genealogy*). Nietzsche speaks, for example, of "engaging" *and* "disengaging" perspectives. As one commentator has noted, there is a critical and undermining aspect to Nietzsche's "perspectivity," which is frequently overlooked in accounts of it (see Richardson 2001: 21; see also Schacht 1983: 96ff.). There is, in fact, a principal "perspective" at work in Nietzsche's thinking, which is that of "life." He stresses that whenever we address values and speak under their inspiration we are always doing so from the perspective of life: "life itself forces us to establish values; life itself evaluates through us *when* we posit values" (*TI*, "Morality as Anti-Nature," 5). If the problem of the "value of life" cannot be touched upon by us – since to do so would require situating ourselves *outside* life – then one of the tasks of thinking is to develop a treatment of different forms and types of life (ascending and descending modes, for example), in which we become attentive to the signs of life. Nietzsche stresses that morality is an *interpretation* of phenomena. The genealogist of morals is at the same time a semiologist of morals, one who appreciates that morality is a sign language and symptomatology, and understands just what is going on in moral judgment, to the extent that the philosopher who places himself "beyond good and evil" has the "illusion of moral judgment" *beneath* him (*TI*, "The 'Improvers' of Humanity," 1). Nietzsche diagnoses moral judgment as, like religious judgment, lacking in knowledge precisely because it lacks the important distinction "between the real and the imaginary," to the point where "truth" on this level designates nothing but "illusions": "Morality and religion belong entirely under the *psychology of error*: in every single case cause and effect are confused;

or truth is confused with the effect of what is *believed* to be true; or a state of consciousness is confused with the causality of this state" (*TI*, "The Four Great Errors," 6).

The new and difficult challenge facing us moderns is that of turning the growth of "neutral" and "indifferent" knowledge into a passion, that is, something we embody, experiment with, and practice as an art and science of living. Nietzsche posits a joining of artistic energies and practical wisdom with scientific thinking that will lead to the formation of a "higher organic system" (*GS* 113). In place of the aim or goal of denial he wishes "to make asceticism natural again." He envisages new ascetic practices involving a "gymnastics of the will" and tests of sovereign individuality (*WP* 915). Even the "stupid psychological fact" of death is to be transformed into a moral necessity in which one will want to die at the right time (*WP* 916).

Nietzsche's thinking on truth and knowledge reaches a position of maturity in 1886–7 as he begins to unravel the "no-saying" part of his task, notably the revaluation of values and all it entails. Any engagement with his stress on the need to incorporate truth and knowledge has to take this development into account. Nietzsche calls for a "philosophical physician" who will be able "to pursue the problem of the total health of a people, time, race or humanity" and push to its limits the suspicion that in all philosophizing to date what has been at stake is not so much "truth," but rather "health, future, growth, power, life" (*GS*, preface, 2). He also describes our desire for truth at any price, "the will to truth," as amounting to bad taste; there is a "youthful madness in the love of truth" (*GS*, preface, 4; see also *BGE* preface). Nietzsche makes it clear that the will to knowledge can only establish itself on the basis of the will to the uncertain (*das Ungewisse*) and the untrue. For him there is no opposition at work here – which would be metaphysical – but rather a refinement of the one will by the other. We need to be cheerful about the fact that the *best* science (*Wissenschaft*) "loves error" because, "being alive," it loves life (*BGE* 24). It is not a question for Nietzsche of philosophy ever being proved right (he notes that to date no philosophy has been proved right). Moreover, the little question marks that the conscientious philosopher places at the end of his mottoes and doctrines – a feature that characterizes Nietzsche's presentation of all his key doctrines – have more value for truth than all the "dignified gestures" he might display before plaintiffs and courts of law (*BGE* 25). The new lovers of knowledge (the gay scientists), therefore, will not become martyrs for the cause of truth; they will not parade themselves as sublime self-torturers who suffer for the sake of it. This is because what guides their love of truth and knowledge is the love of life, especially the superior life, and this life exists, of necessity, outside the social order and the public gaze. This is what the popular "will to truth" fails to appreciate. All the moral prejudices about truth, which abound for Nietzsche in the realm of popular philosophy, need to be overcome (*BGE* 34):

> The indignant man and whoever else uses his own teeth to mutilate and dismember himself (or God or society in place of himself) may stand higher than the laughing and self-satisfied satyr in moral terms, but in every other sense he represents the more common, more inconsequential, more uninstructive case. And only the indignant tell so many lies. (*BGE* 26)

By contrast, the exceptional human being seeks out his secrecy – his truth – only "where he is *delivered* from the crowd, the multitude, the majority," and where he is able "to forget the rule of 'humanity'" (*BGE* 26). It is clear, I think, that what Nietzsche is proposing is a fundamental reform of truth in an effort to entice the coming philosophers (the ones of the future). Part of the free-spirited task of questioning the will to truth involves posing a set of strange questions about it and about our desire for the truth. Nietzsche insists that certain independent questions need to be posed, such as: *Who* is asking the questions in any given context? *What* is it in us that wants to "'get at the truth'" (*BGE* 1)?

In the *Genealogy of Morality* Nietzsche continues this questioning of truth, and argues that it be permitted to be taken as a "problem" (*GM* III. 24). But how do we square this with the fact that so much of his genealogical inquiry is unequivocally informed by a profound *will* to truth, one that shows us that effective truth is necessarily something ugly and frightening, and something that cannot be avoided now that the conscience of truth and the passion of knowledge have taken such deep root in our life-practices? His preferred intellectual habitat is that of a state of cheerfulness (*Heiterkeit*) among "hard truths" (*EH*, "Why I Write Such Good Books," 3). Nietzsche opens the First Essay of the *Genealogy* by paying homage to the "English psychologists" whom he then devotes a significant portion of the book to criticizing (along with English biologists). This motley group of pioneering researchers has held a microscope to the soul and, in the process, come up with a new set of truths: "plain, bitter, ugly, foul, unchristian, immoral . . . " (*GM* I. 1). Although Nietzsche goes on to criticize these psychologists for bungling their moral genealogy and for not carrying out "real" history, it is clear that he feels a deep affinity with their commitment to unchristian and immoral truth. Indeed, he explicitly states that, in contrast to other interpreters, he does not view them as "old, cold, boring frogs" that crawl around men and inhabit a "swamp," but rather as "brave, generous, and proud animals." And throughout the *Genealogy* Nietzsche adds to the unchristian and immoral truths of these psychologists a whole set of his own (the work of these psychologists has its basis in the work of Locke, and in Hume's new approach to the mind which shows that so-called complex, intellectual activity emerges out of processes that are, in truth, "stupid," such as the *vis inertiae* of habit and the random coupling or association of ideas).

So why does Nietzsche take to task the will to truth in the Third Essay of the *Genealogy*? He makes a number of contentions: that modern knowers and free spirits remain "idealists of knowledge"; that these spirits represent the most intellectualized product of the only ideal that has flourished on earth to date, the ascetic ideal; and that our modern faith in science is a *metaphysical* faith. In calling, *tentatively*, for a "critique" of the will to truth Nietzsche is not proposing a negative task but a limiting and refining one. His critical attention is focused on the *unconditional* character of our modern will to truth and on our belief in the *divine* nature of truth. We moderns overestimate truth; such is our faith in truth we take it to be something that cannot be assessed or criticized (*GM* III. 25). In the claim that our commitment to truth supposes a "metaphysical" valuation Nietzsche has in mind such things as the paralogical ideal of knowledge free of presuppositions, a knowledge without a direction, a meaning, and a limit, and a knowledge that renounces interpretation and everything that is essential to it (*GM* III. 24). However, it is clear that the ascetic truth-practices which Nietzsche calls into question prove to be indispensable for his own historical inquiries, including a deep mistrust and skepticism (in *GM* III. 9 Nietzsche lists the drives peculiar to the philosopher and mentions the drives to doubt, to deny, to dare, and to research). The difference between Nietzsche and the free spirits who remain "idealists of knowledge" is that for him *belief* in truth is not sufficient; rather, truth has to be an affair of incorporation.[9] It is here that the "play of life" asserts itself and involves our continued, and necessary, reliance on perspectivist assessments and appearances (*BGE* 34). For Nietzsche it is a question of developing the selection of affects and drives in the direction of a perpetual enhancement of the human being and within the framework provided by the *task* of incorporating truth and knowledge. In other words, the practice of truth and knowledge is to be placed in the service of a new legislation of the human and its future development. Nietzsche envisages a program of cultural engineering which will bring about a new, sovereign species of human that is both intellectually strong and ethically independent. This is what he has in mind when he ascribes to philosophy a "spiritual perception" (*BGE* 252). He criticizes British empiricism for failing to make use of truth in this way; in its timidity with regard to the tasks of cultural discipline and breeding it displays its "plebeian ambition" (*BGE* 213) and allows truth to further the ends only of the transformation of man into a perfect herd-animal.

As early as 1872, in the notebook known as the "Philosophers' Book," Nietzsche defines philosophy as the "selective knowledge drive." He continues to uphold this conception of philosophy in the works of his late period with the difference that philosophy's tasks are no longer conceived on the basis of a disappointment over the end of metaphysics and a turn to the consoling powers of art, as typifies the early work, but on the basis of mature genealogical insights into human evolution and future possibilities. In the *Genealogy* Nietzsche writes of the will to truth becoming conscious of itself, a process that will destroy "morality" (as commonly conceived, that is) and result in a drama that will be terrible and questionable, but also rich in hope (*GM* III. 27; this drama refers to the possible new twist and outcome in the wider "Dionysian drama on the fate of the soul" heralded in the book's preface). We should note something important here: if we are now the beings in whom the will to truth has become aware of itself as a problem, then this is because it is the question of the *value* of truth that now constitutes the most important aspect of intellectual inventiveness. This is not so much to call truth as a virtue into question, but rather to demand that it be made the subject of a practice of incorporation. Why do we *wish* to incorporate truth and knowledge? Nietzsche's answer is because we want to become the ones that we are and because there is a new goal and task, namely, the development of a superior humanity. It is the new incorporation, therefore, that provides truth with the meaning (*Sinn*) it would otherwise lack. To paraphrase Nietzsche from a draft he composed of the discourse on "Self-Overcoming" for *Zarathustra*, if truth does not allow us to build a new world, then what is its value? (See *KSA* 14, p. 302.) The overhuman is the true vision and riddle of Nietzsche's *superior* (noble) empiricism:

> There it was too that I picked up the word "*Übermensch*" and that the human is something that is to be overcome, the human is a bridge and not a goal; counting itself happy for its noontides and evenings, as a way to new dawns. (Z III, "Of Old and New Law-Tables," 3)

Is there not grandeur in this view of life?

See also 6 "Nietzsche's 'Gay' Science"; 9 "The Naturalisms of *Beyond Good and Evil*"; 17 "Naturalism and Nietzsche's Moral Psychology"; 21 "Nietzsche and Ethics"; 26 "Nietzsche on Geophilosophy and Geoaesthetics"

Notes

1   The need for us to practice the incorporation of truth and knowledge as an art and science of living – one that endeavors to remain "true to thc earth" – is at the center of Nietzsche's narration of the drama of Zarathustra's down-going and over-going in *Thus Spoke Zarathustra*. For further insight see Ansell Pearson 2005.

2   Nietzsche uses two terms, sometimes interchangeably, for his teaching: *die ewige Wiederkunft* (from the verb *kommen*, to come) and *die ewige Wiederkehr* (from the verb *kehren*, to turn). In the first 1881 sketch Nietzsche presents the teaching as one of *Wiederkunft*; in the "Lenzer Heide" notebook on European nihilism of 1887 it is given first as one of *Wiederkehr* and then as *Wiederkunft* (see the translation forthcoming in Ansell Pearson and Large 2006). The difference also operates in the presentation in *TI*, "What I Owe the Ancients," sections 4 and 5. In his translation of *TI* Duncan Large follows Walter Kaufmann and translates the two expressions as "eternal return" and "eternal recurrence" respectively (R. J. Hollingdale's translation of the text translates both as "eternal recurrence"). There appears to be no consensus on this issue, however, amongst translators. Joan Stambaugh, for example, translates *Wiederkunft* as *return* and *Wiederkehr* as *recurrence*, and conceives the difference as follows: where "return" stresses a going back and a completion of movement, "recurrence" stresses another occurrence and the beginning of a movement, with recurrence being closer in meaning to repetition than return. She makes the further contentious claim that when he is addressing the nihilistic form of the thought Nietzsche uses the term *Wiederkehr* (which she translates as "recurrence") and that he reserves *Wiederkunft* (which she translates as "return") for its more positive form. Although I am not convinced that this is what is at play in the doubling of *Wiederkehr* and *Wiederkunft* we encounter in Nietzsche, it is an issue well worth chewing over. It can be noted, however, that in *Ecce Homo*, where Nietzsche names eternal return as the highest formula of affirmation attainable, he uses the word *Wiederkunft* for his thought. When Zarathustra's animals declare that Zarathustra's destiny (*Schicksal*) is to be and to become the teacher of the teaching the term used in the text is *ewige Wiederkunft* (Z, "The Convalescent," 2). In a private communication Andreas Sommer has pointed out to me that whereas *Wiederkehr* is a possible equivalent for *Rückkehr* (return), *Wiederkunft* is not such a synonym but rather a word from Christian eschatology (it is the word used in German when speaking of the "Second Coming" of Christ, as Nietzsche is well aware, see *The Anti-Christ*, 41). In this essay I have chosen to refer to Nietzsche's thought as "eternal return" for the most part. For Stambaugh's argument see Stambaugh (1972: 30ff., 2004: 335–42).

3   *KSA* 9 11[141], pp. 494–5. The first complete translation of this sketch will appear in Ansell Pearson and Large (2006). David Krell translates several parts of the sketch without providing a complete translation in his highly instructive reading of notebook M III 1. See Heidegger (1961: 330–1, 1984: 74–5) and Krell (1996: 158–77, esp. pp. 162–4).

4   Nietzsche's own doctrine of freedom centers on viewing what one is as "a piece of fate" in which, "the fatality of one's being cannot be disentangled from the fatality of all that was and will be" (*TI*, "The Four Great Errors," 8). On Nietzsche's request that his readers hear the "halcyon tone" of his wisdom, see *EH*, foreword, 4.

5   According to the commentary found in *KSA* 14 on this note Nietzsche's citations of Spinoza in it are taken from a volume in Kuno Fischer's history of modern philosophy.

6 An exception is the study by Blondel (1991): see esp. ch. 9 (pp. 201–39).
7 See his editor's note to Heidegger 1984 (p. 75), and the editors' note in *KSA* 14, p. 645.
8 In the 1880s incorporation becomes increasingly thought of in terms of the will to power, conceived as a "will" to grow through the extension of power and the assimilation of alien forces (*KSA* 13, 14[192]; *WP* 728; cf. *BGE* 259).
9 One major recent intellectual figure for whom the incorporation of truth became an increasingly important issue was Michel Foucault. He turns to it in his late work, principally his lecture course at the Collège de France of 1981–2 on the hermeneutics of the subject (see Foucault 2005).

Editions of Nietzsche Used

I am grateful to Duncan Large and Diane Morgan for assisting me with some of the translations I have made from *KSA* volume 9.

The Anti-Christ, trans. R. J. Hollingdale (Harmondsworth: Penguin, 1968).
Beyond Good and Evil, trans. Marion Faber (Oxford: Oxford University Press, 1999).
Daybreak, trans. R. J. Hollingdale (Cambridge: Cambridge University Press, 1982).
The Gay Science, trans. Walter Kaufmann (New York: Vintage Books, 1974).
On the Genealogy of Morality, trans. Carol Diethe (Cambridge: Cambridge University Press, 1994).
Human, All Too Human, trans. R. J. Hollingdale, 2 vols. (Cambridge: Cambridge University Press, 1986).
"On the Pathos of Truth" (1872), in *Philosophy and Truth: Selections from Nietzsche's Notebooks from the Early 1870s*, ed. and trans. Daniel Breazeale (Atlantic Highlands, NJ: Humanities Press, 1979), pp. 61–9.
Thus Spoke Zarathustra, trans. R. J. Hollingdale (Harmondsworth: Penguin, 1961).
Twilight of the Idols, trans. Duncan Large (Oxford: Oxford University Press, 1998).
On the Uses and Disadvantages of History for Life, trans. R. J. Hollingdale, in *Untimely Meditations* (Cambridge: Cambridge University Press, 1983).
The Will to Power, trans. Walter Kaufmann and R. J. Hollingdale (New York: Vintage Books, 1967).

References

Ansell Pearson, Keith, and Large, Duncan (2006). *The Nietzsche Reader* (Oxford: Basil Blackwell).
Blondel, Eric (1991). *Nietzsche: The Body and Culture. Philosophy as Philological Genealogy*, trans. Sean Hand (London: Athlone Press).
Canguilhem, Georges (1991), *The Normal and the Pathological*, with an introduction by Michel Foucault, trans. Carolyn R. Fawcett with Robert S. Cohen (New York: Zone Books).
Fink, Eugen (1995). *Sixth Cartesian Meditation*, trans. Ronald Bruzina (Bloomington: Indiana University Press).
Foucault, Michel (2005). *The Hermeneutics of the Subject*, trans. Graham Burchell (New York: Palgrave Macmillan).
Gemes, Ken (2001). "Nietzsche's Critique of Truth," in Brian Leiter and John Richardson (eds.), *Nietzsche* (Oxford: Oxford University Press), pp. 40–59.
Heidegger, Martin (1961). *Nietzsche*, vol. 1 (Pfullingen: Günther Neske).
—— (1984). *Nietzsche*, vol. 2: *The Eternal Recurrence of the Same*, trans. David Farrell Krell (New York: Harper & Row).
—— (2004). *Nietzsche Seminare 1937 und 1944* (Frankfurt am Main: Vittorio Klostermann).

Kofman, Sarah (1993). *Nietzsche and Metaphor*, trans. Duncan Large (London: Athlone Press).

Krell, David Farrell (1996). *Infectious Nietzsche* (Bloomington: Indiana University Press).

Middleton, Christopher (1996). *Selected Letters of Friedrich Nietzsche* (Indianapolis: Hackett).

Moore, Gregory (2002). *Nietzsche, Biology, and Metaphor* (Cambridge: Cambridge University Press).

Richardson, John (2001), Introduction to John Richardson and Brian Leiter (eds.), *Nietzsche* (Oxford and New York: Oxford University Press), pp. 1–40.

Schacht, Richard (1983). *Nietzsche* (London and New York: Routledge).

Stambaugh, Joan (1972). *Nietzsche's Thought of Eternal Return* (Baltimore: Johns Hopkins University Press).

—— (2004). "All Joy Wants Eternity," *Nietzsche-Studien*, 33, pp. 335–42.

Williams, Bernard (2004). *Truth and Truthfulness* (Princeton, NJ: Princeton University Press).

Further Reading

Ansell Pearson, Keith (2005). "The Eternal Return of the Overman: The Weightiest Knowledge and the Abyss of Light," *Journal of Nietzsche Studies*, 30 (Autumn).

Brusotti, Marco (1997). "Erkenntniss als Passion. Nietzsches Denkweg zwischen Morgenröthe und der Fröhliche Wissenschaft," *Nietzsche-Studien*, 26, pp. 199–225.

Canguilhem, Georges (1994). *A Vital Rationalist: Selected Writings*, trans. Arthur Goldhammer (New York: Zone Books).

Cox, Christoph (1999). *Nietzsche, Naturalism, and Interpretation* (Berkeley: University of California Press).

Green, Michael S. (2003). *Nietzsche and the Transcendental Tradition* (Urbana and Chicago: University of Illinois Press).

Hales, Steven D., and Welshon, Rex (2000). *Nietzsche's Perspectivism* (Urbana and Chicago: University of Illinois Press).

Heidegger, Martin (1987). *Nietzsche*, vol. 3: *The Will to Power as Knowledge and as Metaphysics*, trans. Joan Stambaugh, David Farell Krell, and Frank A. Capuzzi (San Francisco: Harper & Row).

Montinari, Mazzino (2003). "Nietzsche's Philosophy as the 'Passion of Knowledge'," in Montinari, *Reading Nietzsche*, trans. Greg Whitlock (Urbana and Chicago: University of Illinois Press).

Müller-Lauter, Wolfgang (2001). *Nietzsche: The Philosophy of Contradictions and the Contradictions of his Philosophy*, trans. David J. Parent (Urbana and Chicago: University of Illinois Press).

Richardson, John (1996). *Nietzsche's System* (Oxford and New York: Oxford University Press).

14

Nihilism and Skepticism in Nietzsche

ANDREAS URS SOMMER

Introduction

While scarcely a doubt remains as to the importance of the nihilism problem for Nietzsche, scholars are by no means clear whether there is a skepticism problem with Nietzsche at all, although Nietzsche is often classified as a "skeptic" in popular contexts (e.g. Fraser 2000: 155ff.). Nietzsche's interest in the skepticism of antiquity has recently received a certain amount of attention (Bett 2000; Sommer 2000a; Brobjer 2001). However, the question of how Nietzsche's experimental skeptical-sounding positions fit in with other elements of his thought remains largely unanswered. The following will not attempt to systematize Nietzsche's skeptical approaches but will discuss how nihilism, as the negation of all moral and metaphysical truth, relates to his skepticism as a provisional negation of a recognizable reality. In this context it will be helpful to analyze the complexes of nihilism and skepticism in two separate sections, each referring to Nietzsche's texts from similar points of view. A brief conclusion will finally attempt to establish a relationship between nihilism and skepticism. In so doing, there is no question of clearing Nietzsche of the charge of nihilism (cf. Danto 1965: 195); I wish only to claim for him instead a "mitigated skepticism" (Magnus 1980). If we define a nihilist, according to Ottmann's suggested résumé of the history of the concept, as "one who no longer believes in anything and can find no comfort in anything" (Ottmann 1999: 330), a skeptic could be one who never has enough reason to believe something is true and whose doubt as to the knowability of truth cannot be set aside. For Nietzsche, nihilism is a modern phenomenon with a long history in which he includes himself and against which he wishes to highlight his own philosophy. To him, nihilism seems to be a symptom of *décadence*, denoting a pathological loss of trust in the world. Skepticism, which often has a positive connotation with Nietzsche, might imply an experimental suspension of trust in the world without necessarily, of course, leading to the amoral, immoral or hyper-moral consequences that are indicative of nihilism. The renunciation of knowledge as practiced by the skeptics need not imply a denial of the moral order or the meaning of the world, only a neutralization of them.

Although Nietzsche occasionally holds a certain type of "weak" skepticism to be an epoch-specific phenomenon of decadence (*BGE* 208), he typically treats skepticism as an epistemological position and only seldom as an expression of specific physiological/ psychological given facts, in spite of the tendency elsewhere in his writings to render intellectual manifestations physiological. Skepticism and skeptical questions are, then, discussed in the traditional sense as questions of philosophical theorization, although nihilism does not involve questions of theory but of life praxis and the loss of direction in practical living. With Nietzsche, then, skepticism and nihilism are arranged on different levels; yet they touch one another in what they consciously or unconsciously bring to expression, namely the end of truth, which for nihilism is also an end of values. But is the renunciation of (any claim to) truth a sign of *décadence* or of intellectual and physical strength? At all events, the notion of truth appears to be indispensable to many people (*KSA* 11, 34[253]).

Bett (2000: 83) has rightly indicated that Nietzsche's rhapsodic and aphoristic style, holding in balance that which is thought, shows similarities with the skeptical language, full of reservations and conscious of the fact that the skeptical concern might possibly be better served by silence, of Sextus Empiricus and Montaigne. The constant intellectual travels that take Nietzsche, wearing a mask, into the proximity of Montaigne forbid any final conclusions. However, this should not leave untouched Nietzsche's treatment of the complex of nihilism and – in the self-referential nature of skeptical language – the complex of skepticism. Nietzsche's pronouncements still stand under the skeptical proviso of the "as if" of experimental philosophy (cf. Kaulbach 1980), which forbids final systemization. Both nihilism and skepticism appear to be neutralizing distancing techniques.

1 Nihilism

At least since Heidegger (1961: vol. 2, pp. 31–256; cf. e.g. Conway 1992) there have been ambitious projects to systematize Nietzsche's deliberations on nihilism (recently, Kuhn in particular [1992]). However, such an approach can easily lead us to forget that with Nietzsche's pronouncements on nihilism we are mainly dealing with posthumous jottings that do not document a systematic process of thought. Instead, they represent repeated new approaches that are either uncoordinated or can only be partially coordinated. I shall take account of this structure of the text by also construing the "metamorphoses of nihilism" (*KSA* 13, 13[1]) as metamorphoses of Nietzschean thought which, after some remarks on questions relating to the treatment of sources, make it imperative to inquire about phases and forms of nihilism. The themes of nihilism and religion, nihilism and morality, and the overcoming of nihilism will be dealt with in separate sections. This thematic focus reflects three main points of view in which nihilism is significant for Nietzsche's thought. The death of God (*GS* 125) represents an essential precondition for the uncompromising stance regarding the diagnosis of nihilism. After Nietzsche, the influence of nihilism has its clearest and most sustained effect in the wide field of morality; finally, the doctrines of eternal return and the will to power are firmly conceived as stratagems for the overcoming of nihilism. In all three areas – religion, morality, and the overcoming of nihilism – a growing universalization of the problem of nihilism makes itself manifest.

251

1.1 Sources of Nietzsche's concept of nihilism

"Nihilists" first emerge in Nietzsche explicitly in the *Nachlass* of the summer of 1880, more precisely in a comment that they had Schopenhauer as their philosopher (*KSA* 9, 4[103]), and in a first mention of "Russian nihilists" (*KSA* 9, 4[108]). The sources for this choice of phrase are the French edition of *Pères et enfants* (*Fathers and Sons*) by Ivan S. Turgenev and the *Lettre à l'éditeur* (1863) written by Prosper Mérimée, as well as Turgenev's novel *Terres vierges* (*Virgin Soil*, 1877). Central influences on Nietzsche's concept of nihilism, which intensified strongly from 1885/6 onwards, were Paul Bourget's *Essais de psychologie contemporaine* (1883), his *Nouveaux essais de psychologie contemporaine* (1883–6), as well as Ferdinand Brunetière's *Le Roman naturaliste* (Paris, 1882–4) (Kuhn 2000: 293f.). Fyodor Dostoyevsky's novels can also be mentioned as an important source for Nietzsche's understanding of nihilism (Ottmann 1999: 332–5). Also important for the development of Nietzsche's own concept of nihilism are the works of Arthur Schopenhauer, Max Müller, Carl Friedrich Koeppen, and Afrikan Spir (Kuhn 1992: 19f.). The reception of French writers such as the poet Charles Baudelaire and the novelist Émile Zola comes into play when nihilism merges with *décadence*; Nietzsche developed his physiological understanding of *décadence* and *dégénérence* from Charles Féré (cf. e.g. Ottmann 1999: 336–9 and the literature cited there). Nietzsche brings a new intensity to the examination of the phenomenon of metaphysical ground-lessness, which, despised and welcomed in equal measure, had gone under the name of "nihilism" since the late Enlightenment (for the general history of the concept see Müller-Lauter and Goerdt 1984).

1.2 Phases and forms of nihilism

Anyone who wants to find a formula for the condition of human realities needs individual cases to which this formula is applicable. Anyone who strives for a *"psychology of nihilists"* (*KSA* 13, 11[332]) must be able to point to nihilists who fit into the proposed psychological pattern. If concrete examples are sparse prior to 1880, they soon multiply so fast that only a few historical phenomena can be found "not guilty" of nihilism. The first concrete examples of nihilism appear as people, beginning with the Eleatics, who were said to be the "best nihilists" among philosophers, having identified being with nothing (*KSA* 11, 34[204]). Then the "typical *décadent*" Socrates (*EH*, "Why I Write Such Good Books," 7 and 8) enters the fray as precursor of nihilistic Christianity (*KSA* 12, 5[50]); a similar thing happens with the "pre-existent-Christian Plato" (*TI*, "What I Owe the Ancients," 2). Greek philosophy since Socrates is supposed to have been in thrall to *décadence* (*KSA* 13, 11[375]) and, with its belief in fictitious realities, on the threshold of nihilism, without, of course, stepping over it, as did the founder of radical skepticism, the "nihilist Pyrrho." Pyrrho appears as a Greek Buddhist (*KSA* 13, 14[85–7], see also 14[99]; cf. Brochard 1932: 75), and it is precisely Buddhism together with Christianity that belongs to the "nihilistic religions" (*A* 20; Sommer 1999). Even Jesus, whom Christianity unjustly claims for itself, would quite possibly "live, teach and speak as a 'nihilist' in today's Europe" (*KSA* 13, 11[280]). In the wake of Christianity, the development of Europe takes a wrong direction, in the course of which "the belief in the categories of reason" arises, which again can figure as a "cause of nihilism" in the narrower sense: "we have measured the value of the world with categories *that refer to a purely fabricated world*" (*KSA* 12, 11[99]; *WP* 12), namely, the categories "Purpose," "Unity," "Being," the elimination of which makes the "world" appear "worthless" (*WP* 48; on this, see Ansell Pearson 1987: 328). In Nietzsche's reading, Kant's theoretical philosophy contributed decisively to the destruction of metaphysical and religious backgrounds and in this way provided an important step in the route of nihilism towards self-consciousness (cf. Kuhn 1992: 122–5), while Kant's practical philosophy merely opened another "hidden path to the old ideal" (*A* 10).

The nearer one comes to the present, the more numerous do Nietzsche's verdicts on nihilism become. Nearly the whole of the nineteenth century, with its "not knowing which way to go," falls into this category, "for example, as romanticism of feeling, as altruism and hyper-sentimentality, as feminism in taste, as socialism in politics" (*TI*, "Expeditions of an Untimely Man," 50). In like manner, idealism is in the process of turning into nihilism (*KSA* 12, 7[54]), while socialism and Christianity are lumped together under nihilistic auspices (*KSA* 13, 11[379]). The contemporary Russian intellectual scene is included almost as a matter of course (*KSA* 11, 26[335]). Richard Wagner (e.g. *CW*, Afterword) and Arthur Schopenhauer (e.g. *TI*, "Expeditions of an Untimely Man," 21) also count as specifically nihilistic manifestations. The sum total of nihilistic trends leaves a strident "Pathos of the 'for nothing'" (*KSA* 12, 9[60]).

When contemporaries are dubbed nihilists, it is essential that nihilism and *décadence* are brought together (*KSA* 13, 17[1]). Nihilism is not seen as a "cause" but as "the logic of *décadence*" (*KSA* 13, 14[86]). Moving on from the particular to generalizations, Nietzsche observes that humankind has only ever "been taught *décadence* values as highest values," as when they come to light, for example, in the "morality of getting rid of the self" (*KSA* 13, 23[3]). But perhaps only the teachers of humankind are supposed to be affected by *décadence*. Nowadays, the threat of a culture of pity and "intellectual exhaustion" heralds a "*nihilistic catastrophe*" (*KSA* 12, 9[82]; *WP* 64). These considerations are found under the title "The Second Buddhism." Other notes see the dawn of a "tragic period for Europe," caused by the fight against nihilism (*KSA* 12, 5[50]). Nietzsche finds in himself a last visible example of the presence of nihilism: in the foreword to a work he never wrote, he sees himself as the "first complete nihilist of Europe, but one who has already lived out nihilism to its end in his own life" (*KSA* 13, 11[411]; *WP*, preface, 3). His declared intention is to set in train a "*movement against*" nihilism with a "revaluation of values."

Nietzsche draws up a large number of work plans with nihilism as the central topic. In *GM* III. 27 he announces a contribution "On the History of European Nihilism" that was intended to be a section of the book *The Will to Power*. According to a number of drafts, the first of four books of this work would have been dedicated to the problem of nihilism "*as the necessary consequence of evaluations hitherto*" (*KSA* 12, 2[100]), that is to say, insofar as former values have been devalued (*KSA* 12, 2[131]; *WP* 69). Nihilism must be overcome by knowledge – the cure will follow the diagnosis. Another work draft reveals that "nihilism is only 'unavoidable' when people fail to grasp its premises," namely, its "valuations" (*KSA* 12, 2[188]). In this notation, Nietzsche pronounces himself confident that a genealogical appraisal of valuations will bring about a critical dissolution: "Genesis of valuations as a critique of those same" (*KSA* 12, 2[188]). However, this confidence does not appear to have been sufficiently strong to bring the project to completion. At the end of his sane life, Nietzsche elevates *The Antichrist* to the complete *Revaluation of All Values* – a text that hopes to banish Christianity and, along with it, nihilism, without honoring the latter with a genealogical examination. Apparently the genealogy of Christian values provided in *The Antichrist* is sufficient. Since Nietzsche thus failed to provide a thorough examination of nihilism in one of his own works, the following will first present a few scattered references on the topic from the published works, and will then discuss particularly striking allusions from the *Nachlass*.

Preliminary considerations in the form of "question marks" are found in the fifth book of *Gay Science*, where the immoral "we" confess to the suspicion "that the coming generations face the alternative: 'either abolish your reverences – or *yourselves*!' " (*GS* 346). Nietzsche writes that the latter is nihilism, "but wouldn't the former also be – nihilism?" Is nihilism unavoidable, whatever the case? According to *GM* I. 12, today's nihilism is expressed by the fact that man is "tired" of humankind. In the ascetic life, which appears to be a self-contradiction (cf. Brusotti 2001: 116–21), the "will to nothingness" is not finally realized as the will to self-destruction; instead, the will is rescued. However, *GM* II. 24 prophesies a "man of the future" who, as anti-Christ and anti-nihilist, will deliver us "from the great nausea, from the will to nothingness, from nihilism."

Kuhn (2000: 296) distils six manifestations of nihilism from the notes in the *Nachlass* that she believes can be objectively differentiated one from another: incomplete, complete, passive, active, radical, and most extreme nihilism. A historically speculative differentiation such as Kuhn's is not, however, always helpful in view of the disparate nature of the texts in question. Even so, the comments selected from the *Nachlass* will be grouped in the following three sections according to comments on Nietzsche's nihilistic philosophical premises, the nature of nihilism, and the origin and development of nihilism.

1.2.1 Nietzsche's nihilistic philosophical premises

Important for the discussion of the topic of nihilism is a comment in the *Nachlass* of 1887 (9[41]), where "the most extreme form of nihilism" is presented as a "*divine way of thinking*" according to which "*every* belief, every 'this is true' is necessarily false: *because there simply is no **true world***" (*KSA* 12, 9[41]; *WP* 15). On display here are Nietzsche's perspectivist premises that treat all former and prospective discussions of the essence, origin, and development of nihilism not as historical truths, but as quasi-skeptical hypotheses. The extreme form of nihilism that Nietzsche ascribes to himself already contains, as a conscious negative dogmatism, an inner contradiction, for a perspectivist cannot possibly know that there is no true world. Correspondingly, this extreme nihilism also appears as a philosophical recreation exercise for the warriors of knowledge (*KSA* 13, 11[108]). Extreme nihilism knows that there is no value in the reality of things – no truth, no absolute state of things, no thing in itself – and therefore imputes an unauthorized value to them that amounts to "a simplification for the purpose of life" (*KSA* 12, 9[35], pp. 351–2).

1.2.2 The nature of nihilism

In the *Nachlass* of 1887 nihilism appears as a normal condition of culture, being determined by the fact that it lacks only "the aim," the answer to the why-question. In general, nihilism signifies that "the highest values" devalue themselves (*KSA*, 12, 9[35]; *WP* 2). At first, Nietzsche presents an active nihilism that could either be a sign of intellectual strength, in so much as it rises above hitherto held convictions of belief, or a sign of deficient strength because it fails to set a new target. Active nihilism expresses itself in destruction and has its counterpart in passive nihilism, which, according to Nietzsche, manifests itself in a retreat from intellectual strength, as a symptom of tiredness that communicates former values as empty and irrelevant. This passive nihilism invents religious, moral, political, or aesthetic palliatives. The *Nachlass* of 1887–8 (*KSA* 13, 11[123]; *WP* 24) documents the fact that the destructive power of nihilism is not just intellectual. The "rigorous nihilism of the deed," which leads to the self-destruction of the weak, counts as useful and worthy of encouragement in other texts, while the condemnable nihilism of Christianity, Nietzsche says, protects "those who have turned out badly" and holds them back from suicide (*KSA* 13, 14[9]; *WP* 51). Another category distinguishes between "complete nihilism" and "incomplete nihilism" – the former as a "necessary result of ideals hitherto," the latter as the dominant form of nihilism (*KSA* 12, 10[42]; *WP* 28).

1.2.3 The origin and development of nihilism

The *Nachlass* note (11[99]) of 1887–8 explains the origin of nihilism as a "*psychological condition*," firstly out of disappointment at not discovering a "*purpose of becoming*" (*KSA* 13, p. 46f.), secondly out of disappointment over the impossibility of a unified "systemization" and "organization" of everything that happens. Thirdly, Nietzsche says that the psychological condition of nihilism occurs when it turns out that the construction of a metaphysical counter-world to the "true world" (*KSA* 13, p. 48) merely owes its existence to the psychic need for compensation, and this insight forbids a further belief in such a metaphysical world (cf. *TI*, "How the 'True World' Finally Became a Fable"). One then had no hold on any further worlds and yet could not bear the given world, since the concepts of "purpose," "truth," and "unity" ruled themselves out for an interpretation of existence, making way for the "feeling of worthlessness" (*KSA* 13, p. 48). "Radical nihilism" (*KSA* 12, 10[192]) then appeared as a consequence of relentless "truthfulness" and was, as such, "a result of the belief in morality." And hence, there lies the point of paradox which extreme nihilism strives to overcome: "in so far as we believe in morality, we *condemn* existence." In this way, morality makes its appearance as denial of the "will to existence" against which Nietzsche mobilizes his critical efforts. "Complete nihilism," characterized by its "great *contempt*," "great *pity*," and "great *destruction*," culminated in a "doctrine" that teaches life itself as "*absolute* and *eternal*" (*KSA* 13, 11[149]). In the comment immediately following 11[150], these observations are developed as "*history of European nihilism*" that began in a "*period of **uncertainty**"* through which nobody could penetrate to a decision between old and new values, while the following "*period of **certainty**"* comprehended the difference between the old values of decline and the new values of life in the ascendancy, which did not mean, however, that people were then strong enough for the new. Next, a *"period of the three great affects"* is envisaged, which represent the three features of nihilism quoted above. And finally, there will follow a *"period of* **catastrophe**" with a "doctrine that will *sieve out* people" (*KSA* 13, p. 71). Earlier versions of the prehistory and history of nihilism are found in the *Nachlass* of 1885–6 (2[127]) (*KSA* 12, pp. 125–7), as well as 2[131] (*KSA* 12, pp. 129–32), where, in addition, details are given of various movements that Nietzsche coopts for "nihilism." Finally, the "Lenzer Heide" fragment relates the history of nihilism with a rather different stress (*KSA* 12, 5[71], pp. 211–17, *LN* pp. 116–21; cf. Riedel 2000; Stegmaier 1994: 49–53).

1.3 Nihilism and religion

Nietzsche's much-varied theme of the death of God is what makes reflection on nihilism possible. (cf. Gerhardt 1992: 162f; a critical view in Gillespie 1999). Only when the belief in God as supreme value has been exterminated does the traditional hierarchy of values of old lose its grip, and one can only view the world in total under the preamble of the purely "for nothing." On the other hand, according to Nietzsche, Christianity itself is already nihilistic in so far as it tries to disguise the given world in favor of a world beyond, and cultivates a "will to the end," "a nihilistic will" (*A* 9). Christianity's ascetic preferences alone place it under suspicion of nihilism (*GM* III. 26), "Nihilist and Christ rhyme, and do more than just rhyme" (*A* 58, cf. Sommer 2000a: 586–99). Christianity's priestly asceticism has bequeathed itself to philosophy, for which Nietzsche finds evidence, for instance, in Arnold Geulincx's hatred of the body: "Ubi nihil vales, ibi nihil velis" (*KSA* 9, 11[194], excerpt from Fischer 1889: 38). In 1888, Nietzsche even promises "historic proof: philosophers are always *décadents*, always in the service of nihilistic religions" (*KSA* 13, 14[137]). Christianity appears as a religion that stems from *décadence* on the one hand (*KSA* 13, 14[10]), but on the other hand makes use of (*KSA* 13, p. 166f.) *"elements of décadence"* (*KSA* 13, 11[371]). Christianity works as a melting-pot for decadence; however, it has, Nietzsche states, also succeeded in incorporating and weakening "the strong races of northern Europe" (*A* 19). In *The Antichrist*, it is made morally responsible for the fact that it condemned the Roman empire and the whole culture of antiquity to destruction (*A* 58–60). The anti-Christian evaluation of Buddhism comes off a great deal better, likewise a nihilistic religion of *décadence*, yet "a hundred times more realistic" than Christianity (*A* 20; cf. Sommer 1999: 200–7). In the jotting of 1885 (34[204]), Nietzsche still welcomed Christianity alongside Buddhism, "to deal the death blow to degenerate and dying races" (*KSA* 11, p. 490). In 1888, a pathologization of religion dominates in the "physiology of nihilistic religions" (*KSA* 13, 14[13]). However, for the analysis of nihilism, the observation of 1885–6 remains essential – that Christianity invited its own downfall when "truthfulness," which expresses itself in its morality, "turns against the Christian God" (*KSA* 12, 2[127]).

1.4 Nihilism and morality

Nihilism is primarily a question of moral (devaluation), not epistemology. It appears "as a result of the moral interpretation of the world" (*KSA* 12, 7[43]); the transition from pessimism to nihilism is described – perhaps in connection with Wellhausen (1883: 105; cf. Sommer 2000a: 244) – as a "denaturalization of *values*" (*KSA* 12, 9[107]): values begin to turn "in self-condemnation against action" (*KSA* 12, 9[107], p. 397), to construct an ideal, ultimately also depraved, counter-world. What remains are the "*judging* values," which are, after all, still the values of extreme nihilism with which Nietzsche, as immoralist, identified. Precisely the strongest no longer subscribed to pity as a "*praxis* of nihilism" (*A* 7), which (according to *GM*, preface, 5) leads to a "European Buddhism." This demonstrates that "every purely moral evaluation" ends in nihilism (*KSA* 12, 7[64]). Hitherto, the "will to power" was lacking in "all the highest values of humankind"; instead "values of decline" have held sway (*A* 6). In contrast, a "counter-movement" springing from extreme nihilism is mustered that manifests itself as "the revaluation of all values" (cf. Sommer 2000c). Then the "Übermensch" appears as the counterpart "to the 'good' man, to the Christian and other nihilists" (*EH*, "Why I Write Such Good Books," 1).

1.5 Overcoming nihilism: eternal recurrence and will to power

Nihilism tends towards "*overcoming of the self,*" in which there are both "*overcomers*" and "*overcome*" (*KSA* 12, 9[127]; cf. *KSA* 12, 9[164]). As early as 1882, the "theory of recurrence as heaviest burden" was supposed to help initiate a collective suicide whereby nihilism is not yet universalized but instead figures as a "small prelude" (*KSA* 10, 2[4]). The "Lenzer Heide" fragment (*KSA* 12, 5[71], pp. 211–17; *LN* pp. 116–21) converts the doctrine of recurrence into a great political act, reducing the doctrine to its politico-instrumental value in the process and ceasing to give structure to Nietzsche's thought as such (cf. Skirl 2000: 229f.). Therefore it hardly plays a significant role in the late work, e.g. *The Antichrist* (cf. Sommer 2000a: 686f.). First, the Lenzer Heide fragment discusses the advantages of the Christian moral hypothesis, which has been undermined by the truthfulness originating from this morality itself. Now God proves to be a "much too extreme hypothesis" against nihilism; instead, the opposite, equally extreme, hypothesis surfaced by which all values, nay, the very possibility of values, are cast into doubt. In section 6, "eternal recurrence," emerges as "the most extreme form of nihilism: nothingness ('meaninglessness') eternally!" – to wit, everything recurring eternally "without meaning or goal" (*KSA* 12, p. 213). Eternal recurrence is hence introduced as a hypothesis equivalent to the hypothesis of God in its function and extremity – and is likely to have "truthfulness" against it just as the latter does, even if the hypothesis of recurrence is also "the *most scientific* of all possible hypotheses" (*KSA* 12, p. 213). This train of thought leads back, after a bow to Spinoza, to the function of traditional morality, which consisted of standing by the oppressed human being against those in power, in other words, against the "*will to power*." The oppressed would fall into complete despair if they lost the "*right*" to a moral "contempt for the will to power" (*KSA* 12, p. 215). But with morality, precisely this right had been disposed of, and now, from an indeterminate vantage point, Nietzsche decrees: "There is nothing in life that has value, apart from the degree of power – providing, of course, that life itself is the will to power." The oppressed would thereby lose their "consolation" and be destroyed by condemning themselves to destruction. Nihilism would then appear as "a symptom of the fact that those who have come off badly no longer have a consolation" (*KSA* 12, p. 216). Those "who have come off badly" are quite decidedly determined by "*physiology*" rather than politics. Here again, the motif of recurrence returns: "The unhealthiest kind of person in Europe [. . .] is the ground of nihilism: that type will construe belief in eternal recurrence as a *curse*: once afflicted, no action is too abhorrent" (*KSA* 12, p. 216). The will to power and eternal recurrence are thus pitched into this struggle as catalysts to establish a new "*rank order of forces*, from the point of view of health" (*KSA* 12, p. 217).

For all that, neither of the two "doctrines" provides final philosophical insights. The "strongest" have "no need for extreme propositions of belief" – in other words, neither God nor recurrence. So, as a final proposition, there remains only the rhetorical question: "What would such a human being think of eternal recurrence?" Possibly, the question is irrelevant for that person. Just as, according to *Nachlass* 1888 (16[32]), "experimental philosophy" does not come to a halt at nihilistic negation (*KSA* 13, p. 492), it will not be detained permanently by "doctrines" like eternal recurrence or will to power. The strongest, who are simultaneously the "most moderate," according to 5[71] (*KSA* 12, p. 217), seem to feel clearly a strong inclination towards skeptical reservations. This inclination also touches upon the diagnosis of nihilism, especially in its most universal form: "pathological is the monstrous generalization, the meaningless conclusion" (*KSA* 12, 9[35]). Not just extreme nihilism is a negative dogmatism, but possibly also the assertion that nihilism is unavoidable and ever present.

2 Skepticism

While Nietzsche speaks at length about nihilism as the devaluation of the highest values only in his late work, skepticism is a theme that is more or less strongly present in the whole of his oeuvre. Thus, the radical concept of truth and metaphors in the clandestine early work "On Truth and Lies in a Non-Moral Sense" can be read – without the idea becoming a pronouncement – as a Pyrrhonian attempt to sublate one's own speech in speech itself. Truth appears as a product of language, "the legislation of language establishes the first laws of truth" (*KSA* 1, p. 877; "Truth and Lies in a Non-Moral Sense," 81; cf. Hödl 1997). The virulence, evident in "On Truth and Lies in a Non-Moral Sense," of the "aporia of the missing epistemological place of a critique that has turned self-referential" (Kaiser 1994: 71; cf. Stingelin 1996: 109), is the unavoidable Pyrrhonic aporia of the sublation of a standpoint. While nihilism is primarily concerned with values, i.e. morality, skepticism doubts that reality can be known. "Extreme nihilism" appears as morally skeptical. It is articulated in the negatively dogmatic assassins' motto: "nothing is true, everything is permitted" (Z, "The Shadow"; *GM* III. 24). In contrast, even in Nietzsche's dealings with his so-called chief doctrines (eternal recurrence, will to power), a Pyrrhonian trait is visible that causes them to count only as perspectivist, situational truths (cf. Kain 1983: 283–7; Sommer 2000a: 524–41; on the other hand, see Gerhardt 1992: 78). Nietzsche argues for an experimental skepticism in his late work.

2.1 Sources of Nietzsche's concept of skepticism

Nietzsche acquired a copy of Viktor Brochard's study *Les Skeptiques Grecs* in 1887–8 shortly after it appeared (cf. Oehler 1942: 10) and studied it thoroughly (cf. Bett 2000; Sommer 2000a). A few jottings from 1888 are connected with the reading of Brochard's work, all of which treat the founding figure of skepticism, Pyrrho of Elis (Brobjer 1997, 2001). Before Brochard, whom he expressly praises (*EH*, "Why I Am So Clever," 3), Nietzsche had studied few monographs on the historical manifestations of philosophical skepticism. His general knowledge of skepticism in the ancient world might have been derived from his reading of ancient doxographs – in particular, Diogenes Laertius, *Vitae philosophorum* IX 11 (Pyrrho) and IX 12 (Timon) – and, on the other hand, from reading general surveys of the history of literature and philosophy, as, for example, Rudolf Nicolai's *Complete History of Greek Literature* (Nicolai 1867: 298–300, 489f.; cf. Oehler 1942: 12), Friedrich Überweg's *Survey of the History of Philosophy from Thales to the Present* (Oehler 1942: 22), or Eduard Zeller's *Philosophy of the Greeks in their Historical Development* (Zeller 1880–1: vol. 3/1, pp. 478–527, vol. 3/2, pp. 1–69). There are no indications that Nietzsche might have read the work of Sextus Empiricus in the original (but cf. Conway and Ward 1992).

In his reading of contemporary philosophical works, Nietzsche was confronted with skeptical considerations in a variety of forms, for example, with Afrikan Spir (cf. D'Iorio 1993; Sommer 2000b: 419f.), Gustav Teichmüller (1882; cf. e.g. *KSA* 13, 21[1]) or with Friedrich Albert Lange. On the one hand, Lange's *History of Materialism* is an expression of radical criticism; on the other, it introduces several skeptical authors of the modern world, from Michel de Montaigne through Pierre Bayle all the way to David Hume, all of whom Nietzsche had also encountered in Kuno Fischer's *History of New Philosophy* (*KSA* 12, 7[4], pp. 259–70 is a Fischer excerpt). Nietzsche studied the works of Montaigne, Pierre Charron, Blaise Pascal, and the French moralists intensively (cf. Vivarelli 1998), while he at least possessed a copy of Hume's *Dialogues Concerning Natural Religion* (Oehler 1942: 19). In so far as skepticism is coupled with the critique of language, Georg Christoph Lichtenberg might have been an important prompt (Stingelin 1996), as well as Gustav Gerber in the early work (Meijers and Stingelin 1988). Skepticism towards religious claims to truth was revealed to Nietzsche in, for example, William Edward Hartpole Lecky's *History of the Origin and Influence of the Enlightenment in Europe*, a book he utilized heavily (cf. Oehler 1942: 20). Nor was intensive study of Jean Marie Guyau's *L'Irréligion de l'avenir* (2nd edn. 1887) and Eugène de Roberty's *L'Ancienne et la nouvelle philosophie* (1887) without its rewards.

2.2 Phases and forms of skepticism

Anyone looking for examples of the philosophical skeptic in Nietzsche would not necessarily find these among the "usual suspects" of popular histories of philosophy. It is noticeable that the "classical" skeptics of antiquity are sporadic before he read Brochard (Brobjer 2001: 14). While it is true that Heraclitus is the prominent philosopher of becoming for Nietzsche, though not figuring as a proto-skeptic, research is divided over the role the Sophists, namely Gorgias, Hippias, Callicles, and Protagoras, play in Nietzsche (Mann 2003, versus Brobjer 2001). On the other hand, Socrates is expressly categorized as a skeptic in Nietzsche's early periodization of Greek philosophy (*KSA* 7, 23[8]); "demolition of the rigidly dogmatic" set in with him (*KSA* 7, 23[14]), though naturally this did not alter the worryingly optimistic tendency of Socratic philosophy. "Socratic skepticism is a weapon against the preceding culture and knowledge" (*KSA* 7, 23[35]). Nietzsche also inserts an early phase of thorough-going skepticism into Plato's development, because, he states, Plato at that time saw everything in "flux" (*KSA* 7 23[27]; cf. Ghedini 1999: 272f.). At the same time, Plato's middle philosophy seems to be completely unskeptical, while a renewed "skepticism" is found in the refutation of the doctrine of ideas in the *Parmenides*. By contrast, in his treatment of Plato in the *Nachlass* of 1885, Nietzsche differentiates between an exoteric and an esoteric point of view: no philosopher ever nursed such an "absolute skepsis towards all given concepts" as Plato; and yet Plato "*taught the opposite*" (*KSA* 11, 34[195]). For the young Nietzsche, it is clear that the "tragic philosopher" is not a skeptic (*KSA*, 7, 19[35]) – while the opposite applies to the academic skeptic Arkesilaos, who was incapable of art (*KSA* 7, 5[21], perhaps after Zeller 1880: vol. 3/1, pp. 496f. n. 4).

Pyrrhonian skepticism is hardly ever found in Nietzsche's early and middle work – apart from in the *Philologica*. Only in "The Wanderer and his Shadow," 213, does Pyrrho emerge in a dialog with an "old man" – a Pyrrho, moreover, who, according to Bett (2000: 67), has nothing in common with the historic figure of Pyrrho of Elis. Pyrrho is portrayed as the "*fanatic of mistrust*" (*WS* 213) who wants to promulgate mistrust towards "everything and everyone," because this is the "only path to truth." During conversation, Pyrrho recognizes that, if he wants to be mistrustful of all words, he is condemned to silence, but he would have to tell people that he must keep silent: "Saying nothing and laughing – is that your whole philosophy? *Pyrrho*: It would not be the worst" (*WS* 213). At all events, aphasia (cf. Zeller 1880: vol. 3/1, p. 488), keeping silent in the face of indecision, is characteristic for the skepticism of the historic Pyrrho (Diogenes Laertius IX 61, 76 [1967: 192, 200]). In structure, Nietzsche's dialog resembles Fontenelle's *Dialogues des morts*, mentioned in *WS* 214, and that of his model, Lukian's *Dialogues of the Dead*. A closer examination of the historical Pyrrho only took place after Nietzsche read Brochard in 1887–8 (1932: 51–76), where the founder of skepticism, to whom Diogenes Laertius (IX. 61 [1967: 192]) imputed familiarity with Indian gymnosophists, appears as a "Greek Buddhist" (*KSA* 13, 14[85]) who acts as a radical critic of the philosophers to the extent that their teachings are unsuitable for life (*KSA* 13, 14[129]). Pyrrho is gripped by a decadent "silence requirement" (*KSA* 13, 15[58]); in a lengthy note (*KSA* 13, 14[99]) we find his "philosophy as *décadence*," which defends itself against "knowledge and mind," no longer wants to believe in the "importance of all things," and ends up as a "final self-overcoming, final indifference." In comparison to the *décadent* Epicurus, Pyrrho is "more traveled, more worn out, more nihilistic." "His life was a protest against the great *doctrine of identity*." Finally, the philosophical way of living even ceased to strive for happiness. However, this does not prevent Nietzsche from suspecting elsewhere that even with Pyrrho, as with Socrates, Aristippus, the cynics and the epicures, a "battle against knowledge" is being fought in favor of "morality" (*KSA* 13, 14[141]).

In defiance of German conformity in things intellectual, Nietzsche in *Daybreak* 207 claims for himself "the southern freedom of feeling" with the Romans and the Greeks, who knew how to fend off "unconditional trust" with skepticism (cf. *GS* 358). Among the skeptical thinkers of the modern age, Montaigne and Pascal play a significant role in Nietzsche's thought (cf. Vivarelli 1998), although a tired skepticism of the present day lays an unjustified claim on Montaigne (*BGE* 208). The "brave and good-humored skepticism of a Montaigne" seems to be of much more serious import to Nietzsche (*KSA* 11, 36[7]), while "the doubt of doubt" surfaces under Pascal's merciless gaze (*D* 46). In contrast, Nietzsche finds Descartes' methodology of doubt insufficiently radical because it builds on something directly certain, which, in his words, is simply "nonsense": "cogito, ergo sum presumes that one knows what 'thinking' is and secondly, what 'being' is" (*KSA* 11, 40[24]) – precisely what one does not know. While Hume plays only a marginal role with Nietzsche (cf. Beam 2001), Kant made the "Englishmen's epistemological skepticism" possible for the Germans by meeting their moral and religious needs, "just as Pascal even made use of moral skepticism to excite the need for faith" (*KSA* 12, 9[3]). Similarly, Kant shows himself to be a "dogmatist through and through" (*KSA* 12, 9[3]) who, "thanks to a mischievously clever skepticism," had even tried to make Christianity irrefutable (*A* 10). By contrast, the early work had allowed Kant's theory of knowledge even greater skeptical explosive force (e.g. *UM III*, "Schopenhauer as Educator"), although Nietzsche points out in the *Nachlass* of 1872–3 that "nobody could live" with Kant's skepticism (*KSA* 7, 19[125]).

While the jotting of the year 1887 (9[157]) imputes to several great individuals (from Caesar through Leonardo and on to Napoleon and Goethe) a skepticism that exists in the "permission to withdraw from a faith" (*KSA* 12, p. 428), the second untimely meditation on history already sketches out a nihilistic-seeming skepticism of the present, prevented from taking any forward-looking action by the epigonic consciousness. "Skeptical historicism" is, according to the *Nachlass* of 1880–1 (*KSA* 9, 10[D88], p. 434), the formula for this.

In parallel with nihilism, I shall now recapitulate first, Nietzsche's skeptical premises; second, the character of skepticism; and third, the origin and course of skepticism, according to Nietzsche, drawing on relevant texts.

2.2.1 Nietzsche's skeptical premises

Already in the *Nachlass* of 1872–3, Nietzsche deduces skeptical consequences from a radicalized critique of knowledge ignited by the problem of causality. However, here as in *The Birth of Tragedy*, the "necessity of art and illusion" is mobilized against "absolute skepticism" (*KSA* 7, 19[121]). In 1875, the philologist counts as a great skeptic with regard to culture (*KSA* 8, 3[76] and 5[55]) – a motif that recurs in the philological Ephexis' speech (*A* 52). At the same time, Nietzsche increasingly guards against a comfortable skepticism associated with tiredness and feeling weak (letter to Romundt, April 15, 1876, *KSB* 5, p. 153). He profiles what is new in his approach as the fact "*that we do not have truth*," whereas earlier, even the "skeptics" had claimed to be in possession of the truth (*KSA* 9, 3[19]). For Nietzsche, skepticism remains essential precisely with regard to every experience (*KSA* 9, 11[293]), even if the skeptic occasionally allows himself to relax in "pleasant raptures" (*KSA* 9, 10[F101], p. 438). The form of skepticism Nietzsche prescribed for himself in the middle period of his creativity is revealed in jotting 6[356] of 1880: "Skepticism! Yes, but a *skepticism of experiments!* Not the lethargy of despair" (*KSA* 9, p. 287). When, in a note on the third part of *Zarathustra*, skepticism counts as "a temptation" (*KSA* 10, 16[83]), in the immediately following note, life itself is understood as "an experiment"; "happiness" lies "in guessing or experimenting (skepticism)" (*KSA* 10, 16[84]): skepticism as the realization of eudaimonia! According to a jotting from the winter of 1882–3, the statement that things are unknowable has a therapeutic component that was also essential for skepticism in antiquity; "Despair abolished via skepticism," whereby the speaking "I" has gained "the right to *create*" (*KSA* 10, 6[1]). These deliberations culminate in *GS* 51: "I salute any form of skepticism to which I am allowed to reply: 'let's give it a try!'" All the same, Nietzsche wants to arm himself against "skeptical arbitrariness." The result of the newly won freedom "from the tyranny of 'eternal' concepts" ought to lead us "to view concepts as experiments, with the help of which certain types of human being" can be bred (*KSA* 11, 35[36]). This should apply to Nietzsche's own new concepts, "will to power" and "eternal recurrence of the same," in particular. Nietzsche's experimental skepticism results in the "capacity to have one's for and against *under control* and to put it on show, or not" (*GM* III. 12). The "perspectivist character of existence" cannot be removed, nor indeed can the possibility that the world "*contains within itself endless interpretations*" be ignored (*GS* 374; cf. Figal 2000). True, this does not mean the denial of knowledge in general (as Schacht 2000 rightly points out), but it does mean the unavoidable perspectivism and situatedness of all knowledge. If one takes Nietzsche's experimental skepticism seriously, one must read the apparently dogmatic late work, particularly *The Antichrist*, as an expression of skeptical strategy as well, that of asserting certain interpretations against others (cf. Sommer 2000a). This procedure is reflected expressly in *A* 54. Without doubt, the experimental skepticism of Nietzsche's late work is far removed from the Pyrrhonian doctrine of withholding judgment (cf. Bett 2000: 81). Precisely through constant judgments, Nietzsche's late texts inject a neutralizing skepticism into his work that becomes clear when these judgments are contrasted with the judgments they attack (e.g. Christian).

2.2.2 The character of skepticism

According to a note of 1873, there are "only" "friends of truth," "*enemies of truth*," or "skeptics" (*KSA* 7, 26[10]). The skeptic is thus constituted by indifference towards the truth. According to Nietzsche, the removal of (metaphysical) truth in turn characterizes the intellectual situation of the present, later to be labeled by him as nihilism. Skepticism then manifests itself in the *Nachlass* in 1880 (6[31]) as "the afterbirth of pride" (*KSA* 9, p. 200), long nurtured by humanity in the metaphysical certainty of its own worth. If this skepticism first shows itself as a powerful self-destruction of human pride, Nietzsche postulates that a phase of exhaustion will follow. But the nature of Nietzschean skepticism is belligerent: "We have become disgusted by the views of the authorities – we would rather starve!" (*KSA* 9, 6[122]); this "skepticism is a passion." In an informative jotting of 1885, the "Ephexis" (Nietzsche means the Pyrrhonian *epoché*) becomes a scientific principle (*KSA* 11, 35[29]; cf. *A* 52, Sommer 2000a: 510–12). The Ephexian characterizes himself through his readiness to keep problems open and through ironic reservation regarding precipitous attempts at explanation. "Thus his conduct stems, not from his weakness but from his strength" (*KSA* 11, p. 521). "Ephexis" is by no means a comfortable attitude; rather, it consists of cultivating a view that is free of illusions, especially when it comes to morality.

2.2.3 The origin and course of skepticism

Important for the historical-genealogical development of perspectivism in skepticism is Nietzsche's differentiation of 1883–4 between a "skepticism of weakness" and one of "courage" (*KSA* 10, 24[30]), though his own adaptation of skepticism aims to connect it with "*heroic* feelings." Nietzsche revises his old thesis of the incompatibility of skeptical and tragic thought. Historically, "the skeptical eras, *suffering* from indecision" (*KSA* 12, 5[17]) are precisely the ones that go over to a "rigid faith." Meanwhile, the "suffering of uncertainty" is introduced as the fundamental origin of systematic thought – a suffering that Nietzsche's experimental, heroic skepticism refuses to engage with systematically. Christianity, he says, grew up in the very midst of a skeptical world (*BGE* 46). Faced with an egalitarian and democratizing skepticism in contemporaries like Sainte-Beuve and Renan, the speaking "we" want to do without being called skeptics from time to time and flirt with the name "critic" or "'criticist'" to articulate yet again the claim to "experimental philosophy" (*KSA* 11, 35[43]). According to Nietzsche, commanding skeptics have obviously appeared only rarely up to now (*KSA* 11, 42[6]); what is needed is the "overcoming of the skeptic of weakness" (*KSA* 11, 26[241]). Finally, *BGE* 208–10 formulates this idea – a passage that defends itself against the comfortable skepticism of the present and lets it be known that Nietzsche's new philosophy will not be the slightest bit satisfied with skepticism as "gentle, pure, soothing opium" (*BGE* 208); instead, it plans "a skepticism of bold masculinity" "that is closely related to the genius for war and plunder" (*BGE* 209). The works of 1888, propagating skepticism as the only form of philosophy worthy of attention (e.g. *A* 12, 54) are born of this kind of skepticism, while the critical views Nietzsche adopted towards skepticism in the ancient world under the influence of his reading of Brochard remain consigned to the notes in the *Nachlass* (Bett 2000: 79). There, skepticism turns out to be, for example, "a result of *décadence*" (*KSA* 13, 14[86]). But this brushing away of the critique of skepticism in the *Nachlass* does not hinge on the fact that, as Bett surmises, Nietzsche suddenly becomes a dogmatist in 1888. Rather, the experimental skepticism favored by Nietzsche is completely different from the retreatist Pyrrhonism, with its complete refusal to make a judgment, that he found described in Brochard.

2.3 Skepticism and religion

If skepticism doubts truth then it naturally stands on a tense footing with religion as an institution of social administration of truth (cf. e.g. Nicolai 1867: 299). Nietzsche thought about this in 1873 when he defined skepticism as an "*ascetic* viewpoint of the thinker" (*KSA* 7, 23[8], p. 624) who denies himself believing in belief (even when he retains the "belief in logic," *KSA* 7, 23[8], p. 625). In 1885 Nietzsche described the appearance of "the inwardly bold skepticism in Germany" (*KSA* 11, 34[157]) as a reaction to the all too close acquaintanceship of philosophers with representatives of

Protestantism – a path that, for example, Nietzsche's most loyal friend, the non-believing Professor of Theology Franz Overbeck, had trod (cf. Sommer 1997, 2003). At all events, Nietzsche admits that Christianity made a contribution to the Enlightenment by its teaching that humankind should be viewed with skepticism (*GS* 122). On the other hand, Nietzsche observes that Christianity, with the help of the Pilate question, used the skepticism of "not being able to know" for gaining converts (*AOM* 8). This does not alter the fact that it was precisely a skeptical insight that eliminated God, especially the Christian one. The "new philosophy," conceived as an "epistemological skepticism," is "*anti-Christian*," albeit "by no means anti-religious" (*BGE* 54). In the *Nachlass* of 1888, Nietzsche remarks that the philosopher becomes a skeptic through the examination of knowledge and comes to an arrangement with the "priest" "so as not to arouse the suspicion of atheism or materialism" (*KSA* 13, 14[194]). The result of this somewhat unflattering description of his fellow practitioners means that no practicing philosophers appear as representatives of a noteworthy skepticism. Instead, Nietzsche refers to politicians such as Frederick the Great (*BGE* 209) or Pilate (*A* 46), who is portrayed as the opponent of Paul and Jesus. Jesus in his anti-Christian "psychology of the redeemer" (*A* 28) does not just resemble Epicurus (*A* 30) but also Pyrrho, as he is described, following Brochard, in the *Nachlass* of 1888, where the close connection to Epicurus is made (*KSA* 13, 14[99]). Jesus and Pyrrho behave in their native land in the manner of Buddha (Jesus: *A* 32; Pyrrho: *KSA* 13, 14[162]): both renounce "*all* [. . .] *bounds and distances in feeling*" (*A* 30), likewise all judgment and denial. In both cases, Nietzsche puts this down to the specific, even pathological, physiological conditions; in the late works, his own experimental skepticism of denial and judgment departs sharply from these models.

2.4 Skepticism and morality

Skepticism remains no mere epistemological exercise. The concept of the genealogy of morality is deeply stamped with skeptical premises (*KSA* 9, 4[37]; *GM*, preface, 5), while morality, in return, objects to the skeptics (*AOM* 71). Looking back, Nietzsche already claimed for himself in the mid-1870s a "moral skepticism" in which pessimism had not only deepened but also criticized itself (*WS*, preface, 1). According to *D* 477 "moral skepticism," which approaches "man" with fundamental mistrust, does not need to be followed by bad temper and weakness: For dialog partner A, "general moral skepticism" is, to all appearances, an elixir of life. Dialog partner B objects that A, having made a denial, has ceased to be a skeptic. To which A replies that he has learned to say "Yes" again. The little dialog illustrates the structure of experimental skepticism within Nietzsche; this is not an ephectic but a judgment-friendly skepticism. Its task lies in the removal of valid "value judgments on people and things": "one would have to overturn all values by means of a radical skepticism, to have a clear path" (*KSA* 9, 3[54]). In 1880 Nietzsche sees in Socrates an epoch-making forerunner of moral skepticism (*KSA* 9, 7[222]) whose time has now come (*KSA* 9, 7[231]). For Nietzsche, "skepticism of morality" counts as a decisive prerequisite in the development of nihilism (*KSA* 12, 2[126]).

Elsewhere, we are instructed that moral skeptics would be well advised to subject their own "mistrust of morality" in turn to a mistrustful skepticism (*KSA* 10, 3[120b]).

Skeptics too easily forget how much they themselves have been infected by morality (*KSA* 11, 34[193]). Radical doubt about morality is potentially self-contradictory. As soon as the skeptic ceases to believe in the truth, the reason for his doubt falls away, except, as Nietzsche says, "*the will to know*" has "*a quite different root yet* [. . .] *from that of truthfulness*" (*KSA* 11, 35[5]). In consequence, Nietzsche presumes in 1885–6 that "no skepticism has arisen without reservation" – and this reservation has so far always been a moral one (*KSA* 12, 2[161]). His examination of the skeptics of antiquity in 1888 does not reach any fundamentally different conclusions: morality remained the highest value for them (*KSA* 13, 14[135, 137]). According to Nietzsche, the Pyrrhonians subject even their epoché to the "herd instinct" and "live like the 'common man'" (*KSA* 13, 14[107]). The new experimental skepticism nurses the strongest aversion to such subordination: it wants to create differences, not do away with them. The "victory of skepticism" over "morality as prejudice" might well hide "a dawn-like happiness" (*KSA* 12, 5[28]). That can only be discovered through hard work, of course: "One should reduce and bound the realm of morality step by step" (*KSA* 12, 10[45]).

2.5 Skepticism and the revaluation of all values

Just as moral skepticism is a requirement for the emergence of nihilism, it also belongs to Nietzsche's late project of a revaluation of all values, which he thought he had finally achieved in *The Antichrist*. Naturally, if the revaluation does not seek to bring about a new form of heteronomy, it can hardly amount to a canon of new values that individuals will have to obey as they did the old one. Then the freedom to create values that Nietzsche, of course, wishes to see granted to strong individuals, would be undermined again. Revaluation of all values – and to that extent, *The Antichrist* really is the complete revaluation – consists precisely in the creation of the freedom to shape one's self and the world, while all the former differences are neutralized through dissonances. In turn, this forces every individual to make unavoidable personal, situational, and perspectival decisions in shaping his or her life and the world, unlike the Pyrrhonians, who had to fit in with what was given. "Ephexis" in *The Antichrist* (*A* 52) is a principle of philological interpretation not intended to make perspectives absolute, but it is no Pyrrhonian suspension of one's own decision; on the contrary, in Nietzsche's experimental skepticism, the epoché is rejected as a basic attitude to life (cf. Obstoj 1985). To that extent, philosophers and skeptics both end up as "*givers of orders and laws*" who say how it should be *for them* (*BGE* 211).

3 Nihilism and Skepticism

My discussion of the complex of nihilism and skepticism has brought into view numerous overlaps and revealed mutual dependencies. The borders between skepticism and nihilism are frequently fluid. In his early work, when the formula for nihilism was not yet available to Nietzsche, occasional phenomena later classified as nihilistic (e.g. *UM II*, 8), are subsumed under the rubric of "skepticism." Later, it is impossible not to detect skeptical resonances, not only when Nietzsche refers to a nihilism that he rejects decisively (e.g. *GM* III. 24; *KSA* 13, 14[74]), but also when he refers to a nihilism that he appears to claim for himself (*KSA* 13, 14[24]). When Nietzsche in 1885 propagates an "ecstatic nihilism" as a possibly indispensable instrument for the philosopher "to make way for a new order of life" (*KSA* 11, 35[82]), nihilism is used just as strategically as are the convictions in *A* 54 that the experimenting skeptic uses for his own purposes. The "most extreme form of nihilism," which, according to the *Nachlass* of 1887 (9[41]), could be *"a divine way of thinking"* (*KSA* 12, p. 354), converges with anti-Christian skepticism in its strategy of neutralizing all forms of conceiving something to be true.

While both nihilism and skepticism as historical manifestations are founded on *décadence* and represent symptoms of degenerating life, extreme nihilism and experimental skepticism are two different names for the strategy that Nietzsche adopts in his last creative period to complete a revaluation of values. Seen against this revaluation, the putative "main doctrines" of "will to power" and "eternal recurrence of the same" appear only as the means, not the ends. Extreme nihilism and experimental skepticism are radical distancing acts towards everything hitherto believed and seen as valid; the inability to gain distance that characterizes the historic forms of nihilism and skepticism is supposed to be overcome here. The diagnosis of nihilism in terms of the philosophy of history is, then, neither a doctrine of belief nor a strong proposition of a hidden metaphysics, but rather a stratagem of that very skepticism that strives for power – power in favor of an individually accountable creation of value and world.

See also 7 "Nietzsche and Philosophical Anthropology"; 8 "Nietzsche's Philosophy and True Religion"; 22 "Rebaptizing our Evil"

Nietzsche's Sources

Brochard, V. (1932). *Les Skeptiques Grecs*, 2nd edn. (1887; Paris: Librairie Philosophique J. Vrin).

Diogenes Laertius (1967). *Leben und Meinungen berühmter Philosophen*, trans. from the Greek by O. Apelt, ed. K. Reich (Hamburg: Felix Meiner).

Fischer, K. (1889). *Descartes und seine Schule*, pt. 2: *Fortbildung der Lehre Descartes's Spinoza*, Geschichte der neuern Philosophie, vol. 1, pt. 2; 3rd, improved, edn. (1865; Heidelberg: Carl Winters Universitätsbuchhandlung).

Lange, F. A. (1905). *Geschichte des Materialismus und Kritik seiner Bedeutung in der Gegenwart*, ed. O. A. Ellissen (1866; 2nd edn. 1873–5; Leipzig: Philipp Reclam Jr.).

Lecky, W. E. H. (1873). *Geschichte des Ursprungs und Einflusses der Aufklärung in Europa*, trans. H. von Jolowicz, 2 vols. (Leipzig and Heidelberg: C. F. Winter'sche Verlagshandlung).

Nicolai, R. (1867). *Geschichte der gesammten griechischen Literatur. Ein Versuch* (Magdeburg: Heinrichshofen'sche Buchhandlung).

Teichmüller, G. (1882). *Die wirkliche und die scheinbare Welt. Neue Grundlegung der Metaphysik* (Breslau: Koebner).

Wellhausen, J. (1883). *Prolegomena zur Geschichte Israels. Zweite Ausgabe der Geschichte Israels*, vol. 1, pt. 2 (Berlin: Georg Reimer).

Zeller, E. (1880–1). *Die Philosophie der Griechen in ihrer geschichtlichen Entwicklung*, vols. 3/1– 3/2: Die nacharistotelische Philosophie 3 (Leipzig: Fues's Verlag [R. Reisland]).

Editions of Nietzsche Used

"Truth and Lies in a Non-Moral Sense," in Daniel Breazeale (ed.), *Philosophy and Truth: Selections from Nietzsche's Notebooks of the Early 1870s* (Atlantic Highlands, NJ: Humanities Press), pp. 79–101.

References

Ansell Pearson, K. (1987). "Nietzsche's Overcoming of Kant and Metaphysics: From Tragedy to Nihilism," *Nietzsche-Studien*, 16, pp. 310–39.

Beam, C. (2001). "Ethical Affinities: Nietzsche in the Tradition of Hume," *International Studies in Philosophy*, 33(3), pp. 87–98.

Bett, R. (2000). "Nietzsche on the Sceptics and Nietzsche as Sceptic," *Archiv für Geschichte der Philosophie*, 82(1), pp. 62–86.

Brobjer, T. H. (1997). "Beiträge zur Quellenforschung," *Nietzsche-Studien*, 26, pp. 574–9.

—— (2001). "Nietzsche's Disinterest and Ambivalence toward the Greek Sophists," *International Studies in Philosophy*, 33(3), pp. 5–23.

Brusotti, M. (2001). "Wille zum Nichts, Ressentiment, Hypnose. 'Aktiv' und 'Reaktiv' in Nietzsches *Genealogie der Moral*," *Nietzsche-Studien*, 30, pp. 107–32.

Conway, D. W. (1992). "Heidegger, Nietzsche, and the Origins of Nihilism," *Journal of Nietzsche Studies*, 3, pp. 11–43.

Conway, D. W. and Ward, J. K. (1992). "Physicians of the Soul: *Peritrope* in Sextus and Nietzsche," in D. W. Conway and R. Rehn (eds.), *Nietzsche und die antike Philosophie* (Trier: WVT), pp. 193–224.

Danto, A. (1965). *Nietzsche as Philosopher* (London and New York: Macmillan).

D'Iorio, P. (1993). "La Superstition des philosophes critiques: Nietzsche et Afrikan Spir," *Nietzsche-Studien*, 22, pp. 257–94.

Figal, G. (2000). "Nietzsches Philosophie der Interpretation," *Nietzsche-Studien*, 29, pp. 1–11.

Fraser, G. (2000). *Redeeming Nietzsche: On the Piety of Unbelief* (London and New York: Routledge).

Gerhardt, V. (1992). *Friedrich Nietzsche* (Munich: C. H. Beck).

Ghedini, F. (1999). *Il Platone di Nietzsche: Genesi e motivi di un simbolo controverso (1864–1879)* (Naples: Edizioni Scientifiche Italiane).

Gillespie, M. A. (1999). "Nietzsche and the Anthropology of Nihilism," *Nietzsche-Studien*, 28, pp. 141–55.

Heidegger, M. (1961). *Nietzsche*, 2 vols. (Pfullingen: Günther Neske).

Hödl, H. G. (1997). *Nietzsches frühe Sprachkritik* (Vienna: Universitätsverlag).

Kain, P. J. (1983). "Nietzsche, Scepticism, and Eternal Recurrence," *Canadian Journal of Philosophy*, 13, pp. 365–87.

Kaiser, S. (1994). "Über Wahrheit und Klarheit. Aspekte des Rhetorischen in 'Über Warheit und Lüge im aussermoralischen Sinne'," *Nietzsche-Studien*, 23, pp. 65–78.

Kaulbach, F. (1980). *Nietzsches Idee einer Experimentalphilosophie* (Cologne and Vienna: Böhlau).

Kuhn, E. (1989). "Cultur, Civilisation, die Zweideutigkeit des 'Modernen'," *Nietzsche-Studien*, 18, pp. 600–26.

—— (1992). *Friedrich Nietzsches Philosophie des europäischen Nihilismus* (Berlin and New York: Walter de Gruyter).

—— (2000). "Nihilismus," in H. Ottmann (ed.), *Nietzsche-Handbuch. Leben – Werk – Wirkung* (Stuttgart: J. B. Metzler), pp. 293–302.

Magnus, B. (1980). "Nietzsche's Mitigated Scepticism," *Nietzsche-Studien*, 9, pp. 260–7.

Mann, J. E. (2003). "Nietzsche's Interest and Enthusiasm for the Greek Sophists," *Nietzsche-Studien*, 32, pp. 406–28.

Meijers, A., and Stingelin, M. (1988). "Konkordanz zu den wörtlichen Abschriften und Übernahmen von Beispielen und Zitaten aus Gustav Gerber: *Die Sprache als Kunst* (Bromberg 1871) in Nietzsches Rhetorik-Vorlesung und in 'Über Wahrheit und Lüge im aussermoralischen Sinne'," *Nietzsche-Studien*, 17, pp. 350–68.

Müller-Lauter, W., and Goerdt, W. (1984). "Nihilismus," in J. Ritter and K. Gründer (eds.). *Historisches Wörterbuch der Philosophie* (Basel: Schwabe), vol. 6, pp. 846–54.

Obstoj, D. (1985). *Skepsis bei Nietzsche*, Ph.D. thesis, University of Hanover.

Oehler, M. (1942). *Nietzsches Bibliothek. Vierzehnte Jahresgabe der Gesellschaft der Freunde des Nietzsche-Archivs* (Leipzig: Hadl).

Ottmann, H. (1999). *Philosophie und Politik bei Nietzsche* (Berlin and New York: Walter de Gruyter).

—— (ed.) (2000). *Nietzsche-Handbuch. Leben – Werk – Wirkung* (Stuttgart: J. B. Metzler).

Riedel, M. (2000). "Das Lenzerheide-Fragment über den europäischen Nihilismus," *Nietzsche-Studien*, 29, pp. 70–81.

Schacht, R. (2000). "Nietzschean Cognitivism," *Nietzsche-Studien*, 29, pp. 12–40.

Skirl, M. (2000). "Ewige Wiederkunft," in H. Ottmann (ed.), *Nietzsche-Handbuch. Leben – Werk – Wirkung* (Stuttgart: J. B. Metzler), pp. 222–30.

Sommer, A. U. (1997). *Der Geist der Historie und das Ende des Christentums. Zur "Waffengenossenschaft" von Friedrich Nietzsche und Franz Overbeck* (Berlin: Akademie Verlag).

—— (1999). "Ex oriente lux? Zur vermeintlichen 'Ostorientierung' in Nietzsches Antichrist," *Nietzsche-Studien*, 28, pp. 194–214.

—— (2000a). *Friedrich Nietzsches "Der Antichrist." Ein philosophisch-historischer Kommentar* (Basel: Schwabe).

—— (2000b). "Philosophie und Theologie des 19. Jahrhunderts," in H. Ottmann (ed.), *Nietzsche-Handbuch. Leben – Werk – Wirkung* (Stuttgart: J. B. Metzler), pp. 412–22.

—— (2000c). "Umwertung aller Werte," in H. Ottmann (ed.), *Nietzsche-Handbuch. Leben – Werk – Wirkung* (Stuttgart: J. B. Metzler), pp. 345–6.

—— (2003). "On the Genealogy of the Genealogical Method: Overbeck, Nietzsche, and the Search for Origins," in I. Gildenhard and M. Ruehl (eds.), *Out of Arcadia: Classics and Politics in Germany in the Age of Burckhardt, Nietzsche and Wilamowitz* [= *Bulletin of the Institute of Classical Studies*], supplement 79, pp. 87–103 (London: Institute of Classical Studies).

Stegmaier, W. (1994). *Nietzsches "Genealogie der Moral"* (Darmstadt: Wissenschaftliche Buchgesellschaft).

Stingelin, M. (1996). *"Unsere ganze Philosophie ist Berichtigung des Sprachgebrauchs." Friedrich Nietzsches Lichtenberg-Rezeption im Spannungsfeld zwischen Sprachkritik (Rhetorik) und historischer Kritik (Genealogie)* (Munich: Wilhelm Fink).

Thiele, L. P. (1990). *Friedrich Nietzsche and the Politics of the Soul: A Study of Heroic Individualism* (Princeton: Princeton University Press).

Vivarelli, Vivetta (1998). *Nietzsche und die Masken des freien Geistes. Montaigne, Pascal und Sterne* (Würzburg: Königshausen & Neumann).

Further Reading

Clark, M. (1990). *Nietzsche on Truth and Philosophy* (Cambridge: Cambridge University Press).

Hill, R. K. (1997). "Ultimate Scepsis. The Self-Overcoming of Cartesianism," *International Studies in Philosophy*, 29(3), pp. 109–19.

Hull, R. (1990). "Scepticism, Enigma, and Integrity: Horizons of Affirmation in Nietzsche's Philosophy," *Man and World*, 23, pp. 375–91.

Kuhn, E. (1984). "Nietzsches Quelle des Nihilismus-Begriffs," *Nietzsche-Studien*, 13, pp. 253–78.

Martin, G. T. (1987). "A Critique of Nietzsche's Metaphysical Scepticism," *International Studies in Philosophy*, 19(2), pp. 51–9.

Molner, D. (1993). "The Influence of Montaigne on Nietzsche: A Raison d'Etre in the Sun," *Nietzsche-Studien*, 22, pp. 80–93.

Morrison, R. G. (1997). *Nietzsche and Buddhism: A Study in Nihilism and Ironic Affinities* (Oxford: Oxford University Press).

Morrisson, I. (2001). "Slave Morality, Will to Power, and Nihilism in *On the Genealogy of Morality*," *International Studies in Philosophy*, 33(3), pp. 127–43.

Müller-Lauter, W. (1999). *Nietzsche: His Philosophy of Contradictions and the Contradictions of his Philosophy*, trans. David J. Parent (1st pub. in German 1971; Chicago: University of Illinois Press).

Parush, A. (1975–6). "Nietzsche on the Sceptic's Life," *The Review of Metaphysics*, 29, 523–42.

Poellner, P. (1995). *Nietzsche and Metaphysics* (Oxford: Oxford University Press).

Schröder, W. (2002). *Moralischer Nihilismus. Typen radikaler Moralkritik von den Sophisten bis Nietzsche* (Stuttgart and Bad Cannstatt: Frommann-Holzboog).

Simon, J. (1984). "Nietzsche und das Problem des europäischen Nihilismus," in R. Berlinger and W. Schrader (eds.), *Nietzsche – kontrovers* (Würzburg: Königshausen & Neumann), vol. 3, pp. 9–37.

Sommer, A. U. (1997). *Der Geist der Historie und das Ende des Christentums. Zur "Waffengenossenschaft" von Friedrich Nietzsche und Franz Overbeck* (Berlin: Akademie Verlag).

—— (2000d). "Vom Nutzen und Nachteil kritischer Quellenforschung. Einige Überlegungen zum Fall Nietzsches," *Nietzsche-Studien*, 29, pp. 302–16.

Stegmaier, W. (1985). "Nietzsches Neubestimmung der Wahrheit," *Nietzsche-Studien*, 14, pp. 69–95.

Thiele, L. P. (1995). "Out from the Shadows of God: Nietzschean Scepticism and Political Practice," *International Studies in Philosophy*, 27, pp. 55–72.

Wilcox, J. T. (1974). *Truth and Value in Nietzsche* (Ann Arbor: University of Michigan Press).

269

Part IV

Philosophy of Mind

15

The Body, the Self, and the Ego

VOLKER GERHARDT

In Zarathustra's fourth speech, entitled "On the Despisers of the Body" ("Von den Verächtern des Leibes"), we find the formula of the "*great reason*" of the body. Although this turn of phrase has never quite achieved the popularity of some others, such as the will to power, the eternal return of the same, the re-valuation of all values, or "*amor fati*," it stands at the undeclared center of Nietzsche's experimental philosophy and bears all the promise connected with these other formulae. Now, there is a certain suspicion that these and other programmatic slogans coined by Nietzsche are ultimately only designed for their emotional and rhetorical effect. What I wish to show here is that this suspicion may only be met by showing *how* the body may be understood as "great reason." I propose to undertake a philosophical interpretation of this formula. In the first part of this essay (section 1) I will begin by analyzing its apparent triviality. In so doing, I will argue that the sense of this formula seems rather to be at odds with the practical relationship between reason and the body – not just on the interpretation of this relation which we find in the tradition of the philosophy of reason, but also in our everyday intuitions about this relation. This picture of the relation between the body and reason, founded upon the assumed dominance of reason, is portrayed in section 2. With that we gain a point of departure for Nietzsche's programmatic slogans which is in keeping with their paradoxical character: the "great reason" of the body can be understood as both provocative *and* uncontroversial; and it can have both a *polemical* and a *systematically foundational* sense. This is the object of section 3. This result is applied to a reading of Zarathustra's speech in sections 4, 5, and 6. First we will inquire as to the status of those "despisers of the body" whose life-contradiction is mentioned in Zarathustra's third speech (section 4). Then we turn to our main topic and interpret the brief passage in which Zarathustra speaks of the "great reason" in the body (section 5). Following this, I shall treat the problematic relation between "body" and "ego" (section 6). It is in this context that the difficulties connected with speaking of the "great reason" of the body and the "small reason" of consciousness become clear. If one wished to take this manner of speaking literally, the only way to make sense of it would be by way of an aesthetic interpretation, which I shall give.

Zarathustra speaks not only of "body" and "ego," but also of "self." This is natural, but also puzzling. Of course, there could be no room for the concepts of "body" and "ego" without some sort of self-relation. The self-organization of the body and the self-reflection of the ego make self-reference unavoidable whenever they are expressed. But is this not simply a crutch of language? Couldn't Nietzsche have treated the "self" just as he did "substance" or "God"? These are both supposed by him to be grammatical illusions with no real reference (see *HH* 18; *TI*, " 'Reason' in Philosophy," 5). In the case of the body's "self," however, things seem to stand differently. "Self" is treated as if it had the same ontological dignity as "body." In fact, the "self" proves to be the thoroughly real mediator between body and ego. As will become apparent, in the end it is nothing other than the *self* that holds body and soul, or body and ego, together. This insight will permit us to derive another, systematic insight from the formula of the "great reason" in the body (section 7).

Many Nietzsche interpreters doubt he had a conception of reason. Yet it is ineluctably clear from his texts that – at least as critic and free spirit – he did have such a conception at his disposal. At any rate, it is only under the assumption of a certain conception of reason that it is possible to attribute to Zarathustra's speeches some reconstructable sense.

1 Reason as an Organ of the Body

At first glance, the formula of the "great reason" of the body seems to express something obvious and thoroughly natural. All human functioning is the expression or work of the human body. Since we know reason – if at all – as a specifically human function, then it too must be connected with the human body. In any case, body and reason are not mutually exclusive; even more: if it is indeed the body which hosts reason, it will not do to pose just any kind of connection or compatibility between the two. One must rather assume that reason belongs to the very blueprint of the body. In order to develop as a bodily capacity in and with the body, reason must somehow inhere in the body. But that means that the body must already contain reason in some way. The organization of the body is such that it leads to the capacities which we know belong to reason, and which we expect from it. Consequently, the body should contain not only reason, but also that which reason serves. For – barring disease, handicap and atavism – a bodily organ is not present without its function. We speak of eye or ear, and we understand these organs in reference to the functions of seeing and hearing. In the case of reason things are a bit more difficult, insofar as we already know its functions, and must draw conclusions on what articulates itself in these. In so doing, we seek to find reason as an organ.

The particulars in the process of inferring an organ from its functions need not detain us here. For the present argument it will suffice to simply ascertain that the capacities of reason also belong to the function of the body, which themselves are present in the organization of the body if they are not implanted from without. And this is evidently not the case, though the development of reason does require certain interactions such as respiration, the use of things, and social activity. Even if all the particular capacities of reason were learned in interaction with the world, its bodily component would still have to be present. The very fact that reasoning can be learned speaks for a certain disposition to its use in the organization of the human body, and this fact makes the superiority of the body apparent: whatever happens, it can always develop itself according to the possibilities inherent in it. That reason should be conceived of as an organ and understood upon the basis of its capacities sounds odd, particularly since we primarily think of things such as lungs, liver, and the gallbladder when we think of organs. Yet this oddness is quickly dispelled when we lengthen the list of organs to include the hand, the voice, or – quite generally – the senses. In fact, reason is generally understood as the "sense" which makes us able to understand. And yet: how could reason ever produce anything which itself is not rational? As we know no answer to this question and can only infer reason from reason, as its "cause," we are compelled to admit reason as the *ground* for reason. It is this very admission which is contained in Zarathustra's formula of the "great reason" of the body: since reason is only found in a certain substrate, namely the body, this substrate must itself be seen as capable of reason. And since the substrate is prior to, and more extensive than, the "rational" capacity it supports, it can indeed be said to be "greater."

In comparison to that substrate, the reason with which we consciously and explicitly understand things is indeed "small." The competence of this kind of reason is limited to what it is conscious of. It is thus consistency that leads Zarathustra to speak of human "spirit" as "small reason." This "small reason" is for him an "instrument" of the body and thus the "tool and plaything" of the "great reason" of the body. We shall speak more of this later.

2 The Body as the Instrument of Reason

So much for that which at first sight might appear self-evident and natural. We know, however, that things are not quite so simple – even barring the questions which must be posed when "reason" is assumed to be "natural." If we recall the tradition from which the concept of reason arose, or even just the manner in which reason appears to us in its use, then there seems to be precious little which would speak for its integration in the organic functions of the body. To the contrary, one could easily understand the formula of the "great reason" of the body as an intended provocation, directed against both the philosophical concept of reason and the concept as it is used in everyday language. For if the body were always rational in all it does, we could leave everything to the body – we would no longer need our "small faculty of reason."

Of course, the body does not prepare us for all eventualities in this way. It is also apparent that we cannot automatically follow many of the momentary inspirations which the body provides. For this reason we cannot leave things to the supposedly "greater" reason in the body. Rather, we are existentially dependent upon the "small reason" of conscious deliberation. Only with the help of "small reason" are we able to consciously know, to distinguish precisely, to exactly define, to deduce consistently, to imagine things in a way comprehensible for others, and to make decisions on grounds accessible to others. Thus reason seems to be a capacity which far exceeds the capabilities of the body: reason goes beyond the body *in principle*. In this way, reason is not simply an extension of bodily capabilities, nor does it consist in an improbable widening of the radius of bodily activity. Reason makes a step *in another dimension*, so to speak. And this dimension seems, in a fundamental way, to no longer be a bodily or physical one. This is especially clear in those cases in which the activity of reason is directed against the activity of the body. When, for example, the body tires of work, rational insight is in certain circumstances necessary, in order that the powers required for the completion of work are mobilized. If pain briefly prevents us from continuing to clean the wound, reason advises us to bear the pain. If pleasure or pain entice us to break a promise, reason tells us that we are to keep our word.

This is not to say that we follow reason in all cases. But, for the purposes of my argument, it is sufficient that reason only hold sway occasionally. In each of these cases – be they ever so rare – reason designs ends for the "entire" body. Even when reason merely advises us seriously, there is a certain assumption that it would be possible to obey it. Even here reason seems more extensive than the body, for it recommends a course of action that affects the body as a whole. Assuming we overcome our fatigue, which is always also a fatigue of the body, it is reason that compels the body as a whole to complete the task at hand. When we resist fear or pleasure and hold our word, then the body "wholly" does reason's bidding. In such cases the manners of speaking in classical ancient philosophy and in everyday language correspond: reason and purpose are said to "rule," and the meaning which reason may justify as rational supplies the goals for the body as a whole. "End," "goal," or "meaning" are *concepts of reason*, even when their extension is modest and their instantiations seem unsound.

From this perspective, it is reason that seems to be "greater" than the body. Reason can expressly exercise power over the body, whereas the body seems only to use its own weakness in order to exercise influence. Though we must not neglect the original, causal role of the body, which carries reason as an organ, one could nevertheless say that body rides, so to speak, on the back of reason. Body supplies the fundament upon which reason rests, and sets the conditions and bounds for that which reason considers meaningful, consistent, or satisfying. But whenever the body expresses itself in passions, feelings, and moods, it is already in a dimension of meaning created by reason; for in these things too there are intuitions, consequences, insights, and deductions: reasonings, in which reason is always involved. Reason rules in the sphere of sense, wherever we are engaged in the processes of perceiving and understanding. In these cases reason is manifestly not the "instrument" of the body, but rather the inverse: Reason rules over the body. Reason provides for the protection and maintenance of the body, gives it poisons (and this not only always against better judgment), puts the body in danger, and can, in extreme cases, arrange for the death of the body, with which reason too will perish. Seen from the vantage point of such capabilities, it is reason which dominates the body, as much as the body may determine the conditions for reason's manifestation. The body may support, underlie, and maintain the faculty of reason, but as soon as the latter is active, it puts the body in its service. By reason's demand to have the body at its disposal, body becomes the instrument of reason.

It is this understanding of the relationship between body and reason that is implicit in all practical and theoretical processes. In distinction from the *intuitive* and *natural* interpretation of this relationship, we may speak here of the *conceptual* relation posed between body and reason. The practical fundament of the conceptual interpretation of this relation brings with it the assumption that reason is to be seen, as a matter of principle, as superior, the body being not just a means to reason's ends, but sometimes indeed an impediment to these. With this interpretation reason becomes so important that, "in the face of" reason, there is occasion to be ashamed of the body. For it is the weight of the body which seems to bring reason back onto the ground of pure factuality. The body distracts reason with its pleasures and fears, and forces it into the yoke of its own habits.

Assuming that one understands the relationship between body and reason in this everyday manner – one characteristic, also, of the philosophical tradition – then it is immediately understandable how one may easily come to despise the body; according to this theory, the body inevitably appears to be the antagonist of reason. And in this role, the body is a hindrance for reason's ends, it is simply a distracting bother, and it makes the grand plans of reason impossible. In this antithesis, the body is the downward falling antipode set over and against an ever upward-striving faculty of reason. And so one wants to see things from the "higher" position of reason, and to look down with contempt upon the "lowering" pull of the body. The low seems so lowly that one can only fend it off with disgust.

3 The Paradox of Aesthetic Concepts

No doubt, it is the second concept of reason which Zarathustra assumes among his listeners. As I have said, this concept fits with a certain commonsense understanding of reason; it also happens to be the concept of reason which is associated with both Platonism and Kant's critical philosophy. In order to upstage this philosophical tradition, Nietzsche counters it with an ancient Persian wise man. For he had already realized, by that time, that the pre-Socratics were also Socratic in their thinking. The logical domination of the world which, in *The Birth of Tragedy*, Nietzsche had once attributed to Socrates, he later came to see as beginning with Thales and Anaximander, and being perfected early by Parmenides (see PTAG). Nietzsche must have recourse to an even older wise man, in order that he may produce an authority for a true alternative to Platonism. There seems to be not a single genuine counter-program to Platonism within the entire European tradition. In *Zarathustra* Nietzsche makes it clear that he knows of no European passage which might finally lead beyond metaphysical territory.

There is little need to argue that Nietzsche's construction of the hatred of the body is historically problematic. In fact, in the European tradition there are other perspectives on the relationship between reason and its bodily substrate – such as Kant's well-known metaphor in which he compares reason with a dove which deludes itself into thinking it could fly better in a vacuum (Kant 1950: B8). Nietzsche surely did not forget how closely Plato connects the productivity of body and soul, and not only in the *Symposium*. These finer historical shades are, however, not to the philosophical point of interest here. That point is rather the paradox involved in the conceptual construction of the "great reason" of the body – a paradox which is evident as soon as we try to conceive of the natural interpretation of the relationship between body and reason from the vantage point of the conceptual interpretation of this relation. For this is exactly what Nietzsche's formula demands.

This is a rather extreme demand, but it is not made on a whim; it lies rather in the nature of the problem. Even if reason were nothing but an organ of the body, as portrayed in section 1, we would only be able to comprehend this state of affairs by means of reason. Yet reason has its main function in the comprehension of its relationship to the body, as argued in section 2; and this is a function in which reason rules all else – including the body. This means that reason rules quite generally, even on the thesis according to which reason is dependent upon the body as an organ is. Reason is the authority before which every possible claim must be justified. We have a paradox which is thoroughly inescapable. *For we cannot abandon the position of the dominance of reason, even if we wish to accept the total dominance of the body.* In order for the position stating the dominance of the body to become intelligible we must first have not just an understanding of reason, but also some consciousness of its rule-abiding application. After all, the claim that reason is an organ of the body can only be arrived at by means of rational argument. "Little reason" is required in order to transform "great reason" into an intelligible expression. Yet even here "little reason" proves to be so dominant that it determines our attention and interest fully. And our attention also includes our senses, at the very least. Thus "little reason" rules the body, even on the thesis that the body is its own "great reason." Whatever magnitude we may ascribe to "great reason," already in the determination of the possible greatness of "great reason" it is under the direction of "little reason."

This paradoxical state of affairs need not make the formula of the "great reason" of the body completely senseless, however. There are many examples of paradoxical expressions which make the context of human experience systematically accessible. Indeed, in one of the areas of human experience which is particularly important for Nietzsche, this theory seems to be forced into a paradoxical formulation if it is to be able to provide a sufficient description of given impressions. Since Nietzsche sees himself closely attached to this realm of experience, it is unavoidable to see some connection here.

It is the experiential context of art to which I refer; and it is a *philosophical* aesthetics which seeks to approach its object in the seemingly contradictory terms we have discussed. This could be shown with reference to Plato, who often repeated the early Greek view that "all things beautiful are difficult" (Greater Hippias I. 304e; cf. *Republic* 435c, 497d; Cratylus 384a). Plato traces this view to Solon, the reformer of old Athens and one of the "seven wise men" of Greek antiquity. We do not know how Solon meant this; it might have been a sigh of dismay, or even a kind of warning. For Plato it is a paradoxical expression. For he knows of the lifting weightlessness in the enjoyment of the beautiful; he refers to this in his definitions, and ironizes the self-deception of the ingenious man who is obsessed with art (*Ion* 534b). He also makes plain, in the mythical portrayal of the *Phaedrus*, to what extent the contemplation of the beautiful is dependent upon the mastery of contradictory human powers. The ascent to beauty requires the greatest effort of all. Yet at the summit of this journey into light, which may be undertaken only through the utmost self-control, the beautiful offers itself to that soul capable of recognizing and knowing it.

It is to this very passage that Nietzsche refers when he has Zarathustra depict the experience of the beautiful:

> To stand with relaxed muscles and unbridled wills: that is the most difficult thing for you all, you sublime ones!

When the power grows gracious and descends into the visible: Beauty do I call such a descension. (Z II, "Of the Sublime Ones")

In all things, Plato is for Nietzsche the most important source. Yet with regard to the paradoxical description of aesthetic experience there is another author who is no less important for Nietzsche. That author is Kant. It is Kant who places his aesthetics in the context of a theory of life and living things. As is well known, the second part of the *Critique of Judgment* contains a theory of the organic. Yet even the first part, in which the experience of the beautiful and the sublime are described and related to the faculties of reason, is contained within a philosophy of life. In fact, Kant founds his aesthetics upon a form of life which animates itself. Spirit (*Geist*), which is as much at work in artistic genius as in the purely receptive judgment of a work of art, is – from the perspective of aesthetics – "the animating principle in the soul." Kant refers to a "power of imagination" which keeps the powers of the soul "purposively in motion" and functions as a kind of "game [. . .] that keeps itself going." Thus an aesthetic experience alway coincides with an "animation" of the powers of cognition. And from this follows that through such experience all the life powers of man come "into motion" (Kant 1987: §49). "Animation" is something which, from the perspective of an animated being, can only be experienced as something psychic, i.e. mental. For it is something "internal," something which does not simply warm, accelerate the pulse, or create goose bumps. It is rather the person as a whole who is gripped and affected. It is, above all, the "mental powers" which are involved, since only these may experience "animation" as a kind of mood or mental state, and express it as such. And yet "animation" could never be conceived without a living body as its subject. Even "enthusiasm" is something which could only properly belong to a living body. "Animation" and "enthusiasm" are thoroughgoing expressions of the living body and what makes the physiological constitution of a living being appear comprehensible: mood or attitude, which only the mind and spirit can grasp, consist in a certain tuning and disposition of the body. For Kant it goes without saying that only the life-powers of the individual are meant here – i.e. the powers of the human "subject" who seeks to become active through his or her "communication" with others. Kant's theory of aesthetics clearly bears witness to the "reason of the body."

Kant speaks of four "moments" of the beautiful. Of course the origin of this word – from the Latin verb *movere* (to move) and the substantive *momen, mominis* (movement) – was present in his mind. In the *Critique of Pure Reason* Kant had used this term specifically for designating the causes of sensations (1950: B254). In the *Critique of Judgment* "moments" denote the causes for changes which are both sensory and mental, and which occur in subjective consciousness under the impression of the beautiful. In order of their occurrence, we find them listed there as *disinterested pleasure, universality without concept, purposiveness without purpose*, and, finally, *subjective necessity*. From the point of view of the faculty of understanding all these formulations contain a manifest contradiction. And yet they are not devoid of sense, for – from the perspective of a kind of reason which embraces man as a whole – they express a change originating in the opposite and opposed powers which take part in such reason. From the conflict of these powers comes a kind of balance which reconciles the antagonists; the seriousness of the opposition between sensory stimulus and mental impulse becomes a game which ensures a dynamic balance. Movement and tension both remain intact; they produce a self-moving unity. The individual, finally, experiences this balancing reconciliation of his best powers, which occurs without conscious effort, as an expansion of his possibilities. His life grows through a contradiction which may be contemplated without constraint. In this entire process the physiological, sensory, and cognitive powers are activated. Yet they do not lead to an inner conflict, but rather – on the contrary – to an increase of individual dispositions through the awareness of their resonance. Thus from contradiction comes the medium of harmony. What is experienced as opposition, both conceptually and in the *modus* of practice, is in aesthetic experience complementary. What is more: the opposing powers which are first created by the organization of life prove to be "favorable" in their organized interaction: in the ever-increasing competition of individual psychic, sensual, and cognitive capacities, the individual becomes open for experiences which seem to come to him from without. The beautiful arises from the "favor" of nature – a favor for which one must be properly disposed.

All that which, in the final passages of the second *Untimely Meditation*, Nietzsche dared to hope in regard to culture as a "new and improved physis," is found prefigured in aesthetic experience. In his concept of culture Nietzsche seeks a "harmonization of life, thought, seeming and willing"; the difference between "without and within" is to be eliminated; there is to be no more "deception" or "convention"; no "ornament hides that which is adorned"; "truthfulness" is the binding moment of both "moral nature" and "true education" *UM II*, 10). Nowhere else is Nietzsche truer to his formula concerning the "great reason" of the body. One might not be surprised if he had spoken of culture as the great reason of nature in this context. Yet the phrase which we actually find in *Zarathustra* sharpens his older position by means of individualization: the conception of culture found in the second *Untimely Meditation* – a conception already completely centered upon the individual – was later to be radicalized. It is no longer education which forms the individual after the fashion of a social reason; it is rather the living body of the individual person, the very bodily organization of the individual, which underlies all living things, which figures as "great reason."

4 Hatred of the Body

Zarathustra's fourth speech stands under the heading "On the Despisers of the Body." Who these despisers are is not specified, and there are only hints as to what their hatred consists in. And yet we immediately think we know who they are: the world-weary ascetics, the "backwoodsmen" to whom the preceding speech refers – these life-weary "preachers of death" who have become tired and thus seek to make one final "leap to the end." The despisers of the body, we learn, wish to "re-learn and re-educate." Accordingly these are people who seek to educate themselves and nevertheless would like, at the same time, to teach others. If their teaching consists in a hatred of the body, as one might reasonably assume, then their "re-learning" would imply that they originally lived in respect for the body, a respect they seek to rid themselves of.

Though this may sound trivial, it is of some import for the systematic content of Nietzsche's critique. Every man exists, originally, in positive acknowledgment of his body; he respects his body, and not only that: through his body he has respect for himself. Because Zarathustra preaches on behalf of this original relationship to the body he speaks of the despisers of the body in the past tense:

> Sick and dying ones were they, who despised body and earth and invented the heavenly and redeeming drops of blood . . . (Z I, "On the Backwoodsmen")

Zarathustra seeks to illustrate the inconsistency of their flight into the heavens beyond:

> They sought to escape from their misery, and the stars were too far off for them. Then they sighed: "Oh, if only there were heavenly ways to glean some other existence and happiness!" – and they invented their little tricks and bloody potations.
> They thought they had escaped their bodies and the earth, those ungrateful ones. Yet to what did they owe the pain and joy of their escape? To the body and the earth. ("On the Backwoodsmen")

The despisers of the body remain within the body's sphere – and yet they do not understand "the meaning [Sinn] of the earth." This they could only understand through a "healthy body": only the "honest and pure" "voice of the healthy body" may speak of the "meaning of the earth" ("On the Backwoodsmen"). Respect for their own body is not possible for them, because they lack health.

A condition for knowledge is introduced which is by no means unproblematic: only the healthy can escape the "preachers of death"; these are able to ignore the "backwoodsmen" and can let the "meaning of the earth" speak for itself through their very own bodies. In the following paragraph Zarathustra thematizes this condition. He speaks of the child whose health we simply assume, the child which says what it thinks in all "innocence." We already know what importance Zarathustra assigns to the child's innocence from his first speech. There, it is the child which, after the camel and the lion, comes as the third form of spirit. The child is the primally natural "wheel rolling out from within itself" and stands for the creative "forgetting" which makes a "new beginning" possible. In the childish "Yes" to life, unfettered by any kind of doubt, spirit finds its way back to the "game of creating" and regains for itself that world which was lost under the weight of obligation and the strenuous one-dimensionality of willing (Z I, "The Three Metamorphoses"). Already in his first speech Zarathustra assumes an interplay between spirit and body: a child is, at first, nothing more than a young body. Through the body of the child, life – which arises from the conditions of the earth – rejuvenates itself through the interplay of two older bodies, those of the parents. It is this rejuvenation upon which the hope in the third metamorphosis of spirit is founded. In the young body, spirit seems to be reborn, free of the weights and cramps of its older form, and careless enough to simply start again, just as every child is a bodily beginning.

In order to maintain this hope one must have deep trust in life's power of regeneration. Since life is only manifest as body, all trust in the future is in fact invested in the body. Whenever we place our trust in a "rational" development (however the term "rational" be construed), we place our trust in the body. It is impossible to conceive of "spirit," or even of that faculty of "reason" which is associated with it, as anything other than alive: in these a *beginning* is made again and again, and both constantly seek to *create something* which is then to be brought to a certain *goal* and *end*.

The expectations which are raised time and again in connection with spirit and reason are shown to have their source in life itself, which renews itself in ever-new individuals. Spirit and reason can only be conceived as living; and living things only occur in the form of living bodies. Thus both occur in connection with the body, but not just externally (and accidentally); rather, they belong originally to it, i.e. already in their most elementary, intelligible functioning. The power of the mind to comprehend problems and solve them; its power to grasp something as present, which underlies all explanation; its capacity, expected in all things, to reach a conclusion through insight and knowledge – all this depends upon the paradigm of the body. If the living body did not provide the determined form which ceaselessly practices its organization, then it would not be in all things the initiator, the process itself, as well as the endpoint of the process. And if there were not the full spectrum of epistemic states between the extremes of *desire* and *satisfaction*, we would have not even a vague idea of what mind and reason could accomplish.

For those who have considered all this, the hatred of the body no longer requires refutation. Such hatred is the expression of a fundamental contradiction of human existence – though it is not a contradiction between mind and body which might be reconciled under other conditions. It is, rather, a contradiction in which the mind catches itself, because it cannot be separated from the physical conditions of its functions.

5 The Meaning of the Body

Once Zarathustra has given the despisers of the body the only advice which they could follow with any consistency, namely to be "dumb," he then cites the speech of a child, though he is well aware that the child's speech is that of most adults, too:

> "Body am I, and soul" – so saith the child. And why should one not speak like children? (Z I, "Despisers")

The distinction between body and soul is thus portrayed as the expression of a naive kind of consciousness. Children speak in this way, and an adult could only adopt this manner of speaking if he were to speak of himself as an artist does – as someone not so much interested in self-knowledge as self-encouragement. The awakened and knowing speaks of himself in a different way:

> Body am I entirely, and nothing more; and soul is only the name of something in the body. (Z I, "Despisers")

In the awakened light of mature consciousness and the perspective of knowledge, the difference between body and soul is evidently no longer defensible. It is important to see that Nietzsche seeks to place himself in the standpoint of a *knower* here. The statements which follow are made from the vantage point of a kind of consciousness the limitations of which he would like to show. A heightened and advanced understanding will recognize that there is only the body – "and nothing else."

Living body is a *totality* beyond which there is nothing else with comparable status. If, in the child's mind, there appears to be something besides the body which is of equal ontological order, i.e. the *soul*, then this is only by way of a misunderstanding: The child interprets an *attribute* of the body as an independent *substance*. In fact, the "soul" should properly be simply a "word" for "something in the body." In a later speech, Zarathustra mentions in passing what such a "something" might be. It is the "courage" with which man, "the bravest animal," lives his life (Z III, "On the Vision and the Riddle," 1). Just as Plato shows in the *Laches* that there are more forms of courage (*andreia*) than the mere physical advantages of the warrior, so too does Nietzsche invoke a specific kind of human behavior in order to make an example of this certain "something in the body."

At first, this kind of talk seems strange. "Something in the body" could be a piece of clothing, a ring, a watch, or an artificial limb. It certainly could also be a humpback, a sore, or some hair. Is "courage" comparable to these? Perhaps not; but if we recall that a certain manner in one's gait, laugh, or speech is often said to be in one's "flesh and blood," then Zarathustra's manner of speaking becomes immediately comprehensible. The characteristic behavior of a person – otherwise known as *habitus* – can and indeed must be seen as something which belongs to "flesh and blood." Derived from the Latin verb *habeo* (I have), *habitus* originally denotes a certain posture and position of the body; it then comes to mean the body's appearance and form, from which the meanings clothing and cloak are derived. Finally, by way of metaphor, the word came to refer to the body's disposition, general state, nature, and character. *Habitus* is thus indeed "something in the body." Zarathustra's phrase happens to approach a formulation found in Aristotle, as well: *sôma gar ouk esti, sômatos de ti* ('[the soul] is not a body, but something of the body': *De anima* I. 414a).

The constitution of a living thing is manifest nowhere else than in its body. Even if we recognize courage in a candid remark, or perhaps in the flashing of the eyes, and even if someone's behavior – as manifest in a laugh or witty remark – seems to be spiritual, all these things nevertheless remain "something in the body." But are they therefore "nothing more"? This is an enormous question which Zarathustra would like to answer by simple authority. And yet the argumentative effort which this costs him suggests that there is more to this "nothing more." For it is evident that reason, which itself must be something in or of the body, has to do primarily with this certain "nothing" – not least on account of the fact that reason must give an account of the meaning of that mere "word" which it uses to refer to the soul.

Yet before Zarathustra comes to mention the type of reason which provides explicit meaning – "little reason" – he introduces "great reason." This he does in the most simple way: by *identifying* it with the body. Body is a *"great reason"*:

> The body is a great faculty of reason, a plurality with one sense, a war and a peace, a flock and a shepherd. (Z I, "Despisers")

It should be noted that Nietzsche does not speak of *the* "great reason" of the body, but rather of *a* "great [faculty of] reason" – one among many. A plurality of "great [faculties of] reason" is thus not excluded. To the contrary: it is suggested that the plurality of bodies corresponds to a *plurality of reason*. For if there is nothing other than the body, and the body is only one among many, then the body's faculty of reason must also be one among many. The question which arises at this point is this: under these conditions, what could "reason" possibly be? For reason can only be *one* – at least insofar as its *use* is concerned, i.e. its manner of manifestation in the body. If this were not so, then there would be a true plurality of reason (i.e. not just various substrates of reason, but truly different functions and instances of it), and one could no longer speak of reason in any particular case. For it is only meaningful to speak of the faculty of reason in a particular person under the condition that this person has the very same faculty which others have at their disposal.

According to a claim made by Zarathustra, reason creates *unity* where there is *plurality*. More specifically, reason gives plurality a *meaning*. What might this mean in relation to the body? Perhaps this question is best addressed with recourse to the vectorial connotation of the German word *Sinn*: in German, the *Uhrzeigersinn* or "clockwise direction" indicates in which *direction* something moves.[1] Thus the specific direction of a body may indicate the particular *Sinn* or "direction" in which a "plurality" may be related to a certain point. One need only think of the endless variety of impulses of motion necessary for one single step in a certain direction in order to immediately apprehend what a "plurality with one sense [*Sinn*]" means in the case of a bodily act. The connection which might be made to the traditional understanding of the faculty of reason is also manifest: assuming that a living body were incapable of following its own sense of direction, and assuming that it would collapse, tumble, spin, or flail at the slightest movement (without, of course, being naturally predisposed to doing so). In that case the body would be, *qua* body, an impossibility, for there would be nothing with which it could orient itself; it could neither find nourishment nor protection, nor could it fight or flee. Its existence would lack the directedness (or *Sinn*) which is contained in its natural processes, and without which the body could not be considered to be such. A body which could not unite the plurality which it contains in a unity of processes – such a body would be quite impossible.

With this step we are already quite close to the classical understanding of reason: the body's sense of direction is the sense of action in the entire being, the sense in which a being first attains its processual unity. If the body is a thing which is "*organized* and *self-organizing*" (Kant 1987: §65), then it is first and foremost nothing other than a *self-producing unity*. Accordingly, it must, in all its processes, be oriented towards itself, and by itself. This is the bare minimum of "sense" for every movement and action of a body. Thus we arrive at a determination of the body as the whole of a plurality which finds its own unity in the harmony of internal and external movement. Seen in this way, the "reason" of the body lies in the consistency of its processes. To rephrase a well-known definition of reason: the body is the "power to reason deductively" (Kant 1950: B355/A299).[2] Depending upon the perspective taken, this deductive reasoning may be considered "mediated" or "immediate." "Mediated" is such reasoning insofar as it is mediated by a plurality of participating organs; "immediate" is such reasoning which the body produces itself in the "conclusions" which it draws in every act of its existence.

284

This *formal* connection between body and reason is supported by the *material* expectations which are always in play when we speak of reason: for both in everyday usage and in philosophical theories we expect reason to accomplish something in accord with some good or value. Such value may be so conceived that only *God* could cash it in. This is surely the oldest option among the theories of reason, and one which Nietzsche thinks is historically overcome. The value associated with reason may also be conceived in such a way as to coincide with a certain *natural order*, or so as to be intimately tied to *the whole of human existence*. It is in this last sense that Kant and Hegel sought to tie reason and reality together.

Nietzsche puts no stock in this scheme of the connection between rationality and reality, a scheme in which these are mediated by a *concept*. For he rightly suspects that here, too, the assumption of a divine being is in play. Thus he calls for another, sensually present reality with which reason may be supported, in order that reason may meet the material condition for rationality. This reality is the *body*. Body is the fully present actuality which realizes itself in its own sense of direction and action. From a systematic perspective, the identification of body with reason fills the gap created by the "death of God." Once the death of God has been declared, all appeals to cosmically given orders, or even to those which have grown historically, are discredited. If we cast a comparative glance at the various functions of the concept of God, the reasons for speaking of the *great* reason of the body become plain. Greatness is, in this case, not simply a comparative adjective, i.e. a magnitude defined in reference to "little" reason; in this attribution there remains something of the old metaphysical claim of reason: that reason be not just *formally* empowered to conceive the whole, but that it also stand *materially* for a divine, natural, and historical whole. With Nietzsche, the body becomes the administrator of this totality; accordingly, the body is "great reason."

Although this might sound far-fetched, it is not. On the one hand, the body is indeed dependent upon, and determined by, the natural and historical conditions from which it comes and by which it necessarily remains bound. On the other hand, the body determines *solely by itself* the beginning and end of the sense and senses at its disposal; through the particular configuration of its organization the body determines the *rhythm* and *time* of the activity it pursues. What stimulus and reaction, desire and satisfaction is determined by the body's organic constitution; and what may be conceived of as a "whole" or some "part" is necessarily related to the body and its constitution. Thus it is in fact the body which provides the order in which the sense of a living existence is attained.

One need not fear that, in this way, the body might become some kind of idealistic consciousness, isolated from the conditions from which it arose and by which it is determined. For living bodies always remain bound to the consistency and regularity of the material body of which they are constituted and with which their metabolism is supported; the body is seamlessly connected with nature, in which it maintains itself. What is more, both the body's physiological constitution and the rhythmical cycles of its organization are connected with the elemental regularity of its environment: the change from day to night and from summer to winter; the supply of nourishment; the size of a certain population; the number and particular character of natural enemies; or – not least – the element in which the organism lives: all these conditions of organic life and living things are given by the earth, and thus also by the particular place which a given living body occupies. True, every living body moves according to its own law, and in this way each body does possess its own faculty of reason. Yet this individual law can only come into being under the mundane conditions determined by its terrestrial environment. The *sense of the body* is thus originally and primarily oriented towards the *earth*, which lets this sense develop. It is on account of this relationship that Zarathustra speaks of the "sense of the earth."

In the course of this brief explanation it will have become clear that the "sense of the earth" is not an alternative to the "great reason" of the body. Rather, the "sense of the body" obtains only under the conditions of terrestrial influence, and it can assert itself only in congruent correspondence with a "sense of the earth." On the other hand, talk of the "sense of the earth" only has meaning if there is sense in the body. Strictly speaking, sense is something exclusively "in the body"; sense can be associated with the earth only insofar as there is something which corresponds to the sense in embodied beings. The sense of the earth refers us back to the reason in the body.

6 The Living Body and its Ego

The extension of the "great reason" in the body, which cannot be meaningfully subsumed under anything else, makes it clear from the very start that everything else in the body necessarily appears "small." It is either a particular organ and part of the total organization of the body or it is an effect and consequence of the body's sense of activity. Whether physical strength, courage, the harmonious flow of motion, or intellectual presence: everything is a certain "something in the body." For the *spirit*, which we habitually conceive as the *totum* of some sort of unity, this insight may amount to a kind of insult. That seems to be of some import for Nietzsche. When he designates the spirit as a kind of mere "instrument," or even "plaything," then he necessarily slights those who would think of themselves as spiritual beings. Those, at least, who justify their actions in terms of reasons, place their own proper *insight* and *intelligence* to the fore, and employ their bodies as the *means* to the ends of their mental faculties. This order, so ineluctable for thinking beings, is inverted by Zarathustra:

> An instrument of thy body is also thy small reason, my brother, which thou callest "spirit"
> – a little instrument and plaything of thy great reason. (Z I, "Despisers")

Here we find one of the refined mechanisms of Zarathustra's speeches: an abrupt switch into direct address. The employment of this strategy here coincides with a shift of thematic focus onto the individual consciousness which is capable of saying "ego." The ego becomes intelligible by way of distinction from some Other. In order to articulate the meaning of "ego," some reference to Thou is inevitable. In direct address, the second person singular is of course already present. In employing this form of address, the new theoretical focus is anticipated, in a kind of prolepsis, by the underlying concepts of the language employed.

Spirit – which comes into the center of focus at this point, and remains there for the rest of Zarathustra's speech – can develop itself only through a relation to a certain, other, ego. By addressing another person as "brother," an accent is placed not only upon a communality founded in embodiedness, but also upon immediate mutual understanding. In connection with such a kind of understanding, particularly among brothers, one is prone to think of a certain feeling or emotion; but if this understanding is to be reliable and founded upon the exact designation of some state of affairs, then it will require the use of a concept. In this connection, a certain restricted concept of spirit – i.e. spirit as the faculty of the Understanding – is indispensable; here, too, is it first required. If there were no concepts, mutual understanding of one and the same thing could never be attained. It is thus the difference between ego and thou which makes spirit – understood as the medium of concepts – necessary.

Spirit in just this sense is the "little faculty of reason" to which Nietzsche refers. He calls it an "instrument" of the body; it is thus supposed to assume a merely subsidiary and instrumental function. However, as the body does not explicitly and unambiguously reveal the ends of its actions, we also do not know what purposes are served by its means. That is why the "instrument" is also a "plaything." It exists for the sake of something which does not persist without it, and which seems to be somehow meaningful in and of itself. As an "instrument" or "plaything" it abides by the rules of the game, the perpetuation of which it helps to support. With regard to game or play, "little reason" is of obvious value; and it proves itself to be useful, even when no purpose above and beyond the perpetual cycle of play can be named. Thus, this instrument is purposive even in the absence of a purpose. The well-known ascription "purposiveness without a purpose" is natural, and suggests itself. In referring to spirit as the "plaything" of the body we find an immediate reference to an *aesthetic relation*.

Spirit is strictly dependent upon the ego. Since Descartes' *cogito* we know this much regarding the knowledge of the understanding; and Kant followed suit in positing the phrase "I think" as one which must be able to accompany all our representations. The ego is already present in the need for coherence and completeness; it organizes both the capacity to deduce and the faculty of understanding; and it cannot be conceptually detached from insight, for the simple reason that it must indicate the satisfaction which comes with knowledge of reason. One could adapt Kant's slogan here and make the claim that all the capacities of reason must be able to be accompanied by the phrase "I understand."

The ego is therefore present in the very "sense" which the spirit "knows." The ego is required in both of these fundamental capacities of the spirit. As it is always present when anything at all is known or recognized, the ego also has a certain pride. Those human capacities which reach farthest, including those with which we regulate ourselves, are not possible without the ego. This is evidently recognized by Zarathustra where he has "spirit" be "proud" of its "ego"; but disillusionment follows closely upon the heels of this recognition. For pride cannot be a sufficient indication of the independence of spirit. To the contrary: pride is rather an expression of the self-deception of the spirit. In spite of self-consciousness, the self-sufficiency and independence felt by the spirit only conceals its dependency upon the body.

Decisive is the fact that Nietzsche does not put the ego at the body's immediate disposal, but rather places the "great reason" of the body between these. *This* is what serves as agent, and not the body, which requires its own "great reason" in order to act in a unified, coherent sense:

> "Ego," you say, and are proud of that word. But the greater thing – in which you are unwilling to believe – is your body with its great faculty of reason; it does not say "ego," but does it. (Z I, "Despisers")

From this passage it is clear that Nietzsche's formula does not entail any kind of reductionism. He easily could have claimed that it is the body which says "ego." Are they not *bodily* instruments which produce those sounds which become intelligible as language? Is it not the lips, tongue, larynx, and vocal cords which work in concert with other organs in order that a person may speak? Certainly. Yet the physical movement of the organs of the human voice do not, by themselves, make any sort of *sense* – nothing which could be *understood*.

The sort of sense which is intelligible requires a specific organ, and for Nietzsche – as for Plato, Kant, or Hegel – this organ is the faculty of reason. Though he does call this organ the "great reason" of the body, he does not equate it with the body, as one might assume on the basis of a casual or superficial analysis. The passage cited above shows, to the contrary, that Nietzsche is at pains to specify the author of the ego as precisely not the *body*, but its own proper *sagacity* or *reason*. It is not at all the case that the body produces referential meaning or intelligible sense *locally*: understanding and reason are faculties which in some way express the *whole of the body*. They are not "something in the body," such as blushing or a sound. Though they are connected to bodily expressions, their particular character lies in the "sense" which they convey. And it is this sense which the body initiates in the modus called *action*. In action, in which a *whole* is always established, it is the body as a whole that is actualized.

A further differentiation is to be found in the circumstance that the reason of the body does not function as the "speaker," but rather the "doer" of the ego: body's reason "does not say ego, but does ego." Here, too, a direct physical or physiological relation is avoided. The competence involved in doing and action is both more profound and more extensive than the competence at play in the spoken word. All speaking can be understood as action; but not all action is spoken word. In this we find a manifest relativization of the foundational character of language. It is a strategy which Nietzsche pursues further in a later speech, "On the Pale Criminal": here the "act" is the actual event, which is to be distinguished both from the "image" which follows upon it, and from the "thought" which accompanies it.[3] The actual event, elsewhere portrayed as originally creative potential,[4] is not the word, but action, the deed. And this is not attributed to the ego, but to the body; more precisely, to the reason of the body. When it is said that the "great reason" of the body has no need to say "ego" because it "does" ego, there is an emphasis of its creative capacity in play. Soon afterwards we find Nietzsche speaking of the "creative self." It creates "for itself respect and spite," "pleasure and pain," "value and the will" and, in all this, also "spirit." Indeed: "most of all" it would like to create "beyond itself" – "that is its only desire" (Z I, "Despisers"). It is thus quite certain that the body is here conceived in analogy to the *artist*. Body is conceived as the creative ground from which all initial energy, all formative power, and, finally, all sensitivity to pleasure and pain spring. The body is *the* instance of creativity; from it come all things capable of having any sense or meaning.

The analogy to the artist also clarifies the distinction between the body and its own proper reason, a distinction which Nietzsche fails to fully elucidate. In his theory of aesthetics, Kant refers to the artist as "nature." Yet the power of nature, which is ultimately expressed in a kind of productivity that is not regulated by conscious rules, is expressly distinguished from the physical and physiological powers of nature. Here, nature expresses itself in "genius," i.e. in a form of *spirit* that is evidently prior to reason, which proceeds by certain rules. When we see that it is the genius of the artist which is to be seen as the original creator of the unity of a given work of art, then the analogy to reason suggests itself: the totality which creative genius produces as a "wheel rolling out from within itself" corresponds to the unity developed by reason, which proceeds consciously and with rules, but upon the basis of its own requirements. The multivalence of a work of art, of which the "aesthetic idea," according to Kant, "provides much material for thought," is inexhaustible. Despite its bound and determined form it contains an infinite *variety of sense* which exceeds the concept of reason. For though the concept of reason also aims at a kind of totality – a totality for which it strives under the constrictions of stringency, consistency, and rigor – it is far excelled by the artwork's never-ending processuality, as well as by its sensible and intellectual abundance.

With this we come to the conclusion that the formula concerning the "great reason" in the body is constructed in parallel to the aesthetic concept of genius. It is a connection which draws on reference to art, a connection in which the concept in the "great reason" of the body has a certain tradition and in which we may appreciate the paradoxes involved in this formula. The body is understood on analogy to a "great artist." If we wish to understand the attribution of "great reason" to the body, we would do well to think of the "greatness" of the great artist's work. It is a greatness which supersedes its author, which is more expansive and inclusive than the artist, and which cannot be simply reduced to him, his origin, his training, or his technique. A great work by a great artist has, at the same time, a kind of unity which escapes all flat attempts at conceptual reduction: as self-contained and complete as it may seem, it nevertheless contains such an endless variety of meanings that it makes its unity seem paradoxical.

The "great reason" in the body is thus to be understood as an aesthetic concept. It is much more than a mere metaphor for the wonderful stringency and succinctness of bodily processes. If one were modest, one could of course leave the interpretation of this formula at that. Yet there is more to it: in the aesthetic concept, the difference between creator and product is also contained. The regular and self-consistent activity of the body becomes distinguishable from the particular forms of activity it occasions. With that we have a true analogy to the specific capacities of reason, which engages in deductions and insights, and which in this way may be compared to the internal consistency of a work of art. Both reason and art have their origin and goal in the senses, though neither may be reduced to these. Thus the paradoxical aesthetic concept of the "great reason" of the body has the merit not only of illustrating the proximity of body and intellect, but also of showing their difference, which begins in the act of production and is actualized in a certain form. Nietzsche does not equate body with reason. Reason is that which makes itself manifest in the expressions of the body – just as the beautiful does in art. Reason is thus only present in the presence of an *observer*.

This means that the reason of the body is established merely as one perspective in a world of multiple perspectives. It occurs as the individual expression of a body, and only for such embodied individuals as are receptive to its impression. A sphere of perception is required in which an expression corresponds to a certain, other, impression. The necessarily individual reason of the body can develop itself only in that space which exists between other individuals. Here, too, the analogy to art holds, which can be received as art only by individuals – and nevertheless only in such space as is accessible to others. In this connection it is no accident that Kant sought in his aesthetics to give the expression *sensus communis* a new twist (Kant 1987: §40). Accordingly, the "great reason" of the body is bound to a kind of sense which is as embodied as it is communal.

7 An "Unknown Wise Man" between Body and Ego

With this demonstration of the independence of body's reason as construed on analogy to art we could end our investigation of the "great reason" of the body. For all that follows in Zarathustra's fourth speech serves, on the one hand, to illustrate the character of consciousness as "instrument and plaything," while providing on the other hand a diagnosis and prognosis for the despisers of the body. These have lost the artistic impulse "to create beyond themselves," and thus have lost trust in the reason of their own bodies. They choose to despise that which they can no longer stand to acknowledge: the body. Their rage towards "life" and "earth," and their "envy" towards every creative engagement with existence, have no future. In the words of Zarathustra: "You are not bridges for me to the overman" (Z I, "Despisers") – a clear sign that this questionable concept, too, is best defined and defended as an aesthetic term.

Besides "body" and "ego" Zarathustra uses another, inconspicuous word to which he assigns an importance which can hardly be ignored. It is the pronoun "self" (*Selbst*), which appears only as a substantive in this speech, and which evidently refers to something between "body" and "ego":

> Sense and spirit are instruments and playthings: behind them there is still the Self. The Self seeks with the eyes of the senses, it listens also with the ears of the spirit.
>
> Ever listens and seeks the Self; it compares, masters, conquers, and destroys. (Z I, "Despisers")

This is a confusing speech: after all that has been said, one would have expected that there be only body "behind" sense and spirit. Body, we were told, "creates" for itself its own "great reason," of which the "instrument" and "plaything" is the "ego" of "small reason." Yet here we find "behind" the ego the very word which, in common usage, serves as a pronoun for the ego. The "self" is, in everyday language, an expression for persons who can say "me": the consciousness of the *ego* is that of the *self*. The pronoun may be used only metaphorically in the case of those unities which are active in analogy to self-consciousness – which function "by themselves" and thus "automatically." Seen in this way, everything which transpires or happens without an external cause happens "by itself."

Yet this is obviously just a circumlocution for the assumed originality and primality of the integrity of a certain unity grasped from without, and nothing more. The "self" indicates the spontaneity of a totality – and thus abbreviates a figure of speech which would have to be much too long if the process were to be described in its actual complexity. And so we say that the larva in metamorphosis moves "by itself," and that in this way a butterfly comes into being. The phrase "by itself" indicates that no immediate, external influence is at work, though we certainly know that many external factors are involved in the metamorphosis which transpires within the cocoon. The opening of the cocoon is easily explained as the consequence of the biting activity originating from the developed butterfly within it. It would be absurd to attribute to this process some "self" which would have to be conceived in the manner of a real subject.

Yet there are two borderline cases in which we use the pronoun without being able to explicitly describe the process that we thus assign. The first of these cases is present in the *ego*. We may be able to describe a process involving some ego in many different ways; yet the ego remains irreplaceable, and with the *ego* also the *self*, which is the ego's linguistic surrogate. Whenever someone consciously does something of his or her own accord, then there is no avoiding the ego and the word "me."[5] The second borderline case is that of the *body*, and of organisms in general. The spontaneity of the processes which occur in organisms endogenously are to this very day only conceivable as self-production (*autopoiesis*) and reflexive activity (*self-organization*). This does not alter the fact that all the materials of metabolism have their origin outside the organism, which is dependent in all its processes upon the homeostatic exchange with its environment. Those processes which are essential, i.e. specific and particular, to a certain organism are the ones which originate in the organism *itself*. The organism is what it is by and through its own activity. Whoever seeks to describe an organic process will not be able to do so without some reference to the whole of an organism, which moves "by itself."

It is certainly no accident that Zarathustra introduces the *self* in the transition of those two fields of activity, a place in which the pronoun is indeed semantically unavoidable: in the transition between *ego* and *body*. Even if one were not disposed to comprehend this usage of the term, one could still take it as further evidence for the human configuration of all knowledge, a point Nietzsche returns to again and again. Everything refers back to man – himself: "We always can only *know ourselves*" (*KSA* 9, 6[419]). This is the case in particular when a process strikes us as particularly familiar, and we can conceive of its originality only in terms of the spontaneity which we experience in ourselves. Herein lies the particular epistemic status of the body, a status from which we can never escape: the body's processes, in which the body finds expression as a whole and as an original unity, can only be understood in analogy to our experience of ourselves. And this means that we understand by analogy to our self: "We have borrowed our concept of unity," we read in Nietzsche's posthumous works, "from our concept of the self – our oldest article of faith" (*WP* 635).

However, this relation will not suffice to explain the appearance of a substantivized self between ego and body. Nothing suggests that Zarathustra seeks to illustrate an epistemological insight. He seems rather to want to make a claim concerning the *real relation of cause and effect* between the body and the ego. It is of little avail if we assign new names to the self, which appears here as an independent agent; in this way we would only give the impression of making this term more intelligible. Of course, there are certain similarities to Schopenhauer's "will," and these might prompt one to understand the "self" which Nietzsche speaks of here as the "will to power." This would fit well with the ruling and commanding functions of the "self," but not so well to the fact that the self "listens," "laughs," and "creates." In his very first speech Zarathustra denies the will the ability to be creatively productive. But "will to power" must, according to Nietzsche, be present in each and every activity. For this reason one cannot deny that the self is active as will to power – if, that is, the self can be thought of as active at all. But this is certainly not the *proprium* of the self. Naturally, we cannot reject out of hand the claim that this usage of the term "self" might refer to that authority which Sigmund Freud referred to as the "subconscious."[6] Yet what does this mean for the "brother" whom Zarathustra addresses and who is not at all familiar with Freud? Before elucidating this term by means of historical parallels, one is well advised to attempt to explain it on the basis of the context in which it is found. Let us hear Zarathustra's speech once again:

> Behind thy thoughts and feelings, my brother, there is a mighty lord, an unknown sage – it is called Self; it dwells in your body, it is your body. (Z I, "Despisers")

The self is, then, a "mighty lord" and "unknown sage." This stands in agreement with the claim that it has "ends," that it keeps the ego on a "leash" and "secretly feeds it" concepts, even tells it when it should feel pain or pleasure. Finally it is the self which has the power to induce "respect and hate," "pleasure and harm." It is thus not merely the expression of the productive function of the body, but also the product of the body's reduced liveliness. It is, after all, the self which seeks to "die" and which "has turned itself away from life" (Z I, "Despisers"). Even so, the ego must follow the self, in order that Zarathustra may tell the despisers of the body that their hatred is only the expression of their life-weary self, itself the expression of a weakened body. They despise the very thing they obey, and in so doing they reveal the most profound contradiction in their form of life. They are caught in this contradiction because they do not know how they are connected with their body – that it is by way of their self.

What, then, is the self? What is this authority which is hardly extractable from the body, but which nevertheless manages its productivity and even its decay and decline? How can the self be grasped, assuming it is no longer mere body and manifestly more than mere consciousness, upon which it nevertheless seems to depend? The affinity between body and self is most apparent; a "creative self" and a "creating body" work hand in hand. A difference or even an opposition between the two seems inconceivable. The self appears to be an *expression* of the body, a *form* which the body may give itself in its dealings with itself and its own kind. The self communicates a (perhaps particular) change in the body in a feeling which becomes an expression of the entire body:

> The Self says to the ego: "Feel pain!" And thereupon it suffers, and thinks how it might put an end to its suffering – and for that very purpose it *is meant* to think.
>   The Self says to the ego: "Feel pleasure!" Thereupon it rejoices, and thinks how it may often rejoice – and for that very purpose it *is meant* to think. (Z I, "Despisers")

Feeling and thinking are the functions of the *ego*. In relation to the ego, the *self* functions as an amplifier in matters which, under certain circumstances, affect the body – matters which may be influenced by means of a change or reinforcement of sensibility. It is striking to what extent the self is charged with concepts, though it of course does not have concepts at its disposal: it has the wisdom of a wise man, exhibits the prudence of an educator (bearing a "leash"), has the intentions of a speaker, possesses ends as a commander might, and is, as the "creative self" of the body, hardly distinguishable from an artist.

In all these relations, the self stands on the threshold of consciousness, a threshold which it – "by itself" – cannot cross. In order to formulate conscious statements and to achieve logically consistent reflection, the self requires the "instrument" and "plaything" of "small reason." The self can and must give "small reason" impulses and commands, though it does not "itself" have any concepts at its command. The feelings and concepts of the ego evidently are related to circumstances in which body finds itself as a whole, and in which it must also be engaged as such. The self shows the body such circumstances; and it does so from within the body. It forms the impulsivity which affects the body as a whole, in order to make this disposition receptive for the condition of the body as a whole.

We can now provide an answer to the question as to the particular characteristic of the self that distinguishes it from body and ego: the self is an *expression of the body understood as a unity*. It is the active configuration of the entire body, and enables the body to *present itself as a unity*. In the self the body creates for itself a form in which it makes understanding of the body as a whole possible. As manifest in such a form, the body is not simply activity or an event; through this form the body translates itself into a meaning which it may have, and which it may share with others of its own kind. This meaning concentrates the sensibility of the organism in such a way as to enable the organism to be perceived, individuated, and controlled in its own "sense." Put simply: *the self transposes the body into a possible sense*. It represents the direction in which the body moves itself. In the self the body possesses a unity which can mean something, and which is thus accessible to conceptual understanding, though the self as such is not a source of concepts. In the self the body is concerned with the communication of its position and condition insofar as the body is disposed to possess a faculty of control which affects it as a whole. Such control, which is explicitly exercised over the body in this way, is exercised in the name of the ego.

It is in this sense that the self stands for "wisdom." It is deceptively similar to the reason of the body. When Zarathustra states that "the creating body [. . .] creates the spirit as a hand of its will" (Z I, "Despisers"), we may take this as a suggestion, at least, of how the body attempts to go beyond itself as a whole by means of the self. We may recognize the integrative and representative function of the self in connection with "great reason." The self enables the body to perform symbolically in situations in which the body acts as a kind of substrate, and in which it may express something only when it is affected as physical body *itself* – i.e. from a *unified perspective*, however that perspective may be conceived. The body finds comprehensible expression only through the authority of the self, which represents the body. It is the body which speaks, and not – as emphasized above – the lips or vocal cords; the author of the spoken word is the person as a whole – the man *himself*. The self is the author of sense and thus most intimately related to "great reason."

Zarathustra is concerned above all with distinguishing the *self* as the author of sense from the *ego*. For this we may give a reason: whereas the self merely supplies the conditions for meaning, the ego is already articulated in a concept. The ego is connected with expressible feelings and thoughts; it is associated with understanding and thinking. Thus it stands in a concrete relation to the use of language; it is – as we can now understand more precisely – an "instrument" and "plaything" of the self. The ego always has the body at its disposal in a certain way; it has an intention to command which is given by its involvement in concepts, and also limited by this involvement. Even when it undertakes an action which affects the body as a whole (such as, for example, when it prescribes some medicine), it remains limited to the perspective of concepts. "Small reason" says "me" because it is embedded in certain communicative relations. The body, on the other hand, "does me" by producing the very self which makes communication possible.

Unfortunately, we learn much too little from Zarathustra regarding the *ego*. He is preoccupied with a critique of the overvaluation of the consciousness of the ego: that is why he refuses to even provide an account of the ego's tasks. But it is quite clear that one cannot do without the "small reason" of the ego, i.e. the conscious functions of concepts and judgments. All of the demands placed on the ego by the self must be fulfilled somehow. Through these demands the ego stands in mediated service of the body. And so it does indeed seem as though the ego could actually serve the body actively, by feeling and thinking. For in this way the ego not only makes the sensibilities of the entire body explicit, it also applies, under certain circumstances, a treatment or action to them which can benefit the body as a whole. The ego "is meant" to think, in order that it may appropriate and name constellations in which the body can develop itself. The ego is most certainly a part of the self. It is the authority of explicitness and of conscious, deductive reasoning. As soon as the ego disregards its integral relation to the body, however, it turns away from life. An ego which denies its bodily duty and raises itself to an authority *sui generis* can only operate with dead concepts. It perceives things all wrong, as the young Nietzsche noted ("On the Pathos of Truth," 65).

If we wish to guard against this mistake, we must admit the active impulses of the self, in which the body enables an expression capable of making a unified impression. Even if the ego cannot avoid appearing self-conscious, it must be cognizant of its position as "instrument" and "plaything" of the body. This is not acknowledged by the despisers of the body. That is why Zarathustra warns against the hubris of self-consciousness, which cuts itself off from the conditions of productivity and thus becomes unfit for life. Nietzsche does not simply aim to show that the despisers of the body are caught in contradiction with their own premises and stuck in opposition with their own bodies. He pursues a more inclusive goal. He seeks to show these despisers that they do not understand themselves properly when they fail to respect the integral relation of body and spirit. The denial of the body necessarily becomes self-denial: here, too, the coherence between body and ego makes itself known, a coherent whole mediated by the self.

See also 4 "Nietzsche on Individuation and Purposiveness in Nature"; 6 "Nietzsche's 'Gay' Science"; 26 "Nietzsche on Geophilosophy and Geoaesthetics"

Notes

1 The German word *Sinn* has an exceptionally wide semantic field, which covers such meanings as "meaning," "sense" – both as the capacity to distinguish stimuli, and as discursive content – "thought," "consciousness," "understanding" of something. In the plural (*Sinne*) the word may also refer to sexual desire.
2 In regard to its formal (i.e. logical) use, Kant defines reason as the "power to deduce."
3 There we read: "The wheel of ground does not roll between them" (Z I, "On the Pale Criminal"). This means that thought and images are linked with action neither by causes nor through necessary conditions. The actual event, which is in fact the act, is accompanied by thoughts, words, and images – without being strictly connected to these. Nietzsche's further reflections on the function of the self, which mediates between – among other things – body and ego, show how the coherence between the act and its conceptual entourage is to be conceived.
4 The child's "creating" is his doing (Z I, "The Three Metamorphoses"). Here too we find a "wheel." It does not stand still, but is in active, spontaneous, and self-created motion.
5 In anticipation of possible objections I would like to emphasize that for the sake of the present argument I assume normal speech practices in Indo-European languages. I do not deny that a stand-up comic may succeed in delivering his routine without saying the word "me." However, it will suffice if I refer only to the language in which Nietzsche has Zarathustra deliver his speeches.
6 On this plausible interpretation, which, however, reveals more about the possible origin of Freud's term than it does about Nietzsche's intended meaning in this context, see Conway 1997: 246ff.

Editions of Nietzsche Used

"On the Pathos of Truth" (1872), in *Philosophy and Truth: Selections from Nietzsche's Notebooks of the Early 1870s*, ed. and trans. Daniel Breazeale (Atlantic Highlands, NJ: Humanities Press, 1979), pp. 61–9.

References

Aristotle (1993). *De Anima* (London and New York: Routledge).
Conway, Daniel. W. (1997). *Nietzsche's Dangerous Game* (Cambridge: Cambridge University Press).
Gerhardt, Volker (1996). *Vom Willen zur Macht* (Berlin and New York: Walter de Gruyter).
Hastedt, H. (1989). *Das Leib-Seele-Problem. Zwischen Naturwissenschaft des Geistes und kultureller Eindimsionalität*, 2nd edn. (Frankfurt am Main: Suhrkamp).
Kant, Immanuel (1950). *Critique of Pure Reason.*, trans. Norman Kemp Smith (London: Macmillan).
—— (1987). *Critique of Judgment*, trans. Werner S. Pluhar (Indianapolis: Hackett).
Kaulbach, F. (1980). *Nietzsches Idee einer Experimentalphilosophie* (Cologne: Böhlau).

Parkes, Graham (1994). *Composing the Soul: Reaches of Nietzsche's Psychology* (Chicago and London: University of Chicago Press).

Plato (1989). *The Collected Dialogues*, ed. Edith Hamilton and Huntington Cairns (Princeton, NJ: Princeton University Press).

Scheier, Claus-Artur (1985). *Nietzsches Labyrinth. Das ursprüngliche Denken und die Seele* (Freiburg im Breisbau: Alber Verlag).

16

Phenomenology and Science in Nietzsche

PETER POELLNER

1 Introduction

The place of phenomenal consciousness in Nietzsche's philosophy of mind and action is notoriously ambiguous.[1] On the one hand we find his eulogy to Leibniz's "incomparable insight [. . .] that being conscious is only an *accidens* of representation, not its [. . .] essential attribute, i.e. that what we call consciousness is only one state of our mental and psychic world [. . .] and does by no means constitute it as such" (*GS* 357; also *GS* 354). Apparently continuous with remarks such as this are his claims that the causes of many of our conscious mental states, in particular our affective and evaluative experiences, are best understood as "physiological" (*GM* III. 15, 17; *TI*, "The Four Great Errors," 2, 3; *WP* 38, 43, 229).

On the other hand, there are a plethora of passages indicating that Nietzsche, even in the later phase of his creative career, regards consciousness as efficacious. The most pervasive evidence that for Nietzsche reference to phenomenal consciousness is not nugatory in the explanation of human comportment comes from the fact that he himself explicitly *uses* explanations in which consciously entertained thoughts, perceptions, evaluations, or desires play a causal role on almost every page of his writings. Prominent examples include his analysis of *ressentiment* (*GM* I. 10, 14), his account of the causes of the belief in freedom of the will (*GM* I. 13), the genealogy of guilt (*GM* II. 16), and the analysis of nihilism (esp. *WP* 1–13). Consider as a final example Nietzsche's apparent alternative to the ascetic ideal which is clearly, whatever its precise content, associated in some way with the idea of an eternal recurrence. The authentic *contemplation* of the possibility of an eternal recurrence of the same is claimed to have momentous psychological *effects* on the subject engaging in it: "If this thought gained possession of you, it would change you as you are or perhaps crush you" (*GS* 341).

What are we to make of these tensions in Nietzsche's utterances on the role of phenomenal consciousness? In this essay I shall develop an interpretation of them suggesting that neither his (implicit or explicit) claims concerning the efficacy of consciousness, nor his advocacy, in other passages, of "physiological" explanation should be understood *metaphysically* as theses about what *really* is the case in an ultimate ontological sense. Rather, both of these approaches should be interpreted as mutually compatible, non-metaphysical, practical methods of understanding and acting on the world within the context of a dominant concern with the *phenomenology of the human life-world*. I shall argue, moreover, that Nietzsche not only pervasively uses and anticipates phenomenological modes of inquiry, but that, perhaps even more importantly, his work contains the most powerful and perceptive statement of the implicit motivations of the "phenomenological turn" in early twentieth-century continental philosophy. These motivations, which have ever since shaped philosophy on the European continent as profoundly as the linguistic turn has dominated much of English-speaking philosophy, have not been fully appreciated in the Anglophone philosophical context even today (one notable exception to this is Cooper 2002). My thesis will be that we need to turn to Nietzsche properly to understand the significance of the phenomenological turn and, with it, of the fission of philosophy for much the twentieth century into several distinct trajectories defined, for the most part, by different concerns.

2 The Idea of Phenomenology

What do I mean by "the phenomenological turn"? Since talk of phenomenology has proliferated in recent years, a demarcation of the specific sense in which the term will be used in this essay is required. Broadly, I shall refer by it to the kind of philosophical approach exemplified by Edmund Husserl (1859–1938) and some of his followers and philosophical descendants, and I take this to comprise the following three basic commitments:

1   The philosophical question which should precede all others is: what is involved in the constitution of a world for a subject? Or: how is it possible that something like a world can manifest itself at all? In order to answer this transcendental question, what is needed is a constitutive analysis of the essential elements involved in such a world-manifestation. This means that phenomenology has to concern itself with questions such as: are there any fundamental data which are involved in the possible encounter of a world by a subject? What is the relation between these elements and other, "founded" aspects of encountering a world – i.e. of what phenomenology calls *intentionality* – such as the representation of objects? Central issues here include the role of self-moving bodily agency for the possibility of perceptual experiences as of persisting spatial objects; the relation between action, conscious perception, and conceptualization; the relation between context-bound ("pre-predicative") and context-independent ("predicative") judgment; and the relation between conscious object representation and *self*-consciousness. In general, phenomenology seeks to give descriptions of the constitutive characteristics of each of these modes, levels, or aspects of intentionality. These descriptions, if carried out properly, will reveal any dependencies of such an aspect or level on others, which then call for description in turn.[2] But what counts as proper or adequate description? Here we need to consider phenomenology's central methodological commitment.
2   In its descriptive enterprise, phenomenology is to accept no data or evidence other than what is given *as* it is given. This methodological demand in fact divides up

into at least the following two requirements. First, no evidence relating specifically to the subject-matter of the investigation is to be accepted at any stage of the analysis if it has not been *self-given* to the investigator in its intrinsic (phenomenal) character, either by way of perception, or as a characteristic of samples or analogs (re-)presented imaginatively or imitatively. One implication of this is that phenomenology is never content with characterizing its subject-matters in terms of only their consequences, or by extraneous marks (however infallibly or necessarily concomitant these may be), or in terms of *merely* symbolic (e.g. linguistic) representations, however much such representations may have a pragmatic use elsewhere. For phenomenology, an item has only been authentically understood once it has been (re-)presented by the phenomenologist as it itself, *qua* phenomenon, intrinsically is. Secondly, the methodological requirement enjoins the provisional "bracketing" or "suspension," i.e. leaving out of account, of any substantive assumptions or beliefs concerning the subject-matter *going beyond* what is given *as* it is thus (self-)given. This procedure itself involves two things: (i) The phenomenologist is, for the purposes of her analysis, not interested in the veridicality or otherwise of any intuitively presented contents she is using or examining. For example, where the phenomenologist is analyzing the general structure of spatial perceptual content, she may be using a perception as of a tree as a sample. But it would not matter to her if the tree subsequently turned out to have been a hallucination. One way of putting this would be to say the phenomenologist is only interested in the level of *sense* (in Husserl's broad understanding of *Sinn*, whereby all intentional contents, not merely linguistic ones, involve senses). She is not interested, *qua* phenomenologist, in the level of *reference*, e.g. in whether some apparent represented object used as a sample really exists. But this temporary suspension of the "natural attitude" is of course not an end in itself, but is engaged in for the sake of a better understanding of the *Sinnstruktur* of our *actual* experiential world (Merleau-Ponty 1964: 44–57). (ii) The phenomenologist is supposed *only* to consider the given as it is given, leaving out of account any *theories* – whether commonsense, scientific, or metaphysical – in interpreting the phenomena. In the history of philosophy such antecedently held theories have often obstructed the correct description of phenomena; for example, the metaphysical idea that secondary qualities as they are experienced do not inhere in the objects themselves has frequently encouraged the misguided description of them as aspects of "inner" representations or of alleged experiential items called "sensations." Now it may seem as if Husserl's distinction between the "given as it is given" and "theory" fails to recognize the conceptually structured, or "theory-laden," nature of ordinary perceptual content. But this is not so. Husserl in fact emphasizes that the "given" of thematic (i.e. attentional) intentional consciousness is for the most part conceptually structured, although it often also contains non-conceptual components. But he distinguishes between sedimented *habitualities* which make it the case that many things are perceived by us non-inferentially under this or that aspect, as a hammer or as a computer, say, and *theories*, which do not thus inform our immediate encounter with the world, and which we are free to examine for their rational credentials and in the light of such examination can grant assent to or withhold it (Husserl 1983: §30, 1973: §§10, 25). All scientific and metaphysical theories are of this kind, while by contrast various everyday commonsense theories have become sedimented in our perceptual habitualities and thus from a Husserlian point of view no longer count as "theories" in the relevant sense. It is only the former type of theory that the phenomenologist is able and required to suspend, and this is in part what it means to describe what is given just as it is given. It should be unnecessary to emphasize that this requirement is very far from implying that the descriptions of phenomenology state the obvious, or that they only express the modest ambition of providing a transparent overview of what we knew already before we started to philosophize. On the contrary, it sees as one of its main tasks the difficult and far from trivial explication of what is only implicitly, or adumbrationally, or horizonally contained in intentional experience, and, at the meta-level, the explication of what such implicitness (etc.) actually consists in. Therefore the claims of phenomenology, while putatively "merely" descriptive, are frequently surprising, striking, and new.

The points made above imply that the familiar (self-)characterization of classical phenomenology as "Cartesian" is potentially highly misleading. What Husserl himself wanted to indicate by imprudently using this epithet for his own approach was only that its focus was to be on the perspective of consciousness and on the world as it manifests itself to it. But Husserlian phenomenology is emphatically *not* committed to various other more substantive and problematic tenets of Cartesian philosophy. In particular, it denies that the contents of consciousness can adequately be described without reference to the *world itself* as it presents itself to consciousness. At the fundamental level of intentionality, i.e. spatio-temporal experience, the intentional objects analyzed by phenomenology are not "inner" objects distinct from the objects populating the real spatial world, but *those very objects* in their manner of presentation (Husserl 1970a: vol. 2, pp. 593–6; cf. Zahavi 2003: 55–60).

But, it may be objected, is not Husserl's idea of a phenomenological "suspension" of beliefs about the actual world nevertheless incompatible with even quasi-phenomenological externalist positions in recent philosophy of mind which insist that the very identity of experiences of certain fundamental kinds, usually perceptual experiences, depends on the actual existence of their objects, since these objects enter into the very content of these experiences themselves (Campbell 2002: 116–20)? Now the claim that the object of a perceptual experience determines the identity of the experience may mean a number of different things. In the present context two interpretations of it might be thought to be relevant. The thesis may be that the presence or absence of some real, objective, third-personal relation between an external object and the subject of an experience goes to constitute the identity conditions of the experience the subject is having as a matter of metaphysical necessity. Evidently, the concept of experience used in externalist theories of this type is not phenomenological but metaphysical. Their claim is that what an experience *really* is may be different from what it presents itself to its subject as being, and even different from what finite evidence that may subsequently become available to the subject can in fact reveal it to her as having been. Since Husserlian phenomenology makes no metaphysical claims, it does not *deny* this point, but suspends judgment on the issue.

Alternatively, the claim that the objects of perception enter into the very content of the perceptual experience may be the conjunction of two theses: (i) external objects are perceived directly, without the mediation of inner representations, and (ii) unless many of a subject's perceptions are veridical, the subject cannot even possess the concept of experience. Hence there can be no coherent investigation of the structure of experience from a first-personal point of view which does not presuppose the existence of a mind-independent world. As we have seen, Husserl himself emphatically asserts thesis (i). With respect to (ii), while he would deny that we can rule out global skepticism about the external world simply by reflection on the concept of experience, he could allow the following as an a priori truth: the concept of experience can only be grasped by a subject who is defeasibly or provisionally justified in taking herself to be experiencing a world of persisting objects whose existence and nature transcend any particular experience of them. The question whether there genuinely is such a conceptual dependence is in fact itself a legitimate topic of transcendental phenomenology. In any event, when Husserl asserts that there could be consciousness even if the world was "annihilated" (Husserl 1983: §49), his point is simply that some kind of rhapsodic phenomenal consciousness is conceptually possible even in the absence of the kind of order in experience that arguably makes possible both conceptualized *self*-consciousness and the belief that there are objects whose existence is independent of any particular state of representing them. Kant would not have demurred from this.

The primary phenomenological concept of experience, then, is of experiences as they (can) present themselves to the subject, or as we might also say in Husserlian language, experiences as individuated in terms of their *senses*. Experiences are here in the first instance identified in terms of what they purport to be of, e.g. "*E* is an experience as of a tree." This fundamental concept of experience is of course not replaced by, but rather *presupposed* by the concepts of experience used by contemporary content externalists. Otherwise one would not even be able to say such things as that, when circumstances are unpropitious, our experiences are different from *what we take them to be* (Campbell 2002: 163).

3   The third central commitment of phenomenology as understood here, unlike the previous two, is not expressly stated in its canonical texts, but it is, I would argue, operative in them. At the level of explicit self-interpretation, classical phenomenology often presents itself as a transcendental discipline, occupying itself with universal conditions of possibility for a world to be encounterable at all. But in fact many of its analyses cannot plausibly be granted such a universal transcendental significance, but seem to be concerned with the conditions of possibility of having a world for beings approximately like human beings in relevant respects. For example, is it really an a priori truth that a world of persisting spatial objects can only be experienced by an embodied subject that is conscious of its bodily agency through something of the qualitative nature of kinaesthetic sensations (Husserl 1989: §18a)? Even if it is granted that self-movement is a condition of possibility of such representations – although even this might be disputed, insisting on the conceptual possibility of appropriate innate capacities – could changes of spatial position of the subject with respect to the object not conceivably be signaled to her

by indices of an entirely different (e.g. visual) character? In short, it could be argued that Husserl is here not so much concerned with uncovering a priori truths applicable to any conscious knower whatever, but with the necessary presuppositions of a certain type of representation for beings with approximately the cognitive endowment and constitution of *human* beings (cf. Smith 2003: 121–5). In other words, the investigation of what might be called the *conditionally* a priori structures of the *human world*, rather than transcendental inquiry into universal conditions of the possibility of representation, becomes a central theme in its own right in Husserlian phenomenology, although this appears to be not sufficiently acknowledged – for whatever reasons – in its "official" self-interpretations.[3]

A similar point applies even more obviously to the Heideggerian variant of phenomenology. While the early Heidegger officially conceives of the task of phenomenology as ontological, rather than transcendental, in practice all the analyses of his early *magnum opus* are concerned with a phenomenological ontology of *human* being or *Dasein*. His declared reason for this initial thematic privileging of the human is that all ontological inquiries concerning beings other than *Dasein* must "arise out of," i.e. presuppose, the "fundamental ontology" of the phenomenal mode of being of *Dasein* (Heidegger 1962: §4). But this substantial and ambitious claim hardly receives any uncontroversial support from the analyses offered in *Being and Time*. What these show at most is that, for example, beings like *us* cannot represent something as context-independent objects without having encountered entities as available in practical dealings with them. They do not show, even on the most generous reading, that there cannot *be* objects independently of there being available equipment (*zuhandenes Zeug*). Moreover, many of the detailed descriptions of the various modalities of inauthentic or authentic being-in-the-world-with-others are hardly necessary for the task of a general ontology. Here also, the conclusion seems inevitable that, whatever the explicit self-interpretation of early Heideggerian phenomenology, it treats of human being as it is revealed in its own self-understanding as a central, perhaps even as the pre-eminent, philosophical theme in its own right.

Of the three fundamental features of classical phenomenology as interpreted here, the first and the third specify *substantial objectives* while the second is essentially a methodological prescription concerning how these objectives are to be attained. The substantial commitments in fact amount to a *fundamental reorientation* of philosophical inquiry in relation to the predominant modern paradigm of philosophy inaugurated by Descartes. Modern philosophy has generally conceived of epistemology and/or metaphysics as the fundamental philosophical disciplines, although in some influential modern philosophers – Kant and some of his successors in particular – questions concerning the rational foundations of morality have challenged this disciplinary hierarchy. In opposition to this, phenomenology, in its own practice and in part also in its self-interpretation, installs the first-personal investigation of how a world can manifest itself in experience, and how, in particular, it does so in human experience, as the fundamental philosophical enterprise. Metaphysical questions and epistemological issues in the traditional sense, by contrast, while not rejected, are at best considered secondary or derivative. Yet neither from Husserl nor from early

Heidegger do we really glean a sufficient explanation or justification of this shift of orientation. Why, we may ask, should the detailed descriptive investigation of the structures of the world as experienced by beings like us come to take priority among philosophical questions?

In fact, I shall argue, we cannot fully grasp the reasons for this shift from the self-reflections of the phenomenologists themselves, but should rather understand it as the philosophical manifestation of a broader cultural transformation that occurred in the last two decades of the nineteenth century and the first decade of the twentieth. No single intellectual figure was more influential in articulating and shaping this cultural transformation than Nietzsche. And it is no accident that phenomenology emerged in the German-speaking countries at a time when Nietzsche's writings were the dominant, omnipresent point of reference in the intellectual discourses of those countries. And despite Husserl's hostility towards what he saw as the irrationalism and psychologism of the – often Nietzsche-inspired – fashionable modes of philosophizing in fin-de-siècle central Europe, it is in Nietzsche that we find the philosophical underpinnings of the phenomenological turn in philosophy.

3 Truth and the Primacy of Life

I have argued that the phenomenological turn in philosophy should in part be understood (going beyond the official self-interpretation of the classical phenomenologists) as the emergence of the human world – the world as it shows up from the human point of view – as the primary topic of philosophical concern in its own right. Most of the modern philosophical tradition from Descartes via the post-Kantians to the mainstream of analytic philosophy has by contrast regarded either metaphysics or epistemology as *prima philosophia*. Its characteristic questions have been either "What is the fundamental nature of reality as it is in itself, irrespective of the finite and specifically human point of view?" or "Do or can human beliefs correspond to the nature of reality as it is independently of that finite and specifically human point of view?" It is an important aspect of the radical character of Nietzsche's work that these questions are dethroned from their traditional position of preeminence. Indeed, more than this, for Nietzsche:

> It is of cardinal importance that one should abolish the *real world*. It is the great inspirer of doubt and devaluator in respect of the world *we are*. (WP 583)

How is this demand to be understood? It is clear that any adequate interpretation of it depends on a grasp of what Nietzsche means by "the real world" (*die wahre Welt*). The most famous use of this expression in Nietzsche's published writings occurs in the section "How the 'Real World' at Last Became a Myth" in *Twilight of the Idols*. Here it denotes, in succession, the Platonic Forms, the Christian God, and the Kantian thing in itself. The passage ends:

> The "real world" – an idea no longer of any use, not even a duty any longer – an idea grown useless, superfluous, consequently a refuted idea: let us abolish it! [. . .]

303

> We have abolished the real world: what world is left? The apparent world perhaps? [...] But no! *with the real world we have also abolished the apparent world!* (*TI*, "How the 'Real World' at Last Became a Myth")

What do the Platonic, Christian, and Kantian concepts of the "real world" have in common that makes them "useless" and *consequently* refuted? The crucial affinities between these conceptions are evidently that (1) according to all of them there is a real world which has a "constitution in itself" independent of human representations of it, and (2) this real world does not reveal itself as it is in itself in ordinary sensory (or otherwise receptive) experience. The real world is supposed to be quite other than what the contents of ordinary human experience present the world as being, and to be inaccessible to such experience in its intrinsic nature. Nietzsche gives a more precise description of the focal target of his objections when explicitly rejecting "things in themselves" in other passages:

> That things possess a constitution in themselves quite *apart from interpretation and subjectivity*, is a *quite idle* hypothesis. (*WP* 560, my emphases)

> "Things that have a constitution in themselves" – a dogmatic idea with which one must break absolutely. (*WP* 559)

It is clear that the idea of things in themselves is considered here, as in the passage from *Twilight*, as the conceptual core of the objectionable notion of a "real world." These notes make it quite explicit that what Nietzsche means by a "thing in itself" is a supposed *intrinsic nature* of reality or parts of it which is or may be entirely independent of, or transcendent to, the way in which this reality reveals itself to humans – to its experiential mode of presentation, we might say. And what makes this idea objectionable, as in *Twilight* and some earlier passages (most importantly *HH* 9), is not that it is somehow unintelligible or otherwise *theoretically* deficient, but that it is *idle* or *useless*. To "abolish" or "break with" the idea of things in themselves means to recognize, and to enable others to recognize, this idea as idle, i.e. to cease granting great importance to it in our intellectual economy.

What also emerges explicitly from these notes is that what Nietzsche rejects is not only Platonist–Christian "two-world" metaphysics, according to which some ordinarily inaccessible reality-in-itself is held to *cause* the world of appearances, but also those forms of one-world metaphysics which maintain that the world's *fundamental properties* – its intrinsic constitution – are not those which are revealed in possible human experience. But *why* should such conceptions be considered "idle" or "useless"? After all, even if Nietzsche is right in opposing two-world metaphysics, does not science reveal properties of our one world to us which are both different from and more fundamental than the properties which are accessible to human sensory experience? And how could it plausibly be claimed that the discoveries of science are *useless*? In order to assess this objection, we need to venture a brief excursion into Nietzsche's reflections on the nature of modern science.

Modern scientific explanations, for Nietzsche, are essentially *incomplete causal explanations*. Causal explanations account for events in part by identifying them as instances of lawlike regularities. To have explained an event B is, at least at the basic level, to have identified a presumptively universal regularity under which it falls: "all As are concomitant with Bs." To allow for the asymmetry of causal relations – i.e. the priority of the cause, which is not necessarily temporal priority – the law has to sustain counterfactuals like: if an intervention had been applied to A, B would have been different, but not vice versa (Mackie 1974: 180). But why should there be this asymmetry? The natural response to this question is that the cause A is prior to the effect B because it compels or necessitates the effect, and this compulsion is matter of certain *powers* being released, whose qualitative nature is efficacious in bringing about the effect. For Nietzsche, this idea of causal efficacy or power is central and indispensable for full or adequate causal explanation (*WP* 664).

According to Nietzsche, the characteristic methodological paradigm of modern science was only fully attained, not in Galileo or Descartes, but in Newton. What crucially distinguishes Newton and his scientific successors from their mechanist predecessors, such as Robert Boyle, is a prescinding from the question of the qualitative character of force or power. The mechanists had thought that in the mechanics of solids, fluids, and gases we are directly acquainted with the actually intrinsic character[4] of causal power: pressure and impact experientially reveal the qualitative nature of operative power to us in any single instance of mechanical interaction (Hume would later famously dispute this claim). Newton, however, found himself compelled to postulate a force of attraction whose mode of operation could not be reduced to mechanical pressure or impact – a force, that is, apparently acting at a distance. His response to the problem was simply to shelve the problem of the intrinsic qualitative character of gravitational force – "I do not feign hypotheses" – and to insist that it was sufficient for scientific explanation to have a mathematical model which enables us to *predict* the celestial and terrestrial motions and the tides of the seas, whatever the non-mathematical intrinsic properties of the force or power responsible for these events. Force, for Newton, is not a myth, but all we need to know about it for the purposes of scientific "explanation" as conceived by him, i.e. for prediction, are its numerical indices. As long as we can *calculate* the magnitude of forces by correlating them functionally with other measurable properties (distances, accelerations, masses), and have suitable correspondence rules by which to correlate these properties to observable phenomena, we can simply ignore the question of the qualitative nature of that which the numerical values of the variable "force" in our equations measure. This revolutionary Newtonian conception of what scientific explanations should concern themselves with has been definitive of modern science up until the present (cf. Cohen 1980: 131). Nietzsche correctly predicts that all scientific explanation will, at the fundamental level, soon follow the Newtonian model in this respect, basing its explanations on the hypothesis of various quantifiable "forces" acting at a distance through empty space (i.e. space not "filled" by anything instantiating non-geometrical categorical properties: *WP* 618). This means that scientific explanation in fact *suspends* the question of what it actually is that is operative in the processes mapped by its functional equations, and scientific explanations are therefore incomplete in this specific sense. Nietzsche often expresses this point by saying that science at the fundamental level does not explain but describe: "It is an illusion that something is *known* when we possess a mathematical formula for an event: it is only designated, described; nothing more"

(*WP* 628; also *WP* 554, 624, *GS* 112). To the possible objection that force, even when actualized, has no intrinsic qualitative properties, and that scientific mathematical models therefore leave nothing relevant out, Nietzsche's reply is concise: " 'Mechanistic interpretation': desires nothing but quantities; but force is to be found in quality" (*WP* 660; also *WP* 564). Indeed, it is obvious that causal efficacy cannot reside in abstract mathematical properties or entities (i.e. in numbers) and the objection to which Nietzsche is responding to here is therefore equivalent to an anti-realist dismissal of the concept of efficacious force.[5] According to Nietzsche, in merely giving us "descriptions" useful for prediction, science is not *deficient*, however. It is not failing to do something it ought to be doing. Rather, it does what it should do, and it does this often extremely successfully:

> "Science" (as it is practiced today) is the attempt to create a common sign language for all phenomena for the purpose of an easy predictability and, consequently, manipulability of nature. (*GOA* XIII. 83)

> Science – the transformation of nature into concepts for the purpose of mastering nature – belongs under the rubric "means." (*WP* 610)

Does this mean that Nietzsche's conception of science is instrumentalist? Yes and no. It is clear that he thinks of the methodology of modern Newtonian and post-Newtonian science as *in fact* (whatever its meta-scientific self-interpretation) determined by the purpose of prediction and as, in this sense, essentially instrumental or technological. However, Nietzsche's conception of modern science is not instrumentalist in the technical sense familiar from contemporary philosophy of science. He is not committed, that is, to the view that scientific theories are mere calculating devices or that the substantival terms in it, unless they can be cashed observationally, do not refer to real entities. It is quite possible that some of these terms, although originally introduced as expressing theoretical assumptions without observational backing, can later be correlated with observables and thus be confirmed as referring to real, "theoretical" entities (such as atoms or genes). But in good Newtonian manner, scientific theory, while ascribing causal properties to such theoretical entities, is not, *qua scientific* theory, concerned with the intrinsic qualitative nature of the powers that are responsible for the causal efficacy of these entities, and it works perfectly well without needing to "feign hypotheses" about this.

If we now return to Nietzsche's claim that the concept of a "real world," of fundamental intrinsic properties the world might have which transcend ordinary human experience, is useless, we can see how a belief in the truth or verisimilitude of modern scientific theories not only does not conflict with this claim, but may serve to make its meaning more transparent. We can divide human cognitive interests or concerns into two mutually exclusive and jointly exhaustive classes: practical and purely theoretical interests. Purely theoretical interests are interests which aim at knowledge of the truth for its own sake, whatever the truth may be and irrespective of whether knowledge of it has a bearing on any other interests. All cognitive interests which are not purely theoretical in this sense I shall call practical interests. They might include aesthetic interests, communicative interests, moral interests, technological-manipulative interests, soteriological interests, and so forth. Nietzsche's point is that knowledge of any supposed non-mathematical fundamental intrinsic properties transcending the sort of experience in fact possible for humans is useless in the sense that it serves no conceivable interest other than a purely theoretical one. As we have seen, modern science *de facto* suspends the issue of what these properties might be: its interests are to this extent precisely *not* purely theoretical. What would be examples of such "useless" knowledge? It is initially tempting to think that all metaphysical propositions would belong to this category for Nietzsche. However, to interpret Nietzsche's point like this would be precipitate. For there are clearly metaphysical beliefs which do affect interests other than purely theoretical ones, for example the Christian belief in an afterlife, or its denial, or the belief in metempsychosis, and others. But there are indeed many other metaphysical beliefs which have no such implications and which therefore satisfy, if any, only purely theoretical concerns. Examples of such "useless" beliefs include the following: the intrinsic qualitative nature of real objects is mind-like or representation-like; the intrinsic nature of the spatio-temporal world does not include consciousness among its properties; the real spatio-temporal world consists of objects with absolute (non-perspectival) properties; being is fundamentally non-objectifiable. Claims like these, which of course make up much of the history of metaphysics and ontology up until the present, are "idle" in the sense that they are all in principle compatible with all our practical interests, and knowledge of them would satisfy only a purely theoretical concern. Metaphysicians have of course usually claimed that their preferred doctrines are "better explanations" of the predictive success of some of our commonsense and scientific theories than others. But since metaphysical claims of this sort do not essentially make any predictions at all, there is no agreement among competent inquirers about what would make one "explanation" of this kind better than another, as long its rivals are not *obviously* incoherent or more limited in scope.

But since Nietzsche, unlike the logical positivists, has no theoretical objections to the very possibility of metaphysics, and since those of its claims he regards as useless and "consequently refuted" are so because their truth or falsity does not impinge upon any practical interests, why should he not simply tolerate them as expressing the harmless if somewhat arcane and idiosyncratic interests of some philosophers? Why should he consider it to be "of cardinal importance that one should abolish the real world" (*WP* 583)? While none of the relevant propositions about a putative "real world" are presupposed or entailed by any propositions associated with human practical interests, the *belief* by others or ourselves either in *particular* "real world" propositions, or the belief in the *importance* of such propositions in *general*, may certainly affect our practical interests. If the people in my environment mostly believe, for instance, that the body is a sign or even a mere epiphenomenon of some mind-like reality, this is likely to be associated with a conviction that the really serious and important matters are those of the mind. Conversely, if the people in my culture predominantly think that conscious states are superficial properties or even mere epiphenomena of processes describable more adequately in a physical idiom, the likelihood is that such a culture will regard the way the world presents itself to consciousness as of relatively little importance and not worthy of one's *really* serious attention. To be sure, none of these evaluative stances are strictly entailed for a fully rational individual by the respective metaphysical beliefs, but that they tend often to be associated with them is amply confirmed by intellectual history. And insofar as one's own practical interests are significantly affected by the evaluative stances common in one's culture, one cannot remain indifferent to the latter. Secondly, the *general* belief in the *importance* of purely theoretical questions concerning the "constitution in itself" of a putative "real world" whose intrinsic qualities may be inaccessible to ordinary human experience obviously also has practical consequences. Given that human capacities are finite, the more my surrounding culture is convinced of the central importance of purely theoretical issues, the less attention and effort will it be able to devote to (broadly) practical questions. In the particular subculture of philosophy, this evaluative hierarchy has, according to Nietzsche, held sway almost since its inception, with deleterious consequences.

In the light of these considerations, how should we interpret Nietzsche's apparent ambivalence noted at the beginning of this essay between his frequent use of *phenomenological* explanations, and his insistence elsewhere on the need for *physiological* explanations for various conscious phenomena? Insofar as both types of explanation are governed by practical interests, broadly construed, there need be no essential conflict between them, and Nietzsche is therefore not being inconsistent in his appeal to both. In many circumstances, in fact probably in most everyday circumstances regarding our own or others' actions and behavior, our cognitive interest will be best satisfied by phenomenological explanations. If I want to know why Paul approached Janet at a party, the sufficient explanation may be that she struck him as attractive. This is not a "superficial" explanation, because there is in fact no other type of explanation that would answer my cognitive interest in this kind of case better than this phenomenological one. There are other cases – for example, certain kinds of depression – where a person's conscious state is not satisfactorily explicable by or responsive to phenomenological considerations. Here the appropriate explanation and treatment may appeal to factors such as a deficiency of neurotransmitters like serotonin and catecholamines in the brain. While this type of explanation may in this instance be the best suited to satisfy the cognitive interest, it is important to remember, as was shown earlier, that such explanations are like phenomenological explanations in at least this respect: they involve no metaphysical claims regarding the intrinsic efficacious properties of whatever causal powers are responsible for, say, the effect of monoamines at the molecular-biological level.

There are, then, circumstances in which someone may be interested in altering her own or somebody else's state of consciousness, not through seeking to alter its intentional contents directly, for example through argument or observation, but indirectly through interfering with consciousness's neural correlates. In the present context, the crucial point is this, however. Even in such cases, where we resort to non-phenomenological, neurophysiological explanations or techniques, there is a sense in which phenomenological considerations remain fundamental. For both the justifications and *motivations* of using such techniques, and the conditions of their *success* need to be specified in terms of human desires and affective states whose relevant features are phenomenological. The alcoholic desires to get drunk to escape his felt unhappiness or *ennui*. The psychiatrist who uses a serotonin treatment for a case of clinical depression normally does so with the aim of producing a hedonically more tolerable state in the patient – of improving his "quality of life." The more general and

308

fundamental point here is that what motivates and justifies our cognitive practices are *values*, that is, experiences or conceptions of something as important or worthwhile. And our concept of value is essentially linked to consciousness. A value is minimally something that, when it is actualized, shows up as mattering to some suitably disposed consciousness. In a world without consciousness there would be no *actual* value. One might of course propose a radical revision of the concept of value which would construe value as conceptually independent of conscious experience. But it is wildly implausible to believe that human beings might be persuaded to adopt such a revised concept with broadly the same pattern of action-guiding use as the current concept of value or worth, but with no essential reference of consciousness. One might express this by saying that human beings are not only attached to various things they value or desire, but to the valuing and desiring, as we currently understand these terms, *themselves*. This is part of Nietzsche's point when he says that what matters most fundamentally to us is not so much what is desired in any given instance, but the desiring itself (e.g. *KGW* VII. 1. 20. 4; p. 661).

Indeed, what would it even mean to say that something should matter to me or be significant to me without this "significance" manifesting itself in any way to my consciousness? Nietzsche is surely right in saying that we cannot even fully conceive what it would be systematically to accept as reasons for our "will" something that does not consciously manifest itself as *meaningful*, as important to us:

> [. . .] *the ascetic ideal offered man meaning!* [. . .] man was *saved* thereby, he possessed a meaning, he was no longer like a sheaf of wind, a plaything of nonsense – the "sense-less" – he could now *will* something; no matter at first to what end, why, with what he willed: *the will itself was saved.* (*GM* III. 28)

The correct description of the cognitive interests that motivate even non-phenomenological explanations therefore essentially requires reference to phenomenological facts – to consciousness and its contents. But it is also worth bearing in mind that in many cases human practical cognitive interests are not concerned with prediction-generating *explanations* at all. Rather, they involve desires to *understand empathetically* the character of others' conscious states and their contents, or to *explicate* and make transparent the contents of our own consciousness, for their own sake. In many of our social interactions, for example, our primary interests are not in predicting or manipulating the behavior of others, but simply in gaining a fuller grasp of the nature of their perspective on the world, and, if things go well, enjoying both what is different from and what is similar to our own. With respect to ourselves, much of our engagement with the world involves attempts to explicate what is implicit in it yet initially opaque to us – for example, why it is that some things attract and others repel us, and what features of the world as it manifests itself to consciousness motivate these responses. Nietzsche's own writings, with their extraordinary richness and detail of psychological observations and analyses, offer many instances of the pursuit of such cognitive interests in a fuller descriptive grasp of the world as it presents itself to consciousness in its own right. Indeed, much of what we call culture consists of comportment governed by such quintessentially phenomenological, *autonomously communicative*, and *explicative* concerns about the world as it is given.

4 Diagnosing the Will To Truth:
A Phenomenological Case Study

What motivates Nietzsche's demand to "abolish" the real world, then, is the opposition of what he calls his "taste" to the privileging of purely theoretical cognitive concerns; of questions, that is, the truth or falsity of any answers to which makes no difference to the way a rational subject can encounter and interact with the world as it can manifest itself in experience. The evaluative attitude that accords a high or even pre-eminent importance to having correct answers to such questions he calls the "will to truth." What also falls under this label is, secondly, the idea that the "real" or deep qualitative character or properties of the world are other than those it normally manifests to human beings, and that it is important for humans to think of themselves and the world in terms of those "real" properties, rather than in terms of the "superficial," or merely apparent, manifest ones.[6] The latter might include, for example, the secondary qualities of worldly objects, or the conscious affective contents of experiences, which underlie our evaluative discourse. Nietzsche identifies the will to truth thus understood as the "core" of the "ascetic ideal" (GM III. 27). A significant proportion of the later writings published by himself is devoted to persuading, or seducing, the reader to develop a similar anti-ascetic taste to his own, and to presenting the will to truth in his sense, not so much as theoretically in error, but as impoverished, dull, and undesirable.[7] The "method" implicit in Nietzsche's critique of the ascetic ideal and its "core," and in his advocacy of non-ascetic ideals, thus consists basically of a careful *phenomenological description* or explication of the form of life that is being opposed, and an *exemplification* of the form of life that is being affirmed.

Nietzsche's own descriptive analysis of the evaluative commitments constitutive of the "will to truth" diagnoses it as essentially expressive of a fundamental lack or deficiency in its adherents' relation to the world as given in possible human experience. Nietzsche's question here is: what would the consciousness of a subject have to be like that, without being *theoretically* confused, is disposed to granting great importance *either* to a knowledge of evidence-transcendent truths which affect no practical interests, *or* to adopting a conception of ourselves and the world according to which their "real" intrinsic properties are systematically other than those which in fact can become experientially manifest to us? His answer is that such a consciousness would have to be characterized, at least, by a relative indifference to the world as it normally affects that consciousness, which in turn is only intelligible if in its interaction with that world it is predominantly disposed towards states such as – in ascending order of negativity – boredom, discontent, or suffering. Nietzsche himself usually stresses the hedonically most negative states in his phenomenology of the will to truth. But his point is a more general one: only a consciousness largely determined negatively in its experiential interaction with the world-as-given is comprehensible to us as a consciousness governed by the will to truth in his sense. This implies that, according to Nietzsche, we cannot understand the intentional objects (or goals) of the will to truth as characterized positively, but only negatively. What the theoretically lucid individual who is subject to the will to truth desires is therefore not adequately or fully described as "the truth for its own sake." Indeed, how could we understand someone's being ruled by such a desire, *irrespective* of what the truth was like?[8] Rather, the truth is in this condition desired because and insofar as it focuses attention away from the world as it is given to consciousness. The truth is desired "*as* liberation [. . .] *as* release from all purpose, all desire, all action" (*GM* III. 17; my emphases), or, more simply, because it is *other* than "the world we are" (*WP* 583), the experiential world of "appearance, change, becoming, death, [. . .] desire" (*GM* III. 28) which Nietzsche often simply calls "life." In the terminology of his analysis of *ressentiment*, the will to truth is *essentially reactive* in relation to life (*GM* I. 10):

> We can no longer conceal from ourselves *what* is expressed by all that willing which has taken its direction from the ascetic ideal: this hatred of the human, and even more of the animal, and more still of the material, this horror of the senses, this fear of happiness and beauty, this longing to get away from appearance, change, becoming, death, wishing, from desire itself – all this means – let us dare to grasp it – *a will to nothingness*, an aversion to life. (*GM* III. 28)

See also 7 "Nietzsche and Philosophical Anthropology"; 9 "The Naturalisms of *Beyond Good and Evil*"; 18 "Naturalism and Genealogy"; 23 "Nietzsche's Fatalism"

Notes

For comments on earlier versions of material contained in this essay, I wish to thank Brian Leiter, John McGovern, and Michael Rosen.

1   I borrow the expression "phenomenal consciousness" from Block (1995) as a label for the qualitative what-it-is-likeness, the character as experienced, of conscious awareness and its contents: in other words, consciousness as it is normally, pre-philosophically understood. But, like the phenomenologists, I take it that the qualitative properties of phenomenal consciousness are for the most part representational. What manifests itself in phenomenal consciousness are mostly not brute non-representational qualia, but properties which *objects* appear as having (e.g. the visual shape and color of *that* tree, as seen from *this* point of view).

2   The common interpretation of phenomenology as primarily concerned with *consciousness* is imprecise and potentially misleading. Phenomenology begins with an analysis of the *contents* of consciousness, i.e. with what are by its lights aspects of the phenomenal *world* as it is encountered, and only secondarily moves on to an examination of the structure of that to which these aspects manifest themselves, i.e. consciousness. See Husserl 1970b: §50.

3   For a similar interpretation of the project of Husserlian phenomenology, see Camus 1975: 44–5. See also Cooper 2002: ch. 5.

4   By the *actually intrinsic* character of power (or force) I mean its properties when actualized as opposed to its dispositional properties when the force is unactualized or merely potential. One might also call this the *categorically intrinsic* character of power, but it is preferable to reserve "categorically intrinsic" for the putative *non-causal* internal properties of objects, i.e. those "primary" properties, like Lockean solidity, which are thought to be both non-dispositional and possessed by objects when they do not act on other objects, and which many philosophers have regarded as the basis of the object's causal powers. Nietzsche, following Lange, rejects this Lockean conception as scientifically obsolete (*WP* 618; Lange 1866: 359–71; cf. also Langton 1998: 174–7). He favors instead a dynamist "Boscovichean" physics according to which the physical world consists purely of forces which are not

based on any corpuscularian or other items with non-geometrical categorically intrinsic properties (*BGE* 12). The *intrinsic nature* of an item, as this expression is used here, includes its categorically intrinsic properties (if any) and any real causal powers it has, whether actual or dispositional.

5 The claim that causation does not involve efficacious forces at all but simply consists in universal, counterfactual-sustaining regularities is often attributed to Hume. There are many powerful reasons for rejecting such regularity accounts of causation. For some of them, see Strawson 1989: esp. 20–31. Nietzsche himself argues that the experience of power is a necessary condition of the possibility of a distinction between the self and a real world interacting with it. For a discussion of this transcendental argument, see Poellner 2001: 100–6.

6 Does Nietzsche's own metaphysics of the will to power, fragments of which are contained in *Nachlass* notes, qualify as an instance of the will to truth? I do not think so. But the issues here are beyond the scope of this essay. For a detailed discussion, see Poellner 1995: ch. 6.

7 Relinquishing the will to truth implies that even if one knew that, say, the conscious affective what-it-is-likeness of one's experiences does not figure among the metaphysically "fundamental" or "real" qualities, this knowledge would leave one's practical self- and world-conception entirely unaffected. The individual who is not subject to the will to truth has no significant purely theoretical interests and is consequently indifferent as to whether her life-world is illusory by the lights of a purely theoretical metaphysical inquiry. This is what Nietzsche means when he says that what fundamentally matters about a worldview is not whether it is (metaphysically) true, capturing the intrinsic qualitative nature of what there is, but its value for life (*BGE* 4; *KGW* VIII. 3, 15[19]). Cf. Leiter 2002: ch. 4.

8 It is important not to conflate the will to truth with the *activity of seeking* the truth. A taste for this activity *per se*, which might in principle be satisfied by other difficult intellectual challenges – such as solving a mathematical problem – obviously need not call for such a negative characterization. Nietzsche, however, is concerned with a phenomenology of valuing what would normally be considered to be the goal of the activity, the *having* of true beliefs about the "real world" (whatever this might turn out to be).

Editions of Nietzsche Used

Beyond Good and Evil, trans. R. J. Hollingdale (Harmondsworth: Penguin, 1973).
The Gay Science, trans. Walter Kaufmann (New York: Vintage Books, 1974).
On the Genealogy of Morals, trans. Walter Kaufmann (New York: Vintage Books, 1967).
Twilight of the Idols, trans. R. J. Hollingdale (Harmondsworth: Penguin, 1990).
The Will to Power, trans. Walter Kaufmann and R. J. Hollingdale (New York: Vintage Books, 1967).
Werke Grossoktavausgabe, ed. E. Förster-Nietzsche, P. Gast, et al. (Leipzig: Naumann/Kröner, 1894–1913).
Werke. Kritische Gesamtausgabe, ed. G. Colli, M. Montinari, et al. (Berlin: Walter de Gruyter, 1967–).

References

Block, N. (1995). "On a Confusion about a Function of Consciousness," *Behavioral and Brain Sciences*, 18, pp. 227–47.
Campbell, J. (2002). *Reference and Consciousness* (Oxford: Clarendon Press).

Camus, A. (1975). *The Myth of Sisyphus* (1942), trans. J. O'Brien (Penguin: Harmondsworth); 1st pub. 1942.

Cohen, I. B. (1980). *The Newtonian Revolution* (Cambridge: Cambridge University Press).

Cooper, D. E. (2002). *The Measure of Things* (Oxford: Clarendon Press).

Heidegger, M. (1962). *Being and Time* (1927), trans. J. Macquarrie and E. Robinson (Oxford: Blackwell).

Husserl, E. (1970a). *Logical Investigations* (1900), 2 vols., trans. J. N. Findlay (London: Routledge & Kegan Paul).

—— (1970b). *The Crisis of European Sciences and Transcendental Phenomenology* (1936), trans. D. Carr (Evanston: Northwestern University Press).

—— (1973). *Experience and Judgment* (1938), trans. J. S. Churchill and K. Ameriks (Evanston: Northwestern University Press).

—— (1983). *Ideas Pertaining to a Pure Phenomenology and to a Phenomenological Philosophy* (1913), *First Book*, trans. F. Kersten (Dordrecht: Kluwer).

—— (1989). *Ideas Pertaining to a Pure Phenomenology and to a Phenomenological Philosophy* (1952), *Second Book*, trans. R. Rojcewicz and A. Schuwer (Dordrecht: Kluwer).

Lange, F. A. (1866). *Geschichte des Materialismus* (Iserlohn: Baedecker).

Langton, R. (1998). *Kantian Humility: Our Ignorance of Things in Themselves* (Oxford: Clarendon Press).

Leiter, B. (2002). *Nietzsche on Morality* (London: Routledge).

Mackie, J. L. (1974). *The Cement of the Universe: A Study of Causation* (Oxford: Clarendon Press).

Merleau-Ponty, M. (1964). "Phenomenology and the Sciences of Man," in *The Primacy of Perception*, trans. J. M. Edie (Evanston: Northwestern University Press), pp. 41–95.

Poellner, P. (1995). *Nietzsche and Metaphysics* (Oxford: Clarendon Press).

—— (2001). "Perspectival Truth," in J. Richardson and B. Leiter (eds.), *Nietzsche* (Oxford: Oxford University Press), pp. 85–117.

Smith, A. D. (2003). *Husserl and the Cartesian Meditations* (London: Routledge).

Strawson, G. (1989). *The Secret Connexion* (Oxford: Oxford University Press).

Zahavi, D. (2003). *Husserl's Phenomenology* (Stanford: Stanford University Press).

17

Naturalism and Nietzsche's Moral Psychology

CHRISTA DAVIS ACAMPORA

In *Beyond Good and Evil* Nietzsche anticipates a future philosophy that will break free of the moral prejudices he thinks cloud not only philosophy's metaphysical pursuits but also the inquiries of science. He announces that "psychology is now again the path to the fundamental problems" and that "psychology shall be recognized again as the queen of the sciences, for whose service and preparation the other sciences exist" (*BGE* 23). If we take "psychology" here to be philosophy of the mind, many contemporary philosophers would agree (even if they would think that Nietzsche has little to contribute to this area). And there is more on which Nietzsche and these like-minded philosophers would agree – this redirection of philosophy to psychology entails a naturalism that requires drawing on the best science available. But Nietzsche and our contemporary philosophers of mind would surely disagree on the sense in which philosophy might usefully be practiced as psychology, and their conceptions of what constitutes naturalization would surely diverge. It is a fairly recent development in secondary literature in the English language to focus on Nietzsche's naturalism as the dominant framework for his thinking generally and his moral views in particular.[1] I shall engage the most prominent literature on that front, suggest an agenda for future research along such lines, and highlight at least one path I see as indicated for developing Nietzsche's moral thinking informed by the psychology that issues from his naturalism and conception of philosophy.

One of the most basic elements of moral philosophy is the conception of the subject upon whom duties rest, to whom rights are granted, within whom virtues are cultivated or potencies are realized. If Nietzsche has a moral theory, and I shall not argue that he does, he must also have a conception of the subject that accounts for its moral agency, its possibilities for action, its potential goods, and its freedom. It is this subject that is my concern in this essay. Since I grant that Nietzsche's conception of the subject largely follows from his naturalism, I shall begin there, summarizing the most prominent contours and the problems it raises. The current trend of highlighting Nietzsche's naturalism presents a number of unresolved interpretative challenges, which I articulate and then indicate some possible ways of resolving. I argue that accounts that associate Nietzsche's naturalism with a strict form of scientism are mistaken and that those that grant a significant role to art in Nietzsche's account are superior to their alternative but nevertheless remain incomplete insofar as they leave relatively empty the concept of artful appropriation that I agree is attributable to Nietzsche. The more specific aim of my essay, then, is to side with interpreters who emphasize the interplay of Nietzsche's naturalism and aestheticism – although I shall suggest Nietzsche anticipates that a time might come when they would not be entirely distinct – and then fill the gap in the literature by providing an example of one way in which artful appropriation might be engaged and its relevance for an ethos of the subject naturalized beyond the poles of good and evil in moral philosophy.

1 Nietzsche's (Artful) Naturalism

What does one mean when one calls Nietzsche a naturalist? In the straightforward sense of granting existence only to things natural and denying the existence of supernatural entities, Nietzsche, who famously proclaims the death of God and seeks to shine a light on his shadow, seems clearly a naturalist. And Nietzsche's broad philosophical projects, and perhaps his more significant contributions, are organized around his effort to "de-deify" nature (GS 109), which includes wringing residual supernatural notions from concepts – especially those relating to matters of truth, knowledge, and goodness – such that traces of the metaphysics he critiques are purged from inquiries that purportedly leave it behind. This is, for example, what leads Nietzsche to hostilely oppose teleological models of organic development and evolutionary theories that utilize teleological concepts, which imply there is some fundamental rational order directing development or some ultimately good end toward which all things progressively strive.

There is a more narrow conception of naturalism that focuses on the relation between philosophy and science such that it claims that philosophy is done best when it models its methods on the empirical sciences or that it ought to draw upon the researches of the empirical sciences, or both. Contemporary philosophy of mind provides a good example of an area that conceives naturalization in this last sense, as both informed by and modeled on sciences of the brain and cognition. It generally considers epistemological issues to revolve (or dissolve) around the researches of these two areas. Those who identify Nietzsche with naturalism must clarify precisely which of these views they are claiming Nietzsche holds.

It is this narrower conception of naturalism that is becoming increasingly popular among Nietzsche interpreters as his interest in and appropriation of his contemporary science becomes better known.[2] The narrower conception of naturalism as applied to Nietzsche commits him to having a (nearly unqualified) positive estimation of science and to model his own philosophical thinking on scientific methods, especially in its goal of identifying *explanatory causes*. Brian Leiter's *Nietzsche on Morality* advances arguments along these lines (Leiter 2002). He begins his book by asserting a dilemma between naturalism and postmodernism. For Leiter this reduces to a distinction between science and literature. A major goal of his book is to offer an account of how Nietzsche follows the first path, and thus why the secondary literature that pursues the second path is hopelessly flawed and lacks merit.[3] In his account of what constitutes naturalism in philosophy generally, Leiter describes naturalists who think philosophy should take its guide from the *methods* of science (whom Leiter labels

"M-Naturalists"), even when it is not obedient to specific scientific methods but still emulates them. Naturalists who emulate the methods of science are called "speculative naturalists" by Leiter, and he includes Hume in this group. He further distinguishes naturalists in terms of holding the following crucial view: "The speculative theories of M-Naturalists are 'modeled' on the sciences most importantly in that they take over from science the idea that natural phenomena have deterministic causes" (Leiter 2002: 5). Nietzsche is also an "S-naturalist" (substantive naturalist) in Leiter's view, insofar as he rejects supernatural agents or causes.

A concern with and an embrace of a particular conception of causation are crucial to Leiter's overall argument and the arguments of those who follow him in asserting that Nietzsche is a naturalist of this sort. Nietzsche's moral psychology, for Leiter, is essentially bound up with a "doctrine of types," according to which "Each person has a fixed psycho-physical constitution, which defines him as a particular type of person" (Leiter 2002: 8). The type of person one is, the type of fixed constitution one has, *causally determines* what one chooses and how one acts. Nietzsche's aim, Leiter asserts, is "to specify 'type-facts'" that serve as *explanations* for developments in the history of moralization – for example, the taking root of the ascetic ideal – and as *explanations* for why people take the actions they do and even why they hold certain ideas. Nietzsche's interest in causation, on Leiter's account, is not limited to this claim about type-facts as causes for human action and the development of moral theories based thereupon. He attributes to Nietzsche epistemological views about the relation between ascertainable "facts" and their status as truths.[4]

Leiter recognizes that his claims about truth and Nietzsche's faith in causation are at odds with other interpretations of Nietzsche that emphasize his apparent critiques of truth and science, which Leiter claims, "involve significant misreadings of Nietzsche" (Leiter 2002: 12). His insistence that Nietzsche maintained a positive interest in truth is more defensible than his view that Nietzsche was skeptical about causation only prior to his overcoming of Kant's (and the neo-Kantians') noumenal/phenomenal distinction (Leiter 2002: 22–3). I shall focus the remainder of my discussion of ways of naturalizing Nietzsche on just this one point (although there are numerous other paths one could pursue) because, as I shall show, it illuminates precisely why a different understanding of Nietzsche's naturalism is warranted and fruitful. For I shall further argue that the failure to appreciate Nietzsche's critical remarks on causation is intimately connected to the failure to appreciate the genuine *depths* of Nietzsche's interest in truth (rather than his rejection of truth). What I shall term Nietzsche's "artful naturalism" addresses this very concern and, once applied, indicates a prominent feature of Nietzsche's moral psychology, namely a different possibility for understanding the prospective moral agent and its possibilities for the activity of creative valuing.

The conclusion at which I am aiming can now be summarized thus: Nietzsche is clearly a naturalist in seeking a focus on natural, observable phenomena for garnering our understanding of the world and our place within it. Empirical science is admirable for Nietzsche because of its rigorous method and its concern to free itself of supernatural and mythological presuppositions. The latter motivation reflects a kind of mental hygiene that for a long time has been recognized as important in philosophy but is rarely achieved, namely to avoid the use of hidden or unjustified assumptions. The problem with science, for Nietzsche, is that it quite often sneaks in principles or articles of faith that smack of the very metaphysical and theological conceptions that it seeks to overcome. Two such ideas that were crucial to the science of his day, and one of which remains the bedrock of scientific inquiry, are the teleological conception of nature and the concept of causation. If we shed these ideas, if development cannot be understood in terms of having discernible purposes or a fundamental goal, and if the common conception of causality is problematic,[5] then much of scientific inquiry is in jeopardy. Without a different conception of naturalism, it seems we reach an impasse and must either retreat to literature or become complete skeptics. But Nietzsche sees another alternative, namely the possibility of naturalizing "cheerfully" to use Richard Schacht's familiar phrase in his treatment of Nietzsche's *Gay Science* (Schacht 1988). I shall call the alternative artful naturalism, which conceives the fruit of philosophical psychology as an understanding of what I shall term *artful appropriation*. This reading of Nietzsche's naturalism emphasizes the centrality of art in his critique and appropriation of science. Adherents of this position are also increasing in number; among them Christoph Cox goes to the greatest lengths in elaborating the relation between Nietzsche's naturalism and his aesthetics, broadly conceived so as to include his interests in interpretation and valuation (Cox 1999).

Unlike Leiter, Cox takes Nietzsche's aestheticism seriously insofar as he grants it a place of primacy in Nietzsche's philosophical project. He similarly defines Nietzsche's naturalism in terms of scientism, claiming that Nietzsche "only criticizes science for its residual theology, its claim to describe pure and unmediated 'facts' about the world" (Cox 1999: 69–70 n. 1). It strikes me, though, that what is intended as a clarification at this point in Cox's statement is, in fact, an *amplification*, one that makes an important difference. Nietzsche is critical of *both* the remnants of theological concepts upon which science relies *and* its pretense to purity or what it calls objectivity (which might very well be one of the ways in which it retains theological ideals in the sense that it claims for itself a "god-like view" on the world, although purity and immediacy need not be limited to theological contexts). Cox's "only" is somewhat misleading, for Nietzsche at times appears to think that the entire scientific project to disclose the "joints of reality" stems from a theological or mythological impulse, that science stills rests upon a "metaphysical faith" in the possibility and value of its ends (e.g., *GS* 344; cf. *BGE* 21, *GS* 112, and *GS* 121). The scientific perspective is preferable to Nietzsche in many respects, particularly for its *method* of inquiry, but there is also much he finds to criticize. Additionally, Nietzsche thinks science can be *improved* by the integration of certain aesthetic values and interests, not because this would make science more like art, but on account of the fact that he sees a significant role that valuation plays in the formation and pursuit of interests and how evaluative processes can be directed, organized, and reformed. Thus, when Nietzsche emphasizes the significance of art, he is not being *less* of a naturalist, as he sees it, but rather *more* of one. It is this key idea that requires a more thorough accounting in Nietzsche interpretation, and it bears tremendously on the enduring value of Nietzsche's philosophy.

As Cox also grants, the point of the criticisms Nietzsche makes of science is to actually *strengthen* science, to make it better at informing us about the nature of the world and how we might better understand ourselves. The route to this *even more rigorous* science – what Nietzsche anticipates at *GS* 113 as a "higher organic system" – is not simply "more" science but rather its amalgamation with the aesthetic. Such a merger, ultimately, does not rest upon a hierarchy of art over science, as seems to be the case in Nietzsche's *Birth of Tragedy*, but rather requires a kind of *reciprocal formation* insofar as the aesthetic is intrinsically involved in the process of interpretation that gives scientific researches their organization and direction. The scientific view is, for Nietzsche, an interpretation – one that is better than most, but an interpretation nonetheless, an "exegesis of the world" in the case of physics (*BGE* 14), a means of determining "our human relation to things" in the case of mathematics (*GS* 246). And, as Nietzsche's perspectivism holds, there is an irreducibility of interpretation. Science cannot some-how escape that fact.[6] A challenge faced by those who at least recognize this feature of Nietzsche's reflection on science and its relation to art is describing the nature of their entwinement, giving it some more substance and vivifying it. That is what I aim to do in the next few sections that describe Nietzsche's critique and revisioning of the supposed moral subject and its future possibilities.

Nietzsche's naturalism prevents him from casting the moral subject in terms of a soul or the creation of a supernatural being. The very same framework cautions him against reifying reason and encourages recognition of the fact that much of human existence is not the product of or under the control of reason. Thus conceptions of the moral subject in terms of a freely reasoning autonomous being are also doubtful. As I shall discuss at length below, drawing upon the sciences of his day, Nietzsche conceives human beings, strictly speaking, as constellations of forces. What we call the self, what we refer to when we talk about consciousness, is simply (although not simplistically or singly) the perspective or perspectives of dominant force(s).

So, if Nietzsche does not embrace the view that human beings are fundamentally free, does this mean that Nietzsche is a determinist? The question is ill formed. In setting aside metaphysical conceptions of the moral subject in terms of souls or rational autonomous beings, one also abandons the related metaphysical and moral concepts appropriate to such entities, including the polarity of free/determined. It is true that Nietzsche does not consider human beings to be free in the way that Kant supposed and Descartes asserted, but it is also the case that the other term in the dilemma falls away as its very basis is undermined. Nietzsche seems to think that the free/deter-mined dilemma is a false one, and that neither concept is appropriate for the kind of beings humans are (cf. *BGE* 21). But how, then, does one make sense of human cap-abilities and potentialities in the absence of this framework? It is on this point that the characterization of Nietzsche's naturalism makes such a difference. Answers to this question appear on the horizon once one gets a better sense of how he conceives of human beings and how he might replace the conceptions of subjectivity he criticizes.

2 The Subject Naturalized

In what are generally described as Nietzsche's "mature writings," namely those at least from *The Gay Science* onward, he links his critique of causality to his critique of the conception of the subject. Roughly put, Nietzsche speculates that our belief in causality significantly influences the conception of the subject – chiefly as willing, causal agent – and its responsibilities and potentialities. In *Beyond Good and Evil* he famously advises:

One should not wrongly reify "cause" and "effect," as the natural scientists do (and whoever, like them, now "naturalizes" in his thinking), according to the prevailing mechanical doltishness which makes the cause press and push until it "effects" its end; one should use "cause" and "effect" only as pure concepts, that is to say, as conventional fictions for the purpose of designation and communication – *not* for explanation. (*BGE* 21)

It is *description* – which is to say *interpretation* – that is accomplished in a causal account (*GS* 112). Cause and effect, Nietzsche suggests in the earlier work *The Gay Science*, are moments selected from a process of change; what we call "cause" and "effect" stem from an interpretation of this process from which we extrapolate a relationship between two entities that we determine as separate and discrete:

> Cause and effect: such a duality probably never exists; in truth we are confronted by a continuum out of which we isolate a couple of pieces, just as we perceive motion only as isolated points and then infer it without ever actually seeing it. The suddenness with which many effects stand out misleads us; actually, it is sudden only for us. In this moment of suddenness there is an infinite number of processes that elude us. An intellect that could see cause and effect as a continuum and a flux and not, as we do, in terms of arbitrary division and dismemberment, would repudiate the concept of cause and effect and deny all conditionality. (*GS* 112)[7]

In calling the cause and effect relationship an interpretation, however, I do not suggest that we are simply free to come up with any other account that we might wish to counter the interpretation Nietzsche critiques. In the passage cited above, Nietzsche speculates that another intellect that had the capability to see things otherwise might very well reject the concept of causality; there would simply be no reason to hold it – another and different interpretation would better describe experience. Our interpretations are, Nietzsche appears to believe, significantly related to our possibilities for experience, and they are not bald fictions as critics of Nietzsche's perspectivism often protest.

Nietzsche's critical comments on morality, especially outside of but also within *On the Genealogy of Morals*, focus on a critique of fundamental concepts of morality such as the nature of the individual and the freedom of the will. And such critiques also make trouble for the (alternative) naturalist's account insofar as they call into question the legitimacy of related concepts such as those of substance and causation. Nietzsche's naturalistic undermining of morality simultaneously destabilizes key tenets of the scientific naturalistic view. Nowhere is this more apparent than in *Twilight of the Idols*, in the collection of paragraphs on "The Four Great Errors." It is worth quoting a portion at length to draw out the numerous ideas it entwines:

> *The error of a false causality.* [. . .] We believed ourselves to be causal in the act of willing: we thought that here at least we caught causality in the act. [. . .] The conception of a consciousness ("spirit") as a cause, and later also that of the ego as cause (the "subject"), are only afterbirths: first the causality of the will was firmly accepted as given, as *empirical*. [. . .] And what a fine abuse we had perpetrated with this "empirical evidence"; we *created* the world on this basis as a world of causes, a world of will, a world of spirits. The most ancient and enduring psychology was at work here and did not do anything else: all

that happened was considered a doing, all doing the effect of a will; the world became to it a multiplicity of doers; a doer (a "subject") was slipped under all that happened. [. . .] The thing itself, to say it once more, the concept of thing is a mere reflex of the faith in the ego as cause. And even your atom, my dear mechanists and physicists – how much error, how much rudimentary psychology is still residual in your atom! Not to mention the "thing-in-itself," the *horrendum pudendum* of the metaphysicians! The error of the spirit as cause mistaken for reality! And made the very measure of reality! And called God!

This reflects Nietzsche's curious account of the anthropocentrism that is deeply rooted in human psychology and which organizes our very scientific inquiries; it affects what constitutes "the empirical" as an organization of "things" in the first place. Here Nietzsche speculates that our self-conscious reflection gives us the impression of willing for which we postulate a cause. The "cause" of our willing has been variously conceived in terms of a soul, a spirit, or, more recently, an "ego," a "subject." Nietzsche's claim is that it was on the basis of this first (and fundamental, unjustified) assumption that we postulated causes behind all actions. Change is cast in terms of the "doing" of "things," which, conceptually, presupposes there is a *doer*. Thus, the empirical world of the scientist is populated by a host of "spirit"-subjects in the form of "doers" or agents. This is the framework in which the concept of causation operates. Although "materialists" or "physicists" would not describe the world and their work in this way, although they would not say that they think the world is inhabited by "spirit-doers," if we scrutinize how they think about causes, we find this conceptual substructure.[8]

If appeals to god(s), soul(s), and rational effective powers are deficient or defective forms of artful supernaturalism, then what are the alternatives? What is an appropriate way to conceive of ourselves, and does this leave any possibilities for a future morality? I shall address the latter question in the concluding section below. The answer to the former is that Nietzsche favors the scientific interpretation (presumably on the grounds that it is least fraught with, which is not to say that it is completely free from, the kinds of errors and ill-formed fundamental concepts mentioned above) that follows a line of thought advanced early on by Boscovich and which he considers to be more recently developed by the founder of evolutionary mechanics, Wilhelm Roux, namely the idea that human beings (indeed, that all that we identify as entities) are collections or organizations of forces (see Müller-Lauter 1999: 161–82).[9] What we call the individual, or "subject," is at best, for Nietzsche, a composite. In his published writings, this idea is explicitly stated in *Beyond Good and Evil* and reiterated in the *Genealogy*:

Boscovich has taught us to abjure the belief in the last part of the earth that "stood fast" – the belief in "substance," in "matter," in the earth-residuum and particle-atom [. . .] one must also, first of all, give the finishing stroke to that other and more calamitous atomism which Christianity has taught best and longest, the *soul atomism*. Let it be permitted to designate by this expression the belief which regards the soul as something indestructible, eternal, indivisible, as a monad, as an *atomon*: this belief ought to be expelled from science! (*BGE* 12) the entire history of a "thing," an organ, a custom can in this way be a continuous sign-chain of ever new interpretations and adaptations whose causes do not even have to be related to one another but, on the contrary in some cases succeed and alternate with one another in a purely chance fashion. The "evolution" of a thing [...] is [...] a succession of more or less profound, more or less mutually independent processes of subduing, plus the resistances they encounter, the attempts at transformation for the purposes of defense and reaction. (*GM* II. 12)

In the second essay of the *Genealogy*, Nietzsche strives to replace the view of the individualized soul with the idea that "our organism is an oligarchy" (*GM* II. 1; cf. *BGE* 19). What we call consciousness is the formation resulting from the struggle between forces of (active) forgetting and remembering (*GM* II. 1–2; cf. *GS* 111). It is a building up of experiences that form as certain other aspects of our experience recede or are purged entirely.

In his notebooks, Nietzsche hypothesizes, on the basis of scientific studies of morphology, that a better description might cast the individual in terms of a complex struggle for power: "It is a question of a struggle between two elements of unequal power: a new arrangement of forces is achieved according to the measure of power of each of them. The second condition is something fundamentally different from the first (not its effect): the essential thing is that the factions in conflict emerge with different quanta of power" (*KSA* 13, 14[95]). There is, fundamentally, a dynamic struggle, with different elements discernible at any given moment and whose components are not stable. What we have is "the mutual struggle of that which becomes, often with the absorption of one's opponent; the number of developing elements not constant" (*KSA* 12, 7[54]). As this process goes, so goes our own appropriation, our own absorption of the world that we call "experience" and our interpretation thereof. Empirical observation is one of the ways in which we are part of the ongoing interpretative process (rather than causal system) that characterizes all of existence for Nietzsche, and, as some have admirably argued, "will to power" is simply the name that Nietzsche gives to this ongoing interpretative and appropriative process (see also Cox 1999: 239–41).

So the critique of causation exposes a prior error in a mistaken postulation of ourselves as subjects or effective agents. For Nietzsche, the idea that there is some "essential self" must disappear along with the appearance/reality distinction. *There are* thoughts and actions. Exercising intellectual conscience, we realize that we simply are not entitled to the postulation of a hidden or core reality that stands behind thoughts and actions as their cause or agent. And just as "the deed is everything" (*GM* I. 13), so there is no subject behind our actions or thoughts, at least not in the way that Descartes and others conceived of such an "I" (cf. *BGE* 16 and 17).

Thus Nietzsche's naturalism leads him to consider replacing belief in the existence of individuals with a conception of the human being as a complex of forces. And, with that, he dissolves the conceptions of the willful human agent and cause and effect, which are more akin to articles of faith than actual knowledge. Nietzsche's concern is that if we remain unquestioningly committed to these ideas and permit them to guide our scientific inquiries, we will retreat further into the subjective anthropomorphic world of the human rather than acquire the knowledge science seeks.

3 Nietzsche's *Artful* Naturalism

Just what is the *artful* aspect of artful appropriation that I have tied to Nietzsche's naturalism? And, in the context in which I have been discussing it, how does this artful activity stand in relation to what is considered the work of science? There are numerous helpful resources on Nietzsche's interest in art and aesthetics, including some that discuss its relation to science.[10] Art is a central interest for Nietzsche throughout his productive life, although his views about art and the contexts in which he considers it shift. Three particular aspects of this broad theme are most relevant to my discussion: (1) the contest between art and science that Nietzsche is keen on elaborating early in his career and which continue to hold his interest in his later writings; (2) his early characterization of artistic forces, which he designates as the Apollonian and Dionysian, and which he conceives not only as driving forces of art but also as evident in the creative and destructive work of nature as a whole; and (3) the connection between art and illusion (or semblance: *Schein*) and its relation to truth. I shall touch upon the first two points in the context of elaborating the third. Once it becomes clearer how Nietzsche thinks art and science stand in relation to each other and the project of truth, I shall revisit the conception of the subject that Nietzsche envisions and what might become of moral valuation in its light.

In describing what Nietzsche calls "the basic will of the spirit" (*Grundwillen des Geistes*) (*BGE* 230), Nietzsche attributes to human existence "needs and capacities [that are] the same as those which physiologists posit for everything that lives, grows, and multiplies." We can gain some additional insight into what Nietzsche might envision as "artful appropriation" as it relates to naturalism when we realize that Nietzsche associates what he describes as fundamental powers (*Kraften*) of *appropriation* and *artful creativity* with all things that "live, grow, and multiply." What we call "science" is a specialized and intensified exercise of these very powers that are basic to all living existence. Some extensive quotation of the relevant portions of the passage facilitate further appreciation of this point:

> The spirit's power to appropriate the foreign stands revealed in its inclination to assimilate the new to the old, to simplify the manifold, and to overlook or repulse whatever is totally contradictory – just as it involuntarily emphasizes certain features and lines in what is foreign, in every piece of the "eternal world," retouching and falsifying the whole to suit itself. Its intent in all of this is to incorporate new "experiences," to file new things in old files – growth, in a word – or, more precisely, the *feeling* of growth, the feeling of increased power.
>
> An apparently opposite drive serves this same will: a suddenly erupting decision in favor of ignorance, of deliberate exclusion, a shutting of one's windows, an internal No to this or that thing, a refusal to let things approach, a kind of state of defense against much that is knowable, a satisfaction with the dark, with the limiting horizon, a Yea and Amen to ignorance – all of which is necessary in proportion to a spirit's power to appropriate.

And these differing and at times opposing drives account for (and circumscribe) our will to deceive and to be deceived, which is countered by the desire or will to know:

> This *Willen zum Schein* [will to semblance], to simplification, to masks, to cloaks, in short, to the surface – for every surface is a cloak – is *countered* by that sublime inclination of the seeker after knowledge who insists on profundity, multiplicity, and thoroughness, with a *will* which is a kind of cruelty of the intellectual conscience and taste.

What Nietzsche means by the *Willen zum Schein* and his frequent praise and even celebration of appearances elsewhere must be understood in this context. In embracing *semblance* (or, as it might otherwise but more problematically be translated, "appearances"[11]), Nietzsche neither rejects *truth* (and thus proclaims the superiority of its opposite), nor gives up on truth altogether (thus celebrating *merely* the play of the apparent). The will to deception, for Nietzsche, is also part of the process of ratiocination insofar as conceptualizing entails overlooking differences and inventing similarities.[12]

These counteracting wills – to deceive and to know, to cover and *discover* – should strike readers familiar with Nietzsche's thought as similar to his account of the opposing artistic forces of the Apollonian and Dionysian in *The Birth of Tragedy*. There, Nietzsche associates the Apollonian with a plastic force that generates illusion and the Dionysian with a form-rending force that aims to dissolve the illusory images the Apollonian creates. Their contest and play of the production and reformation of illusion (or semblance: *Schein*) is what accounts for the tension that generated tragedy. But, in Nietzsche's story, this tension was disrupted with the appearance of Socratism, which, among other things, gave *Schein* a bad name, indeed, an association with moral failing, and it intensified the desire or will to know over and above the will to deceive (and be deceived in the play of the artistic images of the artist).

An excellent discussion of *Schein* in Nietzsche's philosophy, including a brief but very helpful discussion of its relation to discussions of *Schein* in Kant and Schopenhauer, is advanced by Robert Rethy (1991). Rethy convincingly argues that early on Nietzsche, influenced by Schopenhauer, comes to see *Schein* and *Erscheinung* (the latter, for Kant, the appearance that stands in opposition to the "thing-in-itself") as on a continuum rather than in a binary relation of true or false. Whereas Kant associates *Schein* with error (i.e., the mistaken belief that the apparent *is* the real) and with deception to be avoided, Nietzsche attributes a kind of innocence to *Schein* as apparent semblance and play of appearances that can be captivating and willfully pursued in a manner similar to art. In *The Birth of Tragedy* (and later), *Schein* is associated with a kind of "honest deceptiveness," itself a kind of truthfulness. What Nietzsche means by this is that, rather than *mere* illusion or delusion, the deceptiveness of *Schein* discloses something about the proclivity of the world itself (whatever *that* may be) to dissimulate, to bear semblance, to highlight its aspects of unreality (see *BT* 1; Rethy 1991: 61–5).

What is meant by "innocence" here, and what sense could we make of thinking of scientific enterprises, or the pursuit of naturalism, as having truck with *semblance* rather than *truth*? It is at this point that we would do well to take notice of the broader context of Nietzsche's concern. It would be a mistake to think that Nietzsche celebrates semblance *rather than*, or *in opposition to*, truth, in which case one maintains the opposition between *mere appearance* or *illusion* and some (presumably ontologically superior and epistemologically more faithful) *reality* whose understanding constitutes truth. Nietzsche does not simply reduce everything to illusion. Instead, he conceives *Schein* as a kind of self-limitation. It is a reformulation of what constitutes truth, a redefinition of its boundaries and possibilities, rather than an opposition to truth.[13]

In this sense, *Schein* is not *mere* but uncannily *more* – semblance is not the mere appearance of some greater reality but rather something that conveys more than itself. What is this *more*? Nietzsche seems to think of it as a kind of extra or surplus. What is gained for truth (or, for our purposes, for science) in a willful embrace of *Schein*? This pointing beyond that appears to be involved in self-limitation involves recognition of the inventiveness in human rationalization, what Nietzsche associates with mathematics' determination of our human relation to nature (*GS* 246). It calls attention to the artfulness of human cognizing or the fundamental concepts of human thinking (such as causality, as discussed above) that help us to sort through and communicate our experiences. For the Nietzsche of *The Birth of Tragedy*, the artist (and for the later Nietzsche, the future philosopher practicing gay science) calls attention to the *Schein* of the transfiguration that constitutes the making of art, and in so doing thematizes or highlights the *Schein* of experience. This constitutes an intensification of the world-making enterprise in which we all participate. Experience for Nietzsche *is* *Schein*-making, but this does not stand in opposition to some essence whose appearance is transformed (and presumably thereby *de*formed by us). And *Schein*-making is inclusive of (although not exhausted by) the activities of selection, identification, coordination, and classification that are involved in the scientific enterprise. It also includes the embrace of willful ignorance and fascination with ambiguity that seems opposed to science and is more akin to indulgence in the fancy of fiction. The interplay of these two opposing drives, the will to appearance and the will to know, as Nietzsche describes it in *BGE* 230, involves a kind of cruelty (insofar as neither is given satisfaction as its opposite is indulged and pursued). But it is precisely this that Nietzsche appears to associate with a reformulated kind of "extravagant honesty" (*ausschweifende Redlichkeit*) if one wishes to continue to use moral terms, a reformulation of what others call "honesty [*Redlichkeit*], love of truth, love of wisdom, sacrifice for knowledge, heroism of the truthful."[14]

Nietzsche thinks that it is the very "harden[ing] in the discipline of science" that will lead us to recognition of these ideas about *Schein* and the appropriative capacities of human beings, and that this is the business of philosophy. Standing before the rest of nature, seeing himself as the appropriating being that he is because he is a part of nature, because that *is* the basic text of human existence, will lead, Nietzsche thinks, to this reformulated conception (purged of its moral content, its will to be "nice," and the seductive "siren songs of old metaphysical bird catchers") of honesty, truthfulness, and wisdom. Such a reformulation is what is involved in the translation of man back into nature described in *BGE* 230, one that will likely appear both "strange" and "insane" from the standpoint of metaphysics, perhaps even from the standpoint of philosophers driven to naturalism in the very narrow sense that I have been criticizing with Nietzsche.

This seems to be what Nietzsche envisions in *GS* 113 as "the higher organic system of knowledge," a system of knowledge that might further develop the multiple strengths that had to emerge in order for science to become a possibility for us. A curious thing about these different capacities, such as "the impulse to doubt, to negate, to wait, to collect, to dissolve," is that singly they could be quite detrimental, "poisons" that need to be kept "in check" by other capacities and integrated in "one organizing force within one human being." A future time might come, Nietzsche suggests, when science and art, which seem opposed and detrimental to each other, might become similarly integrated: "And even now the time seems remote when artistic energies and the practical wisdom of life will join with scientific thinking to form a higher organic system in relation to which scholars, physicians, artists, and legislators – as we know them at present – would have to look like paltry relics of ancient times." Such a system might be possible to those who do not separate and distinguish the artful from the scientific when accounting for Nietzsche's naturalism.

So, if this conception of naturalism is more appropriate to Nietzsche, and if it is artful appropriation that leads him to call into question the conception of the subject that lies at the heart of moral theories, then what remains of moral values for Nietzsche? If the moral subject as it has hitherto been conceived has no place in a more rigorous scientific, naturalistic account, then must morality similarly be entirely an illusion? Is there no place for talking about the moral subject? Does this mean there is no place for the concept of the soul? I shall address these questions in reverse order, beginning with the question of the soul, suggesting an alternative conception of the subject, and then, by way of conclusion, indicating a future possibility for thinking about values and their relations to this kind of subject.

Concerning the soul, Nietzsche writes:

> Between ourselves, it is not at all necessary to get rid of "the soul" at the same time, and thus to renounce one of the most ancient and venerable hypotheses – as happens frequently to clumsy naturalists who can hardly touch on "the soul" without immediately losing it. But the way is open for new versions and refinements of the soul-hypothesis; and such conceptions as "mortal soul," and "soul as subjective multiplicity," and "soul as social structure of the drives and affects," want henceforth to have citizens' rights in science. (*BGE* 12)

The refinement of "the soul hypothesis," the source for a new conception of the human subject, is one of the prospects and possibilities for artful naturalism. Its conceptual generation is anticipated as engaging an integrative mode of philosophizing in which one draws upon the researches of science, critically testing concepts for unwarranted assumptions along the lines sketched above, while creatively generating alternative concepts when such are found lacking (an activity Nietzsche conceives as artistry).

Nietzsche's reflection upon and ultimate rejection of at least certain kinds of evolutionary theories reflect his concern to reconceptualize the human subject. In the introductory sections of *On the Genealogy of Morals*, Nietzsche is critical of the "English psychologists" who draw upon what he takes to be Darwinian evolutionary theory in their accounts of the evolutionary development of morality out of utility and the advantage (for a group) of altruism.[15] Much like cause and effect are described as isolated moments out of a continuum of experience in *GS* 112, what we have hitherto called the human subject might be an isolated moment in a stream of experience that constitutes human existence. How might we conceive such an entity that is in a perpetual state of change, of becoming, and how would this stand in relation to the more familiar concept of the human subject as "evolved" or even "evolving"? Alan D. Schrift has outlined such a concept in terms of *compound becoming*, an idea he describes as further developed by Deleuze.[16]

The subject as "compound becoming" differs from the kind of subject entailed by evolutionary accounts. An evolutionary path of the subject is marked and measured by beginnings and endpoints, in which case the significance of the passage between is generally diminished or obscured. But compound becoming sets its sights precisely on the process of change, and in so doing the endpoints recede. Schrift describes this difference thus: "Becomings take place *between* poles, they are the in-betweens that pass only and always along a middle without origin or destination" (Schrift 2001: 56). Such a conception of the subject better captures the continuum Nietzsche hypothesizes above. Even a subject naturalized could result in very different models for conceiving human existence. Emphasis on an evolutionary model selects or picks out a different set of concerns and points of interest than a model of compound becoming, which also has a basis in a scientific account of the nature of human existence. So, the choice of conceptual frameworks briefly indicated here is not limited to literature or naturalism but rather suggests different paths that follow different kinds of naturalistic accounts.[17]

What motivates or accounts for the changes that constitute the "becomings" in this alternative model? Nietzsche's answer appears to be that it is the conflict and struggle of the forces we are. Such forces are innumerable, and even if we were able to fix their number at any given point that number would change as some are absorbed and incorporated by others. Nietzsche variously endeavors to capture the sense of the process of the relation of forces by radically simplifying their number and casting their struggle on a grand scale – the struggle between the creative force of the Apollonian and the destructive force of the Dionysian (*BT*), the struggle between remembering and forgetting (*GM*), the struggle between the will to deception and the will to knowledge (*BGE*). Precisely how these forces relate to each other requires greater attention and elaboration than this essay allows, but one thing is clear: Nietzsche appears to think that these conflicts are defining – we *are* the interpretations of these battles[18] – and productive – the outcomes of these struggles account for different stages of development, which have no particular or final direction or end. Nietzsche's agonistic subject is at war with himself – or, to be more precise, *is* a war himself – but unlike Nietzsche's predecessors, who also grant that the human is subject to conflict and who have sought to eliminate this struggle as a way of gaining mastery over the self, Nietzsche often suggests it is the maintenance and sustenance of such discord that constitutes the best life as he sees it. What kind of morality could possibly be generated from this disharmony and dissonance? By way of conclusion, I shall suggest that Nietzsche conceives a possibility of deriving values out of conflict in such a way that it both cultivates the subject characterized in the manner described above, which is to say it provides some organization (without elimination) of conflicting forces, and supplies a mechanism for deriving values that can be flexible and responsive to the *becoming* constituents of the communities such values bind and define.

4 Toward an Ethos of the Agonized Subject

The term "ethos" in the title of this section signals that I think Nietzsche still envisions possibilities for articulating a *way of life* after the overcoming of the subject of morality (that is, once the major terms of the conceptual framework that supports moral thinking generally are undermined). Such an ethos would allow for the production of values (that is, it would not be nihilistic) and would indicate ways of relating to other beings (so it would provide some direction for action). This need not necessarily constitute an ethics that specifies in advance what the values should be or how they should be acted upon and embraced. What widespread competitive interaction might contribute to the development of such an ethos is supplying a mechanism for deriving values and playing a role in constituting subjects, which is to say providing a general framework for distinguishing and integrating subjects in the context of agonistic inter-action. What is generally missing from discussions of Nietzsche's agonism is an account of how contest potentially serves this function for Nietzsche and how it might be relevant to other ethical frameworks.

In keeping with his interests in evolutionary models that are expansive rather than conservative, Nietzsche conceives of virtue as strength and not simply endurance. In *Twilight of the Idols*, he describes physiological vitality a cause of virtue, rather than having virtue follow the reverse order in which case *it* yields the reward of (at least spiritual) strength and good fortune. Nietzsche writes, "first example of my 'revaluation of all values': a well-turned-out human being, a 'happy one,' *must* perform certain actions and shrinks instinctively from other actions; he carries the order, which he represents physiologically, into his relations with other human beings and things. In a formula: his virtue is the *effect* of his happiness [*In Formel: seine Tugend ist die Folge seines Glücks* . . .]" (*TI*, "Errors," 2). Here, happiness is defined physiologically, in terms of a kind of health, keenness of instinct, and integration of the multiplicity of drives that together constitute what we call will: "Every mistake in every sense is the effect of the degeneration of instinct, of the disintegration of will; one could almost define what is bad in this way" (*TI*, "Errors," 2). And, although Nietzsche's characterization cannot rule out the possibility that a person we would consider to be ruthless and cruel could at the same time fit his description of a person who manifests such virtue, it is not limited to such types.

So, what integrates the will, sharpens the instincts, and facilitates directing the aims of human existence? Although such aims will not be specifiable in advance – as there can be no particular end, no particular potentiality, no particular way of life that is fundamentally good and in light of which we should live – it is possible to continuously redefine and reshape such aims in ways that avoid both nihilism and a pernicious relativism. The model for this draws on a conception of social life as organized in a way similar to how Nietzsche thinks "individualized" organic life is organized: agonistically, which involves giving shape and direction to the struggle that characterizes human existence, the constellation of forces described above. Nietzsche's agonistic model can be sketched briefly in order to provide some sense of how this addresses both the issue of how values might be shaped in an ethos of agonism and how such a model bears on what I have described as Nietzsche's artful naturalism.

Nietzsche conceives contestation as an organizing structure in both cultures and individuals. This idea emerges early in his career (for example, *The Birth of Tragedy* and "Homer's Contest") and gets refined throughout such that it appears even as late as *Twilight of the Idols* (for example, in the sections on "The Problem of Socrates" and "What I Owe the Ancients"). Competitive relations serve as an organizing force of culture by bringing together diverse elements, coordinating heterogeneous interests, and providing occasions for the refinement and exercise of judgment. Insofar as competitors with similar but differing abilities vie for the estimation and recognition of superiority by the community of those who would bestow honor upon them, competition provides opportunities for self- and communal evaluation. And such evaluation can be endogenous, the standard emerging from within the relation of the competitors.[19]

The *agon* provided Nietzsche with a graphic image of how meaning could be publicly produced and reproduced. Agonistic contest, for Nietzsche, is a potentially productive force that regulates without subjugating the interests of individuals, coordinating them without reducing them to the interests of the community, and provides a radical openness for the circulation of power that avoids ossification into tyranny. (Nietzsche's interest in what he describes as the origin of ostracism in ancient Greece supports this last point. It originally served the function of expelling a hegemonic force that would shut down any possible competition and was not simply a means for one party or group to rid itself of a more powerful competitor. See "Homer's Contest".)

Moreover, Nietzsche sees contest as a way of mediating the tension between the individual and the group. Participants can distinguish themselves through pursuits in competitive interaction, thereby supplying basis for their claim to individuality. In this way agonized spaces gather the context out of which distinctive performances emerge. Understood in this light agonized spaces quite literally *activate* an ongoing process of individualization. In this way, the *agon* potentially *cultivates subjects*, supplying them with integrity and unity where no such traits might exist otherwise.

The *agon* also *cultivates values*. Competitive interaction supports the activity of value creation as it generates social significance through the relation between the individual and the community of judges who bear witness to and sanction the action produced in agonistic engagement. Nietzsche envisions the best possible situation as one in which these interests are reciprocal and in tension: the community desires the production of greatness cast in terms that it establishes; the most potent competitor achieves the affirmation of the community that provides the conditions for the possibility of her victory, but she also aspires to become the standard bearer, to bring about a reformation of judgment generally.

Finally, Nietzsche admires the radical openness of the circulation of power that well-regulated contests can provide when they widely extend the promise of competitive enterprise and place some kind of cap on competitive dominance that keeps the good of the contest in play. Because the competitive relation can lapse into complacent hubris or destructive and violent aggression, it is a fragile condition to maintain. Sustaining the way of life the *agon* fosters requires preserving the viability of challenge and maintaining sufficient flexibility in generating decisions about excellence that are both relative to past performances and in accordance with new standards that are derived through subjecting the prevailing standards of measure to contest.[20]

Agonistic interaction sharpens by testing the instincts, and it integrates will insofar as it yokes diverse interests under the possibilities presented by the agonistic situation. It is thus that Nietzsche can envision his agonized subjectivity as attaining the new kind of virtue he describes in his first attempt at a revaluation of all values. Such virtue and the prospective route for attaining it are conceived through the application of Nietzsche's artful naturalism, which draws upon a conception of the human

328

being informed by science, described above as the subject naturalized, but whose conceptualization and ultimate realization is creatively amplified, refined, and further vivified in the recreation and reorientation of aims that contestation affords.

See also 3 "The Aesthetic Justification of Existence"; 6 "Nietzsche's 'Gay' Science"; 9 "The Naturalisms of *Beyond Good and Evil*"; 18 "Naturalism and Genealogy"; 20 "Agent and Deed in Nietzsche's *Genealogy of Morals*"; 24 "Nietzsche *contra* Liberalism on Freedom"

Notes

For numerous helpful comments and suggestions on this essay, I am very grateful to Keith Ansell Pearson.

1 "Nietzsche's naturalism" is deployed as the guiding idea behind the selection of materials for the recent edition of Nietzsche, *Writings from the Late Notebooks* (2003). In the introduction, the editor Rüdiger Bittner elaborates what he takes to be Nietzsche's project in light of his own reading of *Beyond Good and Evil*, where Nietzsche famously defines the task "to translate man back into nature" ("den Menschen nämlich zurückübersetzen in die Natur"; *BGE* 230). Bittner has a curious reading of this passage insofar as he considers "translating back" as something different from translation (and, presumably, something different from interpretation), a kind of uncovering or undoing of other translations that have falsified. I discuss the passage in question from *Beyond Good and Evil* below. It is worth mentioning at this point that Bittner does not treat the relevance of Nietzsche's conception of art to his naturalism. In fact, he intentionally ignores it precisely in the place that I argue it is most crucial – with regard to how Nietzsche conceives knowledge.

2 For some examples, see Moore 2002; Small 2001; Moore and Brobjer 2004.

3 See especially Leiter 2002: 1–29. The dilemma appears to be a false one considering that the very thinkers Leiter dismisses as "postmodern" (e.g., Derrida) themselves draw upon various contemporary scientific theories in the organization of their thought.

4 Leiter largely follows Clark's arguments for Nietzsche's interest in and estimation of truth. See Clark 1990.

5 The evidence for this view is offered below in the section on Nietzsche's conception of the individual. As I, joining others who would hardly fit the bill of "postmodern," shall illustrate, Nietzsche is nowhere more suspicious of causation than in the later writings that Leiter and others who are similarly minded deem Nietzsche's "mature" philosophy. Thus, those who hold that Nietzsche's critical remarks about causation are limited to his earlier writings are simply mistaken. I have described Nietzsche's concerns about teleology and his experiments with developing an alternative in Acampora 2004. See also Swift 1999.

6 Cox characterizes this position as Nietzsche "treading paths between relativism and dogmatism": "The apparent relativism of perspectivism is held in check by Nietzsche's naturalism, which offers the doctrines of will to power and becoming in place of all theological interpretations; the apparent dogmatism of will to power and becoming is mitigated by perspectivism, which grants that will to power and becoming are themselves interpretations, yet ones that are better by naturalistic standards" (Cox 1999: 106). On Nietzsche's naturalism and its bearing on the apparent contradiction between Nietzsche's conception of cultivation or breeding (*Züchtung*) and fate (in the imperative of *amor fati*), see Groff 2003. Groff's essay is an admirable response to the challenge Leiter poses to interpretations of Nietzsche that emphasize his interest in creativity and transformation in the sense of

self-overcoming (see Leiter 1998). This also bears on Leiter's emphasis in his *Nietzsche on Morality* on fatalism as he takes it to follow from Nietzsche's theory of types. But if, as I argue below, Leiter is mistaken about Nietzsche's views of causation, then the explanative power Leiter aims to garner from Nietzsche's so-called theory of types (as causally determining a person's thoughts and actions) is lost.

7   Cf. *BGE* 14. Nietzsche might very well have in mind Karl Ernst von Baer's study of perception relative to life span and sensory capacity, which Nietzsche cites in his earlier lectures on the pre-Platonic philosophers. It was Baer's hypothesis that the appearances of change, development, and growth are relative to perception. Creatures perceiving at lower rates of speed have the experience of persistence, but an increase in the speed of perception would result in the phenomenon of constant becoming. See Baer 1862. Greg Whitlock, in his notes to his translation of Nietzsche's lectures on the pre-Platonics, invites comparison of these ideas with *Daybreak* 117. See *The Pre-Platonic Philosophers*, p. 60 n. 35.

8   This is not to say that Nietzsche rejects causation altogether, only that our current way of conceiving it is hampered by these other conceptual presuppositions or "errors" as he calls them. The section from *Twilight of the Idols* addresses what Nietzsche designates as "false causes" and "imaginary causes." He claims that the danger of these is that we accept them over and above the *real* causes: "Thus originates a habitual acceptance of a particular causal interpretation, which, as a matter of fact, inhibits any investigation into the real cause – even precludes it" (*TI*, "Errors," 4). This suggests that Nietzsche endorses some kind of causation but calls into question its conceptual formulation, its place in a conceptual framework organized around various metaphysical abstractions such as subjects and doers. Nietzsche's artful naturalism would seek to craft an interpretation of causality that is at least free of this error.

9   Helpful elaboration of these ideas in their context of other scientific developments and conceptual schemes is found in Moore 2002: ch. 1, "The Physiology of Power."

10   The most extensive treatment in English of Nietzsche's conception of art is Young 1994. The most extensive discussion of Nietzsche's aesthetics as it relates to his conception of science is Babich 1994.

11   Kaufmann actually compounds the problem when he translates this as "*mere* appearance" (emphasis mine).

12   This point is obviously relevant to Nietzsche's discussion of "truth and lies in a non-moral sense" and the metaphorical nature of thought. See "On Truth and Lies in a Non-Moral Sense," pp. 79–97. These ideas have been most elaborately discussed in Kofman 1993: esp. pp. 23–58.

13   Just as Nietzsche calls into question the opposition of appearance and reality, so too he challenges the binary opposition of truth and falsity: "what forces us at all to suppose that there is an essential opposition of 'true' and 'false'? Is it not sufficient to assume degrees of apparentness and, as it were, lighter and darker shadows and shades of appearance – different 'values,' to use the language of painters?" (*BGE* 34).

14   As Rethy demonstrates in his discussion of the evolution of Nietzsche's thought about *Schein*, Nietzsche strives to put *Schein* in a new relation, not in opposition to the thing-in-itself, not in opposition to reality, but rather *as* reality and in opposition to a "truth world," in opposition to *Verstand*. Rethy cites a note written contemporaneous to the writing of *Beyond Good and Evil*: "I thus place 'Schein' not in opposition to 'reality' but rather on the contrary accept semblance as the reality which resists transformation into an imaginative 'truth world'. A more determinate name for this reality would be 'the will to power' " (*KSA* 11, 40[52], [53], p. 654; Rethy's translation on p. 69). Rethy writes, "The new opposition is thus not between *Erscheinung* and *Ding an sich*, but between *Schein* and *Verstand* and the *Berstandsbestimmungen* or Laws of Thought. [. . .] [T]here is [also] the characterization of

Schein as 'the actual and sole reality of things' (*wirkliche und einzige Realität der Dinge*). This surface may be the 'reality' of the *res*, but such a playful self-display does not allow the philosopher's 'going to the depths'; there are no depths, no 'grounds'" (Rethy 1991: 69).

15   Herbert Spencer, mentioned by name, is Nietzsche's main target. See *GM*, preface and I. 1–5. Illuminating and astute accounts of Nietzsche's interest in evolutionary theory are found in Robin Small's introduction to the new translation of Paul Rée's *Basic Writings* (2003); and in Moore 2002: ch. 2. While Nietzsche earlier accepted the account of the utility of altruistic acts as functioning to preserve the group and then becoming incorporated as habits whose utilities were forgotten, he later rejects that view. I am convinced by Moore's account of the development of Nietzsche's ideas about evolution and the physiological issues at stake in his account of morality, in which he claims that Nietzsche does not so much change his mind about the value and significance of science generally between *Human All Too Human* (where he admires and appears to endorse the evolutionary ethics of his contemporaries, but most especially the work along those lines that had been published by Rée) and *On the Genealogy of Morals* (in which he begins by denouncing the English psychologists of morals) as he changes his views about what he understood as the Darwinian basis of evolutionary ethics. Moore traces Nietzsche's arguments against conservation specifically as they develop alongside his reading of the zoologist William Rolph. See Moore 2002: 46–55. Moore elsewhere (1998) catalogs correspondences between Nietzsche's notes and Rolph's works. Thus, Nietzsche changes his mind about evolutionary ethics not because he has second thoughts about the prospects for evolutionary science generally but rather because of his conception of life and its possibilities for development. Ultimately, Nietzsche was concerned about the hidden teleology and anthropomorphism in such accounts, although his own alternative might very well repeat the same errors against which he struggled.

16   Another admirable effort to articulate an alternative conception of the subject in light of Nietzsche's critiques of what he takes to be the traditional subject of philosophy is found in Hales and Welshon 2000: chs. 6 and 7. Hales and Welshon also tackle the concept of causality and logic in light of Nietzsche's perspectivism (see their chs. 4 and 2, respectively).

17   A particularly helpful discussion of different ways of naturalizing philosophy relevant to this point can be found in Hoy 1988.

18   See e.g. Z I, "On the Gift-Giving Virtue": "Thus the body goes through history, a becoming [*ein Werdender*] and a fighting [*ein Kämpfender*]. And the spirit – what is that to the body? The herald of its fights and victories, companion and echo" (my translation).

19   This feature of the *agon* should be compared with the vision of the higher organic system Nietzsche anticipates in *GS* 113 and the struggle between the will to deception and the will to knowledge elaborated in the context of *BGE* 230 discussed above.

20   I have discussed Nietzsche's conception of the *agon*, particularly in terms of its limits, possibilities, and applications, in several articles. The two most relevant to this discussion are Acampora (2002) and Acampora (2003).

Editions of Nietzsche Used

Beyond Good and Evil, trans. Walter Kaufmann (New York: Vintage Books, 1966).
The Gay Science, trans. Walter Kaufmann (New York: Vintage Books, 1974).
On the Genealogy of Morals, trans. Walter Kaufmann and R. J. Hollingdale (with *Ecce Homo*) (New York: Vintage Books, 1967).

The Pre-Platonic Philosophers, ed. and trans. Greg Whitlock (Urbana and Chicago: University of Illinois Press, 2001).

"On Truth and Lies in a Non-Moral Sense," in *Philosophy and Truth: Selections from Nietzsche's Notebooks of the Early 1870s*, ed. and trans. Daniel Breazeale (Atlantic Highlands, NJ: Humanities Press, 1979).

Twilight of the Idols, in *The Portable Nietzsche*, ed. Walter Kaufmann (New York: Viking Penguin, 1954).

Writings from the Late Notebooks (1885–8), ed. Rüdiger Bittner, trans. Kate Sturge (Cambridge: Cambridge University Press, 2003).

References

Acampora, Christa Davis (2002). "Of Dangerous Games and Dastardly Deeds: A Typology of Nietzsche's Contests," *International Studies in Philosophy*, 34(3), pp. 135–51.

——— (2003). "Nietzsche's Agonal Wisdom," *International Studies in Philosophy*, 35(3), pp. 205–225.

——— (2004). "Between Mechanism and Teleology: Will to Power and Nietzsche's 'Gay' Science," in Gregory Moore and Thomas H. Brobjer (eds.), *Nietzsche and Science* (Aldershot: Ashgate).

Babich, Babette E. (1994). *Nietzsche's Philosophy of Science: Reflecting Science on the Ground of Art and Life* (Albany: State University of New York Press).

Baer, Karl Ernst von (1862). *Welche Auffassung der lebenden Natur ist die richtige? und Wie ist diese Auffassung auf die Entomologie anzuwenden? Zur Eröffnung der Russischen Entomologischen Gesellschaft im Mai 1860 gesprochen* (Berlin: August Hirschwald; repr. from Horae Societatis Entomologicae Rossicae, 1861).

Clark, Maudemarie (1990). *Nietzsche on Truth and Philosophy* (Cambridge: Cambridge University Press).

Cox, Christoph (1999). *Nietzsche: Naturalism and Interpretation* (Berkeley: University of California Press).

Groff, Peter S. (2003). "*Amor Fati* and *Züchtung*: The Paradox of Nietzsche's Nomothetic Naturalism," *International Studies in Philosophy*, 35(3), pp. 29–52.

Hales, Steven D., and Welshon, Rex (2000). *Nietzsche's Perspectivism* (Urbana: University of Illinois Press).

Hoy, David Couzens (1988). "Two Conflicting Conceptions of How to Naturalize Philosophy: Foucault versus Habermas," in Dieter Henrich and Rolf-Peter Horstmann (eds.), *Metaphysik nach Kant?* (Stuttgart: Klett-Cotta), pp. 743–66.

Kofman, Sarah (1993). *Nietzsche and Metaphor*, trans. Duncan Large (Stanford: Stanford University Press).

Leiter, Brian (1998). "The Paradox of Fatalism and Self-Creation in Nietzsche," in Christopher Janaway (ed.), *Willing and Nothingness: Schopenhauer as Nietzsche's Educator* (Oxford: Clarendon Press), pp. 217–57.

——— (2002). *Nietzsche on Morality* (New York: Routledge).

Moore, Gregory (1998). "Beiträge zur Quellenforschung," *Nietzsche-Studien*, 27, pp. 535–51.

——— (2002). *Nietzsche, Biology, and Metaphor* (Cambridge: Cambridge University Press).

Moore, Gregory, and Brobjer, Thomas H. (eds.) (2004). *Nietzsche and Science* (Aldershot: Ashgate).

Müller-Lauter, Wolfgang (1999). *Nietzsche: His Philosophy of Contradictions and the Contradictions of his Philosophy*, trans. David J. Parent (Urbana and Chicago: University of Illinois Press).

Rée, Paul (2003). *Basic Writings*, ed. and trans. Robin Small (Chicago: University of Illinois Press).

Rethy, Robert (1991). "*Schein* in Nietzsche's Philosophy," in Keith Ansell Pearson (ed.), *Nietzsche and Modern German Thought* (London and New York: Routledge), pp. 59–87.

Schacht, Richard (1988). "Nietzsche's *Gay Science*, or, How to Naturalize Cheerfully," in Robert C. Solomon and Kathleen M. Higgins (eds.), *Reading Nietzsche* (Oxford: Oxford University Press), pp. 68–86.

Schrift, Alan D. (2001). "Rethinking the Subject: Or, How One Becomes-Other Than What One Is," in Richard Schacht (ed.), *Nietzsche's Postmoralism* (Cambridge: Cambridge University Press).

Small, Robin (2001). *Nietzsche in Context* (Aldershot: Ashgate).

Swift, Paul (1999). "Nietzsche on Teleology and the Concept of the Organic," *International Studies in Philosophy*, 31(3), pp. 29–41.

Young, Julian (1994). *Nietzsche's Philosophy of Art* (Cambridge: Cambridge University Press).

Part V

Philosophy and Genealogy

18

Naturalism and Genealogy

CHRISTOPHER JANAWAY

Most commentators on Nietzsche would agree that he is in a broad sense a naturalist in his mature philosophy. He opposes transcendent metaphysics, whether that of Plato or Christianity or Schopenhauer. He rejects notions of the soul, the absolutely free controlling will, or the self-transparent pure intellect, instead emphasizing the body, talking of the animal nature of human beings, and attempting to explain numerous phenomena by invoking drives, instincts, and affects which he locates in our physical, bodily existence. Human beings are to be "translated back into nature," since otherwise we falsify their history, their psychology, and the nature of their values – concerning all of which we must know truths, as a means to the all-important revaluation of values.[1] This is Nietzsche's naturalism in the broad sense, which will not be contested here.

Brian Leiter has recently offered a more pointed characterization of Nietzsche's naturalism, however, that would give it specific links with the methods and results of science. For Leiter, if we look at "Nietzsche's actual philosophical practice, i.e. what he spends most of his time doing in his books," we find a naturalism that is "fundamentally *methodological*" (Leiter 2002: 6 and n.). Nietzsche is a naturalist, Leiter argues, in virtue of holding a view that "philosophical inquiry should be continuous with empirical inquiry in the sciences" (2002: 3) – a naturalist who

> aims to offer theories that explain various important human phenomena (especially the phenomenon of morality), and that do so in ways that both draw on actual scientific results, particularly in physiology [. . .] but are also *modeled* on science in the sense that they seek to reveal the causal determinants of these phenomena, typically in various physiological and psychological facts about persons. (2002: 8)

I want to suggest that, if we pay attention to Nietzsche's artistic and rhetorical methods and a range of his methodological statements, we may find that this statement risks giving an exaggerated impression of the continuity with science that Nietzsche seeks and achieves.

1 Methodological Naturalism

Let us look at Leiter's claims, starting with the task of "translating man back into nature" found in *BGE* 230. Leiter says that here Nietzsche "calls for man to stand 'hardened in the discipline of science'" (2002: 7). This already involves a slight over-reading. Nietzsche states that as regards the rest of nature we stand before it hardened in the discipline of science; he calls for us in future to stand before ourselves in a similar way, blind and deaf to "the siren songs of old metaphysical bird catchers" whose message is "you are more, you are higher, you are of a different origin" (*BGE* 230).[2] Nietzsche's call urges us to resist the kind of metaphysics that invokes some realm other than the empirical to account for certain aspects of humanity. But it is not a call to do science, rather a call to be *as disciplined as scientists* in our resistance to metaphysics. A similar analogy is made in *GS* 319: "we [. . .] want to face our experiences as sternly as we would a scientific experiment, hour by hour, day by day!" Then, in *GS* 335, Nietzsche urges upon us a particular kind of inquiry into our evaluations:

> Your judgement, "that is right" has a prehistory in your drives, inclinations, aversions, experiences, and what you have failed to experience; you have to ask, "*how* did it emerge there?" and then also, "what is really impelling me to listen to it?"

Nietzsche describes this process of self-questioning with the words "reflect more subtly," "observe better," "study more," and finally "become the best students and discoverers of everything lawful and necessary in the world: we must become *physicists*." But Nietzsche does not mean that we can achieve the requisite self-discovery literally by doing physics. Rather, there is a discipline and depth to the self-study which he finds it fruitful to see as *analogous to* a scientific approach.

That Nietzsche's method is not literally scientific does not matter for Leiter, however, given his fuller statements concerning methodological naturalism. To be methodologically naturalist, philosophical inquiry should either (a) be supported by, or justified by, the actual results of our best science in its different domains; or (b) employ or emulate successful, distinctively scientific ways of understanding and explaining things. Leiter refers to these as "Results Continuity" and "Methods Continuity" respectively (2002: 4–5). But if Nietzsche were to satisfy the requirements for philosophical naturalism solely on the grounds of Methods Continuity, he would not have to employ specifically scientific methods, for instance scientific means of testing theories; it is sufficient that his methods *emulate* scientific ways of understanding the world. And this comes down to explaining various phenomena by locating their causal determinants (2002: 5, 8).

So, for Leiter, if one is a naturalist just on the grounds of a commitment to Methods Continuity, the continuity one advocates with science can in fact be relatively loose, consisting in the giving of explanations of phenomena through locating their causes. A worry here might be that this kind of continuity on its own does not rule out very much, given that belief systems such as Christianity, Satanism, and astrology all attempt to explain various phenomena by locating their causes. If what puts these theories beyond the pale for naturalism is that they do not *use* scientific methods, well

338

and good. But if mere *emulation* of scientific method through the giving of causal explanations is sufficient for naturalism, as it must be to let in Nietzsche as a naturalist on these grounds, then naturalism on the grounds of Methods Continuity looks to be rather a broad church.

This problem can be obviated by invoking Results Continuity. If one is a naturalist by virtue of commitments to both Methods Continuity and Results Continuity, then one will seek to explain phenomena in terms of their causes, and require, in Leiter's words, "that philosophical theories [...] be supported or justified by the results of the sciences" – to which he adds that "theories that do not enjoy the support of our best science are simply *bad* theories" (2002: 4). The attribution of this requirement of "support or justification" lends a much stronger sense to "continuity" with science, but arguably gives rise to problems for Leiter's account, because no scientific support or justification is given – or readily imaginable – for the central explanatory hypotheses that Nietzsche gives for the origins of our moral beliefs and attitudes. For a prominent test case, take Nietzsche's hypothesis in the *Genealogy*'s First Treatise that the labeling of non-egoistic inaction, humility, and compassion as "good" began because there were socially inferior classes of individuals in whom feelings of *ressentiment* against their masters motivated the creation of new value distinctions. This hypothesis explains moral phenomena in terms of their causes, but it is not clear how it is *justified* or *supported by* any kind of science, nor indeed what such a justification or support might be. Other cases fall into the same pattern. Nietzsche's crucial hypothesis about the origin of bad conscience (in the Second Treatise) is that instincts whose outward expression against others is blocked turn themselves inward and give rise to the infliction of pain on the self. What scientific results justify or support this claim is again obscure. If we are to regard the explanations of morality given by Nietzsche as supported or justified by the results of the sciences, the onus is on Leiter to show what that support or justification consists in.

At one point Leiter talks of the continuity between Nietzsche's philosophy and one particular "result" that pre-occupied mid-nineteenth-century Germans: "that man is not of a 'higher . . . [or] different origin' than the rest of nature" (2002: 7). However, the status of this as a "result" is perhaps debatable: it is hard to say whether the exclusively empirical nature of humanity was a conclusion or an assumption of scientific investigation in the nineteenth century or at any time. But let us allow that "man is not of a different origin than the rest of nature" has – and that Nietzsche regards it as having – scientific justification. Then we still face the question whether Nietzsche's explanations of the origins of moral concepts, bad conscience, and so on are themselves supported or justified by "man is not of a different origin than the rest of nature." And rather than saying that this general programmatic claim provides the grounds for Nietzsche's explanations, it is more plausible to say that it functions as a background assumption which constrains what will count as a good causal explanation. This suggests a weaker Results Continuity than Leiter's, namely one that requires simply that explanations in philosophy be compatible with our best science, or not be falsified by appeal to our best science. A theorist who held that any explanation given in philosophy must be continuous with the results of science just to this extent might have some claim to the title of naturalist – at least as much claim as the Methods Continuity theorist who holds merely that philosophy must emulate science by giving causal explanations. I argue that a weaker "naturalism" which requires of its hypotheses that they cite causes to explain the change in value distinctions, and are falsified by nothing from archaeology, history, philology, psychology, biology, or physics, represents Nietzsche's stance in the *Genealogy* better than that which Leiter attributes to him. In other words, Nietzsche is a naturalist to the extent that he is committed to a species of theorizing that explains X by locating Y and Z as its causes, where Y and Z's being the causes of X is not falsified by our best science.

There is also a nagging worry about Results Continuity arising from some of Nietzsche's discussions of will to power – a worry I shall mention here but not pursue fully for lack of space. When Nietzsche recommends translating the human being back into nature in *Beyond Good and Evil*, he is, as numerous references in that same book testify, conceiving nature as will to power (see *BGE* 13, 22, 23, 36, 186, 259). It is by understanding that we, like the rest of organic nature, manifest will to power in a bewildering variety of guises that we will truly penetrate beneath the misleading scrawlings that distance us from the truth about ourselves. The problem is that Nietzsche presents will to power as a counter to what he sees as the dominant paradigm in science, the "plebeian antagonism against all privilege and autocracy" (*BGE* 22), or (in the *Genealogy* now) "the democratic idiosyncrasy against everything that rules and desires to rule," a prejudice about method which "has become lord over the whole of physiology and the doctrine of life – to its detriment [. . .] by removing through sleight of hand one of its basic concepts, that of *activity*" (*GM* II. 12). Nietzsche says that the scientific explanation of organisms' behavior in terms of reactive adaptation to the environment must be rejected in favor of the view that at all levels of the organic world there is spontaneity, active appropriation, interpretation, and the imposition of form and meaning. His statements earlier in the same passage clearly imply that all happening in the organic world is a form of interpretation of one thing by another (since "all happening in the organic world is an over-powering" and "all over-powering is a new interpreting"; *GM* II. 12). On a straightforward reading, Nietzsche goes out of his way to reject Results Continuity with scientific biology – unless he believes that a perfected scientific inquiry would find that relations of over-powering and interpretation were indeed the best models for biological process. But in that case more recent science does not display Results Continuity with Nietzsche.

To go further with this would require more care over the much-discussed notion of will to power than I can devote here.[3] Instead I want to move on to some other, and I think deeper, questions about Nietzsche's methods, methods which in many respects are indeed discontinuous with those of empirical scientific inquiry. Any page of Nietzsche looks starkly unlike scientific literature. He usually does little systematic marshaling of evidence, does not locate the phenomena that compose his explanations precisely in space or time, presents neither clear linear arguments nor unambiguous conclusions, and seems unconcerned about the repeatability of results. Instead he champions a literary, personal, affectively engaged style of inquiry that deliberately stands in opposition to science as he thinks it tends to conceive itself: as disinterested, impersonal, and affectively detached. We might wonder how happy Nietzsche would be to claim methodological continuity with science, given some of his remarks to the effect that failure of affective engagement, failure to personalize one's inquiry into the origin of values, leads to failure to unearth the truth about them. Such a line of thought

340

arises out of explicit contrasts Nietzsche draws between his methods and those of his former close friend, the would-be genealogist of morality, Paul Rée.

2 Nietzsche's Antagonists in the *Genealogy*

In his book *The Origin of the Moral Sensations* (1877) Paul Rée gives an account of our practice of judging egoistic actions and attitudes "bad" and unegoistic actions and attitudes "good." The preface of the *Genealogy* makes plain Nietzsche's preoccupation with Paul Rée as an opponent, and a first glance at the organization of Rée's book sparks the hypothesis that Nietzsche's may be designed as (among many other things) a kind of riposte to his former friend.[4] Rée's first two chapters have titles strikingly similar to Nietzsche's, "The Origin of the Concepts Good and Evil [*Gut und Böse*]" and "The Origin of Conscience." The next two chapters concern other issues central to Nietzsche's discussion: free will (or its absence), responsibility (or its absence), punishment, deterrence, and retribution. Rée presents an unadorned naturalistic picture influenced by Darwin and utilitarian thought and using mental processes such as association and habitual conditioning to explain the origin of our beliefs and other attitudes. Nietzsche calls this "English psychology," and in fact his use of the terms "English psychologists" and "English genealogists" in the *Genealogy* demonstrably refers to Rée.

In outline Rée's account of morality is as follows. "Good" and "bad" (German *gut* and *schlecht*)[5] are terms of approval and condemnation which strictly should be used relative to the utility of an object for human beings: nothing is good or bad in itself. We habitually associate "bad" with behavior that is *egoistic* and "good" with behavior that is *unegoistic*. These associations are learned by repeated conditioning, and mask the true origin of the value terms, which lies simply in their utility in maintaining peace within human communities in the distant past. Natural selection favored those groups of humans who lived together harmoniously because they had the custom of disapproving of egoism. Feelings of conscience or guilt are likewise a case of habitual and socially useful association of a disapproving attitude with egoistic behavior. Punishment owes its existence to its instrumental value in deterring future selfish actions and keeping in check the "menagerie" of rabidly egoistic individuals that every community would otherwise be. But because human beings "forget" the origin of their habitual feelings, they come to regard punishment as a deserved retribution or repayment for a past action, and subsequently believe that retribution is the essence or purpose of punishment. This is a sheer error or illusion, founded on conditioning that breeds forgetfulness of the origins of moral feelings in utility, and on the belief that we can hold agents responsible because they could have done otherwise – which is also false, since humans no more have free will than dogs.

In the preface to the *Genealogy* Nietzsche names only two thinkers as his antagonists: Rée and Schopenhauer. Both had inspired his earlier thought at different stages, but are now evoked as pasts he is happy to disown, embodying that which he had to "struggle almost solely with" and that to which he "emphatically said 'no' [. . .] proposition by proposition" (*GM*, preface, 4 and 5).[6] Both Schopenhauer and Rée reject the metaphysics of Christianity. Both deny that being moral leads to greater happiness, or that genuine moral progress is possible for human beings. Both argue that human individuals lack free will and responsibility for their actions. Schopenhauer, unshackled from Christianity's metaphysics and its inherent optimism, nevertheless retains a transcendent metaphysics of the will to support his accounts of compassion, responsibility, and eternal justice. Rée goes further and rejects all Schopenhauer's transcendent explanations in favor of a scrupulous empiricist naturalism. Rée's mission statement is reminiscent of Nietzsche's: "Today, since Lamarck and Darwin have written, moral phenomena can be traced back to natural causes just as much as physical phenomena: moral man stands no closer to the intelligible world than physical man" (Rée 2003: 87). Rée is also a would-be genealogist, substituting an account of the origin and development of our moral feelings for Schopenhauer's deliberately ahistorical picture of human motivation.

So what goes wrong? On what grounds does Nietzsche object to Rée's results and methods? Most fundamental is the assumption Rée shares with Schopenhauer: that selflessness, or what Rée continually calls "the unegoistic" (*das Unegoistische*), is constitutive of morality. Nietzsche's named antagonists agree in regarding the unegoistic as "value in itself" (*GM*, preface, 4 and 5), and are thus representative of a more pervasive problem, "the prejudice that takes 'moral,' 'unegoistic,' 'désintéressé' to be concepts of equal value" and which "in present-day Europe [. . .] already rules with the force of an '*idée fixe*' and sickness in the head" (*GM* I. 2). Schopenhauer and Rée, along with the rest, assume selflessness has positive *value*. Yet it is this very value that must be called into question, according to Nietzsche.

3 Rée and Selflessness

The well-known culmination of the *Genealogy* charges that the "disinterested pursuit of truth" is but a subtle and disguised manifestation of Christian, ascetic value. I shall suggest that Rée is a target for particular criticism on this score as well. Rée is paradigmatic for Nietzsche of a type of modern thinker who has rejected Christianity, transcendent metaphysics, and even free will, but who clings to selflessness as the prime moral value, and – most importantly in the present context – allows his conception of value to govern his own self-understanding as an inquirer, his conception of method.

A relevant passage is *GS* 345. Nietzsche there alludes to Rée[7] in a covert way as the only person he has attempted to convert from a method of selflessness to one of personal involvement:

> The lack of personality always takes its revenge: a weakened, thin, extinguished personality, one that denies itself and its own existence, is no longer good for anything good – least of all for philosophy. "Selflessness" has no value in heaven or on earth; all great problems demand *great love*, and only strong, round, secure minds who have a firm grip on themselves are capable of that. It makes the most telling difference whether a thinker has a personal relationship to his problems and finds in them his destiny, his distress, and his greatest happiness, or an "impersonal" one, meaning he is only able to touch and grasp them with the antennae of cold, curious thought. In the latter case nothing will come of it, that much can be promised; for even if great problems should let themselves be *grasped* by them, they would not allow frogs and weaklings to *hold on* to them; such has been

their taste from time immemorial – a taste, incidentally, that they share with all doughty females. [. . .] in one single case I did everything to encourage a sympathy and talent for this kind of history – in vain, as it seems to me today. These historians of morality (particularly, the Englishmen) do not amount to much: usually they themselves unsuspectingly stand under the command of a particular morality and, without knowing it, serve as its shield-bearers and followers, for example, by sharing that popular superstition of Christian Europe which people keep repeating so naively to this day, that what is characteristic of morality is selflessness, self-denial, self-sacrifice, or sympathy and compassion.

The allegation is that adherence to the conception of morality as selflessness left Rée, unwittingly, trapped in a sterile mode of investigation that could bring only philosophical failure.

Two metaphors with parallels in the *Genealogy* leap out of this passage. The description "old, cold, boring frogs" is applied at the opening of *GM* I to so-called "English psychologists," the term there a playful reference uniquely to Rée, given that the theory up for criticism is transparently his.[8] Secondly, in the epigram of *GM* III wisdom is a woman who loves only someone "carefree, mocking, violent," the opposite of the "weakened, thin, extinguished" type evoked here.[9] That epigram introduces Nietzsche's essay on the meanings of the ascetic ideal, and points forward to the essay's culminating claim that contemporary objective, scientific method, which prides itself on leaving behind Christianity, theism, and the transcendent altogether, is but another version of an originally Christian, metaphysical faith in ascetic self-denial before something absolute and quasi-divine, namely truth. Rée's "English," baldly empiricist, anti-metaphysical, atheist, Darwinian approach exemplifies the contemporary method that Nietzsche embroils in his complaint against the ascetic ideal.

Confirmation comes from Rée's own words, in a passage towards the end of *The Origin of the Moral Sensations* where he pronounces that "Nothing can be sacred to the philosopher but truth," and continues:

> if disinterested knowledge does not make someone better or more non-egoistic directly, nevertheless a certain utility [*Nutzen*] is indirectly linked with it. That is, knowledge is peaceable by its nature: everyone can devote themselves to knowledge of the same thing without feeling rivalry or hostility. But desire is always warlike: two people cannot desire the same thing without feeling mutual hostility. Hence, the writings and works of art that inspire one to knowledge of the true and beautiful, although otherwise useless, have the utility of leading people away from activities arousing hostility (owing to desire) to peaceable activities. (Rée 2003: 164–5)

Rée is, then, the paradigm, or at least the most intimately known example, of the cold, froglike type who errs not just in adopting selflessness as definitive of morality, but in aspiring to make it definitive of himself as investigator. Nietzsche is simultaneously opposing morality as selflessness and opposing selflessness as a mode of inquiry.

To the extent that scientific inquiry is committed to a vision of itself as affect-free, disinterested, and impersonal, it is, for Nietzsche, an offshoot of the values of selflessness that so urgently need re-valuing. His rigorous self-scrutiny will seek to expose and undermine the affective and historical foundations of our predilection for impersonality in inquiry. Each of us should ask, "How did my attachment to the ideal of an impersonal, affect-free search for truth emerge?" and "What impels me to follow that ideal?" and look for the answers in our inclinations and aversions and their cultural prehistory. Hence to say that Nietzsche wants continuity of method with the empirical sciences is at least over-simple. Given his views about the conception of truth-seeking that predominates in science, his preferred form of truth-seeking will call in question our weddedness to that conception. Hence he can scarcely, without further questions, assume scientific inquiry as his model.

4 Real History

In the same year as the above passage from *The Gay Science* Nietzsche published the preface to the *Genealogy*, including in section 7 some further methodological criticisms of Paul Rée. In both passages Nietzsche says that he vainly hoped to persuade Rée to abandon a poor conception of history for a better one. But it may look as though Rée would have been pulled in two incompatible directions if he had tried to follow both sets of advice. For according to the *Genealogy*'s preface he was to stop his "hypothesizing into the blue" in favor of a "real history of morality," seeing "that which can be documented, which can really be ascertained, which has really existed" (*GM*, preface, 7). How could he have pursued "real history," investigating what really existed, and at the same time have abandoned his cold and clammy objectivity for a personal approach to problems, in which they became "his destiny, his distress and his greatest happiness" (*GS* 345)?

I want to argue that, for Nietzsche, Rée's failure to open himself in the right way to a deep examination of his personal affective states disabled him from doing "real history," and that there are not two methods advocated as preferable to Rée's, but only one. As a first step, we must realize what is meant by "real history" and by "what really existed." Consider an explicit example of something that for Nietzsche "actually happened":

> One will already have guessed *what* actually happened with all of this and *under* all of this: that will to self-torment, that suppressed cruelty of the animal-human who had been made inward, scared back into himself [. . .] who invented the bad conscience in order to cause himself pain after the *more natural* outlet for this *desire to cause pain* was blocked – this man of bad conscience has taken over the religious presupposition in order to drive his self-torture to its most gruesome severity and sharpness. (*GM* II. 22)

To do "real history," judging by this example, is to explain the origins of our present-day attitudes by reconstructing the operation of a multiplicity of mental states, acts, drives, and mechanisms located in past human beings – though not specific, datable human beings, but rather human beings conceived in generic fashion by a kind of projective reconstruction of how a certain psychological type would act and feel in a certain dynamic of power relations and cultural inheritances.

Note especially the emphasis on the affects here: fear, delight in making suffer, severe and sharp pain of self-torture; and, at the end of the same passage, the emphasis on the affects of the inquirer or reader: "There is so much in man that is horrifying!"

and "All of this is [. . .] of such black gloomy unnerving sadness that one must for-cibly forbid oneself to look too long into these abysses." Nietzsche is exemplifying and encouraging the personal relationship to problems that he found lacking in Rée. And so I reach my central question: Might "real history," as Nietzsche conceives it, demand a personal, affective responsiveness in the investigator?

5 Rhetorical Method and the Affects

In a previous essay I argued that Nietzsche's inflammatory rhetoric in the *Genealogy* is a deliberately contrived tool to provoke the reader's affects, and that this provocation is a vital part of the revaluation of values Nietzsche seeks (see Janaway 2003). Here I summarize and extend that argument.

First, when Nietzsche describes the essays of the *Genealogy* in *Ecce Homo*, he uses the vocabulary of discovering psychological truths, but equally strongly presents the achievement of the essays in artistic and rhetorical terms, pointing out their overall musical shape and mood, their ironic deceptions, and the powerful, disorienting emo-tional effects they are calculated to have upon the unsuspecting reader. Thus:

> Regarding expression, intention, and the art of surprise, the three inquiries which con-stitute this *Genealogy* are perhaps uncannier than anything else written so far. [. . .] Every time a beginning that is calculated to mislead: cool, scientific [*wissenschaftlich*], even ironic, deliberately foreground, deliberately holding off. Gradually more unrest; sporadic lightning; very disagreeable truths are heard grumbling in the distance – until eventually a *tempo feroce* is attained in which everything rushes ahead in a tremendous tension. In the end, in the midst of perfectly gruesome detonations, a *new* truth becomes visible every time among thick clouds. (*EH*, "On the Genealogy of Morals")

In the first essay of the *Genealogy* the thuggish behavior of the nobles is portrayed in vocabulary calculated to make the modern, post-Christian reader wince with apprehension and bristle with indignation, at the same time, perhaps, as admiring the psychic health of the self-legislating aristocrat. The slaves are presented so as to arouse contempt, but also to excite admiration for their ability to create new values. In the artistic culmination of the essay, the disgust that we feel for the brutal discharge of power towards the weak is harnessed into a disgust at the ultimately similar discharge of power by means of which the creators of Christianity set out to subjugate their masters, an affective disgust dramatized through the "Mr. Rash and Curious" figure, the reader's representative who descends into the cavernous workshop where moral ideals are fabricated, and leaves because of the bad smell (*GM* I. 14). We can apply the reflections of *Ecce Homo* to the first essay in the following way – if I may be excused for quoting myself:

> The misleading beginning is the discussion of philological and historical origins of words such as "good." This makes it appear that we are in a scientific, objective study of the past, a sort of history or anthropology, cool and *wissenschaftlich*, as Nietzsche says. But [. . .] what will really be transacted is a calling into consciousness of the reader's affects. The uncanny surprise is that what initially seem opposites – the noble mode of evaluation

and the slavish morality of *ressentiment* – will provoke in the reader a similar mixture of disquiet and admiration. Hence the growing unrest. The reader will find his or her own attachment to Christian or post-Christian moral values hard to stomach. Gruesome detonations occur in that the reader can be expected to suffer under the violence of this reversal in his or her affects. The new truth is among thick clouds because these freshly aroused feelings are at first hard to integrate with the rest of the reader's attitudes. (Janaway 2003: 262–3)

The appropriateness of a rhetoric that arouses the affects can be suggested by appreciating that the affects are central in Nietzsche's view of how we come to be attached to morality, a view perhaps at its clearest in *Daybreak*, where he states that at the most fundamental level we inherit not moral concepts, but moral feelings, or aversions and inclinations, feelings "for" and feelings "against" (see D 34, 35; and Janaway 2003: 268–70 for discussion). Moral concepts are *post facto* rationalizations of our relatively more basic inherited feelings, but our feelings themselves are, as he says, "nothing final or original" – we inherited just *these* feelings because of particular moral concepts and distinctions that held sway in the past. Affects enter at two stages in the account. We are not slaves, but we have inherited an affective allegiance to what counted as good in the conceptual scheme of slave morality. And that conceptual scheme in turn arose because it resolved certain affects and drives for its otherwise powerless inventors. Nietzsche will have an interest, then, in showing us (a) that we have such complexes of affects "for" and "against"; (b) that our having such affects is explanatory with respect to our moral judgments and our rational justifications of them; (c) that it is to a variegated past of social and conceptual arrangements that our present feelings and meta-feelings owe their origins; (d) that those past cultural arrangements themselves are explained by their function in discharging, preserving, repressing, or transforming pre-existing affects for those who participated in them.

Incidentally, if this schematic account is somewhere near correct, there are problems for the particular species of naturalist explanation that Leiter makes central in his account of Nietzsche, that is, explanation of moral beliefs in terms of a fixed set of psycho-physical characteristics of the individual, which Leiter refers to as "type-facts." Leiter suggests the following as a "typical Nietzschean form of argument": "a person's theoretical beliefs are best explained in terms of his moral beliefs; and his moral beliefs are best explained in terms of natural facts about the person he is" (Leiter 2002: 9). But we can now suggest a corrective to this view. It is not that my value-beliefs are explained by my psycho-physical constitution; rather, my value-beliefs are rationalizations of my inclinations and aversions; my inclinations and aversions are acquired habits inculcated by means of the specific culture I find myself in; this culture inculcates just these habits because it has a guiding structure of value-beliefs; and this structure of value-beliefs became dominant through answering to certain affective needs of individuals in earlier cultural stages. This suggests two correctives to Leiter: (1) the explanatory facts about me, even if located somehow in my psycho-physiology, are essentially shaped by *culture*: I could not have the specific inclinations and aversions (and perhaps even drives) that give rise to my beliefs except by having learned them culturally; (2) the psycho-physical element in the explanation of my beliefs cannot be given solely in terms of *my* psychology and physiology, but must encompass a huge host of affects, drives, and rationalizations located in human beings *other* than myself.

We saw that to discover the prehistory of our values we require a stern self-examination in which the questions "How did it emerge there?" and "What is really impelling me to listen to it?" must be asked of any value judgment we are inclined to make. Now we see that on Nietzsche's view a large amount of inherited affect is packed into our current attitudes. From this we may conclude that the process of self-examination he urges upon us cannot succeed unless it takes on the task of separating out these many affective strands, in order to discover truths about which inclinations and aversions cause me to hold certain beliefs, which cultural institutions and conventions cause me to have those inclinations and aversions, which drives and affects brought about and sustained those cultural institutions, and so on.

Behind all this lies a more general difference between genealogy and mere history: Nietzsche's genealogy of morality is, unlike much ordinary history but like ordinary family genealogy, restricted to those realities that causally terminate in our specific present-day states, and so is a highly selective exercise, ignoring vast tracts of history from which our current attitudes do not clearly descend. If I am pursuing my own genealogy, my being a descendant of X is decisive in X's being a salient object of study for me. Only tangentially, if at all, do I care to discover who lived in the neighboring plot of land, what were the most significant political events and personages of that age, or how my ancestors fit into wider patterns of change in social attitudes, movements of labor, and so on. Genealogy is a vertical study, rooted in ourselves as the eventual outcome, and so lacking the horizontal spread of interest characteristic of much historical work. So too with Nietzsche's genealogy: it is extremely selective of its past and always guided by the question, "How did *I* come to feel and think in *these* ways of mine?" That is one sense in which the inquiry must be personal for Nietzsche.

But why do the reader's feelings have to be *aroused*, or at least enacted on the reader's behalf through Nietzsche's narrative voice or the voice of an invented character? Does calling the reader into a personal affective engagement have a deeper justification, or is it nothing more than a vivid shock tactic that could be eliminated without real loss to the fundamental enterprise? It seems clear that the revaluation of values Nietzsche seeks is not just a change in judgments but a revision at the level of affects too. After we have learned not to make judgments using "good," "evil," "right," and "wrong," we finally may come, says Nietzsche, *to feel differently* (D 103). And it is plausible that the therapeutic or educative aim of bringing about revised affective habits has the arousal of affects as a prerequisite. But what about the task of understanding our values? Understanding our values properly will require *understanding* the roles of our affects in producing and sustaining our propensity to adhere to certain moral values – but is such understanding conditional upon our *feeling* the affects Nietzsche is bent upon arousing in us? Let us suppose that revaluation has among its instrumental conditions both affective engagement and understanding the history of our values. Then the question is whether the second can be fulfilled independently of the first. If not, Nietzsche implicitly holds to the following methodological principle:

> I properly understand the causal history of my moral evaluations only if relevant affects of mine are engaged in the course of my enquiry.

Does Nietzsche hold to such a principle? Here are a few initial thoughts. First, if Nietzsche held such a principle, his writing style would not be extraneous to his central aims, but a well-judged means towards the task of discovering the causal origins of one's moral evaluations, as he understood that task. Second, there is a point about identifying the true subject-matter of the genealogical investigation. If the target explananda are my moral values, and my specific personal affects are an essential rung on the explanatory ladder, then in order to understand the origin of my values I must recognize that these affects are explanatory, and that they have a cultural-psychological prehistory; and in order to recognize this about my affects I must recognize what my affects are, to do which, arguably, I would first have to feel them consciously. The argument would be that unless we *feel* specific affects we will be unable to identify them as ours, and hence unable to assign them any explanatory role. A third, related consideration is as follows: when one is investigating the nature and origin of morality, acknowledgment of the role of one's own affects is likely to be blocked by rationalization. Without Nietzsche's provocations our temptation might be to rest upon our learned attitudes and concepts, listening to the voice within us that tells us that compassion, equality, humility, and so on are "right," converting them by default into the singular set of positive values at stake and justifying them as our values by argument that we tell ourselves is rational, impersonal, and detached. If, as Nietzsche often reminds us, it is easy for the investigator to be complicit in ignoring the explanatory role of his or her own affects, the investigation can succeed only if I feel and engage with the inherited affects which are at the basis of my attachment to morality. The more we allow ourselves to feel, the better we unlock the causal truth about ourselves, or, as Nietzsche famously put it, "the more affects we allow to speak about a matter [. . .] that much more complete will our 'concept' of this matter, our 'objectivity' be" (*GM* III. 12).

6 Perils of Present Concepts: *Causa fiendi* and False Unity

Further contrasts between Nietzsche's genealogical method and Rée's emerge from the methodological remarks in *GM* II, sections 12 and 13, surrounding the history of punishment. Nietzsche includes in the scope of his criticism here "previous genealogists of morality" who "discover some 'purpose' or other in punishment, for example revenge or deterrence, then innocently place this purpose at the beginning as *causa fiendi* of punishment" (*GM* II. 12). The genealogist who places revenge at the beginning is Eugen Dühring, whom I shall not discuss here;[10] but the genealogist who makes deterrence the cause of punishment's coming into being is Rée. His mistake, for Nietzsche, is to discover a single contemporary purpose or meaning in some human institution and assume it as *causa fiendi*, the cause of the institution's coming into being. Rée proceeds under the false assumption that punishment, useful as a deterrent today, must have originated as a deterrent, indeed as a deterrent to egoism, even though (as Nietzsche would argue) the question whether an action was egoistic, like the question whether an agent could have done otherwise, arrives in human history much later than the institutions of punishment.[11] Rée places present uses of moral concepts – "punishment" for what deters the egoistic, and earlier "good" used as praising the unegoistic – at the origin of morality, and simply gives a glum, deflationary story about why the unegoistic is associated with praise. By offering an explanation in which selflessness features as *the* morality once and for all, Rée's origin-story reinforces the present dominant conception, and the opportunity to *evaluate* the practices of praising the unegoistic and deterring the egoistic disappears.

Related to this *causa fiendi* error is that of supposing that there is a single, readily available meaning for our own present concepts. Nietzsche offers instead the thought that "use," "purpose," or "meaning" are fluid, and can be assigned anew to the same type of punitive act in any number of reinterpretations over time. This history of diverse uses and purposes remains compacted in the concept that we have inherited, making it rich but problematic. "Today it is impossible to say for sure why we actually punish," says Nietzsche profoundly: "all concepts in which an entire process is semiotically summarized elude definition" (*GM* II. 13). Because so much history is compacted into our present concepts, they do not really have a single reliable meaning or definition, merely a "kind of unity" brought about by historical crystallization: and, like a crystal, a concept has now hardened so that its once fluid elements are "difficult to dissolve."

To grasp the real history of our values we require, then, some process that dissolves or explodes our apparently unified present-day concepts into their more primitive psychological components. This, I believe, is where the personal affects and Nietzsche's deliberate rhetorical evocation of them enter the picture. To overcome our reliance on received moral thinking, we must understand it as a result of the diverse affective psychology of past human beings, and realize how much it retains vestiges of that psychology compacted within it. But for Nietzsche – I have argued – this understanding must proceed by way of personal affective engagement. Because our moral concepts are *post facto* rationalizations of inherited affects, to whose explanatory role we may be blind, our own feelings "for and against" need to be aroused and questioned, if we are to grasp the variegated psychological truth behind our concepts.

Note that when Nietzsche accuses previous genealogists of relying on their limited acquaintance with present-day concepts – "their own five-span-long, merely 'modern' experience" – and says that in consequence they "aren't good for anything" and "stand in a relation to truth that is not even flirtatious" (*GM* II. 4), he twice replicates the terminology he used to castigate Rée's methodological selflessness in *The Gay Science*. The two faults – selfless approach to problems and lack of instinct for history – are linked. If they are linked in the way I have suggested, then we can see why it is that Paul Rée could not turn to "real history." He thought of his task as a cold, impersonal inquiry and did not allow his own affective responses, his gut allegiances, fears, admirations, and ambivalences to inform him about the nature of his own values. Thus he missed the enormous psychological complexity behind the concepts "good," "conscience," "punishment," and so on, and assumed that their current commerce with the morality of selflessness was a safe guide to their coming into being. In other words, complicity with the dominant self-image of inquiry as disinterested and impersonal leads to blindness to the truth about the role of one's multiple personal affects in the formation of one's concepts, to a false trust in the unity and serviceability of those concepts for history, and to the error or positing present functions and meanings as causally explanatory when they are not.

7 Conclusion

It is time to return to the issues surrounding naturalism. For brevity's sake, I shall itemize some points that have emerged explicitly or implicitly from the above discussion:

1   Nietzsche can be read as a naturalist in that he seeks explanations that cite causes in ways that do not conflict with science.
2   Nietzsche's commitment to continuity of results with the sciences is put in some doubt by some of his statements about the fundamental explanatory notion of will to power, which may essentially import notions of over-powering and interpretation into the biological realm.
3   Nietzsche's methods, on the evidence of "what he spends most of his time doing in his books" are characterized by artistic devices, rhetoric, provocation of affects, and exploration of the reader's personal reactions, and show little concern for methods that could informatively be called scientific. His "Methods Continuity" with the sciences is thus minimal, amounting merely to a concern to explain morality in terms of causes.
4   If Nietzsche's causal explanations of our moral values are naturalistic, they are so in a sense which includes within the "natural" not merely the psycho-physical constitution of the individual whose values are up for explanation, but also many complex cultural phenomena and the psycho-physiological states of past individuals and projected types of individual.
5   To the extent that scientific method is conceived as an impersonal, affect-free search for truth, Nietzsche is critical of it, because he holds that it disables the identification of one's affects through feeling them, and so obscures the truth about the causal role of affects in the production of one's values.
6   Nietzsche's method of self-scrutiny, in questioning the inquirer's attachment to the values of selflessness, must also question his or her allegiance to the methodology of cool, detached inquiry that tends to characterize science, since this for Nietzsche is a version of selflessness. Nietzsche cannot simply assume scientific practice as a fixed and unproblematic paradigm for his inquiry into values, since he regards scientific practice as imbued with the very values he spends most of his time calling into question.

See also 9 "The Naturalisms of *Beyond Good and Evil*"; 17 "Naturalism and Nietzsche's Moral Psychology"; 21 "Nietzsche and Ethics"

Notes

I should like to thank Ken Gemes for his generous discussions of this essay and related issues through numerous phases. Thanks also to Aaron Ridley, David Owen, Robin Small, and Brian Leiter for comments on different versions.

1   See *GM*, preface, 5 and 6: "Hypothesizing about the origin of morality [. . .] concerned me solely for the sake of an end to which it was one means among many [. . .] The issue for

me was the *value* of morality"; "we need a critique of moral values [. . .] and for this we need a knowledge of the conditions and circumstances out of which they have grown, under which they have developed and shifted."

2   In this instance the translation of *BGE* being referenced is the Walter Kaufmann edition (New York: Vintage Books, 1966).

3   Richardson (2002: 545–7) concedes the unattractiveness of Nietzsche's view of will to power in the passage I have quoted, but holds out for "non-psychic, non-vitalist will to power" that would "play the role of an internal amendment to Darwinism." Richardson argues that Nietzsche at least "*sometimes* takes this view."

4   In 1876–7 Nietzsche spent nearly six months in Sorrento engaged in shared intellectual inquiry with Rée and another friend, Albert Brenner. This collaboration, idealized as a kind of monastic "college for free spirits," was unparalleled in Nietzsche's career. It issued in *Human, All Too Human* and Rée's *Origin of the Moral Sensations*, changed the direction of Nietzsche's philosophy, and lost him former friends, in particular the Wagners. His remarks in *GM*, preface, 4 and 7 acknowledge the debt to Rée, though with carefully contrived dismissive rhetoric. Accounts of Nietzsche's intellectual relationship with Rée can be found in Donnellan 1982; Small 2003: "Translator's Introduction"; and Small 2001: 180–6. See Pfeiffer 1970 for a thorough collection of evidence, much of it bearing on personal relations between Nietzsche, Rée, and Lou Salomé.

5   Rée implicitly treats *böse* and *schlecht* as equivalent – an assumption whose elaborate denial gives *GM* I its basic structure.

6   Aside from points mentioned in the text Nietzsche counters Rée in the *Genealogy* as follows: (1) the evaluations "good" and "bad" have their origins not in a homogeneous human community, but out of differential power relations (*GM* I *passim*); (2) the idea that we forget the utility of praising unselfishness is psychologically implausible (*GM* I. 3); (3) punishment is not predicated upon the notion that the punished party "could have acted otherwise" (*GM* II. 4).

7   The allusion is noted in the most recent translation of *GS* by Josefine Nauckhoff: 202 n.

8   Compare Nietzsche's text with Rée's. Nietzsche (*GM* I. 2): "Man hat ursprünglich [. . .] unegoistische Handlungen von Seiten Derer gelobt und gut genannt, denen sie erwiesen wurden, also denen sie *nützlich* waren; später hat man disen Ursprung des Lobes *vergessen* und die unegoistichen Handlungen einfach, weil sie *gewohnheitsmässig* immer als gut gelobt wurden, auch als gut empfunden – wie also ob sie an sich etwas Gutes wären." Rée (1877: 17): "Das Gute (Unegoistische) [ist] wegen seines Nutzens, nämlich darum gelobt worden, weil es uns einem Zustande der Glückseligkeit näher bringt. Jetzt aber loben wir die Güte nicht wegen ihrer nützenden Folgen, vielmehr erschient sie uns an und für sich, unabhängig von allen Folgen, lobenswerth. Trotzdem kann sie ursprünglich wegen ihres Nutzens gelobt wordern sein, wenn man auch später, nachdem man sich einmal daran gewöhnt hatte, sie zu loben, vergass, dass dieses Lob sich anfangs auf den Nutzen der Gemeinschaft gründete."

9   See Janaway 1997 on the role of this epigram, and pp. 260–1 in particular for a discussion of its parallel with *GS* 345. It is no doubt unworthily "personal" to remark that Nietzsche's friendship with Rée ended because of a disastrous rivalry for the attentions of a real woman, Lou Salomé, who in the end favored Rée. But Nietzsche's metaphors about what women prefer can begin to take on an unpleasant tone if one keeps this fact in mind for too long.

10   See Dühring's *Der Werth des Lebens* (1865: 219–34). On Dühring and Nietzsche, see Small 2001: esp. 171–80, and Venturelli 1986.

11   See Leiter 2002: 168, 198. That Nietzsche is interested in maintaining the pressure on Rée's position as a particular instance of the "*causa fiendi*" error is suggested by the fact that his "most important proposition for history of every kind" concerns *usefulness*

(*Nützlichkeit*): "the cause of the genesis of a thing and its final usefulness, its actual employment and integration into a system of purposes, lie *toto caelo* apart," with *Nützlichkeit* and its cognates recurring a further five times in section 12.

Editions of Nietzsche Used

Beyond Good and Evil, trans. Judith Norman, ed. Rolf-Peter Horstmann (Cambridge: Cambridge University Press, 2002).

Daybreak, trans. R. J. Hollingdale, 2nd edn., ed. Maudemarie Clark and Brian Leiter (Cambridge: Cambridge University Press, 1997).

Ecce Homo, trans. Walter Kaufmann (with *On the Genealogy of Morals*) (New York. Vintage Books, 1967).

The Gay Science, trans. Josefine Nauckhoff, 2nd edn., ed. Bernard Williams (Cambridge: Cambridge University Press, 2001).

On the Genealogy of Morality, trans. Maudemarie Clark and Alan J. Swensen (Indianapolis: Hackett, 1998).

References

Donnellan, Brendan (1982). "Friedrich Nietzsche and Paul Rée: Cooperation and Conflict," *Journal of the History of Ideas*, 43, pp. 595–612.

Dühring, Eugen (1865). *Der Werth des Lebens. Eine philosophische Betrachtung* (Breslau: Eduard Trewendt).

Janaway, Christopher (1997). "Nietzsche's Illustration of the Art of Exegesis," *European Journal of Philosophy*, 5, pp. 251–68.

—— (2003). "Nietzsche's Artistic Revaluation," in S. Gardner and J. L. Bermúdez (eds.), *Art and Morality* (London: Routledge), pp. 260–76.

Leiter, Brian (2002). *Nietzsche on Morality* (London: Routledge).

Moore, Gregory (2002). *Nietzsche, Biology and Metaphor* (Cambridge: Cambridge University Press).

Pfeiffer, Ernst (1970). *Friedrich Nietzsche Paul Rée Lou von Salomé. Die Dokumente ihrer Begegnung* (Frankfurt am Main: Insel Verlag).

Rée, Paul (1877). *Der Ursprung der moralischen Empfindungen* (Chemnitz: Ernst Schmeitzner).

—— (2003). *Basic Writings*, ed. and trans. Robin Small (Urbana and Chicago: University of Illinois Press).

Richardson, John (2002), "Nietzsche contra Darwin," *Philosophy and Phenomenological Research*, 65, pp. 537–75.

Small, Robin (2001). *Nietzsche in Context* (Aldershot: Ashgate).

—— (2003). "Translator's Introduction," in Paul Rée, *Basic Writings* (Urbana and Chicago: University of Illinois Press).

Venturelli, Aldo (1986). "Asketismus und Wille zur Macht. Nietzsches Auseinandersetzung mit Eugen Dühring," *Nietzsche-Studien*, 15, pp. 107–39.

19

The Philosophical Function of Genealogy

ROBERT GUAY

1

It is seldom in dispute that genealogy, or genealogical accounts, are central to Nietzsche's philosophic enterprise. The role that genealogy plays in Nietzsche's thought is little understood, however, as is Nietzsche's argumentation in general, and, for that matter, what Nietzsche might be arguing for. In this essay I attempt to summarize Nietzsche's genealogical account of modern ethical practices and offer an explanation of the philosophical import of genealogy.

Understanding the philosophical function of genealogy presents difficulties. Genealogy offers a story of the *genesis* of contemporary ethical beliefs and practices. The story that Nietzsche gave is obviously a revisionist one, and Nietzsche seldom cites specific historical evidence; although it contains many historical allusions, the presentation is thematic or even mythical. At the same time, Nietzsche's interests were primarily ethical: he seems to be attempting, in some novel way, either to solve or to eliminate philosophical problems about norms and values. In particular, he offered his genealogy as part of a critique of specifically "modern" values and the advancement of an "immoralism" that would take their place. So the difficulties are: it is unclear what status we should accord Nietzsche's stories in particular, and it is unclear what role *any* story about the emergence of modern values can play in an assessment of those values. We need a reason to take Nietzsche's account as particularly authoritative, and then an explanation of how his account bears upon the normative status of "modern values."

We can categorize the standard attempts philosophically to place Nietzschean genealogy by dividing them up into four categories, consisting of two possibilities in each of two dimensions. The categories do not pertain to the interpreter, but to Nietzsche as interpreted. There are no ideal types here, and the interpretations do not come self-identifying. But nearly every one qualifies either as a "Humean" or an "Enlightenment" interpretation, or as a "postmodern" one, and each of these interpretations comes in a "cautious" and a "carefree" version.

According to the Humean or Enlightenment interpretation, the purpose of genealogy is, roughly, to manipulate our attitude towards so-called "higher" values by casting them in an unfavorable light (cf. Danto 1980: 157). By showing that moral values and assessments, along with tradition, superstition, and prejudice, have a "base" origin, we are disabused of any notion that they might possess a privileged status. In the "cautious" version of this interpretation, the influence that genealogy exerts is purely causal, rather than epistemic or normative: genealogy happens to lead us away from defective beliefs. In this way it prepares us to be receptive to genuinely philosophical doctrines or arguments (cf. Schacht 1994: 429): perhaps something about the will to power or eternal recurrence, or, in a recent interpretation, an account of the typology and mechanisms of human nature (Leiter 2002). In the "carefree" version this persuasive task itself takes on philosophical importance: that these ethical beliefs or practices *in fact* have this origin is adequate to discredit them, not merely in the sense of causing us to find them unappealing, but in the sense of determining that they are bad or wrong. "[Nietzsche] intends for [genealogy] to come up with a definitive valuation of the traditional moral virtues and principles" (Hoy 1994: 252).

According to the postmodern interpretation, genealogy is something of an aberration, but is best explained as an attempt to show the ruptures, lacunae, arbitrariness, and randomness in all of our sense-making and ethical practices (cf. Geuss 1999: 13; Nehamas 1985: 107f.). Genealogy, on this account, does not show the continuity of apparently disparate views, but the radical breaks and conclusive failures in humanity's attempts to understand its place in the world. Again, there is a cautious and a carefree version. According to the cautious version, again, genealogy per se does not have any philosophical import; it merely clears the way for the philosophic work proper – in this case, not to argue or interpret anything, but often to *do* something – laugh or play or dance in a manner free from *ressentiment* and unconstrained by the ascetic tradition. In the carefree version, the ruptures which genealogy (playfully) exhibits are themselves philosophical activity: genealogy not only shows us the inescapable failures of our sense-making and self-critical abilities, it returns us to a celebration of unreason or of primal urges or, alternately, to a "radical pluralism" (Deleuze 1983; cf. Nehamas 1985: 104).

But these interpretations carry defects. In the cautious versions, genealogy has no philosophic importance; it is merely preparatory to the "real" doctrines, which are to be found in obscurity elsewhere. This seems implausible because it makes most of Nietzsche's work extraneous to his philosophical position, as if it could all be eliminated without philosophic loss: Nietzsche, on this reading, could have presented his conclusion economically and thus skipped most of what he had to say. The postmodernists tend to suffer from a lack of evidence in general. They take heart from passages such as "the cause of the origin of a thing and its eventual utility, its actual employment and place in a system of purposes, lie worlds apart" (*GM* II. 12). But this seems more like a statement of what gives genealogy something to do rather than what would make it an exercise in futility made manifest. And, as Nietzsche insisted, "It is true that everything in the domain of morality has become and is changeable, unsteady, everything is in flux; but *everything is also flooding forward*, and towards one goal" (*HH* 107).

Moreover, I take it that the cautious positions have only been attractive as attempts at evading the carefree positions. With the notable exception of Georges Bataille (1986), the carefree positions belong to those who take pains to be *unsympathetic* to Nietzsche: Alasdair MacIntyre on the Enlightenment side (MacIntyre 1990: ch. 2), and Jürgen

Habermas on the postmodern side (Habermas 1987: ch. 5). The carefree Enlightenment position is often constructed *as* an example of the so-called "genetic fallacy":
inferring the worth of something from its origin. But Nietzsche took great pains
explicitly to deny that this was what he was doing;[1] he identified such an association
between origin and value as something sick, ascetic (cf. *TI*, "Reason," 4; *BGE* 32). The
carefree postmodernist invites us to witness the consequences of the "self-denial of
reflection" (Habermas 1971: 290): an appeal to mythic origins, the breaking of taboos,
the destruction of social convention, and, of course, totalitarianism. But Nietzsche
seemed to be, if anything, reflective – "questioning and questionable" (*GM* III. 9) – and
his invocation of myth was infrequent and ironic. And it's not clear how much room
there is to interpret *anyone* as both transgressive and authoritarian.

The functioning of Nietzschean genealogy is complex, but, in the account that
I shall present, genealogy recounts the history of ethical "ideals" in terms of their
purposiveness – their directed character – and assesses them in terms of their success
or failure. Nietzsche, that is, argued that ethical ideals are themselves functional:
they serve to structure how persons understand and conduct their lives. Nietzsche's
genealogy, then, does not purport to offer historical facts with inherent normative
implications, but the functional assessment of ideals in terms of their own internal
standards. Genealogy as a specifically historical account is thus necessary in Nietzsche's
philosophic enterprise for two reasons. First, genealogy is needed because Nietzsche
aims to provide an internal examination of the logic of practices rather than a theoretical critique. Since his commitments regarding the "value of truth" seem to render
a refutation unavailable, Nietzsche's strategy is to explain the unity and necessary
failure of certain pervasive ethical practices. Second, genealogy is needed because
its explanatory burden does not relate to a single, static subject-matter, but to transformations in the very standards of what could count as success.

2

Although Nietzsche does not employ the term "genealogy" to describe his work very
often,[2] we should be able to arrive at an interpretation which does not drive us to
cautiousness. That is, we should be able to ascribe philosophical significance to genealogy itself. Nietzsche did devote an entire book to the matter. More importantly,
Nietzsche claimed that genealogy marks off precisely what is distinctive about his
philosophy: the *Genealogy of Morals*, he wrote, is "my touchstone for what belongs to
me" (*CW*, epilogue note). Nietzsche even suggested that not merely the stories of *On
the Genealogy of Morals*, but all of his work, at least from *Human, All Too Human* on, was
genealogical (*GM*, preface, 4).[3]

But other than to call it the "contrary" (or, by implication, the "right-side-up"
version) of English genealogy (*GM*, preface, 4), Nietzsche was not explicit about what,
exactly, his version of genealogy consists in. There are, however, four formal characteristics that can serve to identify his approach. Genealogy, first of all, concerns all that
which Nietzsche places under the rubric of "values": ethical beliefs, practices, institutions, customs, norms, and so on. Nietzsche was interested above all in how people
make assessments and direct their lives, and this is what he wants to put himself in a

355

position to assess. Secondly, the subject-matter of genealogy, in particular, is the *origin* of particular values and norms, not in the sense of a single point or event, but as a long process or history.

The third formal characteristic of genealogy is that it concerns the *purposive* character of values and norms. Nietzsche's stories do not merely report the adoption or rejection of particular beliefs, or the gradual mutation of one code of conduct into another. Ideals, for Nietzsche, are a kind of goal-directed practice: ethical beliefs and practices are themselves attempts to structure the conduct of life in a certain directed way. This is the "psychological" aspect to Nietzsche's work – his insistence on the question, "What were they trying to achieve?" Rather than simply taking them at face value, genealogy considers, for example, preferences or the recognition of a rule as at least partly constitutive of some greater pursuit. The relationship between particular ethical ideals and the overarching purposiveness in which they play a part is always, according to Nietzsche, dynamic and variable. But genealogy is what tracks this changing purposiveness behind ethical ideals.

The final formal characteristic, which is closely connected to the previous one, is that genealogy concerns the *meaning* of ethical ideals: the sense or significance these ideals take on by their relation to human concerns and other things outside themselves. An account in terms of the meaning of ideals, thought Nietzsche, unifies seemingly disparate phenomena: for example, Nietzsche interpreted priests, scientists, artists, and atheistic free spirits all as fundamentally ascetic "types." Conversely, it allows for distinctions among superficially similar phenomena. Without the discriminations that meaning allows, genealogy would lose its present and future relevance: it could not incorporate new phenomena. Meaning, further, represents a dimension of assessment that allows for unlimited specificity. Instead of relying on, say, conformity to law or the realization of given ends, genealogy facilitates assessment in terms of all the *sui generis* concerns that can be brought to bear: typically, whether an ideal is a sign of flourishing, subtlety, health, ambition, desire, and hope, or slavishness, weakness, cowardice, incoherence, and resignation.

We can also identify three functional characteristics of genealogy. Genealogy serves as Nietzsche's central "no-saying" (*EH*, "BGE," 1) or critical activity: it provides the leverage with which to scrutinize and find fault with defective viewpoints. Second, genealogy is what affords self-knowledge to modern humanity. According to Nietzsche we have grown too complex, too polysemous for "direct self-observation" (*AOM* 223), so genealogy is "where the beehives of our knowledge are" (*GM*, preface, 1). Finally, genealogy enables us to assess the "value of values" (*GM*, preface, 6); through genealogy we not only find fault with viewpoints, but also get at the question of what our commitment to particular values should be, and ultimately to the all-important matter of our "health." The question that Nietzsche posed with regard to ethical ideals was: what are they worth to us? For Nietzsche, coming to terms with the status or authority of ethical values was itself a matter of ethical evaluation. One poses higher-order questions about our ideals in order to determine what our commitment to them should be:

> Have they inhibited or promoted human flourishing so far? Are they a sign of crisis, of impoverishment, of the degeneration of life? Or, on the contrary, do they betray the fullness, the force, the will of life, its courage, confidence, future? (*GM*, preface, 3)

Genealogy offers an account in which answers to these sorts of questions can be found, and by so doing provides the means to address the value of values.

Considered in this light, much of Nietzsche's writing can be seen as genealogical in character. More importantly, we can see that genealogy as so conceived serves its philosophical function: providing a descriptive or explanatory account with normative implications. If we look at genealogy as a means of bringing considerations of purposiveness and meaning together with considerations of normativity into a single account, the form of the argument emerges. Nietzsche argued that ethical ideals are functional, and thus, by examining the functional history of ideals, one can assess them in terms of their effectiveness. Ideals serve a purpose: they are a means of structuring one's life and self-understanding. So as a minimal constraint on an ideal it must "work." In particular, Nietzschean genealogy shows the unity and pervasiveness of one ideal, the "ascetic ideal," and argues that this ideal *does not work*, and is thus unavailable to us: it can no longer be affirmed. The ascetic ideal, claimed Nietzsche, is no longer effective on its own implicit terms: it is incapable of serving to explain, justify, or guide action; it does not enable us to distinguish among more and less authoritative reasons; it cannot command adherence; it provides no horizon of sense-making. Genealogy further explains this failure of the ascetic ideal as a conclusive, irremediable one. Nietzsche, in fact, identified it as a "necessary" one. He argued that the internal character of the ascetic ideal led to its demise: its very advancement ultimately brought about its destruction. Finally, Nietzsche tried to show that this unavailability of the ascetic ideal made it impossible for it to be accorded any authority.

3

In what immediately follows I shall lay out some of the details of Nietzsche's genealogical account. Obviously, I cannot give a definitive account here. But this schematic presentation should at least make clear how the phenomena that Nietzsche identified fit into his historical argument, and how the historical argument serves broader argumentative ends. In particular, I hope to illuminate the two ways in which genealogy accounts for its own indispensability: by showing that ideals falter not through theoretical defects but through specifically historical failures, and by showing that historical forms of agency have altered its own possibilities.

We can identify seven basic stages in the genealogy of morals. There are certainly more, since Nietzsche does not present his accounts in a single narrative. But, for present purposes, faithfulness to every detail is less important than capturing the functional outlines of the narrative. And there should be no doubt that Nietzsche's many genealogies comprise *the* genealogy of morals. What unifies the disparate accounts, apart from the many places at which they intersect and their culmination in *GM* III's discussion of the ascetic ideal, is that they form a present perspective on *our* past, on what according to Nietzsche is our moral history.

The first three stages should probably be considered prehistorical, if not mythical: one in which a community is formed in the face of external threats, one characterized predominantly by the "pathos of distance," and one whose distinguishing mark is widespread cruelty. In the first, a "long struggle with essentially uniform *unfavorable*

357

conditions" (*BGE* 262) fixed a social order. Constrained by necessity, a number of persons organized themselves in some determinate way, with rigid social roles, hier-archies, customs, and traditions. The second stage began when threats to the com-munity, both internal and external, had abated. In moments of relative ease the nobles turned to self-glorification and self-reverence (*BGE* 260, 287). Ethics thus begins with a mere "pathos of distance" (*GM* I. 2), a prereflective sentiment of the socially superior of their own superiority. But as pathos it was always tenuous and indeterminate, so in order for such "distance" to be maintained, some means of social propagation was necessary. This led to the third stage. The nobles, according to Nietzsche, took so little heed of others that their spontaneous self-expressions could be vicious and cruel. *Cruelty* was for the nobles first of all a "voluptuous pleasure [*Wollust*]" (*GM* II. 5): it was an "enchantment," a "seduction" in which one indulged if one could (*GM* II. 7). More importantly, cruelty was a means of rendering their assessments, especially their self-ascriptions, the compelling ones. Violence was the sole original means for establishing and maintaining values; to make someone believe in something, adhere to something, or revere something required a tremendous amount of force exerted consistently over a long time. In order to sustain their authority the nobles needed to enforce it publicly, so they made their power manifest to others by giving it a visible sign in someone's pain (cf. *HH* 103).

These first three stages are not very important. The beginning of Nietzsche's genealogy does not impart any great lesson for the simple reason that it has little to do with us. Our lives are not governed by threats to our continued existence, or by childish but vicious nobles. Nietzsche did not glorify origins, praise violence, or applaud unreflectiveness. These are elements of the most remote part of a story. Already, how-ever, the story conveys a point in that each one of these stages represents a *failure*: they are gone, and it is almost inconceivable that they could make a comeback. These ideals are portrayed as, although not self-contradictory, defective: they failed in a way that can only be understood in terms of internal flaws. Nietzsche abstracted from historical particulars in order to make the point that the disappearance of certain phenomena in our historical self-understanding was not due to fortuitous events, but to their own inherent instability. No matter when, where, or how they play out, they fail but lead in a natural way to successively more complex and recognizable attempts to establish something analogous.

The generalized depiction of these historical failures is thus meant to illustrate a minimal constraint on any normative authority. On Nietzsche's telling, authoritative norms and values originally depended on some form of social and political authority. These stages are now lost to us, however, because they lacked the means to sustain themselves in ongoing social existence. Such authority must be able to fulfill a certain public role for it to be what it is, and we can understand the irretrievability of some ethical outlooks in terms of their functional inadequacy in this regard. External threats, merely subjective self-affirmation, and, as we shall see, violence, do not work, so there can be no more authority which relies on them.

The nobles of course lost their power, and their defeat constitutes the fourth stage in Nietzsche's genealogy. With nothing but physical force available to them, the nobles met challenges to their authority exclusively with modulations of cruelty. This pro-voked hostility on the part of the oppressed, but deference and fear prevented them from manifesting it. Out of this "cauldron of unsatisfied hatred" (*GM* I. 11) came *ressentiment*. Those filled with *ressentiment* retaliated by imagining that precisely the characteristics by which the nobles identified themselves were the undesirable ones, and that they themselves were the virtuous ones: they looked at the same facts "but dyed in another color, interpreted in another manner, seen in another way" (*GM* I. 11). The inability to act thus engendered "imaginary revenge." This is not to say that the oppressed imagined themselves to have exacted revenge whenever they could not. Rather, where they could not exact revenge "in deed," they exacted a novel, "subterranean" (*GM* III. 14) sort of revenge, which operated primarily on an "ideal" or "spiritual" level rather than a factual one. Nietzsche identified priests as being the catalysts for this change; they invented ever more elaborate explanatory schemes to support the "priestly mode of valuation" (*GM* I. 7) and show that the nobles' characteristics were to be condemned. But the imaginary revenge of *ressentiment* is first and foremost "an inversion of the value-positing view" (*GM* I. 10). And, claimed Nietzsche, "The slave revolt in morals begins when *ressentiment* itself becomes creative and gives birth to values" (*GM* I. 10).

The oppressed achieved "the ultimate, finest, sublimest triumph of revenge [...] they succeeded in pushing their own misery *into the consciences* of the fortunate" (*GM* III. 14). The weak were more numerous, and out of necessity more devious than the nobles. The nobles, by contrast, were childish, unreflective, even stupid. Their *only* talent was cruelty; thus, after the mere insinuation of inverted values, their downfall became inevitable. The nobles themselves came to doubt whether strength and health were in fact worthwhile, and a new type, the priest, became the ideal: the healer who is himself sick (*GM* III. 15), the impotent master.

Nietzsche's invocation of the so-called slave revolt thus functions primarily as a claim about the impossibility of a way of life regulated entirely by force. The victory of the priestly mode of valuation, claimed Nietzsche, represents the triumph of "cunning" over "violence" (*GM* III. 15). The nobles did not lose power because their strength faltered, but because it became useless when they could no longer make sense of their own authority. The nobles are characterized by perfected instinct (*GM* I. 11), and this is their strength: their physical vitality is untempered by self-doubt or self-examination. Without any capacity for reflection, however, they "could never adequately give information about the reasons for their actions" (*BGE* 191). They were fundamentally incapable of explaining, even to themselves, why they were in charge (*GM* I. 10), and precisely because they could not take seriously the challenge presented by the priests (*GM* I. 11) they eventually lost their good conscience to administer means of holding on to power.

Nietzsche later insisted that all social institutions manifest some form of violence. In fact, our slavish modern ones are in their own manner the most violent of all. But violence by itself is completely inadequate,[4] and the slave revolt marks its demise. The forces that are still effective today have long been "refined" (*D* 30), "spiritualized" (*AOM* 276), "transfigured" (*BGE* 229), "sublimated" (*HH* 137), and "transformed" (*GS* 23); the constraints that have a hold on us are not primarily physical.[5] Violence by contrast is "coarse" and "crude," and Nietzsche referred to those who would rely on it as "retarded" (*HH* 614, 633), that is, as left behind from another age. The "force of reason" (*D* 453) has turned out to be more powerful: the social conditions on the endurance of some putative authority require that it be to some extent *rational*. This rationality is not one of efficient means to given ends, and not one of what Nietzsche calls *Begründung* (*D* 34, *BGE* 186), that is, providing a rational foundation for authority. Rather, authority must be rational in that it can give an account of itself, and provide for some distinction between those reasons that genuinely explain and those that do not. The slaves won because they were able to offer reasons; they could explain that they should be in power and what the source and status of their authority was. The nobles by contrast, strong but sublimely unreflective, always lose (*GM* I. 8).

It is in the fifth stage that things start to get interesting. Here transpires the "greatest event in the history of the sick soul" (*GM* III. 20): the creation of the "bad conscience." Nietzsche contended that the slave revolt in morals, this attainment of imaginary revenge, was also defective. The reason for its shortcomings was simple: the successful revolt perhaps alleviated some arbitrary physical abuse, but it did not make anyone happy. Successfully casting blame on an obvious source of suffering did not suffice for finding a satisfactory life. In fact, with everyone's conscience thereafter "poisoned," the slave revolt in fact made things worse, in that it made everyone less capable of addressing the reasons behind their enduring dissatisfaction.

According to Nietzsche, the weak were directionless without something to react against. But after the slave revolt they had no obvious enemies, so when their dissatisfaction inevitably emerged, it provoked confusion. They consequently sought guidance from the priests, who offered an explanation:

> "I suffer: someone must be to blame for it" – thus thinks every sickly sheep. But his shepherd, the ascetic priest, tells him: "Quite so, my sheep! someone must be to blame for it: but you yourself are this someone, you alone are to blame for it – *you alone are to blame for yourself!*" – This is bold and false enough, but one thing at least is achieved by it [. . .] the direction of *ressentiment* is *altered*. (*GM* III. 15)

The weak needed an object of blame: striking back was their art of self-preservation. But by this time they had assumed power, so there was no one to turn to but themselves. They directed their hostility against the purported source of their suffering, and tormented themselves. Self-torture and self-laceration fed off the perpetual shortcomings in their humility. Their *ressentiment* turned against itself, and the "bad conscience" was invented.

Nietzsche claimed that man "invented the bad conscience in order to hurt himself after the *more natural* vent for this desire to hurt had been blocked" (*GM* II. 22). One had instinctively sought to assert one's will by manipulating the environment; loosing one's energies entailed exerting some control over the world, including over others. But the fear of reprisal restrained aggressive instincts against others. Fear of the nobles prevented some from manifesting their aggressive instincts at all. The accomplishment of imaginary revenge stopped even the "spiritual" outlet for these instincts; the attainment of revenge left no more room for revenge. Once all of these outlets were gone, the only direction in which to unleash one's hostility was back toward oneself, as a reprisal: to hold oneself accountable for all for one's suffering by causing oneself more suffering. This involved, most crudely, literal self-torture, self-flagellation, self-mortification, but much more significantly aggression against one's instincts, the

360

repudiation of one's wants, and hostility toward one's desires, as well as scourging oneself with doubt, guilt, grief. And it was all precipitated by an "*ineluctable* disaster" (*GM* II. 17; emphasis added). Sooner or later self-inflicted suffering was bound to become a familiar human habit:

> I take the bad conscience as the profound sickness that man was *bound to* contract under the pressure of the most fundamental of all changes that he ever experienced – that change which occurred when he found himself definitively closed up inside the confines [*Bann*] of society and of peace. (*GM* II. 16; emphasis added)

Although it emerged out of contingent events, there was nothing arbitrary about the invention of the bad conscience. It was the only possible response to the stress of socialization.[6] Leading a life came to require one to be predictable and sociable, so cruelty was directed back inward until a social animal was the result.

Nietzsche deemed the creation of the bad conscience the most decisive event in the genealogy of morals because of the changes it wrought in human character. According to Nietzsche we cannot look at these changes merely as "organic adaptations" (*GM* II. 17). That is, although the changes were brought about by force of circumstance, they were far more significant than what expedience would have required. Rather than the mechanical effect of a natural process, the creation of the bad conscience marked humanity's self-separation from nature. Human governance rather than environmental adaptations took over the shaping of human character; for the first time human character was itself taken as an object and made what was willed of it. The new potentials this created were so profound that Nietzsche described the change as "a leap and a plunge into new situations and new circumstances of existence" (*GM* II. 16). With the bad conscience the story truly starts to be about us: self-determining, even self-inventing persons, rather than just animals who talk. More than self-inflicted suffering for the sake of socialization, the bad conscience was what created the self-distance needed to take oneself as an object. The inwardness thereby established made it possible for us to revise our beliefs, our ends, and even ourselves:

> the animal soul turned against itself, taking sides against itself, was something so new, profound, unheard of, enigmatic, contradictory, *and pregnant with a future* that with it the aspect of the earth was essentially altered. (*GM* II. 16)

Before the invention of the bad conscience, the world was primarily either hospitable or inhospitable; after, it became profound.

Nietzsche understood norms and values in terms of a certain authoritativeness that arose first out of social and political hierarchies. Gradually such authoritativeness came to be less and less explicitly political until, with the advent of the bad conscience, particular concerns could take on their own "sovereignty of movement" (*BGE* 3). That is, the bad conscience is so important because it occasions the *sui generis* concerns that have become a familiar part of our ethical lives. The most remarkable feature of the history of ethics is, according to Nietzsche, that we have come to take norms and values so seriously. Through the bad conscience certain concerns have come to be seen as bearing completely autonomous authority: irreducible to, for example,

361

prudential considerations or someone's subjective state, and not necessarily requiring justification in terms of anything else. This not only produces novel sorts of concerns, it also represents the advent of objectivity. By making possible concerns that are important independently of anyone in particular taking them as such, the bad conscience integrated the particularities of subjective concern with the generalities of normative status.

The other significant change wrought by the bad conscience is that, by forcibly driving apart inclination and behavior, it rendered human character and human action a matter of self-determination. The bad conscience thus made it possible for the subject-matter of ethics to be how we, although natural beings, could nevertheless come to hold ourselves to self-originating but nevertheless objective standards. Nietzsche, in other words, extended the tradition of construing ethics in terms of freedom, and in particular, in terms of freedom as autonomy. The issue is not escaping from the causal order, but how it is possible to construe a standard of self-determination at all. And Nietzsche offered perhaps the most radical freedom-as-autonomy position. For Nietzsche, "man is the not yet determined animal" (*BGE* 62): everything about us, from our ideals to the character of our agency, is the product of our continuing efforts at self-creation. Our freedom is not merely to act in a particular, free way, but to determine in a free way what the freedom could consist in, and so on. And this, incidentally, is why genealogy is needed, rather than a philosophical anthropology or theory of human nature. We have made ourselves into malleable, historical animals, and what is at stake is not the genetic story of how we got here, but the forward-looking issues of how to construe the meaning of our historical inheritance and the character of our self-determination.

The incredible productiveness that Nietzsche attributed to the bad conscience leads to a central feature of his genealogy, the ubiquity of asceticism. All ethical phenomena of any importance depend upon the self-directed cruelty that the bad conscience represents. The language, not to mention the historical examples invoked, can sometimes be a bit lurid, but the point is basic: a tremendous amount of work had to be done to make ourselves reflective and self-governing, and the impetus to do that work did not come naturally, and did not come exogenously. Nietzsche claimed that we have made ourselves increasingly responsive to and productive of reasons and subtleties of meaning through an accelerating self-discipline. This self-discipline has made us more discriminating with respect to both thought and action. Nietzsche identified "knowledge" as "a form of asceticism" (*A* 57; cf. *GS* 305 and *BGE* 229), in that it involves self-imposed demands that distinguish it from mere belief or impression; similarly, Nietzsche insisted, "Consider whether sacrifice is not present in *every* action that is done with reflection" (*AOM* 34). And this self-refinement and the suffering it has involved cannot be considered as something that happened to us, but rather must be seen as something we have actively committed ourselves to. Precisely as self-refinement it is something *directed*: not merely change, but change in a particular direction, so engaging in it amounts to taking on its purposive character. Nietzsche claimed, that is, that the aspirations toward freedom that constitute so much of our ethical life must be seen as both self-imposed and painful – or, in another word, ascetic.

Asceticism was so readily exploited just because it was so mechanical: it was possible to adopt a routine and achieve an effect. By removing oneself forcibly from the

362

economy of nature one could thereby produce meaning. Pain was something remark-able: as a survival mechanism, a signal for danger, it automatically commanded atten-tion. But it could be introduced arbitrarily into any situation. The original medium for this was others: one directed cruelty against them, and made a spectacle of their pain, as a way of making one's own activity eventful. But this inevitably failed to suffice. Torture was a crude instrument, and one could inflict only so much pain upon others. It was like trying to impress a stamp upon water: irrespective of the force brought to bear, there was a limit to the effect one could produce. But one's own self proved to be a more convenient and tractable medium. There were new disciplines to impose, com-plementing a new expanse of effects: not only could one tyrannize over behavior, but also impulses, dispositions, inclinations, and even thoughts. Ascetic practice provided a forceful, public way to manufacture a sense of purposiveness. Self-inflicted suffering in a public context was a particularly effective means for making it clear that *this* is not worth much but something else strange and hidden is worth all the pain, worth far more than what is forsaken. Asceticism made pain transparent and customary, and since self-inflicted pain only made sense as a means, it created the appearance of some goal, even if the appearance was illusory.

Once this asceticism began, claimed Nietzsche, it accelerated. Since "an improve-ment is invented only by one who can feel that something is not good" (*GS* 243), we rendered ourselves increasingly discontented in the search for some satisfying sense of purposiveness. But the result of this process was that self-estranging ideals *as such* became authoritative. This is the sixth stage of Nietzsche's genealogy, the ascendance of the ascetic ideal. It was not merely the case that ascetic practice spread. When everything else failed to suffice, one adopted ends precisely *because* they were self-abnegating. Nietzsche's claim was that once the search for ethical authority became public and rational, the slide into asceticism was inevitable. He depicted the process as gradually intensifying constraints on what could count as objective. Self-provoked doubts led to ethical crises, in which familiar ideals came to seem artificial or arbitrary. The response was always to look with greater rigor for something that was immune to such worries. Eventually it came to be seen as a requirement on any putatively authoritative ideal or norm that it be completely estranged from human will. Human-kind came to have "faith in a *metaphysical* value" (*GM* III. 24): the hope of finding something exterior to human practice which could validate it conclusively, from without. Nietzsche deemed this to be a remarkable achievement, in that it became possible to take norms and values as authoritative even when they are completely disconnected from one's immediate or idiosyncratic purposes. But at the same time it was tremendously destructive: "When one places life's center of gravity not in life but in the 'Beyond,' – in nothingness – one deprives life of its center of gravity altogether" (*A* 43). By subscribing to the ascetic ideal, we look to some "Apart, Beyond, Outside, Above" (*GS*, preface, 2) for the reasons that structure our lives. We thereby lose touch with our normal receptivity to reasons, and what sense our lives did have. And in turning over our lives to the "nothingness" where our hopes lie, we harm ourselves.

Although the ascetic ideal has been both destructive and unsatisfying, it has proven itself durable. In fact, claimed Nietzsche, its hold on us grew with the passing of time, because it functioned as an "expedient" (*GM* III. 13). The ascetic ideal solved a problem:

> *This* is precisely what the ascetic ideal means: that something was *lacking*, that man was surrounded by a monstrous *void* – he did not know how to justify, to account for, to affirm himself; he *suffered* from the problem of his meaning. He also suffered otherwise, he was in the main a *sickly* animal: but his problem was *not* suffering itself, but that there was no answer to the crying question, "*why* suffer?" (*GM* III. 28)

The ascetic ideal has been so durable because it was needed: it "offered man meaning" (*GM* III. 28). When no other means were available, it provided a general sense of purposiveness which could structure one's reasons, one's ends, and one's sense of self. The "meaning" thus produced was always unstable, but each time the ascetic ideal began to falter, it managed to perpetuate itself still further. Not only was it expedient, claimed Nietzsche, but it also functioned as a "closed system of will, goal, and interpretation" (*GM* III. 23). It furnished a horizon of sense-making, which encompassed not only modes of conduct and reasons, but also motivations and a picture of the world. This set is mutually reinforcing: the picture of the world helps to explain the authority of the norms, and so on. And the ascetic ideal is completely general in scope; it is directed toward the sustaining of purposiveness per se. As such, it is the "*'faute de mieux' par excellence*" (*GM* III. 28): not only has it been the sole option for solving the "problem of man's meaning," but it coopts or destroys any potential rivals.

Despite its durability, the ascetic ideal nonetheless perished, and this brought about the seventh and final stage of Nietzsche's genealogy, nihilism. According to Nietzsche's famous analysis of modernity, we have managed to liberate ourselves more and more from constraint, and yet this liberation is accompanied by a profound sadness and insecurity. And yet, thought Nietzsche, our autonomy depends on finding some authoritative direction of commitment; we need some self-imposed constraint as a condition of our freedom. Nietzsche considered nihilism to be the culmination of our ascetic cruelty. After having given up more and more for the sake of finer and finer subtleties, there was nothing left to do but give up everything for the sake of nothing. Now there seems to be nothing to give any point to what little of our asceticism remains, and yet there is nothing else; there is no direction in which to turn.

Nietzsche claimed not only that nihilism is our contemporary condition, but that we have arrived there out of *necessity*. In fact, the entire route that genealogy traces is, according to Nietzsche, a necessary one: there was no decisive turning point, no crucial missteps, no alternate paths. The various invocations of necessity in Nietzsche – eternal recurrence, *amor fati*, tragic fate – are often ignored or given strange metaphysical readings. But the identification of necessity, especially historical necessity, is central to Nietzsche's philosophical position. For all Nietzsche's attention to lacunae and contingency within historical processes, the focus of his argument was the discernment of an underlying directionality that has determined the present situation. Historical understanding is dependent on finding just such a necessary course:

> What I relate is the history of the next two centuries. I describe what is coming, what can no longer come differently: *the advent of nihilism*. This history can be related even now, for necessity itself is at work here. (*KSA* 13, 11[411]; cf. also *BGE* 203, *GM*, preface, 2 and II. 1)

Not only does necessity alone permit understanding in an otherwise chaotic realm, but it renders history of philosophic interest. Identifying where necessity is at work helps to distinguish that which concerns the internal character of our attempts at self-determination from the occurrence of chance events.

Asceticism culminates in nihilism according to a "relentless inner logic" (Pippin 1997: 259). Nietzsche typically discussed the "self-overcoming of morality" (*BGE* 32; cf. *D* 61) or the "self-contradiction" (*GM* III. 11) inherent in the ascetic ideal in making this claim. So the ascetic ideal didn't just die according to Nietzsche; it killed itself. The basic form of the story is that certain activities, by their very structure, progress in a way that eventually brings about their own unavailability. In the most familiar form of this claim, the "will to truth" destroyed itself. The ascetic ideal, significantly in the form of Christianity, cultivates truthfulness to such an extent that it becomes necessary to reject Christian faith, and much else too:

> One sees *what* has really triumphed over the Christian god: Christian morality itself, the concept of truthfulness taken ever more rigorously, the father confessors' refinement of the Christian conscience translated and sublimated into a scientific conscience, into intellectual cleanliness at any price. (*GS* 357; cf. *GM* III. 27 and *EH*, "Why I Am a Destiny," 3)

In general Nietzsche argued that the very absoluteness of the ascetic ideal made it impossible for it to sustain any concrete allegiance. But the more important form of the argument is the one that runs across the entire genealogy, namely this one. As we have tried to direct ourselves better, this has required the ability to reflect on what we are doing and how we could be doing better. Once this critical self-scrutiny began, it accelerated, taking on independent authority and quickly becoming destructive. And after undermining all other commitments, it turned to examine itself, and found itself wanting. Thus a self-scrutiny that had become pointless was the final commitment, but now this too is gone. Genealogy thus depicts history as one long enterprise, that of our attempts at self-direction. The story of the genealogy is how these attempts were made possible and initiated, but have foundered. And the point of the story is to show that they foundered not because of some accident, but because the very character of the project as pursued was faulty.

4

This is the substance of Nietzsche's philosophical argument: our past attempts at free self-direction are no longer viable. We arrived at the ascetic ideal, and now this, too, has come to an end. And not only has it come to an end, but there was no avoiding it, and no way to have advanced it without contributing to its demise. Nietzsche described ethical commitments as purposive, and the point of genealogy was to show that everything we have tried does not work: even on their own implicit terms they are permanent, irremediable, inevitable failures. And they are not merely inevitable failures, but they are inevitable failures because of internal defects. This is what Nietzsche needs for his historical account to have normative implications. If the failure of the ascetic ideal were reversible then, obviously, it would remain a viable option; if it were irreversible but transpired in an accidental manner then it would be possible to look on it regretfully as a lost but powerful aspiration. Note that an account of causal genesis would be beside the point here: a genuinely internal critique could not rely on historical accident. The failure at issue must be immanent, and for this to be brought to light what is needed is a functional isomorphism between the genealogical analysis and the ideals being critiqued. So Nietzsche claimed that the failure was necessary: the ascetic ideal is internally defective in such a way that it causes its own demise.

Raymond Geuss insists to the contrary that "there is nothing 'necessary' about any of this"; Hegel had such a view but, "If Nietzsche's own views really had this structure he would just have relapsed into the kind of German metaphysics of a 'real, deep structure' partially hidden behind an apparently different surface which it was one of his major achievements to have rejected" (Geuss 1999: 183f.). Nietzsche, however, very concisely disputed both the lack of necessity and the dissociation (on this matter) from Hegel:

> And if *this* book is pessimistic even into the realm of morality, even to the point of going beyond faith in morality – should it not for this reason be a very German book? For it does in fact exhibit a contradiction and is not afraid of it: in this book faith in morality is terminated – but why? *Out of morality!* [. . .] In us there is accomplished – supposing you want a formula – the *self-sublimation* [*Selbstaufhebung*] *of morality.* (D, preface, 4)

Nietzsche's argument here is that the ascetic ideal, particularly in the form of morality, destroys itself: it promotes a moralized conscience that cannot subscribe to the ascetic ideal. "As the executors of its innermost will" (*D*, preface, 4), we come to reject it; the only way to avoid this is to avoid ever embracing it. It is part of the character of the ascetic ideal that it eventually turns against itself, and this explains the necessity of its demise. Or, as Nietzsche asserted in pseudo-Hegelian terms, because of its "contradiction" it "sublimates itself." But just as Nietzsche allied his "German book" with Hegel, he denied having lapsed into a two-tiered metaphysics: "We have accustomed ourselves to believe in the existence of two realms, the realm of *purposes* and *will* and the realm of *chance* [. . . .] The belief in the two realms is a primeval romance and fable" (D 130).

To have both purposes and chance does not require a magical deep structure; it requires only that we have and find purposes. To do so, of course, we need not postulate a deeper reality behind or underneath the causal surface.[7] Finding purposes and appealing to "psychological" explanations only demands that we be able to take certain phenomena as *meaningful*. Nietzsche was not claiming that what was "really" happening was different from what seemed to be happening, but only that when one understood human history in a certain way, one could see that a particular crisis was necessary. This necessity is not the undeviating necessity of mechanism or logic, but that of *meaning*: it did not imply that nothing could possibly have been otherwise, but that if something were otherwise, it would be not what it is. What is at issue is how one understands the regularities that obtain. Culture, character, and narrative stand like laws over their respective domains: they explain, even serve as reasons. If someone is of a particular culture, or has a particular character, she is not merely *very likely*

366

to act in certain ways; she acts in certain ways *because of* who she is. Should she fail to do so, something has gone wrong; one might need to re-evaluate who she is. Similarly, if one considers, say, the increasing secularization of Western society, it is hard to see this as a long sequence of repeated, entirely accidental events, as if one might just as likely wake up to a theocracy tomorrow. There is a necessity in this process in that it would take a radical disruption in our self-image for the process to change direction.

So Nietzsche was not claiming that it would contravene the laws of nature or logic if the ascetic ideal were not to destroy itself; such a claim would serve no argument-ative purpose in any case. Nietzsche's necessity claim was that the process of the destruction of the ascetic ideal was internal, directional, and unrevisable. Something could have intervened to prevent the ascetic ideal from failing: a meteor that ended everything, for example. Nietzsche's point, however, was that the failure of the ascetic ideal was not akin to something falling from the sky. We would not be persons if we saw our deepest commitments as randomly given. Our ideals, in particular, cannot be understood as governed by chance; we have something to do with our holding of them. In general, to take phenomena as *significant* is to see them as stemming from a process governed by mind. When wars begin or markets move, we look for causes, and these causes are not mechanical ones that compel guns to be fired or cause sell orders to be executed, but rational ones: rivalries, a need for resources, the end of a fiscal year. The economic interests that cause a war and the fear of inflation that causes the stock market to go down provide reasons that are sometimes the best, if not the only, available explanation; physics and logic, certainly, are not helpful here.

Similarly, genealogy provides an account of the changes that lead up to our ethical commitments in terms of an underlying directionality. Human history is presented as one long, collective enterprise that moves, if a bit haltingly, toward the capacity for self-determination. In this enterprise, the causes of change stem from human will rather than merely from natural contingency; the process is responsive to and guided by reasons. Accordingly no ancillary factors or special circumstances are needed to explain how it reaches its conclusion, and this is Nietzsche's necessity claim: all that is needed to explain the ascetic ideal's demise is the internal character of the historical, self-correcting striving toward some ideal by which to live. This sort of necessity claim is a ubiquitous feature of our self-understanding. The inevitability of liberal trading regimes, the impossibility of peace without a Palestinian state, someone's destiny for greatness, lovers fated to meet, and the sorry lot of small family-run stores are familiar to us because we understand the underlying processes as somehow directed. What distinguishes Nietzsche's account from these more common ones, apart from its complexity, is the generality of the issues: the status of ideals and autonomous self-determination.

Nietzsche allowed that his assessment of things carried no guarantee: "necessity is not a fact, but an interpretation" (*KSA* 12, 9[91]). In fact, Nietzsche readily conceded that all of his contentions were "interpretive" in character. This did not trouble him: "Supposing that this also is only interpretation – and you will be eager enough to make this objection? [. . .] Well, so much the better" (*BGE* 22). Philosophy should be self-consciously offering interpretations, since matters of ethical concern are filled with a "polysemous character" (*GS* 373). We contend over subtleties that are bound to be underdetermined by any possible neutral description, and just this contentiousness is expressive of the importance they bear. A demand for conclusiveness, or for something external to human practices that would provide us with a definitive reassurance about their worth, might seem to be a neutral constraint on the critical process. But Nietzsche regarded it as representing a pathological need for security: not only is it cowardly and slavish, it is ascetic. Nietzsche, by contrast, by offering an interpretation in which ethical commitment and reflection are themselves credited as purposive, attempted to avoid the ascetic ideal. And this is Nietzsche's primary defense for his interpretations: his, alone, are still possible. There is no alternative that does not demand fundamentally ascetic commitments in order to hold it. The ascetic ideal, Nietzsche said, was a "closed system of will, goal, and interpretation" (GM III. 23): it involved not only commitments about ends and action, but a comprehensive way of making sense of life. Now that it can no longer effectively serve this function, some other meaning must be given to history, and to ethics.

This of course is a regressive[8] argument: Nietzsche supported his interpretation by means of a conclusion drawn from that interpretation, which is in turn presumably to be supported by further, equally disputable interpretations. Nietzsche readily conceded this, too: "And we, pressed this way, we who have put the same question to ourselves a hundred times, we have found and find no better answer" (BGE 230). Nietzsche went out of his way to claim that he was not attempting to refute the ascetic ideal: that would be ascetic once again. Instead, he claimed, "*Looking away* shall be my only negation" (GS 276). How one understands these matters is ultimately a question of the practical commitments one settles on in pursuing self-direction. Nietzsche claimed to offer practical considerations on how one could go about living, so as to be able to make better sense of one's life. Further, he contended that the other side is regressive vis-à-vis genealogy:

> You say the morality of pity is a higher morality than that of stoicism? Prove it! But note that "higher" and "lower" in morality is not to be measured by a moral yardstick [. . .] so take your measures from elsewhere. (D 139)

The idea that there could be any conclusive, non-interpretive basis on which to assess either our collective, historical enterprise of self-determination or the value of competing ways of life cannot itself be supported non-regressively.

Nietzsche's other response to an objection of regressivity is that it must be so; the acuteness of the freedom problem demands it. In the problematic as Nietzsche conceived it, everything falls under the scope of our self-determination: our historical self-understanding, our standards of judgment and of rationality, the norms that we collectively impose on ourselves, the meaning that we attach to particular concerns, the way in which we think of our freedom. Just to characterize ourselves as even potentially spontaneously self-determining when there are other compelling domains of description already requires a confidence that cannot be fully redeemed. In Nietzsche's radicalization of the post-Kantian linkage of judgment and freedom, how one interprets is inextricable from ethical considerations. With everything thus up for revision, there is no fixed point which could serve definitively to resolve questions of norms, purposiveness, or meaning. What remains for philosophy is to show how authoritative norms could emerge within the context of a way of life that sustains attachment.

368

It offers prospective considerations on how we might find a life that we can affirm, and perhaps reassurance that we do not go astray in according weight to the concerns that we take as real, regardless of what their origin might be.

See also 7 "Nietzsche and Philosophical Anthropology"; 14 "Nihilism and Skepticism in Nietzsche"; 16 "Phenomenology and Science in Nietzsche"; 21 "Nietzsche and Ethics"

Notes

I wish to thank the following for helping me to refine and clarify my thoughts on the subject-matter of this paper: Keith Ansell Pearson, Rachel Barney, Kelly Barry, Dan Brudney, Anna Gebbie, Michael Green, Robert Kendrick, Paul Loeb, Emily Nakamura, David Owen, Robert Pippin, and Thomas Pogge.

1   For explicit distinctions between the origin of an ethical ideal, and its sanction or source of value, cf. *HH* 96 and 252, *WS* 3, *D* 44, *GS* 335 and 345, and *Z* III, "Of Old and New Law-Tables," 12.
2   Other than mentions of the title of *On the Genealogy of Morals*, Nietzsche only refers to genealogy per se at *GM*, preface, 4 and 7, *GM* I. 2, and *GM* I. 4.
3   The "History" essay (*UM II*) has some affinities with genealogy, and already in *HH* we can find not only genealogical observations, but also general reflections on what might be considered genealogical method: cf. *HH* 1, *HH* ch. 2 ("On the History of the Moral Sensations"), *HH* 20 ("the historical justification [. . .] and the psychological"), *HH* 450, *AOM* 223, and *WS* 189. Similar reflections appear at *D* 95, *GS* 1, 7, and 335, *BGE* ch. 5 ("Natural History of Morals"), *BGE* 186, *GS*, preface, 2, and *GS* 345.
4   On the inadequacy of force without reflection, see e.g. *HH* 245 and 452, *D* 534, and *TI*, "Morality as Anti-Nature," 1, and "What the Germans Lack," 1.
5   Nietzsche claimed in fact that, even in the case of the nobles, it was "strength of soul" rather than "physical strength" on which they relied for their authority; cf. *BGE* 257.
6   One might be more precise than Nietzsche here and follow Geuss (1999: 4) in saying "urbanization": i.e. the issue is not how persons lived in proximity without trying to kill each other (as perhaps in the earlier stages), but how they lived together in conditions of mutual interdependence.
7   As Joshua Cohen points out (1997: 93), one does not need "deep" metaphysical commitments to make arguments about the "necessary" demise of certain social institutions: in Enlightenment theories of history the injustice of certain social arrangements was related to their lack of viability.
8   Nietzsche in describing his argumentation also used tropes of circularity: for example, "self-propelled wheel" (*Z* I, "On the Way of the Creator"), and "widest circle" (*Z* III, "Of Old and New Law-Tables," 19).

References

Bataille, G. (1986). "On Nietzsche: The Will to Chance," *October*, 36.

Cohen, J. (1997). "Arc of the Moral Universe," *Philosophy and Public Affairs*, 26.

Danto, A. (1980). *Nietzsche as Philosopher* (New York: Columbia University Press).

Deleuze, G. (1983). *Nietzsche and Philosophy*, trans. H. Tomlinson (New York: Columbia University Press).

369

Geuss, R. (1999). *Morality, Culture, and History* (Cambridge: Cambridge University Press).

Habermas, J. (1971). *Knowledge and Human Interests*, trans. J. J. Shapiro (Boston: Beacon Press).

—— (1987). *The Philosophical Discourse of Modernity*, trans. F. Lawrence (Cambridge, MA: MIT Press).

Hoy, D. C. (1994). "Nietzsche, Hume, and the Genealogical Method," in R. Schacht (ed.), *Nietzsche, Genealogy, Morality* (Berkeley: University of California Press).

Leiter, B. (2002). *Nietzsche on Morality* (London: Routledge).

MacIntyre, A. (1990). *Three Rival Versions of Moral Enquiry* (London: Duckworth).

Nehamas, A. (1985). *Nietzsche: Life as Literature* (Cambridge, MA: Harvard University Press).

Pippin, R. (1997). *Idealism as Modernism* (New York: Cambridge University Press).

Schacht, R. (1994). "Of Morals and *Menschen*," in R. Schacht (ed.), *Nietzsche, Genealogy, Morality* (Berkeley: University of California Press).

Further Reading

Bittner, R. (1994). "*Ressentiment*," in R. Schacht (ed.), *Nietzsche, Genealogy, Morality* (Berkeley: University of California Press), pp. 127–38.

Conway, D. (1987). "Nietzsche's Internal Critique of Foundationalism," *International Studies in Philosophy*, 19, pp. 103–10.

—— (1994). "Genealogy and Critical Method," in R. Schacht (ed.), *Nietzsche, Genealogy, Morality* (Berkeley: University of California Press), pp. 318–33.

—— (1995). "Writing in Blood: On the Prejudices of Genealogy," *Epoché*, 3, pp. 149–81.

Foucault, M. (1977). "Nietzsche, Genealogy, History," in D. F. Bouchard (ed. and trans.), *Language, Counter-Memory, Practice* (Ithaca, NY: Cornell University Press), pp. 139–64.

Guay, R. (2002). "Nietzsche on Freedom," *European Journal of Philosophy*, 10, pp. 302–27.

Loeb, P. S. (1995). "Is There a Genetic Fallacy in Nietzsche's *Genealogy of Morals*?," *International Studies in Philosophy*, 27, pp. 125–41.

Owen, D. (2003). "Nietzsche, Re-evaluation, and the Turn to Genealogy," *European Journal of Philosophy*, 11, pp. 249–72.

Pippin, R. (2000). "Deceit, Desire, and Democracy: Nietzsche on Modern Eros," *International Studies in Philosophy*, 32, pp. 63–70.

Reginster, B. (1997). "Nietzsche on *Ressentiment* and Valuation," *Philosophy and Phenomenological Research*, 57, pp. 281–305.

Ridley, A. (1998). *Nietzsche's Conscience: Six Character Studies from the Genealogy* (Ithaca, NY: Cornell University Press).

Soll, I. (1988). "Pessimism and the Tragic View of Life," in R. C. Solomon and K. M. Higgins (eds.), *Reading Nietzsche* (New York: Oxford University Press), pp. 104–31.

Strong, T. (1975). *Nietzsche and the Politics of Transfiguration* (Berkeley: University of California Press).

Wellberg, D. E. (1988). "Nietzsche – Art – Postmodernism: A Reply to Jürgen Habermas," in T. Harrison (ed.), *Nietzsche in Italy* (Calistoga: ANMA Libri), pp. 77–100.

20

Agent and Deed in Nietzsche's
Genealogy of Morals

ROBERT B. PIPPIN

1

In his *On the Genealogy of Morals*, Nietzsche expressed great skepticism about the moral psychology presupposed by the proponents of "slave morality," the institution that we know as anti-egoistic, universalist, and egalitarian morality *simpliciter*.[1] He claimed to identify the foundational claim in such a moral psychology – belief in "that little changeling, the 'subject'" (*GM* I. 13) – and he then offered a historical and psychological narrative about the origin of the notion. His story purported to show why a certain type (the weak) would try to justify its position relative to the stronger type by portraying the master's expression of strength as evil, and the situation of the defeated slave as good. This, in turn, if it was to be an effective *condemnation* rather than a mere report of the facts, had to go one step farther than characterizing those who end up by nature as such overpowering types, one step farther than just characterizing the weak type, those who happen to be in their deeds meek, humble, sympathetic to the suffering of others, and so forth. The real genius of the slave rebellion, according to Nietzsche, lies in its going beyond a simple inversion of value types, and in the creation of a new way of thinking about human beings: the creation of a subject "behind" the actual deed, one who could have acted to express his strength (or virtuous weakness) *or not*, and who thus can be condemned and held individually and completely responsible for his voluntary oppression of others, even as the slave can be praised for his supposedly voluntary and so praiseworthy withdrawal from the struggle, in the service of supposedly higher ends. Nietzsche's psychological narrative points to a distinct motive that explains this ideological warfare and invention – his phrase is, "thanks to the counterfeit and self-deception of *impotence*" – and he draws a conclusion about the realization of this motive, such that the slave can act,

> just as if the weakness of the weak – that is to say, their essence, their effects, their sole ineluctable, irremovable reality – were a voluntary achievement, willed, chosen, a deed, a meritorious act. This type of man needs to believe in a neutral independent "subject," prompted by an instinct for self-preservation and self-affirmation. (*GM* I. 13)

The experience of the two differing motivations cited in these two passages is obviously supposed to be linked. Nietzsche appears to assume that the experience of such impotence itself is, if confronted unadorned, unbearable in some way, threatens one's very "self-preservation," requires a "self-affirmation" if one is to continue to lead a life. Hence the "self-deception," the compensatory belief that one's "impotence" is actually an achievement to be admired. In sum, this invention of a subject (or soul) independent of and "behind" its deeds is what "the sublime self-deception that interprets weakness as freedom, and their being thus-and-thus as a merit makes possible" (*GM* I. 13).

However, as in many other cases, Nietzsche is not content merely to ascribe these psychological motivations to the originators of some moral code. Even if the slaves had such a "need," establishing that would not of itself establish the further claim that this slavishly motivated commitment is actually false, *necessarily* deceived. Nietzsche clearly realized this, and he certainly wanted to establish that further point. He suggests how he intends to demonstrate that in a famous simile proposed in *GM* I. 13, just before the passages cited above. The simile appears to assert an ambitious, sweeping metaphysical claim, all despite Nietzsche's frequent demurrals about the possibility of metaphysics. His main claim is stated right after he notes that there is nothing surprising or even objectionable in the fact that "little lambs" insist that the greatest evil is "bird of prey" (*Raubvögeln*) behavior, and that the highest good is little lamb behavior. Nietzsche goes on:

> To demand of strength that it should *not* express itself as strength, that it should *not* be a desire to overcome, a desire to throw down, a desire to become master, a thirst for enemies and resistances and triumphs, is just as absurd as to demand of weakness that it should express itself as strength [. . .] For just as the popular mind separates the lightning from its flash and takes the latter for an action, for the operation of a subject called lightning, so popular morality also separates strength from expressions of strength, as if there were a neutral substratum behind the strong man, which was free to express strength or not to do so. But there is no such substratum; there is no "being" behind doing, effecting, becoming; "the doer" is merely a fiction added to the deed – the deed is everything. (*GM* I. 13; see also *BGE* 17)

This denial of a subject behind the deed and responsible for it is so sweeping that it immediately raises a problem for Nietzsche. It is the same question that would arise for anyone attacking the commonsense psychological view that holds that a subject's intention, normally understood as a desire for an end, accompanied by a belief about means or a subject's deciding or "willing" to act for some purpose or end, must stand both "behind" and "before" some activity in order for the event to be distinguished *as a deed at all*, as something *done* by someone.[2] We must be able to appeal to such a subject's "intending" in order for us to be able to distinguish, say, someone volunteering for a risky mission from steel rusting or water running downhill or a bird singing. The identification of such a prior condition is, in Wittgenstein's famous words, what would distinguish my arm going up from *my* raising my arm. It is "behind" the deed in the sense that other observers see only the movements of bodies – say, someone stepping out from a line of men – and must infer some intending subject in order to understand and explain both what happened and why the action, someone volunteering for a mission, occurred. If there "is" just the deed, we tend to think, stepping out of

372

line *is* just body movement, metaphysically like the wind blowing over a lamp. A subject's intention is "before" the deed because that commonsense psychological explanation typically points to such a prior intention as the *cause* of the act; what best answers the question, "Why did that occur?"

2

Now Nietzsche is often described as a "naturalist," perhaps a psychological naturalist in his account of moral institutions. Nowadays, naturalism is understood as the position that holds that there are only material objects in space and time, perhaps just the entities and properties referred to by the most advanced modern sciences, and that all explanation is scientific explanation, essentially subsumption under a scientific law. However, even with such a general, vague definition, it is unlikely that Nietzsche accepts this sort of naturalism, especially the latter condition. In *GM* II. 12, he rails against the "mechanistic senselessness" of modern science, and he contrasts what he here and elsewhere calls this democratic prejudice with "the theory that in all events a will to power is operating." But many people think he accepts at least the former condition, and that such acceptance may partly explain what is going on in the denial of any separate soul in *GM* I. 13; i.e. that Nietzsche mostly means to deny "free will."

Nietzsche's descriptions of the strong and the weak in *GM* I. 13 have indeed already expressed the anti-voluntarist view that the strong can "do nothing else but" express their strength. He seems to treat the commonsense psychology just sketched as essentially and wholly derivative from the slave or ultimately Christian compensatory fantasy of self-determining subjects and a "could have done otherwise" sense of freedom. This all does make it tempting to regard him as indifferent to the distinction between ordinary natural events and actions, and as perfectly content to consider the "reactive force" most responsible for the slave rebellion – *ressentiment* – as one of the many natural forces in the world we will need to appeal to in order to account for various social and political appearances. All this is in contrast to a separate subject which could act or not, depending on what it "decides." We could interpret *GM* I. 13 as only denying the possibility of this metaphysically free subject behind the deed and attribute to Nietzsche a broadly consistent naturalism. Nietzsche certainly believes that the free will picture *is* a fantasy (*BGE* 19, 21), and in *GM* I. 13 he obviously thinks that the classic picture of a commanding will and the resultant action give us, paradoxically and unacceptably, two actions, not one, and that it pushes the basic question of origin back yet again.

The trouble with proceeding very far in this direction is that Nietzsche does not seem interested in merely naturalizing all talk of motives, goals, intentions, and aversions; he denies that whole model of behavior. The passages just quoted do not appear to leave room for *corporeal* states causing various body movements, as if, for example, a subject's socially habituated fear for his reputation (where fear is understood as some sort of corporeal brain state or event) were "behind" his stepping out of line and acting in a way he knew would count for others as volunteering. If that model were adopted, we would still be pointing to some determinate causal factor "behind" and "before" the deed. The lightning simile is unequivocal, though, and we would not be following its suggestion if we merely substituted a material *substance* (like the brain or brain states) for an immaterial soul. Moreover, such a naturalist account relies on the material continuity through time of some identical substance in order to attribute to it various manifestations and expressions as interconnected properties. If there were no substance or subject of any kind behind or underlying various different events, it is hard to see how we might individuate these expressions of force, and even if we could, how we might distinguish a universe of episodic, atomistic force-events from the world that Nietzsche himself refers to, a world of slaves, masters, institutions, priests, and so on. He nowhere seems inclined to treat such a world as arbitrarily grouped collections of force-events (grouped together by whom or what?), as if these were either "becoming master" events or "becoming subdued by" events, etc. We thus still need a credible interpretation of the following claim: "But there is no such substratum; there is no 'being' behind doing, effecting, becoming; 'the doer' is merely a fiction added to the deed – the deed is everything" (*GM* I. 13). Materialist or naturalist bloody-mindedness is not going to help.

3

In order to understand what such an extreme claim could mean ("there is no lightning behind the flash and responsible for it," "no subject behind the deed"; there is just the deed), we might turn to Nietzsche's own psychological explanations of the slave revolt, and what appears to be his own general theory about the psychological origins of normative distinctions. In some places, there is certainly language consistent with the anti-agent language of *GM* I. 13, but at the same time and more frequently language immediately in tension with it. In *GM* I. 10 Nietzsche appears to attribute explanatory power to forces themselves, as if events were causally responsible for human deeds: "The slave revolt in morality begins when *ressentiment* itself becomes creative and gives birth to values." It is odd to say that resentment itself could become creative and could *do* something, and not that a subject, motivated by such a feeling of resentment, acted, but perhaps Nietzsche is deliberately looking ahead to his own denial of any causal agent. Nietzsche also speaks of *the noble mode of valuation* as if it were an independent *explicans*, although both these expressions still seem to "substantialize" force and distinguish it from the manifestations they cause. In *GM* I. 13 Nietzsche himself criticizes the scientific language of "force moves, force causes" ("die Kraft bewegt, die Kraft verursacht"), and claims that this language is no improvement on that of subjects causing events by willing them. In his most important statement in *GM* of what appears to be his will to power "doctrine," Nietzsche seems to be trying to deliberately avoid any commitment to an agent-cum-intention causing-the-deed model.

> all events in the organic world are a subduing, a *becoming master*, and all subduing and becoming master involves a fresh interpretation, an adaptation through which any previous "meaning" and "purpose" are necessarily obscured or even obliterated. [. . .] But purposes and utilities are only signs that a will to power has become master of something less powerful and imposed upon it the character of a function. (*GM* II. 12)

Likewise, in the Second Essay, he talks freely of such things as a "struggle between power-complexes" (*GM* II. 11).

On the other hand, Nietzsche would seem to be right in *GM* I. 13 about the *inevitably* substantializing tendencies of language itself, even throughout his own account. Immediately after his claim using resentment as the subject of a sentence, he cannot himself resist parsing *this* as "the *ressentiment* of natures that are denied the true reaction, that of deeds, and compensate themselves with an imaginary revenge" (*GM* I. 10). This reintroduction of the substantive bearer of the property, "natures," who express *ressentiment*, rather than any claim about *ressentiment*-events occurring, is also more consistent with the overall psychological manner of explaining morality. It is hard enough to imagine appealing to something like forces without substrates in which they inhere, of which they are properties, but the core idea of Nietzsche's account is a picture of a *social* struggle, lasting over some time, among *human beings*, not forces, which results in a situation of relative stability, a successful subduing and a being subdued, wherein, finally, the reaction of the subdued finds another outlet of response than a direct counter-force. This last is caused by a feeling that is apparently unbearable, impotence, responsible then for a reaction motivated by an attempt to revalue such impotence. So, as he must, Nietzsche refers both to "the noble mode of valuation" as explicans and directly to "the noble man" as someone with motives, intentions, a self-understanding, a certain relation to the slavish, etc. I say that Nietzsche "must" so refer because, as several others have pointed out (Bittner 2001 with regard to Nietzsche; Honneth 1991 with regard to Foucault), there cannot just "be" *subduing* and *subdued* events. Someone must be subdued and be *held* in subjection, be prevented from doing what he might otherwise do, by the activities of someone else who is not so restricted. Otherwise, we don't have a *Herrwerden*, just a quantitative more or less. Even the "will to power" passages cannot end by pointing to a mere "becoming master" *event*. If such a striving is successful, what we are left with is *a master*, and thereby correspondingly a slave.[3]

Throughout the *Genealogy of Morals* Nietzsche treats his own explanation of the slave revolt in morality as something not acknowledged by, something that would be actively disputed by, the proponents of such a revolt, and for such an account to make sense there must *be* proponents, quite complex proponents, it turns out. That is, while he might invoke the language of psychological naturalism, the language of instincts, to account for this moralizing reaction, he also notes that this instinctual force is not "for itself" what it is "in itself," to adopt a non-Nietzschean form of expression. The "moral reaction" is not experienced by such a subject as what it really is, even though the reaction could not be satisfying unless *also* "experienced," somehow, as some sort of revenge. Morality is a counterfeit and self-deception, and its effectiveness as a weapon against the master would disappear if it were correctly understood by its proponents as a psychological ploy or strategy in the search for an indirect route to power over one's oppressors. In fact, Nietzsche thinks that the Christian imperative to complete honesty about one's motives will eventually precipitate exactly this sort of "crisis of honesty," will make known to its adherents the origins of Christianity in hatred and a desire for revenge on the masters (cf. *GM* III. 27; *GS* 357).

But then, it would seem, it cannot be that "the deed is *everything*." Nietzsche himself, it would appear, is only able to account for the deed being what it is, a reactive, revenge-inspired rebellion, motivated by the frustrations of impotence, by appeal to the standard psychological language of a subject's "true intentions," the struggle to realize those intentions, and the conflict with other subjects that this produces, and, as we have just seen, he must also be able to refer even to the possibility of a *self*-deceived commitment to an intention, acting for the sake of an end one consciously and sincerely would disavow. Nietzsche's claim is that the deed in question *is not* a discovery, or even the attempt at a discovery, of the true nature of good and evil, but a revolt, *because* it is motivated by a vengeful reaction. But if there were "only the deed, not a doer," the question "*What* deed?" would, it appears, be unanswerable, or at least it could not be answered in the "divided subject" way Nietzsche appears committed to. Indeed, in pursuing that question, we are not only back with a "subject" and a subject's intentions behind the deed, but involved in a hunt for true, genuine intentions, lying "back there" somewhere, but unacknowledged.

Finally the whole direction of Nietzsche's narrative seems to depend on what *GM* I. 13 denies. Since the revolt is something the slaves *did*, is a deed, and not something that happened to them, or merely "grew" in them, it is something that can be *undone*, that, in the right situation, can be countered by a new legislation of values, once the "crisis of Christian honesty" occurs. Oddly, this alternative *deed*, or revaluation, seems to be both an idea that Nietzsche accuses the slave of fabricating in order to focus absolute blame on the master, and a possibility Nietzsche himself seems to want to preserve, the possibility of an eventual "self-overcoming." All of this requires not only subjects of deeds, but even possibilities inhering yet unrealized in such subjects. Again, the denial of a causally autonomous soul, the free will, and freely undertaken commitments does not get us very far in understanding Nietzsche's own enterprise in a way that is consistent with *GM* I. 13. And so we need to think again about what "the deed is everything" might amount to.

4

Now it may be that Nietzsche is such an unsystematic thinker that at some point in any philosophical reconstruction one will simply have to pick and choose, follow one of the paths Nietzsche opened up and ignore another, inconsistent path that he also pointed to.[4] But if we reject the substantializing of the will to power, or any substantializing, the social account that results from an application of it would look like so many heterogeneous episodes of conflicting and discontinuous fields of contingent forces and it would resemble not at all the typology that Nietzsche so clearly relies on. Accordingly, Rüdiger Bittner has encouraged us to discard the "will to power" explanation as a dead end, one ultimately wedded to a "creationist" and projective theory of value, and to concentrate on what Bittner thinks is closer to Nietzsche's interest: an adequate account of life and living beings, and therewith the instability and provisionality of any substance claim. To understand the domain of "life," we have to rid ourselves of substance presumptions and concentrate on subject-less "activity" itself. Bittner also wants us to take *GM* I. 13 as the heart of Nietzsche's project, and to abandon completely the language of subjects who create value (Bittner 2001).

But, as we have seen, if we accept *GM* I. 13 at face value, and insist that there is *no* doer behind the deed, we have to give up much more than the metaphysics of the will to power, and its assumptions about exclusively created value. We will make it very difficult to understand the whole of Nietzsche's own attack on the moral psychology of Christian morality, since he appears to rely on a traditional understanding of act descriptions, appears to claim that the act is individuated as an act mainly by reference to the agent's intentions, and he invokes a complex picture of unconscious motives, operative and motivating, but inaccessible as such to the agents involved. Not to mention that we shall be left with little coherent to say about Nietzsche's *BGE* 23 claim about "psychology," "now again the path to the fundamental problems." Without Nietzsche's own, prima facie inconsistent, doer–deed language, the question of *what* is supposedly happening in the slave revolt, which in his account clearly relies on notions of subjection to the will of others, resentment, and even "madness" (*GM* II. 22), will be difficult to understand. Values cannot be said to simply "grow" organically, given some sort of context. For one thing, as Nietzsche famously remarked, we must *make* ourselves into creatures capable of keeping promises, and this requires many centuries of commitment and perseverance and so the unmistakable exercise of subjectivity. It seems a question-begging evasion to gloss all such appeals as really about "what happens *to* us," what madness befalls us, in situations of subjection. There would be little reason to take Nietzsche seriously if he were out to make what Bernard Williams has called the "uninviting" claim that "we never really do anything, that no events are actions" (Williams 1994: 241).

5

However, before returning to *GM* I. 13, the suggestions just made about Nietzsche's reliance on what appears to be some notion of subjectivity should be expanded a bit. Two points are especially relevant. The first concerns Nietzsche's essentially genealogical and so historical treatment of the issue, and the second involves the highly literary or figurative attempt to explain what is involved in what he calls in *GM* II. 2 the historical creation of the "sovereign individual."

His historical narrative of the development of a creature able to make and keep promises makes two substantial if also fairly minimal assumptions about the "nature" out of which such historical development proceeds. As he puts it in the first paragraph of the Second Essay of the *Genealogy*, the problem of breeding an animal capable of promising is a task that nature "has set for herself." His first assumption is that nature "sets the task" that human beings must complete in historical time because any conceivable human situation is one where suffering is unavoidable. His second assumption, manifest throughout the last two essays of the *Genealogy*, is that it is suffering that in effect shocks, forces human beings into a distinct reaction – not just reactions of avoidance and prudence. He gathers whatever historical, anthropological, literary, and philological elements he can muster to try to demonstrate that a species-distinct reaction is also provoked: that is, the burden of the question of the meaning of suffering is taken on. He assumes that we are so disposed that the deepest suffering we can experience is from a lack of any sense in the suffering. Consciousness itself is often treated by Nietzsche as such a reactive phenomenon, as if human beings do not merely suffer, but, given the intensity of their suffering and some sort of disposition to react against it, they can be said also to be jolted into the awareness *that* one is suffering, and this not just as a kind of second-order neutral self-monitoring. Such second-order awareness is originally reactive and negative, seeks to cancel out in some way what injures so meaninglessly. (As in many accounts of origin – by Rousseau, Hobbes, Hegel, and even Freud – the "state of nature" is unbearable and requires its own negation and the creation of a second nature. Being human cannot function like a standard natural predicate, like being white or being an animal, but involves not being, and negating, what our natural endowment would require.) In the case of primitive injuries by others, Nietzsche tries to show that we can retroactively render the act in some way sensible by requiring recompense from the offender. "What suffering means" is that a balance has been upset and can be restored, usually by payment in the suffering of the offender; more precisely and gruesomely, by pleasure in watching the other suffer. His story then develops into the famous account of bad conscience, internalization and sublimation, guilt and debt, the ascetic priest and ascetic ideal (see *GM* III. 15).

The details of this famous genealogy would take us far afield. It is well known that Nietzsche believed that the interpretation of suffering provided by "morality" – that the reason for suffering was the subject's own sinfulness, and the picture of guilt and conscience that such an account requires – actually *succeeded* in creating conditions of commitment, sacrifice, and dedication, but it ultimately exacted far too high a price. It thus eventually left us "a nook of discontented, arrogant, and repulsive creatures" (*GM* III. 11). This double rhetoric is also on view in the laudatory introduction of "the sovereign individual," even as Nietzsche is preparing the reader for the inevitably self-destructive nature of the main weapon "against himself" that permits this admirable sovereignty – conscience, ultimately "bad conscience."

For the moment, the second important element in this narrative of a "subjective" mode of self-understanding is Nietzsche's formulation of just what has been achieved, this "power over oneself." In *Thus Spoke Zarathustra* Nietzsche has Zarathustra announce the advent of nihilism in this way: "Alas the time is coming when man will no longer shoot the arrow of his longing beyond man, and the string of his bow will have forgotten how to whir" (*Z*, prologue, 5). In the preface to *Beyond Good and Evil* he notes that our long struggle with and often opposition to and dissatisfaction with our own moral tradition, European Christianity, has created a "magnificent tension [*Spannung*] of the spirit the like of which never yet existed on earth: with so tense a bow we can now shoot for the most distant goals." But, he goes on, the "democratic enlightenment" also sought to "unbend" such a bow, "to bring it about that the spirit would no longer experience itself so easily as a 'need'" (*BGE*, prologue). This latter formulation coincides with a wonderfully lapidary expression in *Gay Science*. In discussing "the millions of Europeans who cannot endure their boredom and themselves," he notes that they would even welcome "a craving to suffer" and so "to find in their suffering a probable reason for action, for deeds"; that is, "neediness is needed!" (*GS* 56). In sum:

> with the appearance on earth of an animal soul turned against itself, taking sides against itself, something so new, deep, unheard of, enigmatic, contradictory, and full of future

had come into being that the appearance of the earth was thereby essentially changed. (*GM* II. 16)

This "tension" amounts to Nietzsche's term for self-consciousness, the possibility of some distance from oneself that makes possible everything from there being possible addressees of Nietzsche's rhetorical appeals, to rendering intelligible that one could not *be* who one is, and so might have to become, would want to become, who one is. Nietzsche clearly also wants to raise in these terms the question of whether the threshold in accepting our natural situation of ignorance and suffering has come to be significantly lowered in bourgeois Europe, and he is clearly worried that it has sunk far too low, that we have lost the capacity to feel any self-contempt at our animal status.

6

Part of what is involved in the weakening of this tension, failure of desire, or unbending of bows is the central picture of a subject separate from and absolutely responsible for its deeds. Nietzsche has proposed that we need a new way of understanding ourselves, given the historical fate of this Christian notion, one wherein "the deed is everything," and we have been trying to understand the implications of this alternate picture. We might do better, I want now to suggest, to attend more closely to the surface meaning of the claims made in *GM* I. 13. As we see in *GM* II. 12, the notion of an "activity" functions as a "fundamental concept" in what Nietzsche himself claims, and he insists in that passage on a contrast between such an activity and the "mechanistic senselessness" of the ordinary modern scientific worldview. We thus need to return to *GM* I. 13 and appreciate that Nietzsche is not denying that *there is* a subject of the deed; he is just asserting that it is not *separate*, distinct from the activity itself; it is "in" the deed. He is not denying that strength "*expresses* itself" in acts of strength. He is in fact asserting just that, that there is such an *expression*, and so appears to be relying on a notion of expression, rather than intentional causality, to understand how the doer is in the deed. "To demand of strength that it should *not* express itself as strength" is the expression he uses. He does not say, "there are just strength-events." The appeal to expression is quite an important clue. He is not denying, in other words, that there is a deed, and that it must be distinguishable from any mere event. He maintains that distinction. However, because he has introduced the category of deed or activity (his "fundamental concept") so quickly and metaphorically, it is difficult to flesh out what he means. Indeed, there are other such metaphorical expressions which are both striking and somewhat mysterious, as well as indications of how important the issue is to Nietzsche. In *Thus Spoke Zarathustra*, he writes: "Oh, my friend, that your self be in your deed as the mother is in the child – let that be your word concerning virtue" (*Z* II, "On the Virtuous").

This suggests a very different relation between self and deed than cause and effect, but we would first have to know how, for Nietzsche, a mother can be said to be in her child before we can appreciate what is being suggested, and that would require at least a separate essay. Put in terms of the image we have been exploring, we cannot say "there are only deeds," no agents, just as we cannot say that the flash is *just* an electrical discharge in the air. Clearly, a certain *sort* of meteorological event is "expressed," and so a phenomenally identical "flash" might not be lightning, but could be artificially produced. It would be a phenomenally identical event, but not lightning.

In order to understand this claim about a doer "in" the deed, I want to suggest a comparison with another philosopher that will seem at first glance quite inappropriate. Assume for a moment that there is a brotherhood of modern anti-Cartesians, philosophers united in their opposition to metaphysical dualism, to a picture of mind shut up in itself and its own ideas and so in an unsolvable skeptical dilemma about the real world, and opposed as well to the notion of autonomous, identifiable subjects, whose intentions and acts of willing best identify and explain distinct sorts of events in the world, actions. There is a range in such a group, including Nietzsche and Wittgenstein and Heidegger, but surely a charter member is also Hegel. Hegel formulated this issue of how to "find" the agent "in" the deed in a way that suggests something of what Nietzsche may have been thinking. Consider:

> The true being of a man is rather his deed; in this the individual is actual, and it is the deed that does away with both aspects of what is [merely] "meant" to be: in the one aspect where what is "meant" has the form of a corporeal passive being, the individuality, in the deed, exhibits itself rather as the negative essence, which only is insofar as it supersedes [mere] being. Then, too, the deed equally does away with the inexpressibility of what is "meant," in respect of the self-conscious individuality. In such mere opinion the individuality is infinitely determined and determinable. In the accomplished deed this spurious infinity is destroyed. The deed is something simply determined, universal, to be grasped in an abstraction; it is murder, theft, or a good action, a brave deed, and so on, and what it is can be said of it. It is this, and its being is not merely a sign, but the fact itself. It is this, and the individual human being is what the deed is. [. . .] even if he deceives himself on the point, and, turning away from his action into himself, fancies that in this inner self he is something else than what he is in the deed. (Hegel 1977: §322 [pp. 193–5])

And, even more clearly, in §404:

> Whatever it is that the individual does, and whatever happens to him, that he has done himself, and he is that himself. He can have only the consciousness of the simple transference of himself from the night of possibility into the daylight of the present, from the abstract in-itself into the significance of actual being, and can have only the certainty that what happens to him in the latter is nothing else but what lay dormant in the former. [. . .] The individual, therefore, knowing that in his actual world he can find nothing else but its unity with himself, or only the certainty of himself in the truth of that world, *can experience only joy in himself*. (1977: p. 242)

Modern Hegel scholarship owes a great debt to Charles Taylor for having focused so much of our attention on this "expressivist" notion of action, as opposed to an intentionalist or causal account, and it is quite relevant here for understanding how Nietzsche could appear to deny any standard picture of agency and of normal volitional responsibility, and yet still speak of *actions*, and of the expression of a subject in a deed, indeed *wholly* in the deed (Taylor 1977, 1985). The main similarity turns on what might be called a non-separability thesis about intention and action, and a corresponding non-isolatability claim about a subject's intention, the claim that the determinate meaning of such an intention cannot be made out if isolated from a much larger complex of social and historical factors.

According to the first or non-separability thesis, intention-formation and articulation are always temporally fluid, altering and being transformed "on the go," as it were, as events in a project unfold. I may start out engaged in a project, understanding my intention as X, and, over time, come to understand that this was not really what I intended; it must have been Y, or later perhaps Z. And there is no way to confirm the certainty of one's "real" purpose except *in* the deed actually performed. My subjective construal at any time before or during the deed has no privileged authority. The deed *alone* can show one who one is. This means that the act description cannot be separated from this mutable intention, since as the intention comes into a kind of focus, what it is I take myself to be doing can also alter. This is partly what Nietzsche has in mind, I think, when he objects to the way other genealogists search for the origin of punishment, by looking for a fixed purpose which subjects struggle to realize with various means,

> and the entire history of a "thing," an organ, a custom can in this way be a continuous sign-chain of ever new interpretations and adaptations whose causes do not even have to be related to one another but, on the contrary, in some cases succeed and alternate with one another in a purely chance fashion. (*GM* II. 12)

This is why, in the next section, Nietzsche writes that "only that which has no history is definable," and that we must appreciate "how accidental the 'meaning' of punishment is" (*GM* II. 13).

Likewise there is a common "non-isolatability" thesis between Hegel and Nietzsche: attending only to a specific intention as both accounting for why the act occurred and what is actually undertaken distorts what is necessary for a full explanation of an action. In the first place, the conditions under which one *would* regard an intention as justifying an action (or not) have to be part of the picture too, and this shifts our attention to the person's character and then to his life-history and even to a community as a whole or to a tradition. We have to have all that in view before the adoption of a specific intention can itself make sense. Indeed this assumption is already on view from the start in Nietzsche's genealogy, since he treats the unequal distribution of social power as an essential element in understanding "what the slavish type was attempting." The psychology that Nietzsche announces as "the queen of the sciences" is also a social and historical psychology.

In addition, while, on the standard model, the criterion for success of an action amounts to whether the originally held purpose was in fact achieved, on this different model "success" is much more complicated. I must be able to "see myself" in the deed, see it as an expression of me (in a sense not restricted to my singular intention), but also such that what *I* understand is being attempted and realized is also what *others* understand. I haven't *performed the action*, haven't volunteered for the mission, if nothing I do is so understood by others as such an act. We could use Robert Brandom's pragmatic terminology to make this point and say that for an action to be successful the commitments I undertake must be those also attributed to me by others; we thus make room for the original uncertainty "for me" in just *what* I am undertaking, and the unacceptability of any one-sided answer (as in "*just* what others attribute to me": Brandom 1994).

Now Hegel and Nietzsche are going to part company radically very soon in this exposition, but it is important to have in view this way of understanding action as "mine" without our needing to say that some prior "I" caused it by deciding it should happen. On this model, as Hegel notes, we should understand successful action as a continuous and temporally extended, everywhere mutable translation or expression of inner into outer, but not as an isolated and separated determinate inner struggling for expression in imperfect material. Our "original" intentions are just provisional starting points, formulated with incomplete knowledge of circumstances and consequences. We have to understand the end and the reason for pursuing it as both constantly transformed, such that what I end up with, what I actually did, counts fully as my intention realized or expressed.

Thus, if I start out to write a poem, I might find that it does not go as I expected, and think this is because the material resists my execution, my inner poem, and so what I get is a "poorly expressed poem." This is a very misleading picture on this account, as misleading as the commanding will of *BGE* 19. The poem is a perfect expression of what your intention *turned out to be*. To ask for a better poem is to ask for another one, for the formation and execution of another intention. If the poem failed; everything has failed. It, the expression of what has turned out to be the intended poem, just turned out to be a bad poem; not a bad expression of a good poem. As Nietzsche keeps insisting, our egos are wedded to the latter account; but the former correctly expresses what happened.

Now, philosophically, a great deal more needs to be said before this understanding of "the doer in the deed" could be defended. The anti-Cartesian and broadly anti-Christian account asks for something quite unusual. These passages in Hegel and Nietzsche seem to be asking us to relocate our attention when trying to understand an action, render a deed intelligible, from attention to a prior event or mental state (the formation of and commitment to an intention, whether a maxim, or desire-plus-belief, etc.) to "what lies *deeper* in the deed itself" and is expressed in it, where "deeper" does not mean already there, hidden in the depths, but not yet fully formed and revealed. Rather, the interpretive task focuses on a continuing expression or translation of the subject into the actuality of the deed, and conversely our translation back into "who the person is." As Hegel put it in his clearest expression of this anti-intentionalist position: "Ethical self-consciousness now learns from its deed the developed nature of what it actually did" (Hegel 1977: §469 [p. 283]).

This can all sound counter-intuitive because it seems obvious that the final deed may not express the agent simply because some contingency intervened and prevented the full realization, thus reinstituting a "separation" between the subject in itself and the deed that actually resulted, shaped as it so often is by external circumstances and events. Or we easily accept that if someone did something unknowingly and innocently, he cannot be said to be properly "in" the deed, even though the deed came about because of him and no one else, as when someone genuinely does not know that he is revealing a secret, and *does* so, but, we want to say, guiltlessly.

The issues are quite complicated and cannot be pursued here. The central question is: should not Nietzsche be aware that, by eliminating as nonsensical the idea that appears to be a necessary condition for a deed being a deed – a subject's individual causal responsibility for the deed occurring – he has eliminated any way of properly understanding the notion of *responsibility* and a place for criticism of an agent? If strength is not at all "free" to be weak, is not free to express that strength in any way other than by "a desire to overcome, a desire to throw down, a desire to become master, a thirst for enemies and resistances and triumphs," in *what* "responsibility sense" *is* the agent *in* the deed if not "causally" (*GM* I. 13)? A plant's life-cycle might be said to be "expressed" in its various stages, but, as we have seen, Nietzsche rejects such a reductionist reading; he shows no indication of wanting to eliminate his fundamental concept, activity.

Now it is true that sometimes Nietzsche seems content with a kind of typological determinism. People just *belong* to some type or other, whether biological or socially formed, and some just *are* weak, base, vengeful, and ugly; others are strong, noble, generous, and beautiful (cf. *BGE* 265). There is no way to justify these distinctions; that is the ("Socratic") trick the former group tries to play on the latter. The whole point is that you have to *be* a member of the latter group to appreciate the distinction. Nietzsche's own evaluations are not so tied to this fixed typology. About the weak he says: "Human history would be altogether too stupid a thing without the spirit that the impotent have introduced into it" (*GM* I. 7). Likewise, he certainly seems to be criticizing the nobility by contrast when he says:

> it was on the soil of this essentially dangerous form of human existence, the priestly form, that man first became an interesting animal, that only here did the human soul in a higher sense acquire depth and become evil – and these are the two basic respects in which man has hitherto been superior to other beasts! (*GM* I. 6)

Such passages suggest a radical flexibility and indeterminateness in the normative value of such distinctions, an unpredictability in what they "turn out" to mean, as if Nietzsche thinks that such oppositions look one way in one context and another in another context. That raises the question of how this variation works, how this interpretive struggle is to be understood, and what its relation might be to the psychological struggle.

Nietzsche has a great many things to say about this hermeneutical warfare, but we should note that his remarks confirm attributing the "non-isolatability" thesis to him, as noted above, and the second "success" condition for actions, as understood on this alternate model. Not only is the determinate meaning of a subject's intention not a matter of inner perception and sincerity but rather a function in some way of a certain social context, but also "what is going on" in such a context is itself constantly contested among the participants. As he put it in the famous passage quoted earlier, "all events in the organic world are a subduing, a *becoming master*, and all subduing and becoming master involves a fresh interpretation, an adaptation through which any previous 'meaning' and 'purpose' are necessarily obscured or even obliterated" (*GM* II. 12).

He makes the same sort of point about the variability and contestability of the various understandings of punishment (*GM* II. 14) and notes that even the noble man *needs* the appropriate enemies if his actions are to have the meaning he sees expressed in them (*GM* I. 10). In such cases, "the subject" is not absent; he is "out there" in his deeds, but *the deeds are "out there" too*, multiply interpretable. These interpretations are themselves already expressions of various types that cannot be isolated from historical time and from the contestations of their own age. They are not existential "projections," motivated by some sort of self-interest or self-aggrandizement. And we already have good reason to be cautious of interpreters who think that there must be something appealed to, underlying Nietzsche's account, as a kind of criterion: "life" and/or "the will to power," to cite the most frequent candidates. If life must also *turn against itself* to be life, and if we don't know what really counts as *having established power*, or even *what power is*, we have only returned again to a social struggle about the meaning of deeds. In other words, if the most important deed is *the legislation of values*, what *actually* is legislated cannot be fixed by the noble man's strength of resolve *alone*, or guaranteed by his "pathos of distance." There is a difference between "actually" legislating values, that is, *succeeding* in doing so, and, on the other hand, engaging in a fantasy of self- and value-creation.

It is at this point that the similarities between Nietzsche and Hegel end. In a sense one can read Nietzsche's infrequent, published references to the "will to power" as attempts to dramatize the simple claim that there is no best, appropriate, finally reconciling resolution to these sorts of conflicts. "There is" *only the conflict*, at once potentially tragic and ennobling, and potentially dispiriting, a source of nihilistic despair. Hegel of course claims that such conflicts have an inherent "logic," that a developmental story can be told, say, in the *Phenomenology of Spirit*, from the conflict between Antigone and Creon, to the partial overcoming of morality in forgiveness, and that the heart of that story is the ever more successful realization of freedom as a kind of rational agency. There is no corresponding logic or teleology in Nietzsche; just the opposite.

7

I want to conclude by returning to the intuitive difficulties created by *GM* I. 13, especially about responsibility. We should try to understand Nietzsche's own response to the responsibility question – how, on his picture of how an agent is wholly in the deed, not separate from it, such reactions as regret, sorrow about what one did, and so forth, might be understood.

Not surprisingly, given their similarities on so many issues, Nietzsche turns to Spinoza to make his point, and his remarks in *GM* II. 15 are perfectly consistent with, and I think confirm, the position attributed to him above. He muses that Spinoza might one afternoon have asked himself, given that there is no "free will" or separate subject underlying the deed in Spinoza's own system, what could remain in that system of the *morsus conscientiae*, the sting of conscience. This is the very intuitive or commonsense question I posed above. Nietzsche first appeals to Spinoza by making his own attempt at a "becoming master" as a "new interpretation" of Spinoza, invoking essentially Nietzschean language (especially "innocence"), and announcing: "The world, for Spinoza, had returned to that state of innocence in which it had lain before the invention of the bad conscience." But then he notes that Spinoza reinvented this *morsus conscientiae* in *Ethics* III. 18. 1.

> "The opposite of gaudium," he finally said to himself – "a sadness accompanied by the recollection of a past event that flouted all of our expectations." [. . .] Mischief-makers overtaken by punishments have for thousands of years felt in respect of their "transgressions" *just as Spinoza did*: "here something has unexpectedly gone wrong," *not*: "I ought not to have done that." (*GM* II. 15)

So disappointment that I was not who I thought I was, sadness at what was expressed "in" the deed, replaces guilt, or the sort of guilt which depends on the claim that I could have done otherwise. Indeed, it is a kind of regret that depends on my *not* really having had the option to do otherwise; or at least that counter-factual option, on this view, is like considering the possibility that *I might not have been me*, a fanciful and largely irrelevant speculation, a mere thought experiment.

None of this settles the many other questions raised by Nietzsche's position. What are the conditions necessary for rightly identifying what it *was* that I did? What role do the judgments of others properly play in that assessment? Deeds, even understood as expressions, rather than caused results, conflict, express incompatible – if also provisional and changing – purposes. How do we, as non-participants, understand or evaluate such conflicts? Are not our interpretations the expressions of *current* contestations, and if so what would count as success, as prevailing now? How much of "who I am" can be said to be expressed in the deed? How might I distinguish important "discoveries" about myself that I had not known and would have denied, from trivial or irrelevant revelations? If whatever it is that is expressed in such deeds is not a stable core or substantial self, neither as an individual soul nor as a substantial type, what could form the basis of the temporal story that would link these manifestations and transformations?

These are difficult questions, but, I have tried to show, they are the right sort of questions raised by Nietzsche's remarks in *GM* I. 13, and they are very different from questions about metaphysical forces, naturalized psychologies, instinct theories, or existential, groundless choices, leaps into the abyss. Whether Nietzsche has good answers to such important questions is another story.

See also 16 "Phenomenology and Science in Nietzsche"; 17 "Naturalism and Nietzsche's Moral Psychology"; 21 "Nietzsche and Ethics"; 24 "Nietzsche *contra* Liberalism on Freedom"

Notes

1 Although Nietzsche does not treat "morality" as a univocal term and certainly not as a phenomenon with a single necessary essence, it is clear that he has a standard form of nineteenth-century Christian morality often in his sights. See Geuss 1999: 171.
2 That is, deciding what to do, and then deciding to act. See Williams 1994: 242. John Searle (2001) multiplies matters even more, adding our persistence in the deed once undertaken.
3 There are, of course, several other genealogical origins of morality sketched in *GM*: suffering itself seems inevitably to require a compensatory mechanism; there is the feeling of guilt

traced back to debt; the internalization of aggression, turning it towards oneself, and so on. But all of these, I would argue, raise the same problem, the compatibility of their "psychological accounts" with *GM* I. 13.

4 See Williams's remark: "With Nietzsche [. . .] the resistance to the continuation of philosophy by ordinary means is built into the text, which is booby-trapped, not only against recovering theory from it, but in many cases, against any systematic exegesis that assimilates it to theory" (1994: 242).

Editions of Nietzsche Used

Beyond Good and Evil, trans. Walter Kaufmann (New York: Vintage Books, 1966).

The Gay Science, trans. Walter Kaufmann (New York: Vintage Books, 1974).

On the Genealogy of Morals, trans. Walter Kaufmann and R. J. Hollingdale (with *Ecce Homo*) (New York: Vintage Books, 1967).

Thus Spoke Zarathustra, trans. Walter Kaufmann (New York: Penguin, 1978).

Twilight of the Idols and *The Anti-Christ*, trans. R. J. Hollingdale (Harmondsworth: Penguin, 1968).

References

Bittner, Rüdiger (2001). "Masters without Substance," in Richard Schacht (ed.), *Nietzsche's Postmoralism: Essays on Nietzsche's Prelude to Philosophy's Future* (Cambridge: Cambridge University Press), pp. 34–46.

Brandom, Robert (1994). *Making It Explicit: Reasoning, Representing, and Discursive Commitment* (Cambridge, MA: Harvard University Press).

Geuss, Raymond (1999). *Morality, Culture, and History: Essays on German Philosophy* (Cambridge: Cambridge University Press).

Hegel, Georg Wilhelm Friedrich (1977). *Phenomenology of Spirit*, trans. Arnold V. Miller (Oxford: Clarendon Press).

—— (1999). *Hauptwerke*, 6 vols., vol. 2 (Hamburg: Felix Meiner).

Honneth, Axel (1991). *The Critique of Power: Reflective Stages in a Critical Social Theory*, trans. Kenneth Baynes, Studies in Contemporary German Social Thought (Cambridge, MA: MIT Press).

Searle, John R. (2001). *Rationality in Action* (Cambridge, MA: MIT Press).

Taylor, Charles (1977). *Hegel* (Cambridge: Cambridge University Press).

—— (1985). *Human Agency and Language. Philosophical Papers*, vol. 1 (Cambridge: Cambridge University Press).

Williams, Bernard (1994). "Nietzsche's Minimalist Moral Psychology," in Richard Schacht (ed.), *Nietzsche, Genealogy, Morality: Essays on Nietzsche's Genealogy of Morals* (Berkeley: University of California Press), pp. 237–47.

Part VI

Ethics

21

Nietzsche and Ethics

PAUL J. M. VAN TONGEREN

1 Introduction

Friedrich Nietzsche is without doubt one of the most radical critics of morality and ethics in the history of philosophy. But at the same time there is an unmistakably strong moral pathos in his philosophy, even in his criticism of morality and ethics. Nietzsche himself interprets his thoughts on morality as what he calls "a morality for moralists" (*KSA* 11, 34[194]). Both aspects of his thinking, the critique of morality as well as the morality of his critique, are of utmost importance for a correct understanding of his whole philosophy.

His critique of morality plays a basic and founding role in the critical analyses of the other domains of human culture that we find in his work. Morality is not only related to the fields of individual, social, and political activity, but equally to the spheres of knowledge and belief. The moral distinctions of "good" and "evil" also lie, according to Nietzsche, at the heart of religious principles, metaphysical categories, and aesthetic appreciation. But at the same time we can see that in Nietzsche's critique of those cultural domains morality has an important role to play: the Christian God has been undermined by the morality of truthfulness that unmasked the belief in God as a lie, and that same morality of truthfulness plays an important role in the criticism of science, philosophy, and art. Nor can Nietzsche escape this criticism since his own critique is inspired and molded by the morality he criticizes.

Moreover, Nietzsche resembles all those he criticizes, continually holding them up to an ideal of health and fitness that has an unmistakable moral tone. His own thought is certainly no exception to the rule he formulates in *Beyond Good and Evil*:

> Gradually it has become clear to me what every great philosophy so far has been: namely the personal confession of its author and a kind of involuntary and unconscious memoir; also that the moral (or immoral) intentions in every philosophy constituted the real germ of life from which the whole plant had grown. (*BGE* 6)

We have to look for the inner pathos and the moral intentions of the philosopher in order to understand his thinking.

But in order to understand Nietzsche's moral pathos we first have to do justice to his critique of morality. Therefore I will deal with his critique of morality before moving on to the morality of his critique. We will see that the latter does not become much easier after we have completed the former. Quite the contrary, it will become questionable whether and how one can speak about morality at all without becoming entangled in the nets of this "Circe of humanity, which is morality" (*EH*, "Why I Write Such Good Books," 5).

2 Nietzsche's Critique of Morality and Ethics

2.1 The method of the critique: the genealogy

Why, actually, do we speak of a "critique?" How does Nietzsche argue in his criticism of morality and ethics? Is it in such a way that would allow us to speak of a "critique"? And if so, what kind of a critique is it? And what does the word "critique" mean here? We may expect that the term in this framework not only indicates a (predominantly negative) evaluation, but also refers to the philosophical and especially the Kantian concept of "critique" as a (transcendental) search for conditions of possibility, an investigation which shows the limits of the investigated and – since it is a self-investigation – situates itself on these limits. Nietzsche, however, does not speak of a "transcendental" but of a "genealogical" critique. What does that mean?

Let us take as our starting point the preface to his *Genealogy of Morals*. There he calls it his "a priori" to have a suspicious interest in morality. He is interested in the following questions, he says:

> under what conditions did man devise these value judgments good and evil? *And what value do they themselves possess?* Have they hitherto hindered or furthered human prosperity? Are they a sign of distress, of impoverishment, of the degeneration of life? Or is there revealed in them, on the contrary, the plenitude, force, and will of life, its courage, certainty, future? (*GM*, preface, 3)

In the sentence which Nietzsche himself underlined (here italicized), he reveals the evaluative, if not moral, effort of his critique. But in order to understand that effort correctly, we first have to concentrate on the method of this critique. And we find in this passage several important aspects of this method, which in *GM* he calls "genealogy." Nietzsche argues in favor of the study of (1) the originating and (2) the functioning of moral categories, and this in the sense of (3) a critical evaluation of those categories. The three crucial elements of his genealogical method are: (1) history of origin and evolution; (2) analysis of function and effectiveness; and (3) critical evaluation.

Nietzsche gives a particular meaning to the concept of a "genealogy".[1] On the one hand it points to the investigation of the origin and the evolution of a phenomenon; it describes the successive forms the phenomenon adopts, and it is especially interested in the most significant changes or displacements in such an evolution. On the other hand "genealogy" points to the investigation of the psychological, sociological, and physiological conditions, functions, and effects of such an evolution. Thus he first examines the constitutive understanding of the two foundations of morality, i.e. good/

evil and good/bad in *GM* I, then guilt and (bad) conscience in *GM* II, and finally the ascetic ideal in *GM* III. This is done with respect to the origin, development, and physiological and psychological conditions and impact of each. We also find a brief genealogy of morals in the fifth part of *BGE* in which the same elements can be found. Genealogy, or as it is called in *BGE* the "natural history of morals," is history, but a particular kind of history, and it is psychology and physiology, but again, of a particular kind. And so we must ask: what kind?

The historical part of Nietzsche's genealogical analysis can be characterized as follows: it does not so much sanction the power of the analyzed phenomenon (as history often does or is used for), but quite the contrary: it attacks and harms this power. It does so because it shows that the phenomenon as it is investigated is only one out of many possibilities and that it is the product of a completely contingent development, a development without a first origin or predetermined goal, with many changes or displacements, and always alterable (see e.g. *BGE* 188f., 191, 195, 199–201, 203).

The psychological and physiological part of the genealogy tries to reconstruct the moving forces behind the evolution. Again such a psychology and physiology break down the claims of the unity and self-evidence of the phenomenon. Through this psychology and physiology, morality (or a particular moral phenomenon) is being rooted in nature, and nature is shown to be plural and ambiguous. The moral psychologist looks, according to Nietzsche, for the plurality of motivations behind a moral act. While analyzing one particular moral phenomenon he brings to light a plurality of possible moralities (see e.g. *BGE* 187f., 190, 192–4, 196–9). We will see how important this emphasis on plurality is, not only for the critique of morality but also for a correct understanding of the evaluative part of the genealogical method.

Nietzsche's genealogy is not the search for a true origin and essence; his "natural history" is not a foundational reduction of the phenomenon at hand to nature in the traditional metaphysical or scientific sense of the word. It is, on the contrary, the methodology of a philosophy that interprets reality as will to power; it is the "morphology and the doctrine of the development of the will to power" (*BGE* 23). The genealogist "knows" that life is will to power; this enables him to acknowledge the plurality while at the same time "collecting" it in terms of universal structures (e.g. "the ascetic ideal" in *GM* III), and it provides him with a criterion by which he can evaluate what he finds; with this criterion he can even evaluate the traditional (moral) criterion. I will come back to this criterion (see below, section 3.2), and to Nietzsche's thesis on the world as will to power (see below, section 3.1).

2.2 The scope of Nietzsche's critique

Although it may seem so at times, Nietzsche does not criticize only one particular type of morality (the herd, or Christian, or contemporary European morality), but – as he calls it – "everything which has been celebrated as morality on earth so far" (*GM*, preface, 3). Remarkably Nietzsche often speaks about "every morality" (*BGE* 188), "all moralities" (*BGE* 198), "all moral philosophies" (*BGE* 228), or "the whole morality" (*BGE* 291), etc. Whatever traditional distinctions one wants to make between different types of morality or moral philosophy (deontological versus teleological, eudaimonistic versus utilitarian, hedonistic versus duty-based, consequentialist versus intention-oriented, individual versus social, egoistic versus altruistic, intuitionistic versus rationalistic, etc.), one can, for each type to be distinguished, find a passage in Nietzsche's writings in which it is criticized. We are forced to suppose that all different moralities and moral philosophies do have something basic in common which allows Nietzsche to make his generalizing critique.

This remarkable aspect of Nietzsche's critique of morality is particularly important not only if we want to do justice to that critique, but also when we apply it to the morality of the critique itself, because the extent to which the scope of Nietzsche's claims widens makes it more difficult for him to find a place outside the scope of his own critique, a place from which he can evaluate without collapsing under his own critique. Let us therefore look more carefully at this generalizing tendency of Nietzsche's critique of morality. What could this common characteristic or common ground of all moralities and moral philosophies be?

It is my suggestion that this common ground, which allows Nietzsche to speak about "all and every morality" in such a generalizing way, lies precisely in the generalizing tendency that every morality and moral philosophy has, according to him. Nietzsche criticizes all moralities, "because they address themselves to 'all,' because they generalize where one must not generalize. All of them speak unconditionally, take themselves for unconditional" (*BGE* 198). A few sections further on, in a section that is presented as a kind of summary of the chapter, Nietzsche phrases the upshot of his genealogical analyses:

> We have found that in all major moral judgments Europe is now of one mind, including even the countries dominated by the influence of Europe: plainly one *knows* in Europe what Socrates thought he did not know and what that famous old serpent once promised to teach – today one "knows" what is good and evil. Now it must sound harsh and cannot be heard easily when we keep insisting: that which here believes it knows, that which here glorifies itself with its praises and reproaches, calling itself good, that is the instinct of the herd animal [. . .]. *Morality in Europe today is herd animal morality* – in other words, as we understand it, merely *one* type of human morality beside which, before which, and after which many other types, above all *higher* moralities, are, or ought to be, possible. (*BGE* 202)

At this moment of history, according to Nietzsche, there is only one type of morality left, and this morality claims to be the only one: "it says stubbornly and inexorably, 'I am morality itself, and nothing besides is morality'" (*BGE* 202). This is, according to Nietzsche, characteristic of all moralities. No morality "wants there to be many moralities, they want no comparison and no criticism; just absolute faith" (*KSA* 11, 35[5], 510).

This type of morality, which according to Nietzsche is predominant in his age, has succeeded in what all moralities try to do: identify good and bad in a fixed, definite, and everlasting way. Before human history, in paradise, the snake promised Adam and Eve knowledge of good and evil. Now this promise has come true, which means, according to Nietzsche, that human history has ended. There is only one morality left, and this one and only morality dominates everything and everyone. Against this background we can understand why Nietzsche so often *seems* to criticize one particular morality, while – as we saw – he still claims to criticize all morality: the criticized one has become the only one.

But Nietzsche is inspired by a belief in the possibility of other moralities: "We who have a different conviction" (*BGE* 203). In the section I have quoted at length he even speaks of "higher moralities." How is that possible? In what sense can he speak about a higher *morality*, when he criticizes not only every morality, but even the conceptual distinction (good/evil) which seems to be constitutive of morality as such? Before we can attempt to answer this question, we have to go through the critique once more.

2.3 What is at stake in Nietzsche's critique

In *Beyond Good and Evil* Nietzsche describes the human being as it presents itself in this age in which the morality of the herd has become the only morality. The upshot of this absolute and exclusive predominance of only one type of morality is a "degeneration and diminution of man into the perfect herd animal": Nietzsche speaks about a "animalization of man [*Verthierung des Menschen*]" (*BGE* 203).

With this interesting formulation, Nietzsche refers to the traditional definition of the human being as a special type ("species") of (the "genus") animal. In other places he uses this same formula when he defines the human being as a particular kind of animal. For Nietzsche, however, "man is the as yet undetermined animal" (*BGE* 62). On the one hand the human being is an animal: natural, corporeal, driven by instincts, etc. But, on the other hand, the naturalness of this being is not complete and encompassing. Human beings are not completely determined by their instincts, they cannot be classified once and for all into one particular pattern. They do not have a fixed and definite identity, but maintain in themselves many possibilities. Nietzsche more often writes about this "*plurality of characters*" which every human being harbors (cf. *KSA* 11, 25[21], 17). He claims that "the type we are representing is *one* of our *possibilities* – we *could* form many persons – we do have the *material* for that *in us* –" (*KSA* 11, 25[362]). Nietzsche uses the traditional form of the anthropological definition (*per genus et differentiam specificam*) in an ironic way. For him the *differentia specifica* which distinguishes this animal (this species) from the other ones (the other species of the same *genus*) is not its rationality, nor its language, its laughing, its upright stature, or whatever else has been proposed, but precisely its indeterminacy.

In order to better understand what this means, we should acknowledge that the traditional definitions of the human being to which Nietzsche refers were usually meant to be not merely descriptive but also normative. They were always part of some sort of naturalistic teleological ethics according to which human beings must become what they are. This adage has dominated the European tradition since Pindar who, in the second Pythian Ode, exhorted people to self-actualization through self-knowledge. It is the task of people to realize their humanity through actualization of that which distinguishes them from the other animals, i.e. that which appears as the *differentia specifica* in the definition. Nietzsche too stands in the tradition of self-realization of humanity; he lets himself be addressed by the voice that says "You shall become the one you are" (*GS* 270).[2] In an unpublished note we read: "The principle through which humanity became master *over the animals* will probably also be the principle that determines 'the highest man'" (*KSA* 11, 25[459]).

393

But Nietzsche's variation on the traditional form of the definition of humanity changes the "ethic of self-realization" in a dramatic way. The call to become who you are is, for the being whose *being* is not yet determined, paradoxical because it claims that every form to which a human being attaches him or herself at the same time would do harm to what he or she is, i.e. "the as yet undetermined animal."

In one respect a human being cannot live with this indeterminacy, therefore humans are called "as yet" undetermined. Self-determination is required and unavoidable for this "most endangered animal" (GS 354). In another respect every determination is an identification that wrongly conceals its own one-sidedness, and thus is in contrast with the proper nature of this animal. As soon as the human being has become what it has to become and what it is already, it is not what it most properly is, i.e. "as yet undetermined," any more.

According to Nietzsche, every morality reduces the human being to an animal (a particular animal: the herd animal), whereas the human being most properly is *and is not* an animal, or is at least not identical with its animality, because it is "as yet undetermined." Therefore Nietzsche calls it a "paradoxical task that nature has set itself in the case of man": "to breed an animal with the right to make promises," that is, an animal which has become "calculable, regular, necessary" (GM II. 1), or, in other words, which has become determined. That the human being is by essence "as yet undetermined" (BGE 62) and therefore always has to be determined and at the same time should never become determined, that is "the real problem of humankind" (GM II. 1).

2.4 The core element of the critique

When we come to formulate the morality of the critique, having investigated the critique of morality, we will have to find a solution to the problem indicated above, one that allows us to combine the indefiniteness of humanity with an ethic of self-realization. We will look for this solution in the distinction between the different ways in which "self-realization" can be understood and developed, between higher and lower types of self-realization. Among the ways in which the human being identifies itself, those that most comply with its being undetermined, i.e. those that are most open to many possibilities, will be higher. Instead of a morality that fixes humanity to such an extent that it loses that which distinguishes it from other animals and makes the human being "an *animal*, literally and without reservation or qualification," we seek a different morality, one that does justice to this "old faith" according to which the human being is not an animal but "almost God" (GM III. 25). Does not Nietzsche after all oppose the moral and religious fanaticism which is dominated by "a single point of view and feeling," a freedom which is "practiced in maintaining [itself] on insubstantial ropes and possibilities" (GS 347)?

But after having taken notice of the radical and all-encompassing nature of Nietzsche's critique of morality we must be cautious. Will we, with our distinction of higher and lower forms of self-realization, not in fact exclude a certain morality from the critique? And if we can make such a distinction at all, must we not hold ourselves to Nietzsche's own distinction between the morality of herd animals and "the other types, above all *higher* moralities" (BGE 202)? Let us first take another look at the well-known distinction between the two types of morality: the morality of the masters and that of the slaves. I would like to make two observations with regard to Nietzsche's introduction of this distinction.

First, concerning the characteristics of both types of morality. The most important characteristic of the morality of the herd is that it negates all distinctions and all differences between human beings. It is a systematic denial of antagonism, distance, tension, and struggle. The morality of the herd is an ideology of equality. For that reason it cultivates culpability: the subordination under a highest authority to whom everyone is equal. It cultivates charity as a kind of universal brotherhood that unites all human beings. It cultivates unselfishness as an instrument which destroys individuality and difference. The morality of the masters, on the contrary, strengthens these differences. It lives from a "pathos of distanciation."

According to Nietzsche, the distinction between masters and slaves, between those who give and those who take orders, is even constitutive of humanity in a certain respect. The violent overthrow that he places at the beginning of moral and political history really establishes the distinction between animal and human. By this process those who are subjugated develop into the type in whom bad conscience may arise. And those who subjugate develop in such a way that a strong and powerful type may arise. The latter affirm and cultivate this fundamental distancing and, with it, the difference, antagonism, distance, order of rank, tension, and struggle which are denied by the lower type. Nevertheless it is the morality of the herd that has conquered, and which has become the one and only morality in Europe (and in those countries where Europe's influence is dominant).

This victory of the morality of the herd is expressed in many ways: in the popularity of democracy and socialism, which both declare the herd autonomous and which both deny the difference between master and slave; in the ideology of human dignity and (equal) human rights; in the process of assimilation of the contemporary European, in which he loses his own identity, and which yields to mediocrity and makes out of the human being a "useful, industrious, multi-functional and multi-employable herd-animal" (*BGE* 242), "something eager to please, sickly, and mediocre [. . .] the European of today" (*BGE* 62). The fact that morality today always addresses itself in Europe to "the" people, i.e. to all people equally, is a clear manifestation of the victory of herd morality: it denies the original and principal difference among people and moreover creates uniformity where only difference, even antagonism, exists. And with that the herd morality constitutes a threat to the development of humanity.

The second observation is connected here, and is remarkable: Nietzsche does not want to replace the morality of the herd by the morality of the masters. In the place of herd morality he wishes to see a revival of the struggle between the two types as an inversion of the current situation in which only one dominates.

The first essay of the *Genealogy* is one long description of the struggle between these two types of morality and their conceptions of struggle, difference, order of rank, and distance. The strong subject and oppress the weak and to this end, where necessary, battle them. Among themselves there is a power struggle that guarantees that they will compete with mutual respect. The weaker ones, on the other hand, remove themselves from the competition. But secretly and inwardly they tell themselves that they are actually "better" than those to whom they submit. They form a close family in their collective hatred of the strong. But, instead of taking the fight to the strong, they declare themselves victors in the eyes of God, to whom all people are equal; and successfully so.

Whereas for millennia a struggle has raged on earth between competing types of morality, the situation has now almost reached the point where but one type remains. After Nietzsche has once more gone over the history of the struggle in the second-last paragraph of the first essay of the *Genealogy*, he closes the final paragraph with the pathetic question:

> Was that the end of it? Had the greatest of all conflicts of ideals been placed *ad acta* for all time? Or only postponed, indefinitely postponed? Must the ancient fire not some day flare up much more terribly, after much longer preparation? Still more, must one not desire *this* with all one's might? even will it? even promote it? (*GM* I. 17)

And in one of the last sections of the Third Essay he writes:

> What is the meaning of the *power* of this ideal, the monstrous nature of its power? Why has it been allowed to flourish to this extent? Why has it not rather been resisted? The ascetic ideal expresses a will: *where* is the opposing will that might express an *opposing ideal*? The ascetic ideal has a *goal* – this goal is so universal that all the other interests of human existence seem, when compared with it, petty and narrow; it interprets epochs, nations, and men inexorably with a view to this one goal; it permits no other interpretation, no other goal; [. . .] Where is the match of this closed system of will, goal, and interpretation? Why has it not found its match? – Where is the other "one goal"? (*GM* III. 23)

Nietzsche's critique attacks every morality, but especially that kind of morality which rules as if it were the only one. Not only because it is in fact predominant, but also because – more than any other type of morality – it denies the existence of other types. If Nietzsche pleads for another type of morality, it is in the framework of and as a precondition for the struggle between moralities.

It is as if we are forced to conclude that Nietzsche's critique of morality is inspired by a morality which says that there should be other moralities, several different moralities that are in conflict with each other. What strange kind of morality is this?

3 The Morality of the Critique

In order to explore this Nietzschean morality we will have to make a brief detour through what one could call "Nietzsche's metaphysics" (even if this is a metaphysics between quotation marks). Let's have a quick look at his thought of the will to power.

3.1 Will to power and struggle[3]

From *Zarathustra* onwards, Nietzsche states in different formulations that everything, i.e. the world, is will to power. On the one hand this obviously sounds like a metaphysical statement. It does what metaphysics always tries to do: it says something about all reality. But on the other hand it can be misleading to call it a metaphysical statement, because calling it that could reinforce the idea that Nietzsche reduces all reality to one metaphysical principle, or that he interprets the world in terms of the metaphysical distinction between appearance and reality-as-it-is-in-itself, e.g. the Schopenhauerian "will." In order to prevent this incorrect interpretation, we should remember that according to Nietzsche there is no ultimate metaphysical entity. There is one reason for this, which is that, according to Nietzsche:

> All unity is unity *only* as *organization and co-operation* – not different from how a human community is a unity – thus *opposed* to an atomistic *anarchy*, therefore a *pattern of domination* that *signifies* a unity but *is* not a unity. (*KSA* 12, 2[87])

> Everything that enters consciousness as "unity" is already tremendously complex: we always have only a *semblance of unity.* (*KSA* 12, 5[56])

If Nietzsche says that all reality is will to power, he means that reality is the interaction of wills in the plural. Even these wills are no ultimate entities, but figures of the interaction of wills, and so on without there being an ultimate reality. Reality is what is happening between wills to power.

What else could happen between wills to power than struggle and contest? Power is power over another power. Wills to power try to overpower each other. This means that every willing of power presupposes the resistance of another will to power, another figure of will to power. Will to power is therefore necessarily a plural concept; and the relation between wills to power is necessarily one of struggle or contest.

Nietzsche sees himself as an heir of Heraclitus: reality is becoming, and becoming is interpreted as struggle: *polemos pater panton*. But a struggle can have different outcomes, and different appearances: one of those possibilities is the balance of powers or the armistice. What we usually call an entity, what we perceive as more or less enduring unities, these are – according to Nietzsche – such situations of a balance of powers. In reality they are only transitory moments in an ongoing struggle.

There is another difference between Nietzsche's "metaphysics" of the will to power and what we generally see as metaphysics. Nietzsche puts his thesis forward not so much as a statement about what the world is, but rather as a particular *interpretation* of the world. Even when he categorically states "*This world is the will to power – and nothing else!*" he calls this "a *name* for this world" (*KSA* 11, 38[12]; cf. also *BGE* 36). Nietzsche opposes his interpretation of the world as will to power to other interpretations, e.g. to the scientific interpretation of the world. But science does not see its own interpretation as an interpretation; it considers it to be a description of the facts. Nietzsche on the contrary writes: "There are no facts, only interpretations" (*KSA* 12, 7[60]). He goes even further when he writes: "One should not ask: '*who* then interprets?' but interpreting itself, as a form of will to power has existence" (*KSA* 12, 2[151]).

Nietzsche presents his thesis of the will to power as a perspective, as his perspectival interpretation, and he opposes it to other perspectival interpretations of the world. This means that the "theory" of the will to power is itself a figure of what it says: it realizes itself in a struggle between interpretations that try to impose themselves on the world. The "theory" of the will to power is homologous to, or in accordance with, the struggle that it describes.

Nietzsche takes reality to mean living (cf. *KSA* 12, 2[172]) and that means doing so in a continual struggle (cf. *BGE* 259). For this reason living is "wanting to be other than this nature" (*BGE* 9), and so the pathos of distance that the strong or higher type represents (cf. *GM* I. 2) is the patent adherence to living thus understood. Through this we can begin to see the connection between the metaphysical and the ethical in Nietzsche's thought, or, better still, the connection between his "metaphysical" hypothesis of reality as will to power and his engagement with a struggle against the one morality which denies the struggle.

3.2 The moral commitment of Nietzsche's thought

In *BGE* 227 Nietzsche calls himself one of the last Stoics. This is not in contradiction with his being the heir of Heraclitus nor with the critique of the Stoics which he also and more often formulates. According to Nietzsche, "the Stoics inherited almost all of their principal notions from Heraclitus" (*EH*, "BT," 4), and what he criticized was mainly not their basic ideas but their perverted interpretation of their own ideas (cf. *BGE* 9). Nietzsche is especially interested in this famous highest moral ideal of the Stoics: the *homologoumenos tei physeizen*, living in accordance with nature. But while he shares this ideal with the Stoics, he disagrees deeply with their interpretation of the *physis*. For Nietzsche nature is not order and harmony but rather chaos and struggle. In an important note we read how Nietzsche tries to interpret this ideal in the light of his metaphysics of the will to power:

> Imagine that the world were false, life could only be understood as based on illusion, under the veil of illusion, in light of illusion: what would "living according to nature" then mean? (*KSA* 11, 40[44]; cf. also *BGE* 9)

This is the key to Nietzsche's ethics: the ideal of living in accordance with nature as being will to power: "The affirmation of passing away *and destroying*, which is the decisive feature of a Dionysian philosophy; saying Yes to opposition and war" (*EH*, "BT," 3).

Stoic ethics prescribes the affirmation of life, nature, reality, as they are: *amor fati*. But reality is will to power, as is the human being who has to affirm reality. The morality that is being criticized by Nietzsche does not affirm reality as it is, but tries to transcend it and arrive at another more true reality, one in which there is no change but eternity, in which there is no struggle but only peace. Where this morality rules as if it were the only one, reality is being petrified into one interpretation. Reality that is not a conflict of interpretations is like a battle that is settled by only one of the parties: it is over. On behalf of life, Nietzsche commits himself to the struggle, the struggle that has no goal outside of itself: "the struggle for the sake of the struggle" (*KSA* 11, 26[276]), the struggle that does not aim at peace, but for which peace is only "the means to new wars" (*KSA* 11, 37[14]).

Even if we recognize the theme of multiplicity and struggle throughout Nietzsche's work, it is not immediately clear what being unified toward reality (*homologoumenos tei physeizen*) could mean if reality is to be taken as struggle. It is clear that in his work Nietzsche always seeks confrontation. Not only is the *Genealogy* "A Polemic" as the subtitle states, but his thought as a whole is substantially polemical. He criticizes "every philosophy that ranks peace above war" (*GS*, preface, 2). But isn't his polemic still an engagement *in* a struggle? The ideal of a wholly integrated, unified, or homological life seems to suggest that we ought to engage with the struggle itself! But what could that mean?

Nietzsche describes the noble as the ideal of such a way of living. Therefore we have to ask the question that is the title of part 9 of *Beyond Good and Evil*: "What is noble?"

3.3 Nobility

In the first part of *BGE* 9 we find a genealogy of nobility: the history of its origins and development, and a psychological and physiological description of "the noble." In the ancient aristocratic societies of which he speaks (cf. *BGE* 262 and *GM* I. 11), groups faced each other in continual struggle. In a later phase of development stability arose and the groups ceased to threaten one another. But as a result the possibility of a new form of struggle developed: competition between individuals: "a splendid, manifold, jungle-like growth and upward striving, a kind of tropical tempo in the competition to grow" in which "savage egoisms [. . .] have turned, almost exploded, against one another" (*BGE* 262). This new form of competition or struggle makes a new form of nobility possible; it creates an aristocracy of the spirit.

Still later, in contemporary Europe, the competitive multiplicity has turned still further inward. In a period such as our own, in which differences between groups and individuals are played down, a type has developed which accommodates *in* itself the variety that used to exist *between* people. Many histories, cultures, and tastes come together in the modern "individual." It goes without saying that such an inner disunion is more distressing and more painful than previously adopted forms. As such it offers a still more sublime form of "nobility." But a morality that tries to avoid or escape such pain eliminates this as a possibility. It would deny the multiplicity and present to humanity but one of the possibilities. "Everything that is imperative in morality addresses itself to the *many masks* we have in ourselves, it wants to bring one to the fore and another not" (*KSA* 11, 40[18]). And we have seen how successful that morality has been and how much it has reduced humanity to an animal that is determined in one fixed direction. Hence the question must be asked once more and in a new and precise fashion: what can "nobility" mean in our time? Nietzsche asks: "what does the word 'noble' still mean to us today? [. . .] under this heavy, overcast sky of the beginning rule of the plebs that makes everything opaque and leaden?" (*BGE* 287).

The uniformity of this overpowering morality stands in stark contrast to the possibilities that we have at this very moment. We gather in ourselves all the possibilities that the richness of history and of cultures offers; we gather all kinds of beliefs, convictions, and tastes. But – the predominant morality forbids us to realize this plurality in a fruitful, which is to say in an agonal or contesting, way. We gather all those possibilities in ourselves, in the same way as we do in our museums. There we bring together ages and cultures that could not tolerate each other. We walk from one room to the next, and we enjoy everything, or at least we find it all interesting. This "postmodern" identity is our proper ignobility, according to Nietzsche. But at the same time it has the capacity in itself to develop a special kind of nobility. Nietzsche explains both sides of this postmodern condition:

> In an age of disintegration that mixes races indiscriminately, human beings have in their bodies the heritage of multiple origins, that is, opposite, and often not merely opposite, drives and value standards that fight each other and rarely permit each other any rest. Such human beings of late cultures and refracted lights will on the average be weaker human beings: their most profound desire is that the war they *are* should come to an end. Happiness appears to them [. . .] as the happiness of resting, of not being disturbed, of satiety, of finally attained unity [. . .] – But when the opposition and war in such a nature have the effect of one more charm and incentive of life – [. . .] then those magical, incomprehensible, and unfathomable ones arise, those enigmatic men predestined for victory and seduction [. . .] They appear in precisely the same ages when that weaker type with its desire for rest comes to the fore: both types belong together and owe their origin to the same causes. (*BGE* 200)

Our age is one in which there is more plurality than ever before. But we do everything possible to escape from the tension that should be included in this plurality. Our predominant morality and our predominant faith make us dream of the happiness of eternal rest; they make us believe in tolerance as a kind of indifferent attitude towards plurality and difference. We turn ourselves into museums, and hide our lack of taste behind our collection of different kinds of taste; or we become scientific and strive for objective knowledge about what we have gathered in order to forget about ourselves; or we use all kinds of narcotics as anesthetics in order not to feel the tension that we harbor (according to Nietzsche, Wagner's music was such a narcotic); or we become desperate when, standing before our wardrobe, we find out that we have disposed of all the costumes of history but have none of our own (cf. *BGE* 223).

But with all this we also have at least the possibility of realizing the final and highest form of nobility: the possibility of realizing the struggle within ourselves. At the end of the First Essay of the *Genealogy of Morals* Nietzsche writes that "today there is perhaps no more decisive mark of a '*higher nature*,' a more spiritual nature, than that of being divided in this sense and a genuine battleground of these opposed values" (*GM* I. 16).

We reach a paradoxical conclusion: nobility in our age means to realize in oneself the struggle between different possibilities that one harbors (even when these different possibilities are themselves typologized in the duality of noble and ignoble). Nobility in our age is living in a continuous struggle within oneself, and thus in a continuous self-overcoming. Nietzsche's moral ideal seems to refer to a being that can be compared to a stretched bow:

> The highest man would have the greatest plurality of instincts, and also in the greatest relative measure which can still be endured. Indeed: where the plant man shows itself strong, there we find the instincts powerfully acting *against* each other. (*KSA* 11, 27[59])

> The wisest person would be the one who is *richest in contradictions*. (*KSA* 11, 26[119])

Maybe we should compare this type to a person who plays chess, or another board game, against him or herself. The players must make both parties as strong as they can. As soon as they win, they lose. In playing a game, such a scenario is more or less possible. It is, however, extremely difficult where ways of living or ideals are concerned: egoism and altruism, individualism and sense of community, peacefulness and aggression, proud self-assuredness and humility, purity and voluptuousness, individual hedonism and solidarity. We can (and we will when we are honest) acknowledge all these possibilities in ourselves. But it seems very questionable whether we can commit ourselves to the struggle between them. Has Nietzsche anything to say about this problem, this apparent impossibility?

3.4 Measure and radical transcendence

What Nietzsche has to say on this heads in two different directions, which can be summarized in the words "higher type" and *Übermensch*.

A struggle without any rules or measure is the specter against which many philosophers have aimed their weapons. And Nietzsche's intensification of the struggle – the idea of the "(in)dividual" as itself a conflicting plurality – seems to bring us (or him) close to madness. Therefore it seems that some measure of the plurality and the conflict is necessary. But at the same time, this measure should not be itself a threat to the living core of all reality, which is struggle and plurality. It should not so much limit the struggle, but rather enable it and promote it. What kind of a measure could this be?

In an unpublished note we read, "the measure of our ideal morality is the measure of our power, under the presupposition that we can raise this power" (*KSA* 9, 4[104]). Human beings can be measured according to the extent to which they manage to keep their controlling force and their inner plurality in balance. Only then will there be the possibility of a continuous overcoming of each and every stage or figure. For any measure should be open to growth and self-overcoming. The forces that are being managed and measured by some standard should not be reduced and weakened, but rather strengthened. Or, more precisely, they may be reduced only temporarily, as long as it is needed for the organization of the whole. But the perspective of this arrangement should always be towards growth and strengthening. In an unpublished note Nietzsche speaks about "the pleasure of maintaining measure" (*KSA* 11, 25[420]). There he compares this pleasure with the "pleasure of the horseman on a fiery horse!" The horseman is of greater quality to the extent to which he is able to ride more fiery horses. And the better horseman will not so much reduce the forces of his horse, but rather stimulate them while keeping them under control. The ideal is not control, but the greatest multiplicity and strength of forces that are still under control. In other words, the ideal is to be able to endure a tense plurality without reducing it along the lines of the ascetic ideal, and without the weakening *laisser faire* of the (post)modern measurelessness.

In the two citations above I left a few words out of the text. More completely (but what can one call "complete" as regards an aphorism?), the notes run as follows:

> The highest man would have the greatest plurality of instincts, and also in the greatest relative measure which can still be endured. Indeed: where the plant man shows itself strong, there we find the instincts powerfully acting *against* each other (e.g. Shakespeare), but measured. (*KSA* 11, 27[59])

401

> The wisest person would be the one who is *richest in contradictions*, who has, as it were, a feel for many types of humanity: in amongst his great moments of grandiose harmony. (*KSA* 11, 26[119])

These texts are concerned with the "highest" or "wisest" man. But in spite of the superlatives, this is not an indication of the final goal. We must therefore look to the other, more radical direction that Nietzsche's answer indicates.

This more radical answer to the question of whether Nietzsche's ideal is humanly possible points to the possibility that it is indeed impossible, and that it is so by design. And with that, a final fundamental characteristic of each morality up to now is criticized and dropped: for why should an ethic per se aim at the survival or well-being of humanity, let alone humanity as we now know it? Why should the *type* "human" be the measure of reality?

We have seen that the idea of the will to power plays an important role in Nietzsche's thought on morality. This will to power has already created many forms of reality and destroyed them as well. Humanity is only one of those forms. It is not only possible but likely that this same will to power will produce new forms, even new forms of life. And why shouldn't it be possible that these new forms surpass humanity, that they should indeed be "*Übermensch*-like"?

Übermensch does not mean "superman," but "overman." There are many examples of this "transcending" movement in Nietzsche's thought. Just a few examples should suffice here: "A people is a detour to get to six or seven great men. – Yes, and then to get around them" (*BGE* 126). The ultimate goal is not identified, but only hinted at, alluded to. *Übermenschlich*, according to Nietzsche himself, is "not to be realized by humanity, only approximated at best" (*KSA* 13, 11[54]). Therefore Zarathustra says: "Never yet has there been an overman" (Z II, "Of the Priests").

Earlier we saw that Nietzsche sought a morality that did justice to this "old faith" according to which the human being was not an animal but "almost God" (*GM* III. 25). The *Übermensch* is frequently connected with God. That does not mean that the old God lives again in the *Übermensch*, but that in the *Übermensch* transcendence is conceived without identification: neither as God nor as humanity. It is an open possibility, which leaves humanity behind. On one occasion where Nietzsche presents this "overhuman" possibility, he refers to the story of Dionysus. Dionysus is the god who seduces human beings and lures them to transcend their limits and to enter his labyrinth (cf. *BGE* 295). Towards the end of his own thinking life, Nietzsche often signed his writings "Dionysus." Can we see it as a final hint by the disappearing thinker that, at that same time that his individuality was falling apart "he" identified himself with many different persons?

See also 7 "Nietzsche and Philosophical Anthropology"; 13 "The Incorporation of Truth: Towards the Overhuman"; 17 "Naturalism and Nietzsche's Moral Psychology"; 19 "The Philosophical Function of Genealogy"; 24 "Nietzsche *contra* Liberalism on Freedom"; 29 "Life and Self-Overcoming"

Notes

1 Cf. also Hill 2003, which seeks to show that the "three pillars of Kant's moral philosophy" (i.e. "rational reconstruction, justification and metaphysical explanation") are echoed in Nietzsche's three essays of the *Genealogy of Morals*.
2 Kaufmann translates: "You shall become the person you are." A "person," however is always only one of the possibilities, as Nietzsche indicates in *KSA* 11, 25[362].
3 This interpretation of the "will to power" is based on that developed in Müller-Lauter 1999.

Editions of Nietzsche Used

Beyond Good and Evil, trans. Walter Kaufmann (New York: Vintage Books, 1966).
Ecce Homo, trans. Walter Kaufmann (New York: Vintage Books, 1967).
The Gay Science, trans. Walter Kaufmann (New York: Vintage Books, 1974).
On the Genealogy of Morals, trans. Walter Kaufmann (New York: Vintage Books, 1967).
Thus Spoke Zarathustra, in *The Portable Nietzsche*, ed. Walter Kaufmann (New York: Viking Penguin, 1954; pbk. edn. 1959; repr. 1976), pp. 103–439.

References

Hill, R. Kevin (2003). *Nietzsche's Critiques: The Kantian Foundation of his Thought* (Oxford: Oxford University Press).
Müller-Lauter, Wolfgang (1999). *Nietzsche: His Philosophy of Contradictions and the Contradictions of his Philosophy*, trans. David J. Parent (Urbana and Chicago: University of Illinois Press).

22

Rebaptizing our Evil: On the Revaluation of All Values

KATHLEEN MARIE HIGGINS

In what do you believe? – In this, that the weights of all things must be determined anew.

(*GS* 269)

In his final year of writing, Nietzsche uses the slogan "revaluation of values" (*Umwerthung aller Werthe*) as a rallying cry:

> *Revaluation of all values*: that is my formula for an act of supreme self-examination on the part of humanity, become flesh and genius in me. It is my fate that I have to be the first *decent* human being; that I know myself to stand in opposition to the mendaciousness of millennia. (*EH*, "Why I Am a Destiny," 1)

Nietzsche's vehemence when suggesting that the historical moment has come for such a revaluation has led some commentators to believe that his idea of revaluation is essentially a matter of the current need for a cultural shift of worldviews. This shift would involve the ousting of reigning moral values and the project of supplanting them with others. The revolutionary tenor of Nietzsche's remarks insinuates that revaluation is an unprecedented historical step, which will lead to Western culture's opting for a new stage of its evolution, one characterized by "living dangerously" (*GS* 283).

Certainly, Nietzsche does propose a reconsideration of many of the moral values in our standing repertoire. He is convinced that if many of our fixed moral ideas were reconsidered, their hold on us would be undermined. Even allowing that these values may have served society (or some component of society) well when they were adopted, Nietzsche believes that the bedrock of our moral presuppositions could not survive thoughtful scrutiny.

Walter Kaufmann interprets Nietzsche's negative agenda as the essence of the revaluation project:

> the "revaluation" means a war against accepted valuations, not the creation of new ones. [...] The "revaluation" is not a new value-legislation but reverses prevalent valuations that reversed ancient valuations. It is not arbitrary, but an *internal* criticism: the discovery of what Nietzsche refers to as "mendaciousness," "hypocrisy," and "dishonesty." (Kaufmann 1974: 111–12)

The revaluation is thus the alleged discovery that our morality is, *by its own standards,* poisonously immoral. (Kaufmann 1974: 113)

One of the perplexities about Kaufmann's reading is how "revaluation of values" relates to another of Nietzsche's recurrent images, that of "the self-overcoming of morality" (*EH*, "Why I Am Destiny," 3). If Christian morality, on its own, will eventually self-destruct, it is not obvious that any new evaluation is necessary in order to accomplish this. Nevertheless, Kaufmann sees the revaluation enterprise as being one with Nietzsche's critique of the Christian moral value scheme, "revaluation" being a term for his attempt to undercut its basic assumptions.

Edgar Sleinis, by contrast, argues that revaluation involves a positive agenda. Revaluation is negative insofar as it functions "to eliminate from the system those artificial value constructs and those modes of organizing and directing life that have been taken to embody genuine values, but that in fact operate to diminish real value overall" (Sleinis 1994: 12). However, the positive objective is already implicit in this description of the negative task. Sleinis sees the objective of revaluation to be an enhancement of aggregate value, with the goal of optimizing it. This task presupposes certain higher-order values which flow directly from Nietzsche's understanding of reality; on naturalistic terms, Nietzsche assumes the value of life and its flourishing.

Sleinis does not restrict revaluation to the project of undermining the Christian moral worldview. He takes Nietzsche to be literally calling for a revaluation of *all* values. This interpretation invites the challenge that the revaluation project is not obviously coherent for it presupposes commitment to certain values as the criteria for judgment. Sleinis responds, "Nietzsche utilizes an extensive array of strategies for investigating the phenomena of valuation that do not rely on the antecedent embrace of values or substantive values" (1994: 21). Sleinis acknowledges that values are involved in the formulation of an evaluation of current values. For example, even when one determines that one or more of the values upheld by the tradition are internally or mutually inconsistent, one relies on cognitive values. The cognitive values on which such an assessment depends must themselves be recognized as open to revaluation if "all values" are really to be revalued. Nevertheless, Sleinis submits that "not every kind of strategy has to work against every kind of value" (1994: 197), and he defends the internal consistency of the revaluation project. One might consistently use cognitive values in the course of revaluing certain values, so long as one subjects these cognitive values to examination in a separate moment of revaluing.

I agree with Sleinis that Nietzsche's conception of "revaluation" is a much richer and more positive project than Kaufmann admits. I also agree that revaluation involves a variety of strategies. Yet I think that Sleinis's account, largely owing to its abstract character, insufficiently acknowledges the role of the individual reassessment in Nietzsche's revaluation project. I will interpret the project in a manner that differs from those of both Kaufmann and Sleinis, for I will focus on the role of personal revaluations in Nietzsche's project. I am convinced that Nietzsche's authorial strategies quite often aim to prompt individual reconsiderations on the part of his readers, and that these efforts at incitement are an important part of his own efforts at revaluation.

Seen in this way, the revaluation of values is something more than the agenda for society that Nietzsche announced in his last year of sanity but ultimately failed to realize. On my view, revaluation is fundamental to Nietzsche's positive agenda, the effort to re-naturalize spirituality and to seek naturalistic strategies for giving one's life meaning in the context of the current, disillusioned, modern world.

At this juncture I should comment on what I mean when I call Nietzsche's aims and strategies "naturalistic," for "naturalism" is understood variously by different Nietzsche scholars. "Naturalism" as I understand it stands in contrast to "supernaturalism." Nietzsche asserts that any value that has significance for human beings has value in earthly terms, not on the basis of some purported otherworldly goal. I do not agree with the construal of Brian Leiter, therefore, that Nietzsche's naturalism should be understood as requiring that "philosophical inquiry [. . .] should be continuous with empirical inquiry in the natural sciences" (Leiter 2002: 3). That is, I disagree with this view of Nietzsche's naturalism if "continuous with" means that the natural sciences (as currently understood) are to set the standards for philosophical research. I have no problem with attributing to Nietzsche a weak form of "methodological naturalism" (in Leiter's vocabulary) in that Nietzsche favors open-ended empirical observation and experimentation. "Naturalism" in this sense proposes for philosophy an approach with a generic resemblance to that involved in the sciences. Philosophy, according to Nietzsche, seeks insight into how we might best live in the context of the natural world, the world that science aims to describe.

I think it is a mistake, however, to insist that Nietzsche's "naturalism" takes the natural sciences as its primary philosophical paradigm. In the first place, this is something of an anachronism. The term *Wissenschaft*, which is translated "science," has a broader scope than "the natural sciences," and includes the approaches of many traditional fields in the humanities. Nietzsche's comments referring to "scientific" method in connection with philosophy call for intellectual rigor and honesty, as well as openness to discovery through observation. At times he does praise the insights of particular natural sciences or scientists (for example in *The Gay Science* section "Long Live Physics!", although he even there he uses "physics" so broadly that one might construe it to mean "the study of nature," as Kaufmann suggests) (GS IV. 335n.: 267). But I see little evidence that Nietzsche favored the methods of the sciences over those of the arts for philosophy. I interpret his references to the arts and the sciences in connection with philosophy as provocative images, not as clarifications of disciplinary boundaries.

Secondly, Nietzsche is also quite critical of adopting science as the center for interpreting our life in the terrestrial world. Nietzsche did express strong enthusiasm for science at certain points, particularly during the period when he wrote *Human, All Too Human*, and he retained an admiration for experimentation (although the experimentation he encourages is more often that of lifestyle and psychological stance than that of the laboratory). However, he was also critical of the scientific worldview. By the time he wrote *The Gay Science*, which appeared not long after *Human, All Too Human*, he had already become concerned that the scientific worldview was a new mythology that harbored "shadows of God" in the wake of God's "death," i.e. the Western world's abandonment of its former God-centered understanding of reality. The scientific worldview, according to Nietzsche, provides a basis for people to belittle themselves, much as they did in considering their relationship to the God of monotheism. Human beings are no longer interpreted as "sinners," but as mere epiphenomena of natural forces in an undistinguished part of the universe.

406

Nietzsche sees science, when glorified as the source of truth, as an instrument for avoiding the psychological consequences of the death of God while reinforcing the negative view of human powers that belief in God instilled. Far from promoting a naturalism that takes science as paradigm for relating to the world, Nietzsche explicitly calls for his new naturalism in opposition to some of the slogans of science in his time. In *The Gay Science*, after urging his readers to beware of scientific images such as "natural law," nature as a machine, and the "organic processes" of nature, he proposes an alternative: "When will all of these shadows of God cease to darken our minds? When will we complete our de-deification of nature? When may we begin to 'naturalize' humanity in terms of a pure, newly discovered, newly redeemed nature?" (GS 109).

The image of humanity as seen against the background of a newly redeemed and innocent nature is an image of paradise as experienced by humanity before its confrontation with God. Nietzsche urges a spiritually renewed outlook, not burdened with the baggage of either a religious tradition that always interprets human beings as lacking or its scientific replacement. Far from insisting that modern humanity understand itself in scientific terms, Nietzsche presents this option as one of its gravest dangers. Nietzsche is a naturalist in that he interprets the natural world as our home. He is not urging that we see ourselves in terms of the abstract world theorized by scientists.

In order to gain a sense of what revaluation of values might mean on a personal level, let us consider one of Nietzsche's aphorisms from *Beyond Good and Evil*: "The great epochs of our life come when we gain the courage to rechristen our evil as what is best in us" ("Die grossen Epochen unsres Lebens liegen dort, wo wir den Muth gewinnen, unser Böses als unser Bests umzutaufen") (*BGE* 116). The terminology of this statement is evocative. I will focus on three of its terms: "great epochs," "rechristen," "evil."

The aphorism's concern with "great epochs" in our lives imaginatively compares the dramatic structure of one's individual life to that of the history of peoples. As Nietzsche envisions societies, the culture of any particular people has its own unfolding and eventual decline. No society endures for ever, and each is in a transient state throughout its existence. The achievement to be desired in a society is not absolute invulnerability; instead, a society's life is genuinely valuable if during its trajectory the society achieves its own kind of greatness.

By employing the image of a personal life's "great epochs," Nietzsche portrays the individual's experience similarly, as a quest for its own greatness. We encounter here an idealized mode of self-assessment, one in keeping with the theatrical idealization of ourselves that Nietzsche praises in *The Gay Science*.

> Only artists, and especially those of the theater, have given men eyes and ears to see and hear with some pleasure what each man is himself, experiences himself, desires himself; only they have taught us to esteem the hero that is concealed in everyday characters; only they have taught us the art of viewing ourselves as heroes – from a distance and, as it were, simplified and transfigured – the art of staging and watching ourselves. Only in this way can we deal with some base details in ourselves. (GS 78)

Art enables us to appreciate our potential for greatness in part by distracting us from ugly facts. Yet Nietzsche is also asserting that a hero *is* concealed in our everyday characters, like Michelangelo's hero concealed in the rock he sculpts. To fulfill one's individual potential in a positive way, it is first necessary to see it. The impact of recognition here is comparable to that involved in the observation of Nietzsche's Zarathustra, "That which we recognize in a person we also inflame in him" (Z I, "On the Flies of the Market Place"). Zarathustra is warning his listeners here that attending to a fault in another person tends to draw it into operation. The passage on artistic self-idealization indicates that Nietzsche is convinced that positive evaluations are also galvanizing. The aphorism about "our great epochs" hints at why this may be so.

In the aphorism we are considering, the recognition of one's own potential for greatness arises in the context of "rechristening." This image is rather surprising given Nietzsche's rejection of much of his religious heritage. Yet Nietzsche here, as elsewhere, sees that heritage as offering insight into the conditions for meaning in life (even if he rejects its specifically religious views). The aphorism draws on the traditional characterization of baptism as a sacrament of radical transformation, which is to have repercussions for the entire future of the baptized individual. Baptism marks a radical change, a new beginning that puts a previous mode of experience behind one. It not only marks such a change, it initiates it. Baptism opens a sacred dimension for the baptized person, which is to enlarge the person's conception of their experience henceforth. The baptized individual begins a new stage of experience, whatever direction their life might take. In this respect, baptism is both forward-looking, and open-ended. It reveals new possibilities and at the same time *prepares* the individual for coping with future eventualities.

Baptism readies the individual for the adventure of a new life, and it does so by *declaring* the person ready. The words used in baptism constitute, in the jargon of twentieth-century philosophy, a performative act, in which the ritual pronunciation of words brings about a new state of things. Words accomplish the baptismal transformation, and a word, in the form of a conferred name, also signals that such a transformation has taken place.

Significantly, the community symbolically acknowledges baptismal transformation through the use of the baptismal name (even though this is most often the same as one's secular name). In this respect christening resembles the process by which values take their place as part of the standard operating procedures of a society, a process that Nietzsche describes with some concern in *The Gay Science*.

> This has given me the greatest trouble and still does: to realize that what things *are called* is incomparably more important than what they are. The reputation, name, and appearance, the usual measure and weight of a thing, what it counts for – originally almost always wrong and arbitrary, thrown over things like a dress and altogether foreign to their nature and even to their skin – all this grows from generation unto generation, merely because people believe in it, until it gradually grows to be part of the thing and turns into its very body. What at first was appearance becomes in the end, almost invariably, the essence and is effective as such. How foolish it would be to suppose that one only needs to point out this origin and this misty shroud of delusion in order to *destroy* the world that counts for real, so-called "*reality*." We can destroy only as creators. – But let us not forget this either: it is enough to create new names and estimations and probabilities in order to create in the long run new "things." (GS 58)

The terminology of "performative acts" was not in vogue in Nietzsche's time, but he marvels at the conjuring power of words, and at the solidity of "things" brought about so contingently. Words enable one to draw attention to some aspect of experience, drawing particular features of some phenomenon into the foreground of awareness while leaving others in the background. Creating abstract boundaries around a "thing," according to Nietzsche, involves an imposition of foreign categories onto it. But as time passes, the name and the thing become organically conjoined in a linguistic culture's imagination.

The act of appropriation involved in the creation of "new things" by naming depends on human judgments, both the namer's judgment that something is worth identifying and the confirming judgment of others who accept the new coinage. The creation of things by means of new names is itself a matter of evaluating, indeed of *revaluing*, some field of reality that was previously construed differently. In this *Gay Science* passage, Nietzsche himself is drawing attention to something hitherto unidentified: the highly contingent nature of value "creation" and the social dimension of any value judgment that "takes." Values come to be through human invention, but they become part of a society's standard operating procedure when the act of naming is accepted across a group. As we will see, these two moments of individual selection and societal acceptance are relevant to Nietzsche's understanding of revaluation generally.

Already in the passage on renaming, revaluation is presented as an ongoing feature of human experience, both individually and culturally. Insofar as individuals express themselves in an innovative fashion and others accept their innovations as meaningful, revaluation is a fundamental and recurring feature of our linguistic mediation of the world. This passage is counter-evidence to the view that Nietzsche's conception of the ideal mode of legislating values is completely solipsistic. Insofar as human beings continue to make new efforts to interact more effectively or simply freshly with the environment, and use language to do so, they will engage in revaluation. Nietzsche's ambivalence about the ease with which people can transform the world through language is not, I think, a fundamental doubt that such transformation must happen interpersonally. Instead, I see it as reflecting his distaste for the herdlike way in which most of us agree with any judgment that others accept. Indeed, he thinks we all do this too easily, himself included, and his admonitions that would-be creators of values should go into solitude are offered as antidotes to this tendency (e.g. GS 50). Nietzsche presupposes that the individual interacts with society to such an extent that we need to exercise our individual uniqueness lest it atrophy. By comparison with the person who develops his or her individuality, the herd member is actually more solipsistic. The herd member's performance has so completely collapsed into the forms demanded by the group that the socially vitalizing tension between individual perspective and group outlook is pre-empted.

Despite his worries about the effects of linguistic conjuring, Nietzsche does not renounce the practice, but instead expresses his hope that people might become more conscious of this process. Perhaps, just by recognizing how contingent our revaluations are, we will recognize them both as our own handiwork and as subject to revision.

To return to the aphorism from *Beyond Good and Evil*, we are now in a position to make sense of what Nietzsche means by "one's evil."

Immediately following the reference to "christening," this reference to "evil" is the kind of inversion that we have learned to expect from Nietzsche. The traditional practice of baptism does indeed "christen" a person who is tainted by evil, at least (as in infant baptism) the evil of "original sin." Indeed, the notion that human beings are "evil" is presupposed by the sacrament. Yet the "evil" itself is not renamed by Christian baptism. Baptism involves the individual's explicit rejection of evil, through the performative act of pronouncing vows.

According to Nietzsche, the notion of "evil" is one of the "things" that human names have brought into being. Quite consistently, he uses the term "evil" to indicate negative value judgments that have gained traditional acceptance. In his accounts of master and slave morality, for example, Nietzsche distinguishes "evil" (the resentful, slavish judgment that one ascribes to the persons and traits of those with advantages over oneself) from what is "bad" (the "masterly" judgment that something or someone is inimical to the achievement of one's goals). After analyzing the differences between the kinds of "goodness" opposed by "bad" and by "evil," Nietzsche remarks,

> Whoever begins at this point, like my readers, to reflect and pursue his train of thought will not soon come to the end of it – reason enough for me to come to an end, assuming it has long since been abundantly clear what my *aim* is, what the aim of that dangerous slogan is that is inscribed at the head of my last book *Beyond Good and Evil*. – At least this does *not* mean "Beyond Good and Bad." (*GM* I. 17)

Indeed, Nietzsche thinks that prudence dictates that we avoid certain types of actions, whether or not the tradition has labeled such actions "evil."

> It goes without saying that I do not deny – unless I am a fool – that many actions called immoral ought to be avoided and resisted, or that many called moral ought to be done and encouraged – but I think the one should be encouraged and the other avoided *for other reasons than hitherto*. We have to *learn to think differently* – in order at last, perhaps very late on, to attain even more: *to feel differently*. (*D* 103)

Nietzsche denies that he wants to recharacterize categories of action hitherto deemed evil as desirable across the board. Murder and cruelty, paradigmatic evil categories, do not become good if we reject the judgment "evil." Instead, Nietzsche urges more particularized and more thoughtful evaluation of such actions. Sometimes, instances of behaviors and attitudes deemed "evil" by the moral tradition are better understood as symptoms of vitality instead. But to recognize this requires judgment.

"Evil," as Nietzsche uses the expression, is a conventional, human invention. As he most often uses the term "morality" (taking it to be equivalent to Christian, "slave" morality), "evil" is the moral judgment *par excellence*. The moral tradition uses "evil" as its term of moral condemnation. "Evil" is a deeply incorporated term, as Nietzsche understands it. The moral tradition names a behavior or attitude as inherently repugnant by calling it "evil," and we actually do feel revulsion, on cue, in many instances. Moreover, the Western tradition implies with its term "evil" that something is objectionable on absolute grounds.

Nietzsche's remark about refraining from certain actions for different reasons than hitherto indicates his grounds for rejecting judgments of "evil." First, he does not think that actions can be judged as a class on absolutistic grounds. Particular actions should be assessed in the context of particular circumstances and with respect to the goals of all parties concerned, some of which are more fundamental than others. Revaluation in this sense involves taking a fresh look at actions that have traditionally been dismissed as whole categories, and assessing them in the context of particular situations.

Second, Nietzsche is concerned about the extent to which we have absorbed the tradition's rejection of certain types of actions on a visceral level, as a kind of "second nature." This concern is related to his general ambivalence about the power of language to produce effects in the world. By means of categorizing actions as "types" and labeling some of these types as "evil," we have physically incorporated unconscious, programmed responses to whatever behavior is conventionally analyzed in this way. Nietzsche thinks that consciousness should be used to reassess actions that are now categorically rejected on the level of inculturated "gut responses."

What kind of "evil," then, does Nietzsche propose should be rebaptized? I do not think he is proposing that actions should continue to be evaluated in general terms, so that what the tradition calls "evil" should now be called "good." That would be a revaluation, of course, but a simple-minded one. The broad sweeps with which moral judgment has been made and those with which it has been criticized in some quarters strike Nietzsche as a reason why revaluation is so important. He comments dismissively of his contemporaries, seemingly allies, who join him in trying to assess morality historically in Book V of *The Gay Science*:

> These historians of morality [. . .] do not amount to much. [. . .] Their usual mistaken premise is that they affirm some consensus of the nations, at least of tame nations, concerning certain principles of morals, and then they infer from this that these principles must be unconditionally binding also for you and me; or, conversely, they see the truth that among different nations moral valuations are *necessarily* different and then infer from this that *no* morality is at all binding. Both procedures are equally childish. [. . .] Even if a morality has grown out of an error, the realization of this fact would not as much as touch the problem of its value.
>
> Thus nobody up to now has examined the *value* of that most famous of all medicines which is called morality; and the first step would be – for once to *question* it. Well then, precisely this is our task. – (GS 345)

The kind of "evil" that is rechristened in Nietzsche's aphorism is a trait that is understood to be one's own (perhaps but not necessarily shared with others), one that has been traditionally assigned the judgment "evil." In other words, such a trait is deemed by the reigning moral worldview to be a fundamental deficiency on absolute criteria. To recognize "evil" in oneself is a long-standing practice in the Christian tradition. One must recognize one's moral failings in order to repent and become receptive to God's grace. Nietzsche proposes a reconsideration of this scenario.

In the first place, Nietzsche does not think it is much of an accomplishment to "recognize" evil in oneself. As Christian institutions have evolved, they have entrenched the basic value scheme of good and evil so completely and hegemonically that one would be hard put not to identify oneself as a "sinner." Luther's characterization of the spirit and the flesh at war with one another inside the soul is one formulation of a basic presupposition of Christian self-examination. One has good features, evil features, and some that might go either way. One's moral vocation can only be accomplished if one ensures the victory of the good over the evil, ideally enlisting the help of traits that could go either way.

Nietzsche, however, thinks that this way of approaching one's character and one's life stunts one's growth as an individual. Too much energy is consumed in self-loathing, and for relief, one usually seeks some external standard, often in the form of some "more evil" person by comparison with whom one can feel morally superior. This strategy contradicts the supposedly "loving" approach that Christianity preaches; thus Nietzsche accuses the typical Christian of moral hypocrisy. On more naturalistic criteria, self-hatred is hardly good for one's health; instead, it makes one more likely to fail (on any front) because failure was what one was expecting. The "good and evil" method of approaching self-understanding obscures certain subtle discoveries about one's capacities, for one keeps flipping between the two extremes of self-judgment, like someone playing "he loves me/he loves me not."

Nietzsche urges us to recognize that our "evil" traits have become so because we have lost sight of the fact that they can be anything but deficits. The great moments come when we consider our personal traits as a complex system, and recognize that each has multiple potentials, depending on how one uses it in the larger context. When we rechristen our "evil" to the extent of rejecting the ascription "evil," we eliminate the self-torturing mechanism of seeking the "truth" about our characters, as if such a "truth" could be established once and for all: "Am I good? Am I a bad person?" This mechanism, although it might seem a sign of moral sensitivity, is actually a means of dulling our capacity for judgment, as Nietzsche sees it. This mechanism is the moral equivalent of only looking to the bottom line, with little appreciation for how one gets there. If we stop judging some characteristic as "evil" or our inner "demon," Nietzsche suggests, we can see it as part of who we are (at least at this point in time), and as part of our wherewithal for dealing with our experiences. We should stop imagining that our ethical work is done when we judge ourselves good or evil. Instead we should consider our "evil" trait's full range and try to develop our skill in fine-tuning the way we use it. We would embark on this effort if only we dropped the "evil" judgment from thinking about the trait.

When we rechristen our "evil" as that which is *best in us*, however, we do more. We take a view of ourselves that is thoroughly different from the one we've developed or assimilated. It is easy enough to think of some of Nietzsche's self-doubts in this light. His biography suggests that he had looked for some fault in himself when he experienced religious doubts, and that he sometimes questioned whether he wasn't profoundly self-indulgent for pursuing the life of a solitary writer instead of that of a respectable householder. At moments when he rebaptized one of these "evils," he seems to have felt reborn. "Then my life hasn't been a mistake?" Nietzsche writes to Peter Gast, who had just written to praise his *Zarathustra* (*Selected Letters*, 211).

Of course, Nietzsche was no foreigner to melodrama, and one might take this remark as par for the course (and also self-indulgent). Yet Nietzsche appears to have certainly asked himself this question – "Is my life a mistake?" – rather frequently. I think this is the kind of question that prompts him to write the aphorism about rechristening one's evil. To judge one's traits "evil" ensures that one will judge one's life a "mistake" in some serious sense. To rebaptize one's supposedly "mistaken" tendency as one's greatness is to overcome the question.

Although rebaptizing one's own evil sounds rather bizarre, we rebaptize the evil of others with some frequency, especially when we overcome some hostility or resentment toward them. Loung Ung, a Cambodian author who has published her memoirs of her childhood during the reign of the Khmer Rouge, claims that for many years she thought her mother a terrible mother (Ung 2000). The reason was that her mother told her children to leave home and head to a distant orphanage. Only later did she realize what superhuman love it must have taken. Her father had been killed by the Khmer Rouge, and her mother recognized that all of their lives were in peril. She sent her children away from home and into danger, while trying not to frighten them, because she knew that this was their only chance to survive.

Such a revaluating realization about someone else can be transformative. It can be the thought that coincides with the more complex psychological process of forgiveness. Certainly, such a realization dissolves some internal rigidity in one's attitude. What Nietzsche tells us is that this can happen with ourselves, too.

Examples of such rechristenings are bound to be deeply personal, for they presuppose a situation of psychological rigidity and negativity toward oneself. I will consider some illustrations of rebaptizing evil that he suggests, not always in so many words, in part with the aim of displaying the variety of forms such revaluations can take.

One instance of "rebaptizing one's evil" that Nietzsche proposes is that of the "dreamer," the poet who has developed an inferiority complex toward those "men of action" who really "make something of themselves." Clearly including himself among such dreamers, Nietzsche comments,

> Whatever has *value* in our world now does not have value in itself, according to its nature – nature is always value-less, but has been *given* value at some time, as a present – and it was *we* who gave and bestowed it. Only we have created the world *that concerns man!* – But precisely this knowledge we lack, and when we occasionally catch it for a fleeting moment we always forget it again immediately; we fail to recognize our best power and underestimate ourselves, the contemplatives, just a little. We are *neither as proud nor as happy* as we might be. (*GS* 301)

Nietzsche reiterates, in large measure, his assessment of the artist mentioned above, as one who has enabled all of humanity to recognize the hero within. However, Nietzsche is here reminding the artist and the contemplative person to recognize his or her own value and essential role in the human community. Precisely because you are a contemplative, he tells himself along with others, you are a man of action.

Another illustration of a revaluation, this time a humorous one, is suggested by Nietzsche's notes regarding his plans for *Thus Spoke Zarathustra*. He considered titling the book "Zarathustra's Idleness," and he remarks "Zarathustra's idleness is the beginning of all evil" ("Zarathustras Müssiggang ist aller Laster Anfang") (*KSA* 9, 12[112]). The joke here is a joke on the moralist, again with the suggestion that the dreamer should not feel inferior on that account. Zarathustra, the prophet who announced the distinction between good and evil, was historically "the beginning of evil." It was his judgment, his declaration, that brought about this "thing" (see *EH*, "Why I Am a

Destiny," 3). Ironically, however, later moralists, building on this invention, promote endless activity, lest one be tempted in any pause to engage in evil behavior. This is ironic since Zarathustra, as Aristotle might have remarked, had to have leisure, or idleness, to introduce moral value into the world. The modern moralist who is in some sense Zarathustra's descendant could only judge the precondition for the division between good and evil – Zarathustra's idleness – evil (see Higgins 1997: 82–98 and 2000: 151–66).

A third revaluation of a personal sort that Nietzsche considers is that concerning the moralistic outlook on pursuing one's own agenda. Nietzsche's repeated defenses of "selfishness," in which "selfishness" seems to be self-determination of one's own direction in life, suggest that he had real ambivalence about his strong sense of his personal direction, his "vocation." Although he has many arguments against pity (which he seems to see as the kitsch approach to morality), one of his challenges to a morality centered on pity is that it shows no respect for the person who protects his time and energy in order to pursue his own vocation. He contends, for example,

> Indeed, those who now preach the morality of pity even take the view that precisely this and only this is moral – to lose one's own way in order to come to the assistance of a neighbor. I know just as certainly that I only need to expose myself to the sight of some genuine distress and I am lost. And if a suffering friend said to me, "Look, I am about to die; please promise me to die with me," I should promise it; and the sight of a small mountain tribe fighting for its liberty would persuade me to offer it my hand and my life – if for good reasons I may choose for once two bad examples. All such arousing of pity and calling for help is secretly seductive, for our "own way" is too hard and demanding and too removed from love and gratitude of others, and we do not really mind escaping from it – and from our very own conscience – to flee into the conscience of the others and into the lovely temple of the "religion of pity." (GS 338)

Nietzsche concludes that the enthusiasm with which young men enlist when a war breaks out can be explained similarly:

> Rapturously, they throw themselves into the new danger of death because the sacrifice for the fatherland seems to them to offer the long desired permission – to dodge their goal; war offers them a detour to suicide, but a detour with a good conscience. (GS 338)

If we recall these various discussions, I think we might revalue some of Nietzsche's least appealing comments, such as those on poverty in *The Gay Science*. These fairly repugnant remarks include the following:

> It is raining, and I think of the poor who now huddle together with their many cares and without any practice at concealing these: each is ready and willing to hurt the other and to create for himself a wretched kind of pleasure even when the weather is bad. That and only that is the poverty of the poor. (GS 206)

> He is poor today, but not because one has taken everything away from him; he has thrown away everything. What is that to him? He is used to finding things. It is the poor who misunderstand his voluntary poverty. (GS 185)

414

"There is no lack of courtesy in using a stone to knock on a door when there is no bell"; that is how beggars feel and all who suffer some sort of distress; but nobody agrees with them. (*GS* 204)

One interpretation of this set of passages is that Nietzsche is advocating that the well off ignore the poor, and even saying that the poor bring on their own problems. Either sentiment would be offensive, even if, as I think we should recognize, Nietzsche was rather naive about poverty, not having BBC or CNN News or photojournalistic documentation of the dehumanizing conditions under which some people in the world live. (On the other hand, given his contempt for Zola's attempts to portray human misery realistically, Nietzsche might not have found our news networks to be fonts of insight either.) Nietzsche presents "voluntary poverty" like his own (his choice not to pursue material wealth) a reasonable illustration of poverty, even though one would hope that he recognized that some people were involuntarily without certain basic material supports.

I think this set of passages is a case, a rather extreme one, of Nietzsche's provocative challenges to the reader. I cannot imagine that he thought his readers would not take umbrage. A particular range of his possible readership would surely find this distasteful, among them the "socialists" of his era, with whom he continually takes issue.

In these passages, Nietzsche is certainly re-evaluating some of the socialists' judgments, if not his own, particularly the view that class structure determines who are allies and who are enemies. The voluntary poverty remark indicates his own view that one's possessions or lack thereof are not the determining factor of whether one's way of life is satisfactory.

However, Nietzsche does not deny that the poor are poor. The rainy days passage asserts that they are poor, but that the standard Lord or Lady Bountiful has no conception of their real plight. Nietzsche is no doubt naive to assume that the poor are not really unable to make ends meet. But supposing that one's having or lacking possessions is not the primary standard of one's well-being, as he suggests, one needs to look elsewhere to understand poverty. Those who are impoverished to a serious degree are more spiritually than materially undermined, he suggests.

When one feels deprived and incapacitated, according to Nietzsche, one is motivated to demonstrate one's potential to affect things, even if one is only in a position to needle those around one. Far from forming a community of class-consciousness, deprivation motivates one to alienate precisely those with whom one shares an unfortunate set of circumstances. Far from feeling solidarity with other members of one's economic class, one becomes so desperate to feel effectual that one will needle one's dearest friend just to feel a bit of power. In part, Nietzsche is offering an account of the psychology of deprivation.

As the comment about the beggar and courtesy indicates, he is also suggesting that one's orientation toward society as a whole is transformed by poverty, in a way that is self-undercutting. The beggar, whose very approach to staying alive involves interacting with and persuading those who are materially better off than he or she is, is overwhelmingly conscious of being deprived. This overwhelming awareness is the internal aspect of what John D. Jones has called the "social death" involved in profound poverty (Jones 1986–7).

The beggar in Nietzsche's story has abandoned civility toward others because he or she feels that others have abandoned civility first (not offering the beggar a doorbell). This reasoning, so presented, makes some sense. And yet Nietzsche points out that it is absolutely unpersuasive toward those the beggar wants to summon. The beggar's sense of victimization, however justified by objective circumstances, exacerbates the situation that the beggar finds objectionable. His gesture is tantamount to burning the bridge before anyone has had a chance to use it (or perhaps biting a hand before it has the chance to feed him).

Nietzsche's remarks are overstated, and yet they do offer a perspective from which we can reconsider the interactions between the poor and the wealthy, and perhaps diagnose the impasses often involved. They also illustrate Nietzsche's strategy of provoking reassessments on the part of his readers. We can imagine a variety of tones of voice in which Nietzsche might make these remarks (cynical, non-emotional, self-justifying, etc.), the variety corresponding to a range of ways in which we might be offended. What is clear is that they prompt a response from the reader and a reconsideration of what Nietzsche just said. Many of Nietzsche's aphoristic works operate similarly. They incite something akin to a conversation in which the reader is baited to reply, at least sometimes, "Wait a minute! I don't know about that! Surely that overstates the point."

Aphorisms *always* overstate the point, and Nietzsche's do so more than most. They function in Nietzsche's project of revaluation in at least two ways. First, they cause the reader to do double takes. Second, they create a facsimile of a conversation between Nietzsche and the reader, and eventually between the reader in the first moment of response and the reader who has reconsidered. Each judgment that Nietzsche makes in such writing is limited in its scope, and many are barbed. They are thus geared to prompting the reader's challenges – but also the reader's further reflections on why Nietzsche (or his persona) might make such a disagreeable claim. Aphorisms are designed to prompt reverberating reassessments (the more so because they are relatively easy to recall and to reconsider again and again). As an authorial strategy, they are particularly good at provoking the ongoing activity of revaluation that Nietzsche encourages.

None of the revaluations Nietzsche proposes are absolute, even if he is firmly convinced that certain long-standing values cannot survive critical reassessment. What I have tried to indicate by considering various modes of revaluing one's evil is that Nietzsche includes as part of his revaluation strategy reconsiderations that are highly personal and evolving. Nietzsche does not consider the individual transformations effected by such rebaptizing to be either anti-social or entirely predictable. Indeed, they may be interpersonally jarring, for they can involve organic changes in one's outlook that affect how one proceeds. Yet such transformations provide the potential for a more "live" interaction between the individual and the larger human world. Rebaptizing one's evil eliminates a motive for narrowly egotistical power plays at others' expense, the sense that one is deficient, which inspires the desire to see deficiencies in others as well. It thus allows one the flexibility to judge with less encumbrance and thus more appreciatively. In this respect, it makes the boundaries between oneself and others more porous, because one is able to move in imagination more freely.

Nietzsche believes that the imaginative freedom to feel connected to all humanity while engaged in one's personal heroic adventure is the key to life's meaning. It is also the only wealth available that really nurtures human beings. This, at any rate, is how I read *GS* 337, the passage with which I will close.

> Anyone who manages to experience the history of humanity as a whole as *his own history* will feel in an enormously generalized way all the grief of an invalid who thinks of health, of an old man who thinks of the dreams of his youth, of a lover deprived of his beloved, of the martyr whose ideal is perishing, of the hero on the evening after a battle that has decided nothing but brought him wounds and the loss of his friend. But if one endured, if one could endure this immense sum of grief of all kinds while yet being the hero who, as the second day of battle breaks, welcomes the dawn and his fortune, being a person whose horizon encompasses thousands of years past and future, being the heir of all the nobility of all past spirit – an heir with a sense of obligation [. . .] if one could burden one's soul with all of this – the oldest, the newest, losses, hopes, conquests, and the victories of humanity; if one could finally contain all this in one soul and crowd it into a single feeling – this would surely have to result in a happiness that humanity has not known so far; the happiness of a god full of power and love, full of tears and laughter, a happiness that, like the sun in the evening, continually bestows its inexhaustible riches, pouring them into the sea, feeling richest, as the sun does, only when even the poorest fisherman is still rowing with golden oars! This godlike feeling would then be called humaneness.

See also 2 "Nietzsche and the Art of the Aphorism"; 6 "Nietzsche's 'Gay' Science"; 17 "Naturalism and Nietzsche's Moral Psychology"

Editions of Nietzsche Used

Beyond Good and Evil, trans. Walter Kaufmann (New York: Vintage Books, 1966).
Daybreak, trans. R. J. Hollingdale (Cambridge: Cambridge University Press, 1982).
Ecce Homo, trans. Walter Kaufmann (New York: Vintage Books, 1967).
The Gay Science, trans. Walter Kaufmann (New York: Vintage Books, 1974).
On the Genealogy of Morals, trans. Walter Kaufmann and R. J. Hollingdale (with *Ecce Homo*) (New York: Vintage Books, 1967).
Selected Letters of Friedrich Nietzsche, ed. and trans. Christopher Middleton (Chicago: University of Chicago Press, 1969).
Thus Spoke Zarathustra, trans. Walter Kaufmann (New York: Viking, 1966).

References

Higgins, Kathleen Marie (1997). "Waves of Uncountable Laughter," in John Lippitt (ed.), *Nietzsche's Futures* (London: Macmillan), pp. 82–98.
—— (2000). *Comic Relief: Nietzsche's "Gay Science"* (New York: Oxford University Press).
Jones, John D. (1986–7). "Poverty as a Living Death: Toward a Phenomenology of Skid Row," *Philosophy Research Archives*, 12, pp. 557–75.

417

Kaufmann, Walter (1974). *Nietzsche: Philosopher, Psychologist, Antichrist*, 4th edn. (Princeton: Princeton University Press).

Leiter, Brian (2002). *Nietzsche on Morality* (London: Routledge).

Sleinis, Edgar (1994). *Nietzsche's Revaluation of Values: A Study in Strategies* (Urbana: University of Illinois Press).

Ung, Loung (2000). *First They Killed My Father: A Daughter of Cambodia Remembers* (New York: HarperCollins).

23

Nietzsche's Fatalism

ROBERT C. SOLOMON

My conception of freedom. [. . .] What is freedom? That one has the will to assume responsibility for oneself.

(*TI*, "Expeditions of an Untimely Man," 38)

It is now commonly supposed that Nietzsche subscribes to a number of striking doctrines which might be described as "fatalism" if not as a kind of "biological determinism." Fatalism, strictly understood, means that nothing could be other than it is, and Nietzsche's much-quoted comments in *Ecce Homo* provide some good evidence that he might, sometimes, have believed this: "that one wants nothing to be different, not forward, not backward, not in all eternity. Not merely to bear what is necessary [. . .] but to *love* it"(*EH*, "Why I Am So Clever," 10). His persistent emphasis on "instincts," "drives," and "physiology" suggests biological determinism while he famously ridicules both the Kantian–Schopenhauerian notion of "will" and the idea of "free will." He sometimes insists that each of us has a particular "nature" which (whether actualized or not) cannot be altered, thus defending a particularly strict version of determinism. Of course, fatalism and determinism are two very different theses, the latter still philosophically respectable, the former not so. But many commentators have argued that Nietzsche holds both theses, often by conflating them.

And yet, Nietzsche is often classified and taught along with the "existentialists," in part because he is an early advocate of "self-creation." Like Søren Kierkegaard and Jean-Paul Sartre, Nietzsche defends what one might call "the existential self," the individual who "makes himself" by exploring and disciplining his particular talents and distinguishes himself from "the herd" and the conformist influences of other people. Nietzsche seems to attack the very idea of freedom and with it the existentialist idea that we are free and responsible to make ourselves, but I think his views are more subtle than his bolder statements would suggest. Nietzsche may celebrate the ancient concepts of "fate" and "destiny" that Sartre, in particular, rejects as exemplary of "bad faith," but the question is whether Nietzsche's many comments and occasional arguments in favor of "the love of fate" (*amor fati*) and against "free will" undermine any interpretation of his philosophy in terms of "self-creation."

I want to argue that Nietzsche's fatalism and Nietzsche's "self-making" are ultimately two sides of the same coin and not at odds or contradictory. I will argue that Nietzsche embraces rather than dispenses with the notion of responsibility and, in particular, the responsibility for one's character and "who one is." Thus I want to defend the imperative tone of one of Nietzsche's most oft-quoted comments: "What does your conscience say? – You shall become the person you are" (*GS* 270).

Nietzsche on Freedom and Fatalism

If one interprets what Nietzsche has to say about self-making along the lines of Kant and the infamous free will problem, then the combination of fatalism and self-making surely will appear to be at odds. And if one interprets Nietzsche's conception of fatalism along the lines of the thesis of scientific "determinism" one will also find that there is little "wriggle room" for the kind of self-making thesis that Nietzsche advocates. True, Nietzsche is an enthusiastic advocate of the scientific method (during some periods of his career, at least). But it does not follow that he is a determinist. Indeed, he has some incisive skeptical comments on the concept of causality. Most important, however, are the differences between determinism and the scientific outlook, on the one hand, and fatalism and Nietzsche's concept of fate on the other. In brief, fatalism is not determinism, and Nietzsche's acceptance of the former has almost nothing to do with the latter. It is rather a harking back to the ancient Greek notion of *moira*, or fate, and has little to do with modern scientific thinking.

Whatever else it may be, self-creation is not a human version of what Nietzsche thinks is impossible even for God, namely creation *de nihilo*. We cannot act as a *causa sui*, "bootstrapping" our way into selfhood. Nor does it require or involve any break from natural laws, like Kant's noumenal subject, the target of many of Nietzsche's most ferocious attacks. Self-making, which is ultimately a kind of self-cultivation, is by no means independent or separable from one's native talents, one's "instincts," one's environment, the influence of other people and one's culture. It is not a matter of "making oneself" on a basis of absolute ontological freedom (as Sartre famously insists) but of "becoming who you are." This strongly suggests that self-making ("becoming") already embraces fatalism ("who you are"). Self-becoming does not involve "free will," but, nevertheless, Nietzsche, like Sartre, is a staunch believer in personal responsibility.

I do not see any conflict (much less a "paradox") between Nietzsche's fatalistic and self-making themes, but rather an excellent example of his "perspectivism." Fatalism and self-making represent two complementary perspectives on ourselves and on human life. On the one hand, there is our familiar view of ourselves as (more or less) autonomous beings, deliberating, making choices, acting on our desires, sometimes reflecting on and weighing our desires, sometimes conscientiously denying our desires (or refusing to be motivated by them). It is from this perspective that we normally hold people (and ourselves) responsible for their (our) actions and declare them (and ourselves) to be the "authors" of their (our) actions. On the other hand, we cannot but recognize that we are all "thrown into" our circumstances, born with (or without) certain talents and abilities to varying degrees and with or without dispositions to certain physical liabilities and limitations. We are all products ("victims" some would say) of our upbringing, our families, our culture. Even without bringing in such spooky words as "fatalism," we recognize in ourselves and in others the heavy baggage of our backgrounds and the fact that our choices and our so-called autonomy are both quite limited. We take up one or other of these perspectives, often sequentially, even simultaneously, but I do not see this as a problem or a "paradox" (Leiter 1998: 217). It is, rather, just "the human condition." We see ourselves as both free and constrained, which is not quite (yet) to say "fated."[1]

One powerful argument in favor of Nietzsche's strong sense of responsibility, quite apart from any thesis regarding free will, is his heavy use of what I call the *blaming* perspective, according to which people are held accountable as the authors or agents of their actions. Of course, their actions can also be praised and they can be forgiven, but I think "blame" best captures the essence of this perspective, both as Nietzsche pursues it and, admittedly, as he sometimes exemplifies it as well. The blaming perspective presupposes a robust sense of agency. It thus tends to emphasize responsibility and be suspicious of excuses. To be sure, in *On the Genealogy of Morals* Nietzsche urges us both to get "beyond good and evil" (Essay I) and to get over our felt need to judge, to blame, and to punish (Essay II).[2] But it would be difficult to read virtually any of Nietzsche's writing without noticing the harsh denunciations that permeate his style. Nevertheless, it would be a mistake to simply assume that the blaming perspective necessarily presumes the heavy metaphysical baggage of "subject," "Will," and "free will" that Nietzsche also so frequently criticizes.

Nietzsche expresses disgust with the blaming perspective, but he nevertheless exemplifies it as no other philosopher. He holds people responsible for what they do, but as exemplary of their "natures" and their virtues and not so much because of their choices and decisions. Thus one can blame a person and ascribe responsibility without at the same time insisting on the truth of those metaphysical theses summarized under the heading of "free will" just as one can recognize that a person is bound by his or her "nature" without subscribing to the "hard" thesis of scientific determinism.

Fatalism, Determinism, Destiny

Nietzsche's "fatalism" should be distinguished from "determinism," although, as I shall argue, the two are interestingly connected. "Determinism," of course, has been interpreted in very sophisticated ways, depending on the causal or scientific paradigm. "Fatalism," by contrast, has been interpreted in a great many dismissive ways.[3] Fatalism has been taken to be just the tautological thesis "what will be, will be" (rendered more romantically by Doris Day *en Español* as *Ché sera sera*" in Hitchcock's *The Man Who Knew Too Much* of 1956). Literally interpreted, of course, this saves the thesis at the expense of rendering it trivial and utterly uninteresting. But this is not what it means. It is rather a note of resignation, acceptance of what has happened or will happen. Thus fatalism has been interpreted in terms of "God's will" and "predestination," though this is clearly not what Nietzsche meant by it. It is also worth noting that many Christian thinkers and theologians have sharply distinguished God's will, grace, and providence from any sense of fate or fatalism, which they associate with paganism. And this, of course, is just what makes it so appealing to Nietzsche.

Fatalism, unlike determinism, is an ancient thesis (or set of theses). It is sometimes interpreted in terms of some sort of agency called "Fate" or, more atavistically, it is interpreted as the intervention of "the Fates," assuring the relegation of fatalism to ancient mythology and now representing only a quaint bit of poetic license. Thus

Daniel Dennett expresses the overriding current view about fatalism when he dismisses it as the "mystical and superstitious" thesis that "no agent can do anything about anything" (Dennett 1984: 123). Fatalism has been given a metaphysical interpretation, for instance in Mark Bernstein's 1992 study, *Fatalism*, but Nietzsche's fatalism is clearly not a metaphysical thesis. It rather harks back to his beloved pre-Socratic Greek tragedians. It is an *aesthetic* thesis, one that has more to do with literary narrative than with scientific truth. In this sense, fatalism has little to do with determinism. There need be no specifiable causal chain. There is only the notion of a necessary outcome and the narrative in which that necessity becomes evident. Thus Oedipus was "fated" to do what he did, whatever causal chain he pursued.

Determinism and fatalism would seem to make two quite different claims. The first insists that whatever happens can (in principle) be explained in terms of prior causes (events, states of affairs, inherent structures, plus the laws of nature). The second insists that whatever happens *must* happen, but there need be no effort to specify the causal etiology behind the modal "must," although it would also be a mistake to interpret fatalism as *excluding* any such effort. To be sure, Oedipus's behavior and its terrible outcome can be explained, step by step, as one event causing another. But that would surely miss the point of the narrative, which is that the outcome is fated but the path to the outcome is not. Thus it is important that we neither reduce fatalism to determinism nor oppose the two in such a way that determinism becomes the respectable scientific thesis while fatalism is relegated to ancient mythology and poetry. For example, to insist that fatalism depends on the whims of the gods or frivolous fates or any other mysterious force is to render ridiculous (and in any case most un-Nietzschean) a sensible and defensible philosophical concept.

Sensible? Defensible? Fatalism doesn't have to be mythology. Nietzsche's favorite "pre-Socratic" philosopher Heraclitus presented such a sensible vision when he declared, "Character is fate" (*Fragments* 104, in Kahn 1981). This is a perfectly plausible and easily defensible notion of fate. It is not in any way incompatible with a causal or scientific explanation, but it also entails the narrative structure that is essential to fatalism. So, too, Aristotle based his theory of tragedy on the notion of a "tragic flaw" or *hamartia* in the tragic hero's character, and today the tragedy of Oedipus is still "explained" by appeal to his obstinacy, his refusal to listen to Teiresias, or his tyrannical arrogance (see Bowra 1945; Nussbaum 1986). Hume's answer to the free will problem, and later Mill's as well, was to say that an act is "free" if it "flows" from a person's character (Hume 1973; Mill 1874). One might object to the vagueness of "flow" here, but I would suggest that it suits the issue far better than "cause," which too readily separates cause and effect, character and action. One might try to assimilate fatalism to determinism by restricting one's focus on "fate" to dispositions both to behave in certain ways and to get oneself into certain kinds of situations. But this, I think, is only half of the picture. Fatalism, in contrast to determinism, begins at the end, that is, the outcome, and considers the outcome as in some sense necessary, given the nature of the person's character, which in turn entails a protracted narrative which, all things considered, encompasses the whole of that person's life, culture, and circumstances.

Determinism's emphasis on causality introduces a distortion and a narrowing that neither the ancients nor Nietzsche would have countenanced. Nietzsche, of course, expresses multiple and often profound concerns about the status of causality and causal relations, especially in his late work, *Twilight of the Idols*. But even earlier, when he was fully within the orbit of science, for example in *Gay Science*, he expresses deep doubts about the abuse and overuse of such concepts (*GS* 112). A number of commentators have written at considerable length about Nietzsche's "naturalism" and his various attempts to reconcile science, his perspectivism, and his theory of interpretation, and I will not try to summarize them here (see Cox 1999). But at the very minimum, what "Nietzsche's naturalism" excludes is any reference to God, miracles, supernatural explanations, or any notion of divine purpose or design (including those in Greek mythology). What we need for Nietzsche, therefore, is a "naturalistic" conception of fate and fatalism.

I think we find one, clearly stated, in one of the texts of Nietzsche's so-called middle period, *Daybreak*:

> *What we are at liberty to do.* – One can dispose of one's drives like a gardener and, though few know it, cultivate the shoots of anger, pity, curiosity, vanity as productively and profitably as a beautiful fruit tree on a trellis; one can do it with the good taste of a gardener and, as it were, in the French or English or Dutch or Chinese fashion; one can also let nature rule and only attend to a little embellishment and tidying up here and there; one can, finally, without paying attention to them at all, let the plants grow up and fight their fight out among themselves – indeed, one can take delight in such a wilderness, and desire precisely this delight, though it gives one some trouble, too. All this we are at liberty to do, but how many know that we are at liberty to do it? Do not the majority not *believe* in *themselves* as in complete *fully developed facts*? Have the great philosophers not put their seal on this prejudice with the doctrine of the unchangeability of character? (*D* 560)

I would compare this to Nietzsche's better-known, slightly later comment that one should "give style to one's character" (*GS* 290), where Nietzsche again pushes the idea of "cultivation" and perhaps also to *Twilight of the Idols* "Morality as Anti-Nature" (section 1), where he talks about "the spiritualization of passion." The gardening metaphor is an old favorite in the naturalism literature (leaving aside for the moment the rather difficult question of the will and ways of the gardener). But it makes clear that Nietzsche does not abandon any notion of control or responsibility in his defense of naturalism, and it makes equally clear that he does not endorse the "prejudice" or the philosophy that would "seal" it that our fates are "fully developed facts," which is what the cruder forms of determinism would suggest.

Considering the garden imagery, it should also be clear that Nietzsche's naturalism does not exclude the concept *teleology*. I would argue that his concepts of fate and fatalism are naturalistically teleological. Nietzsche criticizes *theological* teleology as a mode of explanation, but there are also the purposes that are evident in every living thing. (Indeed, Nietzsche's notion of "the will to power" would be unintelligible without teleology in this sense, as would all of his talk of "drives" and "instincts.") Thus it is important not to make determinism and teleology into incompatible competitors as modes of explanation. Biology is full of examples in which teleology and determinism complement one another. To mention only the standard example: the heart pumps in order to circulate the blood throughout the body *and* the heart pumps because it is made of innervated muscle. Nietzsche, like Aristotle before him, is a biologist. He is always asking about the purpose and function of human attitudes, beliefs, and behavior. One might object that he is also a Darwinian, and that natural selection undermines purposiveness, but this is again a rejection of only the notion of some *external* purpose, or some purpose that rules the whole of evolution, not the rejection of purposes as such. (We might also note that insofar as Nietzsche embraced Darwinism – a complex and interesting question in itself – it was before Darwinism had been definitively severed from teleological thinking.)

The teleology of fatalism is clearly captured in those places where Nietzsche dramatically speaks of "*destiny*," a concept that was quite popular in the nineteenth century. (Consider the American imperialistic concept, "Manifest Destiny.") In *Ecce Homo*, Nietzsche considers his own life and career under the rubric, "Why I Am a Destiny." Destiny is not just a necessary outcome. It is an outcome that is necessary given some larger sense of purpose as well as the character, abilities, and circumstances of the person. And it presupposes culture and history, a context in which destiny can play itself out. Thus it was Goethe's destiny to be the first great German internationalist and it was Einstein's destiny to turn the world of physics on its head. But one cannot imagine a Goethe without a European world in which literature was just becoming international and Germany was gaining respect in the artistic world, or Einstein in a world that was not ready to consider the implications of relativity and the possibilities of weapons of truly mass destruction. To be sure, one can restate these claims by analyzing how Goethe's and Einstein's respective genius *resulted in* their respective successes. But it is worth noting what is lost thereby. What gets lost is the purpose-driven *significance* of the narrative. One cannot understand destiny just by understanding how (causally) the outcome came about.

So, too, Nietzsche's destiny is unimaginable without understanding not only his tremendous talent but his character – including his occasional megalomania – and his culture, which was indeed at the cusp of a revaluation due to what Nietzsche famously called "the death of God." One can explain, as many biographers and commentators have done, why (causally) Nietzsche may have written such-and-such a work at such-and-such a time, given his previous works, his mind-set and aspirations, and what was going on in his life (e.g. the break with Wagner, his disappointment with Lou Salomé, his various illnesses). But the strategy and tone of such accounts is rarely just by way of "explanation." It is also by way of celebration of Nietzsche's astounding posthumous success and how he got there. It was Nietzsche's fate to be famous, and to be abused by his sister, and consequently to be enormously misunderstood. We can debate to what extent he may have brought this on himself and to what extent he was a victim, but in doing so we are largely debating the *significance* of Nietzsche's destiny, not its causal etiology.

Whatever Nietzsche's views on science and scientific determinism (and I do not think that these are by any means either clear or consistent in the textual evidence), his "fatalism" consists almost entirely in his intimate and enthusiastic engagement with the fatalism of the ancients (Sophocles, Aeschylus, Heraclitus) and as a rich way of viewing our lives in which we are neither victims of chance and contingency nor Sartrean "captains of our fate." One might even say, alluding to another of Nietzsche's better-known bits of euphoria, that we are more like the oarsmen of our fate, capable of heroic self-movement but also swept along in a sometimes cruel but open sea.

424

Nietzsche's Classical Fatalism

In ancient tragedy, a staggering variety of curses and wars was usually due to the intervention of gods and goddesses. Thus ancient fate and destiny are straightforwardly teleological, that is, they serve the (often petty and whimsical) purposes of the Olympians. In Christian "predestination," similarly, the outcome is determined by God according to his purposes, mysterious though they may be. But in the ancient world, fate was distinct from the gods, and the gods are often depicted as themselves constrained by fate (though not usually its victims). And though fate is clearly presented as necessity, it is by no means clear that it involves anything like agency or any person's (or divinity's) purpose. Only occasionally is fate personified as "the Fates," in which case both agency and purpose can be presumed, but Nietzsche would obviously reject this, even as metaphor, as he would reject any "otherworldly" conception of fate. It is worth noting that in Christian thought fate and fatalism are pointedly opposed to free will, which is defended as the hallmark of the Christian worldview, certain famous paradoxes notwithstanding. Thus in defending fatalism Nietzsche is by no means buying into Christianity nor is he in any way compromising his naturalism. On the contrary, his embracing fatalism is just one more aspect of his rejection of the otherworldly. Ancient fatalism is by no means to be equated with the purposive behavior of divine agency.

The greatest Western text on fate, Homer's *Iliad*, makes many striking observations which surely influenced Nietzsche's thinking on these matters. It is worth noting that for Homer, as for Nietzsche, there was no emphasis at all on the distinction between fate and fatalism. Homer speaks solely of fate. Belief in the Judeo-Christian God, by contrast, insofar as it involves a version of fatalism (for example, in the notion of "God's will"), is distinctively opposed to any notion of fate (that is, of any agency or ultimate significance of what happens apart from God). Fate, for Homer, cannot be gainsaid. Not even the gods – not Zeus himself – can countermand fate.[4] So, too, Nietzsche suggests that our fate cannot be countermanded, and our only option is therefore to "love it."

But fate, in both the *Iliad* and in Sophocles' *Oedipus Tyrannus*, does not make men do what they would not do. Rather, fate (like the gods) arranges circumstances such that what a man would "naturally" do determines the inevitable outcome, for example, when proud and hot-headed Oedipus encounters Laius on the narrow crossroad near the foot of Parnassus. Achilles, grieving over the death of Patroclus, tells his men that he like his friend is "fated to redden the selfsame earth with [his] blood, | Right here in Troy I will never return home" (Homer 1998: 18. 350–1). Hector, at the beginning of the *Iliad*, has made a similar speech, to the effect that no one will send him to Hades before his time, though to be sure he is fated like all the others (6. 512–13). Nietzsche, in line with these ancient models, talks frequently of fate (as in *amor fati*) but really refers only to fatalism. That is, he urges us to appreciate the necessity and significance of outcomes without reference to any mysterious agency. Here he clearly sides with Heraclitus, and he might be argued to be equally opaque with regard to the extent to which character is agency and regarding how character and specific actions are related. One might say that, for Nietzsche, character *is* agency and thus embodies both

425

freedom and necessity (a position associated with David Hume as well: Hume 1973: 400ff.).

Nevertheless, Nietzsche goes out of his way to avoid agency-talk even regarding intentional action. Thus his fairly frequent "quantum of energy" talk (e.g. *GS* 360), where the metaphor of a quantum that "discharges itself" can be assimilated to the more commonsense picture of character as the underlying force that manifests itself in any number of actions (in which conscious purposes may be irrelevant or merely secondary). In *BGE* 232 Nietzsche writes of that "granite of spiritual *fatum*, of pre-determined decision," thus rendering even decisions as fatalistic and not clearly matters of agency. In *Beyond Good and Evil*, too, Nietzsche relishes talk of "physiology," thus lending his views to a kind of materialistic reductionism in which agency plays no role. At the far extreme of Nietzsche's thinking, he comments in the *Nachlass* (and I always suspect the status of anything that is only in the *Nachlass*), "everything has been directed along certain lines from the beginning" (*WP* 458). This is, indeed, not only fatalism but a victimized way of thinking about the utter pervasiveness of fate.

But "directed" *by whom?* No gods or God, to be sure. Here Nietzsche has surely gone beyond his ancient mentors suggesting not that *some* acts, events, or outcomes are necessary but rather that *all* are. I am tempted to simply dismiss this as one of Nietzsche's more outrageous and unsuccessful (and unpublished) thought experiments, except that it highlights in its extremity a sensibility that is evident throughout the mature Nietzsche, and its source is not hard to find. The sensibility is that there is some pur-poselessness "behind" the conscious agency of our actions. For Schopenhauer, of course, this purposelessness was located in the impersonal and irrational Will. For Nietzsche, this purposelessness is attributed to more scientifically respectable processes, notably "instinct," "drive," and other biological "agencies," much as it is, nearly 50 years later, in Freud's later works (regarding the ego, id, and superego). I think that both Freud and Nietzsche would be horrified at the mechanization of these concepts in what is now sometimes called "psychic determinism" or, in Nietzsche, various deterministic revisions of his so-called "will to power" (see Richardson 1996). Contrary to adopting an impersonal determinism, Nietzsche quite enthusiastically accepts an ancient Homeric conception of fate that sees a personal and, if not benevolent, then at least neither malevolent nor "indifferent" (as in Camus), determination of our possibilities and their outcomes. When he speaks of his own "destiny" (in *Ecce Homo*), whether ironic or not, he makes it clear just how enthusiastic he is in his "love of fate," not as an abstract philosophical thesis but as a very real and palpable way of thinking and feeling about one's own life.

Nietzsche's Watchword, "Become Who You Are"

Nietzsche's watchword is "Become who you are." (Cf. the subtitle of *Ecce Homo*, "Wie man wird, was man ist.") This short phrase captures Nietzsche's position in a non-paradoxical way. One *is* insofar as one has predetermined and limited possibilities – one's talents, abilities, capacities, disabilities, limitations. A child at an early age (perhaps almost from birth) displays a real talent for music, for language, for special relations, for gymnastics, for dancing, for leadership. But it is perfectly obvious that these promising possibilities are no more than that, that they require development, encouragement, training, practice, and dedication. But one *becomes* what one is, and thus cultivating one's character goes hand in hand with Nietzsche's conception of fatalism. If one believes that we are all talented and limited in different ways (including what we might call our meta-talents, such as self-discipline, which have to do with our ability to foster our talents), then it more or less follows that we are free to develop (or not) our talents (free, that is, insofar as we have the talent). Thus Nietzsche's existential imperative tracks Kant's famous example of the categorical imperative, the "duty" to realize one's talents.

We may not be free regarding what talents we have and, therefore, what talents we might choose to develop, but it does not follow that we are not free or responsible. Moreover, most people have more than one talent and are therefore free to choose among them. Nor is this to deny that the development of any talent can be thwarted by any number of external and internal factors, such as lack of opportunity, the absence of adequate role models or exemplars, a paucity of praise and encouragement or (worse) an excess of discouragement and even ridicule, or a debilitating mishap or accident. What's more, one does not always know whether or not one has a talent, and in most disciplines one can develop some approximation of talent even without it. Sometimes one must choose among competing talents, and the resulting clash of talents may result in an inability to choose them. But, again, this is no argument that we are not free or responsible for developing our talents. Nietzsche tells us to "create ourselves" and with that "invent new values," but always *in accordance with* our inborn abilities and limitations.

The notion of self-creation admits of many variations. At one extreme, there is the Kantian (some would say Sartrean) "bootstrapping" version that would have it that we create ourselves *de nihilo*, by sheer will or decision. We act as an original cause for which there are no prior determining causes, presuming that "there are in the world causes through freedom" (Kant 1996: B472) Regarding any such detached and metaphysically suspect sense of self-making, it is clear that Nietzsche has no tolerance for it. But I see no evidence that even the most gung-ho advocates of Nietzschean self-creation, for example, Alexander Nehamas and Richard Rorty, entertain any such position. At the other extreme, there are those hard determinist interpretations, to the effect that all that is meant by "self-creation" is the development or "unfolding" of the self. Just as an acorn grows into an oak, albeit within the determining network of life-supporting factors in the environment (water, weather, soil quality, surrounding flora, marauding fauna), a person's character manifests itself in actions, subject to the action-determining factors of the environment. Of course, to make sense of such a position, some of these factors will have to be conventional rather than causal, that is, determining what a bit of behavior "counts as" rather than what effectively brings it about. But self-creation thus means just the development of the self, nothing more.

The Kantian conception of the noumenal self is too extravagant, and the determinist account of self-creation too stingy, to capture either the conceptual complexity of self-creation or the richness of Nietzsche's proposals. I think a large part of the problem is due to the fact that the self-creation issue is too often conflated with the notorious free will problem. The purported analyses of self-creation track one or another of the "determinist-compatibilist-libertarian" resolutions of the free will problem and this leads

427

to the entire issue getting sucked into the black hole of the very metaphysics Nietzsche so clearly denounces. I do not think that Nietzsche has anything to say about *that* problem. Rejecting a philosophical issue is not the same as taking a stand on it. Thus Nietzsche on "free will." In his nomadic (though hardly "free-wheeling") life and in his wildly unrestrained works no one is more appreciative of freedom than Nietzsche. But for the philosophical debates surrounding "free will" and the uses to which this very technical notion has been put Nietzsche has nothing but contempt. To confuse this with some thesis to the effect that Nietzsche "rejects freedom" would be absurd.

Nietzsche surely accepts the commonsense vision, summarized in Goethe's simple but elegant phrase "freedom within limitations." There are, as Daniel Dennett suggests, notions of freedom that are well worth defending, but the metaphysical paradoxes surrounding the *causa sui* are not among them. I think that Nietzsche would even accept something like the Kantian thesis, which I think lies at the heart of Sartre's theory too, that "every being who cannot act except under the idea of freedom is by this alone – from a practical point of view – really free" (Kant 1982: 100). Nietzsche would add, to be sure, that this is "only an interpretation," perhaps therefore a "fiction" as well, but it is from such a "practical point of view" that Nietzsche's account must be understood, and "fiction" is by no means always a term of abuse in Nietzsche, as we all know.

Any advocate of perspectivism, and I think Kant in his fashion was one, will find no fault with such a view. Sometimes, for instance when we take ourselves to the doctor, we view ourselves under the rubric "physiological system in distress." But most of the time, when we are deliberating and deciding what to do in particular, we take our bodies for granted as "instruments" and "we act under the idea of freedom." To do so is in no way to reject the truth of determinism.[5] All of this gets terribly confused when the determinism in question involves such social and psychological issues as one's upbringing and "influences," or such issues as victimization, but the supposed paradox or contradiction – *determinism or free will?* – seems not to be either a paradox or a contradiction at all, just one more manifestation of the phenomenologically curious fact that we are not just objects in nature but conscious of ourselves and our role in nature and society.

"Free will" (construed as some sort of metaphysical or ontological claim) is not necessary for freedom, nor for self-making. All that we need is a robust concept of *agency*. But agency is by no means a simple concept, and the literature on this subject has become as technically complex as the literature on free will. Indeed, for obvious reasons, the two tend to overlap and mutually refer to one another. But I would suggest that here, as so often in philosophy, there is no single concept of agency and the concepts of agency employed depend on a number of different contrasts, for example, between something being imposed and something being chosen, between an action being coerced and an action "freely" (that is, non-coercively) chosen, between behavior that is habitual or "automatic" and behavior that is the result of deliberation. As an abstraction, I am not sure that "agency" means much of anything, except as a general contrast with, say, the natural processes described in physics, physiology, and chemistry or the "behavior" of a computer. Nietzsche writes, "Do we really want to permit existence to be degraded for us like this – reduced to a mere exercise for a calculator?" (*GS* 373).

428

Agency requires the actions of a self (and self, I think, requires the notion of agency). Thus people create themselves through their actions, many of which may not be the products of deliberation or any conscious volition. Indeed, it is with something of a shock that most of us wake up, some late morning well into life, and realize what we have made of ourselves. The process of "making" has been filled with intentional actions, to be sure, but there may well have been no intention to become what one has become. Alternatively, "one should be careful what one wishes for," for the shock may be precisely that one *has* become what one intended, and now the haunting question is why one ever would have wanted that in the first place! Thus we create ourselves, not, for the most part, consciously or even attentively, but gradually, as Aristotle insisted, by cultivating our character and our "excellences" (or vices). There need not be any "bootstrapping" or mysterious acts of will, nor need there be any problematic commitment to one or another kind of "subject." It is on the basis of one's nature that one has talents, virtues, abilities, and purpose in life, and one's ability to cultivate his or her character or develop his or her talents may itself be subject to abilities and talents with which one is either blessed or not. But what is not in question is the need to cultivate one's character and develop one's talents and take some responsibility in doing this.

Nietzsche on "Free Will"

The question of responsibility might be (cautiously) separated into two aspects: first, the global sense – how one becomes who one is – and, second, what it is to be responsible for a particular action. (It should be assumed that this brief formulation includes "acts of omission" as well as responsibility for events and states of affairs which one's actions – or inaction – bring about.) One way of dealing with Nietzsche's concept of self-creation is to insist that it is the global sense of self-cultivation that concerns him, not responsibility for particular actions. This neutralizes the supposed antagonism with fatalism just because it is obvious, as indicated above, that one creates oneself through his or her actions *whether or not these actions are knowingly so directed*, indeed, whether or not these actions are even fully intentional.

But although Nietzsche (unlike Sartre) says relatively little about responsibility for particular actions, I think that it is important to insist that he does suppose a robust sense of agency and thus responsibility with regard to particular actions. The complication is the idea of "compulsion," which may have seemed clear to Aristotle but certainly not to Freud. Nietzsche sometimes seems to suggest that all of our behavior is compelled, perhaps not so much by external forces (what Aristotle had in mind) nor by forces from the unconscious (what Freud had in mind) but by one's nature and what Nietzsche misleadingly calls our "instincts." Thus the birds of prey in *Genealogy* I cannot help but act like birds of prey, and lambs cannot help but act like lambs. A strong person cannot but be strong, and a weak person cannot but be weak, and the particular actions they perform are thus "compelled" by their natures. Nevertheless, they are responsible for these actions. And it does not much matter whether they deliberate over them (as Nietzsche suggests the slaves often do although the nobles usually do not) or even whether they are fully conscious of what they are doing (which, Nietzsche assures us, the nobles are but the slaves are not).

429

But acting out of one's nature may by itself be ample warrant for ascribing responsibility. David Hume argues this, in the face of the Newtonian determinism of his day. Harry Frankfurt has made a now famous distinction more recently that helps make this clear (Frankfurt 1988: 23). Frankfurt calls a "free action" simply one in which one acts according to his or her desires. If we take it (as Frankfurt does) that free action implies responsibility, then a person who acts in accordance with his or her desires is responsible for that action. This may eliminate compulsive actions and (with some fine-tuning) coercive actions but it includes many "thoughtless" acts and, with some further argument, unintended acts (so long as the outcome is in accordance with one's desires).

But the story does not stop there. Frankfurt distinguishes a "wanton" from a full-blooded person, where a wanton acts *thoughtlessly* on his or her desires. But a full-blooded person is not a wanton. He or she also has "second-order desires," "desires about acting in accordance with one's desires." A person who acts not only in accordance with his or her (first-order) desires but also in accordance with his or her second-order desires acts not only freely but has "free will," according to Frankfurt. This set of distinctions is important in reading Nietzsche for at least two reasons.

First, Nietzsche is often read (on the basis of seemingly clear textual passages) as an "instinctualist," urging us to act "out of instinct" instead of with reflection and deliberation. In the first essay of the *Genealogy*, Nietzsche suggests that the "masters" act like this and it is one aspect of their virtue. Elsewhere, he suggests that the virtues more generally are much more matters of instinct than they are of calculation or reflection. (In *Ecce Homo*, he confesses that he is "an atheist by instinct.") But if acting on instinct is taken to mean acting thoughtlessly or without further motivation or (in Frankfurt's language) without second-order desires, then this is a crude and highly misleading interpretation of Nietzsche.

Even if Nietzsche (like Kierkegaard) harshly criticizes action that is strangled and eviscerated with an excess of deliberation and reflection, he surely urges us to act in accordance not only with our natures (that is, with our first-order desires born of that nature) but with second-order, "higher" goals and aspirations. That is to say, Nietzsche tells us to follow our instincts and not to get distracted by impersonal theories (especially *moral* theories) *but not to the exclusion of higher-order desires and reflection.* We may not be free to change our natures, according to Nietzsche, but that does not mean that we are limited to thoughtlessly acting on their most immediate (and often stupidest) manifestations.

Second, and more directly to the point in question, one might well say that Nietzsche believes in, even insists upon, our "free will," so long as this does not imply some suspicious notion of the subject, as in both Kant and Lutheran Christianity more generally. But "free will" in Frankfurt's sense need not imply any particular view of the subject (apart from the capacity to have and act on higher-order desires) nor any mysterious faculty called "the Will" (see Greenspan 1999). Thus, following Frankfurt, we can interpret Nietzsche as holding that we are free and responsible insofar as we act not only in accordance with our desires, "instincts," and character but in accordance with our higher-order desires (also derived from our character, if they are to be "our" desires). Thus to have free will it is not necessary to deliberate nor even to make a decision.[6] It is enough to act in accordance with one's highest aspirations.

Nietzsche on Responsibility

Nietzsche does not often use the term "responsibility" (*Verantwortung*), and when he does it is more often critically than with Sartrean exultation. But I do not think that it is at all a misreading or a bad interpretation of Nietzsche that places the existentialist thesis of "responsibility for self" at the very heart of his philosophical mission. Nietzsche actually discusses responsibility at some length in at least two places, where, as usual, he is both sarcastic and critical of the concept's history and its abuses without saying much about its positive value (*GM* II. 2; *TI*, "Four Great Errors," 3–7). Nevertheless, it is hard not to see that, as so often, Nietzsche's scorn is mixed with tremendous respect.

In *Genealogy*, it receives its best-known and most protracted treatment:

> Precisely this is the long history of the origins of *responsibility*. As we have already grasped, the task of breeding an animal that is permitted to promise includes, as condition and preparation, the more specific task of first making man to a certain degree necessary, uniform, like among like, regular, and accordingly predictable. (*GM* II. 2)

Responsibility is cited as a "privilege," as a hallmark of individual "freedom" and "sovereignty," awakening "trust, fear and reverence." Its "proud knowledge [. . .] has sunk into his lowest depth and become instinct," what the "sovereign human being calls his *conscience*" (*GM* II. 2). The sneer quotes surrounding such terms as "freedom" and "sovereignty" should be interpreted with some care. Insofar as they point to or presume a Kantian notion of self, they are, to be sure, intended sarcastically. But insofar as they indicate precisely the self-mastery that Nietzsche advocates, they should be treated with appropriate respect. The mixed description of people as "necessary, uniform, like among like, regular, and accordingly predictable" suggests very different images and analyses.

What does "necessary" mean in this context? Is this an allusion to Kant's deontology? "Uniform," "like among like," and "regular" are, of course, intended as insults, but how else would one "breed" animals who can trust one another, and would Nietzsche suggest that trust and reverence (let's put aside fear) are untoward sentiments in any social setting? Does predictability necessarily point to slavish attitudes? I would think, to the contrary, that one of the dangers in dealing with the weak and resentful is their unpredictability, the likelihood that they will act precisely contrary to their own self-interest out of spite. (Consider Dostoyevsky's "underground" man.) And are noble types so unpredictable, by contrast, or does their "virtue" rather require consistency?

The use of the phrase "sunk into his lowest depth" referring to instinct is curious in several ways, not least in the fact that it is unusual (in biology, at least) to speak of *acquiring* an instinct (Nietzsche's Lamarckianism, the inheritance of acquired characteristics?). In what sense are the instincts "low"? This is not Nietzsche's usual way of speaking about them. And assuming that one is talking about the species and not individual acquisition, Nietzsche seems torn between chastising responsibility as "unnatural" (a familiar complaint with him) and criticizing it for *becoming* natural, an odd pair of complaints.

431

I think that the whole paragraph, which turns on the odd phrase "permitted to promise," should be read as a much more neutral piece of anthropology, on the one hand, and as a barbed bit of admiration and wonder on the other. Isn't it remarkable, Nietzsche is telling us, that human beings have so mastered their sense of themselves that they can commit themselves into the future and take responsibility for what they have done in the past? What higher praise could be offered, and what could be more necessary in the breeding the "future philosophers" and even the *Übermenschen* that Nietzsche so breathlessly anticipates? Does it make sense to suppose that the *Übermensch* would not be "permitted to promise," or that he would be in some unusual sense free to break his promises? (On the other hand, "Neither Manu nor Plato nor Confucius nor the Jewish and Christian teachers have ever doubted their right to lie": *TI*, "The 'Improvers' of Mankind," 5).

The other passage that deals with responsibility in some depth, the "Four Great Errors" section of *Twilight of the Idols*, from "the error of a false causality" to "the error of free will." In section 7, Nietzsche supplies "the psychology" of "making responsible," tracing the compulsion to look for "responsibilities" to the "instinct of wanting to judge and punish." So, too, the notion of freedom: "the origin of every act had to be considered as lying within the consciousness." And here Nietzsche trots out once again his incontinent campaign against judgment, guilt, and punishment. ("Christianity is a metaphysics of the hangman"). But notice that there is an enormous difference between the notion of responsibility discussed in *Genealogy* and the one discussed under the rubric of the "error of free will." The first does not presume any particular notion of the subject (though, as I suggested, Nietzsche may allude to Kantian notions). Indeed, to point out that a responsible being is "necessary, uniform, like among like, regular, and accordingly predictable" and acting out of acquired "instinct" is precisely to avoid any mention of particular motive or origin. The *Twilight* version, however, is all about a particular notion of self, and one can quite clearly reject that notion of self without rejecting, in the first sense, Nietzsche's notion of responsibility.

So what does "responsibility" mean for Nietzsche? One might be instrumental in cultivating one's character only in the more or less trivial sense that it is one's character that is being cultivated, as one might say that the acorn is instrumental in its development into a tree. But even this trivial account has the virtue of distinguishing self-generation and growth from external shaping and molding, and some such distinction is undoubtedly at stake here. Insofar as one develops one's talent for, say, playing the piano only because one has been threatened and coerced into doing so, one might be said not to have taken responsibility for developing one's talent at all. Insofar as one has developed one's talent for playing the piano only because one has been bribed and rewarded – Alasdair MacIntyre's example of an "external" as opposed to "internal" reward system for a practice, we hesitate to talk about responsibility at all.

But it does not follow that an "internalist" account of taking responsibility needs to include anything like an act of will or a special "subject" or any willful overcoming of counter-inclinations or any other specific obstacles. It need not involve deliberation or "practical reasoning." It means, in classical terms, that one's wishes, intentions, aspirations, and actions are all in harmony, that the trajectory of one's development is in tune with one's talents and the practices or institutions that sustain them. All of this might well be accompanied by those "feelings of delight of [one's] successful executive instruments" that Nietzsche suggests might easily be confused for a volition or an act of will (*BGE* 19), but to say that responsibility may thus be severed from the Kantian notion of Will is not for a moment to say that it must also be distinguished from agency and responsibility in this larger and more ordinary sense. We can take Nietzsche seriously in his critique of "free will" without compromising our or his insistence on responsibility.

Nietzsche writes, "What alone can our teaching be? – That no one *gives* a human being his qualities: not God, not society, not his parents or ancestors, not he himself" (*TI*, "The Four Great Errors," 8). Nevertheless, having those qualities, whether as gift or as curse, it is our responsibility what we do with them.

See also 5 "The Individual and Individuality in Nietzsche"; 20 "Agent and Deed in Nietzsche's *Genealogy of Morals*"; 24 "Nietzsche *contra* Liberalism on Freedom"

Notes

1   I thus liken Nietzsche's so-called paradox to Kant's third and most famous antinomy (Kant 1996: B480), which has the *appearance* of two contradictory claims but in his view turn out to be the expressions of two different "standpoints." This is quite independent of such Kantian notions as "Will as a kind of causality" or "thinking of oneself as free" or "as members of the intelligible [or supersensible] world."

2   At the beginning of Book IV of *The Gay Science* Nietzsche celebrates *amor fati* and declares: "I do not want to accuse; I do not even want to accuse those who accuse. *Looking away* shall be my only negation. And all in all and on the whole: some day I wish to be only a Yes-sayer." (*GS* 276) Nietzsche often resolves not to be so "judgmental," but we can probably agree that he does not succeed in this. He emerges from his writings as one of the most judgmental of philosophers – one would not go wrong in calling him "moralistic" in his tone. Some commentators will object to calling Nietzsche a "moralist," reminding us that he preferred to describe himself as an "immoralist" and that his objections are less often moral objections than they are aesthetic objections ("Socrates was ugly," "Goethe was beautiful") or diagnostic, even physiological ("Carlyle was dyspeptic"). And, of course, many of Nietzsche objections have the unmistakable tone of mockery ("Oh, you Stoics . . .").

3   Dennett ridicules fatalism as the "mystical and superstitious" thesis that "no agent can do anything about anything" and whose only virtue is "the power to create creepy effects in literature" (Dennett 1984: 123, 104).

4   Nevertheless, Zeus, at least, seems to have ample "elbow room" with regard to fate. For instance, there is a remarkable passage (16. 470–96; Lombardo trans., p. 318) where Zeus is contemplating saving Sarpedon, one of his favorite sons, despite the fact that "Fate has it that Sarpedon, whom I love more | Than any man, is to be killed by Patroclus." Hera, warns him against contravening fate and Zeus backs down. Thus the extent to which Zeus is "bound" by fate – as opposed to the clear "binding" of mere mortals – is left ambiguous.

5   I have elsewhere argued that Sartre sustains a full-blooded determinism in his philosophy, untouched by his adamant insistence that we must, even ontologically, consider consciousness as free, and free from causation.

6   Both Frankfurt (1988) and Greenspan (1999) have some clever arguments against the need to invoke either decisions or the possibility of "acting otherwise" in the analysis of freedom.

433

Editions of Nietzsche Used

Beyond Good and Evil, trans. Walter Kaufmann (New York: Vintage Books, 1966).
Daybreak, trans. R. J. Hollingdale (Cambridge: Cambridge University Press, 1982).
Dissertation of 1868 on Teleology (Urbana: NANS, 2000).
On the Genealogy of Morals, trans. Walter Kaufmann (New York: Vintage Books, 1967).
Twilight of the Idols, in *The Portable Nietzsche*, ed. Walter Kaufmann (New York: Viking Penguin, 1954).

References

Bernstein, Mark H. (1992). *Fatalism* (Nebraska: University of Nebraska Press).
Bowra, Cecil M. (1945). *Sophoclean Tragedy* (Oxford: Clarendon Press).
Cox, Christoph (1999). *Nietzsche, Naturalism, and Interpretation* (New York: Oxford University Press).
Dennett, Daniel (1984). *Elbow Room* (Cambridge, MA: MIT Press).
Frankfurt, Harry G. (1988). *The Importance of What We Care About* (Cambridge: Cambridge University Press).
Greenspan, Patricia (1999). "Impulse and Self-Reflection: Frankfurtian Responsibility Versus Free Will," *Journal of Ethics*, 3, pp. 325–40.
Homer (1998) *Iliad*, trans. Stanley Lombardo (Indianapolis: Hackett).
Hume, David (1973). *Treatise of Human Nature*, ed. L. A. Selby-Bigge (Oxford: Clarendon Press).
Kahn, Charles H. (1981). *The Art and Thought of Heraclitus* (Cambridge: Cambridge University Press).
Kant, Immanuel (1982). *Grounding the Metaphysics of Morals*, trans. J. Ellington (Indianapolis: Hackett).
—— (1996). *Critique of Pure Reason*, trans. W. S. Pluhar (Indianapolis: Hackett).
Leiter, Brian (1998). "The Paradox of Fatalism and Self-Creation in Nietzsche," in C. Janaway (ed.), *Willing and Nothingness: Schopenhauer as Nietzsche's Educator* (Oxford: Clarendon Press).
Mill, John Stuart (1874). *A System of Logic* (New York: Harper & Row).
Nussbaum, Martha (1986). *The Fragility of Goodness* (Cambridge: Cambridge University Press).
Richardson, John (1996). *Nietzsche's System* (Oxford: Oxford University Press).
Solomon, Robert C. (2003). *Living with Nietzsche* (New York: Oxford University Press).

Further Reading

Kane, Robert (1999). "Responsibility, Luck, and Chance," *Journal of Philosophy*, 94(5), pp. 217–40.
Raphals, Lisa (2001). "Fatalism, Fate and Stratagem in China and Greece," in Steven Shankman and Stephen Durrant (eds.), *Early China, Ancient Greece* (Albany: SUNY Press).
Sartre, Jean-Paul (1956). *Being and Nothingness*, trans. Hazel Barnes (New York: Philosophical Library).
Strawson, P. F. (1962). "Freedom and Resentment," *Proceedings of the British Academy*, 48, pp. 1–25; repr. in *Studies in the Philosophy of Thought and Action* (Oxford: Oxford University Press, 1968).

Part VII

Politics

24

Nietzsche *contra* Liberalism on Freedom

HERMAN SIEMENS

1 Introduction

Nietzsche's thought confronts us with the task of reassessing the place and value of conflict in ethical and political life. Because of the devastation so often caused by conflicts, moral and political philosophy have tended to neglect the dynamic, product-ive, and socializing qualities of conflict, concentrating instead on ways to prevent or to resolve conflict in favor of consensus and security. In Nietzsche's philosophy of life, however, conflict, struggle, and tension are not just a matter of contingent, local dis-turbances to be avoided or resolved; they are an essential and all-pervasive condition for life, from the smallest organism or cell to the historical struggle between master and slave moralities. How far can this position reasonably be taken? And what exactly are the ethical and political implications of Nietzsche's ontology of conflict? Is there a way to acknowledge conflict and struggle as part of the "deep structure" of human existence and interaction, and to affirm them for their valuable qualities *without* simply condoning devastation or oppression as a consequence?

One way to tackle this question is through a confrontation between the liberal and Nietzschean concepts of freedom. Typical of liberalism is the negative concept of freedom as freedom *from* external obstacles that would inhibit or prevent me from doing what I want. For Nietzsche, by contrast, obstacles, resistance, and antagonism are the *sine qua non* for the exercise of freedom. In this essay these radically opposed concepts of freedom will be played out against one another with a view to assessing the strengths and weaknesses of each. This will be done by situating the question of freedom within the broader antagonism between Nietzsche's thought and liberalism.

The term "liberalism" covers a whole gamut of diverse positions with roots in quite distinct traditions and political histories. For our purposes, liberalism can be identified above all with two values: a commitment to individuals as free and equal persons; and a commitment to individual diversity, closely linked to the values of pluralism and tolerance. The first commitment to individual freedom and equality makes for a characteristic attitude to political authority: on the one hand, the defining liberal move is to place *limits* on political authority so that the state does not infringe upon indi-vidual freedom and equality; on the other hand, there is the argument for the *necessity* of political association and, specifically, for a state with the coercive powers needed to guarantee the widest possible range of individual freedom compatible with freedom for all. Typically, this ambivalence has led liberals to formulate a *contractarian* justification of political authority: the legitimacy of the state resides in the free consent of individuals who come together (hypothetically) and transfer (some of) their powers to the state in exchange for the freedom to pursue their own ends. The boundaries of political authority are often inscribed in the contract as inviolable, individual rights (e.g. to life, liberty, property).

The second liberal commitment to individual diversity is motivated by the belief that each person has his or her own unique conception of what makes life worth living and is entitled to pursue that conception. It is often expressed as a commitment to pluralism, that is, the equal freedom of all individuals to pursue their moral commitments, values, or ends. This value is of particular importance in connection with Nietzsche for two reasons. The first is that Nietzsche is above all a pluralist thinker who starts out from the infinite diversity of life-forms, the uniqueness of each, and the value of each in its uniqueness.[1] The second reason is that pluralism is a potential source of conflict between individuals, and conflict is for Nietzsche an essential condition for freedom. In its starkest formulation, pluralism means that there is no shared concept of the good, so that social life is opened up to competing, potentially conflicting views of the best life. The problem of liberalism is how to establish peaceful coexistence among individuals with differing conceptions of the good (Mouffe 1996: 248). Liberalism affirms or at least accepts pluralism, while seeking to minimize conflict in favor of harmony. The question, as Mouffe (1995: esp. 39–45; 1996) has forcefully argued, is whether one can genuinely value pluralism if one denies (potential) conflict.

In his book *Nietzsche, Politics and Modernity* (1995) David Owen has made a valuable contribution to the antagonism between Nietzsche's thought and liberalism in the broad sense described. Focusing on the liberal idea of personhood, he asks about the participants in the contract that legitimates political authority in the liberal state. Taking his bearings from Rawls's influential formulation of liberal theory in *A Theory of Justice*, he argues that they are persons whose identities are prior to or independent of any specific commitments and any association with others. In Rawls's version of the hypothetical contract, the participants are separated from their conceptions of the good – their beliefs about how best to lead their lives – by the so-called "veil of ignorance." This ignorance expresses Rawls's liberal commitment to freedom conceived as the right to choose freely our conceptions of the good. Specific conceptions of the good are ruled out in favor of purely formal freedom to choose (any) good or end. By separating the individual from its ends, Rawls conceives the person as autonomous chooser of ends. But this implies that a person is what he or she is independently of the ends or values he or she freely chooses; as persons, we are "antecedently individuated" in the sense that the ends we choose are not constitutive of who we are, of our identities. A second, equally dubious, implication concerns our relations as persons to others. Rawls's hypothetical contract also implies that as persons, our ends are formed prior to, or independently of, association with others. Society does not inform a person's identity, values, or ends, but is rather the outcome of a contract between individuals whose ends are already given; as persons we are "asocially individuated."[2]

According to Owen (1995: 138), Nietzsche offers a powerful critique of these presuppositions. In the first place, Nietzsche shows that our conception of the self as an antecedently individuated subject is not a metaphysical truth, but a cultural artifact produced in contingent circumstances to express the practical interests of a specific group; what Nietzsche calls the "slave revolt of morality" in essay one of the *Genealogy*. In the second place, the *Genealogy* also shows that our capacities – especially our capacity for sovereign agency – are socially constituted and the product of a long pre-history. In a similar vein, Volker Gerhardt writes, of Nietzsche's "sociological insight," that the "freedom and self-responsibility of the 'sovereign individual' are due to the stringency and severity of centuries of moral coercion [*sittlicher Zwänge*]" (Gerhardt 1992: 28f.). But according to Owen, Nietzsche also offers an alternative, positive conception of personhood. This turns on the constructive counterclaim that the maintenance and cultivation of our capacities – especially "our capacities for autonomous reflection and agency" – is dependent on communal practices of contestation.

All three points will be taken up and developed in the next section by focusing not on personhood, but on Nietzsche's concept of freedom. To begin with, I shall consider a *Nachlass* text from 1881 which contains an explicit and direct critique of liberal assumptions.

2 Nietzsche's Socio-Physiology and the Question of Sovereignty

In note 11[182] (*KSA* 9, p. 509) Nietzsche offers a naturalistic account of the history and social constitution of our capacities as sovereign individuals (cf. Owen's second claim). The text begins with an organismic model of sovereignty in which our capacities are conceived as qualities or "functions" of the organism, where the organism is characterized above all by processes of internal organization and self-regulation (Nietzsche is here following Wilhelm Roux: see Müller-Lauter 1999):

A strong free human being feels *the qualities of the* **organism** towards [*gegen*] everything else

1   self-regulation: in the form of *fear* of all alien incursions, in the *hatred* towards [*gegen*] the enemy, moderation etc.
2   overcompensation: in the form of *acquisitiveness* the pleasure of appropriation the craving for power
3   assimilation to oneself: in the form of praise reproach making others dependent on oneself, to that end deception cunning, learning, habituation, commanding incorporating [*Einverleiben*] judgments and experiences
4   secretion and excretion: in the form of revulsion contempt for the qualities in itself which are *no longer* of use to it; communicating [*mittheilen*] that which is superfluous goodwill
5   metabolic power: temporary worship admiration making oneself dependent fitting in, almost dispensing with the exercise of the other organic functions, transforming oneself into an "organ," being able to serve
6   regeneration: in the form of sexual drive, pedagogic drive etc.

It is, however, a mistake to *presuppose* these capacities as somehow intrinsic to human beings (as they are in liberal contract theory). They are rather the very late fruit of a long social history which Nietzsche then recounts. He does so from a *socio-physiological*

439

perspective in which the social origins of the sovereign individual are focused not on our reason (emphasized by liberal contract theories), but on our affects and drives. The thesis is that our drives are not "natural," but learned and assimilated from society or the state.

In the first phase of Nietzsche's story we are but organs of a larger, self-regulating social organism to which we belong ("society"/"the state"). In the second phase, sovereign individuals are formed when the organs cease to be organs and become instead autonomous organisms (in place of society or the state). This transition, Nietzsche argues, is made possible by a process of learning, assimilation, or incorporation (*Einverleibung*). In the first phase, where human beings are organs, their actions and impulses are determined by the needs of the organism to which they belong: they feel the "*affects of society* towards [*gegen*] other societies and single beings [. . .] and *not* as individuals"; there are *only* public enemies. But as an organ, the human being also assimilates the interests and needs, the "experiences and judgements" of the organism, so that later, "when the ties of society break down," it is able to reorganize itself into an autonomous individual or organism. Nietzsche speaks of the "*reorganization and assimilation excretion of drives*" needed to transform the human being from an organ into an organism.

In a central passage of the note Nietzsche takes issue with liberal assumptions on three counts:

1 Society first educates the single being [*das Einzelwesen*], pre-forms it into a half- or whole individual, it is *not* formed *out of* single beings, not out of contracts among them! Rather, an individual is needed at most as a focal point (a leader) and this one will only be "free" in relation to the lower or higher level of the others. So:
2 The state does *not* in its origins somehow oppress the individuals: these do not even exist!
3 It [the state] makes the existence of human beings at all possible, as herd-animals. Our *drives affects* are first *taught* to us from there: *there is nothing originary about them!* There is no "state of nature" for them! As parts of a whole we take part in the conditions of existence and functions of the whole and *incorporate* [*einverleiben uns*] *the experiences and judgements made in that process.*

Nietzsche's criticisms of liberal contract theory can be enumerated as follows:

1 Society is not formed out of pre-existing individuals by way of a contract; rather, it is society that educates and forms individuals, so that they are the product of society.
2 Since individuals are the product of the society or state to which they belong, the state cannot be understood as a threat to pre-existing individuals. In particular, the liberal concept of individual freedom as a primordial power or "natural right" of individuals in need of protection against the artificial construct of the state is ruled out.[3]
3 Nietzsche's socio-physiology forbids the abstraction of our capacity to reason from our affective, embodied existence. Not only are our "experiences and judgments" incorporated and learned from the state; so too are our very affects and drives.

440

Together, they are pre-formed by the interests and functions of the social organism to which we originally belong. This rules out not only those liberal contract theories that presuppose our capacity for reason or autonomous reflection (e.g. Rawls), but also those that presuppose primordial affects and drives on the individual's part, such as Hobbes's fear of death and desire for self-preservation. (Hobbes 1991: chs. 13 and 14, pp. 90, 99)

Clearly, all of this implies a critique of the liberal notion of freedom as the right to choose one's concept of the good, where this right is attached to an asocial, antecedently individuated person. But it also raises the question: what sense of individual freedom or sovereignty does Nietzsche's socio-physiology allow for? That Nietzsche wishes to advance a viable alternative to the liberal concept of freedom is clear from the organismic model of sovereignty that opens the text. In its concluding passage he gives us two further clues to his conception of sovereignty.

The first clue comes from Nietzsche's account of how Socrates and the moral philosophers first emerged. In this, the second phase of Nietzsche's story, "when the ties of society break down," the first experimental individuals or *Versuchs-Individuen* assert themselves as sovereign. This process is described as the transformation of an organ into an autonomous organism, a painful "*reorganization and assimilation excretion of drives*":

> The times when they emerge are those of de-moralization [*Entsittlichung*], of so-called corruption, that is, all drives now want to go it alone and, since they have not until now *adapted* to that personal utility [i.e. the interests of the individual], they destroy the individual through excess [*Übermaass*]. Or they lacerate it in their struggle [*Kampfe*] with one another.

The destructive conflict of the drives unleashed by their emancipation from bondage to the social organism moves the moral philosophers to commend a reactionary path of bondage:

> The ethicists [*Ethiker*] then come forward and seek to show human beings how they can still live without suffering so from themselves – mostly by commending to them the *old conditioned way of life* under the yoke of society, only that in place of society it is [the yoke of] a concept – they are *reactionaries*.

The individual is saved (from suffering at least), but not its sovereignty. Such a path is, in any case, unavailable to us moderns. Unlike Socrates' audience, we are too alienated from our erstwhile bondage to the social organism for a reactionary ethic of social conformity to work: "We, however, have long been *misshapen* [*Missgestalten*], and to that there corresponds the far *greater malaise* of individuals who are in the process of becoming free [*frei werdenden Individuen*]." What, then, would be an adequate or appropriate ethic for us, as modern individuals?

The second clue to Nietzsche's concept of sovereignty comes almost as an afterthought in his account of the reactionary ethos of the first moral philosophers: "Their claim is that there is an *eternal moral law* [*ewiges Sittengesetz*]; they will not

441

acknowledge the individual law [*das individuelle Gesetz*] and call the effort to attain it immoral and destructive." Against the belief in an "eternal moral law" promoted by the moral philosophers, especially Socrates, Nietzsche here suggests the alternative of *radically individual self-legislation* (*das individuelle Gesetz*). The importance of this ideal for Nietzsche's positive ethics cannot be overestimated, as the work of Volker Gerhardt (1992), above all, has shown. In this essay the discussion will be restricted to its bearing on the problem of freedom or sovereignty; there seems to be little sense in speaking of any ethic without presupposing freedom in some sense, and yet it is not clear what space, if any, Nietzsche's socio-physiology leaves for individual sovereignty or freedom.

In the following sections I will argue that, against Socrates, Nietzsche advocates not the elimination of conflict through conformity, but the transformation of *unmeasured destructive conflict* – the mutual destruction of competing drives, and with them the individual they inhabit – into *productive measured conflict*. Nietzsche's socio-physiology suggests an ideal of sovereignty that turns on an *inner* plurality of drives in productive conflict, sustained by and interlocked with an *outer* plurality of sovereign beings or organisms in productive conflict. In other words, freedom is thought of by Nietzsche as the maintenance of a measured inner antagonism through a measured external antagonism with others. Put in this way, the argument develops Owen's (third) point that for Nietzsche the maintenance and cultivation of our capacities depends on communal practices of contestation. The underlying claim that needs to be examined is that there is no genuine freedom or plurality without a measure of conflict.

3 Nietzsche versus Liberalism on Freedom and Resistance

Preliminary orientation for Nietzsche's concept of freedom can be gained from a well-known passage in the early text of 1872, "Homer's Contest." Regarding the attitude of the ancient Greeks to human ambition Nietzsche writes:

> Now for the ancients the goal of agonal education was the welfare of the whole, the state society. Every Athenian, for example, was supposed to develop his self in the contest to that degree which would be of greatest advantage to Athens and do it the least harm. It was no ambition into the unmeasured and immeasurable, as is mostly the case with modern ambition: it was of the well-being of his maternal city that a youth thought when running or throwing or singing in the contests; it was her fame that he wanted to increase through his; and the wreaths which the judges of the contest placed in honour upon his head, he dedicated to the gods of his city. Every Greek felt from childhood on the burning wish within himself to be an instrument for the good of his city in the contest of the cities: therein was his egoism enflamed, therein it was also checked and bounded. That is why the individuals in antiquity were more free, because their goals were nearer and closer at hand. Modern humans, by contrast, are everywhere overtaken [lit. crossed: *gekreuzt*] by infinity, like the quick-footed Achilles in the allegory of Zeno the Eleatic: infinity inhibits him, he cannot even catch up with the tortoise. (*KSA* 1, p. 789)[4]

One cannot but be struck by a paradox in Nietzsche's reasoning here. Where the individual sees himself as a mere instrument for the good of the community, he is free;

to be free, an individual's actions must be under the constraints, the pressure imposed by the interests of the community. Where, by contrast, the individual's actions are free from constraint or limits, where he sees himself as an autonomous end-in-itself rather than a means, he cannot be free; the lack of constraint or of obstacles acts as a constraint, an insuperable obstacle to genuine freedom. Why does Nietzsche make this utterly paradoxical claim?

By way of an answer, this passage suggests four theses on freedom. The first is that *freedom requires tangible goals*. Freedom can only mean freedom *for* something – in this passage the "maternal city." In general, the ends of freedom – the question: Free for what? (*Wozu?*) – cannot be abstracted or separated from the claim to freedom. Underpinning this thesis is something like Charles Taylor's remark that "freedom is important to us because we are purposive beings" (Taylor 1985: 219). This thought returns in emphatic terms when Zarathustra says:

> You call yourself free? Your governing thought [*herrschende Gedanke*] is what I want to hear, and not that you have escaped a yoke [. . .]
> Free from what [*Frei wovon*]? What does Zarathustra care about that! But your eye should tell me clearly: free *for* what [*Wozu*]? (Z I, "Of the Way of the Creator")

This claim places Nietzsche in a twofold opposition to liberalism. In the first place it is clear that Nietzsche advocates a "positive," against a merely "negative," concept of freedom. In the second place it rules out the kind of abstraction performed by Rawls's veil of ignorance, that is, the exclusion of specific ends or concepts of the good in favor of the purely *formal* freedom to choose *any* end or good on the part of an antecedently individuated person.

The second thesis on freedom in the passage from "Homer's Contest" is that *freedom attaches to deeds or works*. Freedom cannot be abstracted or separated from acting or doing itself, from the actual exercise of our capacities for agency, any more than it can be separated from our goals or "governing thoughts." At stake for Nietzsche, as he puts it in the opening paragraph of "Homer's Contest," is the question of "humanity, in impulses deeds and works [*Regungen Thaten und Werken*]." This suggests a twofold alignment on the part of Nietzsche's concept of freedom. The first is with what Charles Taylor (1985) calls an "exercise-concept" of freedom, against the so-called "opportunity-concept" typical of liberalism. Freedom as opportunity corresponds to the negative notion of freedom espoused by classical liberal theory (Locke, Hobbes, Bentham), that is: freedom as the absence of external (physical or legal) obstacles. It is what Nietzsche in "Homer's Contest" calls freedom without limits, the characteristically modern sense of freedom that is ultimately crossed or crossed by the limitless. In the opportunity-concept of freedom, the absence of external obstacles is important because being free means "being able to do what you want"; it is "a matter of what we can do, what is open to us, whether or not we exercise these options." In the exercise-concept, by contrast, freedom requires the actual exercise, the realization of certain capacities (Taylor 1985: 215, 213). In "Homer's Contest" Nietzsche's exercise-concept of freedom is clearly inscribed in the demand, the guiding imperative of Greek pedagogy: "Every gift or capacity *must* unfold through contestation ("Jede Begabung *muss* sich kämpfend entfalten": *KSA* 1, p. 789; emphasis added).

443

Nietzsche's emphasis on doing itself suggests a second alignment, this time with Hannah Arendt and her performative concept of freedom as an attribute of doing, against the metaphysical tradition she opposes and its inward notion of freedom as an attribute of the will and thought (Arendt 1968, 1998: 178ff.; see also Villa 1992; Siemens 2005). This alignment brings to light an important feature of Nietzsche's understanding of freedom. Even if the ends (the *Wozu?*) of freedom are essential to the claim to freedom, Nietzsche does not conceive freedom as an attribute of the will and thought, on the model of free will (*liberum arbitrium*), whereby the intellect chooses the right end and calls upon the will to command its execution (Arendt 1968: 151f., 163). That is because for Nietzsche, as for Arendt, free action has *external sources*.

Before considering this point, it is worth noting that the twofold alignment described involves a tension, one that goes to the heart of Nietzsche's thought on freedom. As Taylor points out, the exercise-concept of freedom revolves around the ideal of self-determination; it is about realizing those capacities that give one control over one's life (Taylor 1985: 213, 215). Arendt's performative concept, on the contrary, is an attempt to think of freedom as non-sovereignty, for it is, in her view, the effort to retain control over one's actions from beginning to end that motivates Platonic and post-Platonic philosophy and distorts the original, political meaning of freedom (Arendt 1998: 220–7). Without question, control, mastery, and self-mastery (*Herrschaft, Zucht*) are important figures in Nietzsche's thought and essential to his ethical ideal of individual self-legislation. On the other hand, Nietzsche's thought is relational in character, and the individual is unthinkable in abstraction from socio-physiological relations of power and resistance (cf. *KSA* 9, 11[182]; see section 2 above).

This implies that for Nietzsche, as for Arendt, individual action is interactional and non-sovereign, bringing us to the third thesis on freedom in the passage from "Homer's Contest." In the context of agonal deeds or works, *freedom as activity or doing is essentially public and interactional*. For Arendt, free action falls into an "already existing web of human relationships, with its innumerable, conflicting wills" (1998: 184); because it is interactional in this sense, it is unpredictable and boundless (non-sovereign). Typically, exercise-concepts of freedom also insist that we cannot realize our capacities in isolation, outside of society of a certain kind (Taylor 1985: 217, 229). For Nietzsche, too, freedom depends on a specific kind of society or social relations. In all three cases, freedom is radically opposed to the liberal concept of freedom as the right of an asocial individual. But what exactly are the kinds of social relation or interaction that make free agency possible for Nietzsche?

Limit or measure is a crucial ingredient in the kind of interaction that makes for agonal freedom. In the passage from "Homer's Contest," Nietzsche contrasts the constraints or limits imposed by the Greek community with modern, limitless freedom. But that is only one side. When describing individual ambition he writes that is *both* "enflamed" (*entflammt*), *and* checked or bounded (*umschränkt*) by the communal good or interest. The good of the community is not just a source of pressure or limits on action; it is also a stimulant, what first moves the individual to distinguish himself. According to Hartmut Schröter (1982: 111f.), what fascinated Nietzsche in the agon was that the *same* conditions that unleashed the individual in his or her spontaneity and particularity also generated the limits or measure needed for social life. This is encapsulated in the dynamic character of action or interaction in the agon which

Nietzsche describes as a plurality of forces (*Kräfte*) or geniuses who "provoke or stimulate [*reizen*] one another to action, as they also hold one another within the bounds of measure" (*KSA* 1, p. 789). Or again, to return to the principle of Greek pedagogy: "Every capacity must unfold through contestation" (*KSA* 1, p. 789). This imperative presupposes a specific social ontology: if every capacity must unfold through contestation, it is because each capacity can only become what it is through antagonistic striving against others. That is to say, each capacity needs antagonistic relations with others in order to become what it is. In the context of the agon, then, free action needs the resistance of others as *both* a stimulant towards self-realization *and* a limit on the forms it can take.

Let us take stock of the picture so far. If freedom for Nietzsche attaches to the exercise of capacities, to activity itself or action, and if action for Nietzsche means *interaction*, then the nature of this interaction can now be spelled out as the fourth thesis on freedom in the passage from "Homer's Contest": *freedom is located in the space between reciprocal stimulation and reciprocal limitation, between the provocation to excess (hubris) and the imposition of measure.* Or, from the perspective of the agent: exercising freedom requires resistance or obstacles, where resistance or obstacles are conceived as *both* a stimulant *and* a limit. This formulation helps to clarify why it is that Nietzsche rejects negative freedom (without limits) and what it is that divides his concept from the liberal concept of freedom. If freedom as opportunity – typical of liberalism – requires the absence of external obstacles, it is because obstacles are seen to *inhibit* freedom. For Nietzsche freedom presupposes resistance or obstacles, because obstacles do not act as an inhibitor. Without doubt, obstacles impose a limit, but the resistance they offer is what first calls free action forth. The agon begins with reciprocal stimulation, where ambition or envy of the other sets in motion a dynamic of mutual provocation or empowerment. It has external sources in the sense that each antagonist is moved to act from without, in response to the other. Free action is, to borrow Arendt's phrase, "inspired from without" (1968: 152). This understanding of antagonism and resistance *as a stimulant to free action, not as an inhibitor* is what divides Nietzsche most sharply from the liberal concept of freedom. That external obstacles limit what I can do is acknowledged by Nietzsche. But it is the resistance offered by others that first compels me to exert myself, to define myself against them in new and unknown ways.

On the basis of these four theses on freedom, an answer can now be given to the question posed at the beginning of this section. Why does Nietzsche advocate the paradoxical notion of (true) freedom under constraint, against the (false) freedom as the absence of constraint? It is because freedom is thought of by Nietzsche as activity, as the actual *exercise* of our capacities, and not as freedom of opportunity in the absence of obstacles. Moreover, the exercise of freedom requires *tension* or *conflict*: resistance or obstacles of the kind that work *both* as a stimulant to deeds *and* as a limit on those deeds.

Why, then, does Nietzsche insist on tension or conflict as the *sine qua non* for the exercise of freedom? As mentioned above, the opportunity-concept of freedom typical of liberalism is concerned above all with keeping open the space for free action, whether or not we exercise our options; in Taylor's words, "[i]t is a matter of being able to do something or other, of not having obstacles in one's way, rather than being a capacity

445

that we have to realize" (1985: 214). In many versions of liberalism, our capacity to realize freedom is simply assumed, and thought is given only to its external conditions. According to the exercise-concept of freedom, this capacity cannot simply be assumed. As a consequence, the question of freedom is profoundly complicated, since it now becomes bound up with the problems of self-knowledge, the discrimination between different capacities and desires, and self-control. What counts as realizing my freedom? Which of my capacities and desires are essential to my self-realization, and which are not? (Cf. Taylor 1985: 215.)

Like the exercise-concept theorists, Nietzsche holds that our capacity to realize freedom cannot simply be assumed. And in his reflections on freedom, the same problems of moral discrimination, self-control, and especially self-knowledge are recurrent preoccupations.[5] For Nietzsche, like Taylor, they pose the most important challenge to the realization of freedom. But Nietzsche is far more emphatic than Taylor about our incapacity to realize freedom, and for this there is a distinctively Nietzschean reason. It goes back, at least in part, to our condition in (late) modernity, to the generalized crisis of values and forces that he calls nihilism.

In a well-known fragment on nihilism (*KSA* 12, 9[35]; *LN* 146f.), Nietzsche begins: "Nihilism a **normal** state. Nihilism: the goal is lacking; the answer to the 'Why?' is lacking." Already here one can see why we are incapable of realizing freedom: the ends of freedom – the *Warum?* the *Wozu?* – are lacking, the ends without which freedom is unthinkable for Nietzsche. As a *physiological* phenomenon of modernity, nihilism, or at least "passive nihilism," names an affliction or sickness, what Nietzsche calls exhaustion (*Ermüdung, Erschöpfung*). It is "a sign of *insufficient* strength to *posit* productively [*produktiv*] a goal again, a why? a belief for oneself." One of the symptoms of modern nihilism is an incapacity to create. Under nihilistic conditions, we have lost the creative capacity to posit credible goals, and as a result we need stimulants, the provocation and tension of conflict, in order to realize the productive capacities essential to freedom.

This is the reason, or at least one reason, why Nietzsche insists on tension or conflict as the *sine qua non* for the exercise of freedom. It would be wrong, however, to reduce the connection between conflict and freedom in Nietzsche's thought to nihilism. Rather, nihilism is an extreme and highly visible instance of a more general phenomenon for Nietzsche, one that has its roots in his "ontology" of tension or struggle. There are countless texts in which Nietzsche advances the thesis that *creativity requires tension*. To cite just one:

> The better the state is organized, the lamer humanity [becomes].
> To make the individual uncomfortable: my task!
> Stimulus for the liberation of the single being in conflict! (*KSA* 8, 5[178]; cf. 5[188])

4 Freedom and Resistance in Nietzsche's Later Thought

The theses on freedom were taken from an early text on Greek culture, and Greek culture lost its unconditional, binding character for Nietzsche in the course of his development. Nonetheless, his early work on the Greeks does retain a special significance for his later work, one that goes beyond the theme of Greek culture. It is as if certain key themes and problems of the later work are rehearsed on the stage of Greek culture, from which they are subsequently transposed. This goes, for example, for the balance between knowledge (probity) and art advocated in *GS* 107, which takes up the principle of "equilibrium" among social powers, thematized in *Human, All Too Human* as the origin of justice (cf. Gerhardt 1984: 384), which in turn is first rehearsed in the concept of the Greek agon as a balance of more or less equal forces in "Homer's Contest." It also goes for Nietzsche's theses on freedom. Their development in his later work will be traced in this section.

BGE 224 deals with a peculiarly modern virtue, the virtue of "the historical sense," and ends with a passage that takes up and sharpens the thought of freedom expressed in the passage from "Homer's Contest":

> Perhaps our great virtue of the historical sense stands in a necessary opposition to *good* taste, at least to the very best taste, so that we are only able to take up [*in uns nachbilden*] the small, brief and highest moments of good fortune and transfigurations of human life, as they appear every now and then, badly, hesitantly and only by forcing ourselves: those moments and miracles where a great force [*Kraft*] willingly [*freiwillig*] held back in the face of that which is without measure or limits [*Maasslosen und Unbegrenzten*] –, where a surplus of fine pleasure was taken in a sudden binding and petrifying, in standing fast and fixing oneself [*Feststehen und Sich-Fest-Stellen*] on a ground still trembling. *Measure* [*Das* **Maass**] is alien to us, let us admit it; our thrill is precisely the thrill of the endless, unmeasured [*das Unendliche, Ungemessene*]. Like the rider on a steed tearing at the bit, we let go our reins before the endless, we modern humans, we half-barbarians – and are only really in our element, where we are most – *in danger*.

Here true freedom is associated with measure (*Maass*) against the modern predilection for the endless and unmeasured and our concept of freedom without limits or measure. One can clearly recognize in this contrast, the contrast from "Homer's Contest" between the tangible goals imposed on the individual by the Greek *polis* and the freedom without limits ascribed to moderns. However, Nietzsche does not draw a simple opposition between freedom as measure on one side, and unfreedom as the lack of measure on the other. Rather, freedom is described in terms of the pleasure of "standing fast" in the face of the measureless and unlimited (*Maasslosen und Unbegrenzten*), of "fixing oneself on a ground still shaking," still trembling with unmeasured desires. Freedom is not simply identified with measure against excess; it is located in the space between absolute measure (a definitive fixing-of-oneself: *Sich-Fest-Stellen*) and absolute unmeasure (*das Maasslose*). Nietzsche's point seems to be that freedom involves a tension or antagonism between *measure* and *excess* (*Maas* – *Übermaas*). This formulation is a mature and sharper version of the fourth thesis in "Homer's Contest" that freedom is located in the space between the provocation to hubris and the imposition of measure.

The antagonistic concept of measure returns in one of Nietzsche's best-known texts on freedom in *Twilight of the Idols*, entitled "My Conception of Freedom." David Owen has remarked (1995: 164f.), this text offers a clear formulation of Nietzsche's exercise-concept of freedom:

> Liberal institutions immediately cease to be liberal as soon as they are attained: subsequently there is nothing more thoroughly harmful to freedom than liberal institutions. One knows, indeed, *what* they bring about: they undermine the will to power, they are the levelling of mountain and valley exalted to a moral principle, they make small, cowardly and smug – it is the herd animal that triumphs every time. [. . .] As long as they are still being fought for [*erkämpft*], these same institutions produce quite different effects; then they actually advance freedom in a powerful way. Seen more closely, it is war [*der Krieg*] that brings forth these effects, the war *for* liberal institutions, which, as war, gives endurance to the *illiberal* instincts. And war is a training in freedom. [. . .] The highest type of free man would have to be sought there where the greatest resistance [*Widerstand*] is continually being overcome: five steps from tyranny, up against the threshold of the danger of bondage [*Verknechtung*]. This is true psychologically, if under the "tyrant" one understands relentless and fearsome instincts which call for a maximum of authority and discipline towards [*gegen*] themselves – finest type Julius Caesar –; this is also politically true, one has only to take a look at history. (*TI*, "Expeditions of an Untimely Man," 38)

In these lines freedom is defined as the *exercise of self-control*, whereby the tyrannical "relentless and fearsome instincts" call forth "a maximum of authority and discipline towards [*gegen*] oneself." Here, as in *BGE* 224, freedom is defined in terms of an antagonism or tension between excess ("relentless and fearsome instincts") and measure or total control. For it is important to note that the exercise of self-control does not involve the *extirpation* of tyrannical instincts; rather, it involves a form of control that "remains five steps from tyranny, up against the threshold of the danger of bondage." This concept of self-control does not, however, exhaust the exercise-concept of freedom developed in the text. The passage cited explicitly connects the inner or "psychological" conditions for the exercise of freedom with its outer or "political" conditions: in both cases the exercise of freedom is greatest "where the greatest resistance is being overcome." The measure of freedom, Nietzsche argues, is given by the resistance to being overcome, whether this be the inner resistance of tyrannical drives, or the outer resistance of other individuals or communities.

In general terms, then, the exercise of self-control is situated within a broad concept of freedom, as the exercise of warfare, struggle, antagonism (*Krieg, Kampf*) both within and without; the overcoming of resistance both within and without; and the exercise of mastery over such resistance. This broad concept of freedom serves Nietzsche to launch an attack on modern liberal institutions as a threat or obstacle to freedom. His argument is that the institutionalization of liberal values – we may think here of the protection of equal rights to basic liberties against external constraints (à la Rawls) – leads in practice to the breeding of uniformity among herd animals; that is, it leads to unfreedom. At the heart of this argument is a critique of the liberal opportunity-concept of freedom, what Nietzsche elsewhere identifies as the modern *laisser aller* concept of freedom, freedom without limits or measure. To institutionalize the opportunity-concept of freedom by eliminating external obstacles through the institutional guarantee of equal rights to liberty, is, in effect, to promote the exercise of unfreedom in the sense of uniformity among herd animals who know only how to obey, not to command (cf. *BGE* 242; *KSA* 12, 10[17]). Against this, the real exercise of freedom is defined by Nietzsche as warfare or struggle; that is, as the exercise of martial – Nietzsche says explicitly "illiberal" – instincts.

448

It seems clear, then, that the concept of freedom advanced in this text is explicitly and implacably opposed to modern liberal democracy. Yet this judgment falls short, because something crucial has so far been omitted, something which is integral to Nietzsche's understanding of freedom from the very beginning: the ends of freedom, the wherefore (*Wozu?*), Zarathustra's "governing thought." In its proper formulation, Nietzsche's concept of freedom is not the brute exercise of warfare or struggle, but rather the struggle *for freedom*, or in his words: "the war *for* liberal institutions" (*der Krieg* **um** *liberale Institutionen*). Nietzsche's argument against liberal democracy must therefore be reformulated as follows: if freedom means the struggle for freedom, for equal rights to basic liberties, then the institutional guarantee of these rights (by eliminating the exercise of struggle and promoting uniformity) undermines freedom. In these terms, Nietzsche's exercise-concept of freedom is still implacably opposed to liberalism and, specifically, to the institutional safeguards against the conflict between different values or ends in liberal democracy. However, as the "war *for* liberal institutions," it opposes liberalism *for the sake of* liberal values, as a preparation or "training" for their realization. This reading suggests that Nietzsche's exercise-concept of freedom (as warfare) intends an *immanent critique* of liberalism: what liberalism claims to advance, the interests of the individual, it ends up undermining through the uniformity and conformity engendered by liberal institutions. Nietzsche's counterclaim is (in agreement with liberalism) that freedom attaches to the individual in its particularity, in its difference from a plurality of other individuals, but (*contra* liberalism) that it is conflict, obstacles, resistance, and *not* the protection against them that promotes particularity, difference, and genuine pluralism.

5 On the Necessity of Conflict for Freedom: Nietzsche's Critique of the Subject

In *TI*, "Expeditions," 38, we once again find Nietzsche advocating an exercise-concept of freedom that is bound up with antagonism and conflict (both within and without) and conditional upon resistance or obstacles (within and without), obstacles of the kind that must be absent according to liberal concepts of freedom. His opposition to liberalism on this point is radical and cuts across Taylor's distinction between "crude" opportunity-concepts (e.g. Hobbes, Bentham) and those with exercise-components (e.g. Mill), for neither allows for obstacles or antagonism as having a positive role for freedom or self-realization. By way of recapitulation, this section will focus on the question of conflict: why does Nietzsche advocate conflict, obstacle, resistance as the *sine qua non* of freedom? Why in particular does he connect inner and outer antagonism?

The first answer (see section 3 above) is that our capacity to realize freedom cannot simply be assumed, as it is in opportunity-concepts of freedom. Freedom cannot be conceived in abstraction from the specific goals or "governing thoughts," and under modern nihilistic conditions our creative capacity to posit credible goals has withered. This claim, moreover, instantiates a more general, "ontological" thesis that *creativity requires tension*. It is only under pressure of external obstacles, of antagonism and resistance, that we are compelled to come up with the "governing thoughts" needed for the exercise of freedom. This thought recurs across Nietzsche's writings under various rubrics, such as "freedom under the law" or under "pressure," and "dancing in chains," to name a few (see *GS* 290; *BGE* 188; *WS* 10).

The second answer, given in *TI*, "Expeditions," 38 (see section 4 above), is that freedom attaches to the individual in its particularity and difference from others, and it is tension, antagonism with external obstacles – *not* the elimination of such obstacles through liberal institutions – that makes for particularity and difference. In Nietzsche's words: "war is a training in freedom. For what is freedom! That one has the will to self-responsibility. That one holds on to the distance that divides us."

A third answer goes back to Nietzsche's mature formulation of inner antagonism as self-control in *Beyond Good and Evil* and *Twilight of the Idols*, that is, self-control as the tension or antagonism between measure and excess (see section 4 above). If we ask: why does Nietzsche insist on self-control in this sense as a condition of freedom? we find a straight answer in a subsequent aphorism in *TI*, "Expeditions," entitled "'Freedom, As I Do *Not* Mean It . . .'." Here Nietzsche recurs to his diagnosis of modern nihilism as a physiological phenomenon: we moderns are "a kind of chaos" (*BGE* 224), "a physiological self-contradiction" in whom "the instincts contradict, disrupt, destroy one another" (*TI*, "Expeditions," 41; cf. *CW*, Epilogue, *KSA* 12, 9[35], and *LN* 147 on "passive nihilism"). (This condition bears a certain similarity to the second phase of Nietzsche's socio-physiology of the individual considered in section 2 above, that is, the quasi-nihilistic conditions of "demoralization" (*Entsittlichung*), in which the conflict of drives asserting their demands in an absolute, unmeasured way destroyed the first "experimental individuals"). Under these conditions, Nietzsche argues, no discipline would be too severe, and yet our modern, negative concept of freedom asserts the opposite: "the claim to independence, to free development, to *laisser aller*" (*TI*, "Expeditions," 41). In this context, we can see that Nietzsche's concept of freedom as self-control or the inner antagonism between measure and excess is his response or counter-proposal to the modern concept of freedom as an expression of inner, uncontrolled antagonism.

In my closing remarks, I shall sketch a fourth answer to the question why antagonism is to be viewed as the condition of freedom. I shall focus on the connection between inner and outer antagonism central to of Nietzsche's concept of freedom. This answer goes back to Nietzsche's critique of the modern concept of the subject as a substantive unity. From a range of extraordinary notes from the *Nachlass* of 1880–1 (*KSA* 9), we can reconstruct an argument along the following lines:

1   The modern concept of the unitary subject as substance is derivative of our phenomenal sense of ourselves as subjects, the "I" experienced or "felt" in self-consciousness, what Nietzsche calls *Subjekt-Empfindung* (subject-feeling) (*KSA* 9, 11 [270]).
2   This "I" of self-consciousness or *Subjekt-Empfindung* is not an end-in-itself, but a means of survival; a myth, an error, whose value lies *not* in its truth, but in its selective value for the kind of organism or "life-system" that we are (Nietzsche's *naturalism*).[6]
3   In truth, we are not individuals, but "dividua" (*HH* 57; *KSA* 11, 25[159]): a plurality of antagonistic drives and feelings formed through the internalization of social practices and norms (Nietzsche's *socio-physiology*).[7]

4   We cannot therefore eliminate the antagonism of the plurality of drives and feelings that we are. And since we cannot eliminate the antagonism of drives and feelings, the question arises: how best to manage this inner antagonism?

5   One strategy would be to seek to reduce to a minimum the vehement antagonism of our feelings towards their opposites; in this way, we might overhear the inner antagonism and get the impression that we are entirely at one with ourselves (*KSA* 9, 6[58]). The advantage of this strategy, as Socrates saw (cf. *KSA* 9, 11[182]), is to save the individual, or rather the dividuum, from suffering.

6   However, *eudaimonia* or happiness in this sense carries a high cost: it is a kind of "euthanasia, entirely unproductive" (*KSA* 9, 6[58]) that promotes uniformity. As we have seen, creativity is contingent upon tension.

7   The alternative strategy is to maintain inner tension, the vehement antagonism between our feelings and their opposites. But this then raises another problem: how to avoid the complete loss of unity, our nihilistic disintegration as individuals through the unmeasured conflict of drives?

8   Nietzsche's answer is to connect strong inner tension with outer, interpersonal tension as its condition. In the above-cited note (*KSA* 9, 6[58]), he goes on to contend that it is through relations of tension and antagonism with others that the antagonism of inner drives is best contained, so that the dividuum can attain unity, or maintain itself as an individual. In modern liberal society, he writes: "the oppositions among individuals are reduced to a sublime minimum: so that all inimical tendencies and tensions, *through which the individual maintains itself as individual* can barely be perceived" (*KSA* 9, 6[58]; emphasis added).

   This strategy carries the supreme advantage of making the exercise of freedom possible. Freedom, as we saw, attaches to each of us only in our particularity, and requires the creative capacity to posit credible goals or "governing thoughts." By stimulating *and* containing the inner antagonism of drives and feelings, this strategy promotes the uniqueness of each being in its difference or distance from others, as well its creativity.

   From the early 1880s on, this is one of the main motivations for Nietzsche's ideal of individual sovereignty as the maintenance of a measured inner antagonism through a measured external antagonism with others. It is also, I believe, his strongest argument against the liberal concept of freedom and for the necessity of conflict, antagonism, resistance, and obstacles as the *sine qua non* of freedom.

See also 17 "Naturalism and Nietzsche's Moral Psychology"; 20 "Agent and Deed in Nietzsche's *Genealogy Of Morals*"; 21 "Nietzsche and Ethics"; 23 "Nietzsche's Fatalism"

Notes

1   The standard view of Nietzsche sees him as locating absolute and exclusive value in an elite of higher men or geniuses (see e.g. Rawls 1971: 325). In *UM III*, however, Nietzsche makes it clear that he ascribes value to any human existence in its uniqueness: "At bottom every human being knows quite well that, as a unique being [*Unicum*], he is but once in the world and that no imaginable chance will for a second time bring together such a wonderfully

variegated assortment as he is into one"; it is the artists who reveal the secret "that every human being is a one-time wonder, they dare to show us the human as it is, uniquely itself right down to every movement of the muscles, and what is more, that in this strict consistency of its uniqueness [*Einzigkeit*], it is beautiful and worthy of contemplation, new and incredible like every work of nature, and not the least tedious." Concepts like "the herd" and the "masses" do not simply serve Nietzsche to dismiss the value of the majority of humankind in favor of an elite. The problem with the herd-like existence of the majority is that it submerges diversity, distance, and the uniqueness of each member.

2 These criticisms have been made by "communitarian" critics of Rawls, notably Sandel 1998. For an account of the debate and a critical assessment of these charges, see Mulhall and Swift 1992. After *Theory of Justice*, Rawls's position takes account of these criticisms. On the later Rawls, see Owen 1995: 154–64, Mulhall and Swift 2003, and Mouffe 1996: 248–55.

3 By the same token, the notion of equality as a primordial or metaphysical feature of preexisting individuals is also ruled out. This passage suggests instead that as a value, equality has its origins in society or the state, which dictates that individual members act and feel in the same manner: namely, as "herd animals" in the interests of the state. While equality is opposed by Nietzsche to his counter-principle of hierarchy [*Rangordnung*], it should be noted that his criticisms do *not* preclude an affirmative concept of equality, where it include difference and distance. Evidence for this is to be found in Nietzsche's accounts of the Greek agon and of aristocracies (e.g. *BGE* 259). See also the moving note: "Inter pares: a word that intoxicates, – it contains within it so much happiness and unhappiness for him who has been alone his whole life; who came across no-one who belonged to him, even if he searched on many a way [. . .]" (*KSA* 12, 2[12], p. 71).

4 An English translation of this essay can be found in *On the Genealogy of Morality*, trans. Carole Diethe (Cambridge, 1994), 187–95.

5 See e.g. *UM II*, 10 on the need to distinguish "authentic" needs from false (*Schein*) needs; *UM III*, 1 and *GS* 335 on the necessity and difficulty of self-knowledge; *TI*, "Expeditions," 38 on self-control or discipline.

6 On the distinction between the "life-system" that we are and individual self-consciousness, see *KSA* 9, 11[7]: "But I distinguish: the imaginary individuals and the true 'life-systems' which we are each and every one of us – they are conflated, whereas 'the individual' is but a sum of conscious feelings [*Empfindungen*] and judgments and errors, a *belief*, a small part of the true life-system or several small parts conceived together and confabulated [*zusammengedacht und zusammengefabelt*], a 'unity' that does not hold up. [. . .] To learn step by step to cast off the *supposed individual*! To expose the errors of the ego! To see *egoism* as *error*! But not to mistake altruism for its opposite! That would only be love for *other supposed* individuals! No! To go *beyond* 'me' and 'you'! *To feel cosmically!* [*Kosmisch empfinden!*]."

7 See also the following important note: "the I is not the position of One being [*Eines Wesens*] to several (drives, thoughts etc.), but rather the ego is a multiplicity of person-like forces, of which now this one, now that stands in the foreground as ego looks out towards the others, like a subject looks towards an influential and determining outside world. The subject jumps around, we probably feel the degrees of forces and drives as nearness and farness and interpret for ourselves as a landscape and plane what in truth is a plurality of quantitative degrees. [. . .] We treat ourselves as a multiplicity and bring to these 'social relations' all the social habits which we have towards humans animals things. [. . .] – To refer all social relations back to egoism? Good: but for me it is also true that all egoistic inner experiences can be referred back to our ingrained [*eingeübten*], learned positions towards others. What drives could we have, which did not bring us from the very start into a position towards

other beings, nutrition, e.g. the sexual drive? What *others* teach us, want from us, what they tell us to fear and to pursue, [all this] is the original material of our spirit [*Geist*]: others' judgments [*fremde Urtheile*] about things. It is they that give us our *picture of ourselves*, according to which we measure ourselves and are well or ill at ease with ourselves! Our very own judgment is only a development [*Fortzeugung*] of combined judgments of others [. . .]" (*KSA* 9, 6[70]).

Editions of Nietzsche Used

"Homer's Contest," in *On the Genealogy of Morality*, trans. Carole Diethe (Cambridge: Cambridge University Press, 1994), pp. 187–95.

References

Arendt, Hannah (1968). "What is Freedom?," in *Beyond Past and Future* (London: Penguin), pp. 143–72.
—— (1998). *The Human Condition*, 2nd edn. (Chicago: University of Chicago Press).
Gerhardt, Volker (1983). "Das Prinzip des Gleichgewichts," *Nietzsche-Studien*, 12, pp. 111–33.
—— (1984). "Von der ästhetischen Metaphysik zur Physiologie der Kunst," *Nietzsche-Studien*, 13, pp. 374–93.
—— (1992). "Selbstbegründung. Nietzsche's Moral der Individualität," *Nietzsche-Studien*, 21, pp. 28–49.
Hobbes, Thomas (1991). *Leviathan*, ed. Richard Tuck (Cambridge: Cambridge University Press).
Mouffe, Chantal (1995). "Democratic Politics and the Question of Identity," in John Rajchman (ed.), *The Identity in Question* (London: Routledge), pp. 33–45.
—— (1996). "Democracy, Power and the 'Political'," in Seyla Benhabib (ed.), *Democracy and Difference: Contesting the Boundaries of the Political* (Princeton: Princeton University Press), pp. 245–56.
Mulhall, Stephen, and Swift, A. (1992). *Liberals and Communitarians* (Oxford: Blackwell).
—— (2003). "Rawls and Communitarianism," in S. Freeman (ed.), *The Cambridge Companion to Rawls* (Cambridge: Cambridge University Press), pp. 460–87.
Müller-Lauter, Wolfgang (1999). "The Organism as Inner Struggle: Wilhelm Roux's Influence on Nietzsche," in id., *Nietzsche: His Philosophy of Contradictions and the Contradictions of his Philosophy*, trans. David J. Parent (Urbana and Chicago: University of Illinois Press), pp. 161–83.
Owen, David (1995). *Nietzsche, Politics and Modernity* (London: Sage).
Rawls, John (1971). *A Theory of Justice* (Oxford: Oxford University Press).
Sandel, Michael (1998). *Liberalism and the Limits of Justice*, 2nd edn. (Cambridge: Cambridge University Press).
Schröter, H. (1982). *Historische Theorie und Geschichtliches Handeln* (Mittenwald: Mäander).
Siemens, Herman. W. (2005). "Poiesis and Praxis in Nietzsche and Arendt," *International Studies in Philosophy* (forthcoming).
Taylor, Charles (1985). "What Is Wrong with Negative Liberty?," in *Philosophical Papers*, vol. 2 (Cambridge: Cambridge University Press), pp. 211–29.
Villa, Dana (1992). "Beyond Good and Evil: Arendt, Nietzsche, and the Aestheticization of Political Action," *Political Theory*, 20(2), pp. 274–308.

Further Reading

Gerhardt, Volker (1996). *Vom Willen zur Macht. Anthropologie und Metaphysik der Macht am exemplarischen Fall Friedrich Nietzsches* (Berlin: Walter de Gruyter).

Gschwend, L. (1999). *Nietsche und die Kriminalwissenschaft* (Zurich: Schulthess Polygraphischer Verlag).

Kerger, Henri (1988). *Autorität und Recht im Denken Nietzsches* (Berlin: Duncker & Humblot).

Müller-Lauter, Wolfgang (1988). "Nietzsches Auf-lösung des Problems der Willensfreiheit," in S. Bauschinger, S. L. Cocalis, and S. Lennox (eds.), *Nietzsche Heute. Die Rezeption seines Werkes nach 1968* (Bern: Francke), pp. 23–74.

Ottmann, Henning (1987). *Philosophie und Politik bei Nietzsche* (Berlin: Walter De Gruyter); 2nd edn. 1999.

Roth, F. (1997). "Die absolute Freiheit des Schaffens," *Nietzsche-Studien*, 26, pp. 87–106.

Siemens, Herman (1998). "Philosophy, Destruction, or the Art of Limited Warfare," *Tijdschrift voor Filosofie*, 60, pp. 312–42.

——(2001). "Nietzsche's Political Philosophy: A Review of Recent Literature," *Nietzsche-Studien*, 30, pp. 509–26.

Stegmaier, Werner (1994). *Nietzsches "Genealogie der Moral"* (Darmstadt: Wissenschaftliche Buchgesellschaft).

25

Nietzsche and National Identity

DIANE MORGAN

Trade and industry, the post and book-trade, the possession in common of all higher culture, rapid changing of home and scene, the nomadic life now lived by all who do not own land – these circumstances are necessarily bringing with them a weakening and finally an abolition of nations, at least the European: so that as a consequence of continual crossing a mixed race, that of European man, must come into being out of them. (*HH* 475)

At first sight Nietzsche's opinion of national identity might seem to be crystal clear: it is an artificial construction, an old-fashioned concept, which is rapidly becoming anachronistic. The affirmation of national identity in Nietzsche's nineteenth-century world – particularly, as far as he was concerned, in the guise of Prussian nationalism – was to be considered a regression to earlier times. The powerfully transformative technological, economic, and cultural tendencies driving the evolution of the modern world were to be seen as forcing nationalism from the forefront of political agendas probably all over the globe, but at the very least within Europe.

Nietzsche scholars have been eager to insist on such a reading of the philosopher's standpoint on national identity.[1] Understandably they have wanted to distance his works from the attempts of sympathizers with National Socialism to pressgang them into the service of the Third Reich.[2] However, in this essay I want to suggest that Nietzsche's analysis of national identity was far more complex, nuanced, and ambivalent than is generally recognized. It does not suffice to present Nietzsche merely as a "good European" who espoused the adoption of the "supranational" and nomadic "homelessness."[3] Rather than simply jettisoning the concept of national identity in favor of that which supersedes its boundaries, he instead combined his interrogation of the relevance of the nation-state in a changing context with an appreciative analysis of cultural specificity and nascent independence movements. That is to say, Nietzsche can be seen not only as engaging with most topical issues relating to "transnationalism," but also as contributing towards thinking on emerging national identities within an interrelated global community. These two movements of his thought give us some insight into the major political and social turbulences of Nietzsche's own age, as well as providing us with a means to analyze more recent political and social shifts, such as those that have taken place in Europe since 1989.

Since the fall of the Berlin Wall, new nation-states have emerged or re-emerged all over Europe. However, they do so within the complex context of an expanding European Union *and* within the ever-increasing globalization of economies, of communications, of culture, of politics. Hence a thinker who combines all of these strata in his analysis of identity has a valuable contribution to make to contemporary debates. Consequently, this essay will maintain a double focus wherever possible: it will situate Nietzsche's thinking on national identity within his historical context, particularly stressing the ways in which his writings appealed to the nascent independence movements of "the East" at work within the empires of Austro-Hungary and Russia; it will also draw parallels with issues currently being discussed within what could become a "New Europe." This emphasis on eastern Europe and its reception of Nietzsche's writings breaks with the usual stress on Nietzsche's connections with southern Europe, with the Mediterranean, as pitted against the north. It is hoped that this refocusing of debate will draw out a different aspect of his thinking, one that is not only of historical but also of contemporary interest.

The first section evaluates those passages from *Human, All Too Human* which support what one could call the "straightforward" reading of national identity as something negative and unproductive that has to be overcome, either in favor of a European identity and culture, or in favor of the trans-national and global. I will draw attention to the limitations of this view and demonstrate how it leads to various dead ends because of its unidirectional focus (*away* from nationally based identity *towards* the wider European, global identity). Thomas Mann's important essay, "Nietzsche's Philosophy in the Light of our Experience," will then be introduced as a way of revisiting the idea of national identity in the second section. This involves developing a more sophisticated understanding of the topic.

1

In the passage on "European Man and the Abolition of Nations" in *Human, All Too Human* cited above, Nietzsche certainly associates "national states" with negative attributes. For example, they are seen as producing noxious hostilities both without and within themselves. Between nations tensions arise precisely because such belligerent friction is useful for keeping the artificial construct, which is the nation, mobilized and thereby intact. Its precious borders, which mark out the difference between the "us" and the "them," also create inner ethnic conflicts by attempting to enforce a specific, homogenized identity on the population. As Nietzsche says: "the entire problem of the *Jews* exists only within national states" (*HH* 475). With a more fluid conception of belongingness, one that does not try to bind nationality together with a particular cultural and biological "identity," one that could countenance the prospect of unspecified people in transit, or those with multiple identities and allegiances, such constitutive "problems" might not arise. The eruption of divisive "*national* hostilities" in Nietzsche's late nineteenth-century world was nevertheless deemed by him to be a mere "temporary counter-current" to the modern "mixing" process which inexorably works towards the eventual "amalgamation of nations."

Later on in *Human, All Too Human*, Nietzsche considers how the enthusiastic feeling of possessing a national identity expresses itself more often than not as nationalism. This by-product, which leads to the mass slaughter of young men on battlefields, is considered to be a wasteful depletion of natural energy reserves that could otherwise be put to good cultural use. When the body politic is mobilized around the "lusting after political laurels," each individual's attention is likewise absorbed; energy which could be directed in a concentrated fashion towards more focused cultural preoccupations is dissipated in the general "inflorescence and pomp of the whole" (*HH* 481). The continuous flag-waving, the breathtaking blowing of trumpets and chanting of patriotic songs, as well as the monotonous marching and the bloody fighting itself, all expend vast quantities of valuable physical, psychic, and nervous energy, with little left over for other intellectual, artistic, and spiritual undertakings, which demand "great concentration and application." Hence, the result of such a "political blooming of a people" must inevitably be an overall "spiritual impoverishment and enfeeblement." Here too, national identity – at least one motivated by an expansionist, empire-building drive, the wish to become a daunting political "colossus" – is considered to be a collective manifestation which is uninteresting, superficial, and tacky (Nietzsche refers to "the coarse and gaudy flower of the nation"). Its militaristically fueled search for geopolitical recognition is ultimately counterproductive inasmuch as, far from strengthening the nation, the body politic is spiritually depleted and thereby rendered vulnerable.[4]

Nietzsche implicitly continues his critique of national identity and the symbolically charged and sentimentalized value it places on a specific territory in his celebration of the "The Wanderer" (*HH* 638). This section in effect reminds us that humans are not born with roots but with feet to walk with.[5] "The Wanderer" enjoys this capacity for mobility to the full. He actively expresses his freedom from ties of all sorts (personal, local, regional, cultural, national), as he takes to the road, his bold stride challenging the fixity of national borders, geographical boundaries, city limits. Thriving on "change and transience," as well as stoically living through the difficulties which all adventurous travelers have to face, he epitomizes a person whose identity is not defined by where he comes from, or indeed by where he is heading to. Nietzsche makes it clear he is not "a traveller *to* a final destination," doggedly pursuing some predetermined goal. He is, rather, someone whose identity is composite, hybrid, always in the process of being constructed by his various experiences and encounters. He may not let his heart adhere too firmly to any individual thing, so if he does decide to settle in one particular place, his putting down of roots is an active choice, the culmination of the "radical selections *we make for ourselves*" (Rushdie 1999: 414; my emphasis). Some vague biologically determined hankering after a long-lost "homeland" does not prompt his sedentarization. Additionally, even when nominally settled in one place, he is not at rest; there is still "something wandering" growing within him which delights in the unusual, the new, and the transitory and that is not solely gratified with what is perceived as homely and familiar. In his resistance to conventional codes which strive to bind people to fixed identities, identifying their belongingness with a particular nationality, associated with a precisely defined territory, the Wanderer embodies what Deleuze calls "nomad thought" (Deleuze 2002: 351–64).

In part 2 of *Human, All Too Human*, one's potential to be a modern citizen is predicated on writing well (*WS* 87). Nietzsche suggests that, just as the Greek model of the city state has been replaced as a political ideal with a grander scale for political activity, one that encompasses the whole planet, so too has oral culture necessarily been replaced by the written word. One's ability to communicate with one's fellow citizens is no longer defined by one's ability to project one's voice audibly to the outward perimeters of the gathered community. As the exchange of ideas now takes place *internationally*, indeed *trans-nationally*, the modern citizen of the world has to use the written word in order to reach his fellow freethinkers.

Evidently, Nietzsche's proposed shift from the oral to the written medium does not anticipate recent developments in global communications. The deficiencies of the human voice are now easily overcome by amplifying technologies. Oral exchanges no longer have to take place face to face: the orator's audience itself may well be physically dispersed or deferred, the impact of the speech, its sound still biting, hitting them at a later date. The oral medium is far from becoming redundant; indeed it could be said that it is the written word that is more than ever under threat. Obliged to mimic the sloppy colloquialisms of the oral in SMS, blurted out sentences hastily dispatched in email, the written word scarcely seems to be respected and nurtured as the creator and vehicle of "things worth communicating." "Writing well" has never appeared to be of less importance. The potentially world-wide exchange of books, pamphlets, and letters, which constituted the strong intellectual and amicable links of the humanist *Leserwelt*, might not be as essential nowadays as Nietzsche makes out.[6] His equation of speaking with "the national," and of the written with the global, maybe strikes one as an attractive, but rather quaint proposition. As more recent commentators, such as Sloterdijk, have made clear, "The friendly model of the literary society" is no longer the "civilizing" force the Enlightenment assumed it would be, nor an adequate analogy for today's vast political and economic networks (Sloterdijk 1999: 3). Also, in the world of global capitalism national boundaries and differences, instead of becoming redundant anachronisms to be jettisoned as quickly as possible, can instead be highly useful tools for multinational companies: pitted against one another, they can be exploited so as to stimulate "market forces" and heighten "competition." Multinational companies can displace, or threaten to displace, factories from one nation-state to another, playing different workforces off against each other. "National characteristics" can be used to justify the relocation and concomitant "laying off" of hundreds of employees in search of cheaper, "more flexible" workforces elsewhere. It would therefore be overhasty to adopt Nietzsche's assumptions in this passage that the becoming-global of the links between humans equates either with the growing importance of the pen (with its long history as repository of humanist, cosmopolitan value) or with a supersession of the nation-state.

In the same section (*WS* 87), Nietzsche also seems to be overtaken by cultural and political developments in his assumption that the "good European" – he who has broken free of the shackles of the national – has facing him the task of managing the cultural health of the globe. After a twentieth century largely characterized by war and by colonial, totalitarian, and genocidal crimes, one would probably hesitate to confer "the direction and supervision of the total culture of the earth" solely on Europeans, however apparently free-spirited they might strike us.[7] Here again his "unidirectional" abandonment of the national in favor of the wider mode of belongingness, in this case the European, fails to satisfy.

In relation to the topics of "fashion and modernity" Nietzsche further expresses his clear disdain for the national:

> Wherever ignorance, uncleanliness and superstition are still the order of the day, wherever communications are poor, the landscape is meagre and the priesthood powerful, there we still also discover *national costumes*. (*WS* 215)

Sartorially itching to distance themselves from their otherwise all too conspicuous origins, modern folk are reaching for the anonymous internationalism of fashion. The complicatedly belted and pleated traditional costumes induce mental and physical sluggishness. Just as national identity itself becomes a carcass hindering new development, so does folkloric attire consist of cumbersome garments hampering movement. By contrast, the bold, easy-wear, slick designs of the great metropolises are able to accompany a liberatingly accelerated speed of life and thereby promote mental and physical agility.

This section is most notable for the definition it gives of Europe, one that is of topical interest:

> Here, where the concepts "modern" and "European" are almost equivalent, what is understood by Europe comprises much more territory than geographical Europe, the little peninsula of Asia: America, especially, belongs to it, insofar as it is the daughter-land of our culture. On the other hand, the cultural concept "Europe" does not include all of geographical Europe; it includes only those nations and ethnic minorities who possess a common past in Greece, Rome, Judaism and Christianity. (*WS* 215)

Whereas national identity is usually designated by mapping out a particular region within which a specific people is assumed to dwell, Europe presents us with a different logic. Nietzsche partly dissociates Europe from any clearly demarcated land mass. Europe, understood in strictly geographical terms, is a mere "little peninsula of Asia." There is a non-alignment between this somewhat negligible promontory and what "Europe" means here. The idea of "Europe" is cultural and for this reason it also has to include its "natural" extension, its "daughter-land," America.[8] Likewise it also excludes, for Nietzsche, Islam. The Muslim populations of Bulgaria, Bosnia, or Romania are not considered to be "European" according to this definition. Additionally, if Nietzsche's criteria were to be adopted, Turkey could not be considered for entry into the entity now called the European Union, unless it were partitioned in such a way that what used to belong to the Greco-Roman dominion of Thrace could be incorporated. Here Nietzsche reveals a conventional and restricted notion of Europe's composition, one predicated on conventional ideas of the "Western" and, as such, over-simplistic in its understanding of the nature of the "common past" informing Europe.[9]

"Europe" also has a problematic relationship with Russia, as Nietzsche indicates in an aphorism entitled "Most Dangerous Form of Emigration" (*WS* 231). Russia figures throughout Nietzsche's writings as both "occidental," part of Europe, and "oriental," foreign to Europe. The latter aspect, called "Asia," provides both constitutive sources

459

for European culture and an alien force against which Europe defends itself and by so doing consolidates itself.[10] Geographically Europe joins the vast Asian continent, and it is only culturally separated from it to a vacillating extent. Through an ongoing process of confrontation, taming, conversion, and incorporation, Asian elements can nourish the dynamism of European culture. Indeed, to give a prime example, Asia is the source of the cult of Dionysus. However, the potential of the Dionysian for revitalizing and deepening culture could only make itself felt in Greece, where, once "moderated," it entered into a most beautiful "*Bruderbund*" with the Apollonian (*KSA* 1, p. 583).[11] Otherwise, in its raw, unmediated state, Asia permanently threatens to engulf Europe with "barbarism." A similar diagnosis is echoed in this section from *Human All Too Human*: furious about being drained of intelligence as "good books" increasingly entice its thinking population towards Europe, "the spirit of the deserted fatherland [is turned] into the extended jaws of Asia that would like to devour little Europe." Russia is characterized as a volatile entity, whose biopolitical balance can change and whose disposition towards Europe can fluctuate. The ascendancy of the Asiatic for Nietzsche spells a menace for "civilization," for things "Greek" (*HH* 114). However, this threat can provide an opportunity for reinvigorating cultural resilience; the world-weary Europeans are obliged to tap into dormant energy reserves so as to mobilize a defense of their heritage and their future. Russia is considered by Nietzsche to be a key consideration when discussing European matters, including the fate of nation-states – as indeed it still is today.[12]

In his essay "Nietzsche's Philosophy in the Light of our Experience" Thomas Mann draws on a late section of *The Wanderer and his Shadow* to present Nietzsche as a surprisingly far-sighted analyst of the changing political tide. This political clairvoyancy is most unexpected, Mann suggests, given that Nietzsche was "the most perfect and irredeemable aesthete, that history has ever known" (Mann 1997: 87). Despite his basic political indifference and naivety, Nietzsche nevertheless prophesies the future emergence of a "European League of Nations." Mann does concede that this prospect is not "not exactly" greeted "with enthusiasm" by Nietzsche; it is rather that, ahead of his time, he foresees this development to be "a consequence of an increasingly victorious democracy" (Mann 1997: 85). Within such a federation the importance of nation-states will necessarily be scaled down, "each individual nation, delimited according to geographical fitness, will possess the status and rights of a canton" (*WS* 292). In his commentary on this passage, Mann draws our attention to the "purely European" perspective adopted by Nietzsche. He then suggests an interesting – but somewhat ill-grounded, in my opinion[13] – shift in Nietzsche's thought towards a more global point of view:

> During the next decade [according to Mann's calculation this would be the 1880s] his perspective expands to include the global and universal. [Nietzsche] talks of the unavoidable, imminent administration of the economy of the world as a whole. He calls for as many international powers as possible "to acquire a global perspective." His belief in Europe wavers [. . .] (Mann 1997: 85)[14]

Interestingly, one of the citations Mann uses to support his thesis of a more engaged, more humanistically minded Nietzsche, whose interests extend beyond the European, would necessitate a re-evaluation of place of Asia and the Asian in Nietzsche's thinking. Mann draws our attention to the following remark from the 1884 *Nachlass*: "Europeans basically imagine themselves to represent the higher human [*den höheren Menschen*] on earth. But the Asians are a hundred times more impressive [*grossartiger*] than the Europeans" (Mann 1997: 85; see *KSA* 11, 26[319] and 11, 36[57]).

Another passage, also from the 1884 *Nachlass*, which Mann does not cite, reinforces this thesis of a wider outlook, one that includes a more positive – though no less "orientalist" – interest in "Asia." Nietzsche tells himself: "I must learn to think *in a more oriental way* [*orientalischer*] about philosophy and knowledge. *An Eastern overview* [*Morgenländischer Überblick*] over Europe" (*KSA* 11, 26[317]).

Mann extrapolates from the 1888 *Nachlass* when he ties Nietzsche's proposed "excursion into the world-political" with the philosopher's dynamic conception of global forces, one that, "purely intuitively, anticipates the investigations of modern physics": "For the world, a new self-forming world-picture [*Weltbild*], is a unity, and wherever, to whatever side, such an enormous hypersensitiveness turns and explores, it experiences the new, the oncoming, and registers it" (1997: 85–6).[15]

Highlighting Nietzsche's reservations about a mechanistic preconception of the world, which in its search for predictability seeks to tie all that happens down to the laws of causality, Mann presents the alternative vision of a incalculable world consisting of antagonistic forces. Their ever ongoing struggle produces completely new states, "new arrangements of forces," which cannot be interpreted as mere predetermined "effects" (Mann 1997: 86). In this interesting reading of Nietzsche's political views alongside, or rather through, his intuitions about physics, Mann presents the philosopher as closely involved in the radically changing world. Far from being just a solitary genius, whose inspired thoughts can only be of minor interest to a traumatized, post-World War II generation, Nietzsche is to be regarded as of contemporary relevance. Mann lays stress on Nietzsche's commitment to life, to the future, and to the destiny of humanity as a whole. To address a German and American public in 1947 with an essay on the tainted Nietzsche is already a bold gesture. To "redeem" Nietzsche, Mann needed to demonstrate not only the inaccuracy of the National Socialist reading of his works, but also highlight aspects of Nietzsche's philosophy which could be of topical interest to those seeking answers to such urgent questions as: What do we understand by "human nature" after all we have seen?[16] To what extent might the human species be transformed by its terrible and violent past? What aims should now be set for a reconfigured humanity, one that can invent a "higher form of being"? (see *WP* 866 and 898).

At the beginning of his essay Mann describes the "desperate cruelty" with which Nietzsche talks about "*everything* he deemed worthy of respect: about Wagner, about music in general, about morality, about Christianity – I almost said: also about Germanness [*Deutschtum*]." Far from really wanting to offend these cherished, "highly esteemed values and forces," his "furious, critical fits" against them were, asserts Mann, "a form of homage" (1997: 64). Indeed, as far as *Deutschtum* is concerned, he goes to some lengths to show how Nietzsche's pro-European, globally concerned stance is compatible with his nationality, with his sense of what it means to be a German. Evidently, the form of national identity in question is not one that defines itself against Europe and against the world, but one that is able to retain or construct a cultural

461

specificity while "thinking and feeling" that which is "beyond the nation" (Cheah and Robbins 1998). It is this logic that we will now develop in relation to the other works of Nietzsche. This will enable us to explore a view of national identity which is not straightforwardly dismissive of it, as has up to now been the case, but which instead necessitates a multi-scaled maneuver between the national, the supra- or trans-national, and the global.

2

Nietzsche's numerous, vituperative remarks about Germans and Germany – those same remarks that seem to hurt Mann's sensibility, still committed as he evidently is to his German cultural heritage – are a good if unexpected starting point for revisiting the theme of national identity in Nietzsche's work. As we will see, it is these same remarks, so merciless in their criticism, which will curiously lead us to a more nuanced, more sophisticated, understanding of national identity than the straightforward rejection of it outlined so far.

To be sure, it is certainly not difficult to find examples of Nietzsche's unsparingly negative descriptions of his "countrymen." For example:

> The German *drags* his soul, he drags everything he experiences. He digests his events badly, he is never "done" with them; German profundity is often only a sluggish "digestion." (*BGE* 244)

Unmasking the "myth" of German *Innerlichkeit* (inwardness) as the product, not of philosophical acuteness of mind, but of all too bodily dumplings and stodgy puddings seems to be a clear enough statement of contempt. Indeed, for Nietzsche, German national identity does appear to encapsulate all that is wrong with national identity per se. Its indigenous (*heimisch*) customs induce a self-satisfied, beer-bloated inertia which results in a "sickness of the will" (*BGE* 208). Having just recently emerged as a nation-state after one decade of strategically calculated warmongering on the part of Bismarck, Germany also epitomizes the lamentable tendency of Europe as a whole. Ever since the Peace of Westphalia (1648), the model dominating the international order had been one based on relations between sovereign states.[17] In 1815, after the defeat of Napoleon, the Treaty of Vienna carved up the continent to feed the expansionist appetites of England, Austria, Prussia, and Russia. Thus consolidated, those nation-states dominated political power in Europe to the misfortune, particularly, of the Polish, but also of other ethnic groups all across the territory. Nietzsche's lamentation of the decline of Napoleon, albeit romanticized and historically inaccurate, marks the mourning of the project to unite Europe beyond the petty divisions of parochially minded nation-states. "*Europe wants to become one*" he proclaims, and the thwarting of this will for a "new *synthesis*" means that Europe is deprived of its future (*BGE* 256). In Nietzsche's eyes, this glorious vision of trans-national European unity seems to be receding in a continental Europe where bulky, belligerently defensive nation-states are increasingly determining the evolution of the continent. Indeed nationalism, "this anti-cultural illness and unreason [. . .] this *névrose nationale*" which pumps up through

German veins, also emits the discordant tone within Europe as a whole (*KSA* 14, p. 503).

However, there are exceptional Germans, such as Goethe. Not just a poet but also a dramatist, novelist, painter, and experimental scientist, Goethe was unusual for his eagerness to seize life in all of its manifold guises. He "aspired to totality," claimed Nietzsche, and this intense wish for more ran counter to an age and a nation that was content with itself, with its limited vision and its abstractions (*TI*, "Expeditions of an Untimely Man," 49). Goethe wanted to maximize his life experiences, but this large appetite led, not to a gnawing insatiability, to a perpetually dissatisfied restlessness, but rather to a generously full-bodied, active participation in the world. Unappreciated by his compatriots, Goethe was not assimilable to the prevailing definition of *Deutschtum*. But then, Nietzsche exclaims, how could any national identity ever incorporate such an exceptional citizen? No *Volk en masse* could ever live up to such a model of human plenitude: "How could a people ever be equal to Goethean *spirituality* in *wellbeing and well-wishing!*" (*AOM* 170). Indeed, Goethe was an exception to the dominant German rule and, in addition, incompatible with any average national character (*GS* 103). In fact, his conspicuous superiority to the norm was not just a sign of the spiritually impoverished times, as he would always remain a cultural anomaly regardless of the particular age and, by extension, of the national culture in question: "Goethe stood above the Germans in every respect and still stands above them: he will never belong to them" (*AOM* 170; see also *GS* 103).

However, Goethe's incongruent untimeliness is also curiously representative of the quintessential German. Or rather, to be more precise, the epitome of Germanness would be someone who "[eludes] *definition*" as his identity is not fixed; it cannot be tied down to an essence. A German is always in the process of becoming himself. Nietzsche defines the undefinable German in the following manner: "The German himself *is* not, he *is becoming*, he is developing" (*BGE* 244). This not uncritical comment appears in a passage where Nietzsche accuses Germans of befuddled and mystificatory obscurity. They stand out as a nation because of their extreme lack of clarity: "the Germans are more incomprehensible, more comprehensive [*umfänglicher*], more full of contradictions, more unknown, more incalculable, more surprising, even more frightening to themselves than other peoples are" (*BGE* 244).

This national "identity," which scarcely emerges from the shifting sands it consists of, which can only be pinpointed by a piling up of epithets, some negative, some positive, is complex and contradictory. As well as deluding themselves that obscurity is "profound," the Germans' lack of clarity leads to a more laudable quest for self-knowledge and a more all-encompassing (*umfänglicher*) exploration of the world than is the case with nations whose identity is more stable. Rather than being sure about his ancestral roots and his place on this planet, the German interrogates his nature and his destiny. For him national identity is no obvious natural given. Instead it is more or less imperfectly produced through a long (historical, ideological) process. It is an identity that is constructed artificially and piecemeal.[18] Goethe can come to represent the perfect German inasmuch as his identity too was imperfect, contradictory, and inconsistent.

Indeed, even Goethe's world-famous "masterpiece," *Faust*, is flawed. In the 1882 *Nachlass* Nietzsche exclaims: "Faust, the tragedy about knowledge? I laugh about Faust!" (*KSA* 10, §406, p. 102). Four years earlier, in *Human, All Too Human* (1878), he had already made clear, in a parodic synopsis of the storyline, why Goethe's "Faust Idea" failed miserably to attain the tragic dimensions it laid claim to:

> A little seamstress is seduced and dishonoured; a great scholar of all the four faculties is the miscreant. But that surely cannot happen in the right nature of things? No, by no means! Without the assistance of the Devil in person, the great scholar could not have brought it about. Is this really supposed to be the greatest German "tragic idea," as the Germans say it is? (WS 124)

In their commentary on this passage, Colli and Montinari add these even more wickedly satirical remarks by Stendhal (1838) about the Faust plot: "Goethe gave the devil friend to doctor Faust and with such a powerful auxiliary, Faust manages to do everything that we all already did at the age of twenty: he seduces a seamstress" (*KSA* 14, p. 192).

Nietzsche (and Stendhal) present Goethe as being just too soft to carry through his plans for a grand-scale tragic drama about one man's desperate striving to overcome human limitations and grasp the essence of things, to penetrate through to "was die Welt | Im Innersten zusammenhält" (Goethe 1991: I. 382–4). Goethe is ineffectual because, unlike "Schopenhauer the educator," he cannot "get really angry for once in order that things shall get better," and the result is that the play *Faust*, despite its epic pretensions, flops back into becoming a rather trite, sordid and banal story of seduction and ultimate loving reconciliation beyond the grave, a big metaphysical cop out" (*UM III*, 4). The *content* is unequal to the scale of the project (*tant pis* for the seamstress! who cares about her!), it is *formally* a mess (Part II especially is unwatchable and unbearable), and it reveals the limited, feeble vision of its author.

Indeed, Nietzsche explains that "every factor which is given as a reason for Faust's suffering in the first scene is erroneous, because of metaphysical fabrications." In the first scene of the play, Faust complains of his stuffy academic life, dedicated to the antiquarian world of books, to past authorities. He feels detached from life, from the real world: his ascetic, over-intellectualized existence leaves him feeling unhappy, so he calls upon the spirits of the other world to give meaning to this one. In *Faust* Goethe is seen as letting down his "good German moments" and "lapsing back into the damp moods" ("fiel er selber wieder in die feuchten Stimmungen zurück": *KSA* 11, 34[97]), which are described as typical of the underlying German predilection for all that is foggy, dark, brooding, musty, bleak, unclear, and chaotic (*BGE* 244).

However, despite – or because of – these very faults, Goethe is a compellingly enigmatic figure. Whatever negative reactions he provokes, he is nevertheless a figure who pushed himself to his limits and continually strained himself to evolve in new directions. In exploring the world, Goethe overhauled his self: at times he was able to distance himself from the worse morbid excesses of his national culture, and in so doing he embodied the best aspects of his national identity. Our reactions to Goethe are therefore not just negative; they are necessarily ambivalent. So too, then, are our reactions to national identity as Goethe encapsulates the enigma of this strange tie.

What has emerged from the above analysis is a more intricate understanding of national identity at work in Nietzsche's writing, which precludes a straightforward rejection of the issue. Hence we now turn back to *Human, All Too Human* and to a passage therein which gives a more elaborate account of national identity than the others analyzed above from this same book. Counteracting the simplistically negative remarks initially extrapolated from this text, Nietzsche elliptically gives the title "To be a good German means to degermanize oneself" ("Gut deutsch sein heisst sich entdeutschen": *AOM* 323). This phrase suggests that a good German, such as Goethe, moves gracefully away from his embarrassing national roots into the freer air of, for instance, European culture, but in so doing he remains typically German.[19] The folkloric dress and customs of a nation can all too easily become a straitjacket hampering growth and stultifying expression. He who breaks through this imprisoning "girdle" thereby helps to further the aims of the despised tradition whose shackles he was supposed to have discarded. The *Volk* need a demolition man to smash down the otherwise petrifying and debilitating crust that accrues on their cultural forms of self-representation: in repudiating his origins, he thereby liberates them, obliging them to outgrow the stereotypical modes of behavior that determine them and to imitate his new model. Nietzsche insists that national identity should not be seen as something permanent. It is not a natural, immutable given, but is instead a reflection of "varying *stages of culture*." Nietzsche concludes:

> He therefore who has the interests of the Germans at heart should for his part see how he can grow more and beyond what is German. That is why a *change into the ungermanic* [*Die Wendung zum Undeutschen*] has always been the mark of the most able of our people. (*AOM* 323)

Far from offering a straightforward dismissal of national culture, Nietzsche is here reformulating its nature and scope. He suggests that great men like Goethe are able to tap the potential for dynamic change that national culture contains. Instead of remaining locked into the senseless repetition of redundant customs, an evolving national identity can become a rich source of energy for a "forward-moving people."

Another passage from *Human, All Too Human*, deliberately left unexamined earlier on, also introduces material for a more positive stance on national identity than one might imagine to be the case. In "Whither We Have To Travel," Nietzsche gives a very different account of cultural traditions than, for example, in the section "Fashion and Modernity" (*WS* 215) previously discussed. Instead of espousing the liberating influence of modern city life, he here gives a sensitive account of the richness of regionalism. Nietzsche begins by insisting on the importance of time-traveling: this can either take the form of physically moving between cultures – as each one evolves at a different speed and in a different way from the others – or by absorbing the various historical "strata" which pulsate through a locality that has preserved its cultural past:

> The last three centuries very probably still continue to live on, in all their cultural colours and cultural refractions, *close beside us*: they only want to be *discovered*. In many families, indeed in individual men, the strata still lie neatly and clearly one on top of the other: elsewhere there are dislocations and faults which make understanding more difficult. A venerable specimen of very much older sensibility could certainly have been more easily preserved in remoter regions, in less travelled mountain valleys, in self-enclosed communities. (*WS* 223)

465

The exploration of the "savage" ages which still resonate within isolated cultures unspoilt by the hardening processes of the modern world, is seen to *open up* not to shut down the ego – for Nietzsche considers that it is the "ego" which goes adventurously traveling through these latent past eras.[20] This analysis of the historically informed self is most positive, even utopian: the "processes of becoming and transformation" which are activated by such adventures through time, if not necessarily across space, are regarded as leading in turn to an eventual overcoming of the self towards a higher plane. Nietzsche writes:

> Thus self-knowledge will become universal knowledge with regard to all that is past: just as, merely to allude to another chain of reflections, self-determination and self-education could in the freest and most far-sighted spirits, one day become universal determination with regard to all future humanity. (*WS* 223)

A trip into the mind of the narrowest of circumscribed individuals, provided that that person relates symbiotically to his environment, will open up varied worlds which might stretch back to ancient Greece and beyond, encompassing hereditary tales of intrepid seafarers or dignified Venetian merchants. A reawakening of past cultural forms, songs no longer sung, dances no longer danced, though remembered deep down, might tap into drives searching for expression which span temporal and spatial divides. Interestingly, such an exploration is not of mere antiquarian interest (the wish to preserve a common past); it is *future-oriented*, working towards the ultimate conflation of boundaries between the self, the particular culture, and the rest of humanity.

Nietzsche begins this section by evoking Heraclitus' conundrum, "Does time flow through us or do we flow through time?" He then asserts that "we ourselves are, indeed, nothing but that which at every moment we experience of this continued flowing [of the past]" (*WS* 223). Regions where the past still resonates are regarded as extending to full span the nature of the human, whereas the past is regarded as sterilely fossilized in urban museological mausoleums. Hence one's quest for self-knowledge might well find fertile sustenance among "savage and semi-savage" peoples who live modestly and traditionally in a remote rural locations, far from the disenchanted, dehistoricized urban centres.

Thoughts such as these provided inspiration to the numerous independence movements at work in late nineteenth- and early twentieth-century "east Europe," often perceived as more "primitive," less "developed," than the west. Indeed the contributors to the important volume *East Europe Reads Nietzsche* present Nietzsche as *the* key figure for those ethnic minorities who were militating against their imperial oppressors and searching for their identity and freedom. "The luminaries of East European modernism," it is claimed, had very "distinctive readings" of Nietzsche which in turn entail a reassessment of the place national identity holds within his oeuvre (Freifeld et al. 1998: p. v). For the Romanian, Polish, Czech, Slovakian, Hungarian, and Bulgarian avant-gardes were indeed well acquainted with his works, which were devoured by them in German, as well as rapidly translated into their native tongues.[21]

Reading Nietzsche through the optic of the east shifts the overriding emphasis of most critics who, while exploring the philosopher as a "good European," tend solely to stress the north–south axis in his work. They concentrate solely on the thinker's flight from the beer-bloated and petty provincialism of German places such as Schulporta and Naumburg to the mountainous freedom of Switzerland and on to the inland and coastal health of sunny Italy (see Krell and Bates 1997). They thereby consider only Nietzsche's drive to "Mediterraneanize" thinking, to the exclusion of the Adriatic and the Black Sea, and of the vast neighboring area of the Austro-Hungarian empire. This oversight is regrettable because, as Peter Bergmann makes clear, it was "along the east–west axis [that] the unresolved tensions of [Nietzsche's] time [ran]" (Freifeld et al. 1998: 24). Evidently these same tensions went on to determine the major political events of the twentieth century. It is therefore interesting and important to read Nietzsche in the light of his reception in the other half of Europe. This new perspective on Nietzsche's influence goes against the dominant preoccupation amongst western Nietzsche readers (and on the part of Nietzsche himself) with the south, as defined and pitched against the north. Brushing against the grain of such orthodoxy, the editors of *East Europe Reads Nietzsche* lay claim to the importance and distinctiveness of the reception of Nietzsche in the Slav world, emphasizing how he "provoked [his readers there] to voice their individuality in their native languages while connecting them to an international avant-garde" (Freifeld et al. 1998: p. vi).

For this other world, Nietzsche was not just a cosmopolitan thinker[22] but also an oft-cited and discussed "linchpin for a national cultural awakening in the Slavic world" (Freifeld et al. 1998: p. vi). Adopting this different point of view on the reception of Nietzsche's ideas brings with it the added advantage of rectifying the illusion that modernism just "flowed through the Vienna gate" out to its satellite cities and towns as if these other places – Budapest, Prague, Bratislava, Cracow, etc. – were mere passive recipients of European culture and not already avidly reading and discussing the works for themselves (Freifeld, in Freifeld et al. 1998: 4). As Alice Freifeld writes:

> The Nietzsche reception in East Europe did not emanate from Vienna, rather Nietzschean modernism was embraced, rejected and debated independently in the other metropolises of the empire. The discourse of intellectuals was a cosmopolitanism addressed *beyond* the borders of the monarchy rather than amongst the peoples *within* it. (Freifeld et al. 1998: 5)

She goes on to stress that "the Viennese Nietzsche reception reflected the political decline of Vienna," and indeed it was Budapest that was "the fastest growing city in Europe" (with Prussian Berlin also threatening to usurp the Viennese cultural hegemony) (Freifeld et al. 1998: 2–3). Intellectuals in the east generally tended to be heavily implicated in politics and public life, whereas the predominantly Jewish intelligentsia of Vienna was, as Zweig and others point out, excluded from such realms and hence became "the guardians and protectors of culture" as their sole means of exerting any influence (Zweig 1988: 35–6). In *The Garden and the Workshop*, a comparative study of socio-cultural life in Budapest and Vienna at the turn of the nineteenth century, Péter Hanák suggests that Vienna was a city marked by Baroque "illusionism and an adoration of beauty and ornamentation," whereas Budapest grew up under classicism. This meant that "art for this [Budapester] public was not an expression of piety and sensuality, nor the stage an evocation of the illusion of reality. They were media for awakening national consciousness – effective tools for educating the nation" (Hanák 1988: p. xxi).

This seems to be true of the other regions of the empire which had been affirming their specific and shared (pan-Slavic) identities at least since 1828 when the Slovak, Kollar, published *Wechselseitigkeit* (*Reciprocity*), an analysis of the "common linguistic stock" informing and underlying the various Slavonic dialects which it was incumbent on "every educated Slavonian" to be familiar with (Krasinski 1848: 108).[23] To give just some indication of the cultural swings and negotiations of the period, whereas in 1848 Prague and Budapest were overwhelmingly German-speaking, by 1914 Czech or Hungarian were the dominant languages (Freifeld, in Freifeld et al. 1998: 8). The tide was even audibly turning.

It might be thought quite strange that Nietzsche, who, as we have seen, constantly inveighs against the stupidity and artificiality of nationalism and against *Kleinstaaterei* (*GS* 377), against the formation of petty states bristling across the face of Europe, which interfere with its wish to become one (*BGE* 256), should be read with enthusiasm, if at times qualified, by those nineteenth- and early twentieth-century Europeans involved in national independence movements. Doesn't Nietzsche make it clear that "the time for small scale politics is over" (*BGE* 208)? Doesn't he embrace the *über*national and push for the nomadic life of free spirits unattached to any homeland, donators to European cultural hybridity (to the European *Mischrasse*) (*HH* 475)?

This is all true, but Nietzsche also constructs a mythic ancestral past for himself, that of a Polish nobleman. This alternative national identity is seen as preventing him from lapsing into being a mere *Reichsdeutsche*. He claims that his adoption of "the East" opens up a vision of what lies "beyond the simply local, beyond the simply nationally conditioned perspective" (*EH*, "Why I Am So Wise," 3; see also *KSA* 14, p. 472).[24] It is his embroidered Slavic connection which is seen as putting him in touch with a future-oriented Europeanism, thereby opening a rich "imaginative field" in which to reorientate himself (Freifeld, in Freifeld et al. 1998: 4). Nietzsche also speaks in favor of an adversarial, militant, all-questioning culture; he calls on energetic youth to overturn the traditional – read imperial – values and beliefs foisted on them in the name of self-affirmation. His analysis of the military successes of major powers, such as Bismarckian Germany, are radically critical, dismissing any equation of political clout with cultural vitality (see the analysis of *HH* 481 above). All these elements come together to form an empowering discourse for would-be nations, looking for cultural expression and social justice. Those who were not so much interested in empire-building as in affirming their will, and who felt in need of a strong thinker to overcome the intimidating specters of Prussian and Austro-Hungarian domination, enthusiastically adopted Nietzsche as their spokesperson.[25]

Indeed Nietzsche's virulent anti-Germanness became for east Europeans a model of, to use Alice Freifeld's term, "higher patriotism." That is to say, a patriotism willing and able to judge the nation that was in the process of being constructed, rather than just following in its trail. "Higher patriotism" is capable of interrogating the very idea of national identity, while being willing to exploit the most productive reserves that the cultural tradition contains. The idea of a "higher patriotism" also necessitates a refusal to isolate the nation from outside influence, to lock culture up within an insulated, discrete identity. It asserts itself in and through an evolving articulation with a more inclusive and complex (cosmopolitan) supra-identity – in this case "European." Nietzsche's sustained fascination with the figure of Goethe contributes to this new formulation of national identity: as we saw, Goethe is praised as a European event and yet as one of the last great Germans, a de-Germanized German. In this manner, national identity is informed and reworked by a trans-national idea of belongingness. A similar sophisticated negotiation faces many newly emerged nation-states today in the new Europe. While feeling disoriented by what has been called their "postcolonial syndrome," they are inventing or rediscovering their own particular cultural heritage and national identity *while* thinking and feeling European, *while* rediscovering what they see as their European past, *within* a global (economic, political, cultural) context.[26] This nurturing of national and cultural singularity, within both a European and a global framework, is a delicate, critical and self-critical, future-oriented process which differs radically from any reclaiming of some pre-given, retrievable past identity. Nietzsche's meditations on questions of national identity and its relationship to a trans-national culture can be perceived as timely and pertinent to such a context.

To the restless militants of the late nineteenth century who sought national and cultural affirmation, Nietzsche also appeared to offer intellectual support. They were sensitively alert to passages such as "Whither We Have To Travel," discussed above, where Nietzsche condemned modernized society, criticizing the expanding Prussian capital of Berlin for only churning out "washed out and hard boiled" (*ausgelaugt und abgebrüht*) citizens in whom ancient and rich historical strata no longer reverberated. Drawing a contrast with the psychic desiccation of efficiency-driven industrialized society, Nietzsche praised geographical locations more propitious to the continued cultivation of a "much older sensibility." Inspired by his celebration of vibrant tradition, inhabitants of the furthest corners of the empire, far removed from the glitzy splendor of the cities of the Dual Monarchy, could feel vindicated that history was flowing even, or especially, through their remote towns and villages. Nietzsche could be understood as reminding them that there was no need to emulate metropolitan culture, no need to travel "thousands of miles" as the "last three centuries still continue to live on, in all their cultural colours and cultural refractions, *close beside us*, they only want to be *discovered*" (cited above).[27]

One such example of an avid reader of Nietzsche who came from one of the remote places evoked by the philosopher, a small village in Transylvania (which belonged to the Austro-Hungarian empire until the end of World War I), was the philosopher and poet Lucian Blaga. Hitchins writes that Blaga "participated fully in post-war debates about the ethnic nature of Romanians and their place in Europe" (Freifeld et al. 1998: 164). He constructed his own version of a Zarathustra prophet-figure in Zamolxe (1921), who encourages his people to free themselves from obsolete beliefs and to reappropriate their rich Slavic and Dionysian Dacian heritage which lies under the superimposed classical, Latinate stratum. This working through and affirmation of national particularity eventually led Blaga to the heart of the cultural elite of the post-1918 national state, when Transylvania became part of the Kingdom of Romania.[28]

Nietzsche's support for contemporary independence movements in the subjugated regions of Europe was far from being unreserved. His reservations about the prospect of new nations forming across Europe are evident in the following scathing comment in the 1885–6 *Nachlass*:

we are in the middle of a dangerous carnival of nationalities-madness, where all finer reason has crept to one side and the vanity of the gruffest backwater-people [*der ruppigsten Winkel-Völker*] shout for their right to a special-existence and self-magnificence. (*KSA* 12, 2[3])

However, he nevertheless goes on to concede that, at least in the case of Poland, his pet nation, it was difficult to deny the people their aspirations for self-governance: "how can one hold it against the Poles, the most distinguished outcrop of the Slavic world, to entertain hopes [. . .]" (*KSA* 12, 2[3]). This fragmentary comment testifies to a reluctant acknowledgment that, in an age of raging imperialist nationalism, there is a case to be made for tentatively emerging or re-emerging nations. But ambivalence accompanies such an acknowledgment, and this ambivalence should be, for Nietzsche, a constitutive element of our national identity: as we saw, this concomitant ambivalence informed Goethe's relation to Germany and, in turn, our relation to Goethe and the German culture he both represented and did not represent.

In the *Uses and Disadvantages of History for Life* Nietzsche analyzed the different types of historicity appropriate to, or noxious for, different cultural and political periods. This account of the shifting, sometimes physical "horizons" which accompany our psychic negotiation with historical processes provides, maybe, the most fertile ground for mustering support from Nietzsche for an affirmation of national and cultural identity. We are told that "The Greeks gradually learned *to organize the chaos* by following the Delphic teaching [i.e. to know thyself] and think back to themselves, that is to their real needs and letting their pseudo-needs die out. Thus they again took possession of themselves [*So ergriffen sie wieder von sich Besitz*]" (*UM II*, 10, p. 122).

It is here that I locate the boldest statement of Nietzsche in favor of assertive national identity as the mastery of the personal and collective self. But again, to conclude, the "organization" must be recognized as provisional, "fictive," artificial, not as eternal and natural. National identity is also not to be regarded in isolation, as that which separates a people from the outside world, but is rather reflexively constructed through and by a communication with the trans-national. It does not suffice to dismiss the search for national identity as a mere regression to primitive times.[29] Rather than presenting us with a unidirectional rejection of national identity as solely anachronistic, Nietzsche's works can be seen as contributing in interesting ways to the self-formulations of nineteenth- and early twentieth-century national independence movements in the east. They are also apposite to discussions currently being held in east Europe. To use Mann's phrase, it remains possible to read Nietzsche's ideas on national identity "in the light of our experience."

See also 26 "Nietzsche on Geophilosophy and Geoaesthetics"

Notes

1 An example of this presentation of Nietzsche's stance on national identity is Kofman 1994. A recent exception to the rule is Crépon 2003.
2 One of the most notable examples of such a "pressganging" of Nietzsche's work into National Socialist ideology is Richard Oehler's *Friedrich Nietzsche und die deutsche Zukunft*

(*Friedrich Nietzsche and the German Future*). According to Oehler's reading, Nietzsche and Hitler speak with one voice in affirming the importance of attaining national unity, the "unity of thought, feeling, wishing" (1935: 1). Oehler presents Nietzsche as extolling the virtues of all that is complete and perfect, over that which is still in process of development. Viewed in this light national identity is the accomplishment and consolidation of a state of being-together as a united, homogeneous national and cultural entity. This is, however, a most inadequate reading of Nietzsche's views. As we will see, his far more interesting understanding of national identity places the emphasis very clearly on national identity as an ongoing development which constitutes cultural and national bonds *while interrogating* the nature of those same bonds. National identity is to be regarded as a creative fiction that is continually reinventing itself.

3   See, for instance, Kofman 1994: 16: Kofman draws her support from passages in Nietzsche such as *BGE* 254 and *KSA* 11, 31[10].

4   However, Nietzsche also characteristically contradicts himself in passages such as *HH* 477, where he advocates the indispensability of warfare.

5   Here I am evoking Rushdie 1999: 414: "So this is what they feel like, I thought: roots. Not the ones we're born with, can't help having, but the ones we put down in our own chosen soil, you could say the radical selections we make for ourselves."

6   For the structural importance of the "world of scholars," the "reading public" within humanist thinking, see Kant 1999: 55.

7   For a careful analysis of the role Europe has nevertheless still to play in evolving global politics, see Derrida 1992 and the transcript of the last public speech he made in France before his death, "Une Europe de l'espoir" (Derrida 2004).

8   Evidently times have changed, and however much some might want to push the "special relation" Europe has, or at least particular members of the European Union have, with the United States, it would certainly be going too far to name the latter a "daughter-land." Indeed many more recent commentators precisely define the idea of Europe *against* "America," symbol of global capitalism, without necessarily intending to be anti-*American*. Again, see Derrida 2004.

9   See e.g. Blockman, "Europe? Which Europe?" in Plessen 2003: 18: "For about four centuries [. . .] a large part of central and south-east Europe lived under a tolerant Islamic empire. Those who believe that Christianity is the main hallmark of European culture overestimate its penetration before the Counter-Reformation in the sixteenth century, and they overlook the continuing prominence of Islam on the continent, from the early seventeenth century onwards." For a more sympathetic account of this Nietzsche passage than mine, see Crépon 2003: 23.

10   Just how historically inaccurate Nietzsche can be in his remarks about "Asia" is evident in the following passage from *Human, All Too Human*: "Reason in school has made Europe Europe: in the Middle Ages it was on the way to becoming again a piece and appendage of Asia – that is to say *losing the scientific sense* which it owed to the Greeks" (*HH* 265; my emphasis).

11   Here Nietzsche follows a stereotypical differentiation evident in much Western philosophy between a primitive formal beginning ("oriental") and the ("occidental") origin. For an account of this logic with regard to Quatremère de Quincy and Hegel see Morgan 2000: 25–30.

12   For Nietzsche's references to Russia and how they contribute to the nineteenth-century debate about pan-Slavism, see Morgan, "Outside the Gates of Vienna: Nietzsche and National Independence Movements in the Austro-Hungarian Empire," in Golomb 2004: 153–5.

13   Mann gives 1875 as the date for Nietzsche's prediction of a "European League of Nations." However, the quotation he uses is to be found in "The Wanderer and his Shadow," initially

published in 1880 and subsequently included in the revised edition of *Human, All Too Human* in 1886. I remain unconvinced that there is a significant shift in Nietzsche's thinking on geopolitics away from a Eurocentric perspective towards a suddenly more enlightened, more "humanist" global preoccupation, however appealing this idea might be.

14 The source for Mann's proof of Nietzsche's more mature cosmopolitical stance is *Nachgelassene Werke*, vol. 13 (Leipzig: Naumann, 1903), §891. The whole quotation reads: "Möglichst viel *internationale* Mächte – um die Welt-perspektive *einzuüben*."

15 The Nietzsche passage Mann appears to be drawing on is *KSA* 13, 14[95], but see also *KSA* 11, 26[410].

16 Mann was finishing off what he called his "Nietzsche novel," *Doktor Faustus*, about a man's pact with the devil, while he was writing his Nietzsche essay.

17 The shift away from the Westphalian model towards a different conception of international relations (the UN Charter model), which places restrictions on some aspects of state sovereignty and takes into consideration the "myriad of relations" between nations, only occurs after 1945. See Held 2002: 77–84.

18 For Nietzsche's suggestion that nations should always be regarded as the artificial products of processes, not as natural givens, see *BGE* 251: "that which is called a 'nation' in Europe today and is actually more of a *res facta* than *nata* (indeed sometimes positively resembles a *res ficta et picta* –) is any case something growing, young, easily disruptable." He goes on to offer advice which will be especially pertinent for emerging and recently established nation-states: "these 'nations' should certainly avoid all hot-headed rivalry and hostility very carefully!" Instead of falling into the same nationalistic trap (cultural retrenchment, political expansionism, xenophobia) as the older, imperialist powers, newer nation-states should remember the fragility of their creation. The nation is a vulnerable and exotic (not rooted, not homely) germination.

19 See Morgan, "'Made in Germany': Judging National Identity Negatively," in Deutscher and Oliver 1999: 219–34, for a full exploration of this conundrum.

20 See Morgan, in Golomb 2004: 144–57, for a comparison between Nietzsche's emphasis on the affirmative ego when discussing cultural history and identity and Freud's analogy with the unconscious. For the latter the cultural and national awakenings of the post-World War I period were taken as a sign of the dark and unpredictable stirrings of the unconscious. Nietzsche, by contrast, provides a more positive and sympathetic account of independence movements. However, one would also have to consider Nietzsche's playful concatenation of the ego with the bovine (Io) in *AOM* 223.

21 For example, a Czech translation of the *Anti-Christ* was published in instalments in 1898, *Zarathustra* in 1901; Radulescu-Motru introduced the Romanian literary public to Nietzsche's works as early as 1895.

22 The proposition in itself is worthy of discussion, considering Nietzsche's often dismissive remarks about cosmopolitanism and its enlightened tradition. For his disparaging remarks about cosmopolitanism, see e.g. *UM II*, 5 and *KSA* 7, 29[109].

23 For a more detailed discussion of the stakes surrounding the pan-Slavic movement, Krasinski's opposition to it and of Nietzsche's views on Russia, see Morgan in Golomb 2004: 153–4.

24 See Kofman 1992: 189–213 for an interesting analysis of Nietzsche's "fantastic genealogy" in *EH*. However, her analysis is exclusively psychoanalytically/philosophically driven and she therefore does not pick up on the *historical* importance of adopting a Polish identity in the 1880s, i.e. after the 1830 and 1863 Polish uprisings and after many militant members of the Polish intelligentsia had been forced into exile. Obviously the fortunes of the Polish were to influence the major events of the twentieth century, so it was no negligible gesture on Nietzsche's part to celebrate his – much thicker than blood – relatedness with them.

25 However, those who were struggling for independence from Russia might well have disliked many of Nietzsche's positive comments about that empire's "barbarism" and Europe's need to be overwhelmed by its power.

26 See e.g. Ankrava, "The Postcolonial Syndrome and Identity Crisis in Latvia," in Cimdina 2004: 24–35, and Moore 2001.

27 See also Conway 1997: 48 for the contribution folk culture can be seen as making in Nietzsche's work "to the delicate, capillary network of ethical life in the political microsphere."

28 However, Nietzsche might well have had problems with this assimilation of culture into a concluding statehood; all talk of a culminative *Kulturstaat* was a sham in his eyes, genius being "incompatible with the ideal state" and cultural flowerings the result of political decline, not ascendancy (*HH* 235).

29 For example, Renata Salecl reproaches the "West" for the inadequacy and indeed arrogance of its position on nationalism, as manifested in the former Yugoslavia: it was unable to comprehend the complexity of the situation and remained content to label events as evidence of an eternally recurring Balkan irrationalism. Instead of comprehending the volatile search for identity within radically transformed times, the West perpetuated the ahistorical myth of primitivism (Salecl 1996: 161).

Editions of Nietzsche Used

Beyond Good and Evil, trans. R. J. Hollingdale (Harmondsworth: Penguin, 1990).

Ecce Homo, trans. Walter Kaufmann (New York: Vintage Books, 1967).

The Gay Science, trans. Walter Kaufmann (New York: Vintage Books, 1974).

Human, All Too Human, trans. R. J. Hollingdale, 2 vols. (Cambridge: Cambridge University Press, 1986).

Twilight of the Idols, trans. R. J. Hollingdale (Harmondsworth: Penguin, 1968).

Untimely Meditations, trans. R. J. Hollingdale (Cambridge: Cambridge University Press, 1983).

References

Cheah, P., and Robbins, B. (eds.) (1998). *Cosmopolitics: Thinking and Feeling Beyond the Nation* (Minneapolis: University of Minnesota Press).

Cimdina, A. (ed.) (2004). *Literature, Folklore, Arts*, vol. 666 (Riga: Acta Universitatis Latviensis).

Conway, D. (1997). *Nietzsche and the Political* (London and New York: Routledge).

Crépon, M. (2003). *Nietzsche: L'Art et la politique de l'avenir* (Paris: PUF).

Deleuze, G. (2002). *L'Île déserte et autres textes: Textes et entretiens 1953–1974*, ed. D. Lapoujade (Paris: Éditions de Minuit).

Derrida, J. (1992). *The Other Heading: Reflections on Today's Europe*, trans. P.-A. Brault and M. B. Naas (Bloomington: Indiana University Press).

—— (2004). "Une Europe de l'espoir," in *Le Monde Diplomatique*, November, p. 3.

Deutscher, P., and Oliver, K. (eds.) (1999). *Enigmas: Essays on Sarah Kofman* (Ithaca, NY: Cornell University Press).

Freifeld, A., Bergmann, P., and Rosenthal, B. G. (eds.) (1998). *East Europe Reads Nietzsche* (New York: East European Monographs).

Goethe, J. W. (1991). *Faust*, ed. E. Trunz (Munich: C.H. Beck).

Golomb, J. (ed.) (2004). *Nietzsche and the Austrian Culture* (Vienna: Vienna University).

Grosser, J. F. G. (ed.) (1963). *Die grosse Kontroverse. Ein Briefwechsel um Deutschland* (Hamburg: Nagel Verlag).

Hanák, P. (1988). *The Garden and the Workshop* (Princeton: Princeton University Press).

Held, D. (2002). *Democracy and the Global Order: From the Modern State to Cosmopolitan Governance* (Cambridge: Polity).

Kant, I. (1999). *Political Writings*, ed. H. Reiss, trans. H. B. Nisbet (Cambridge: Cambridge University Press).

Kofman, S. (1992). *Explosions I* (Paris: Galilée).

—— (1994). *Le Mépris des Juifs* (Paris: Galilée).

Krasinski, Z. (1848). *Panslavism and Germanism* (London: no publisher given).

Krell, D. F., and Bates, D. L. (1997). *The Good European: Nietzsche's Work Sites in Word and Image* (Chicago: University of Chicago Press).

Mann, T. (1997). *Meine Zeit: Essays*, vol. 6, *1945–1955*, ed. H. Kurze and S. Stachorski (Frankfurt am Main: Fischer Verlag).

Moore, D. (2001). "Is the Post- in Postcolonial the Post- in Post-Soviet? Toward a Global Postcolonial Critique," *The Modern Language Association of America*, 116(1), pp. 111–28.

Morgan, D. (2000). *Kant Trouble: The Obscurities of the Enlightened* (London and New York: Routledge).

Oehler, R. (1935). *Friedrich Nietzsche und die deutsche Zukunft* (Leipzig: Armanen Verlag).

Plessen, M.-L. von (ed.) (2003). *Idee Europa. Entwürfe zum "Ewigen Frieden"* (Berlin: Deutsches Historisches Museum/Henschel).

Rushdie, S. (1999). *The Ground Beneath Her Feet: A Novel* (New York: Henry Holt).

Salecl, R. (1996). "See No Evil, Speak No Evil: Hate Speech and Human Rights," in J. Copjec (ed.), *Radical Evil* (London: Verso).

Sloterdijk, P. (1999). *Regeln für den Menschenpark*, available at <http://www.zeit.de/archiv/1999/38.sloterdijk3_.xml>.

Zweig, S. (1988), *Die Welt von Gestern* (Frankfurt am Main: Suhrkamp).

Part VIII

Aesthetics

26

Nietzsche on Geophilosophy and Geoaesthetics

GARY SHAPIRO

Nietzsche aspires to an immanent or naturalistic view of humans (and of *Übermenschen*) and his descriptions of even the most "abstract" of thinkers signal this with pithy geographical analyses or philosophical weather reports, as when he situates Kant's conception of the true world: "(At bottom, the old sun, but seen through fog [*Nebel*] and skepticism. The idea has become sublime [*sublim*], pale, Nordic, Königsbergian)" (*TI*, "How the 'Real World' Finally Became a Fable"). The question arises whether we could construct a map of human thought, a way of understanding philosophy – past, present, and future – in terms of how it describes, redescribes, and inscribes itself within territories and spaces. It is this project, rather than Nietzsche's accounts of his travels, his love or hate of specific sites, or the meticulously recorded responses of this human barometer to climates and micro-climates, that lead Deleuze and Guattari to call Nietzsche the inventor of geophilosophy (Deleuze and Guattari 1994: 102). They take as exemplary Nietzsche's inquiries into the national characters of English, French, and German philosophy and his analysis of how the Greek milieu provided a ground on which philosophy could flourish. Deleuze and Guattari take part of the meaning of his notion of the "untimely" (*unzeigetmäss*) to involve the opening of a geographical rather than a historical perspective, one which ironically renders more accessible the possibility of discerning the structures of a "new people and new earth" (which I take to be their version of Nietzsche's "direction [*Sinn*] of the earth"). The map of thought will involve the imagining of a future for the earth in artistic terms.

Reading Nietzsche as a geophilosopher has no doubt been impeded by the suspicion that such readings render Nietzsche's thought too vulnerable to appropriation by various nationalisms and racisms. A less threatening approach sees Nietzsche's concern with the geographical sense of living on the earth as the confession of personal tastes and idiosyncrasies, however charming or dramatic they might be. Deleuze and Guattari provide an example (not the only one) of how philosophy might take as its slogan "geography rather than history," without leaving it more open to appropriation by noxious ideologies than any other philosophy of site and place. If Nietzsche gives us some tools for a geography of the self as contrasted with a *Bildungsroman* (with a sample sketch in *Ecce Homo*), he also provides suggestions for constructing a geophilosophical map of thought. Nietzsche looks at Europe, he says, with a "trans-European eye" (letter to Paul Deussen, January 3, 1888: *KSB* 8, p. 222). This does not mean only that he gives serious thought to non-European histories, but that he questions the primacy of the European historical approach, with its ethnocentric emphasis on "development" (made into explicit philosophical method in Hegelian thought); the latter is a recipe for failing to understand the multiplicity of peoples, the diversity of philosophies, and the art and culture of the globe. Nietzsche sees the misleading and parochial character of teleological philosophies of history (whether Hegelian or positivist) and so we can say that he counters these by choosing geography over history.

Nietzsche not only thinks about places on the earth, he suggests a vocabulary for thought that draws on resources from geology, geography, and meteorology. In *Beyond Good and Evil* he asks whether we are right to regard Cesare Borgia and his like as "pathological" or, on the contrary, should recognize them as "the healthiest of all tropical monsters and growths." Why not think of the life-world as divided into various interdependent and agonistically related zones of intensity? When we do, we realize that European moralists favor models appropriate to the moderate rather than the tropical (or polar) zones:

> Could it be that moralists harbor a hatred of the primeval forest and the tropics? And that the "tropical human" [*tropische Mensch*] must be discredited at any price, whether as sickness and degeneration of man or as his own hell and self-torture? Why? In favor of the "temperate [*gemässigte*] zones"? In favor of temperate men? Of those who are "moral"? Who are mediocre [*Mittelmässigen*]? – This for the chapter "Morality as Timidity." (*BGE* 197)

If we are truly committed to science, we would hardly exclude the tropics from our study of biological life, environmental science, history, and geography. If moralists don't want to flout the scientific way of thinking, then they must think *tropically* (and we must note that "tropic zones" are also zones of "troping," of turns or twistings away from a standard). Thinking geographically in terms of zones means being sensitive to such complex formations or assemblages as climates. Presumably the moralist accepts the requirement to know the whole; this entails minimizing any tendency to locate reference points prematurely. It is those who *must* measure who are most likely to establish such premature measures. The geographical analogy offers an example of a way of thinking that pursues as wide a range as possible of singularities in their series, spectra, and groupings. History, as argued in the second *Untimely Meditation*, can obscure differences by subordinating them to ideological narrative. Geography is good to think with, because it articulates differences from a perspective relatively free of such metanarratives. However much Nietzsche acknowledges the power of physical geography, he does not endorse any form of geographical reductionism or determinism. Such views were common in the nineteenth century, especially among positivists and those influenced by them, such as the cultural historian Hyppolite Taine, whom Nietzsche greatly respected. Even Zarathustra's poetic formulas, read carefully, do not amount to such reduction. In the discourse of *Thus Spoke Zarathustra* entitled "On the Thousand and One Goals" he says: "Once you have recognized the need and land and sky and neighbor of a people, you may also guess the law of their overcomings, and why they climb to hope on this ladder." Need, land, sky, neighbor: here is an inventory of the context which helps us to understand, but not to predict, what a people deem good and evil. Their actual values are overcomings of this context, and these overcomings will reveal, to the careful observer, the way in which the people deterritorialize themselves in response to the context. In terms borrowed (and hastily schematized) from Deleuze and Guattari, the people inhabit or territorialize a certain area or space; they deterritorialize by identifying themselves with certain values and norms; they reterritorialize by making the claim that these values "come with the territory." This is the law of their overcomings, by which their habitation becomes a human earth (Menschen-Erde) (cf. Z III, "The Convalescent," 2). So the Greeks, Zarathustra says, have a law which is itself a dual principle of agonism and friendship: "You shall always be the first and excel all others: your jealous soul shall love no one, unless it be the friend" (Z I, "Of the Thousand and One Goals"). This is a schema for life within the polis, and for war or competition with other Greek cities or other peoples, one stated succinctly in "Homer's Contest." Deleuze and Guattari offer an elaboration of this and some of Nietzsche's other observations on the Greeks in their attempt to understand how philosophy reterritorializes itself in the Greek world, in which they explain how philosophy emerges as an activity responsive to the situation of cities separated by mountains and valleys, yet joined by the sea. The Greek philosopher must be an isolated comet until this world of competition and friendship, community and distance, provides a space for the general activity of philosophy (Deleuze and Guattari 1994: 43–4, 86–8, 93–8).

As with many of his crucial concepts, we must reconstruct Nietzsche's conception of the earth from his various uses of the term, including especially in this case what might be called poetic or metaphorical uses. The distinctive note in the geophilosophical Nietzsche is the alternative it provides to an overly interiorized reading of this thinker. Geophilosophy recognizes that thinking takes place, not between subject and object, but "in the relationship of territory and the earth" (1994: 85). Whether philosophical or pre-philosophical thought involves a process of territorialization, deterritorialization, and reterritorialization through which it takes up a variety of positions in relationship to the plane of immanence, understood in its most immediate and familiar manifestation as the earth, conceived as the ground of life and thought. To give a necessarily skeletal summary: We (and all living things) territorialize by staking out a space, a place: we settle down, we cultivate a field, we mark the borders of our situation, whether it is the areas that the Australian aborigines trace with their songlines, or the homeless person's little stretch of sidewalk or space under the bridge. Deterritorialization consists in an idealizing movement by which actual, physical space becomes subsumed within some structure requiring a more conceptual definition. A political state, an empire, now declares that the meaning of a certain assemblage of people, land, and resources consists in a unified structure. Ancient Athens, as it showed in the battle of Salamis, was able to conceive of itself in deterritorialized fashion by thinking of itself as a mobile political structure that was not absolutely tied to a fixed place. Think of reterritorialization as a "back to the land" movement, the reclaiming of a territory that had previously been absorbed by a deterritorialized entity. Although Deleuze and Guattari do not limit the use of these notions to their most literal applications to earth and the land, this is surely one of their primary senses, and it is the one I will follow here. In their view, philosophy aims at absolute deterritorialization, but it has, they say, been reterritorialized three times: in the past on the Greek world of the polis, in the

479

present on the modern democratic capitalist state, and in the future on the emerging new people, new earth.

While Nietzsche never used the term "geophilosophy," Stephan Günzel has extensively documented his knowledge of contemporary geographical theory and has shown how it colors his work at least as early as the essay *On the Advantage and Disadvantage of History for Life* (Günzel 2001). While rejecting the geographical determinism of some of these theories, Nietzsche used them to develop a conception of culture and language on the earth, a *Menschen-Erde*. BGE 268 sketches a conception of culture as effecting a linguistic shorthand for registering the common experiences of a people who have long lived together under "similar conditions (of climate, soil, dangers, needs, and work)." For Nietzsche, as for Deleuze and Guattari, the aesthetic is a significant avenue for exploring the possibilities of earthly life. In contrast with the idealism of Kant and Hegel, and in opposition to Schopenhauer's view of aesthetic experience as purely contemplative, Nietzsche sees the aesthetic as the way in which fully embodied agents affectively respond to and alter their environments. Against Kantian and Schopenhauerian claims of the disinterest necessary to the aesthetic, he champions Stendhal's saying that the beautiful is "the promise of happiness" (GM III. 6); in his later preface to the *Birth of Tragedy* he redescribes the project of that book as seeing science with the optics (or perspective) of the artist, and art with the optics of life (BT, "Attempt at a Self-Criticism," 2). When Nietzsche speaks of his project of a "physiology of aesthetics" he alerts us to the fact that it is "practically untouched and unexplored so far" (GM III. 8). This project should not be understood in an exclusively individualistic way, as if it were a question of discerning the ascending or declining signs of life in specific works, artists, or audiences. I suggest that this physiological aesthetics would also deal with, and perhaps focus on, the aesthetics of the earth, the constructions of the *Menschen-Erde*. If we hold up our heads proudly, Zarathustra says, we will have an earthly head (*Erden-Kopf*) that will create the sense of the earth (Z I, "On the Afterworldly"). Nietzsche's texts are sprinkled with many allusions to architecture, including what we would call landscape architecture, in which he foresees this art as producing a new earth. For example, speaking of "the coming age of architecture" he anticipates that "men will work for a few hundred years to beautify nature herself," imagining such projects as redesigning and perfecting the Alps (KSA 9, 4[136], p. 135; see section 4 below).[1]

In what follows I focus selectively on four aspects of Nietzsche's geophilosophy, with suggestions for reading some of his major writings from a geophilosophical perspective. I first situate Nietzsche's geophilosophy within the incipient globalization of his time, noting the contrast between a phenomenology of the earth and the scientistic, positivistic, and imperialist subjection of the earth's time and space to mathematical and technological measure. Second, I sketch a geophilosophical reading of *Thus Spoke Zarathustra*, concluding with an analysis of the chapter "On Great Events," which is explicitly oriented to the politics of the earth. The third section turns to *Beyond Good and Evil* as the "no-saying" contemporary counterpart of the affirmative, mythicizing *Zarathustra*. It explores Nietzsche's analysis of national modes of thought and art (chiefly music) and his projection of the "good European" as a possible direction for the human earth. Finally, I consider some of Nietzsche's thoughts on landscape design which suggest a geoaesthetics unbound by either Kantian idealism or the sentimentalism typical of the eighteenth-century English garden; this, I suggest, could initiate a discussion of how art, in a broad sense, can explore the *Sinn der Erde*.

1 Geo-Metrics: Man as the Measurer

Nietzsche's talk of the earth, as in *Thus Spoke Zarathustra*, should be contextualized in terms of the globalization of space and time, the consolidation of a striated perspective on the earth through an apparatus of measurement, transportation, and control of speeds and flows. The question of the sense or direction of the earth is raised in Zarathustra's first speech in the marketplace:

> "Let your will say: the *Übermensch shall be* the *Sinn* of the earth! I beseech you, my brothers, *remain faithful to the earth*, and do not believe those who speak to you of otherworldly hopes!" (Z, prologue, 3)

I prefer to think of *Sinn* as direction, rather than meaning, which may tend to suggest something relatively static and fixed. It is the earth to come, the transformed *Menschen-Erde* or post-human earth.

Could it be that raising this possibility of the earth-to-come as the earth of the *Übermensch* has something to do with the conceptions of measurement, valuation, and exchange associated with the marketplace? In *On the Genealogy of Morality* Nietzsche argues on the basis of a somewhat shaky Sanskrit etymology that the name of the human, *manas* or *Mensch*, means the measurer, esteemer, and value-giver. This claim was made as early as *Human, All Too Human*, in an aphorism entitled "Man as the Measurer" ("Der Mensch als das Messende") (*WS* 21). Zarathustra's speech "On the Thousand and One Goals" seemingly echoes Protagoras' "man is the measure of all things, of those that are and are not." The earth, as experienced, encountered, shaped, constructed, territorialized, deterritorialized, and reterritorialized by *Menschen*, is a measured, measurable, striated earth, the subject of geo-metry. So far the direction of the earth, the *Menschen-Erde*, has been to be measured, calculated, and controlled.

In his speech in the marketplace Zarathustra denounces the overly measured world of the last man:

> "The earth has become small, and on it hops the last man, who makes everything small. His race is as ineradicable as the flea-beetle; the last man lives longest." (Z, prologue, 5)

During the composition of *Zarathustra* the world was indeed becoming markedly smaller through a market-driven excess of measurement. We should look more attentively at the space and time of industrial capitalism in which Nietzsche was fashioning his crucial ideas, including specifically his rethinking of time and space. Nietzsche was perhaps the first railway philosopher; not only did he live an itinerant, nomadic life traversing the European continent and staying in touch with his many correspondents through a mechanized postal system, but his thought is also shaped by and in response to the globalization that the railways, telegraph, and telephone were spearheading during his lifetime. In his working notes for *Daybreak* Nietzsche strategizes how to present aphorisms to the modern, mobile, traveling reader (*KSA* 8, 23[196], pp. 473–4; cf. *D* 454). "Who will be the lords of the earth?" is a question whose resonances must be heard in terms of those captains of industry, their strategists, and theorists, who were providing their own answers to this question through a global technology of time, space, and measurement.

In *On the Advantage and Disadvantage of History for Life* Nietzsche's now largely forgotten target was Eduard von Hartmann, whose philosophy of history, with its strange combination of Hegelian development and Schopenhauerian pessimism, was perhaps as close as the nineteenth century got to producing a theory of the end of history *and* of the last man. In the historical part of his treatise, devoted to showing humanity's gradual ascent to self-knowledge by realizing the impossibility of happiness, whether in religious or secular form, von Hartmann explains that the modern age must lead to a world connected by commerce and communication. The white races of the northern hemisphere will skillfully exercise rule over the rest of the world, wherever possible provoking the other peoples of the earth to eliminate each other (von Hartmann 1931: esp. vol. 2, pp. 1–45, vol. 3, pp. 94–119). However successful these First World people are at providing themselves with the opportunity for a fully secular happiness, they will finally see that it is not possible to live happily on the earth and that there is no other life to look forward to. Nietzsche took this early theory of globalization, however shallow, to be symptomatic of the last man's possible hegemony over the earth.

An important aspect of the globalization theorized by von Hartmann and others is the fusion of space and time which minimizes earthly differences and diversity. A recent book on the global standardization of time in the later nineteenth century calls the years from 1875 to 1885 "the decade of time" (Blaise 2002: esp. ch. 5). It was then that the local time that had hitherto prevailed everywhere throughout the earth came to be seen as an obstacle to the requirements of speed, transportation, and communication. In local time, as marked by a sundial, for example, noon is fixed by the daily high point of the sun, the time of "the smallest shadow" as Nietzsche says. But since every 12 miles of the earth's circumference marks a difference of a solar minute in local time, each city would have its clocks set differently. Britain was the first nation to adopt a standardized time in 1850, due largely to the internal expansion and density of its rail system. In 1869 the United States completed the transcontinental railway when the Golden Spike was driven in a remote area of Utah. But the cities linked by rail were separated by an anarchic time system, so that a traveler, in making plans, might have to calculate using five or six different local times. In the following years, as Nietzsche was writing and publishing the successive parts of *Zarathustra*, there was a series of international meetings which sought to resolve the dilemmas caused by the collision between the new technologies of speed and communication and the continued plurality of local times. The final result was the establishment of the 24 global time zones that we have now, keyed, with some variation, to lines of longitude. The standardization of time involved the striation of space associated with the state form, and then with an emerging global system; if the railroads offered Nietzsche some of the nomadic possibilities of smooth space, they also demonstrated to him the ominous power of number, weight, and measure, which, as Blake says, should be taken out only in years of dearth. If the human completes a certain trajectory in a total measurement of the earth, then the post-human (*Übermensch*) could be the agent whose excess (*Übermass*) involves abandoning such limited forms of measure.

2 *Thus Spoke Zarathustra*: A Philosophical Landscape Poem

Nietzsche's Zarathustra calls upon his listeners to ask what the sense or direction (*Sinn*) of the earth will be, commands them to be true to the earth, teaches that the *Übermensch* is the *Sinn der Erde*, reminds us that we think with an *Erdenkopf*, and speaks of the immanent horizon of life that is the *Menschen-Erde*; in the song of the earth called "The Seven Seals" we hear that "the earth is a table for gods and trembles with creative new words and gods' throws." Until recently such language was typically taken to be a poetic evocation of a this-worldly existence, functioning to affirm a life of the body and the passions. With few exceptions, little philosophical connection was seen between this dimension of Nietzsche's thought and his concern with questions having to do with nationality, states and peoples, the geopolitics of Europe, race, climate, and other "geographical" topics.

Zarathustra himself reflects on the failure of his addresses in the marketplace, with their calls for "new people, new earth." He attributes this disconnection to his having employed a solitary discourse of the wilderness in the town: "I seem to have lived too long in the mountains; I listened too much to brooks and trees; now I talk to them as to goatherds" (Z, prologue, 5). We remember Socrates, who ventures outside the city walls in the Platonic dialogs only once, in the *Phaedrus*, and there thematizes the distinction between country and city discourses. For Zarathustra, city-talk is the exception rather than the rule. This self-criticism helps to explain a relative decrease in the prominence of the earth in Zarathustra's speeches in the town Motley Cow, although the theme hardly disappears. It is as if he had formulated a teaching about the sense of the earth which needs to be recast for eyes and ears constricted by an earth grown small; he must compromise with those whose conceptions of self, other, and world are governed by an implicit urban, northern, industrial perspective that privileges the interiority of state and subject. Having an *Erden-Kopf* involves a "thought of the outside" (Maurice Blanchot) that deploys concepts not rooted in interiority, subjectivity, and the state, but that borrow from the domains of atmosphere, climate, geography, and geology.

This prologue that frames Nietzsche's landscape poem speaks of the relation between language and the earth. It begins with Zarathustra's invocation to the sun and ends with the burial of the tightrope walker in a hollow tree, moving from stellar energy source to organic decomposition, from solar hymn to burial ritual. We read the call for the *Übermensch* as involving a critique of the figure of the *Mensch* as measurer, as geo-metrician rather than geo-philosopher. In contrast, the wisest among Zarathustra's audience are said to be conflicts and crosses among "plants and ghosts," terms that name two different ways of being on the earth. The first simply grow where they are planted, with no spirit of adventure; the second linger on earth in detached fashion, pursuing an impossible project of disembodiment, shrinking from engagement with the earth's movements and flows. The prologue is a Nietzschean geography lesson, with its descent from solitary mountain peak and cave, through the forested heights inhabited by the solitary hermit whose songs make him akin to the animals, to the town on the forest's edge, and then on a weary journey, passing gravediggers and begging food, until he reaches the hollow tree in the depths of the forest where he has laid the corpse. Burial is a ritual that says something about our relations with the earth. Nietzsche probably knew Zoroastrian practices concerning death. Zoroastrians do not bury or burn their dead; the bodies are left in towers to be devoured by vultures, so that their elements may return to the earth in natural fashion. If Zarathustra were to die alone on his mountain, something like this would very possibly be his fate. Burying the dead in a hollow tree encourages scavenging and picking clean of the body, as does the Zoroastrian practice. In notebooks from the time of *Zarathustra*, Nietzsche reflects on the fact that human beings are three-quarters water and contain many inorganic minerals, concluding "To be released from life and to become dead nature again can be experienced as a *festival* – of the one who wants to die! To love nature! Again to revere what is dead!" (*KSA* 9, 11[125], p. 486).

Zarathustra preaches earthly virtue and admonishes the listener to hold up proudly his *Erden-Kopf*, for it is the earthly head that creates the direction of the earth. Even here, landscape functions as a figure for the state of the spirit, as in the praise of sylvan solitude in opposition to the flies of the marketplace. The firm distinction between state and people shows that Nietzsche understands the *Menschen-Erde* as having possibilities that lie not only beyond the imagination of nineteenth-century geopolitics, but outside the confines of the state-oriented philosophy of thinkers like Kant and Hegel (see Deleuze and Guattari 1987: 374–80).

Once Zarathustra has finished his teaching in the town Motley Cow, the landscape, seascape, and skyscape become more insistent dimensions of the story, both as setting and as subject of thematic exploration. Part II begins in the solitude of a mountain cave, where Zarathustra's "wild wisdom became pregnant on lonely mountains; on rough stones she gave birth to her young [. . .] Now she runs foolishly through the harsh desert and seeks gentle turf" (Z II, "The Child with the Mirror"). Now this "wild" wisdom (outside the striated space of the state) inspires a journey of sea voyages, stays on the blessed isles and isle of tombs, and a flying visit (perhaps by projection of a simulacrum) to the heart of the earth through the cone of a fiery volcano. Geographically, the setting is an archipelago, a series of islands with distinctive attractions and problems. They are the singularities of the earth. Seas, deserts, caves, and mountainous terrain all become forms of smooth space, fields of unconstrained movement of bodies and of thought. In "On the Land of Culture [*Bildung*]" Zarathustra presents himself as a nomad against his will, driven out of cities, fatherlands, and motherlands. He thus rejects the nation-state, a place that would claim its inhabitants by a parental model of natality, for the sake of a new people and new earth, that is his "*children's land*, yet undiscovered in the most distant sea" (*TI* II, "On the Land of Culture"). The Soothsayer challenges this hope, teaching that the earth has become exhausted – fruit turned rotten, soil cracked, wells dried, wine poisonous, sea become shallow swamp. And it is this picture of the earth that motivates Zarathustra's dream of revived life, and the analysis of temporality and fragmentation in the crucial chapter "On Redemption."

Part III begins with Zarathustra acknowledging himself as wanderer and mountain-climber. These are simultaneously narrative and spiritual characterizations of this stateless nomad. As he climbs a mountain ridge, and a new perspective opens on a fresh sea, the climber reflects on the alternation of perspectives, on turning things upside down, and on the need to discern grounds and backgrounds, not merely the foregrounds that appear to those who look with overly obtrusive eyes. Zarathustra invokes geological time to suggest a general pattern of analysis:

> "Whence come the highest mountains? I once asked. Then I learned that they came out of the sea. The evidence is written [*geschrieben*] in their rocks and in the walls of their peaks. It is out of the deepest depth that the highest must come to its height." (Z III, "The Wanderer")

These strata are forms of writing, codings of the earth; this provides a model for understanding how human singularities emerge from their own depths and for reading the inscriptions of their movements and speeds. The earth is a text that we must learn to read.

"The Seven Seals" is a geophilosophical rhapsody. In opposition to the apocalyptic geography of the supremely otherworldly biblical book of Revelation, with its conjuring of earthquakes and the end of the world, this anti-Christian paean to the earth celebrates the earth's immanent divinity, as in the third stanza:

> "if I ever played dice with gods at the gods' table, the earth, till the earth quaked and burst and snorted up floods of fire – for the earth is a table for gods and trembles with creative new words and gods' throws: Oh, how should I not lust after eternity and after the nuptial ring of rings, the ring of recurrence?"

Each stanza is an answer to the question of what the meaning of the earth shall be; the whole is a vision of smooth space that must be heard as an anti-Copernican response to space and time as striated by rapidly growing globalization that makes the earth small and wants to breed the last men who hop like fleas:

> "The coast has vanished, now the last chain has fallen from me; the boundless roars around me, far out glisten space and time; be of good cheer, old heart!"

Like Zarathustra, Nietzsche welcomes the dice game of the gods (alluding to the sayings of Heraclitus), including earthquakes, which remind us that all foundations are fragile and contingent. In February 1887, he writes to Reinhard von Seydlitz, after surviving a severe earthquake in Nice:

> we are now living in the interesting expectation of *perishing* – thanks to a well-meaning earthquake that has everyone here baying at the moon, and not just the hounds. What pleasure it is when these ancient houses rattle over our heads like coffee grinders! (KSB 8, pp. 31–2)

"Well–meaning" earthquakes are salutary messages confirming the earth's process and the ad hoc character of the arrangements of the *Menschen-Erde* (Nietzsche would have welcomed plate tectonics, which demonstrates that the earth is much more mobile than the nineteenth century was able to guess). "On Great Events" carries the theme forward by using the figure of an island volcano to address the politics of the earth. Commentators typically read "On Great Events" as directed against state-oriented politicians, especially Rousseauian enthusiasts. These are allegorized as the "fire-hound" who lives on this volcanic island, where Zarathustra was seen arriving by flying over the sea. The fire-hound is an ego puffed up with a desire to expand its power in the state (elsewhere Nietzsche identifies the dog as a figure for such a restricted "I").[2] The narrative raises the question, then, of what the relation is of earth, state, and "I." The inflated egos of state politics are said to be at most "ventriloquists of the earth," producing the illusion of a politics speaking incontestably from the ground of our being. They give the impression that it is the earth, as reterritorialized by the state, which constitutes a nation's true identity. The secret unknown by the fire-hound (and the state philosophy he represents) is that *the heart of the earth is gold.* This explicitly geographical and geological chapter insists that the resources of the *Menschen-Erde* are rich in possibility. It is constituted by passionate human bodies, their combinations, and their transformations in, by, and through the earth.

So far we could think of Zarathustra as Empedocles *redivivus*, and indeed his discourse to his disciples is a story of elemental love and strife, a geology of morals. As he explains:

"The earth [. . .] has a skin, and this skin has diseases. One of these diseases, for example, is called '*Mensch*.' And another one of these diseases is called 'fire-hound.'"

The earth is a complex of strata; we tend to ignore its intricate stratigraphy because we are deafened by the voice of the fire-hound and the commotion raised by those who let it set the agenda. The earth's interior is mineral, sometimes molten. Humans interfere with the biosphere (the skin) in many ways, mineralizing the surface in stone, concrete, and brick, and releasing noxious materials into its atmosphere. Today they pave the earth with highways and parking lots for oil-driven vehicles. They turn the earth inside out seeking oil and minerals. The new assemblages function as an autoimmune disease, the earth being further disrupted by wars for mineral resources, drawing on these same sources of energy.

To understand the rebellious fire-hound, Zarathustra has conducted a full analysis of its elemental dimensions: not only fire, but sea, smoke, and earth (mud). Now he knows that the fire-hound's noise is not a "great event." Political rebels accept an unquestioned context of state and self, limiting their contestation of received values. True events, singularities, arise in those stillest hours when we become aware of new values. In contrast the state (or churches, those quasi-states) are fire-hounds, bellowing ventriloquists of the earth proclaiming their own absolute importance. Another fire-hound, Zarathustra continues, "really speaks out of the heart of the earth. He exhales gold and golden rain." This beast is at home in elemental extremes, like "ashes and smoke and hot slime"; he knows that "*the heart of the earth is of gold.*" Gold, we know, is glowing and giving, the sign of the *schenkende Tugend* (Z I, "On the Bestowing Virtue"). The molten, radiant core of the earth has an affinity to the sun. Geological flow is what the earth is about. Ordinary politics takes place among skin diseases, the superficial flows of humans and states. On the horizon is the project of a geology of morals, one sketched by Deleuze and Guattari. "Who does the earth think it is?" is a question that must be taken seriously, whenever there is a discourse of nation or national identity, and where ownership of land and the limits of ownership are at issue. Zarathustra's claim that the heart of the earth is gold was rephrased in *A Thousand Plateaus*, by Professor Challenger, who "explained that the Earth – the Deterritorialized, the Glacial, the giant Molecule – is a body without organs. This body without organs is permeated by unformed, unstable matters, by flows in all directions, by free intensities or nomadic singularities, by mad or transitory particles" (Deleuze and Guattari 1987: 40).

3 Peoples and Fatherlands: Songs of the Earth

The diagnoses of specific national forms of philosophy and art in *Beyond Good and Evil* can be read as a critical account of how thinking takes place in the relation between earth and territory. It would then be a geo-logic, a systematic inventory of the ways in which humans construct the *Menschen-Erde* and an evocation of their futurity on earth. The preface reminds us that strange and monstrous forms of thought like "astrology and its 'supra-terrestrial' claims" have had the most stupendous effects on the lived earth, as in "the grand style in architecture in Asia and Egypt," and it proceeds to invite the reader to identify herself as a *"good European"* who will give a new sense to life on what Nietzsche elsewhere calls a little peninsula of Asia. Nietzsche sees these earliest monumental architectural forms as ways of establishing political and religious domains, assigning sacred meaning to specific territories. These efforts rely on misunderstandings of what thinking can do, so far as they attribute divine status to the stars or take the planet or a local capital to be the center of the cosmos. Yet Nietzsche admires these creations insofar as they show thought's power of thinking with the earth, even in its perversity. Both dogmatic philosophy and "the grand style of architecture" demonstrate that "all great things first have to bestride the earth in monstrous and frightening masks in order to inscribe themselves in the hearts of humanity with eternal demands." Accordingly, the argument of *Beyond Good and Evil* proceeds by undermining the residues of philosophical and religious dogmatism before its analysis of the specific, current earthly situation of humans. Like Hegel's *Logic*, *Beyond Good and Evil* moves from the abstract to the concrete; here, from the thoughts and fancies of philosophers and free spirits to the situation of scholarship, art, music, and other cultural formations in the context of "Peoples and Fatherlands." In that chapter (and not only there) Nietzsche discusses a variety of earth-relations, including empire; addiction to the soil; the national characteristics of Germans, French, English, and Russians; the place of the Jews in Europe; the development of supra-national and nomadic humans; how "the pathological estrangement which the insanity of nationality has induced" could be relieved by "Europe's desire to become one"; and the necessary consequences of our historical sense having, as moderns, put us in contact with "the labyrinths of semi-Barbarian peoples" (*BGE* 224). The labyrinth is not only a figure of internalization, but a way of spatializing the earth.

While much of "Peoples and Fatherlands" deals with what seems to be the most ethereal, least earthly of the arts, music, this is not inconsistent with its geo-logical orientation. Here the body's musical expression is also a "song of the earth." Consider the contrast of Nietzsche's concept of music with Hegel's. For the latter, music is the art which definitively breaks with space and externality; it unfolds the inward realm of the spirit in time. Nietzsche turns the tables on Hegel, arguing that his philosophy and Wagner's music (which he calls its artistic equivalent) must be understood geographically; speaking of this pair he explains their similarities by claiming that "the German loves clouds and everything that is unclear, becoming, twilit, damp, and overcast" (*BGE* 244). The claim to transcend and sublate geography in Hegel's philosophy of history is itself a function of a cloudy climate of ideas.

In Deleuze and Guattari's conception of the refrain as a marking of territory we find a structurally similar if more explicit attempt to understand how music establishes a meaningful space (1987: "The Refrain"). This account, like that in "Peoples and Fatherlands," is a geophilosophical analysis emphasizing the interrelations of music, territory, and the political. Deleuze and Guattari distinguish three typical forms (not successive stages) of the relation between sonority and territory. (1) A child might sing to itself in the dark, creating an elementary if fragile sense of safety and shelter; this is what they call the classical mode, aimed at wresting order from chaos. (2) A wall of sound may be created in order to provide the sense of a more permanent home, constructing an interior space; Deleuze and Guattari call this Romantic, describing it as the search for a genuine territory. (3) Music can begin to open up toward the outside, to the future and the cosmos. This "modern" form is adventurous and exploratory insofar as it is not irrevocably tied to a specific territory. Deleuze and Guattari cite Nietzsche's refrain of eternal return as a model of cosmic music, thus recognizing its contribution to the *Sinn der Erde*.

Reading "Peoples and Fatherlands" in this perspective, we see that its attempt to understand national models of thought as closely tied to musical (and other artistic) expressions does more than reflect political prejudices and idiosyncratic aesthetic interests. Rather than evaluating these observations in terms of the accuracy of Nietzsche's "predictions" (e.g. forecasts of important European futures for Jews and Russians), we can ask what principles or methods they exemplify. While Nietzsche's assessments of national tendencies in philosophy, art, and culture are typically couched with reference to climate and physical geography, he does not approach these themes in a reductionist spirit, as if such conditions necessitated specific cultural formations. Both "peoples" and "fatherlands" are constituted, confirmed, modified, and (on occasion) surpassed through expressive works, of which music is the most emblematic. Nietzsche might be described as an "inter-culturalist" (rather than a "multiculturalist"), who sees cultural formations as in constant development through agonistic interaction with their neighbors. What are taken to be ideas of an era are identified genealogically and geographically as the ideas of a specific people, as in Nietzsche's claim that the Germans acquired "modern ideas" such as empiricism, positivism, and utilitarianism from the French, who have in turn adapted them from the English. There are, then, no national essences and the ideology of nationalism, with its nostalgia for the soil or "fatherlandishness," is not only politically regressive but ontologically suspect. The opposition between such nostalgic nationalism and an openness to the future is played out in the contrast between Romantic music, with its longing for an authentic homeland, and other forms which would be "supra-German, supra-European" (*BGE* 255) and would transcend Romanticism by knowing "how to love the south in the north and the north in the south" (*BGE* 254). If Schumann showed that German music was in danger of "losing *the voice for the soul of Europe*," Mendelssohn and Bizet herald the possibility of a music of the "good European" (*BGE* 245, 254). Nietzsche sees such music and the work of figures like Goethe, Beethoven, Stendhal, Heine, Schopenhauer, and even Wagner as "anticipat[ing] experimentally the European of the future." In declaring that "*Europe wants to become one*" his position is supra-nationalistic, but is not a universalistic cosmopolitanism. While Zarathustra asks what the direction of the earth will be, *Beyond Good and Evil* asks in a more limited, but still geophilosophical, vein what Europe's direction will be.

Europe does not name a timeless cultural ideal, but an emergent formation of the *Menschen-Erde* (retaining contrasts with Asia and America, for example). In Deleuze and Guattari's terms: Nietzsche understands Romanticism and nationalism as aspects of a project that attempts to establish a mendacious unity and interiority corresponding to political boundaries, or a reterritorialization of thought and culture on the national state; this tendency stands in the way of the "new people, new earth" that Europe wants to become. If *Zarathustra* offers a poet's proleptic vision of preparing the earth for the *Übermensch*, the analysis in *Beyond Good and Evil* helps to explain the ineluctable poetic dimension of human constructions of the earth. These paired tendencies of poetic apprehension, on the one hand, and critical hermeneutics on the other are not confined to these two exemplary books, and each of these texts contains aspects of both. Given Nietzsche's own pairing of the two in terms of yes- and no-saying, however, focusing on the pair aims at showing the way in which Nietzsche's invention of geophilosophy requires these two mutually imbricated projects.

4 Thinking with the Earth: Toward Geoaesthetics

We might hope that Nietzsche would have complemented the poetic and critical aspects of his geophilosophy with specific analyses of some significant ways in which humans have constructed aesthetic models of the earth. He knew by the 1880s that the categories of the Apollonian and Dionysian did not suffice for a comprehensive "physiognomy of aesthetics." We can speculate that this project would have involved an exploration of the most enveloping works of art, and indeed we find him often describing architecture and landscapes with the question of whether they embody the "grand style." Space does not allow a catalog of such texts, but it may be useful to focus on the genre of the garden, which seems to be the central aesthetic form in which humans so far have concentrated their thinking with the earth and one to which Nietzsche was sensitive. In the dialog he conducts with his animals, the "convalescent" Zarathustra twits them for reducing his thought to a "hurdy-gurdy song," but agrees with them on a few things. One is his acceptance of their invitation: "Step out of your cave: the world awaits you like a garden." Welcoming their "chattering," he replies: "where there is chattering, there the world lies before me like a garden." The garden, of course, is a strongly entrenched topos for the union of nature and art in (at least) the European tradition. More broadly, we can say that the changing forms of garden aesthetics embody distinctively different ways of thinking with the earth; they are models of different forms of the *Menschen-Erde* (think for example of the differing

489

models of the formal French garden and the informal English one, one ideologically an expression of sovereignty and hierarchy, the other meant – no less ideologically – to embody nature and liberty).[3]

Consider, then, Nietzsche's comments on the English garden and on the form of landscape architecture he found in Genoa. When he was hatching the first sketches of eternal recurrence and beginning to envision the book which was to be his "greatest gift to humanity," Nietzsche was not only hiking daily in the Swiss mountains or along the coast near Rapallo, but also rereading Jacob Burckhardt's *Cicerone*, a guide to Italian art, which was his constant companion (see Shapiro 2003a: 89–92, 97). He took some notes on the landscape aesthetics to be found there. Now there is an interesting tension or distinction in Burckhardt's landscape aesthetics that is echoed in Nietzsche. The *Cicerone* ends with a passionate expression of devotion to the ideal landscapes of Claude Lorrain, which are based rather fancifully on the Roman Campagna and the Italian seaside. Nietzsche loved those paintings which had become models for many English landscape gardens.[4] Those gardens, with their seemingly endless horizons, their play with picturesque effects of variety and intricacy, offered a vision of harmony between nature and art. The German tradition recognizes the importance of the genre, as in Kant's seeing it as a paradigmatic fusion of nature and art. In his *Critique of Judgment*, he praises the "natural look" of the style, its participation in the "purposiveness without purpose" which is the hallmark of the aesthetic, while also remarking on the possibility that "the English taste in gardens, or the baroque taste in furniture" can carry the "imagination's freedom very far, even to the verge of the grotesque" (Kant 1987: 242; see also 225, 243, 323; page references to Akademie edition). Burckhardt implicitly decouples the paintings of Claude from their use in English landscape design and architecture when he rejects the latter in favor of Italian Renaissance styles: a rather un-English and also un-Kantian gesture. In fall 1880 Nietzsche approvingly makes this notebook entry based on Burckhardt.

> The taste of the *English* art of gardening – "to imitate free nature in its contingencies" J.B. – is the completely modern taste. Such people wish to be poets: while it is quite a different aim that those people have who "want to make the laws of art useful." NB I have to wean myself from the elegiac sentimentality for nature. "The contrast of free nature, which shines into the Italian garden from the outside" J.B. Essential condition of the impression. Such *people of style* are most effective in a *semi-wild* environment. (*KSA* 9, 6[222])

The passage that Nietzsche cites from Burckhardt occurs in a section on "Villas and Gardens" which describes several important structures and designs. Burckhardt emphasizes the architectural character of the Italian garden, as well as that of the work of André LeNotre, the chief gardener for Louis XIV, known for Versailles, Vaux-le-Vicomte, and other gardens. The lines that Nietzsche quotes above come from a long paragraph in which he muses on what he takes to be the highest expression of "the system of Italian garden art" at the end of the sixteenth century. Our notions of "landscape architecture" or "the art of the garden" do not quite capture the possibility of seeing *Gartenkunst* as aspiring to the status of *Gesamtkunstwerk* and not merely an accessory to others. But the seventeenth and eighteenth centuries were able to see the garden or park as a way of thinking with the earth. Burckhardt praises these perfected

Italian gardens for having confined motley and minor things, curiosities such as water-organs, artificial winds, and puzzling paths to grottoes or subordinated them to the overall plan or eliminated them altogether. He contrasts the weak, modern, English taste for "crooked paths, hermitages, Chinoiserie, straw huts, ruined castles, gothic chapels, and so on" with "the great, synoptic, symmetrical division of spaces with determinate character" of the Italian garden (Burckhardt 1964: 379–80). Burckhardt also acknowledges, as is reflected in Nietzsche's citation, that the effect of the Italian garden is enhanced by the sight of free nature – mountains and sea coast, for example – beyond its bounds. The burden of Burckhardt's contrast is that the English garden represents a false sentimentality; we see through its artificial waterfalls, for example, and so cannot take it seriously. This parallels Nietzsche's criticism of Rousseau, an admirer of the "natural garden," for his fetishization of a contrived nature. Burckhardt admires the sense of power and command in the grand Italian garden, allowing a productive tension between its structure and its other or "free nature." This bit of aesthetic criticism throws some light on Kant's treatment of the garden, in which he favors the English style (so long as it is not carried to grotesque extremes), while classifying landscape architecture in general as a form of painting, "for the eye only." If a garden is to be seen as a painted composition, then it is already from the outset understood to be a creation of artifice. (It is telling that the English garden is typically constructed by means of a hidden frame, a sunken ditch or ha-ha, which obscures the fact of its framing.) What Burckhardt and Nietzsche admire in the Italian garden is its forthright exhibition of its powerful style, its foregrounding the gesture of the artist. But as the history of the reception of the English garden shows, there is a deep tendency to imagine its aesthetic form as a kind of natural beauty, as when children or the naive think of a carefully designed park as unspoiled nature. As Nietzsche's note makes clear, he sees this as a self-deceptive, sentimental construction of nature. In the language of Deleuze and Guattari, we could say something like this: The state transforms a relatively unstructured territory into land dedicated to measurable production, as it transforms free activity into regulated work, and exchange into a system of money and taxation. The English park, private property of a gentleman, was the result of a general enclosure of common land that forced a peasant population into the cities. It disguises this situation (hence its "sentimentality") by creating the illusion of sheer territory, that is of a pastoral utopia before the threefold apparatus of capture of land, work, and money. In terms borrowed from Deleuze and Guattari's analysis of the refrain, it is a form of the Romantic, but one that testifies to its own fragility and discloses its lack of a people. It fails to be true to the earth.

There would be no single Nietzschean style of landscape design, for different climates, topographies, and cultures set different conditions. Yet Nietzsche's observations about the specific historical constructions of the *Menschen-Erde*, as well as the fantastic landscapes of *Zarathustra*, emphasize the way in which human habitations can be open to the unbounded or cosmic. In *The Gay Science* Nietzsche entitles an aphorism after the city of Genoa, where he took the cited note on Burckhardt. He says in part:

> For a long while now I have been looking at this city, at its villas and pleasure gardens and the far-flung periphery of its inhabited heights and slopes [. . .] I keep seeing the

builders, their eyes resting on everything near and far that they have built, and also on the city, the sea, and the contours of the mountains, and there is violence and conquest in their eyes. All this they want to fit into *their* plan and ultimately make their *possession* by making it part of their plan [. . .] what you find here upon turning any corner is a human being apart who knows the sea, adventure, and the Orient; a human being who abhors the law and the neighbor as a kind of boredom and who measures everything old and established with envious eyes. (*GS* 291)

Nietzsche emphasizes the optical dimension of his own experience here, and also sees projectively through the eyes of the others, the builders. This is what a city can be, an adventurous, inventive structure through which the daring of its artists is reflected back to them and which also opens out to the wild exterior of sea, mountains, and strange and distant lands. These houses and gardens, the geoaesthetics of Genoa, constitute what Deleuze and Guattari would call a "modern" art, one open to the cosmos as opposed to the "sentimental" or Romantic mode of the English garden. So when Zarathustra, a year later, raises the question "Who will be the lords of the earth?" and counsels "be true to the earth," we do not hear him calling for the total mobilization of a state war machine, but as beginning to articulate a geophilosophy and an eco-aesthetics that will not be complicit in the technocratic construction of land. Yet the south, real or imaginary, as in the Italy of Claude Lorrain, was one model for a landscape architecture in the grand style. So Nietzsche was able to admire the paintings, as when he compares his experience of Turin to "a Claude Lorrain extended to infinity," while rejecting the falsity of the "picturesque" garden that sought to model itself on these pictorial views. We can imagine that Nietzsche would be receptive to some of the land or earth art that has emerged since the 1960s, especially in Anglophone countries, insofar as these works redraw the lines of exterior and interior, frame and content, or site and non-site.[5] Some of these may prefigure a post-human form of constructing the earth, some may offer critical perspectives on environmental crisis or globalization, and could be construed in the spirit of Zarathustra's saying "I love him who works and invents to build a house for the *Übermensch* and to prepare earth, animal, and plant for him" (Z, prologue). Nietzsche's attempt at a fully immanent thought, involving a geophilosophy and a geoaesthetics has a role to play (recognized by Deleuze and Guattari and others) in thinking critically and creatively about the direction of the earth.

See also 11 "Nietzsche and Cosmology"; 13 "The Incorporation of Truth: Towards the Overhuman"; 15 "The Body, the Self, and the Ego"; 25 "Nietzsche and National Identity"

Notes

1   There is a useful compendium of many of Nietzsche's texts relevant to architecture in Kostka and Wohlfarth 1999: 333–46.
2   I suggest that a dog in Nietzsche often represents the ego as limited by excessive individuation – as in Nietzsche's jotting "And wherever I climb, my dog follows me everywhere; he is called 'ego'" (*KSA* 10, 4[188], p. 165). See Shapiro 2003b.

492

3 For a survey see Barlow Rogers 2001; cf. Shapiro 2005.

4 For a brief account of the role that the paintings of Claude, Poussin, and others played in eighteenth-century English landscape design, see Crandell 1992: 94–9, 116–17, 142–7; see also Shapiro 2003a: 41–9, 53–8.

5 See Kastner 1998 for a comprehensive survey of recent developments, including some theoretical texts.

Editions of Nietzsche Used

The Birth of Tragedy, trans. Walter Kaufmann (New York: Vintage Books, 1967).
The Gay Science, trans. Walter Kaufmann (New York: Vintage Books, 1974).
Thus Spoke Zarathustra, trans. R. J. Hollingdale, 2nd edn. (Harmondsworth: Penguin, 1969).

References

Barlow Rogers, Elizabeth (2001). *Landscape Design: A Cultural and Architectural History* (New York: Harry N. Abrams).

Blaise, Clark (2002). *Time Lord: Sir Sandford Fleming and the Creation of Standard Time* (New York: Random House).

Burckhardt, Jacob (1964). *Der Cicerone* (Stuttgart: Alfred Kröner Verlag).

Crandell, Gina (1992). *Nature Pictorialized* (Baltimore: Johns Hopkins University Press).

Deleuze, Gilles, and Guattari, Félix (1987). *A Thousand Plateaus*, trans. Brian Massumi (Minneapolis: University of Minnesota Press).

—— —— (1994). *What Is Philosophy?*, trans. Hugh Tomlinson and Graham Burchell (New York: Columbia University Press).

Günzel, Stephan (2001). *Geophilosophie. Nietzsches philosophische Geographie* (Berlin: Akademie Verlag).

Kant, Immanuel (1987). *Critique of Judgment*, trans. Werner Pluhar (Indianapolis: Hackett).

Kastner, Jeffrey (ed.) (1998). *Land and Environmental Art* (London: Phaidon).

Kostka, Alexandre, and Wohlfarth, Irving (eds.) (1999). *Nietzsche and "An Architecture of Our Minds"* (Los Angeles: Getty Research Institute).

Shapiro, Gary (1991). *Alcyone: Nietzsche on Gifts, Noise, and Women* (Albany: State University of New York Press).

—— (2003a). *Archaeologies of Vision: Foucault and Nietzsche on Seeing and Saying* (Chicago: University of Chicago Press).

—— (2003b), "Dogs, Domestication, and the Ego," in Christa Acampora and Ralph Acampora (eds.), *A Nietzschean Bestiary* (Lanham, MD and Oxford: Rowman & Littlefield), pp. 53–60.

—— (2005). "Territories, Landscapes, Gardens: Toward Geoaesthetics," *Angelaki* (forthcoming).

von Hartmann, Eduard (1931). *Philosophy of the Unconscious*, 3 vols., trans. William C. Coupland (London: Kegan Paul).

Further Reading

Bachelard, Gaston (1988). *Air and Dreams: An Essay on the Imagination of Movement*, trans. Edith R. Farrell and C. Frederick Farrell (Dallas: Institute of Humanities and Culture).

Bertram, Ernst (1918). *Nietzsche* (Berlin: Georg Bondi).

Drenthen, Martin (2002). "Nietzsche and the Paradox of Environmental Ethics," *New Nietzsche Studies*, 5(1/2), pp. 12–25.

Günzel, Stephan (2003). "Nietzsche's Geophilosophy," *Journal of Nietzsche Studies*, Spring, pp. 78–91.

Irigaray, Luce (1991). *Marine Lover of Friedrich Nietzsche*, trans. Gillian C. Gill (New York: Columbia University Press).

Krell, David Farrell, and Bates, Donald (1997). *The Good European: Nietzsche's Work Sites in Word and Image* (Chicago: University of Chicago Press).

Posth, Sebastian (2002). *Der meteorologische Komplex bei Nietzsche* (Bochum: Germanistisches Institut).

27

Nietzsche, Dionysus, and the Ontology of Music

CHRISTOPH COX

Music, Science, and the Interpretation of Existence

Nietzsche is among a handful of philosophers for whom music was a powerful force and an abiding influence. A pianist, improviser, and composer, he contemplated a career in music before abandoning it to pursue philology and philosophy. His stormy relationship with Richard Wagner – the man and his music – found ample expression in Nietzsche's philosophical writing, from his first book, *The Birth of Tragedy*, to one of his last, *The Case of Wagner*. And remarks on the music of Beethoven, Bizet, Berlioz, Bach, Handel, Mozart, Schumann, and others are sprinkled throughout Nietzsche's corpus. Late in his career, Nietzsche bluntly concluded: "Without music, life would be an error" (*TI*, "Maxims and Barbs," 33).

But just what is music for Nietzsche? And what is it about music that he found so important and philosophically compelling? In a telling passage, he explains how one might wrongly answer these questions and, in so doing, suggests the route to a more adequate response. Entitled " 'Science' as Prejudice," section 373 of *The Gay Science* is framed by the claim that "scholars, insofar as they belong to the spiritual middle class, can never catch sight of the really great problems and question marks." Among such scholars, one particular group is singled out for its intellectual inadequacy:

[S]o many materialistic natural scientists rest content nowadays [with] the faith in a world that is supposed to have its equivalent and its measure in human thought and human valuations – a "world of truth" that can be mastered completely and forever with the aid of our square little reason. What? Do we really want to permit existence to be degraded for us like this – reduced to a mere exercise for a calculator and an indoor diversion for mathematicians? Above all, one should not wish to divest existence of its *rich ambiguity*: that is a dictate of *good* taste, gentlemen, the taste of reverence for everything that lies beyond your horizon. That the only justifiable interpretation of the world should be one in which *you* are justified because one can continue to work and do research scientifically in *your* sense (you really mean, *mechanistically?*) – an interpretation that permits counting, calculating, weighing, seeing, and touching, and nothing more – that is a crudity and naivety, assuming that it is not a mental illness, an idiocy. Would it not be rather probable that, conversely, precisely the most superficial and external aspect of existence – what is most apparent, its skin and sensualization – would be grasped first

– and might even be the only thing that allowed itself to be grasped? A "scientific" interpretation of the world, as you understand it, might therefore still be one of the *most stupid* of all possible understandings of the world, meaning that it would be one of the poorest in meaning. This thought is intended for the ears and consciences of our mechanists who nowadays like to pass as philosophers and insist that mechanics is the doctrine of the first and last laws on which all existence must be based as on a ground floor. But an essentially mechanical world would be an essentially *meaningless* world. Assuming that one estimated the *value* of a piece of music according to how much of it could be counted, calculated, and expressed in formulas: how absurd would such a "scientific" estimation of music be! What would one have comprehended, understood, grasped of it? Nothing, really nothing of what is "music" in it!

The musical example turns up at the end of this passage in what might seem to be a passing illustration of the main argument against reductionist, mechanistic science. Yet I think that the example is more than incidental to the passage and that, if we read it carefully, it will begin to open up not only Nietzsche's conception of music but, indeed, his ontology more generally.

The central contrast laid out in the passage is one of horizons, perspectives, and interpretations. The text focuses on "scholars" such as "materialistic natural scientists" who are criticized for being constitutionally myopic, superficial, and reductionist in their interpretations of the world and of existence. These scientists inhabit a merely "human" horizon, according to which what exists is strictly what is sensible and discrete, what can be grasped and quantified by empirical science. Nietzsche calls this conception of the world "mechanistic" insofar as it reduces the world to the causal interactions of bounded entities or parts. He scoffs at the idea that mechanistic science adequately describes the way the world is. The musical example is aimed at revealing the inadequacy of such an interpretation, for no one who truly understands music would allow that a purely mathematical or physical interpretation would grasp its essential meaning.

What would be left out by such an interpretation? In a brief analysis of the passage, Brian Leiter offers this reply:

> [I]t is a fatal problem for materialistic accounts that they omit the *qualitative* or *phenomenological* aspect of experience, e.g., what it is like to *experience* a piece of music as *beautiful*. It hardly seems plausible, though, that the beauty of a late Beethoven quartet is expressible solely in physical or mechanical terms – and yet it is beautiful nonetheless. (Leiter 2002: 25)

Leiter goes for the traditional philosophical alternatives, contrasting the quantitative with the qualitative, the physical with the phenomenal, the objective with the subjective. But I think this reading misses the mark. For the distinctions Nietzsche offers, in the passage quoted above and elsewhere, are different ones. To see this, we need to read the musical example in the context of the key contrast presented in the passage as a whole: the contrast between various ways of interpreting "the world" or "existence."

Nietzsche is blunt, direct, and explicit in his criticisms of the "scholarly" and "scientific" worldview. But he is more elusive (and allusive) about the alternative in relationship to which this worldview is found wanting. Employing a signature rhetorical strategy, he directs his hints at a select audience, one presumably comprising the "spiritual upper class," a rare breed of like-minded philosophers capable of a more viable world-interpretation. What are the traits of such an interpretation? The passage suggests that it would surpass the narrow, limited, human horizon. To such an overhuman, *übermenschlich*,[1] perspective, the world would reveal itself as ambiguous. Ontologically, Nietzsche continues, this interpretation would not be superficial but profound, countenancing entities other than the discrete, measurable objects of ordinary sense experience. The musical example presented at the end of the section links the human/overhuman opposition with another key Nietzschean opposition, that between science and art, and alludes to an argument Nietzsche develops more fully elsewhere: namely that the aesthetic interpretation of the world is more viable than the scientific interpretation.[2] Indeed, contrary to Leiter's commonsense reading of the musical example, I think it ought to be read as making a deep ontological claim. It is significant that the musical example appears as the coda to a passage that concerns competing ways of interpreting the world, for I think Nietzsche is suggesting that music is a guide to both hermeneutics and ontology, to world-interpretation and to the way the world is.

As such, the passage leads us back to *The Birth of Tragedy*, in which Nietzsche's philological argument concerning the origins of Greek tragedy rests on an ontological argument (derived from Schopenhauer) according to which music models the "essence of nature" (*BT* 2). From the perspective of Nietzsche's mature work, *The Birth of Tragedy* is often seen as a problematic text. Its rich philological insights notwithstanding, the text seems to endorse a Kantian–Schopenhauerian dualism of appearance and thing-in-itself that, in his mature work, Nietzsche virulently repudiates. *The Birth of Tragedy* also notoriously celebrates the renewal of tragic culture in the music of Richard Wagner, whom Nietzsche would later consider his "antipode" (*NCW*, preface, "We Antipodes"). The mature Nietzsche himself often criticizes *The Birth of Tragedy* on these counts; yet he does not reject it, and neither should we. Indeed, in a retrospective preface added in 1886, Nietzsche criticizes the language and conceptual tools employed in the book, but not its core insights. "How I regret now," he writes,

> that in those days I still lacked the courage (or immodesty?) to permit myself in every way an individual language of my own for such individual views and hazards – and that instead I tried laboriously to express by means of Schopenhauerian and Kantian formulas strange and new valuations which were basically at odds with Kant's and Schopenhauer's spirit and taste! [. . .] To be sure, apart from all the hasty hopes and faulty applications to the present with which I spoiled my first book, there still remains the great Dionysian question mark I raised – regarding music as well: what would music have to be like that would no longer be of romantic origin, like German music – but *Dionysian*? (*BT*, "Self-Criticism," 6)

The later Nietzsche may disown some youthful formulations and aesthetic evaluations; but arguments and attitudes central to *The Birth of Tragedy* remain important to Nietzsche throughout his career. He continues to use the term "Dionysian" to name his naturalist and anti-metaphysical[3] ontology and epistemology; indeed, that term becomes particularly important in his final books. Nietzsche also continues to celebrate the tragic, to criticize Socrates and Socratism, to insist on the superiority of aesthetic to scientific world-interpretation, etc. For our purposes, there is one other crucial reason why *The Birth of Tragedy* remains a key text: it presents Nietzsche's most sustained consideration of music and of musical ontology in particular.

I want, then, to return to *The Birth of Tragedy* in an effort to recover this musical ontology and its relationship with ontology more generally. To unpack Nietzsche's musical ontology, we will need to unpack the notion of the Dionysian, with which, in *The Birth of Tragedy* (and beyond), music is so closely associated. Heeding Nietzsche's own remarks, I will try to read this text in light of his mature work. Along the way, I will also draw upon the work of a late twentieth-century Nietzschean, Gilles Deleuze, who, I think, provides distinctions and concepts that help us to see what is really at issue in *The Birth of Tragedy*.

Dionysus and Apollo

Nietzsche contra Hegel, Kant, and Schopenhauer

The Birth of Tragedy is driven by the famous contrast between Apollo and Dionysus, "the two art deities of the Greeks," and by the "tremendous opposition, in origin and aims, between the Apollonian art of sculpture and the nonimagistic Dionysian art of music" (*BT* 1). Nietzsche aims to show that Attic tragedy represents the truce between, and the union of, Dionysus and Apollo, and that it also resolves an assortment of other oppositions in Greek theology, art, culture, psychology, and metaphysics that can be keyed to the Dionysian/Apollonian opposition: the Titans/the Olympians, lyric poetry/epic poetry, the Asiatic-barbarian/the Hellenic, music/sculpture, intoxication/dreams, excess/measure, unity/individuation, pain/pleasure, etc.

It is this fondness for oppositions and their dialectical resolutions that prompted Nietzsche to say, in *Ecce Homo*, that *The Birth of Tragedy* "smells offensively Hegelian" (*EH*, "BT," 1). Yet, Nietzsche's assessment notwithstanding, the central opposition between Dionysus and Apollo is surely not properly dialectical. Were it so, the Dionysian would be sublated in a higher form. But tragedy does no such thing. Rather, it thoroughly affirms the Dionysian, which is made sensible through Apollonian figures and forms. "[W]e must understand Greek tragedy," Nietzsche writes, "as the Dionysian chorus which ever anew discharges itself in an Apollonian world of images [. . .] Thus the drama is the Apollonian embodiment of Dionysian insights and effects" (*BT* 8). "In the total effect of tragedy," he writes later in the text, "the Dionysian predominates" (*BT* 21). Moreover, the overarching argument of *The Birth of Tragedy* is that, in spite of its historical eclipse, tragic pessimism is fundamentally superior to the optimism and progressivism of Socratic dialectics, of which the Hegelian dialectic is clearly a late flowering.

Dionysus and Apollo, then, ought not to be figured as a Hegelian thesis and antithesis.[4] Nor ought they to be figured as Kantian noumena and phenomena or thing-in-itself and appearance. Of course, Nietzsche explicitly adopts this Kantian terminology in his presentation of the Dionysian/Apollonian pair. But we should remember and take heed of Nietzsche's remark that, in *The Birth of Tragedy*, he "tried laboriously to express by means of Schopenhauerian and Kantian formulas strange and new valuations which were basically at odds with Kant's and Schopenhauer's spirit and taste." Derived from Schopenhauer, Nietzsche's usage of the appearance/thing-in-itself dichotomy is twice removed from Kant. Indeed, Schopenhauer's own adoption of the dichotomy is peculiarly un-Kantian. Kant's distinction draws the line between nature and reason, between what can be empirically experienced and what, beyond nature and experience, can be rationally thought. Schopenhauer's thing-in-itself, however, is not an item (or domain) of thought or reason but one of direct physical experience. "Thus it happens to everyone," writes Schopenhauer, "that the thing-in-itself is known immediately in so far as it appears as his own body, and only mediately in so far as it is objectified in the other objects of perception" (Schopenhauer 1969: 19). In place of Kant's distinction between experience and thought, Schopenhauer marks a difference between two different kinds of experience or knowledge: the experience of the object and the experience of the subject, knowledge of the outside and knowledge from the inside, extension and intension. Kant's aim is ultimately to argue for the existence of a moral and theological realm that is super-natural, apart from the realm of nature and experience – "to deny *knowledge*, in order to make room for *faith*," as he famously put it (Kant 1929: 29). Schopenhauer has no such moral or theological designs and, indeed, openly scoffs at Kant's ethics and theology (Schopenhauer 1965: ch. 2).

Schopenhauer, then, goes some way toward naturalizing Kant's distinction between appearance and thing-in-itself. Yet, in Schopenhauer's hands, this distinction remains curiously and problematically metaphysical insofar as he accepts Kant's description of the thing-in-itself as outside of space and time. This last vestige of metaphysical dualism disappears from Nietzsche's account. On that account, the Apollonian and the Dionysian (which play, respectively, the roles of appearance and thing-in-itself in *The Birth of Tragedy*) are thoroughly immanent to nature. Indeed, before they are figures that describe human artifacts such as music, sculpture, and drama, the Apollonian and the Dionysian are natural forces, "artistic energies which burst forth from nature herself, *without the mediation of the human artist* – energies in which nature's art impulses are satisfied in the most immediate and direct way" (*BT* 2; cf. 4, 5, 6, 8). For Nietzsche, then, nature herself is an artist who forms individuals and dissolves them in turn; and art consists in the "imitation of nature" not insofar as it offers realistic representations of natural entities but insofar as it reiterates these "*art impulses of nature*" (*BT* 2). In affirming art and nature in the same breath, Nietzsche radically departs from Schopenhauer. For, in Schopenhauer's aesthetics (which, in many respects, follow Kant's), the role of art is to offer a temporary respite from the natural, phenomenal world, a "contemplation without interest" that disengages the will. On Nietzsche's account, however, art exists as a thorough affirmation of nature and nature's power. His celebration of art is, then, a celebration of nature and an affirmation of existence.

We need, then, to find a way of construing the Dionysian/Apollonian distinction that does not revert back to metaphysical, anti-naturalist distinctions – *ontological* distinctions between a "true" and an "apparent" world or *epistemological* distinctions between an unknowable given and ordinary experience or knowledge. To be sure, the

Kantian–Schopenhauerian language Nietzsche often employs in *The Birth of Tragedy* can be read as endorsing these metaphysical dualisms. Yet this does not sit well with Nietzsche's insistence that the Dionysian and the Apollonian are "forces of nature." Nor does it square with his later assessment of *The Birth of Tragedy* as, ultimately, anti-Schopenhauerian and anti-Kantian, or with his claim that, in this text, "there is only one world" and "[t]he antithesis of a real and an apparent world is lacking" (*WP* 853). I want to suggest, then, that we read the Dionysian/Apollonian opposition in terms of a thoroughly naturalist opposition that plays a central role in Nietzsche's later writing: namely, the opposition between becoming and being. Doing so will not only shed light on the central opposition in *The Birth of Tragedy*; it will also contribute to the larger task of this essay: to grasp the notion of music that Nietzsche so closely associates with the Dionysian, and to understand the meaning of music and existence hinted at in *GS* §373.

Becoming and being

We know that the Dionysian and the Apollonian are "*art impulses of nature*," "artistic energies which burst forth from nature herself" (*BT* 2). But what are the characteristics of these natural impulses (*Triebe*) and energies (*Mächte*)? The Apollonian affirms the *principium individuationis*, "the delimiting of the boundaries of the individual, *measure* in the Hellenic sense" (*BT* 4). The Dionysian, by contrast, affirms "the mysterious primordial unity" (*BT* 1 and *passim*), "the shattering of the individual and his fusion with primal being" (*BT* 8). The Apollonian is associated with "moderation" and "restraint," the Dionysian with "excess" (*BT* 4, 21). The Apollonian is concerned with pleasure and the production of beautiful semblance, while the Dionysian is fraught with "*terror*," "blissful ecstasy," "pain and contradiction" (*BT* 1, 5 and *passim*). The Apollonian celebrates the human artist and hero, while the Dionysian celebrates the individual artist's dissolution into nature, which Nietzsche calls the "primordial artist of the world" (*BT* 5; cf. 1, 8). The Apollonian is a gallery of "appearances," "images," and "illusions," while the Dionysian consists in the perpetual creation and destruction of appearances. "In Dionysian art and its tragic symbolism," Nietzsche writes, "nature cries to us with its true, undissembled voice: 'Be as I am! Amid the ceaseless flux of appearances, I am the eternally creative primordial mother, eternally impelling to existence, eternally finding satisfaction in this change of appearances!'" (*BT* 16, cf. 8; *WP* 1050).

What Nietzsche is offering in these poetic descriptions is an ontology: an account of what there is, of the genesis of individuals from pre-individual forces and materials. This account is strikingly similar to accounts he offers in his later work, where he contrasts becoming with being(s) and explains the genesis of the latter from the former.[5] In *Twilight of the Idols*, for instance, Nietzsche insists on the reality of "alteration," "change," and "becoming," noting that only a "prejudice of reason forces us to posit unity,[6] identity, permanence, substance, cause, thinghood [and] being" (*TI*, "'Reason' in Philosophy," 5; cf. *GS* 110, 112, 121). A few pages earlier, Nietzsche calls unity, thinghood, substance, and permanence "lies," praising Heraclitus "for his assertion that being is an empty fiction," and praising the senses for telling the truth by showing "becoming, passing away, and change." Indeed, assessing *The Birth of Tragedy* in *Ecce*

Homo, Nietzsche explicitly connects the Dionysian with Heraclitean becoming, commenting that, in Heraclitus, one finds an "affirmation of passing away *and destroying*, which is the decisive feature of a Dionysian philosophy; saying Yes to opposition and war; *becoming*, along with a repudiation of the very concept of *being*" (*EH*, "BT," 3).

It might be objected that, despite superficial similarities between Nietzsche's earlier contrast of the Dionysian with the Apollonian and his later contrast of becoming with being, the latter is resolutely anti-dualist – insisting that there is only one world: the world of becoming – while the former is dualist – affirming the existence of two worlds: the world of appearance and the world of the thing-in-itself. Moreover, in *Twilight of the Idols*, Nietzsche claims that "the 'apparent' world" is "the only one" (*TI*, "'Reason' in Philosophy," 2), while, in *The Birth of Tragedy*, he asserts that Apollonian "appearance" is "illusory" and that there is a deeper, true realm of things-in-themselves. There is really no contradiction here. Again, the Dionysian/Apollonian opposition endorses no dualism. Rather, it affirms a basic ontology of becoming – the Dionysian as an incessant process of creation and destruction, a "powerful unity" that precedes and exceeds individuals – and explains how individuals, subjects, and objects come to be articulated as such by a series of "illusions" – the dream world of the Apollonian. Moreover, though it might seem that *Twilight of the Idols* praises appearance as "true" while *The Birth of Tragedy* deems it a realm of "illusion," what is affirmed in both texts is "the ceaseless flux of appearances," and the force of becoming that "eternally impel[s] to existence, eternally find[s] satisfaction in this change of appearances" (*BT* 16).

Admittedly, Nietzsche's rather critical language of "lie" and "prejudice" in *Twilight* contrasts sharply with his praise of Apollonian "illusion" in *The Birth of Tragedy*. Yet this is a question of rhetorical context and interpretive perspective. In *Twilight*, Nietzsche is offering a criticism of rationalism, which wrongfully subordinates becoming to being. Elsewhere, however, the later Nietzsche praises the will to deception, error, lies, prejudice, and illusion much in the manner of *The Birth of Tragedy*: as an aesthetic impulse. In the *Genealogy of Morals*, for example, he endorses art as the anti-ascetic discourse *par excellence* – "art, in which precisely the *lie* is sanctified and the *will to deception* has a good conscience" (*GM* III. 25; cf. *GS* 107). Similarly, in his 1886 preface to *The Birth of Tragedy*, Nietzsche repeats his affirmation of life, noting that "all of life is based on semblance, art, deception, points of view, and the necessity of perspectives and error" (*BT*, "Self-Criticism," 5; cf. *GS* 344, *BGE* 4). This dual attitude toward the deceptions and illusions of being is helpfully explained by another passage, *Gay Science* 370. In this passage, Nietzsche accounts for the way in which, in *The Birth of Tragedy*, he mistook Wagner's and Schopenhauer's romanticism for a tragic sensibility. He explains that "the desire to fix, to eternalize, the desire for *being*" (and, presumably also, the desire for lies and illusions) is ambiguous.

> It can be prompted, first, by gratitude and love; art with this origin will always be an art of apotheosis [...] But it can also be the tyrannic will of one who suffers deeply, who struggles, is tormented, and would like to turn what is most personal, singular, and narrow, a real idiosyncrasy of his suffering, into a binding law and compulsion – one who, as it were, revenges himself on all things by forcing his own image, the image of his torture, on them, branding them with it.

In ontological and moral terms, the desire for art, illusion, and being can be prompted by an affirmation of the creative, procreative power of nature's becoming or by a rejection of it, an attempt to erect another, better world of being. Though *The Birth of Tragedy* essentially endorses the former view, Nietzsche tells us, it mistakenly enlists the forces of Schopenhauer and Wagner, who endorse the latter view.

Nietzsche's ambiguous attitude toward empiricism and sense experience also comes into play here and requires some explanation. In *Twilight*, he has nothing but praise for sense experience. "[T]he senses [. . .] do not lie at all," he writes.

> What we *make* of their testimony, that alone introduces lies; for example, the lie of unity, the lie of thinghood, of substance, of permanence. "Reason" is the cause of our falsification of the testimony of the senses. Insofar as the senses show becoming, passing away, and change, they do not lie [. . .] Today we possess science precisely to the extent to which we have decided to accept the testimony of the senses [. . .] The rest is miscarriage and not-yet-science – in other words, metaphysics, theology, psychology, epistemology. (*TI*, " 'Reason' in Philosophy," 2–3)

In other passages, however, for example *GS* 373 (the passage cited at the outset), Nietzsche criticizes the basic empiricism of materialistic natural science, which "permits counting, calculating, weighing, seeing, and touching, and nothing more," and, as such, grasps only "the most superficial and external aspect of existence – what is most apparent, its skin and sensualization" (*GS* 373). Similarly, in *Beyond Good and Evil* Nietzsche scoffs at "the canon of truth of eternally popular sensualism," and praises "the Platonic way of thinking," which "consisted precisely in *resistance* to obvious sense evidence" (*BGE* 14). Elsewhere I have offered an account of the epistemological reasons for Nietzsche's complex attitude toward empiricism (Cox 1999: 86–101). But there are ontological reasons as well. Nietzsche takes rationalism to task for criticizing the deceptiveness of the senses, which reveal a world in constant flux, an ever-changing array of appearances (*TI*, " 'Reason' in Philosophy," 1). A thoroughgoing naturalist, Nietzsche comes to the defense of empiricism and the world of becoming and appearance to which it bears witness (*TI*, " 'Reason' in Philosophy," 2–3). Yet Nietzsche is also aware that everyday sense experience is imbued with the "erroneous articles of faith" produced by the intellect over the course of its evolutionary history: namely, the illusions "that there are enduring things; that there are equal things; that there are things, substances, bodies; that a thing is what it appears to be [. . .]," etc. "[S]ense perception and every kind of sensation," he notes, has "worked with those basic errors which ha[ve] been incorporated since time immemorial" (*GS* 110).

And it is for this reason that Nietzsche resists crude empiricism and positivism. Instead, he endorses what, following Gilles Deleuze, we might call a "transcendental empiricism," which looks to becoming as the very condition of possibility for being, that is, for those entities that everyday sense experience takes as given: things, subjects, objects, causes, effects, etc. (see Deleuze 1994: 56–7, 143–4; 2001: 25–33). For Nietzsche and Deleuze, what is real is not being and identity but becoming and difference: the differential forces that drive the becoming and change that are characteristic of the natural world.[7] For Nietzsche and Deleuze, the semblance of being (of things, subjects, objects, etc.) is produced by the coarseness of our senses, by slow speeds of

502

change that elude direct perception, or by the illusions of reason, consciousness, and language. "Cause and effect," Nietzsche writes in *The Gay Science*:

> such a duality probably never exists; in truth we are confronted by a continuum out of which we isolate a couple of pieces [. . .] there is an infinite number of processes that elude us. A consciousness that could see cause and effect as a continuum and a flux and not, as we do, in terms of an arbitrary division and dismemberment, would repudiate the concept of cause and effect and deny all conditionality. (*GS* 112)

In the *Genealogy of Morals* Nietzsche reiterates this point of view, which places becoming and difference before being and identity:

> A quantum of force is equivalent to a quantum of drive, will, effect – more, it is nothing other than precisely this very driving, willing, effecting, and only owing to the seduction of language (and of the fundamental errors of reason that are petrified in it) which conceives and misconceives all effects as conditioned by something that causes effects, by a "subject," can it appear otherwise [. . .] there is no "being" behind doing, effecting, becoming; "the doer" is merely a fiction added to the deed – the deed is everything. (*GM* I. 13; cf. *TI*, " 'Reason' in Philosophy," 5)

The virtual and the actual

Becoming, then, is a realm of pre-individual, a-subjective, forces and processes that drive natural change. Insofar as it dissolves the boundaries between individuals and the distinction between subjects and objects, the early Nietzsche calls it a "primordial unity." Yet this language is misleading, for it suggests a kind of undifferentiated, immobile mass, pool, or ether – a description that does not adequately characterize either the Dionysian or becoming. For the early Nietzsche, the Dionysian is "the eternal and original artistic power" (*BT* 25), "dissonance" (*BT* 17, 24–5), "struggle" (*BT* 16), "the contradiction at the heart of the world" (*BT* 9), a force associated with "excess" (*BT* 4), creation and destruction (*BT* 16, 8 and *passim*), "extravagant sexual licentiousness" and "savage natural instincts" (*BT* 2). Clearly, the Dionysian is a dynamic field characterized by forces, energies, and drives in tension with one another. The later Nietzsche qualifies his talk of "unity," describing the Dionysian in terms of difference, tension, force, energy, and power. "And do you know what 'the world' is to me?" he asks in a note from 1885.

> This world: a monster of energy, without beginning, without end; a firm iron magnitude of force that does not grow bigger or smaller, that does not expend itself but only transforms itself; as a whole, of unalterable size, a household without expenses or losses, but likewise without increase or income; enclosed by "nothingness" as by a boundary; not something blurry or wasted, not something endlessly extended, but set in a definite space as a definite force, and not a space that might be "empty" here or there, but rather as force throughout, as a play of forces and waves of forces, at the same time one and many, increasing here and at the same time decreasing there; a sea of forces flowing and rushing together, eternally changing, eternally flooding back, with tremendous years of recurrence, with an ebb and a flood of its forms; out of the simplest forms striving toward the most

503

complex, out of the stillest, most rigid, coldest forms toward the hottest, most turbulent, most self-contradictory, and then returning home to the simple out of this abundance, out of the play of contradictions back to the joy of concord, still affirming itself in this uniformity of its courses and its years, blessing itself as that which must return eternally, as a becoming that knows no satiety, no disgust, no weariness: this, my *Dionysian* world of the eternally self-creating, the eternally self-destroying, this mystery world of the twofold voluptuous delight, my "beyond good and evil," without goal, unless the joy of the circle is itself a goal; without will, unless a ring feels good will toward itself – do you want a *name* for this world? A *solution* for all its riddles? A *light* for you, too, you best-concealed, strongest, most intrepid, most midnightly men – *This world is the will to power* – *and nothing besides!* And you yourselves are also this will to power – and nothing besides! (*WP* 1067)

The Dionysus of *The Birth of Tragedy* is indeed a precursor to the later Nietzsche's most important ontological doctrines: becoming, will to power, and eternal recurrence. In *Beyond Good and Evil* Nietzsche more soberly develops the notion of will to power as a play of drives and forces in a passage that helpfully contributes to our elucidation of the connections between Dionysus/Apollo and becoming/being.

Suppose nothing else were "given" as real except our world of desires and passions, and we could not get down, or up, to any other "reality" besides the reality of our drives [. . .]: is it not permitted to make the experiment and to ask whether this "given" would not be *sufficient* for also understanding on the basis of this kind of thing the so-called mechanistic (or "material") world? I mean not as a deception, as "mere appearance," an "idea" (in the sense of Berkeley and Schopenhauer) but as holding the same rank of reality as our affect – as a more primitive form of the world of affects in which everything still lies contained in a powerful unity before it undergoes ramifications and developments in the organic process [. . .] – as a kind of instinctive life [*Triebleben*] in which all organic functions are still synthetically intertwined along with self-regulation, assimilation, nourishment, excretion, and metabolism – as a *pre-form* of life [. . .] Suppose, finally, we succeeded in explaining our entire instinctive life as the development and ramification of *one* basic form of the will – namely, of the will to power, as *my* proposition has it; [. . .] then one would have gained the right to determine *all* efficient force univocally as – will to power. The world viewed from inside, the world defined and determined according to its "intelligible character" – it would be "will to power" and nothing besides. – (*BGE* 36)

Here Nietzsche once again expresses his basic ontology in terms of a "powerful unity." But this "unity" is now expressly a dynamic play of drives, affects, passions, and forces.[8] Nietzsche is trying to construct an ontology in which forces, powers, movements, tensions, affects, and events precede the individual subjects and objects to which they are ordinarily attributed. In *The Birth of Tragedy*, he describes Apollonian individuals as temporary emissions ("image sparks": *Bilderfunken*) from the Dionysian ferment. The later Nietzsche offers a similar account, describing subjects and objects as particular condensations and concretizations of forces and affects, particular instances and trajectories of will to power.

Wrongly pegged to the traditional metaphysical distinctions between noumena/phenomena, thing-in-itself/appearance, chaos/order, and content/form, Nietzsche's oppositions between Dionysus/Apollo and becoming/being are more aptly characterized by Deleuze's distinction between the virtual and the actual (Deleuze 1994: 208ff., 279; 2002: 148–52). Deleuze's distinction is meant to mark the difference between the realm of (actual) empirical subjects and objects, and the (virtual) flux of pre-individual, impersonal differences, becomings, forces, and affects that constitute these subjects and objects while also preceding and exceeding them. Deleuze often refers to the virtual as "transcendental" insofar as the processes and forces it encompasses (for example, geological pressures and movements, genetic codes and flows, relations of power or desire, etc.) are not given as such in actual, empirical experience. Yet he is careful to note that the "transcendental" status of the virtual implies no "transcendence," nothing that transcends nature or matter. Rather, for Deleuze, there is only one plane of being and reality that he often calls "the plane of immanence," which encompasses both the virtual and the actual, each of which is, for him, fully "real." A variegated domain populated by forces in tension, the plane of immanence produces (or, in Deleuze's idiom, "actualizes" or "differentiates") distinct entities through temporary condensations or contractions of forces and materials. The relative stability and durability of these entities can produce an "illusion of transcendence" (Deleuze and Guattari 1994: 73, 47). But, just as, for Nietzsche, being is an effect of becoming, so, for Deleuze, transcendence is an effect of immanence, and the actual made possible by the virtual.

Deleuze's notion of "the virtual" can help us in our appreciation of Nietzsche's configuration of the Dionysian. Indeed, Deleuze himself links the two concepts. The *virtual*, Deleuze tells us, is both distinct and obscure. It is distinct because it is composed of myriad "differential relations and singularities [that is, particular powers of becoming]"; yet the virtual is also obscure insofar as it is "not yet 'distinguished,' not yet differentiated [in actual entities]." By contrast, the *actual* is clear and confused, "clear because [virtual forces have been] distinguished or differentiated [in actual entities], and confused because it is clear, [that is, because the actual carries with it traces of the entire domain of the virtual from which it emerged and with which it corresponds]." "Distinctness-obscurity," Deleuze continues, "is intoxication, the properly Dionysian Idea. Leibniz nearly encountered Dionysus at the sea shore or near the water mill. Perhaps Apollo, the clear-confused thinker, is needed in order to think the Ideas of Dionysus" (Deleuze 1994: 213–14).

In this characteristically dense and difficult passage, Deleuze draws a parallel between his conception of the virtual/the actual and Nietzsche's conception of Dionysus/Apollo. The Dionysian is the realm of the virtual, the "inchoate, intangible" (*BT* 5) flux of forces and energies that actualizes or differentiates itself in the Apollonian, whose "precision and clarity" (*BT* 10) must, according to Nietzsche's theory of tragedy, bear traces of its obscure origins in the Dionysian. At the end of the passage, Deleuze suitably relates the virtual and the Dionysian to a musical, or at least sonic, example: Leibniz's oft-repeated example of listening to a waterfall, a watermill, or the sea. Leibniz writes: "Each soul knows the infinite – knows all – but confusedly. It is like walking on the seashore and hearing the great noise of the sea: I hear the particular noises of each wave, of which the whole noise is composed, but without distinguishing them" ("Principles of Nature and Grace": Leibniz 1989: 211).[9] Like Nietzsche's Apollonian figures, the clear but confused experience of the seashore's white noise opens up for us the virtual domain of the Dionysian. And this felicitous example brings us back, finally, to music.

The Music of Dionysus

The Birth of Tragedy is centrally concerned with music. Its original title, *The Birth of Tragedy out of the Spirit of Music*, announces this from the start. The book explains that tragedy emerged out of, and remains true to, the dithyramb: lyric song performed in the orgiastic worship of Dionysus, the Greek god of music. To the pre-Socratic Greeks, Dionysus expressed himself in music; and, Nietzsche argues, he does so to us moderns as well.

That said, Nietzsche has little specific to say about music – Greek or modern – and what in it discloses the Dionysian, tragic conception of life and its profound ontological insight. For the most part, Nietzsche simply repeats the general ontological claim that music expresses the primordial essence of things, and the claim that it is associated with the Dionysian half of the Dionysian/Apollonian duality. Here and there, Nietzsche makes some brief, though unhelpfully vague, attempts to concretize his claims about music. He describes pre-Dionysian, Homeric music as centered on "the wave and beat of rhythm, whose formative power was developed for the representation of Apollonian states," and as "a Doric architecture in tones, but in tones that were merely suggestive, such as those of the cithara [or lyre]." He contrasts this with "the essence of Dionysian music (and hence of music in general)," namely "the emotional power of the tone, the uniform flow of the melody, and the utterly incomparable world of harmony" (*BT* 2). He associates Dionysian music with the strophic form of lyric poetry and the folk song, the "continuously generating melody" that "scatters image sparks all around, which in their variegation, their abrupt change, their mad precipitation, manifest a power quite unknown to the [Apollonian] epic and its steady flow" (*BT* 6). Later in the text, he proposes to offer "a single example from our common experience," an analysis of Act III of Wagner's *Tristan and Isolde*. Before doing so, he tells us that he will "not appeal to those who use the images of what happens on the stage, the words and emotions of the acting persons, in order to approach with their help the musical feeling"; rather, he will address those who "speak music as their mother tongue," "those who, immediately related to music, have in it, as it were, their motherly womb, and are related to things almost exclusively through unconscious musical relations" (*BT* 21). Yet the analysis that follows seems to violate Nietzsche's own prescription. Strikingly general, its only direct comments about *Tristan* are, in fact, brief quotations from the libretto and quick descriptions of the actions of characters.

Perhaps we can account for this reticence by referring to Nietzsche's claim that "language can never adequately render the cosmic symbolism of music," that "*language*, as the organ and symbol of phenomena, can never by any means disclose the inner-most heart of music" with which it is only in "superficial contact" (*BT* 6). Yet Nietzsche does offer several hints that can begin to clarify what sort of music a Dionysian music might be and how such music might relate to a more general ontology. The Dionysian, Nietzsche tells us, affirms "the joyous sensation of dissonance in music" (*BT* 24). What it "beholds through the medium of music is in urgent and active motion" (*BT* 6). In Dionysian music, we hear "the roaring desire for existence pouring from [the heart chamber of the world will] into all the veins of the world, as a thundering current or as the gentlest brook, dissolving into mist" (*BT* 21). In these poetic fragments, Nietzsche seems to be describing *becoming* itself, becoming as movement of differential or dissonant forces. Quoting Schopenhauer, Nietzsche takes us further along this path:

> "For melodies are to a certain extent, like general concepts, an abstraction from the actual. This actual world, then, the world of particular things, affords the object of perception, the special and individual, the particular case, both to the universality of concepts and to the universality of the melodies. But these two universalities are in a certain respect opposed to each other; for the concepts contain particulars only as the first forms of abstracted perception, as it were, the separated shell of things; thus they are, strictly speaking, *abstracta*; music, on the other hand, gives the inmost kernel which precedes all forms, or the heart of things. This relation may be very well expressed in the language of the schoolmen, by saying, the concepts are the *universalia post rem* [universals after things] but music gives the *universalia ante rem* [universals prior to things] and the real world the *universalia in re* [universals in things]." (*BT* 16)

Concepts, then, are abstractions *from* particular things.[10] Music, on the other hand, *precedes* particulars, which actualize the forces it puts into play. Though Schopenhauer's language here is Platonistic, we know that the Nietzsche of *The Birth of Tragedy* is a naturalist for whom there is only one plane of being: that of becoming and the Dionysian, out of which Apollonian beings are actualized or differentiated, and back into which they eventually return. What Nietzsche is, once again, affirming here is something very much akin to Deleuze's realm of the virtual: a natural, material flux of differential forces that is actualized in empirical individuals.

Yet *how* does music manifest this virtual power of becoming? And *what sort of* music exemplifies this virtual power? In *The Birth of Tragedy*, of course, Nietzsche found it in "*German music*" (*BT* 19), and, most fully, in the music of Wagner. Yet we also know that Nietzsche later retracted this claim and renewed his question: "what would a music have to be like that would no longer be of romantic origin, like German music – but *Dionysian*?" (*BT*, "Self-Criticism," 6). For the most part, Nietzsche left this question unanswered. It is, I think, an untimely question, one not well answered by the nineteenth-century symphonic music that was Nietzsche's milieu. Rather, I think, the question looks (or listens) ahead to a very different music, one that would gradually develop over the course of the twentieth century.

The music of the French American composer Edgard Varèse begins this trajectory (Cox 2003). In the early decades of the twentieth century, Varèse continually expressed dissatisfaction with classical music as it had come into existence since the Renaissance. In the 1920s he abandoned the term "music" in favor of the phrase "organized sound," calling himself not a musician, but "a worker in rhythms, frequencies, and intensities." At the same time, he complained that "the conventional orchestra of today precludes the exploitation of the possibilities of tone colors and range" and that "the division of the octave into twelve half-tones is purely arbitrary" (Varèse in Cox and Warner 2004: 20). Though he continued to compose for strings, brass, woodwind, and percussion, he began to introduce novel instruments such as sirens, theremins, and ondes martenot that would give his music a greater fluidity. Varèse was after a different sort of music: no longer a music of discrete tones and beautiful melodies but a deeply physical music of powerful flows and forces in tension. In a 1936 lecture he wrote:

> When new instruments will allow me to write music as I conceive it, the movement of sound-masses, of shifting planes, will be clearly perceived in my work, taking the place of the linear counterpoint. When these sound-masses collide, the phenomena of penetration and repulsion will seem to occur. Certain transmutations taking place on certain planes will seem to be projected onto other planes, moving at different speeds and at different angles. There will no longer be the old conception of melody or interplay of melodies. The entire work will be a melodic totality. The entire work will flow as a river flows. (Cox and Warner 2004: 17–18)

Varèse would later discover such a sound world in electronic music, to which he dedicated himself from the early 1950s until his death in 1965.

Electronic music made a decisive break with the musical tradition. Dispensing with traditional musical sonorities and the various discrete instruments and instrumental families that produce them, it affirmed the univocity of sound, generating the entire musical field out of a stream of electrons emitted by an oscillator. Electronic music is a music of forces and flows, of mobile electronic particles contracted or dilated by filters and modulators. As such, it is often criticized as "cold," "impersonal," "dehumanized," "abstract." These descriptions are apt, for electronic music opens music to something beyond the human, the subject, and the person: the non-organic life of sound that precedes any actual composition or composer, the virtual realm of pre-individual and pre-personal forces and flows.

Another decisive break was made by *musique concrète*, which emerged slightly earlier in Pierre Schaeffer's Paris studio. *Musique concrète* exploited the resources of newly developed recording technologies – initially the wax cylinder and, by the early 1950s, the tape recorder. Effectively dissolving the distinction between "music," "sound," and "noise," recording tape provided a neutral surface that could register any sound whatsoever and make it the raw material for composition. Hence, works of *musique concrète* freely mixed the sounds of percussion instruments and pianos with the sounds of train whistles, spinning tops, pots and pans, and canal boats. Though they began with documentary material, however, Schaeffer and his compatriots celebrated the fact that tape music could give access to sound itself, liberated from any reference to musical instruments (see Schaeffer in Cox and Warner 2004: 76–81). Via various techniques (eliminating a sound's attack or decay, slowing it down or speeding it up, running it backwards, etc.), *concrète* composers succeeded in abstracting sounds from their sources, thus eliminating all referentiality and short-circuiting the auditory habits of listeners. Their ability to do this was aided by the fact that tape music was "performed" without any visual element to speak of: no performers or instruments, just pure sonic matter emanating from loudspeakers.

John Cage moved even further along this path. He explicitly attempted to liberate music from human subjectivity, thereby opening up a transcendental or virtual field of sound.[11] Cage insisted that music precedes and exceeds human beings. "Music is permanent," he wrote; "only listening is intermittent" (Cage in Cox and Warner 2004: 224).[12] "Chance" and "silence" were his transports into this virtual domain. "Chance" procedures allowed the composer to bypass his subjective preferences and habits in order to make way for sonic conjunctions and assemblages that were not his own, or, indeed, anybody's. And "silence," for Cage, named a sort of musical plane of immanence: not the absence of sound (an impossibility, he pointed out), but the absence of *intentional* sound – a plane on which dance liberated sound particles.[13] In his famous "silent" composition, *4′33″*, Cage invites the audience to hear the flow of non-intentional, environmental sound – wind, rain, shuffling feet, creaking chairs, humming appliances, etc. – as a musical event. By offering a composition that, paradoxically, abdicates the role of the composer, Cage opens music to the Dionysian element, for, as Nietzsche puts it, "Only insofar as the genius in the act of artistic creation coalesces with this primordial artist of the world, does he know anything of the eternal essence of art" (*BT* 5). That "primordial artist" is, of course, the plane of immanence of nature itself. And composition of this sort is "imitation of nature" – not a reproduction of nature's actual forms but an imitation of its virtual power, or, as Cage often put it, "imitation of nature in her manner of operation" (see Cage in Cox and Warner 2004; on this notion of "imitation of nature" as the imitation of the "*art impulses of nature*" see *BT* 2).

Since the mid-twentieth century the experiments of Varèse, Schaeffer, Cage, Karlheinz Stockhausen, and others have given rise to a new sonic or audio culture that considers music-sound as a natural flow on a par with other such flows (geological, genetic, linguistic, etc.). In the noise composition of Merzbow, the *concrète* performances of Francisco López, the soundscape recordings of Chris Watson, and the electronic signals that course through the work of Carl Michael von Hausswolff and Kaffe Matthews, and in so much experimental music today is disclosed the field of musical becoming, the virtual domain of music that, in his first book, Nietzsche called "Dionysian." Like the white noise of the seashore in which Leibniz and Deleuze heard the Dionysian, experimental music today offers "a musical mirror of the world" (*BT* 6): an aural image of the distinct-obscure world of natural becoming, the dissonant play of forces that makes possible the world of empirical particulars.

Music, Science, and the Interpretation of Existence (Reprise)

With this, we can finally return to and unpack the passage with which we began. Recall that, in *GS* 373, Nietzsche criticizes "scholars" for "never catching sight of the really great problems and question marks." Among these scholars, he singles out "mechanistic material scientists" for their merely "human" horizons, interpretations, and perspectives. Such interpretations take the world to be composed solely of discrete, sensible, and quantifiable entities. And they take natural change to be a matter of the causal interactions of these entities. Such positivist, reductionist, and mechanistic interpretations, Nietzsche insists, are superficial, stupid, meaningless, and worthless. At the end of the passage, he briefly notes that music provides a potent counter-example, asserting that, insofar as it cannot account for music, positivist and mechanist science fails to provide an adequate interpretation of the world.

At the outset, I urged that we take this musical example to be making not merely a phenomenological point or a point about aesthetic value, but a deep ontological claim about the way the world is. Here, as elsewhere, Nietzsche is urging us "*to look at science in the perspective of the artist, but at art in that of life*" (*BT*, "Self-Criticism," 2), arguing that aesthetic interpretations of the world are better, richer, and more naturalistic than scientific ones. More specifically, I take him to be pointing back to his thesis in

509

The Birth of Tragedy that music is an ontological echo that provides us with an aural representation of the very nature of things. What music shows us, I have argued, is that the domain of individuated, actualized, fully constituted, empirical subjects and objects is premised on the domain of becoming: a virtual, transcendental realm of differential forces. In *The Birth of Tragedy* Nietzsche calls this domain the Dionysian. Such a domain precedes and exceeds the horizon of the human and calls for a "transcendental empiricism in contrast with everything that makes up the world of the subject and the object" (Deleuze 2001: 25). Aptly enough, the symbol of Dionysus is the satyr, "that synthesis of god and billy goat" (*BT*, "Self-Criticism," 4), a creature at once post- and pre-human. Tragedy (literally, goat-song) affirms nature and becoming as virtual powers that generate and supersede the human along with every other actual entity. "Dionysian art," Nietzsche writes,

> wishes to convince us of the eternal joy of existence: only we are to seek this joy not in phenomena, but behind them. We are to recognize that all that comes into being must be ready for a sorrowful end; we are forced to look into the terrors of the individual existence – yet we are not to become rigid with fear: a metaphysical comfort[14] tears us momentarily away from the bustle of the changing figures. We are really for a brief moment primordial being itself, feeling its raging desire for existence and joy in existence; the struggle, the pain, the destruction of phenomena, now appear necessary to us, in view of the excess of countless forms of existence which force and push one another into life, in view of the exuberant fertility of the universal will. (*BT* 17)

Gay Science 373, then, offers an ontology, an ontology alternative to the ontology of positivistic science, an ontology guided by music, which, Nietzsche suggests, provides an image of natural becoming or, in other words, "will to power" as a *pre-form* of life." The passage perhaps invites the objection that Nietzsche, the perspectivist, has no right to offer such an account of the way the world really is. To which Nietzsche would no doubt respond, as he does in another passage in which he presents the will to power as an interpretation counter to that of mechanistic science: "Supposing that this also is only interpretation – and you will be eager enough to make this objection? – well, so much the better" (*BGE* 22).

See also 3 "The Aesthetic Justification of Existence"; 6 "Nietzsche's 'Gay' Science"; 8 "Nietzsche's Philosophy and True Religion"; 9 "The Naturalisms of *Beyond Good and Evil*"; 12 "Nietzsche on Time and Becoming"; 30 "Nietzsche's Theory of the Will to Power"

Notes

I thank Keith Ansell Pearson for insightful comments and suggestions that prompted this essay and shaped its argument, and Daniel W. Smith for helpful comments along the way.

1   This term is only suggested in the passage. Yet Nietzsche first introduces the term *Übermensch* earlier in *The Gay Science* (§143); and Book V, in which *GS* 373 appears, was added in 1887, following the publication of *Thus Spoke Zarathustra*, in which the *Übermensch* is a central figure.

2   The argument that art trumps science is a key feature of *The Birth of Tragedy* and remains important throughout Nietzsche's corpus. See e.g. *BT*, "Self-Criticism," and *GM* III. 25. For more on this issue, see Cox 1999: ch. 1, esp. pp. 63–8.

3   In the literal, etymological sense in which Nietzsche often uses this term: *meta*: beyond or above; *physics*: nature.

4   For a more sustained anti-Hegelian reading of *The Birth of Tragedy*, see Deleuze 1983.

5   For Nietzsche, "being" has two related meanings. On the one hand, it names distinct and subsistent empirical particulars, individual entities. On the other hand, it names meta-physical entities that are not affected by becoming or change. As a naturalist, Nietzsche holds that there is only becoming and change and, hence, that, strictly speaking, there are no autonomous, subsistent empirical particulars. The illusion of empirical beings, Nietzsche holds, is due in part to the Platonist projection of metaphysical being into the empirical.

6   This notion of "unity" or "unit-hood" (*Einheit*) is surely different from that of the "primordial unity" (*Ur-Eine*) spoken of in *The Birth of Tragedy*. The former clearly refers to the (Apollonian) illusion of unity and individuation characteristic of empirical beings, while the latter refers to the indistinctness characteristic of the realm of becoming or the Dionysian. Aware of this potential confusion, the later Nietzsche qualifies his talk of becoming and the Dionysian as "unities," describing them instead as continuums or multiplicities.

7   For a rich, Deleuzian and Nietzschean-inspired analysis of natural becoming, see De Landa 1997.

8   The passage invites comparison with Deleuze's conception of being as both "univocal" and "multiple." See Deleuze 1994: 35ff., 1990: 177–80.

9   This example (and the associated examples of the waterfall and watermill) are recurrent in Leibniz's corpus. See also *Discourse on Metaphysics*, §33 (1989: 65), Letter to Arnauld (April 30, 1687) (1989: 81), and preface to the *New Essays on Human Understanding* (1989: 295–6).

10 The same is true of words, according to Nietzsche. See *BT* 6 and 19, for example. On the connection between concepts and words as abstractions, see also TL 81–4.

11 A composer, Cage remarked, should "give up the desire to control sound, clear his mind of music, and set about discovering means to let sounds be themselves rather than vehicles for man-made theories or expressions of human sentiments" (1973: 10).

12 Compare Deleuze and Guattari: "music is not the privilege of human beings: the universe, the cosmos, is made of refrains" (1987: 309).

13 "There is no such thing as an empty space or an empty time. There is always something to see, something to hear. In fact, try as we may to make a silence, we cannot" (Cage 1988: 8). "[T]o me, the essential meaning of silence is the giving up of intention" (Cage 1988: 189).

14 In his 1886 preface, Nietzsche, the rigorous naturalist, corrects the Schopenhauerian phrase "metaphysical comfort," replacing it with "*this-worldly* comfort" (*BT*, "Self-Criticism," 7).

Editions of Nietzsche Used

Basic Writings of Nietzsche, ed. and trans. Walter Kaufmann (New York: Modern Library, 1967; repr. 1992).

Beyond Good and Evil, in *Basic Writings*.

The Birth of Tragedy, in *Basic Writings*.

Daybreak, trans. R. J. Hollingdale (Cambridge: Cambridge University Press, 1982).

Ecce Homo, in *Basic Writings*.

The Gay Science, trans. Walter Kaufmann (New York: Vintage Books, 1974).

CHRISTOPH COX

On the Genealogy of Morals, in *Basic Writings*.

"On Truth and Lies in a Non-Moral Sense," in *Philosophy and Truth: Selections from Nietzsche's Notebooks of the Early 1870s*, ed. and trans. Daniel Breazeale (Atlantic Highlands, NJ: Humanities Press, 1979).

Twilight of the Idols, in *The Portable Nietzsche*, ed. Walter Kaufmann (New York: Viking Penguin, 1954; pbk. edn. 1959; repr. 1968).

The Will to Power, ed. Walter Kaufmann, trans. Walter Kaufmann and R. J. Hollingdale (New York: Vintage Books, 1967).

References

Adelson, Robert. Liner notes to Elliott Carter, *A Symphony of Three Orchestra* and Edgard Varèse, *Déserts/Ecuatorial/Hyperprism*, New York Philharmonic/Ensemble InterContemporain, conducted by Pierre Boulez (Sony SMK 68334).

Cage, John (1973). "Experimental Music," in *Silence: Lectures and Writings by John Cage* (Hanover, NH: Wesleyan University Press).

—— (1988). *Conversing with Cage*, ed. Richard Kostelanetz (New York: Limelight Editions).

—— (2004). "Introduction to *Themes & Variations*," in Christoph Cox and Daniel Warner (eds.) *Audio Culture: Readings in Modern Music* (New York: Continuum).

Cox, Christoph (1999). *Nietzsche: Naturalism and Interpretation* (Berkeley: University of California Press).

—— (2003). "Wie wird Musik zu einem organlosen Körper? Gilles Deleuze und experimentale Elektronika," in Marcus S. Kleiner and Achim Szepanski (eds.), *Soundcultures: Über digitale und elektronische Musik* (Frankfurt: Suhrkamp Verlag).

Cox, Christoph, and Warner, Daniel (eds.) (2004). *Audio Culture: Readings in Modern Music* (New York: Continuum).

De Landa, Manuel (1997). *A Thousand Years of Nonlinear History* (New York: Swerve/Zone).

Deleuze, Gilles (1983). *Nietzsche and Philosophy*, trans. Hugh Tomlinson (New York: Columbia University Press).

—— (1990). *The Logic of Sense*, trans. Mark Lester (New York: Columbia University Press).

—— (1994). *Difference and Repetition*, trans. Paul Patton (New York: Columbia University Press).

—— (2001). "Immanence: A Life," in *Pure Immanence: Essays on a Life*, ed. John Rajchman, trans. Anne Boyman (New York: Zone).

—— (2002). "The Actual and the Virtual," trans. Eliot Ross Albert, in Gilles Deleuze and Claire Parnet, *Dialogues II* (New York: Columbia University Press/Continuum).

Deleuze, Gilles, and Guattari, Félix (1987). *A Thousand Plateaus*, trans. Brian Massumi (Minneapolis: University of Minnesota Press).

—— —— (1994). *What Is Philosophy?*, trans. Hugh Tomlinson and Graham Burchell (New York: Columbia University Press).

Kant, Immanuel (1929). *Critique of Pure Reason*, trans. Norman Kemp Smith (New York: St. Martin's).

Leibniz, Gottfried Wilhelm (1989) *Philosophical Essays*, ed. and trans. Roger Ariew and Daniel Garber (Indianapolis: Hackett).

—— *Discourse on Metaphysics*, in *Philosophical Essays*.

—— Letter to Arnauld (April 30, 1687), in *Philosophical Essays*.

—— Preface to the *New Essays on Human Understanding*, in *Philosophical Essays*.

—— *Principles of Nature and Grace, Based on Reason*, in *Philosophical Essays*.

Leiter, Brian (2002). *Nietzsche on Morality* (London: Routledge).

Schaeffer, Pierre (2004). "Acousmatics," in Cox and Warner (eds.), *Audio Culture*.

Schopenhauer, Arthur (1965). *On the Basis of Morality*, trans. E. F. J. Payne (Indianapolis: Bobbs-Merrill).

—— (1969). *The World as Will and Representation*, vol. 1, trans. E. F. J. Payne (New York: Dover).

Varèse, Edgard (2004). "The Liberation of Sound," in Christoph Cox and Daniel Warner (eds.) *Audio Culture: Readings in Modern Music* (New York: Continuum).

Part IX

Evolution and Life: The Will to Power

28

Nietzsche and Evolutionary Theory

GREGORY MOORE

Nietzsche's writings betray a profound and enduring interest in the far-reaching implications of the theory of evolution for the traditional areas of philosophical inquiry. In
Human, All Too Human his point of departure for a radical reassessment of conventional values is the claim that "everything *essential* in the development of mankind
took place in primeval times [. . .] everything has become: there are *no eternal facts*,
just as there are no absolute truths" (*HH* 2). And the impetus of his later thought, as
expressed for example in *On the Genealogy of Morality* (a book whose very title attests to
the post-Darwinian preoccupation with the question of descent), issues from an appeal
to the explanatory power of a newly confident biology to demonstrate the inferiority of
prevailing ideals and to overturn them. Yet though Nietzsche was immersed in debates
about the mechanisms of evolution and evidently believed in the mutability of organic
forms; though he recognized that the structures of human knowledge are biologically
determined; though he insisted that human morality and artistry are merely modifications of animal behavior, his published works and notebooks contain a number of
critical reflections on Darwin and the theory of natural selection. How should we explain
the rejection of Darwinism on the one hand and the commitment to evolutionism on
the other? Nietzsche returns to the English naturalist at strategic points in the development of his thinking; clearly the figure of Darwin and the refutation of what Nietzsche
took to be his theory were important to him. What did Darwin represent for him? In a
word, he believes Darwinism fatally misconstrues the essence of life (and of human
being in particular), and this is because it is imbued with false values propagated by
the "damnable Anglomania" that has come to dominate modern culture (*BGE* 253).
Nietzsche's own conception of life and of the processes that shape it – which ultimately
finds expression in the concept of the will to power – is an alternative to that underpinning Darwinism. Nietzsche's long campaign against Darwin, then, is both a critique of
the dominant view of nature and of the culture in which it originated.

The Non-Darwinian Revolution

The prominence of Nietzsche's observations on evolution in his writings has tempted
many readers to interpret his thought in the light of Darwinism. Some of Nietzsche's

earliest critics interpreted the *Übermensch* narrowly as a response to the debates about the future of human evolution that Darwinism inevitably provoked, even if Darwin himself studiously avoided such speculation. Despite Nietzsche's irritated side-swipes at those "learned cattle" who suspect him of Darwinist sympathies (*EH*, "Why I Write Such Good Books," 1), the idea was common among a great many subsequent commentators – especially social Darwinists and eugenicists – and remains, stubbornly, a popular misconception (Tille 1895; Stone 2002). Nevertheless, some early twentieth-century critics were prepared to embark upon more careful investigations of Nietzsche's relation to Darwinism and biological concepts more generally. Claire Richter's 1911 book *Nietzsche et les théories biologiques contemporaines* was the first to address the issue in terms of Nietzsche's reading of particular biologists, though many of her conclusions are speculative. Nevertheless, her argument that Nietzsche's thought (albeit unconsciously) owes more to a Lamarckian than to a properly Darwinian understanding of evolution would prove influential, resurfacing periodically over the years, most notably in Charles Andler's six-volume study, *Nietzsche, sa vie et sa pensée* (Andler 1920–31), which also explored the influence of what he called (somewhat anachronistically) "neo-Lamarckian" biologists on Nietzsche's ideas, such as Ludwig Rütimeyer, William Rolph and Wilhelm Roux. A more contemporary and detailed discussion of Nietzsche's extensive borrowings from Roux was undertaken by Wolfgang Müller-Lauter (1978), one of the most important contributions to the debate on Nietzsche's relationship to Darwinism. Müller-Lauter's essay was one of the first fruits of efforts made by scholars to ascertain and quantify the influence of particular authors – including a number of biologists – whose books Nietzsche is known to have read, part of the ongoing re-evaluation of his unpublished notes begun with the Colli–Montinari critical edition of his works. If Keith Ansell Pearson's *Viroid Life* (1997) drew on this philological work in order to examine the significance of the Nietzschean response to biology for the future of the "transhuman condition," followed more recently by John Richardson's work (Richardson 2004), other writers (see e.g. Moore 2002) have sought to examine Nietzsche's reception of evolutionary thought within the historical context of the nineteenth century. Such an approach, which draws on recent revisionist trends in the historiography of the biological sciences, allows us to do greater justice to the complexities of Nietzsche's evolutionism, to understand its apparent idiosyncrasies, and to transcend the inadequate labels of "Darwinism" or "Lamarckism" that in the past have been employed to characterize his thinking. It is this position that I shall summarize here.

The myth of the "Darwinian revolution" has fostered the belief that the publication of *The Origin of Species* in 1859 swept away the old theological certainties overnight. But throughout the latter half of the nineteenth century evolutionary biology was riven by confusions and controversies. There were many staunch evolutionists who, like Ernst Haeckel, the leading apostle of evolutionism in Germany, hailed *The Origin of Species* as "epoch-making" and yet harbored doubts about the sufficiency of natural selection as a means of accounting for organic change. This strangely ambivalent response to Darwin's work, together with the further confusion surrounding the concept of struggle, the genealogy of organisms, the nature and vehicle of heredity, and the patterning of the evolutionary process, is symptomatic of what has been called the "non-Darwinian revolution" in biology (Bowler 1988). Darwin, in other words, succeeded in converting the vast majority of biologists to some form of evolutionism, but not to Darwinism as such.

This was especially the case in Germany. Even though some German biologists openly proclaimed themselves to be "Darwinians," their thought often turns out to be little more than a blend of Darwinian rhetoric – usually the evocation of the struggle for existence – with attitudes that are in reality a legacy of a pre-Darwinian view of nature. This may have been due to the fact that, even before the publication of the *Origin of Species*, many German naturalists were already evolutionists in the sense that they accepted the gradual unfolding or *Entwicklung* of a purposeful trend in the history of life, ideas which had their roots in the dynamic view of nature fostered by Romantic and pre-Romantic *Naturphilosophie*. While there were some German scientists who followed Darwin in holding that natural selection was the mechanism of species muta-tion, a significant number of prominent biologists either wholly rejected Darwin's theory of natural selection or believed it played only a secondary role in evolution. Friedrich Lange, for example, whose book *History of Materialism* constituted Nietzsche's first introduction to the issues surrounding the theory of evolution, thought natural selec-tion was symptomatic of "that splendid and so often successful one-sidedness which we find with especial frequency amongst Englishmen" (Lange 1925: vol. 3, p. 53). Instead, many German thinkers (Lange included) articulated a *pre-Darwinian basic com-mitment to non-adaptive models of evolutionary change*. Loyal to the vitalistic traditions of their science, nineteenth-century German biologists resurrected the concept of the *Bildungstrieb*, and held an internal directive or transformative force to be the main engine of evolution. This is at the heart of the "organic theory of development" pro-posed as a replacement for Darwinism by Eduard von Hartmann, perhaps *the* most widely read philosopher in late nineteenth-century Germany, and certainly one of the first to incorporate evolutionary theory into his thinking. In a book which Nietzsche once owned, he argued that the theory of descent and the doctrine of the unity of nature belonged, not to natural science but to *Naturphilosophie*. He claimed that the "supporters of the theory of descent in Germany," and Ernst Haeckel in particular, were shaking off the spell of Darwinism and working towards "a view more appropriate to our nation of thinkers" (Hartmann 1875: 148–9). Evolution had become for Hartmann an expression of national identity, and it is significant that he was making these demands in the early 1870s, when nation-building was high on the political agenda in Germany. Haeckel himself had already gone down this road, regarding evolutionary biology as an objective foundation for nationalism and an ideology of social integration. Where Hartmann saw Kant as a forerunner of the evolutionary worldview, Haeckel, in his best-selling work *Generelle Morphologie der Organismen*, declared Goethe to be the "*independent founder of the theory of descent in Germany*" (Haeckel 1866: vol. 2, p. 160). Haeckel was not alone; there were many in Germany who downplayed Darwin's achievements in favor of Goethe.

These very same attitudes underpin Nietzsche's own evolutionism, and in particular his anti-Darwinian statements from at least the mid-1880s onwards. He never read anything by Darwin himself (with the possible exception of the essay "Biographical Sketch of an Infant," published in *Mind* in 1877), though he did read an impressive number of books on the subject, including specialist biological treatises as well as works of popular science. All of these, without exception, represent a non-Darwinian

519

understanding of evolution and influenced his ideas to a greater or lesser degree. For a start, he did not regard Darwin as the originator of a new worldview; rather, the theory of evolution is for him merely an "after-effect," an echo of the philosophy of becoming first expounded by Heraclitus, Empedocles, Lamarck and, tellingly, Hegel – a sign of how widespread already was the notion of "development" or *Entwicklung* in pre-Darwinian German *Naturphilosophie* (*KSA* 11, 34[73]). In *The Gay Science* Nietzsche even suggests that Hegel anticipated Darwinism when he introduced the idea that "the species concepts develop *out of each other* [. . .] without Hegel there could have been no Darwin" (*GS* 357). And in a poem Nietzsche even implicitly compares Darwin's supposedly impoverished vision of nature to the grandeur of Goethe's: "Darwin neben Goethe setzen / heisst: *die Majestät verletzen*" (To rank Darwin beside Goethe is *lèse majesté*) (*KSA* 11, 28[45]). More importantly, and in common with the vast majority of his contemporaries, Nietzsche insists that adaptation is "a second-rate activity" (*GM* II. 12), and is therefore not sufficient to account for the development of the individual organism or the species as a whole. Instead of emphasizing the organism's relationship to its environment or the influence of the struggle for existence, Nietzsche locates the primary motor of evolution in an active, creative force inherent in nature itself: "The influence of 'external circumstances' is *exaggerated* by D[arwin] to a ridiculous extent; the essential thing in the vital process is precisely the tremendous shaping force which creates forms from within and which *utilizes*, *exploits* the 'external circumstances'" (*KSA* 12, 7[25]). This force, of course, is what Nietzsche calls the "will to power." Nor is Nature frugal, as Darwin supposed; organisms do not fight amongst themselves for scraps of food like guttersnipes of the urban proletariat – here Nietzsche claims to catch the whiff of "the musty air of English overcrowding" wafting around Darwin's theory (*GS* 349). Anyway, in such an unseemly struggle, it is not the fittest, the strongest, the remarkable individuals who prevail, but the rabble, the herd, the weak – through sheer weight of numbers. We shall look at these arguments in detail below.

It ought to be borne in mind that Nietzsche does not advance a plausible or systematic refutation of Darwinism, let alone a consistent alternative theory of evolution. Many of his frequent allusions to this topic made between the early 1870s and the last months of his intellectual life often take the form of asides or points intended to illustrate entirely different arguments or unpublished notes. There is a danger of imposing an artificial structure upon these sometimes contradictory discussions and remarks; but they can nevertheless reveal much about the original idiosyncrasies and time-bound limitations of his thought, especially if we approach them chronologically. For Nietzsche's response to "Darwinism" itself evolved over time.

1870–1880: The Struggle for Existence and Cultural Evolution

Oscar Schmidt, whose book *The Doctrine of Descent and Darwinism* Nietzsche owned, called the struggle for existence the "badge and common property of our age" (1875: 140); indeed, the slogan became synonymous with Darwinism itself and the apparently new view of nature it represented. Even if the majority of Victorians could not accept that such ubiquitous conflict was entirely without purpose, it naturally appealed to Nietzsche, in whose thinking (like that of Schopenhauer) strife and struggle occupies a central place. Perhaps it is unsurprising, then, that the earliest evidence of Nietzsche meaningfully engaging with the implications of the theory of evolution is his invocation of the concept of the struggle for existence in notes written between 1870 and 1871. Significantly, Nietzsche is concerned here with social or cultural evolution – as he would largely continue to be until he began to study biological texts in earnest in the 1880s. Just as a plant only blossoms when it is removed from the remorseless struggle for existence (*Kampf ums Dasein*), which frustrates Nature's "will to beauty," he argues, so the human being can only flourish when he escapes the exigencies of the struggle for life by combining with others to form communities. The state is a means of transcending the Hobbesian *bellum omnium contra omnes* (a phrase Nietzsche would always use interchangeably with the Darwinian struggle for existence); its function is to provide the conditions for the development of exemplary men; the state is an "institution for the protection and cultivation of individuals, for the genius" (*KSA* 7, 7[121]; cf. *KSA* 7, 7[25], 8, 41[42]). What is particularly noteworthy here is that Nietzsche already views the evolutionary process as a means for the production of rare, superior, yet fragile individuals.

It is at this time that Nietzsche makes his well-known remark about the "horrible consequence of Darwinism, which, by the way, I consider to be correct" (*KSA* 7, 19[132]; *Unpublished Writings*, 44). The horrible consequence of Darwinism – by which he means the theory of evolution in general rather than Darwinian natural selection – is the recognition that all human values are vertiginously contingent and lack any basis in some metaphysical realm. He returns to the issue in *On the Uses and Disadvantages of History for Life*, where he describes as "true but deadly" the "doctrines of sovereign becoming, of the fluidity of all concepts, types and species, of the lack of any cardinal distinction between man and animal," and suggests that, should these teachings find a wider audience, the fabric of society would disintegrate as moral and legal codes lost their binding force (*UM II*, 9, p. 112). But as his earlier diatribe against David Friedrich Strauss's book *The Old Faith and the New* shows, he was already acutely aware that the true and lethal implications of evolutionism were being suppressed by the very men who were its most vociferous champions. One of the many follies for which he lambasts Strauss is the latter's attempt to reconcile the moral teachings of Christianity with the new evolutionary worldview rather than rising to the challenge of devising a "genuine Darwinian ethic, seriously and consistently carried through." Instead of grasping the opportunity to derive "a moral code for life out of the *bellum omnium contra omnes* and the privileges of the strong," Strauss perversely praises the English naturalist as one of the "greatest benefactors of mankind" for having established a non-transcendental groundwork for ethical conduct (*UM I*, 7, pp. 29–30). But Strauss, Nietzsche would soon discover, was not the only thinker to shrink from making the radical break with traditional systems of morality which the theory of evolution would seem to demand.

Soon afterwards, Nietzsche began his own attempts to account for the genesis of moral values in evolutionary terms in *Human, All Too Human*. What is significant is that the "history of the moral sensations" which he outlines in various aphorisms in that work draws heavily on the ideas not only of the Englishmen Walter Bagehot and John Lubbock (Thatcher 1982, 1983), but those of his Anglophile friend Paul Rée, whose own thought was in turn influenced by Spencer and Darwin's *The Descent of Man*. Following Rée and Spencer, Nietzsche's theory is that the accumulated experiences of many human generations have given rise to habits which are expressed in judgments about what is good and bad, and that these judgments are abbreviated in their form, so that things are described simply as "good" and "bad," rather than as good or bad for fulfilling our purposes or interests, which would have been the lesson of the original experiences (*WS* 40). It is this theory that Nietzsche would later deride in the preface to *On the Genealogy of Morality* and accuse of thoroughly misapprehending the nature of moral evolution. Nevertheless, at this stage of his intellectual development Nietzsche was happy to subscribe to it.

In *Human, All Too Human* Nietzsche also shows the first signs of developing his own ideas about the mechanisms and processes of evolution. This is most clearly seen in the aphorism entitled "Ennoblement through Degeneration" (*HH* 224). Interestingly, the preparatory notes for this passage, written in 1875, appear under the rubric "On *Darwinism*"; indeed, Nietzsche's theory of "ennoblement through degeneration" is explicitly conceived as an anti-Darwinian theory of (social) evolution and represents his first extended meditation on the topic of Darwinism. The "celebrated struggle for existence," which Nietzsche consistently misunderstood as a conflict resolved by mere brute force, is consequently dismissed as a "philosophy for butcher boys" and is anyway "not the most important principle" (*KSA* 8, 12[22]). There are, he claims, others ways of explaining the evolution of both race and individual. According to Nietzsche, the strongest and most healthy organisms, upon whom Darwin supposedly lays such emphasis, only preserve the "type." It is through the weak that evolution actually takes place: "Degenerate natures are of the highest significance wherever progress is to be effected. Every progress of the whole has to be preceded by a partial weakening" (*HH* 224). Evolution takes place through a dialectical process of augmentation and consolidation of the "stabilizing force" within a community, which is then partially undermined and weakened by the appearance of certain pathological individuals – Nietzsche is again thinking of the genius here – without whom the community would stagnate. The community has to be robust enough to tolerate this influx of infirmity, this temporary "loosening"; and the health of the social organism, like that of the individual organism, can be measured by its capacity to assimilate degenerate elements. There are two points of interest here. The meaning of "weak" and "strong" organisms gradually changed in Nietzsche's mind (Mostert 1979). The indispensable characteristics of those he called weak in 1875 later became, in his last notes on a Darwinian theme in 1887/8, the essential features of the "strong" (*KSA* 13, 14[123]). Secondly, in the original notes for this passage Nietzsche declares that he wishes to "confine [himself] to man and to refrain from drawing conclusions about animal development from the laws of human improvement," which nevertheless would be more admissible than drawing conclusions from the laws of animal behavior for human society, "as do Mr Haeckel in Jena and D. Strauß and his ilk." When Nietzsche speaks of evolution he almost always has in mind human evolution.

1880–1882: Nietzsche *contra* Spencer

It was after 1880 that Nietzsche became increasingly critical of what he saw as the largely "English" version of the theory of evolution that had gained currency, as well as the egalitarian and democratic ideology of industrial Britain more generally. The British way of life, with its good-natured bad taste, comfortable *laisser faire*, its resolutely unheroic aspirations, and indigestible food was anathema to Nietzsche and seemed to him to be the modern breeding ground of the herd instinct. But the figure whom Nietzsche came to see as perhaps the most characteristic British thinker was not Darwin but Herbert Spencer. Spencer combined Mill's utilitarianism and Darwin's evolutionism to create a doctrine according to which the "greatest happiness of the greatest number" was the inevitable end of evolution, a wholly necessary development brought about by the increasing social adaptation and progressive natural selection of the morally fit. This involves the greater refinement of primitive altruistic impulses, and ultimately leads to the reconciliation of egoism and altruism: all selfish (pleasure-seeking) acts serve to maximize the collective happiness and all altruistic acts benefit the individual members of society. This development runs parallel to biological evolution, and culminates in what Spencer calls the "ideally moral man." The members of this future race will exist in a state of perfect internal adaptation to both their physical and social environment and will have achieved the greatest general good, equal freedom and eternal peace, upheld by the harmonious cooperation of all members of a society.

It was by reading Spencer's *Data of Ethics* – at first enthusiastically then with greater skepticism – and taking issue with the fundamental ideas underpinning his system of thought that Nietzsche was first able to sharpen his critique of "Darwinism" and develop his own brand of evolutionism. Indeed, in some respects Nietzsche simply turns Spencer's thinking on its head. Whereas Spencer posits a gradual advancement from egoism to altruism, Nietzsche argues the opposite: organic change is a process of progressive individuation, an "evolution towards the individual" (*KSA* 9, 6[163]). Both moral and biological evolution lie for Nietzsche in the development and refinement of egoism, which, in phylogenetic terms, represents "something recent and still exceptional" (*KSA* 9, 11[185]). Altruism, as an underdeveloped form of egoism, the egoism of the herd, must gradually become extinct. The human being is for Nietzsche the only life-form which is not yet fully adapted to its conditions of existence, the only one which still has the potential to evolve further. Yet any future evolution would be compromised by the "Spencerian ideal of the future," which is geared toward uniformity and fixity. For its true prerequisite is not, as Spencer claims, the increasing complexity and heterogeneity of life, but rather that "*greatest similarity* between all human beings" which makes altruism possible: because altruism can only exist when "one actually sees oneself in the other," he seeks to erase the natural distinctions between individuals and their needs (*KSA* 9, 11[40]). This inner conformity, this accommodation to the status quo is what the Spencerian notion of adaptation is all about, and it represents an evolutionary cul-de-sac: "the complete *adaptation* of all to all and each person within himself (as with Spencer) is an error" (*KSA* 9, 11[73]). Rather, such a state would represent stagnation, a leveling off, a "higher Chinadom," as Nietzsche would later put it (*KSA* 12, 10[17]). Nietzsche desires self-development and diversity, but he does not want it subjected to a trend defined by the general good. Only "evil" – as the bovine adherents of herd morality mistakenly call natural egoistic acts – promotes and stimulates organic evolution, the "permanent *dissimilarity* and greatest possible *sovereignty* of the individual" (*KSA* 9, 11[40]). This process of progressive individuation culminates in the *Übermensch* – or at least in his precursor, to whom Nietzsche refers in some jottings of 1881 (two years before the *Übermensch* would be heralded by Zarathustra) as the "liberated man" (*freigewordener Mensch*) (*KSA* 9, 11[182]) or the "exceptional man" (*Sondermensch*) (*KSA* 9, 11[209]) – and who is conceived, as his notes would appear to suggest, as the antithesis of Spencer's "ideally moral man." Where Spencer's "ideally moral man" is the embodiment of herd consciousness, Nietzsche's future human being can master the conflicting perspectives and impulses that constitute his existence, who has emancipated himself from the alienating experience of serving ends which are not his own, and who is thus free to posit his own goals and values. (We ought to keep in mind that for all his talk here of the individual organism and the herd or species, Nietzsche elsewhere subjects both to a rigorous critique: they are perspectivalist fictions. See e.g. *KSA* 12, 9[144].)

These early ideas about the primordiality of egoism, an "evolution toward the individual" are carried over into the concept of the will to power.

1883–1888: The Will to Power as *Bildungstrieb*

The concept of the will to power – of an endogenous, creative force operative in nature – began to take shape in Nietzsche's mind in 1880–1, but by 1883 it had acquired cardinal importance for his thinking. Only recently has it become apparent to what extent Nietzsche's ideas in this regard were inspired in large part by works on biology that he read in the 1880s. Some of the earliest outlines of his projected major work, *The Will to Power*, clearly show that he intended this agency to explain not only "the evolution of organic beings" (*KSA* 11, 39[13]), but also *all* organic processes: "With the animal it is possible to derive all of its drives from the will to power: likewise, all functions of organic life can be derived from this one source" (*KSA* 11, 36[31]).

As Nietzsche came to realize from reading the work of such men as Ludwig Rütimeyer and Spencer, nineteenth-century biology was almost universally committed to some form of progressionism. The Swiss botanist Carl Nägeli, whose 1884 work *Mechanisch-physiologische Theorie der Abstammungslehre* (Mechanico-Physiological Theory of Descent) Nietzsche bought in 1886, even introduced as the chief driving force of evolution a "perfection principle" (*Vervollkommnungsprincip*), whereby organisms are impelled to develop increasingly sophisticated forms independently of the environment and of natural competition. It is understandable, then, that Nietzsche should complain that Darwinism – at least as it was understood in the nineteenth century – is one of the last attempts to project "reason and divinity" on to nature (*KSA* 12, 2[131]); that in modern concepts such as "nature," "progress," "perfection," "Darwinism" and "selection," he sees merely the persistence of Christian ideas of providential Design (*KSA* 12, 9[163], 10[7]). Human beings do not, for Nietzsche, represent any significant advance over other species or organisms. Nor is evolution, human or otherwise, an unfolding towards a predetermined *telos*: "Humanity has no goal, just as little as the dinosaurs had one; but it has an *evolution*: that is, its end is *no more important* than any point on its path!" (*KSA* 9, 6[59]). Evolution is neither progressive nor is it a linear development. It is a movement which is random, confused, and conflicting, continually oscillating between both synthesis and dissolution. Yet in emphasizing the open-endedness of the evolutionary process, Nietzsche is hardly striking a blow at Darwin himself (or at his theory as it has has come to be understood by modern biologists), but only at the vast majority of contemporary scientists and thinkers who refused to countenance the full implications of the post-Darwinian world.

Nevertheless, Nietzsche does not dispense with the concept of perfection altogether; he seeks only to redefine it. In common with most biologists, Carl Nägeli, in a passage underlined by Nietzsche in his own copy of the botanist's *Mechanisch-physiologische Theorie der Abstammungslehre*, characterized "perfection" as a tendency to greater organizational complexity and specialization in the organism: "Perfection in my sense is therefore nothing other than the progression towards a more complex structure and to greater division of labor" (Nägeli 1884: 13). Nietzsche accepts – to a degree – this definition of perfection: "greater complexity, sharp differentiation, the contiguity of developed organs and functions with the intermediate members disappearing" (*KSA* 12, 7[9]). However, he does not understand organic perfection solely in terms of increasing structural complexity and quantitative expansion. The concept of "perfection" entails "*not* only greater complexity, but also greater *power*" (*KSA* 12, 2[76]). Nietzsche sees both power *and* complexity as indices of perfection; or rather, greater organic complexity is the result of a more fundamental will to power in the organism: " '*Perfection*': reduced to *the type's increase in power*" (*KSA* 12, 6[26]). In other words, Nietzsche replaces Nägeli's *Vervollkommnungsprincip* with his own will to power.

Nietzsche understands Darwin and Spencer to be exclusively concerned with the origin, formation, and preservation of *species*. The focal point of Nietzsche's evolutionary thought, on the other hand, is *not* the group, but rather the solitary organism: "*Fundamental errors* of biologists hitherto: it is *not* a matter of the species, but of *bringing about stronger individuals*" (*KSA* 12, 7[9]). For Nietzsche, evolution is a process of differentiation taking place within particular individuals. The species as a whole does not advance. Thus, within a given species or population, Nietzsche distinguishes two conflicting loci of evolution. First, there is the strong, solitary, "higher" (that is, more complex) individual, for whom, and only for whom, there exists the real possibility of evolution in the truly Nietzschean sense: the limitless expansion and development of life's creative energies. Second, there is the type or "herd" – the groupings of individually weak centers of power whose forms endure apparently unchanged (*KSA* 13, 14[133]). On the one hand, then, Nietzsche conceives evolution as individual leaps beyond the ambit of the type which have no influence on the history of the species. For while higher forms evolve, they do not – and cannot – maintain or perpetuate themselves; only the "type" is heritable. What is more, their existence is more precarious than that of the herd. Like the genius, they represent a brief, ephemeral flowering; as a result, the "level of the species is *not* raised" (*KSA* 13, 14[133]). On the other hand, Nietzsche envisages slow, regular progress towards morphological stability in the herd; that is, in the greater mass of weaker, yet more fecund and durable, organisms.

Nietzsche's focus on the individual organism as the locus of evolution was also supported by his reading of Wilhelm Roux. Like Nägeli, Roux was convinced that Darwin's theory of natural selection was not sufficient to explain the development of organs or the functional harmony of an organism, and located the primary process of evolution in the internal activity of organisms. In his 1881 treatise *Der Kampf der Theile im Organismus* (The Struggle of the Parts in the Organism), Roux proposes that organs, tissues, cells, and even molecules of organic matter are found in an unceasing struggle for existence with one another for food, space, and the utilization of external stimulation. As the copious entries in Nietzsche's notebooks attest, Roux's physiology had a profound effect on his thinking, both on his "anti-Darwinism" and his formulation of the will to power more generally (Müller-Lauter 1999). Nietzsche makes his own Roux's conception of the organism as a spontaneously self-organizing complexity, a nexus of antagonistic forces, a "plurality of living beings which, partly struggling with one another, partly adjusted and subordinated to one another, unintentionally affirm the totality by affirming their individual existence" (*KSA* 11, 27[27]). Expanding on Roux's own military metaphors, Nietzsche was able to develop an "aristocratic" understanding of physiology diametrically opposed to the dominant model that stressed the accommodation and cooperation between an organism's constituent parts. Radically opposed to what, in *On the Genealogy of Morality*, he disparages as the "democratic idiosyncrasy" prevalent in contemporary biology – and here Spencer's emphasis on internal adaptation is again his target – he complains that such egalitarianism traduces nature as will to power, conjures away life's essential activity, and overlooks "the prime importance which the spontaneous, aggressive, expansive, re-interpreting, re-directing and formative powers have" (*GM* II. 12).

By emphasizing the dynamic nature of organic forms, Nietzsche believes he is able to sidestep Darwin's principle of utility – the assumption that variations are selected on the basis of their survival value in the struggle for existence – to which, like many non-Darwinians, he is staunchly opposed. Darwin's position struck many as being implicitly teleological, for, in seeking to assign a use to each and every organ, he appeared to suggest that this use somehow explained the development of that organ; that all variations arose solely in order to meet a prior functional requirement. One of the most consistent themes in Nietzsche's writings on biology – and which is supported by almost all of the biologists whose works he read – is his frequently repeated assertion that an organ's present function cannot account for its development; to regard the eye as made for seeing or the hand for grasping is naive. He believes instead that form is anterior to function. This means that, since organic structures are in a perpetual state of flux and have passed through various intermediate stages of development, the function which those structures perform is also constantly evolving and changing. While organs evolve through an aggregation of random variations, and thus do not develop in direct response to a functional requirement, the struggle of the parts ensures that newly occurring forms "do not remain for long without being related to a partial use," because they are integrated into a system and a function is immediately imposed upon it by the victorious and dominant part; these structures then develop further through enhanced functional activity, as the new form, "according to its *use*, develops itself more and more completely" (*KSA* 12, 7[25]). This process has no end: as the whole grows, any equilibrium achieved in the struggle of the parts is disturbed, the struggle begins once more and so the function of the individual organs also shifts. But this activity is not restricted to the evolution of organs within an organism; it is characteristic of the will to power wherever it is manifested, whether in biological or cultural evolution:

> anything in existence [. . .] is continually interpreted anew, requisitioned anew, transformed and directed to a new purpose by a power superior to it [. . .] everything that occurs in the organic world consists of *overpowering, dominating*, and in their turn, overpowering and dominating consist of re-interpretation, adjustment, in the process of which their former "meaning" and "purpose" must necessarily be obscured or completely obliterated. [. . .] every purpose and use is just a *sign* that the will to power has achieved mastery over something less powerful, and has impressed upon it its own idea of a use function. [. . .] The "development" of a thing, a tradition, an organ is therefore certainly not its *progressus* towards a goal [. . .] instead it is a succession of more or less profound, more or less mutually independent processes of subjugation exacted on the thing [. . .] The form is fluid, the "meaning" even more so [. . .] (GM II. 12)

Despite the central importance of this passage as a statement of the activity of the will to power, there is little to commend it as an argument against Darwin (even if we overlook the non-Darwinian concept of a spontaneous, endogenous force). Nietzsche's argument recalls what modern evolutionists call "pre-adaptation" – that is, the use of an organ adapted to one function for a different function, such as the development of air-breathing lungs from the bladders providing fish with buoyancy (Dennett 1995: 465). Moreover, Nietzsche's emphasis on the contingency of the evolutionary process may be a well-aimed volley if Spencer is intended to be the sole target, but it would leave Darwin himself entirely unscathed. Finally, it is difficult to see how replacing concepts such as "natural selection" and "adaptation" with the "will to power" results in any less anthropomorphic and thus metaphysical a perspective than the one Nietzsche seeks to overcome (Ansell Pearson 1997: 105–6).

For Nietzsche, life as will to power is nothing but the accumulation and discharge of force; instead of seeking primarily to sustain and consolidate itself, life is a ceaseless movement toward expansion and growth. In developing this aspect of the will to power, Nietzsche drew heavily on the ideas of an obscure Anglo-German zoologist called William Rolph. In his *Biologische Probleme* (*Biological Problems*), which Nietzsche probably acquired in mid-1884, Rolph seeks to refute the orthodox Darwinian conception of the "struggle for existence," and proposes a novel mechanism by which to explain the origin of variation and diversity in nature. For Rolph denies the existence of an instinct for self-preservation – or at the very least rejects the notion that such a drive represents the principal motivation of animal behavior. Rather, life seeks primarily to expand itself, driven by an involuntary "urge to assimilate" to increase its intake of nutriment. All organic functions, from nutrition and reproduction right up to evolution, can be explained by, and reduced to, what Rolph calls the principle of "insatiability."

From 1884 onwards, Nietzsche's notebooks are littered with jottings and comments which suggest that Rolph's influence on him was no less profound than that of Roux. Indeed, it is no exaggeration to say that Nietzsche incorporated all the basic premises of Rolph's biology into his own thought. The principle of insatiability becomes the will to power, which Nietzsche views as a process of assimilation, and even, echoing Rolph's terminology, as an "insatiable appropriation [*unersättliche Aneignung*]" (*KSA* 12, 2[76]). Following Rolph, Nietzsche maintains that this insatiable acquisition of nutriment – and thus power – would suggest that organisms are not driven by an instinct for self-preservation: "one cannot derive the most basic and primordial activity in protoplasm from a will to self-preservation: for it takes in absurdly more than would be necessary for survival" (*KSA* 13, 11[121]).

Like other non-Darwinian biologists, Rolph insists that natural selection is a purely secondary phenomenon in evolution, a claim based on his mistaken assumption that Darwin regarded the "struggle for existence" *primarily* or *exclusively* in terms of a Malthusian intra-specific competition for scarce resources (mistaken because Darwin never saw the scarcity of resources itself as the engine of change, but primarily as a means to eliminate less well adapted organisms). Malthus had argued that human population growth, if unchecked, tended to expand in geometrical progression, while food supply increased at best arithmetically. In practice, however, population was constantly controlled by famine, disease, and war. According to Rolph, Darwin's debt to the Malthusian law of population means he is unable to explain how variations in organic structure arise, because such variations demand an increase in energy and consequently an increase in available nutriment. For if an organism is driven only by an impulse for self-preservation it acquires only sufficient food to survive and cannot cover the physiological costs of evolution. Yet resources are in fact plentiful, so any advance in organization can only be explained by the automatic, insatiable "assimilative activity" fundamental to all life, an innate tendency to grow, to expand, to appropriate. So the struggle for existence is not a defensive struggle for mere survival, which would retard evolution – or even bring about the decline and extinction of a species. Rather, it is a "war of aggression": "While the Darwinists hold that no struggle for existence takes place where the survival of the creature is not threatened, I believe the life-struggle to be ubiquitous: it is first and foremost precisely such a life-struggle, a struggle for the increase of life, but not a struggle for life!" (Rolph 1884: 97).

Nietzsche incorporates all the main points of Rolph's anti-Darwinian argument – the claim that the struggle for existence is an exception, occurring only in rare conditions of scarcity; that there is in fact an abundance of resources to fuel the rapid evolution of organisms; that the basic impetus in nature is towards an increase in life – into aphorism 349 of *The Gay Science*, in the fifth book that was added to the second edition of 1887. The only significant change he makes is to translate Rolph's terminology into his own, with the latter's term the "increase of life" (*Lebensmehrung*) becoming the more recognizably Nietzschean "expansion of power" (*Machterweiterung*):

> The wish to preserve oneself is the symptom of a condition of distress, of a limitation of the really fundamental instinct of life which aims at the *expansion of power* and, wishing for that, frequently risks and even sacrifices self-preservation. [. . .] [I]n nature it is not conditions of distress that are *dominant* but overflow and squandering, even to the point of absurdity. The struggle for existence is only an *exception*, a temporary restriction of the life-will [*Lebenswille*]. The great and small struggle always revolves around superiority, around growth and expansion, around power – in accordance with the will to power which is the will of life. (*GS* 349)

With slight modifications, and under a more explicitly anti-Darwinian rubric, the same argument reappears the following year in *Twilight of the Idols*: "life as a whole is *not* a state of crisis or hunger, but rather a richness, a luxuriance, even an absurd extravagance – where there is a struggle, there is a struggle for *power* [. . .] Malthus should not be confused with nature" (*TI*, "Reconnaissance Raids," 14).

What all this means is that organic change is for Nietzsche – as it is for Rolph – merely the by-product of the acquisition of power. This perspective allows him once again, he believes, to circumvent the issue of utility. For Darwin, as we have seen, the use of a particular adaptation is determined by its value in securing an advantage in the struggle for existence. Nietzsche, on the other hand, is not at all concerned whether an organism survives or not – indeed, the truly evolving organism precisely does not endure, but is inevitably destroyed by its own pregnant potency. He understands evolution not in terms of the gradual accretion of adaptive and self-preservative variations, but as the sudden eruption of life's creative energies:

> "Useful" in the sense of Darwinian biology – that means proving itself advantageous in the struggle with others. But it seems to me that the feeling of increase [*Mehrgefühl*], the feeling of *becoming stronger*, is itself, quite apart from its utility in the struggle, the real *progress*: only from this feeling does the will to struggle arise. (*KSA* 12, 7[44])

However, only by positing this universal striving for power is it possible, Nietzsche believes, to account for what Darwin refuses to acknowledge: that the "struggle for existence" does not always result in the survival of the "fittest" – by which Nietzsche means the "stronger, better constituted." In fact, as the history of humanity attests, the very opposite is the case: "the elimination of the strokes of luck, the uselessness of the more highly developed types, the inevitable ascendancy of the average, even the *below average* types" (*KSA* 13, 14[123]). How does the will to power explain this topsy-turvy state of nature, this "*inverted* struggle for existence"? The answer lies in the fact that both the strong and the weak seek to improve the conditions of their existence, to obtain power. But, on the one hand, higher forms are rare and radically unstable. Such is their profligacy in expending the energy which they so voraciously acquire, such is their immanent diversity, that these exquisite creatures are prone to disintegration and thus short-lived. On the other hand, the weak tend to congregate in herds, thereby consolidating and increasing their collective power as compensation for their individual impotence. Against these organized herd instincts, the "strong" are relatively powerless. The weak, then, prevail not through brute strength, but by sheer force of numbers and as a result of developing various adaptive strategies for survival – pre-eminently, of course, morality.

Conclusion

Nietzsche's evolutionism was expressed in an intellectual climate which favored non-Darwinian concepts of organic development and which circumvented and subverted the more radical proposals put forward by Darwin. In many ways, Nietzsche's anti-Darwinism, his refusal to accept a view of nature which he saw as an expression of a peculiarly "English" spirit, has much in common with the prejudices shared by the many contemporary German biologists who retreated into a Romantic (and supposedly more German) vitalism. By and large his criticisms of Darwin are ineffective, either because the arguments are miscast or because they are rooted in the misunderstandings surrounding the nature of evolution in the late nineteenth century. How far this was a matter of concern to Nietzsche is unclear: for what was most important to him was to formulate a conception of life firmly opposed to that which underlay "Darwinism" and to purge the theory of evolution of the false concepts of adaptation, self-preservation, progress, democracy, utility, and scarcity.

See also 4 "Nietzsche on Individuation and Purposiveness in Nature"; 5 "The Individual and Individuality in Nietzsche"; 24 "Nietzsche *contra* Liberalism on Freedom"

Editions of Nietzsche Used

Beyond Good and Evil, trans. Marion Faber (Oxford: Oxford University Press, 1999).
Ecce Homo, trans. R. J. Hollingdale (Harmondsworth: Penguin, 1979).
The Gay Science, trans. Walter Kaufmann (New York: Vintage Books, 1974).
Human, All Too Human, trans. R. J. Hollingdale, 2 vols. (Cambridge: Cambridge University Press, 1986).
On the Genealogy of Morality, trans. Carol Diethe (Cambridge: Cambridge University Press, 1994).
Twilight of the Idols, trans. Duncan Large (Oxford: Oxford University Press, 1998).
Unpublished Writings from the Period of "Unfashionable Observations", in *The Complete Works of Friedrich Nietzsche*, vol. 11, trans. Ronald T. Gray (Stanford, CA: Stanford University Press, 1999).
Untimely Meditations, trans. R. J. Hollingdale (Cambridge: Cambridge University Press, 1983).

References

Andler, Charles (1920–31). *Nietzsche, sa vie et sa pensée*, 6 vols. (Paris: Bossard).
Ansell Pearson, Keith (1997). *Viroid Life: Perspectives on Nietzsche and the Transhuman Condition* (London: Routledge).
Bowler, Peter J. (1988). *The Non-Darwinian Revolution: Reinterpreting a Historical Myth* (Baltimore: Johns Hopkins University Press).
Dennett, Daniel C. (1995). *Darwin's Dangerous Idea: Evolution and the Meanings of Life* (Harmondsworth: Penguin).
Haeckel, Ernst (1866). *Generelle Morphologie des Organismen*, 2 vols. (Berlin: Reimer).
Hartmann, Eduard von (1875). *Wahrheit und Irrthum im Darwinismus. Eine kritische Darstellung der organischen Entwickelungstheorie* (Berlin: Duncker).
Lange, Friedrich (1925). *The History of Materialism*, 3 vols. (London: Routledge).
Moore, Gregory (2002). *Nietzsche, Biology and Metaphor* (Cambridge: Cambridge University Press).
Mostert, Pieter (1979). "Nietzsche's Reception of Darwinism," *Bijdragen tot de Dierkunde*, 49, pp. 235–46.
Müller-Lauter, Wolfgang (1978). "Der Organismus als innerer Kampf: Der Einfluss von Wilhelm Roux auf Friedrich Nietzsche," *Nietzsche-Studien*, 7, 189–223.

—— (1999). "The Organism as Inner Struggle: Wilhelm Roux's Influence in Nietzsche," in Wolfgang Müller-Lauter, *Nietzsche: His Philosophy of Contradictions and the Contradictions of his Philosophy* (Urbana, IL: University of Illinois Press), pp. 161–82.

Nägeli, Carl (1884). *Mechanisch-physiologische Theorie der Abstammungslehre* (Munich: Oldenburg).

Richardson, John (2004). *Nietzsche's New Darwinism* (Oxford: Oxford University Press).

Richter, Claire (1911). *Nietzsche et les théories biologiques contemporaines* (Paris: Mercure de France).

Rolph, William (1884). *Biologische Probleme, zugleich als Versuch zur Entwicklung einer rationellen Ethik* (Leipzig: Engelmann).

Schmidt, Oscar (1875). *The Doctrine of Descent and Darwinism* (London: King & Co.).

Stone, Dan (2002). *Breeding Superman: Nietzsche, Race and Eugenics in Edwardian and Interwar Britain* (Liverpool: Liverpool University Press).

Thatcher, David S. (1982). "Nietzsche, Bagehot and the Morality of Custom," *Victorian Newsletter*, 62, pp. 7–13.

—— (1983). "Nietzsche's Debt to Lubbock," *Journal of the History of Ideas*, 44, pp. 293–309.

Tille, Alexander (1895). *Von Darwin bis Nietzsche* (Leipzig: Naumann).

Further Reading

Smith, C. U. M. (1987). " 'Clever beasts who invented knowing': Nietzsche's Evolutionary Biology of Knowledge," *Biology and Philosophy*, 2, pp. 65–91.

Stegmaier, Werner (1987). "Darwin, Darwinismus, Nietzsche: Zum Problem der Evolution," *Nietzsche-Studien*, 16, pp. 264–87.

29

Life and Self-Overcoming

DANIEL W. CONWAY

1 Life as Will to Power

We find in the following passage one of Nietzsche's clearest statements of what he means by *life*:

> Physiologists should think before putting down the instinct of self-preservation as the cardinal instinct [*Trieb*] of an organic being. A living thing seeks above all to *discharge* its strength [*Kraft*] – life itself is *will to power*; self-preservation is only one of the indirect and most frequent *results*. (*BGE* 13)

Three elements of this account warrant further elaboration. First of all, Nietzsche presents his teaching of will to power as manifestly superior to a rival theory of life. As this comparison indicates, moreover, some of his most illuminating discussions of life unfold within the context of his (largely dismissive) consideration of popular appeals to *self-preservation* as the essence of life and the goal of evolution. Despite his well-known antipathy to the operation of reactive forces, that is, he is often at his best when reacting to the flawed views of rival theorists.[1] His dependence on competing theories to provoke the articulation of his own hypothesis of will to power thus provides us with an instructive example of the productive strife that he locates in the basic processes of life itself.

Second, we learn that Nietzsche too knows, and apparently wishes to promulgate, what Zarathustra learned when he "crawled into the very heart of life" (Z II, "On Self-Overcoming") – namely, that life is will to power. In its most familiar formulations, the hypothesis of will to power suggests an amoral, chaotic cosmos, whose unceasing flux is organized by nothing more than the impulse of its constitutive "quanta" to reorganize themselves into transient configurations, which promise, at any given moment, the greatest possible expression of power. Although best known as a proposed contribution to physics and/or cosmology, Nietzsche's hypothesis of will to power is also meant to account for the basic processes of life itself. He thus describes life as a shifting nexus of elemental, contestatory forces, mutually engaged in overlapping struggles for domination and preponderance. Every living being, he maintains, blindly pursues the optimal circumstances under which it might express its native "strength" and thereby achieve the desired "feeling of power." The hypothesis of will to power thus presents life itself as essentially active, aggressive, and formative. Or, as he puts it in an oft-cited (and oft-reviled[2]) passage, "Life itself is essentially appropriation, injury, overpowering of what is alien and weaker; suppression, hardness, imposition of one's own forms, incorporation and at least, at its mildest, exploitation" (*BGE* 259).

Rejecting the traditional ontological distinction between animate and inanimate beings, Nietzsche distinguishes instead between organic and anorganic expressions of the will to power. Whether animate or inanimate, he insists, every being both shares in and articulates a will to express its native power. In anorganic beings, "every power draws its ultimate consequences at every moment" (*BGE* 22). In the case of living beings, however, the coincidence of power and the expression of its ultimate consequences is not instantaneous. In life, *laws* are needed to guide each organism to its final incarnation, via a repeatable series of regular developments. (As we shall see, Nietzsche identifies *self-overcoming* as the most basic "law of life.")

Hence both nature and life are essentially will to power, in the sense that organic and anorganic beings strive above all else to expend their disposable power. In the case of anorganic beings, the discharge of power is instantaneous, so no reserves are stored for future expenditures. In the case of living beings, however, expenditures are mediated (and so postponed) by the various law-like developments that deliver an organism to its optimal form and its maximal discharge of strength. Over the course of these developments, some residual stores of strength are accumulated in reserve, to be expended (or "squandered") only in the self-expression of the organism in its final incarnation.

Third, Nietzsche situates his hypothesis of will to power in the emerging deep psychological framework that informs his post-Zarathustran writings.[3] This framework is intended, in part, to accommodate his claim that an organism discharges its strength by availing itself of an invisible network of unconscious drives and instincts.[4] Nietzsche thus identifies the involuntary, instinctual discharge of strength as the uniquely organic activity of the will to power.[5] *Kraft* is *Macht* become animate.

Whereas the involuntary discharge of strength is essential to the life of any organism, living beings are not indifferent to the qualitative nature of their expenditures. Nietzsche thus explains that

> Every animal – therefore *la bête philosophe*, too – instinctively strives for an optimum of favorable conditions under which it can expend all its strength [*Kraft*] and achieve its maximal feeling of power [*Machtgefühl*]; every animal abhors, just as instinctively and with a subtlety of discernment that is "higher than all reason," every kind of intrusion or hindrance that obstructs or could obstruct this path to the optimum (I am *not* speaking of its path to "happiness," but its path to power, to action, to the most powerful activity, and in most cases actually its path to unhappiness). (*GM* III. 7)

Nietzsche's appeal here to a subjective measure of organic activity – notoriously, one's "feeling of power" need not correspond to one's actual capacities or prospects for the exercise of power – thus allows him to introduce a qualitative variable into his alternative theory of life. An organism strives above all to discharge its accumulated stores of strength, but it also does so in such a way that promises to maximize its attendant "feeling of power."

Nietzsche's stipulation concerning this qualitative variable furthermore steers his *Lebensphilosophie* into closer conformity with his more familiar characterizations of will to power. When organisms succeed in discharging their strength under "favorable conditions," they are rewarded with a "feeling of power." This means that the organism experiences its discharge of strength (*Kraft*) *as if it were* an anorganic expenditure of power (*Macht*). Nietzsche thus suggests that inanimate nature serves as an orienting model for the vital activity of organic beings. The "favorable conditions" of discharge sought by an organism turn out to be those that are most conducive to an experience of itself as lawless and free. In this context, it is interesting to note how often Nietzsche likens great, exemplary human beings to inanimate forces or "pieces" of anorganic nature, for example the swollen river, the bolt of lightning, the crashing boulder, the gathering storm, and so on.

Although organisms often act and react in ways that secure their self-preservation, this is not their primary aim. Organisms strive above all else to discharge their accumulated stores of strength in spontaneous outward expressions of their native vitality. Doing so often has the effect of preserving the life of the organism, but this is not always the case. Indeed, living beings often place themselves at risk precisely in order to exhaust their native vitality:

> The really fundamental instinct of life [. . .] aims at *the expansion of power* and, wishing for that, frequently risks and even sacrifices self-preservation. [. . .] The struggle for existence is only an *exception*, a temporary restriction of the will to life. The great and small struggles always revolve around superiority, around growth and expansion, around power – in accordance with the will to power which is the will of life. (*GS* 349)

It is for this reason, in fact, that Nietzsche takes a particular interest in those organisms and species whose natural cycles of growth ultimately place them at mortal risk. Hence his fascination, for example, with the emergence of a new form of life, the butterfly, from the cocoon in which the caterpillar naturally encases itself (*GM* III. 10). If the primary instinct of the caterpillar were simply to preserve itself, then its successor forms, including the chrysalis, would never develop. Nietzsche's interest in mortal expenditures of strength also encompasses those human beings whose will to power is so strong that it obviously overrides the instinct for self-preservation. Whereas an appeal to self-preservation may adequately account for the behavior of most human beings, especially under conditions of pandemic decay, only the hypothesis of will to power can explain the behavior of those exemplary human beings who cannot help but "squander" themselves as they expend their native stores of strength (*TI*, "Skirmishes of an Untimely Man," 44). Nietzsche thus promotes his hypothesis of will to power not only for its superior explanatory power, but also as a hedge against the continued reduction of humankind to its lowest common denominator.

2 Nietzsche *contra* "English Darwinism"

Many of the passages cited thus far trade on an explicit contrast between Nietzsche's *Lebensphilosophie* and the conventional wisdom of his contemporaries. As we have seen, he develops his hypothesis of will to power in response to the popular theory that life aims above all else at self-preservation.

To his ears, "self-preservation" rings suspiciously reactive, as if life timidly awaited the cues and promptings of anorganic stimuli. He takes particular exception to the position – at least as he understands it – popularly espoused by Herbert Spencer, who, he claims, defines

> life itself [. . .] as a more and more efficient inner adaptation to external conditions (Herbert Spencer). Thus the essence of life, its *will to power*, is ignored; one overlooks the essential priority of the spontaneous, aggressive, expansive, form-giving forces that give new inter-pretations and directions, although "adaptation" follows only after this; the dominant role of the highest functionaries within the organism itself in which the will to life appears active and form-giving is denied. (*GM* II. 12)

How could Spencer et al. mistake a secondary expression of life – self-preservation through serial adaptation – for its very essence and primary expression? The answer, Nietzsche suspects, is that these rival theorists cannot bear the likely implications of any hypothesis that dares, like his, to locate "spontaneous, aggressive, expansive, form-giving forces" at the heart of life itself. Unable to behold life as will to power, they focus instead on "evidence" – however dubious – that allows them to emphasize more familiar and less threatening characteristics of life. He thus detects in the currency of this unscientific enthusiasm for "self-preservation" an expression of the general decline that afflicts European modernity:

> The democratic idiosyncrasy [. . .] seems to me to have already taken charge of all physiology and theory of life – to the detriment of life, as goes without saying, since it has robbed it of its fundamental concept, that of *activity*. (*GM* II. 12)

As this passage indicates, the disagreement between Nietzsche and his rivals is not merely academic. Their theoretical deficiencies illuminate a real, practical concern that commands his attention. He believes that the currency of reactive theories of life reflects, *and perhaps even precipitates*, the ongoing extinction of active forces. As we shall see, his perception of life as vulnerable – in this case, to the vampirism of philologically suspect "theories of life" – serves as both the impetus for and the limit to his advocacy. Like Zarathustra, he promotes life only on the unstated condition that life requires his unique assistance.

Nietzsche's explicit references here to Spencer and Huxley, as opposed to Darwin himself, enable us to specify more precisely the intended target of his criticisms.[6] As many scholars have noted, Nietzsche's understanding of Darwin is at best sketchy and at worst uninformed. It is not clear that he ever undertook a careful study of Darwin's theories, and he was far more concerned in any event to combat the pernicious influence of these theories – distorted or not – on "all physiology and theory of life."[7] For Nietzsche, then, the status of Darwin's actual theories and writings was largely beside the point. The real obstacle to progress in the life sciences (and, by extension, in ethics and politics) was posed by those followers of Darwin who asserted the primacy of reactive forces in the microcosm of molecular biology and in the macrocosm of European culture.

As the following passage confirms, in fact, Nietzsche means to take issue with "the whole of English Darwinism," which, he alleges, projects onto the basic processes of life its own decadent experiences of "struggle and distress." By way of contrast, *his* theory of life conforms more closely to nature itself, and thus honors the methods and criteria of the emerging methodology of scientific naturalism:

> The wish to preserve oneself is the symptom of a condition of distress, of a limitation of the really fundamental instinct of life which aims at *the expansion of power* and, wishing for that, frequently risks and even sacrifices self-preservation. [. . .] The whole of English Darwinism breathes something like the musty air of English overpopulation, like the smell of the distress and overcrowding of small people. But a natural scientist should come out of his human nook; and in nature it is not conditions of distress that are *dominant* but overflow and squandering, even to the point of absurdity. The struggle for existence is only an *exception*, a temporary restriction of the will to life. (*GS* 349)

By opposing his unblinkered naturalism to the nookbound anthropomorphisms circulated by his rivals, Nietzsche confirms the affiliation of his theory of will to power with a particular, superior view of nature, in which conditions of "overflow and squandering" prevail. His rivals are wrong about life, he thus implies, *because they are also wrong about nature.* The better view of nature is conveyed, of course, by his own hypothesis of will to power, which he proposes to employ, as in the passage cited above, to deliver a more fully naturalized account of the basic processes of life. At least when responding to "the whole of English Darwinism," that is, he aims to model life as closely as possible on nature, which he figures as amoral and indifferent.

As we shall see, however, his stirring exhortation to the "natural scientist" also betrays his own ambivalence about the naturalism to which he aspires. While it perhaps makes sense for a scholar to renounce the narrow, ethnocentric "nook" that is suggested by Nietzsche's critique of English culture, abandoning the anthropocentrism of the "human nook" may turn out to be more difficult than he allows in this passage. From the standpoint of scientific naturalism, in fact, his exhortation to the "natural scientist" is potentially dangerous, especially if the "absurdity" of nature's "squandering" proves intractable to the concepts and categories at the scientist's disposal. In that event, even the most iconoclastic "natural scientist" would be obliged to resort, even if unwittingly, to the stock fictions of speculative metaphysics. The most obvious alternative to the anthropocentrism of the cramped "human nook," after all, would be the kind of titanic perspective that supposedly affords one a god's-eye view of nature. As we shall see, in fact, Nietzsche's own case confirms the tenacity of the anthropocentric prejudices native to the "human nook" and the folly inherent in any campaign simply to refuse them.

3 Life as Self-Overcoming

In his polemics against "the whole of English Darwinism," Nietzsche is primarily concerned to forward a more fully naturalized account of life. Toward this end, he vows to strip away the superstitions and pieties that insulate his meek rivals from an experience of life as it is – namely, as will to power. In other contexts, however, he is primarily concerned to *distinguish* life from nature and, so, to isolate what is most unique about living beings. Since both life and nature are expressions of will to power, the putative contrast between them may shed clarifying light on the distinctive characteristics of life itself.

In a representative statement of this contrast, Nietzsche takes issue with the ethical injunction to "live according to nature." He thus admonishes the Stoics to

> Imagine a being like nature, wasteful beyond measure, indifferent beyond measure, without purposes and consideration, without mercy and justice, fertile and desolate and uncertain at the same time; imagine *indifference* itself as a power – how could you live according to this indifference? Living – is that not precisely wanting to be other than this nature? Is not living – estimating, preferring, being unjust, being limited, wanting to be different? (*BGE* 9)

Here he apparently concedes that human beings are likely to have very different experiences of life and nature, despite the common provenance of each in will to power. He goes so far – albeit in a rhetorical question – as to define "living" as "wanting to be other than this [i.e., indifferent] nature." Living organisms, he thus implies, cannot afford the luxury of nature's profligacy. To live is to make precisely those interested calculations and selections that are antithetical to the blind indifference of nature. (As we shall see, in fact, it is these calculations and selections that enable an organism to accumulate disposable strength and, subsequently, to overcome itself.) He consequently ridicules the Stoics' wish to live "according to nature" as either trivially accomplished or as betraying a masked death wish.

If Nietzsche wishes to avoid the mistake he implicitly imputes to the Stoics,[8] then he must elaborate further on the distinction suggested here between life and nature. In doing so, however, he must also avoid recourse to the kinds of unscientific vanities that mar the theories advanced by his rivals. In order to preserve the validity of his claim that "the essence of life is will to power," that is, he must beware of fashioning life in his own, flawed image, lest he simply produce yet another de-natured account of life. As we shall see, he is not entirely successful in this endeavor.[9]

Nietzsche's dispute with his rivals ultimately turns on his alternative account of evolution, at the center of which he places his daring hypothesis of the will to power. Although his rivals claim to endorse a fully scientific theory of evolution, they are in fact unwilling to acknowledge the amoral, aggressive forces that actually govern the basic processes of organic development. In its blind impulse to transform itself, life is neither efficient nor economical and in fact resembles nature itself:

> The "evolution" [*Entwicklung*] of a thing, a custom, an organ is thus by no means its *progressus* toward a goal, even less a logical *progressus* by the shortest route and with the smallest expenditure of force – but a succession of more or less profound, more or less mutually independent processes of subduing, plus the resistances they encounter, the attempts at transformations [*Form-Verwandlungen*] for the purpose of defense and reaction, and the results of successful counteractions. The form is fluid, but the "meaning" [*Sinn*] is even more so. (*GM* II. 12)

537

In light of his rejection of these popular models of (supposedly) natural teleology, we might be surprised to learn that he nevertheless detects an "actual *progressus*" at work in nature. (For that matter, we might be surprised that he would retain a word like "evolution," even in scare quotes, which has been so conducive to the proliferation of unwarranted anthropomorphisms.) This *progressus*, he coldly observes, does not favor quantity or mass, but actually threatens to "sacrifice" large masses in order to harvest the entropic power they possess but cannot meaningfully discharge:

> It is not too much to say that even a partial *diminution of utility*, an atrophying and degeneration, a loss of meaning and purposiveness – in short, death – is among the conditions of an actual *progressus*, which always appears in the shape of a will and way to *greater power* and is always carried through at the expense of numerous smaller powers. The magnitude of an "advance" can even be measured by the mass of things that had to be sacrificed to it; mankind in the mass sacrificed to the prosperity of a single *stronger* species of man – that *would* be an advance. (*GM* II. 12)

This *progressus* may be difficult to characterize, inasmuch as it aims at no end other than the articulation of ever greater amplifications of power. This *progressus* may also be difficult to embrace, for it offers neither solace nor redemption to those featherless bipeds who must see themselves as the pinnacle and *telos* of natural evolution. To the extent that it is discernible, however, this *progressus* bolsters Nietzsche's contention that life overcomes itself, for this *progressus* (supposedly) expresses the non-random development of living beings toward ever greater amplifications of power.

Nietzsche's alternative account of evolution thus hinges on the "actual *progressus*" that he discerns within the otherwise chaotic whirl of will to power. While all things, organic and anorganic, partake of the constitutive flux of the cosmos, living beings develop according to an immanent principle of self-transformation. In its unrelenting struggles with external forces and alien entities, an organism is gradually transformed into its *other*. And although these transformations may often appear random, or even whimsical, they are in fact governed by law and always strive to achieve the same goal. According to Nietzsche, an organism or species continues to progress toward ever greater amplifications of power until it arrives at the full and final expression of its native strength. The irrepressible surge of life thus legislates the continual obsolescence of formerly vital forms and the concomitant creation of new forms.

Nietzsche's preferred term for the law-governed process of organic development is *self-overcoming (Selbstüberwindung)*, the "necessity" of which he associates with "the law of life" (*GM* III. 27). Zarathustra learns about self-overcoming from Life itself, in the form of a "secret" whose truth he cannot independently verify (*Z* II, "On Self-Overcoming"). That Life sees fit to add this "secret" to what Zarathustra already has learned on his own indicates that the process of self-overcoming is neither identical nor reducible to will to power. Indeed, the self-overcoming of life suggests a region or disposition of the cosmos in which the unceasing, random flux of will to power is organized toward the non-random production of ever greater amplifications of power. *Self-overcoming* thus names the uniquely organic manifestation of the activity of the will to power.

Nietzsche's decision to divulge Life's "secret" presents us with a formidable interpretive difficulty. If life is will to power, then it belongs to the lawless, random, unceasing flux that characterizes the natural cosmos. If life *also* overcomes itself, however, then the flux to which it belongs is organized, however subtly, to accommodate the development of ever greater (as opposed, say, to different) amplifications of power. At first glance, then, Nietzsche would appear to have it both ways: Evolution both does and does not admit of a teleological ordering principle. If he is to avoid this charge, then he would do well to explain why the "actual *progressus*" he detects in life is not liable to the same objections he levels against more popular accounts of "natural" teleology.

4 The Case of Nietzsche

For all its importance to Nietzsche's *Lebensphilosophie*, his account of the process of self-overcoming remains disappointingly vague and underdeveloped. He spends very few sentences explaining what he actually means by "self-overcoming," and he generally deputizes his readers to furnish the details of its operation. Much like Life in her lessons to Zarathustra, in fact, Nietzsche tends to use the term in a way that already presupposes a general context of understanding. He provides scant elaboration on the mechanism and process of self-overcoming, and he offers very little empirical evidence of its supposed activity. One might be tempted to conclude, in fact, that his preferred use of the term is more properly rhetorical than philosophical.

In any event, Nietzsche's account of self-overcoming is unusually reliant for its elaboration on the specific examples to which he appeals. Not surprisingly, moreover, especially in light of his enduring fascination with himself, most of his specific references to self-overcoming pertain to the developmental trajectory of his own life. Virtually the whole of *Ecce Homo* celebrates his labors of self-transformation, including his plucky convalescence from a debilitating bout with Romantic pessimism. This book furthermore emphasizes his prudent attention to "the little things" that philosophers and educators typically ignore, including the vicissitudes of place, climate, nutrition, and recreation (*EH*, "Why I Am So Clever," 3). His point here is that small, incremental changes in personal regimen (e.g., no alcohol or coffee, long walks in clear mountain air) may eventually contribute, under propitious circumstances, to qualitative evolutionary advances (e.g., the emergence of a post-ascetic mutation of the priestly type).

The philosophical upshot of Nietzsche's self-overcomings is that he is now endowed, or so he claims, with a duplex nature and a uniquely expansive critical perspective. It is to his "*dual* series of experiences, this access to apparently separate worlds," in fact, that he owes his copious "wisdom" (*EH*, "Why I Am So Wise," 2). His experience with different forms of life furthermore attests to the success of his self-overcomings thus far. Although he is now "healthy," for example, he commands ready access to the perspective of illness; although now "opposed" to Wagner, he retains an appreciation for a distinctly Wagnerian (i.e., decadent) experience of life; and so on. Nietzsche's own case thus confirms that the process of self-overcoming does not obliterate predecessor forms of life as it sponsors the evolution of new forms. Subsumed within each successor form are vestiges and inheritances of its various predecessors. He furthermore maintains that, in his case, at least, these vestiges and inheritances are in some sense functional, such that he may draw upon them even in his current incarnation. As his own case is meant to indicate, in fact, access to these predecessor forms endows an evolved organism with unique capabilities and growing reserves of disposable strength.

Nietzsche thus presents his struggle with Wagner as both a cause and a consequence of the amplification of disposable strength that attends his renascent health:

> Interspersed with many jokes, I bring up a matter that is no joke. To turn my back on Wagner was for me a destiny [*Schicksal*]; to like anything at all again after that, a triumph. Perhaps nobody was more dangerously attached to – grown together with – Wagnerizing; nobody tried harder to resist it; nobody was happier to be rid of it. A long story! – You want a word for it? – If I were a moralist, who knows what I might call it? Perhaps *self-overcoming* [*Selbstüberwindung*]. – But the philosopher has no love for moralists. Neither does he love pretty words. (*CW*, preface)

Nietzsche may "love" neither "moralists" nor their "pretty words," but he uses one such word – *Selbstüberwindung* – to describe his own evolution. In the course of explaining why he is a "destiny," in fact, he employs this term to link his own personal triumph to the revolutionary teachings (and heroic self-overcomings) of Zarathustra:

> The self-overcoming [*die Selbstüberwindung*] of morality, out of truthfulness; the self-overcoming [*die Selbstüberwindung*] of the moralist, into his opposite [*Gegensatz*] – *into me* – that is what the name of Zarathustra means in my mouth. (*EH*, "Why I Am a Destiny," 3)

That this discussion occurs in the context of his attempt to reckon his own "destiny" (*Schicksal*) furthermore suggests that self-overcoming involves not merely the *recognition* of one's "destiny," as if determined by external forces or internal directives, but also the possibility of playing an *active* role in this process, of embracing, cooperating with – perhaps even ensuring – one's "destiny." As we shall see in the next section, Nietzsche's "destiny" apparently includes his contribution to the destruction of Christian morality.

5 The Law of Life

As we have seen, Nietzsche occasionally distinguishes between life and nature on the basis of the former's reliance on, and the latter's independence from, law. The function of law, he maintains, is to ensure the eventual coincidence of power with its ultimate consequences (*BGE* 22). This understanding of the function of law apparently serves as the backdrop for his pronouncement that

> All great things bring about their own destruction through an act of self-sublation [*Selbstaufhebung*]: thus the law of life [*das Gesetz des Lebens*] will have it, the law of the necessity of "self-overcoming" [*Selbstüberwindung*] in the nature of life – the lawgiver himself eventually receives the call: "*patere legem, quam ipse tulisti*" ["submit to the law which you yourself have decreed"]. (*GM* III. 27)

This passage presents two, presumably coeval, formulations of the "law of life." The first formulation decrees that all "great things" will bring about their own destruction. The cited example of "great things," that of Christian morality, indicates that Nietzsche has in mind the grand structures, institutions, and movements that have dominated the course of European history. The second formulation is already familiar to us from Life's secret to Zarathustra (Z II, "On Self-Overcoming"): the "necessity of 'self-overcoming' in the nature of life," as evidenced by the lawgiver's receipt of the call to submit to his own commands. The "law of life" thus ordains submission in all things, great and small. Every great thing must destroy itself through an act of *Selbstaufhebung*, and every small thing must overcome itself and thereby surrender its current incarnation.

This passage also forwards the intriguing suggestion that in certain instances, the self-overcoming required of all living organisms may actually contribute to the inevitable destruction of something great (through an act of *Selbstaufhebung*). On the strength of this suggestion, we see that Nietzsche's envisioned "destiny" involves him in a personal regimen of self-overcoming that will catalyze the destruction of Christian morality. That this destruction is *necessary* apparently does not detract from his enthusiasm for it and for playing a decisive role in it. The tantalizing possibility of a convergence of *Selbstüberwindung* and *Selbstaufhebung* may also account for his distinctly approbative use of the term *self-overcoming*. While all living things must overcome themselves, not all do so in a way that also, and so obviously, contributes to transformations on a world-historical scale.

Nietzsche thus envisions his own labors of self-overcoming as contributing to the historical extinction of Christian morality. Just as surely as Christian morality banished Christian dogma, so, he predicts, Christian truthfulness will – and indeed *must* – destroy Christian morality (GM III. 27). He hopes to expedite the arrival of this anticipated moment of destruction by offering himself as the vessel or site of *Selbstaufhebung*. This means that Nietzsche, the self-styled "immoralist" and "Antichrist," will represent "Christian truthfulness" in its finest hour, bodying forth a mortal challenge to the continued viability of "Christian morality." Through *his* efforts and urgings, he thus implies, Christian truthfulness will be compelled to draw its "*most striking inference*," which he identifies as "its inference against itself" (GM III. 27). In *him*, that is, the "will to truth" will finally become "conscious of itself as a *problem*" (GM III. 27). As it does so, Christian morality "will gradually *perish*" (GM III. 27). "This great spectacle," he prophesies, will occupy Europeans "for the next two centuries" (GM III. 27).

What is perhaps most fascinating about Nietzsche's account of his envisioned role in this process is his confidence in the impending convergence of his own regimen of self-overcoming with the world-historical self-sublation of Christian morality. By dint of his otherwise unremarkable efforts at self-overcoming, that is, he will insert himself into the larger historical processes now under way and thereby fulfill his "destiny." Regardless of what we may think of it, his anticipation of the impending convergence enables us to appreciate the urgency he attaches to his otherwise pedestrian efforts to overcome himself. Although his self-overcomings are neither heroic nor grand, his timing, by virtue of which he arrives at the center of world-historical change, is indeed fortuitous. He lives, writes, and overcomes himself at what he elsewhere calls the "right time," the time of "the *kairos*" (BGE 274).

541

As it turns out, however, Nietzsche is not quite prepared to make good his offer to host the destruction of Christian morality. On his own, he is not yet a suitable vessel or site for *Selbstaufhebung*. Before he can become what he is, he must resign his vaunted individuality and immerse himself in a collective consciousness or agency. He has told us that he must find "scholarly, bold, and industrious comrades" (*GM*, preface, 7), and now we understand why this is so: his final, consummatory act of self-overcoming must be accomplished by a "we." No "I" on its own terms is equal to the task of inaugurating the destruction of Christian morality. Dutifully shifting his preferred form of self-identification, he thus acknowledges that "*his* problem" is in fact "our problem, my *unknown* friends" (*GM* III. 27). He goes on to acknowledge that the "meaning" (*Sinn*) to be derived from participating in this world-historical event is to be reaped and held collectively, by the "we" to which he hopes soon to belong. Once gained, this meaning would be the possession of "*our* whole being [*unser ganzes Sein*]" (*GM* III. 27).

Embedding himself in this unknown "we" is the final step toward the purported convergence of his own private labors of self-overcoming with the larger processes of historical transformation. As he elsewhere elaborates,

> In us [viz. we immoralists, we godless men of today] there is accomplished – supposing you want a formula – the *self-overcoming of morality* [*die Selbstaufhebung der Moral*]. (*D*, preface, 4)

This passage is similar to the one cited above (from *EH*, "Why I Am a Destiny," 3), but with several important differences. There the agency was singular – Nietzsche's own – and the activity described as that of *Selbstüberwindung*. Here the agency is plural and the activity is described as that of *Selbstaufhebung*. The mysterious, as yet unformed "we" is furthermore named: "we immoralists, we godless men of today." His final self-overcoming, which coincides with that of the "we" to which he does not yet belong, will catalyze the (eventual) destruction of Christian morality. He, they, and it will perish in the process, only to be taken up and carried forward in the incarnation of the as yet unknown other of Christian morality. In that event, the post-moral future that Nietzsche envisions would bear his stamp, perhaps even his name, such that he might someday be hailed for initiating the demise of Christian morality. In that event, his wish would be granted and he would be "born posthumously" (*A*, foreword).

6 Concluding Critical Remarks

Zarathustra begins his life lessons by seeking out "the living" and listening to their "speeches" (Z II, "On Self-Overcoming"). Boasting that he has "crawled into the very heart of life and into the very roots of its heart" (Z II, "On Self-Overcoming"), he subsequently dispenses his teaching of will to power. So far, so good. Zarathustra presents his teaching of will to power as a general empirical claim pertaining to all living beings, which is observable in principle by anyone who undertakes a similarly intrepid investigation of life and "the living."

Despite the success of this investigation, however, Zarathustra aspires to go further. He longs to hear directly and privately from life itself, which he ultimately cannot help but personify and place in dialogic juxtaposition to himself (Z II, "The Dancing Song"). He thus shifts the focus of his attention from life to Life, whom Nietzsche personifies, engenders, and eroticizes as a dispenser of unverifiable "secrets." It is from Life that Zarathustra learns what his empirical investigation of "the living" did not (and could not) disclose – namely, that life is "*that which must always overcome itself* [*was sich immer selber überwinden muss*]" (Z II, "On Self-Overcoming"). Having received the favor of this "secret," moreover, he cannot resist the further temptation to imagine Life as his exclusive possession, as a lover perfectly complementary only to *him*. His wish to discern the basic processes of life is thus displaced by his need to be the only one to do so, as determined by Life herself.

In the end, however, he cannot bear the vulnerability that necessarily accompanies his asymmetrical dependence on Life. No longer content simply to receive Life's secrets, Zarathustra dares to whisper into Life's ear something that, according to Life, "nobody knows" (Z III, "The Other Dancing Song," 2).[10] Of course, he gathers the courage to do so only after deciding to pursue a less vulnerable relationship. He promptly jilts Life to woo a more constant lover, known to him as Eternity (Z III, "The Seven Seals").[11]

The progression of Zarathustra's life lessons may also describe the development of Nietzsche's *Lebensphilosophie*. Nietzsche too teaches that life is will to power, which he similarly presents as an empirically verifiable claim about all living beings.[12] He furthermore teaches that life is "that which must always overcome itself," but, again like Zarathustra, he treats this teaching as if it were an unverifiable, incommunicable "secret," for which he provides no credible account. As we have seen, however, this teaching is no good to Zarathustra and Nietzsche if it remains a "secret." It must be disseminated to others and incorporated into the defining practices of the emerging life sciences.

The problem, however, is that neither Zarathustra nor Nietzsche is able to divulge this "secret" without resorting to the kinds of anthropomorphisms they otherwise seek to avoid. As "that which must always overcome itself," life becomes for Zarathustra an unreliable, non-reciprocating lover, while for Nietzsche life becomes a suspiciously transcendent agency possessed of "interests" that it mysteriously fails to protect. In their zeal to hear life's intimate "secret," that is, and thereby distinguish themselves from all other advocates of life, Zarathustra and Nietzsche stray from their naturalism and eventually join their supposed rivals in the ancient game of dueling anthropomorphisms. Owing to their need to know something about life that no one else knows, they end up promulgating something that "nobody knows" (Z III, "The Other Dancing Song," 2).

As this Zarathustran parallel suggests, the unsecured teaching of self-overcoming strains Nietzsche's naturalism and licenses his metaphysical transgressions. This is not to say, of course, that something like a doctrine of self-overcoming cannot be squared with Nietzsche's commitment to the emerging paradigm of scientific naturalism. Nor is it to say that his teaching of self-overcoming is therefore false, irrecuperably speculative, or otherwise incompatible with the findings of evolutionary biology. It is simply to acknowledge that neither Zarathustra nor Nietzsche proves equal to the "secret" dispensed by Life. Simply put, neither of them fully believes that life overcomes itself in its unrelenting pursuit of ever greater amplifications of power. They wish and hope that this were true, but their experience, especially of declining forms of life, suggests otherwise. Life's "secret" thus remains a secret even to them. They may go through the motions of sharing this "secret" with us, but they cannot divulge what they do not sincerely believe to be true.

Here we might gain even greater precision. While Zarathustra and Nietzsche may believe that life overcomes itself, they are not convinced that it does so in such a way that will accommodate *their* allegiance to health, growth, and vitality. As far as they are concerned, life tarries far too long with degenerate organisms and declining species. In particular, life displays a galling indifference to protracted periods of decay, which it subsequently allows to postpone the renascence of growth that is, supposedly, its *raison d'être*. As it turns out, in fact, life is surprisingly neglectful of its own "highest interest" (*TI*, "Skirmishes of an Untimely Man," 36). (Which may lead us to wonder in what sense it qualifies as an *interest* at all.) In this respect, life is too much like nature, with which it shares a common provenance in the will to power.

Zarathustra and Nietzsche are anxious for the trajectory of decadence to complete its descensional arc, so that the trajectory of growth might renew its familiar, ascendant arc. It is not enough for them that life overcomes itself, recuperating death and decay as conditions of future life and growth. Life should furthermore adapt its overcomings to accommodate their timetable, as determined by their mortality. Decadent epochs like late modernity should disintegrate more quickly and efficiently, so that the few noble souls stranded therein may witness – and not merely foretell – the renascence of health. This is why Zarathustra and Nietzsche arrogate to themselves the task of protecting the "highest interest" of life, vowing to save life from its own lapses into indifference. While their biological clocks wind down, however, life sets its leisurely tempo to the glacial creep of geological time. Of such frightening disparities metaphysical systems are born.

In this light, we might wonder how Zarathustra and Nietzsche came to discern, much less to champion, the "highest interest" of life. As we have seen, Nietzsche points proudly to his success thus far in overcoming himself. He claims to speak for life not by means of an acrobatic leap of transcendence, but by dint of immersing himself in its organized flux, regarding it from opposing perspectives, and participating eagerly in its self-overcomings. He appeals so confidently to the "highest interest" of life, that is, because this interest has gradually, painfully, become his own. As we have seen, his regimen of self-overcoming has steered him into happy compliance with the "law of life" and willing submission to his own decrees. Having managed "not merely [to] bear what is necessary, much less conceal it [. . .] but [to] *love* it," he thus exemplifies *amor fati*, which he proposes as his "formula for greatness in a human being" (*EH*, "Why I Am So Clever," 10). He has become one with life and has affirmed himself in the world-historical convergence that awaits the "we" to which he hopes soon to belong.

Nietzsche's account of his radical immersion in the well of life may be stirring, but it is not entirely persuasive. He certainly flatters himself if he means to present *his* modest portfolio of experiences as somehow representative of the full plenum of life. Even if we restrict our focus to the range of *human* life, further granting him the heroic terms he prefers for his gritty "convalescence," we are not likely to find the breadth and variety of his experiences particularly impressive. Despite possessing, perhaps, "a soul that craves to have experienced the whole range of values and desiderata to date" (*GS* 382), he is certainly no Faust. While it is true that he displays a preternatural appreciation (and capacity) for the myriad modes of human suffering, he is not so intimately acquainted with life's triumphs, apotheoses, peaks, and overcomings. Well versed in disappointment, illness, and despair, he knows their counterpart conditions largely by negation and analogy. In his occasional efforts to articulate his vision of growth, health, plenitude, and ascendancy, for example, he tends to favor Romantic idealizations that depart from the naturalism to which he otherwise aspires. His exaggerated valorization of the ideal of the "great health" provides sufficient evidence of his relative lack of familiarity with the "ascending line" of life (cf. *EH*, "Thus Spoke Zarathustra," 2; *GS* 382).

Nietzsche's lack of familiarity with life in its plenitude is perhaps most evident in his self-serving presumption that life *needs* a spokesman or advocate. Does life not pursue its own "highest interest" and assert its own claims, independent of what its host organisms (including Nietzsche and Zarathustra) think of it? Nietzsche's full-throated affirmation of life may be exhilarating for him to express, but what could it possibly add to life itself? It is not as if life is an underachieving side that would benefit from timely cheerleading, or a shy maiden who might profit from the attention to be sparked by inventive matchmaking. If life is "that which must always overcome itself" then it requires no external or internal assistance to sustain itself in its abiding dynamism. In truth, life as Nietzsche longs to affirm it has no need for Nietzsche, Zarathustra, or any other of its fickle advocates. Life made this perfectly, painfully, clear to Zarathustra (Z III, "The Other Dancing Song," 2), which is why, I believe, he eventually jilts her for Eternity (Z III, "The Seven Seals").

But if life neither requests nor requires Nietzsche's intervention on its behalf, then the specific need addressed by his affirmations of life must ultimately reside in him. He is able to affirm life, it would seem, only in the event that life somehow requires, or at least acknowledges, his exertions on its behalf. He thus needs life to reciprocate in some capacity and, ideally, to need him in return. Like Zarathustra, perhaps, he needs life to need an avenging hero, *and* he needs to be known as that hero. In contriving for himself a role as advocate for the "highest interest" of life, even if this role is restricted to exhorting others not to apportion productive social resources to degenerate organisms and species (*TI*, "Skirmishes of an Untimely Man," 33), Nietzsche in fact reveals the limits of his advocacy. As it turns out, he cannot promote life as will to power and self-overcoming if doing so obliges him to fold himself unceremoniously into the anonymous flux.

Like Zarathustra, Nietzsche is keen to promote the amoral dynamism of life only so long as *other* organisms are used and discarded as conduits of self-overcoming. When it comes to *him*, however, he requires that his otherwise unmemorable labors of self-overcoming converge wondrously with the world-historical *Selbstaufhebung* of Christian morality. As we have seen, he also needs to postpone his final act of self-overcoming until such time as he is firmly embedded in the appropriate "we." In light of his pathological recoil from actual communities and collectivities, this further condition on his final *Untergang* may buy him quite a bit of time.

Here, however, he runs the risk of echoing the pet anthropomorphisms of his supposed rivals, the "English Darwinists." Just as they project onto life their own conditions of "distress" (*GS* 349), so he diagnoses life as beset by a species of distress that only he can remedy. According to Nietzsche, life needs him to champion its cause, to protect it from unguarded lapses into indifference, and to legislate against attenuated periods of unnecessary decay. It is difficult to see, moreover, why it would be preferable for Nietzsche to depict life as needing his assistance than for Spencer et al. to figure life as primarily adaptive. Life is anthropomorphized (that is, cheapened and demeaned) in either event. And even if Nietzsche's caricature of life is in some sense preferable to theirs, he is nevertheless presumptuous to believe that his advocacy might provide life with the completion, redemption, wholeness, or finality that, supposedly, it otherwise lacks. In short, the life that would require the succor of his advocacy would not be the life that he attempts to honor in his teachings of will to power and self-overcoming.

See also 8 "Nietzsche's Philosophy and True Religion"; 26 "Nietzsche on Geophilosophy and Geoaesthetics"

Notes

1   Here I follow the suggestive interpretation of Ansell Pearson 1997: 97–101.
2   For a representative criticism of the political views ostensibly expressed in *BGE* 259, see Warren 1988: 207–11.
3   My understanding of Nietzsche's depth psychology, and the related discussion that informs this essay, are indebted to Parkes 1994, especially chapters 8 and 9.
4   Clark maintains that this restricted, psychological interpretation of the will to power, as what she calls "a second-order drive that [Nietzsche] recognizes is dependent for its existence on other drives," is all that he may "claim knowledge of" (1990: 227). The extensions and applications of this account, especially into the realms of metaphysics and cosmology, may be more famous and influential, but they amount to unwarranted "generalizations" of his basic psychological thesis (1990: 227).
5   See Parkes 1994: 313–18.
6   Nietzsche's interpretation of Spencer and Huxley are treated at length in Ansell Pearson 1997: 86–92.
7   See e.g. the excellent discussion in Ansell Pearson 1997: ch. 4, "Nietzsche contra Darwin."
8   Clark points out that Nietzsche's own account of philosophizing indicates that he cannot avoid "want[ing] nature to live only after his own image, as an eternal generalization and glorification of what he finds valuable" (1990: 224).
9   For an account of Nietzsche's failure to avoid anthropomorphisms of life and nature, see Ansell-Pearson 1997: 105–6; Clark 1990: 223–5.
10 Lampert (1986: 238–9), Clark (1990: 263–4), and Gooding-Williams (2001: 262–7) all reasonably conclude that Zarathustra's whisper has something to do with his love of life, as expressed in his affirmative embrace of the teaching of eternal recurrence. In doing so, however, these commentators diminish the import of Life's response – namely, that "nobody [including, I would add, Zarathustra] knows" what his whisper is meant to convey. In contrast to these commentators, I take quite seriously the literal interpretation of Life's response to Zarathustra: she both contradicts his claim to knowledge and admonishes him that he has dared to tell her something that she knows to be either demonstrably false or indemonstrably speculative.
11 Lampert's suggestion – that "in marrying Eternity [Zarathustra] marries Life, but in the act of marrying bestows upon her a new name" (1986: 240) – either denies or ignores what I take to be Zarathustra's obvious recoil and flight from Life, which, I believe, furnishes the

dominant dramatic structure of Part III and requires the later addition of Part IV (here I follow Staten 1990: 174–8).

12   For a persuasive statement of the objection that Nietzsche already goes astray in presenting life as will to power, see Clark 1990: 218–27.

Editions of Nietzsche Used

Beyond Good and Evil, trans. Walter Kaufmann (New York: Vintage Books, 1966; repr. 1989).

The Birth of Tragedy and *The Case of Wagner*, trans. Walter Kaufmann (New York: Vintage Books, 1967).

Ecce Homo, trans. Walter Kaufmann (New York: Vintage Books, 1967; repr. 1989).

The Gay Science, trans. Walter Kaufmann (New York: Vintage Books, 1974).

On the Genealogy of Morals, trans. Walter Kaufmann and R. J. Hollingdale (New York: Vintage Books, 1967; repr. 1989).

The Portable Nietzsche, ed. and trans. Walter Kaufmann (New York: Viking Penguin, 1954; pbk. edn. 1959; repr. 1982).

Sämtliche Briefe: Kritische Studienausgabe Briefe, 8 vols., ed. G. Colli and M. Montinari (Berlin: Walter de Gruyter; Munich: dtv, 1986).

References

Ansell Pearson, Keith (1997). *Viroid Life: Perspectives on Nietzsche and the Transhuman Condition* (London: Routledge).

Clark, Maudemarie (1990). *Nietzsche on Truth and Philosophy* (New York: Cambridge University Press).

Gooding-Williams, Robert (2001). *Zarathustra's Dionysian Modernism* (Stanford, CA: Stanford University Press).

Lampert, Laurence (1986). *Nietzsche's Teaching: An Interpretation of "Thus Spoke Zarathustra"* (New Haven, CT: Yale University Press).

Parkes, Graham (1994). *Composing the Soul: Reaches of Nietzsche's Psychology* (Chicago: University of Chicago Press).

Staten, Henry (1990). *Nietzsche's Voice* (Ithaca, NY: Cornell University Press).

Warren, Mark (1988). *Nietzsche and Political Thought* (Cambridge, MA: MIT Press).

30

Nietzsche's Theory of the Will to Power

JAMES I. PORTER

The so-called theory of the will to power is one of the most contested aspects of Nietzsche's writings, and rightly so. The theory presses the idea of a naturalistic moral psychology to startling extremes. It flatly disposes of traditional metaphysical categories and beliefs passed down, with variations, from Plato to Kant to Schopenhauer, such as (free) will, substance, unity, appearance and reality, body and soul, causality, and so on (see *HH* 1–5; *GS* 110). It calls for a radical revision of our concepts of self and reality, in ways that will become clear below. Concepts like the sublimation of the instincts, the affirmation of life, and holism float across its surface like so many bright images of a life better conceived. And yet, for all its brilliance, the will to power presents difficulties of interpretation that often appear insuperable. Modeled on a line of argument that nowhere seems to get off the ground or ever to reach a conclusion, the theory of the will to power is nowhere spelled out as such, being oracular when it is expounded and otherwise seemingly presupposed rather than felt to merit explanation. Worse, even if the presence of the will to power in the finished writings is undeniable, the primary evidence for the theory is found in the controversial and fragmentary *Nachlass* material, representing a work that was never brought to completion and possibly was abandoned (*KSA* 14, pp. 29–35; Montinari 1982; Magnus 1988). Finally, the will to power quickly becomes entangled in the very problems of representability it would denounce, in part by conjuring up problems of representation at three levels, and allowing these to collide with one another:

1   The will to power, as a theory, is a representation – a depiction – of a reality, even if only as a matter of "hypothesis."
2   The theory claims to get at a reality that exceeds the human capacity for representation (depiction, conceptualization, imagination), even as Nietzsche mocks this pretension of the theory and of anyone that would accept it.
3   Nonetheless, will to power as a reality crucially and constitutively involves representational calculations – perspectival viewings and reckonings by the "willing centers" that make up its field.

The claims of (2) clash with that of (1). But the calculations found in (3) are troublingly close to the kinds of faculties critiqued in (2) (more on all of this below). But these are perhaps only worries if we presuppose that the will to power constitutes an argument at all. It is not clear that it does.

A further difficulty has to do not with where the will to power appears in Nietzsche's corpus, but when it appears. When, exactly, does the will to power appear for the first time? Accounts vary, although the consensus view today is that this startling *novum* is announced (Kaufmann would say "discovered") during Nietzsche's last productive decade, while refinements to the concept are made, possibly culminating in 1888. Of course, how one characterizes the will to power will determine how one dates the conception, irrespective of its explicit mentions by Nietzsche (Förster-Nietzsche 1895–1904: vol. 2/2, p. 682; Kaufmann 1974: 178–207; Magnus 1988: 224–6; its first occurrence is in a notebook dating already from the end of 1876 to mid-1877: *KSA* 8, 23[63], p. 425). And this makes the problem not only of defining but also simply of locating the will to power even harder than it appears to be. An argument could be made, for instance, that there is nothing fundamentally novel about the will to power wherever it does occur in the later writings. Indeed, I believe that the problems associated with the will to power were encountered in all their essentials in writings from around 1870/1, where Nietzsche's critical and parasitical demolition of Schopenhauer, his critique of foundational concepts in the metaphysical tradition, his deployment of atomism in that critique, and his writerly practice throughout (his penchant for depicting conceptual "primary scenes," but also the rhetorical posturing of his arguments) were seen to flow together in unexpected and elaborate ways (Porter 2000a: 57–73, 126–31, 2000b: 103–6). All these features of the notebooks from the time, which in fact look back to Nietzsche's university days (for instance, to his 1868 essay, "On Schopenhauer," to the sketch from a month later, "Teleology Since Kant,"[1] or to the notes on the pre-Socratics), can be shown to repeat themselves in the notebooks and the published writings from the 1880s, the materials that will form the basis of this discussion. Further comparisons between these two disparate sets of material will be reserved for below.

If I am right, evidence of Nietzsche's view on the will to power tends to be sought out in the wrong places. Look for it in the presumed reality the theory describes, whether you take that reality to be ontological or psychological, and you will miss the point. In fact, these two options tend to amount to the same thing. In reducing the world to the primitive, instinctual "pre-form of life" and to the reality of our drives (*Triebleben*) as in *BGE* 36, or to the peculiar landscape of "willing centers" as in the *Nachlass* (see below), the psychological reading effectively ontologizes psychology. But the reverse is also true: ontological readings invariably lapse into psychologism. Nietzsche's exposition of the will to power crucially relies on this very dilemma. In short, the tendency in the past has been to focus on the positive contents of Nietzsche's account. Attending to Nietzsche's presentational strategies, I believe, can help us see how we might reassess not only the contents but also the nature and especially the purpose of his account. A few representative views of the will to power will illustrate this point briefly in what follows, starting with Nietzsche's own.

"Claims to Power"

In its most impressive form, the will to power is nothing less than the (somewhat diffusely argued) amorphous nature of the world and the totality of its activities, presented under a terrifying aspect. It is "the tyrannically inconsiderate and relentless enforcement of claims of power," a power so "vividly" conceived that it makes the very notion of tyranny pale into effeteness, leaving it "unsuitable" as a term, no more than "a weakening and attenuating metaphor – being too human" (*BGE* 22; cf. 259). This vision rests on the (monistic) supposition that "all organic functions," indeed the world entire, "could be traced back to this [one] will to power" (*BGE* 23 and 36). What Nietzsche's picture of the will reveals, or rather holds forth like a promise, is a vision of uninhibited exertion and excitement. There is something intuitive and irresistible, not to say seductive, about that picture, with its talk of epidemic, contagion, physiological excitation, eruption of desire, "inability to prevent reaction," the overwhelming incapacitation before "the stimulus of life" – a feeling of potency, fullness, approaching, even, completion, if not perfection (*WP* 811; cf. *TI*, "Expeditions of an Untimely Man," 9 and 10). At its literal extreme, Nietzsche's "idea" (*WP* 636) promises to take in much more than unconscious forces roiling beneath the surface of consciousness, and haunting it as well. "In the actual world" we find an exhilaration of a perhaps more intellectually satisfying kind. Things are "the sum of [their] effects" or relations, and "everything is bound to and conditioned by everything else" in a mutually implicating whole, in which "to condemn and think away anything means to condemn and think away everything" (*WP* 551 and 584). In the words of one recent and influential commentator, "the will to power is then an activity that affects and in fact constitutes the character of everything in the world and that is itself the result of such effects" (Nehamas 1985: 80). And that activity occurs even without the presence of a subject, although it at least appears to have larger implications for defining what a subject is and how it should regard itself (although just what these are is a matter for interpretation). At a final level of abstraction, everything that exists reduces down to mere "quantities" of force or will characterized by a single trait: their endless striving towards a higher condition, or rather, towards an ever greater disposal of ever greater power.

The lure of these various conceptions, I believe, partly lies in their imprecision. The problem is that in each of them Nietzsche places two incompatible demands on us: the world must be intrinsically featureless, conceivable without a subject, yet it has to exhibit the features, and indeed the effects, of a subjective presence. A featureless world would be inert, suspended, and without relations (even without any meaningful relation to itself); but what is wanted is, precisely, the force that actively constitutes relations, effects, and so on. Interpretation and subjectivity *are* essential; they furnish the world with relations, and therefore endow it with features – or so Nietzsche seems willing to concede at least some of the time (e.g., *WP* 560 and 564). But where do these activities occur? The answer is in the will to power, the activity that selects and arranges things from a perspective, and whose effects condition the whole. Will and power are supposed to bring the extra element of "interpretation and subjectivity" to the problem, only there seems to be no subject on hand to supervise such activity: features, relations, and effects just are what interpretation and subjectivity are, or so it seems, and as a consequence the true place of the subject is never acknowledged as such (Nehamas 1985: 81). Either there just is will to power, diffused throughout Nietzsche's holistic conception, or we have its concentrated instances, "centers" or "units" (or else mere "quanta") of force exerting themselves upon their perspectival worlds. The one seems to provide reality with a pulse and a rhythm (although at times terrifyingly); the other is too fantastical even to imagine. Plainly, Nietzsche's view of reality can be as romantically compelling as it is radically estranging, even if it is designed to offer a glimpse into a condition that can only be called, in Nietzsche's own term, "inhuman" (*GS* 382; *EH*, "Z," 2) But the inhuman is itself a romantically compelling notion, and any worries as to how these vagaries of the imagination might be resolved tend to be swept aside in heady assertions of "Nietzschean affirmation," of the sort found in Derrida, Deleuze, and others.

Here, for example, is how Derrida describes "Nietzschean affirmation": it is "the joyous affirmation of the play of the world and of the innocence of becoming, the affirmation of a world of signs without faults, without truth, and without origin which is *offered to an active interpretation*" (Derrida 1978: 293; emphasis added). But to whom is the world offered? Deleuze provides one answer: "a subjectivity of the universe which is no longer anthropomorphic but cosmic" (Deleuze 1983: 44). Evidently, the passage "beyond man and humanism" doesn't get us very far: we land back in subjectivity, but of what sort? Why a cosmic subjectivity should somehow be free of the defects of subjectivity as we know it (the undisputed aim of Nietzsche's will to power) is nowhere clarified. And how this is to be squared with a claim like the following is not easy to see: "There is no will: there are treaty drafts of will [*Willens-Punktationen*] that are constantly increasing or losing their power" (*WP* 715). The model is strange, to say the least, and not easily captured by accounting for the will to power as a joyous affirmation of life. How does one joyously affirm a dot? The very idea bleaches even the most robust concepts of the self as "style." Translate the metaphor back into the organic realm of neural synapses ("stimuli," *A* 14) and it fares no better.

Having reduced opposition to an oscillation, and the subject of sensation to sensation without a subject ("*Who* feels pleasure? *Who* wants power? – Absurd question," *WP* 693), Nietzsche puts us in an uncomfortable position. Less hyperbolic readings, content somehow to envisage the will to power as a basic world-shaping activity, face the same consequence, namely that the will to power is structured like a subject in every way but one: it is not a subject, but the antithesis of one, indeed its critique. Not only is it hard to conceive a subject that is not a subject, it is hard to see how a critique at times so literally invested in what it would displace, namely the manifestly subjective – indeed, anthropomorphic – features of the will to power, can function as a critique of anything at all. Finally, a view that serenely contemplates the world conceived as the sum of its interconnections and seemingly without origins is insufficiently troubled by the violence that underlies Nietzsche's conception – part of which is indicated by its self-refuting character, for instance the claim (which is in fact incoherent) that a thing is the sum of its effects (on which see below). And in general "affirmationist" readings of the will to power, which tend to resolve every conceivable tension through an all-embracing sublimation ("self-overcoming"), fail to reckon with the consequences of "the tyrannically inconsiderate and relentless enforcement of claims of power." And that is to fail to describe the will to power at all.

What is missing from Nietzsche's picture of things, conceived in these ways, is precisely the frame that enables the picture to appear to us at all: ourselves. Shying away from the category of the subject, in the wake of Nietzsche's relentless critique of it as a mere deposit of interpretive activity, we go wrong if we head in the opposite direction, and in fact, as we have begun to see, that way lies no real escape at all. But surely this is Nietzsche's point: there is no escaping the category of the subject. One of his earliest insights, and a point he had made good against Schopenhauer, it is also one he never repealed: "A representing agency cannot 'not represent' itself, cannot represent itself away" (*KSA* 7, 26[11]); and "not-Being is unthinkable" (*KSA* 7, 3[91]), which implies the ineffaceable continuity of thought and being. Together, these provide the complement to a later fragment (*WP* 584): "To condemn and think away anything means to condemn and think away everything" – apart, that is, from the subject of the thinking (cf. *WP* 569).

Nietzsche's point about a representing agency needs to be reapplied to his account of the will to power as represented by us in our own minds (its relevance to Schopenhauer will be made evident below). Identifying with the truth of the will to power, we fail to identify ourselves as its co-authors. Simply to conceive the will to power, a subject must take up a "view from nowhere" and thus eliminate herself as a constituent of the world – an incoherent prospect. Thus, the radical destitution of the subject does not occur at all within Nietzsche's picture, even when he requires that it should; it occurs in ourselves, whenever we try to picture what he is describing. And as for the real source of the violence of Nietzsche's image, it is not at all in the scenarios he describes. It is in the way we imagine them, and in imagining them, delete ourselves as the subjects of the representation we behold. *We* become the missing subjects of Nietzsche's conception and its leftovers: *we* are its premise, which must be obliterated and forgotten for that conception to exist.

This also happens to be where Nietzsche's apparent doctrine that a thing is the sum of its effects (*WP* 551) goes awry: it is not a complete sum, because it leaves out a remainder; it subtracts from the sum the condition of its possibility. Attractive on the surface, eliminating substance and swapping *effects* for *things* is delusive. "Effects" assume the logical status that "things" once had. But more to the point, it is not quite the case that "if we eliminate the effects, hoping to isolate the thing as it 'really' is, we will have nothing left" (Danto 1965: 219; Nehamas 1985: 80). This position echoes *WP* 567 ("as if a world would still remain over after one deducted the perspective"). But in one respect it crucially does not, for it leaves unanswered the question of agency in the "deduction" that is made. In what way can effects be eliminated if they are not thing-like? What makes it certain they even can be eliminated? Of course, to presume to talk about things as "effects," even if only of "will" (*BGE* 36), is to forget that effects are *themselves* the result (the effect) of their having been posited (*GM* I. 13). And so, too, it is not the case that nothing will remain if we eliminate all presumed effects. Second, *who* does the elimination? The answer given in the preceding paragraph tells us that there is indeed something left and what that leftover is: here, it is "we" – the actual source of the positing, the source of the putative totality and its parts. (Cf. also *HH* 9: "*Metaphysical world.* – [. . .] We behold all things through the human head and cannot cut off this head; while the question nonetheless remains what of the world would still be there if one had cut it off. This is a purely scientific problem and one not very well calculated to bother people overmuch.") In depicting the peculiar agency of the will to power, Nietzsche is attacking much more than our integrity and self-conception as subjects. He is showing us, in the most painful demonstration conceivable, how such an attack can only be carried out by someone who is irretrievably a subject, and on herself. (The connection between this kind of violence and the less abstract violence that Nietzsche so often seems to ennoble, but which is sublimated out of existence in the affirming accounts of his philosophy, cannot be gone into here.) There is a limit to self-transcendence, and subjectivity is this limit.

The Rhetoric of the Will to Power

Considerations of this kind reveal something about the rhetorical construction of the will to power, the connotations of Nietzsche's language, and the effects these have upon his readers – effects he could and did count on. This, in turn, raises the question whether Nietzsche's will to power is a theory at all, coherent in itself and offering a coherent image of the world it depicts, or whether it is not in fact a *strategy* aimed at disguising and at times revealing the obvious fact of its construction, but, even more importantly, aimed at implicating its readers in that construction. The will to power, I will be proposing, does not describe the nature of the world, or rather of the reality that underlies everyday appearances. Rather, it describes a process of misrecognition, the poetic manufacture of the world; and it does this by rendering itself circular and incoherent, and its objects inconceivable. It is this circular strategy which in fact invites us, as readers, to participate in a form of misrecognition just by asking us to imagine and construe the will to power.

The same is true of Nietzsche's proposition, "a 'thing' is the sum of its effects," as a glance at its context shows: "Interpretation by causality a deception – A 'thing' is the sum of its effects, synthetically united by a concept, an image" (*WP* 551). A "thing" comes about not wherever there is a sum of effects, but whenever a sum like this has been *postulated* (the sum is itself "a concept, an image," a synthetic unity). This helps account for the meaning of the following: "We take the sum of [a thing's] properties – 'x' – as cause of the property 'x' – which is utterly stupid and mad!" (*WP* 561). To "take" things in this way is "utterly" stupid and mad because the logic is twice invalid: the second fallacy lies in getting the causal property wrong; but the first fallacy lies in the initial positing of x itself – not of the object, but of the alleged sum of the object's properties. "*Causa* is a capacity to produce effects that has been super-added [more literally, "imputed," *hinzuerfunden*] to the events" – namely, by a subject (*WP* 551). Note that Nietzsche does not explicitly denounce the fallacy. Instead, he *commits it himself*, by designating the sum of a thing's properties at all ("x"), thus involving himself, and his readers, in circular reasoning. But the circularity comes about only because the interpretive nature of the proposition has been concealed by the proposition itself. Thus, Nietzsche's proposition repeats the very error it is designed to eliminate: the thing is actually being viewed as a *causa sui* (already a heresy for Nietzsche), when in fact nothing exists, or has effects, except in the mind of a subject. (Differently, Nehamas [1985: 87–93, esp. p. 87], assuming the existence of a "totality," and Müller-Lauter 1971, *passim*, affirming and denying such a synthetic instance [or finality, *Letztes*].)

"In short: the will to power. Consequence: if this conception [*Vorstellung*; sc. the will to power] is *hostile* towards us, why do we give into it? On with the beautiful simulacra! Let us be the imposters and embellishers of humanity! —" (*KSA* 11, 43[1]). A hypertrophy of the will that "has been pushed to its utmost limit (to the point of non-sense, if I may say so)," the will to power is thus not only self-subverting, as Nietzsche occasionally allows (*BGE* 36) – even here one has to recognize "untruth as a condition of life" (*BGE* 4) – but it requires its readers to be self-subverting too. One of the subtler flaws in attempts to rescue Nietzsche from the fantastical nature of his own hypothesis (or myth) lies in assuming that the "bad 'philology'" with which he equates his proposed interpretation of the world as will to power refers to his own, and not our, "bad 'philology'" (*BGE* 22; see Clark 1990: 239–44; more satisfactorily, Clark 1983: 465, and MacIntyre 1990: 48–9).

Of course, Nietzsche nowhere labels the will to power a "myth." In fact, the latter term derives not from Nietzsche's discussion of the will to power, but from his discussion of *Schopenhauer's* theory of the will in *GS* 127. Which brings us to another shared assumption in current scholarship on Nietzsche – only here the agreement is explicit, in addition to being all but universally shared: Nietzsche's will to power, whether the theory or the reality that constitutes the theory's explanandum, must be dissociated at all costs from Schopenhauer's account of the world as will and representation. The effort required to make this dissociation is considerable: after all, Nietzsche's own theory is likewise an account of the world as will and representation. And although there are marked differences in their respective views of the world, at least on the surface (for instance, Schopenhauerian pessimism and Nietzschean optimism, to cite the most familiar contrast), taking note of these still leaves intact the premise of the will's primacy as the key to the intelligibility of the world (cf. *BGE* 36; Schopenhauer 1969: vol. 2, ch. 18). Indeed, the two views of the world might be regarded as tantamount to two distinct attitudes towards the will, the one abhorring the will's activities (which make up the world), the other joyously affirming them (cf. *WP* 1005). Does Nietzsche's difference from Schopenhauer come down to a difference in his evaluation of the Schopenhauerian will, which is to say of the Schopenhauerian project – its correction even?

The ghost of Schopenhauer is not so easily thrown off. Nietzsche's counter-claim, held against his metaphysical opponent, that "life simply *is* will to power" (*BGE* 259), could be paraphrased without loss of meaning as "all that has being is only a willing" which is the very mythology he would oppose (*GS* 127). One immediate reason for suspicion is, to borrow a phrase from Nietzsche (who in turn borrows the phrase from Schopenhauer, e.g. 1969: vol. 1, ch. 22), the persistence of the "one word, 'will'" in Nietzsche's own discourse. It has been suggested that the word "will," presumably taken over from Schopenhauer, was not well chosen, because it carries suggestions which were unintended (cf. Hollingdale 1965: 82, 219–20). We are right to feel uneasy with the term but wrong to rule out that Nietzsche's aim was, precisely, to create this sense of unease (the concept of the will is termed a "paroxysm of nonsense" at *GM* II. 22 and impugned again as a "projection" and "only a word" at *TI*, "'Reason' in Philosophy," 5). Why does Nietzsche invite confusion with his "reinscription" of will? "Perhaps Nietzsche used the word 'will' so as to permit an analogy between it and our ready-made psychological concept" (Danto 1965: 219). Or perhaps there is more than analogy at stake. The question why something like analogy appears in Nietzsche's account of the will is best turned around in the form of another question: why do we *need* the analogy (and not just the disanalogy) to make sense of Nietzsche's "will"? And the same could be said about the categories (or are they merely analogies, too?) of causality and explanation, which plainly are not erased by Nietzsche's alternatives (as at *BGE* 36). As we shall see below, the apparently discarded features of the metaphysical subject are anything but inert in Nietzsche's account of the will to power.

My larger point, however, is that the word "will" can never appear in Nietzsche's writings without invoking this problem of its indebtedness to what the will to power purportedly refuses, in the very same way that the category of the subject is not effaced but merely translated into another dimension by the will to power. To put the point differently, Nietzsche's "will" is legible only through the registers of meaning that the word "will" commonly and philosophically has. And that confusion of meanings, the impossibility of "will" to signify outside its inherited significations, is, I want to argue, crucially bound up with the meaning of Nietzsche's own writing of the will to power. Not the least of these inherited significations is the connotation of Schopenhauerianism, which Nietzsche not only cannot avoid but actively courts. Kaufmann's worry (1974: 178) that Nietzsche's conception is "primarily a perverse development of Schopenhauer's 'will'" is thus real. The perversity lies not in the mere idea that Nietzsche's theory should be distorting Schopenhauer, as if from a safe distance. What is truly perverse is the relation of mimicry established by Nietzsche between the two worldviews, which raises the question whether Nietzsche is able, or even wants, to extricate himself from Schopenhauer in the way that he is generally thought to have done (even including the essays in Janaway 1998, which represent a welcome break from the entrenched orthodoxy of the past).

Nietzsche's statements on the will to power, I am suggesting, are in fact strategies that create dilemmas of interpretation like the one just mentioned. Several important consequences flow from this way of looking at Nietzsche. First, the will to power is no longer to be viewed as a celebration of the interrelatedness of everything imaginable in the world, of perspectivism, of an affirmative stance towards life, of prodigious Dionysian energy, or of an achieved greatness of self and soul. Although undeniably vital to Nietzsche's generalized critique of modernity, his proprietary conception of will (which is opposed to the received notion of will – the view that human action arises in the first instance out of a center of agency that is conscious, volitional, rational, and straightforwardly simple) is no less vulnerable to that same critique. From this, it follows that the will to power is best viewed not as a positive antidote to the failed pretensions of the modern world, but as their repetition. Thus, Nietzsche's account of the will to power actually functions something like an allegory of the modern subject. As I have argued elsewhere (Porter 1998), the will to power is a faintly disguised genealogy of the modern subject and its fascination with the one trait it absolutely lacks: power. This is not to deny that the will to power offers a radical critique of the subject. It does. But then it also critiques itself. Here we may at last begin to see why some of the difficulties with reading Nietzsche's will to power can never be smoothed off. Inconsistencies do abound. But these are a reflection of the conditions of modernity, of which the will to power is to be seen as a symptom, with its delusions of uninhibited power and of agency untrammeled by the constraints and illusions of subjectivity, its self-affirmation, "the cheerful asceticism of an animal become fledged and divine, floating above life rather than in repose" (*GM* III. 8), concealing its own fragility and impotence from itself ("the richest and most complex forms [. . .] perish more easily," *WP* 684; cf. Müller-Lauter 1971: 123), and so on. With these considerations in mind, we may now examine in greater detail Nietzsche's strategic analysis of power as will.

"The world viewed from inside": Nietzsche's Later Atomism

Consider the mind, the body, and their objects in the barest of "physiological" terms, even below the level of neural excitations, and the world immediately takes on an entirely transformed aspect. Suddenly, we have to entertain the fiction of quantities, units of differential force (*Machtverschiedenheiten*) or quasi-corporeal entities spread out over a pseudo-continuum, whose attributes, defined by difference and relative position, constitute their only "qualitative" differences or "values," and whose engenderment reproduces on a primordial micro-level all the agonal effects familiar from the world's largest dissensions, summarized by Nietzsche as the struggle between active and reactive forces. It is the business of these quantitative units of force, which exist at a level that can only be called "atomistic," to generate in turn, or rather to vanish into, effects on a perceptible level of macro-phenomena: appearances, sensations (like pain and pleasure), moral sentiment, and artistic rapture. Such are the primary ingredients and features of Nietzsche's celebrated account of "the will to power," which offers a gripping spectacle of the conditions that show knowledge to be an illusion.

Heidegger's response is the obvious one: "This is a chemical description, but scarcely a philosophical interpretation" (Heidegger 1961: vol. 1, p. 136). Nor is this response the only one of its kind (Kaufmann 1974: 262; Nehamas 1985: 153–4). If we were to accept its premise, by the same token a good deal of Nietzsche would be rendered impertinent – all his accounts, familiar from the published writings, of organic reactions, of "energy," "stimulus," "accumulation," "discharge," and "intoxication," and generally speaking all of what falls under the rubric of "physiology." (A further irony: if we accept the dictum "everything is bound to and conditioned by everything else" [*WP* 584], how can one consistently "think away" Nietzsche's view of physiology? As it happens, the paragraph that opens with this dictum concludes with another: "Physiology teaches us better!") But it would be wrong to assume that the quantitative view of power is a feature peculiar to the notebooks. That the vision of the world as a struggle of forces exerting themselves like molecules under a microscope is actually *presupposed* by the finished works is put beyond doubt by Nietzsche's peculiar "physiological" accounts of, for example, declining and ascending forms of power (as in *TI*, "Expeditions," 37: "*Declining* life, the diminution of all organizing power, that is to say the power of separating, of opening up chasms, of ranking above and below," etc.; cf. *TI*, "Expeditions," 38), or by a passage like the following: "A quantum of force is equivalent to a quantum of drive, will, effect" that is subordinated to a single means, "namely as a means of creating *greater* units of power" (*GM* I. 13, II. 11). The instinctual and energetic basis of life is its will to power as well (cf. *BGE* 36; *TI*, "Expeditions," 41, 44; *TI*, "What I Owe the Ancients," 3). In short, "Long live physics!" (*GS* 335). But his "physics" is of a peculiar variety.

At the core of Nietzsche's conceit is its basic postulate, that of minuscule and myriad "centers of force," each endowed, at first sight, with all the characteristics of a Schopenhauerian will exercising its blind urgency to powerful self-satisfaction. In purely formal terms, these force-centers recall the Leibnizian monad, though with a vengeance, for each center is a perceptual focus tyrannically commanding the confines of a given perspective, and therefore anything but blind, but rather intelligent, calculating, and dangerously cunning. Either way, their sole purpose is the gradual construction of empires of power out of increasingly complex "arrangements" of force (WP 636: "they conspire together"). The "reduction" of "the 'apparent world'" to "a specific mode of action on the world" (WP 567) is simultaneously a disavowal of subjective consciousness ("the absurd overestimation of consciousness [. . .] [viewed as] something that feels, thinks, wills," WP 529). The aim is to depict the way the world looks when our point of view has been subtracted from it: "the world, apart from our condition of living in it, the world that we have not reduced to our being, our logic and psychological prejudices" (WP 568). This picture of things is undoubtedly alienating. Whether Nietzsche actually achieves his aim of repulsing the subject is another question.

But now he adds a further twist, by (as it were) alienating alienation. Least welcome as visitors, on Nietzsche's account, are those who might relish more than anyone else the prospect of a world finally rid of that obtruding presence, man – namely, the "physicists," and above all the atomists, whose physical world is premised on the primary existence of lifeless material elements or forces, such as atoms, which in turn are related by mere mechanical action and nothing more. Nietzsche critiques the atom in all its stripes for being just what it is: an importation of Parmenidean metaphysics (being, unity, impassibility, etc.) – or more crudely, of idealism – into the physical world (cf. WP 507 and 442). The atom is the despicable equivalent of a *Ding an sich*. These arguments are by no means new. They in fact continue Nietzsche's critique of Greek atomism, which runs without break from the late 1860s (Porter 2000b: introduction and ch. 1). Further extensions of the same argument are Nietzsche's aversion to "mechanistic senselessness" in *GM* II. 12 and in *GS* 373.

The same holds for the culminating move in that critique. For in the end Nietzsche's harshest critique of the atom is as consequential as it is highly paradoxical: the atom is if anything too "conceivable": it conceals the hallmarks of subjectivity in its very construction. The concept of the atom smuggles phenomenal traits, properties derived from subjective experience (such as size, weight, shape, density, and motion, the anthropomorphisms of attraction and repulsion), back into conditions which purportedly lie waiting to be "discovered" in some objective sphere (cf. WP 552b). And so if anything the atom is all *too* conceivable and imaginable, too much a "semiotic" of the subject who authored these fictions. The anthropomorphisms of atoms exist "to make it possible for us to form an image of the world, no more!" (WP 621), and so atomism is an insult not to objectivity (which it wants but cannot attain) but to subjectivity. It is a reproach that brings to mind all too vividly the intrinsic limits of the human imagination, in two distinct ways: in the alternative picture of the world that it draws, an image so abhorrent that no imagination would wish to fathom it (for "what does Greek particle theory have to do with the meaning of life?", KSA 8, 3[63]), and in the logically flawed and incomplete attempt to depict the undepictable (cf. WP 552b). Nietzsche, in revenge, effectively sets out to "complete" the project of atomism

(*WP* 619), by laying bare its contradictory impulses and then by making a remarkable move, by absorbing atomism into the very form of the will to power.

First he negates atomism, by rejecting its primary postulate: "There are no durable ultimate units, no atoms, no monads" (*WP* 715). Then he predicts its logical culmination, in a system that surprisingly curves back on atomism itself: "The evolution of the mechanistic-atomistic way of thinking is today not yet conscious of its necessary goal. [. . .] They will end up by creating a system of signs: they will renounce explanations, and abandon the concept of cause and effect" (*KSA* 12, 2[61]). This is a *vaticinium ex eventu*.[2] The completed evolution he has in mind is in fact his own conception of the will to power. The atomists took man out of the picture. Nietzsche claims that they unwittingly imported the "subject" back in. So, on the one hand, he merely draws out the consequence that the atomists shrank back from, by willfully reinstalling the subject in the atomistic scenario, enlivening the picture with the traits of its own construction, populating it with anthropomorphisms (perspectival centers of will and force):

> The victorious concept "force," by means of which our physicists have created God and the world, still needs to be *completed*: *an inner world must be ascribed to it*, which I designate as "will to power," i.e., as an insatiable desire to manifest power. (*KSA* 11, 36[31], emphasis added; cf. *WP* 619)

But surely the will to power is more than a logical extension of atomism – or is it? A closer look at the details of Nietzsche's counter-concept is needed.

A "force-center" (*Kraftzentrum*) or "force-point" (*Kraft-Punkt*), in Nietzsche's vocabulary, is synonymous with a "quantum" of power or of will to power, the amount or degree of force exerted by each center. Quantitatively reduced, a center of force can also be called – surprisingly, and with no loss of semantic substance – a *Kraft-Atom*, or "atom" of force (*WP* 634 and 637; cf. *KSA* 12, 2[69]: *Kraft-Punkt* ("force-point"), and *KSA* 11, 40[36] on the "force-point world" of conventional physics that he opposes):

> A quantum of power is designated by the effect it produces and by the effect it resists. [. . .] Not self-preservation: every atom works [literally, "has an effect"] upon the whole of being: it [*sc.* the atom] is thought away if one thinks away this radiation of power-will [*Machtwillen*]. That is why I call [the atom] a quantum of "will to power." (*WP* 634)

Quanta of force are defined by way of the resistance that they occasion or meet, as they inevitably will, because centers of willing just are the elements of a multiply constituted field of forces (or relations), and because they are projections of points of view that by definition can never completely overlap or "agree." We have to imagine "points" of minimum (or no) extension arrayed "atomistically" across some spectrum, each constituted by (or as) a different window onto the world; the world's "being is essentially different from every point [*Punkt*]; it presses upon every point, every point resists it – and these summations [*Summirungen*] are in every case quite *incongruent*" (*WP* 568; emphasis added). The "summations" are the collective impressions that each point makes or takes concerning its field of view; totaled, they are equivalent to the "world" – its world. But such a world is a *discrepant* total, never equal to itself, because it is never identically viewed from the different viewing centers that can in principle compose it. A sum total of the individual summations (a *summa summarum*) is impossible, in part just because the individual sums are incommensurable with each other. But even assuming such a calculation could be made, who would make it? The assumption requires introducing a further viewpoint, which remains partial at best, and at worst generates an absurd regress. Now we can see why Nietzsche's claim that a thing is the sum of its effects is in fact self-refuting: *the presupposition of a sum total is incoherent*. There is no way to capture the totality of "everything in the actual world" without betraying either the world or oneself. It is not even clear that the world exists in a total state at all. How could it, if the will to power is an account of the conflictual and unarbitrated struggle to define just what the world is?[3]

Nietzsche says that the summings-up are "incongruent" not only as a whole, but "in every case." Thus there is a deeper reason for doubting the quantifiability of every center. To begin with, each center lacks self-identity: this is a direct consequence of its relational identity.[4] But there is more. A viewing center is dynamically constituted in its eccentric relation to a world (the world it sees), which in turn is and is not identical with the individual viewing center that beholds it. It would seem that both the viewing center and its world are constituted together – in the same perceptual act, but as other and different from each other. For just as "there is no such thing as 'willing,'" but only a willing *something*," so too "to be an object is to be a perception" (*WP* 668; *KSA* 7, 7[168]: "the one world-will is simultaneously self-perception: and it sees itself as world, as appearance"; cf. *GM* III. 12: "seeing becomes seeing something"); and yet, the something that is willed by a force-center is the world it sees and resists. How, then, can what is viewed also constitute a "pressure" of the world, a "resistance," when it looks to be internal to the act of viewing? One way it can is in the feeling of an increment in power that accompanies the "growth" of a center of force.

"The Logic of Feeling"

The mere reflection of its own (and arguably doubtful) existence ought to suffice to give the first spurt of this feeling, to "mark" a force-center with the signature of its own quantity. As we saw, "a quantum of power is designated [*bezeichnet*] by the effect it produces and by the effect it resists" (*WP* 634); and these two effects are in fact temporally and formally one, all rolled up into the act of seeing or willing – or rather, *feeling* – something, "a feeling of difference [*Differenz-Gefühl*], presupposing a comparison," *WP* 699). (It is worth noting that the very first occurrence of the expression "the will to power" in Nietzsche's writings [*KSA* 8, p. 425; see the introductory discussion to this essay] is coupled with another: "the *feeling* of [. . .] *power*.") In other words, a quantum of power doesn't exist as such *until* it has been semiotically marked; indeed, it is no more than the "degree" of resistance it meets or feels, because to be a quantity at all is to be already signed, or measured, by a degree of difference in force and resistance. A quantity can never meet with no resistance, unless it should cease to produce (and to "feel" or sense) any effects at all. "The will to power can express itself *only* through resistances" (*WP* 656); and since the will exists only insofar as it is expressed, the will is at the very least crucially dependent on the resistances it meets, and possibly is nothing more than the resistances it posits, or presupposes, in order to discover them.

"The feeling of power, of struggle, of resistance persuades that there *is* something that is here being resisted" (*WP* 533). Resistance is not given, but presupposed, or in more familiar and acceptable language, "interpreted." To illustrate this, we need to rethink the "continuum" of the world posited on Nietzsche's scenario. For the world of forces is not only scarcely fixed but is instead constantly in flux, or rather moving in a flux of ever-changing relations (which is to say, interpretations). The flux consists in the fact that quantities are ever being recast in new form, as new qualities, by the constituent atoms of will, which are *themselves* the very quantities and qualities in question. The conversion of quantity into quality is in fact the activity most proper to the will to power, its most basic perceptual judgment. "The desire for an increase in quantum grows from a *quale*," by which is meant the *perception* that answers to the question, What is the quality in front of me, and what is my own? (*WP* 564). In this way, identities are "fixed," if only *en route* to ever larger, more powerful identities, against the background of a postulated "whole"; differences in quantity and quality are established, displayed, and altered in the very process of their establishment. But, again, these features (and changes) are mere perceptions, and perceptions, being partial by definition, never agree with each other or even with themselves within a stable framework of identity-relations. *Thus, a quantity of force will be internally incongruent just by possessing the quality of a quantity, which is to say, just by representing to itself a qualitative difference from all quantities, including its own.* "Quantitative differences [. . .] are *qualities* which can no longer be reduced to one another" (*WP* 565). To be a quantity is to be a difference, a "difference of quantity"; it is to display the "quality" of a differential force (*WP* 563–5).

How, and why, do qualities come into existence? Nietzsche's answer is complex: "[M]ere *quantitative differences*," which result from a comparative judgment, "are something fundamentally distinct from quantity" in some absolute sense; that is, they are *qualities* (*WP* 565). This "law," which is that of an irresistible constraint, is in fact the law of a subjective impression: "*we cannot help feeling*" that this is so, which is why "qualities are insurmountable barriers *for us*" (*WP* 565; emphasis added). The same point was available in 1872/3, again in the context of a theory of will, conceived as varying quantities of "centers of sensation": "We can free ourselves from *qualities* only with difficulty" (*KSA* 7 19[159]). Qualities (evaluative distinctions) are a way – apparently the only way – of viewing quantities. A quantity is merely the register of a perceived relative difference, not an objective "amount." Indeed, the idea of a totality or whole amount is itself a qualitative grasp of a quantitative difference. But quantities are not totalizable, or "fixed," until they are grasped *as* qualities (that is, in their relations); and until that moment, they cannot even be grasped as *quantities* (that is, totalized as such). Quantities exist, one might say, simply in order to be a sign of qualities (*KSA* 12, 2[157]). And signs exist only for a subject. Plainly, there are no objective amounts and no objective qualities (for "the same quantum of energy means different things at different stages of evolution," *WP* 639). The difference between quantity and quality is a weak one; it is internal to the system of conveniences that enables the distinction to emerge at all. The difference between them is the sign of a perspectivally induced *illusion*.

Now the question naturally arises, for whom is the illusion effective? Here, Nietzsche's account of force-centers wavers meaningfully. Qualitative differences, which is to say differences in force, enliven the scenario of a world that otherwise, were it composed of quantities and no qualities, would be "dead, stiff, motionless" (*WP* 564), just as a world without features would be inert, lacking in all relationality, and suspended. (The mechanistic view of nature is one such attempt to achieve, as near as possible, a world of pure quantities.) So on the one hand, this enlivening is brought about by the force-centers themselves, as they calculate their relative worth, in the conversion of quantities into qualitative, evaluative differences (starting with the very premise of a quantity itself); and that conversion is crucially *retroactive* in nature. What a force-center sees is differences in "rank," order, or value – it has, in other words, a perception of *qualities* – before it can reflect these back onto a perception (or feeling) of quantities of force.

On the other hand, the reduction of a world to pure quantities, Nietzsche insists, is conceptually and psychologically impossible – for *us*. Clearly, if the will to power has any meaning at all, it is only in relation to the intrinsic limitations of its intended spectator, Nietzsche's all-too-human reading subjects, whose limitations just happen to coincide with those of the objects of the spectacle they take in, the force-centers themselves, their distant relations (analogs). Plainly, the will to power is not an account of the world as it is, nor is it an account of Nietzsche's personal view of the world. It is a view that has been projected, in parable form, as a mirror of mankind. "Qualities are our own human idiosyncrasy" (*WP* 565; cf. *WP* 584). And centers of force both mirror and mimic this psychology in their own behavior (a behavior we can be sure has been enlivened thanks to the projections of our more familiar perspectives). Force (power) is what quality represents, and nothing more; it is a *retrospective* perceptual glimpse of the world, validated as a feeling. By now it should be clear that force is constructed as a phantasm of the subject – the subject that any center of force in fact represents. And so, too, the consistency of the world taken in by a center of force (its view of the "whole," epitomized in the dictum that "everything conditions everything else") attests to nothing but *the consistency of a phantasm*. A premise of this picture is the supposition "that the world ha[s] a certain quantum of force at its disposal" (*WP* 638), in other words, a sum of forces. But that premise, we have seen, is false.

The will's power is the retroactive product of a perceptual act. Can it not be said of the will to power too, as it can be said of the world of subjects, objects, and doers that is the misbegotten product of *our* misdescription of the world, "let us not forget that this is mere semiotics and nothing real [. . .] already a translation into the sense language of man" (*WP* 634) – in other words, that the will to power is a mere, or if you like false, perception, made in the first instance by each willing-center, and in the last instance by ourselves? If this is right, then the "errors" of the anthropomorphic perspective – that is, "the logic of the perspectivism of consciousness" that was "left out" of the contents of the physicists' picture of the world (although that logic was everywhere present in its *frame*) – are not so much exposed by Nietzsche's fantastic scenario of willing-centers as they are written into it as its operative, if somewhat concealed, premise (*WP* 636). How strange – or is it? – that the repressed "perspectivism of consciousness" should return, as Nietzsche's version of perspectivism, as "precisely this necessary perspectivism by virtue of which every center of force – *and not only man* – construes all the rest of the world from its own viewpoint, i.e., measures, feels, forms, according to its own force" (*WP* 636; emphasis added). Nietzsche's having concealed things like this has nothing to do with secretiveness. Quite the contrary, he is demonstrating, in Edgar Allen Poe's term, a "hyperobtrusive" fact, one so obvious it escapes notice. What is more, the strategy has a point. For hiding in the light in this way itself constitutes one more analog of the phenomenalist error that Nietzsche detects in all mortal judgments, which conceal their anthropomorphisms in a variety of ways, but most of all by acting as if they did not exist. The will to power is itself deeply anthropomorphic, and a projection of the *constitutive* limits of the subject.

See also 4 "Nietzsche on Individuation and Purposiveness in Nature"; 5 "The Individual and Individuality in Nietzsche"; 12 "Nietzsche on Time and Becoming"; 20 "Agent and Deed in Nietzsche's *Genealogy of Morals*"

Notes

This essay is excerpted and adapted from a book in progress entitled *Nietzsche and the Seductions of Metaphysics: Nietzsche's Final Philosophy*. My thanks to Keith Ansell Pearson for incisive editorial comments.

1   Both of these early pieces can be found in translation in Crawford 1988.
2   A prediction made after the event.
3   See also *WP* 708, where it is shown how the very idea of a "total value" as applied to the world is a meaningless concept, and esp. *WP* 711: "in the 'process of the totality' the labor of man is of no account, *because a total process* (considered as a system –) *does not exist at all*; [. . .] there is no 'totality' [*Ganzes*]; [. . .] the world is [. . .] chaos" (emphasis added). The idea of a total state is a human projection (as is that of chaos – which is another story).
4   The logic of relational identity has been misstated in the past. A "'thing'" may be "the sum of its effects" or relations (*WP* 551), but this does not mean that their sum can be totaled up, or that some unintegratable remainder won't always be left over at the end of the process. It is not just that the relations of a thing keep slipping away from us in the form of a leftover whenever we try to establish the thing's identity: a thing's identity *just is* this leftover itself – whether the thing in question is a "thing," an event, a relation, "everything in the world," or, if you like, the will to power itself, construed as any of these possibilities. There is no whole, no consistent sum, to which the will to power as a feature (or the only relevant feature) of the world might correspond: the presupposition of a sum total is incoherent.

Editions of Nietzsche Used

Beyond Good and Evil, trans. Walter Kaufmann (New York: Vintage Books, 1966).
Ecce Homo, trans. Walter Kaufmann (New York: Vintage Books, 1967).
The Gay Science, trans. Walter Kaufmann (New York: Vintage Books, 1974).
On the Genealogy of Morals, trans. Walter Kaufmann (New York: Vintage Books, 1967).
Human, All Too Human, trans. R. J. Hollingdale, 2 vols. (Cambridge: Cambridge University Press, 1986).
Twilight of the Idols, trans. R. J. Hollingdale (Harmondsworth: Penguin, 1968).
The Will to Power, trans. Walter Kaufmann and R. J. Hollingdale (New York: Vintage Books, 1967).

References

Clark, Maudemarie (1983). "Nietzsche's Doctrines of the Will to Power," *Nietzsche-Studien*, 12, pp. 458–68.

—— (1990). *Nietzsche on Truth and Philosophy* (Cambridge: Cambridge University Press).

Crawford, Claudia (1988). *The Beginnings of Nietzsche's Theory of Language* (Berlin and New York: Walter de Gruyter).

Danto, Arthur C. (1965). *Nietzsche as Philosopher* (New York: Macmillan).

Deleuze, Gilles (1983). *Nietzsche and Philosophy*, trans. H. Tomlinson (New York: Columbia University Press).

Derrida, Jacques (1978). "Structure, Sign, and Play," in *Writing and Difference* (Chicago: University of Chicago Press).

Förster-Nietzsche, Elisabeth (1895–1904). *Das Leben Friedrich Nietzsches*, 2 vols. in 3 (Leipzig: C. G. Naumann).

Heidegger, Martin (1961). *Nietzsche*, 2 vols. (Pfullingen: Günther Neske).

Hollingdale, R. J. (1965). *Nietzsche: The Man and his Philosophy* (London: Routledge & Kegan Paul).

Janaway, Christopher (ed.) (1998). *Willing and Nothingness: Schopenhauer as Nietzsche's Educator* (Oxford: Clarendon Press).

Kaufmann, Walter (1974). *Nietzsche: Philosopher, Psychologist, Antichrist*, 4th edn. (1st pub. 1950; Princeton: Princeton University Press).

MacIntyre, Alasdair C. (1990). *Three Rival Versions of Moral Enquiry: Encyclopaedia, Genealogy, and Tradition* (Notre Dame: University of Notre Dame Press).

Magnus, Bernd (1988). "The Use and Abuse of *The Will to Power*," in R. C. Solomon and K. M. Higgins (eds.), *Reading Nietzsche* (New York: Oxford University Press), pp. 218–35.

Montinari, Mazzino (1982). *Nietzsche Lesen* (Berlin and New York: Walter de Gruyter).

Müller-Lauter, Wolfgang (1971). *Nietzsche. Seine Philosophie der Gegensätze und die Gegensätze seiner Philosophie* (Berlin and New York: Walter de Gruyter). English translation (1999): *Nietzsche: His Philosophy of Contradictions and the Contradictions of his Philosophy* (Urbana: University of Illinois).

Nehamas, Alexander (1985). *Nietzsche: Life as Literature* (Cambridge, MA: Harvard University Press).

Porter, James. I. (1998). "Unconscious Agency in Nietzsche," *Nietzsche-Studien*, 27, pp. 153–95.

—— (2000a). *The Invention of Dionysus: An Essay on "The Birth of Tragedy"* (Stanford: Stanford University Press).

—— (2000b). *Nietzsche and the Philology of the Future* (Stanford: Stanford University Press).

Schopenhauer, Arthur (1969). *The World as Will and Representation*, 2 vols., trans. E. F. J. Payne (New York: Dover).

Further Reading

By far the most perceptive works on the will to power are:

Gerhardt, V. (1996). *Vom Willen zur Macht. Anthropologie und Metaphysik der Macht am exemplarischen Fall Friedrich Nietzsches* (Berlin and New York: Walter de Gruyter).

Haller, F. W. (1976). *Zum Problem des Wertschätzens. Eine ontologische Auslegung der Wertschätzungslehre Nietzsches* (Bonn University); a little-cited dissertation.

See also Müller-Lauter (1971) *above.*

Also of interest:

Gaède, E. (1962). *Nietzsche et Valéry: Essai sur le comédie de l'esprit* (Paris: Gallimard).

Grau, G. G. (1984). *Ideologie und Wille zur Macht. Zeitgemässe Betrachtungen über Nietzsche* (Berlin: Walter de Gruyter).

Hamacher, W. (1997). " 'Disgregation of the Will': Nietzsche on the Individual and Individuality," in *Premises: Essays on Philosophy and Literature from Kant to Celan*, trans. P. Fenves (Cambridge, MA: Harvard University Press), pp. 143–80.

Porter, J. I. (1999). "Nietzsche et les charmes de la métaphysique: 'La logique du sentiment,' " *Revue germanique internationale*, 11 ("Nietzsche moraliste"), pp. 157–72.

Williams, B. (1995), "Nietzsche's Minimalist Moral Psychology," in *Making Sense of Humanity and Other Philosophical Papers, 1982–1993* (Cambridge: Cambridge University Press), pp. 65–76.

31

A Critique of the Will to Power

HENRY STATEN

Nietzsche's theory of will to power is pulled by two contradictory imperatives. On the one hand, based on the physicist's concept of physical force, it undoes the teleological modes of thinking that Nietzsche considered to be the prime intellectual error of Christianity and idealist philosophy. On the other hand, will to power itself is through and through a *nisus* (intrinsic tendency) toward "life at its highest state" (*WP* 639), and represents the internal reality of force, which scientific concepts capture only in its external aspect (*WP* 619; *BGE* 36). In accord with modern science, will to power has no aim; yet, lacking an aim, it must nevertheless operate unilinearly *von Innen her*, outward from the inside in bringing forth new biological and cultural forms. Hence Nietzsche rejects Darwinian "natural selection" on the grounds that natural selection involves the organism's *outside* as an essential factor in the complex process of form-generation, attributing the fundamental impulse of the complex whole to a self-determining power in the constitutive centers of force. As Wolfgang Müller-Lauter pointed out in a groundbreaking essay, Nietzsche theorized that even the forces that are appropriated by a more powerful force must carry through the consequent alteration in themselves out of their own spontaneity (Müller-Lauter 1978: 214–15). No matter how complex the syntheses into which it enters, a unit of force must not, for Nietzsche, become only one element in an "assemblage" that would be illimitably porous to the influence of forces from what indeed could no longer be strictly determined as its "outside."[1]

As Gregory Moore has recently pointed out, will to power is "essentially a *Bildungstrieb*," reminiscent of *Naturphilosophie* and "virtually indistinguishable from the widespread crypto-idealism of contemporary German biology" (Moore 2002: 55).[2] But Nietzsche's commitment to a biological *Bildungstrieb* is clearly overdetermined by his commitment, at the level of his cultural theory, to his latently Romantic-idealist conception of the "higher type" of human. Hence he ascribes the very origin of the state-form to the spontaneous, instinctive, form-producing violence of the "blond beasts" who exemplify will to power in its archetypal human expression (*GM* II. 17–18), and in a famous passage in *Ecce Homo* describes his own development as the operation of a great "organizing 'idea'" that infallibly guided him past all "wrong roads" before he had any "any hint" of the "aim" (*EH*, "Why I Am So Clever," 9). Nietzsche seeks to anchor the will to power of the superior human in something that cannot be affected in its essence by the influence of the social outside, and looks for this anchor in the intrinsic nature of the higher type's biological drives.

Much of even the most up-to-date Nietzsche scholarship has been curiously respectful of this outmoded notion of drives, ignoring the problems with the Romantic-idealist biologism on which it is based.[3] I argue in this essay that the notion of will to power at the level of human action needs to be, and can be, stripped of biologism and aligned with the contemporary sense that human biological endowment is transformed into agency *essentially* and *only* through the mediation of social forms. Once the theory of will to power is revised in this way, it can make a valuable contribution to the further development of the sociological theory of human agency.

A Biological Basis

The voiding of intrinsic purposiveness from nature by science is not for Nietzsche, any more than it is for Kant, a conceptual terminus; rather, it presents a problem to be overcome. *The human will must have a goal*, Nietzsche insists in the *Genealogy of Morals*; it must affirm itself as will in the act of willing, and this self-affirmation of will is in danger of being paralyzed by the sense that the world has no meaning, no goal. Nietzsche sees it as his task to create a new system of valuation such that the human will can once more have a goal; yet this new goal must not be, as in Kant, grounded in the supersensible but in the sensible. It is right that man should be translated fully and without remainder back into nature, the scientific interpretation of the world must be carried to its most radical conclusion in the negation of all teleology of any classical sort; but this conclusion must be the basis of a new conception of purpose. Will to power is pure quantum of energy that "that is waiting to be used up somehow, for something," but which is indifferent to any specific goal (*GS* 360), yet this indifferent tendency toward discharge must somehow replace purposiveness in Nietzsche's world-interpretation. Like the physicist's concept of force, on which Nietzsche's concept of power is based, power is utterly impersonal and unpurposive, and yet power must constitute the matrix out of which all forms of willful striving coalesce. Hence it must possess an additional, "internal" element that physical force does not have, a *nisus* toward expansion, involving overcoming and appropriation of whatever external forces might stand in the way of this expansion.[4] Somehow, out of the conflict of distinct centers of will to power, Nietzsche theorizes, a system-organization would emerge, one in which the strongest of the contending wills would assume command, on the basis of a complex synthesis in which the weaker forces would assume subordinate roles.

Nietzsche's quest for a teleology that would be intrinsic to the blind causality of nature is paradoxical as long as one's notion of physical causality is restricted to what Nietzsche derides as the "push-pull" model of mechanical transmission of force among solid units of matter. But science even in his time offered more sophisticated models of causation on which Nietzsche relied for his own speculations, in particular the physics of Boscovich and the physiological theory of Wilhelm Roux. These thinkers theorized the field of causation as constituted not by the impact of particles but by the interaction of forces. Nietzsche's recourse to physics was sketchy at best; but Roux's physiology by contrast offered a rich model by which the operations of will to power could be scientifically conceived within the realm of life. Roux theorized that the organism is a multiplicity of parts that struggle for dominance, and that it is out of the drive to dominance of each part, which Roux called "overcompensation," that the functional organization of the organism emerges. This functional organization operates in a holistic way, guided by a principle of "self-regulation" that keeps the struggle of parts subordinate to the needs of the whole organism. Roux's model thus seemed to provide exactly what Nietzsche needed: an apparently non-teleological, naturalistic derivation of a higher-level organization out of a warring multiplicity.

Yet, as Müller-Lauter shows, Nietzsche's encounter with Rouxian physiology follows a tortuous course. Nietzsche holds that teleology must be absolutely rejected; mechanistic explanation is methodologically indispensable. Yet mechanism isn't ultimately deep enough; a richer account is required of the forces that science describes mechanistically. The richer account nevertheless must remain free of teleology. But this third way, neither mechanistic nor teleological, remains elusive; the richer account veers toward teleologism, in the form of Nietzsche's new account of the will. Nietzsche thinks hunger plays too large a role in Roux's account; he requires a more active, spontaneous, force within the organism that will not depend, as the drive for the means of survival does, on external "selective" forces of a Darwinian type. The driving force should be one that produces form *out of itself*, not by the action of external forces. Hence he posits the will to power as the most fundamental organic drive – the purely spontaneous movement toward the hierarchical subordination of all other centers of will to power. The principle of self-regulation is no longer to be linked to the function of nutrition but to those of "command" and "obedience," and Nietzsche experimented with the idea that this process of command and obedience would reach all the way down to the most elementary organic functions in the primary units of the organism. Everything organic possesses "memory and a sort of spirit" (Müller-Lauter 1978: 211), "all organic forms participate in thinking, feeling, and willing" (1978: 215).[5]

We must keep firmly in mind that underlying all of Nietzsche's speculations of this type is a profound, career-long skepticism regarding the ability of language to deliver the truth about the world; Müller-Lauter reminds us that the teleological form of expression is for Nietzsche ultimately "a preliminarily indispensable means of representation and nothing more" (1978: 220). However, it is also true that for Nietzsche there is nothing to contrast with mere means of representation, no language of truth to which this sort of talk would be a supplement; the theory of will to power, however hypothetical it might be, is his best attempt to render language, inadequate though it ultimately is to the true nature of things, as adequate as it can be made. It is therefore of considerable significance that in his attempt to put will to power on the rigorous basis of contemporary physiology we find him returning to a mode of thought that is recognizably continuous with *Naturphilosophie*.[6] Despite his acutely critical stance toward teleologism Nietzsche cannot quite give up the idea that, after all, there *is* some push toward form already there in the original bits that compose the struggle, that will to power from the beginning, in its essence, aims at form and at the raising and refining of forms to higher levels. The obedience of the subordinate parts is "no blind, still less a mechanical, rather a choosing, intelligent, thoughtful obedience" (Müller-Lauter 1978: 219).

Eliminating *Vorstellung*

The key to sorting out Nietzsche's relation to teleology is the notion, derived from *Naturphilosophie* generally and more specifically from Schopenhauer, of *purpose without mental representation (Vorstellung)*.[7] Nietzsche's opposition to teleological explanation was not fundamentally to the notion of purpose as such but to that of consciously imaged and intended purpose; hence the persistence in his thinking of *naturphilosophisch* notions of some more profound, unconscious sort of purpose that would operate without a representation of its goal.

The premodern, prescientific picture of the world, the picture Nietzsche wants to put finally to bed, was a Christian elaboration of Aristotelian teleology. According to this picture, the order and intelligibility of the world are underpinned by the intention of the divine craftsman who created it. Kant was acutely aware of the contemporary bankruptcy of this notion, and it is this awareness that drives the project of the *Critique of Judgment*. Kant writes that "we call purposive [*zweckmässig*] that the existence of which seems to presuppose a representation [*Vorstellung*] of that same thing" (2000: 19): in other words, when it is the artifact of a conscious artificer. Nature, therefore, conceived in terms of the empirical laws of nature, cannot be held to be purposive. Yet in order for the whole of nature to be understood as systematic lawfulness the judgment "necessarily carries with it *a priori* a principle of the *technique* of nature," according to which nature is thought "in accordance with the analogy with an art" and its forms understood not as objectively purposive but *as if* they had been constructed according to a purpose. Hence in the concept of the purposiveness of nature "the end [*Zweck*] is not posited in the object at all but strictly in the subject." This positing does, however, find a foothold in nature itself, because there is one special subclass of natural objects that defies understanding on the basis of mechanistic causation: living things. For Kant, as for Aristotle, biological organisms provide an intermediate conceptual step by which to effect the transition from the craftsman model to the workings of inanimate nature. For Kant, organisms, like artifacts, cannot be explained entirely in terms of mechanistic causation, and require the invocation of the concept of purpose. Kant is aware of the problematic character of the step from the teleological nature of organisms to his speculations about purpose in inanimate nature; still, the final result of the "Critique of the Teleological Power of Judgment" is that somehow on the basis of the functional organization of living things something like a teleology of the whole can be at least entertained, and this teleology continues, as in Christian teleology, to be anchored (though now quite indirectly) in the notion of purpose as *Vorstellung* in the mind of an artificer.

Nietzsche too has recourse to the model of organism for his teleological speculations. Unlike Kant, however, he thinks that if we are to rediscover purpose in the world it must be on the basis of the workings of nature in a strictly naturalistic sense. He thinks that because the main problem with teleology is its anchoring in the concept of conscious *Vorstellung*, eliminating this concept would open the way to conceiving a natural purposiveness that has no aim. Nietzsche thus proposes to go straight from biology to purposiveness, without recourse to the model of production on the basis of a concept, and it is the clue to this direct route that he thinks he finds in Roux. But he runs into all the difficulties that Müller-Lauter points out, because the problematic of consciousness is entangled with that of teleology in a way that Nietzsche never gets quite clear.

In the pre-modern picture, the purposiveness of nature is derived, through the mediation of the image of the divine artificer, from the idea of conscious human purpose; but once the analogy has been made, the intrinsic teleology of nature comes to be seen as the *ground* of that human purposiveness *from which in fact it was originally derived*, and human purposes come to be seen as making metaphysical sense only in a world that is itself endowed with a purpose. Hence when modern science reinterprets the world as bereft of purpose, human action itself comes to be felt as purposeless and the crisis of nihilism ensues. So much is clear to Nietzsche. But because for him the problem of teleology is practically identical with that of conscious, *Vorstellung*-directed volition, it is only fitfully clear to him that there remains a problem with interpreting nature teleologically *even if we do it without recourse to aim-as-Vorstellung.*

Neither Kant nor Nietzsche engages Aristotle's metaphysics in a sustained way, which might have introduced a good deal of clarity into their thinking on teleology – at least, if they had been able to look past his teleology of nature into his account of *techne*, "craft" or "method," the original formulation of the craftsman analogy.[8] The importance of this original formulation for the present discussion is that, even though Aristotle did indeed conceive nature on the basis of such an analogy, *he did not conceive the teleology of craft itself in terms of Vorstellung.* For Aristotle, the true cause of an artifact is the *eidos*, idea or essence, which is, like a *Vorstellung*, in the soul of the artificer, but, unlike a *Vorstellung*, not as a psychological entity; it is an objective essence that resides primarily *in the techne itself* by means of which the artificer makes the object. Like Kant's "concept," the *eidos* pre-exists and is the ground of the being of the artifact, but the primary residence of the *eidos* is elsewhere than in human consciousness; taking our cue from Aristotle and translating his notion into modern, non-metaphysical terms, we could say that the *eidos* is in the trans-individual *social practice*. From here it is transferred by training into the psyche of the craftsman, from where it exerts its causal influence – not, however, as a function of something about the conscious intention of the artificer but as a function of the productive power of the social practice in accord with which the artificer acts. With the development in modern Western thought of the idea of mental representation, however, Aristotle's objective *eidei* were reinterpreted as something specific to the human mind and as sharing its nature. A mental representation, *Vorstellung*, is an image that the human mind holds before it in order to "view" it with the mental eye; the "substance" of *Vorstellung* is wakeful consciousness itself (although of course it might be *Vorstellung of* an objective something in the world).

The *Vorstellung* idea together with the Christian notion of free will yields the picture of an autonomous volitional self against which Nietzsche is dead set, and which determines the shape of his assault on teleology. But, still ensnared in the dualism of spirit and nature, Nietzsche imagines that, if purpose is not transcendent to nature, it must be immanent within it, which for him leads to the idea that it must be present in some primordial form in the elementary biological force-units. What he can't imagine – and I will develop this alternative in the second half of this essay, with the help of Aristotle – is that the locus of intelligence might be entirely *elsewhere* – neither

569

in (transcendent) consciousness nor in (natural) drives, but in historically evolved social structures *external* to the organism.

What puts such unbearable strain on Nietzsche's naturalism is the fact that he wants immanent will to power to not be teleological yet to achieve what teleology achieves. As Müller-Lauter cautions (1978: 218–20), the repeated recourse to teleological language we find in the *Nachlass* is always fenced off as merely a way of picturing things in the absence of a better account, while Nietzsche tries to figure out that better account; but the fact that this way of framing the problem is necessary to him even as a temporary expedient shows that he wishes to preserve something essential to the teleological account, only putting it on firmer ground. It is impossible for him to put teleology truly to rest because for him the ultimate source of form must be *within* the primordial forces and must not, as in Darwinism, require some form-producing (but not purposive) action from the *outside*.

Thus, on the one hand, because he eliminates *Vorstellung* from purposiveness, Nietzsche produces his still influential account of human action as continuous with natural processes in general. This account purportedly deconstructs the idea of agency as the naturalistically uncaused action of an autonomous spiritual substance, a self endowed with a free will. Yet to the degree that the theory of will to power is designed to insure that form must ultimately come from the *inside* it remains alien to the main trends of modern naturalism, including obviously Darwinism but also, and more important for the purposes of this essay, ethology and social theory. In Nietzsche's conception of it, human action would be as necessary, as spontaneous, agentless, and innocent, as the operation of natural forces – there would be no conscious intention behind it; yet he tries to rig the picture so that this spontaneity will be intrinsically oriented "upward," toward greater constellations of power that would be integrated according to more refined syntheses of force emerging from the naturalistic inter-action of lower-level forces, without anything essential being contributed to this emergence from the contingencies, at the biological level, of the natural environment, and, at the psychological level, of the socio-historical outside. The highest kind of culture, say that of classical Greece, and the highest kind of person, say the state-builder or the genius, would be expressions of this intrinsic tendency of will to power. I stress that Nietzsche never succeeds in reassuring himself that this intrinsic tendency toward the higher type will prevail in the end; he remains all too aware of the power of "natural selection" by which the outside tends to prune organic forces in a way that shapes them into a mediocre norm. Yet even if the victory of the higher type is rare, this victory is, according to the essential presuppositions of his theory, rooted in the *essence*, and Nietzsche can dream that in certain special cases, such as his own, the essence would be so strong that nothing from the outside could deflect it from its proper course.

Explosive Quantum

A good deal of obscurity is introduced into our attempts to grasp the theory of will to power by the fact that Nietzsche at different times proposes quite different models of its operation, models that are sometimes inconsistent with each other but which can be called in by the commentator in an ad hoc way that, loosely considered, makes them seem to remedy each other's deficiencies. In particular, the "discharge" model to which Nietzsche frequently recurs seems to throw a monkey wrench into any attempt to detect teleology in will to power. However, Nietzsche's most widely quoted account of the discharge model, in *GS* 360, is logically incoherent in a way that alerts us to the larger problems his theory encounters.

The argument of *GS* 360 is intended to eliminate the notion of a conscious purpose that "directs" the movement of energy: the essential phenomenon in willing is said to be not the purpose but the pure tendency of energy to express itself. Hence he describes the purpose as merely "a match" compared to which the energy-quantum is "a ton of powder." Energy, even if goalless, must of course move in a given direction, but Nietzsche thinks he can show that directionality is merely "accidental" to the directionless explosiveness of energy. The notion of conscious representation of the direction/ purpose is not explicitly mentioned, but it is implied in the metaphor of the helmsman, whose direction-giving capacity is denied in favor of the "current" into which the boat accidentally drifts. But Nietzsche's argument gets away from him with the boat-and-current analogy, because even if the boat (the quantum of energy) drifts into this particular current by accident, the notion of the directing current takes us far beyond the match-and-powder analogy. The application of the match is a punctual occurrence that causes discharge as another punctual occurrence. By contrast, if energy follows a current it embarks on a temporally extended course that is determined not by its own pressure to discharge but by the structure of the pathway that it follows. If drive-quantum is caught in a current, however accidentally, then the "must" – which explicitly refers not to the necessity of discharge but to the necessity of going *in this direction* – is that of the energy and structure of the current, not of the pure directionless thrust of drive-quantum.

Moreover, not even the initial moment at which the discharge of energy becomes caught in a given current can be, as Nietzsche suggests, merely accidental. Nietzsche seems to be thinking that the drive-quantum "must" take this path because it is the one that offers discharge, and consequently the pressure to discharge is the prior, compelling necessity; the implication is that any old opportunity of discharge will do. But the link between force-quantum and its pathway of discharge cannot be merely random, as Nietzsche suggests; even a keg of dynamite needs a quite specific type of external stimulus in order to explode. Nietzsche makes his analogy look plausible by ignoring the structural relation that must hold between the specific nature of the force-quantum and the specific types of forces on the outside that are capable of occasioning its discharge. This is true even of a simple explosive compound, and *a fortiori* true of drives, which most emphatically do not discharge purely by accident, but are structured in such a way as to be responsive only to specific objects and situations in the outside world. So if a drive-quantum is going to get caught up in a current that it "must" then follow, this is inescapably because there is some sort of *structure of the drive* that is wired into the organism, and this drive-structure is the residue of some historical relation to the world that must be renewed every time the drive is reactivated. As we have learned from modern ethological theory, the shape of drive, and the causal factors in its activation, are distributed between the inside of the organism and the outside of its environment.[9]

Nietzsche's argument here illustrates the point I have been making about the way in which his focus on conscious *Vorstellung* distracts him from other, equally pressing, questions. He is so intent on denying the necessity of the helmsman that he does not notice the complex structure of the alternate model his analogy suggests; instead, he takes the analogy to show the primacy of the pure tendency to discharge. In fact, despite his repeated statements regarding the ability of force to produce form entirely out of its energetic quantity, Nietzsche often finds it necessary to attribute to drives an aim-directedness that goes beyond the mere need for discharge. The *Nachlass* speculations of the 1880s develop the idea that force is structured by its relation to the other forces with which it struggles, and units of force must retain a "memory" of previous interactions with other units. But if force is directed into specific channels by the history of previous interactions this means it is now not pure quantum but *structured* quantum. This structure conditions the directionality of new interactions, which are then incorporated in their turn, building a further level of structure. Yet in such a case, the later, highly structured forms of will to power would contain a maximum of determination by past interaction with the outside, and this way of deriving form from internal physiological force would be bought at the cost of attributing a very small role indeed to the alleged form-producing power of force. Such speculations are, in fact, "evolutionary" in form and highly compatible with the type of Darwinian account to which Nietzsche was trying to offer an alternative.[10] By the time we get any distance at all in evolution, we are very far indeed from the primitive "explosion" model – which doesn't mean we must now posit free will; it means that our account must focus on the historically derived structurations of discharge-pathways: first in biological evolution; later, for humans at least, by what has come to be called the "cultural construction of the subject." Yet Nietzsche keeps trying to discern some primordial, irreducible tendency that would somehow persist throughout later developments as the principle that keeps the whole thing on track and is somehow the essence of the whole.

The Social Construction of Drives

Nietzsche is an exceptionally astute observer of the formative power of social forces; the *Genealogy of Morals*, for instance, is fundamentally an account of the causal primacy of social dynamics over individual psychology. Just how his commitment to inside-out causation keeps him from a clear understanding of his own sociological insights is visible in the most comprehensive recent account of the theory of will to power, that of John Richardson in *Nietzsche's System* (1996). Unlike most contemporary interpreters of Nietzsche, Richardson unapologetically embraces the teleological nature of will to power, treating drives primarily not as physiological primitives but as historically arising syntheses of more elementary drives. This approach enables Richardson to track the profound formative influence on drives of *historically evolved social practices* that provide drives with their "aims." In his attempt to do justice to Nietzsche's sociological insight, in fact, Richardson verges on a "cultural construction" account. He remarks that drives are not "some common human endowment, they're those particular practices I've been [. . .] trained up into" (1996: 48). And yet in the end, faithfully following the trajectory of Nietzsche's thought, Richardson comes back to the primordial aim-directedness of pre-cultural drive: "As directed at ends," Richardson writes, "even the most primitive wills 'intend' those ends and so exhibit an 'intentionality'; this includes both a view of a goal and a view of surroundings or circumstances in and through which that goal is being pursued" (1996: 188). This primitive "knowing" (1996: 207) that is built into physiological drives guides the course of the organism's life at the most essential level: drives have an immanent, unconscious "'reason'" or "power of discernment," that makes them "trustworthy judges" of sickness and health (1996: 206).

Thus, even though the primitive drives are educable by the social web of thought – notably by Nietzsche's teaching – this education can in the end only unfold the intrinsic purposiveness-without-*Vorstellung* of the drive itself. This unconscious original knowledge is horrendously difficult to bring to the level of reflection; the active individual capable of an "independent long will" (*GM* II. 2) is the product, Richardson says, of "long social engineering" (1996: 213), the historical process of training of the will that Nietzsche describes in the *Genealogy*. But this social engineering doesn't really "construct" the will of the active individual; it seems, rather, on this account, that the historical process merely *releases* an intrinsic tendency of will to power, freeing it from its captivity in the half-sleep of the primitive drives, so that it can at long last attain its metaphysical destiny. Although he does not say so, Richardson, like other recent interpreters, reads Nietzsche as following in the tradition of German idealism; on Richardson's telling, the theory of will to power is a modified Hegelianism, a story of "spirit rising" that doesn't as in Hegel end in the return of spirit to itself but keeps spirit immanent in nature, yet with its unconscious purposiveness height-ened to the utmost degree by the ministrations of reflective consciousness – a reflective consciousness aware that its job is to become conscious of what the unconscious drive already knew and in this way to educate the drive more fully about its own nature. "Nietzsche's spiritualization [of the will to power] is a certain intensification [. . .] of [the] intentional aspect" that is already present in even the most primitive wills or drives (1996: 188).

In the end, on this account, the physiological drives must contain the essence of the whole process within themselves, for the education of the drives is possible only in certain kinds of people, those who have the right kind of drives to begin with – *healthy* drives. The teleologism of Nietzsche's thought, and derivatively, if covertly, of Nietzsche scholarship, always comes back to the quite uncritical founding dichotomy of sickness and health. Everything we do is given its pattern of activity by social practice, and yet the *determining essence* of drive must in the final analysis be something independent of social practice, and there remains an irreducible, undialectical duality between social practice and individual will to power. Hence on the one hand Richardson, expounding Nietzsche, construes subjective agency as constituted *almost* all the way down by the patterns of social practice: "the meaning in what I do lies not in my individual doing but in that template or pattern from which my life is merely an offprint." But, on the other hand, he locates the *real being* of the person elsewhere: "the herd [. . .] is the real being here [. . .] my identity [. . .] [lies] above all in the way that I'm unlike [the herd]" (1996: 161). In order to have such a separate reality, I must not merely participate in one of the "waves or movements" that run through the social mass,

Richardson argues, but originate a new movement of my own, one that *shifts the practice* as it existed before I came along (1996: 161).

The notion of "shifting the practice" is the crux of Richardson's reconstruction of Nietzsche's argument about human agency. If I am to be real *qua* me, I must manifest a quantum of pure individual form-originating force that does not belong to the form of social practice as it is already constituted. Freedom is "activeness," and Nietzschean activeness is defined as "a will's ability or tendency to cleave to its own viewpoint, to press and develop what distinguishes it, and not to be [. . .] swayed or jostled away from this by other forces" (1996: 213)). There is *no being* for the individual except to the degree that agency comes somehow out of the individual's *own*, or we might say, *ownmost* Being. And this originative force-being cannot merely move in a new direction by the accident of its idiosyncrasy; it cannot be like the swerve of Epicurus' atoms; it must be endowed *with its own immanent purposiveness*; it must *off its own bat stipulate the goal of its seeking and the way to this goal*.

Richardson's account articulates in a particularly illuminating way an element that is at the core of Nietzsche's thought. The internal aim-directedness of the most primordial units is designed to ground a kind of non-Kantian "autonomy" of the individual. Nietzsche overthrows the conscious autonomous I (this is what the post-structuralist reading noticed) but still demands that it be me *qua* me who acts, and this "me" is privileged in a way that yields nothing to the most extreme form of romanticization of the self (an aspect of Nietzsche's thought the post-structuralists utterly ignored). There is nothing new about the excision of consciousness and free will; in Western thought since long before Romanticism there has existed alongside the free, rational I another, daemonic I that *does not choose* but is the channel of some unconscious, trans-individual power variously conceived as God or the Muses or spirit-in-nature. Nietzsche's theory of drives is bedeviled by the persistence in his thought of this archaic mystifying trend, which in its most extreme manifestation takes the form of the ideology of genius – an ideology that Nietzsche came to reject, just as he rejected teleologism, yet which generates the idea of the absolutely originative individual act to which Nietzsche is wedded. Despite its naturalistic trappings, this absolute origin of new form is ultimately as mysterious in Nietzsche's account as it was in that of the rhapsode Ion.

On *Techne*

Undeniably there exist cultural circumstances under which social practices are pervasively experienced as a threat to the reality of the individual self; but is this a structural inevitability, something about social practices as such, or something about a culture that has gone wrong? Nietzsche's concept of the herd suggests that social practices are *essentially* static, that they prescribe fixed patterns of thought and action that cannot bring forth the new without the irruption of extra-cultural form-producing force originating in a superior individual.

But why do we need to posit the historically constituted will as having a core of difference from anything in the practices that trained it? After all, in one sense, all individual actions within practices, no matter how typed and repetitive they might be, are stamped with all the particularity of the individual event and are as such irreducibly singular; in another sense, all individual actions can only have the identity and effectuality of moves within a practice to the degree that despite their newness they still count as repetitions of the type. No doubt we can and should distinguish the broad scale of possibilities of action ranging from least to most original; but why must we, how can we, draw a *boundary of essence* between ordinary action and one very special sort performed by a very special human being that will alone count as a real individual action?

Richardson's account puts us in a position to see exactly what is needed for a sociological theory of action that is conceived in terms of will to power yet freed from both the dualism of individual and society and notions of a creative principle intrinsic to nature. We need a conception of social practices that would attribute to them not only the power to repeat themselves in their "typed" form *but also to effect shifts in the type.* According to such a conception, there would be in the human subject no power or purposiveness worth the name that would not be contained primarily, overwhelmingly, in the forms of social practice and only in a highly derivative form in the individual; power would be as it were "deposited" in these practices in a potential form, awaiting activation by the individual actor. It is this aspect of social practice that was given its classical analysis by Aristotle under the heading of *techne*. *Techne* of any type whatsoever – whether arrow-making, harp-playing, mathematics, poetry – is a residue of innumerable and immemorable acts of discovery by bygone individuals, retained in cultural memory as deposits of potential power with which new generations can then be endowed. *Techne* both posits the goal of an action and proposes the means toward its attainment; it is therefore the true repository of the qualities that Nietzsche ascribes to drives.

Aristotle's account will not of course do in its original form (in particular, the notions of *eidos* and *telos* need to be strictly historicized, as follows); but it provides essential clues toward a strictly materialist account of the phenomena of human purposiveness that Nietzsche tries to derive directly from natural process. These clues were taken up from Aristotle by Nikolai Hartmann and then developed along Marxist lines by Georg Lukács in his final, widely ignored work, *The Ontology of Social Being* (Lukács 1980). "For Marx," Lukács argues, "labour is [. . .] the only point at which a teleological positing can be ontologically established as a real moment of historical actuality" (1980: 8), because it is only in the labor process, and never in nature itself, that purposiveness is embodied in materiality. Yet the purposiveness of the labor process does not arise from an action of mental representation by the *technites*, "wielder of the *techne*." This embodiment, of which the tool is the paradigmatic manifestation, arises out of a dialectical interaction between human purposes and the objective qualities of the materiality out of which need and desire must be satisfied. These objective qualities must be respected, the lines along which they can be shaped to human use discovered, if the endeavor is to be successful; and when they are slowly discovered over history these discoveries are stored up as a social possession, as knowledge of the pathways that lead to the goal in question.

By contrast, Nietzsche's account of the origins of the sense of obligation and of the state in the *Genealogy of Morals* are unhistorical in a way that undermines his theory, because there never was nor could there ever be any such formless human matter as these accounts postulate at any point in history. By the time history begins, human beings have already been formed into social groups with very sharply outlined customary practices which form the identities and patterns of activity of the individuals in these groups.

At the material base of all these patterns of activity are the *technai* that are formed in direct interaction with nature, by means of which the group assures its continuing physical survival: the practices involved in, and evolving from, the labor process as described by Lukács. There is another genealogy of morals, older, more rudimentary, and more fundamental than the one Nietzsche describes, that is rooted here. The labor process is characterized by its orientation toward worldly effectuality, its direction toward objects and materials in their resistant materiality, with the aim, under the ineluctable imperative of need, of discovering their real qualities and adapting human action to them, devising each act correctly in its context in a whole correct sequence of acts, with correctness measured in relation to the goal that is to be achieved, and, under primitive conditions, under pain of death in the event of failure. If there is a fundamental will to power in human action, surely the primitive labor process is its primordial expression. Here the awakening power of the human soma-psyche bit by bit extends its formative and appropriative influence into the external world. Nietzsche in *Human, All Too Human* describes how "in nature" human beings seek to feel the pleasure of their own strength by "breaking branches, loosening stones, fighting with wild beasts" (*HH* 103), as though "in nature" human beings needed to indulge in such random exercise of their muscles to feel strong. Lukács's account by contrast encourages us to focus on how in the early stages of the evolution of culture human beings learn not to break sticks but to *sharpen* them, and not in order to "feel" the strength of their muscles but to *extend their force and reach.* The invention of tools must occupy a central place in any theory of will to power that is held responsible to the actual historical conditions under which the forms of human action are formed.

The correctness of action is in each case specific to the *techne* in question – let's say arrow-making – and the muscles and nervous system of the *technites*, "wielder of the *techne*," are in each case disciplined with a corresponding specificity. Unlike the practices of terror by which Nietzsche tells us formless humanity was endowed with calculation and calculability, achieved *techne* embodies historically evolved end-directedness and the effectuality by which the end can be achieved; it can thus be considered *objectified will to power*, objectified not as blind tendency but as fully equipped with the knowledge of both what is to be attained and the pattern of activity by which it can be attained. *Techne* is the social inscription of the successful results of a historical process of discovery involving trial and error with a high admixture of serendipity; a socially evolved *pathway toward a goal* that embodies the effectuality for which it has been evolved because it consists precisely of a typed set of *effectual actions* to which the body is trained and which then informs the "judgments of the muscles" (*WP* 314). I can have the largest muscles in the world, and all the energy in the world, and I can flail about as much as you like, and in the absence of the appropriate *techne* never succeed in so much as tying my shoelaces. Much less would I be able to produce an arrowhead, an arrow, a bow, and the ability to kill animals with them, things the most ordinary member of a Neolithic culture can do without a second thought. Clearly, then, it is the knowledge or *cunning* embodied in the pathways of *techne*, and not anything about the subject's physiology, that is the depositary of power not as *Kraft* but as *Macht*, effectuality or effective-force. Social practices are not just types or patterns of activity, they are "force-creating forms," intrinsic principles of effectuality, the power that both proposes the goal and does the heavy lifting, while the human operator of the practice plays an indispensable but strictly subordinate role. And, as Lukács emphasized, the labor process in general disciplines the entire human drive synthesis, as the impulse toward satisfaction of need learns to take the long detour toward the goal that the labor process constitutes. This overall discipline is the substructure of the "long will" of which Nietzsche speaks.

Self-Shifting Practices

Lukács's account allows us to see beyond the *Vorstellung* model of purposiveness that underlies both Kant's and Nietzsche's concepts of teleology because it describes *the production of the productive process itself*. Once a *techne* has evolved, it will sometimes be the case that an artifact can be produced more or less in the way Kant describes, as the embodiment of a *Vorstellung*. But this is an entirely derivative phenomenon – derivative from the effective form of the *techne* and ultimately of the process by which the *techne* itself came to be, a process that is not based on a pre-existent *Vorstellung*. Those in whom the *techne* evolved had to hearken to the qualities of materiality, to follow the objective pathways in material or social reality in order to arrive at the practices by which their results could be reliably repeated by their successors. The signifier might be as arbitrary as you like; but there is nothing arbitrary about the means by which an arrow is sent to its mark or an edge rendered true. And once they are established these practices embody the knowledge of these pathways in a way that has no *essential* relation to conscious representation, although of course conscious representation always might play a role. As Wittgenstein stressed, a practice can in principle be taught purely by example, without the intervention of an explicit rule; furthermore, as Stephen Turner has decisively shown, there is no reason to think that a practice, in order to be propagated as "the same" among different individuals, need involve any kind of sameness in the internal representations of those individuals; it need not even involve any common *unconscious* or "tacit" representations (Turner 1994). The "pathways" leading to the goal are inscribed in the exemplary repetitions of the practice by those who have learned them from preceding exemplary repetitions; the *techne* as such exists only as the pattern of these repetitions (a pattern that is, however, supplemented by written or other inscriptions, pedagogical techniques and institutions, and so forth).

I argued earlier for the importance of *techne* on the basis of the claim that it is the form of human effectual force (*Macht*); but so far I have focused on material practices and hence on the relation between human effectuality and the body of nature. Richardson's point regarding how practices can be shifted, however, concerns mainly the realm of cultural production; the question is not how to move matter but how to give new form to the symbolic mediations by which the social substance acts upon itself. Material practices, once they successfully achieve their goal, seem to be more or less fixed in place by the nature of material reality, and when they are altered or replaced it is normally because a better route to the end is discovered; the situation is quite different in the realm of the arts or philosophy. Here one can have the illusion that, rather than discovering what is there, the *technites* "brings forth" more or less *ex nihilo*, or at any rate out of the creator's own unique being. If, however, a *techne* has no intrinsic form of unity, existing only in and as its propagation by exemplary repetitions, the problem of the new looks rather different than it does when we conceive a practice as a unitary "type pattern" the result of which is "herd being"; one no longer has the suffocating sense of being trapped in the type. Practices are woven of multiple strands, none of which has a predetermined end point, and each repetition of a type-act within a practice is potentially an essential divergence from the type because it does not repeat the type absolutely identically, and any difference, no matter how small, is potentially a term in a new series.[11]

The power of such small unintended variations should not be underestimated. They can have large effects, perhaps imaginable by analogy with the "cascading" effects described by chaos theory; and certainly modern artists and art theorists have not underestimated the potential of the "aleatory" to generate new forms.[12] But it does seem likely that artists and philosophers also jump to very large-scale new intuitions of form; and this type of innovative procedure might seem to lie beyond the theory of *techne*. The crucial point of the theory is not, however, that forms are generated mechanically, beginning as small variations or not, but that *the art is greater than the artist*, or, as Aristotle says, "the *techne* is the prior cause" (*Physics* 2), and, whatever the scope or type of the achievement, it can be understood on this basis. Rare individuals do indisputably bring forth in a way that strikes us as radically new and that initiates major new lines of cultural production; but the agency of these individuals is, like that of any other *technites*, "agencied" by the *techne* involved. The fact that the practiced artist "spontaneously" produces valid new gestures creates the illusion that there is some creative power native to the person who does the creating; but such spontaneity can be less mysteriously explained as a measure of the artist's successful incorporation of the art involved. Unlike a vital force that would produce form out of its formless vitality, *techne* is formative because it has been formed to be so by the historical process out of which it arises; having been so formed, the ensemble of its components projects a very large field of formal possibilities, and to master an art means to be able to actualize some subset of this field (where the *potential* that is actualized belongs structurally to the field itself and only contingently to the artist).

The structuralists, with their notion of the generative combinatory, had an essential insight into the generative power of a *techne* ensemble, but they created a new mystery because the productive power of a formal combinatory by itself is *too* great: it produces a practically infinite number of forms, a "library of Babel." The notion that the poet is just an "empty site," as Barthes famously had it, negates Romantic-humanist subjectivism, but leaves acute the problem of understanding how this empty site produces more than what Daniel Dennett calls a "vanishingly small" number of valid forms in an infinity of nonsense (Dennett 1995: 109). Astonishingly, neither Barthes nor even his inspiration, Mallarmé, seems to have had a consistent sense of the necessity of positing, between the individual poem on the one hand and the generalized field of the blind combinatory called "language" on the other, the mediation of a *techne* of poetry that would filter out the small subset of valid forms from the infinite field of possibility. This filtering cannot happen mechanically, as an abstract machine that subsists of

itself, but only in terms of a "pragmatics" that functions at the level of the incorporation of the *techne* as an idiolectic variation by an individual who is located at an
absolutely particular place in socio-historical time-space, and who interacts with all
the contingencies of a specific medium.[13]

On this account, the distinctiveness of the "great" artist arises from two factors. The
first is that he finds his productive *nisus*, quite by historical accident, more proximate
than other men's to a nexus of forces in the possibility-field of his art that are ready to
coalesce in strikingly new or large-scale ways – as, for example, Homer, or the two or
more poets who came to be folded under that name, came upon Greek poetry at the
moment when its ancient verse forms (dating back to Indo-European poetry), the
development of the Troy story by generations of poets, and the availability of the *techne*
of writing made it possible for the *Iliad* and the *Odyssey* more or less suddenly to
coalesce into new, much larger and more powerful forms than anything that had
preceded them in their tradition.[14]

The second factor is that the great artist as a rule (though not always) disposes of an
uncommonly great *quantum of energy*. Here we come back to Nietzsche and the theory
of will to power: there is no way around the sheer facts of sustained effort against all
obstacles and prodigal production of new forms that characterize those who succeed
in leaving a deep mark on cultural practices. We might say that the great artist by
dint of his superior quantum of energy penetrates further into the possibility-field
of his *techne* than do weaker artists. This sounds like the idea of genius, but differs
from it on the essential point: it does not attribute an intrinsic formative power to the
artist, whose "demonic" energy functions here *only* as the "efficient cause" by which
the "formal cause," the art itself, is actualized. The separation between the energetic
quantum and the form-producing field furthermore de-biologizes the notion of the
energetic quantum. The locus of effectual force is primarily the *techne*, and the
energetic quantum of the artist must be conceived as a complex, variable function of
the interaction of certain indeterminate potentials given in his biology with the
potentials latent in the *techne*, which not only gives this energy determinate form but
also diminishes or amplifies its quantity.[15] If Nietzsche had lived in a small group of
hunter-gatherers, there would have been no world-historical task to call forth his
heroic striving. Nietzsche himself notes that the energetic quantum of the "great man"
is culturally accumulated, perhaps over centuries; but in his characteristic way he
thinks of this as an accumulation of explosive force (*TI*, "Expeditions of an Untimely
Man," 44). By contrast, I am suggesting that energy accumulates in the formal system
of a *techne*, and that the "great man," at least *qua technites*, does not "squander" this
energy but disposes of it to amplify his own, of itself negligible, biological quantum.

Concluding Observations

Against Nietzsche, I have argued the structuralist-inflected point that the form-
producing action of even the most exceptional individual must be understood in terms
of the structuring effect of social forms. Against structuralism, I have argued the
Nietzsche-inflected point that the essential fact about social forms is not their structure
as such but the effectual force for the sake of which these structures have been

historically evolved, which they now embody, and with which they endow individuals, in such a way as to be constitutive of the individual's will to power.

This account leaves open questions regarding the possibility that entire cultures can "go wrong," such that their *technai* become "unhealthy" and no longer offer their most potentially creative members a means to satisfy their wills to power. Nietzsche turned to biology to define an extra-cultural standard on the basis of which entire cultures and cultural practices could be diagnosed as healthy or unhealthy. But there are no extra-cultural standards of value; Nietzsche was in fact generalizing from cultural models that he found in history (notably that of classical Greece) and in his own experience, and doing so in ways that were a development of the philosophical *techne*-tradition of Romantic idealism. Nietzsche's own practice-shifting ideas, like anybody else's, belong to the generative field of the *techne*, or coalescence of *technai* (and symbolic *technai* are always coalescing), the potential power of which he actualized. This did not prevent him from finding a standpoint from which to mount a radical critique of his own culture.

See also 4 "Nietzsche on Individuation and Purposiveness in Nature"; 6 "Nietzsche's 'Gay' Science"; 24 "Nietzsche *contra* Liberalism on Freedom"

Notes

1   The critique of Nietzsche on the basis of the Deleuzian notion of "assemblages" is developed in Ansell Pearson 1999: ch. 3.
2   Cf. Kevin Hill, who argues that "Nietzsche's thought [. . .] seeks to establish nostalgic relations with German Idealism" (2003: 91).
3   Leiter (2002: 91ff.) argues, for example, that human action is explicable in terms of immutable "type-facts" about an individual's physiology and unconscious drives. Richardson's more nuanced account (1996) turns out to be based in the same kind of biologism.
4   On Nietzsche's insistence that there must be an "internal" aspect to force, see Poellner 1995. Deleuze noted that in Nietzsche's theory an internal "complement" to force is necessary if forces are not to remain "indeterminate" (Deleuze 1983: 51). This is indeed a fundamental problem for Nietzsche; he declares that forces determine each other reciprocally, but, as Poellner points out, this leads to an infinite regress (Poellner 1995: 278–84). Deleuze's attempted justification of the internal "complement", which exerted enormous influence on the post-structuralist reading of Nietzsche, does not confront the problem articulated by Poellner.
5   Even what appear to be his distinctive modifications of Roux's theory are apparently derived from his reading in physiology. Moore points out that the idea that "volition [. . .] is present even in unicellular organisms" was put forth in the *Text Book of Physiology* (1877) by Michael Foster, a translation of which Nietzsche owned; and the rejection of the "struggle for existence" in favor of a principle of insatiable expansion was drawn from William Rolph's *Biologische Probleme* (1884), from which Nietzsche liberally borrowed (Moore 2002: 39, 47).
6   As early as 1868 Nietzsche had articulated a very precise critique of the teleologism and idealism of *Naturphilosophie*; see Hill 2003: 83–94. And yet, as Müller-Lauter notes (1978: 219), as late as 1885 Nietzsche was still toying with the idea of a "purposiveness" (*Zweckmässigkeit*) inherent in the workings of nature.

7 According to Schopenhauer, "absence of all aim [. . .] belongs to the essential nature of the will in itself, which is an endless striving" (1961: 164). I have discussed Nietzsche's engagement with this aspect of Schopenhauer in Staten 1990: 204–7.

8 The best brief account of Aristotle on *techne* is that of Klaus Bartels (1965).

9 Modern ethological research suggests that not even elementary drives like hunger and thirst can be described as drives-in-themselves. According to Slater, "Rather than thinking of animals as having a number of discrete drives, it is usual nowadays to think of them as having overlapping behavioral systems, each of which is responsible for a group of related behaviour patterns" (1985: 69); each of these overlapping systems is "a complex of different actions which may be quite differently caused, though they are superficially similar" (1985: 55), and their activation "is dependent on a variety of internal and external causal factors" (1985: 69). There is thus in this picture no unitary drive-energy that constitutes a drive, and the complex system that we group together with one name, hunger or thirst or aggression, has causal factors that are distributed between the inside of the organism and the external world.

10 The latest results of the study of genetics support this restriction of the power of the physiological "inside" to produce external form. See Ridley 2003: 229–48.

11 See my fuller account of this notion, much influenced by Darwin's conception of species: "The minute change that occurs from one gradation to the next contains an increment of essential or specific change: the transition to a new category has already begun in the slightest individual variation. Yet it is only when we take terms some distance apart in the series that we can see category differences" (Staten 1984: 97).

12 For an extensive survey of the poet's attempt at aleatory generation of forms see McCaffery 2001.

13 On the mistake in the analogy between poetics and linguistics committed by the formalists and then picked up by the structuralists, see Pratt 1977.

14 The Homeric epics demonstrate conclusively – certainly much better than any structuralist theorizing – the power of poetic *techne* to generate large-scale new form. Contemporary Homeric scholarship in the Parry–Lord tradition does not even speak of "Homer" but rather of the "Iliadic tradition" and the "*Odyssey* tradition." See e.g. Nagy 1979.

15 There is some obscurity in my exposition here because of the difficulty of defining "energy" in its various forms in terms of the *techne* model. I feel sure that clarifying this definition involves an adaptation of Aristotle's notions of *dynamis* "potential" and *energeia* "actualization," but it is a difficult problem. For a sense of the depth of the problem, see Heidegger 1995.

References

Ansell Pearson, Keith (1997). *Viroid Life: Perspectives on Nietzsche and the Transhuman Condition* (London: Routledge).

—— (1999). *Germinal Life: The Difference and Repetition of Deleuze* (London: Routledge).

Bartels, Klaus (1965). "Der Begriff Techne bei Aristoteles," in Hellmut Flashar and Konrad Gaiser (eds.), *Synusia. Festgabe für Wolfgang Schadewalt* (Pfullingen: Neske).

Deleuze, Gilles (1983). *Nietzsche and Philosophy*, trans. Hugh Tomlinson (London: Athlone Press).

Dennett, Daniel (1995). *Darwin's Dangerous Idea* (New York: Simon & Schuster).

Heidegger, Martin (1995). *Aristotle's "Metaphysics ⑨ 1–3": On the Essence and Actuality of Force*, trans. Walter Brogan and Peter Warnek (Bloomington: Indiana University Press).

Hill, Kevin R. (2003). *Nietzsche's Critiques: The Kantian Foundations of his Thought* (New York: Oxford University Press).

Kant, Immanuel (2000). *Critique of the Power of Judgment*, trans. Paul Guyer and Eric Matthews (Cambridge: Cambridge University Press).

Leiter, Brian (2002). *Nietzsche on Morality* (London: Routledge).

Lukács, Georg (1980). *The Ontology of Social Being*, vol. 3: *Labour*, trans. David Fernbach (London: Merlin Press).

McCaffery, Steve (2001). *Prior to Meaning: The Protosemantic and Poetic* (Evanston: Northwestern University Press).

Moore, Gregory (2002). *Nietzsche, Biology, and Metaphor* (Cambridge: Cambridge University Press).

Müller-Lauter, Wolfgang (1978). "Der Organismus als inneren Kampf. Der Einfluss von Wilhelm Roux auf Friedrich Nietzsche," *Nietzsche-Studien*, 7, pp. 189–223.

Nagy, Gregory (1979). *The Best of the Achaeans* (Baltimore: Johns Hopkins University Press).

Poellner, Peter (1995). *Nietzsche and Metaphysics* (New York: Oxford University Press).

Pratt, Mary Louise (1977). *Toward a Speech Act Theory of Literary Discourse* (Bloomington: Indiana University Press).

Richardson, John (1996). *Nietzsche's System* (New York: Oxford University Press).

Ridley, Matt (2003). *The Agile Gene: How Nature Turns on Nurture* (New York: Perennial).

Schopenhauer, Arthur (1961). *The World as Will and Idea*, vol. 1, trans. R. B. Haldane and J. Kemp (Garden City, NY: Dolphin Books).

Slater, P. J. B. (1985). *An Introduction to Ethology* (Cambridge: Cambridge University Press).

Staten, Henry (1984). *Wittgenstein and Derrida* (Lincoln: Nebraska University Press).

—— (1990). *Nietzsche's Voice* (Ithaca: Cornell University Press).

Turner, Stephen (1994). *The Theory of Social Practice* (New York: Columbia University Press).

Index

revaluation of values, 404
will to power, 565
education of Nietzsche, 2–3
ego–body relation, 273–4, 286–94
egoism
altruism and, 156, 523–4
Rée's account, 341, 342, 348–9
electronic music, 508
emotions, *see* affects
Empedoclean science, 66, 67, 68, 190–1
empiricism, 151, 154–5, 159–60
ontology of music, 502–3
toward the overhuman, 246
energy-quantum, will to power, 570–2, 579
Enlightenment position, genealogy, 353–5
Epicurean science, 67
epistemological skepticism, 136–7
error, psychology of, 19, 243–4
errors
the error of, 241
incorporation of truth, 236–40, 241,
244
of the individual, 87
in life's time, 219–20, 223
naturalism and moral psychology, 319–20
responsibility, 432
esotericism, 135–6
eternal return/recurrence, 8–9, 171–84,
189–204
anthropological mode, 190
awareness of, 172, 173–5
coherence, 172, 183–4
cosmological mode, 190
Dionysian mode of thought, 201–4, 223
evidence of, 172, 175–8
from final state to, 195–8
and individuality, 83–5, 92–3
Nietzsche's first sketch of, 231–4
nihilism, 190, 201–2, 251, 257–8, 266
optimism, 201
pessimism, 201
phenomenal consciousness, 297
significance of, 172, 178–80
time, 172, 180–4, 185; finitude of,
192–5, 196, 197–8; Nietzsche's
"theory" of, 209, 222–5; possibility
and, 198–201
toward the overhuman, 230; incorporation
of truth, 231–4, 238–9, 242
use of term, 247 (n2)

ethics, 12
agent–deed relation, 371–85
agonism, 326–9
cosmology and, 189–90, 203–4
fatalism, 419–33
gay science, 102
individuation, 78–9
Nietzsche's critique, 389–403
philosophical function of genealogy,
353–69
revaluation of all values, 404–17
of seeing suffering as beautiful, 55–6
self-legislation, 442
see also morality
ethos of the agonized subject, 326–9
Europe
geophilosophy, 477–8, 487, 488–9
national identity, 455, 456, 458–65,
466–70, 487, 488–9
Nietzsche's travels in, 7
evaluation, 9
of human nature, 115–31
see also hierarchy of values; problem of
values
evil, rebaptizing, 407, 409–17
evolution, 517–30
anthropocentrism, 70
cosmology and, 203
cultural evolution, 520–2
egoism–altruism reconciled, 156, 523–4
"English," 523–4, 530, 534–6, 545–6
human temporality, 221–2
incorporation of truth, 236–7, 238–9,
246
naturalism and moral psychology, 315,
320–1, 325, 327
non-Darwinian revolution, 517–20
philosophical anthropology, 129–30
Spencer, 522, 523–4, 535
struggle for existence, 520–2, 527–9
theory of time and, 208, 221–2, 226
will to power, 520, 524–9, 535, 537–9,
565
exegesis, art of, 3, 32–6
existence
aesthetic justification, 4–5, 41–56
eternal return, 8, 83–5, 92–3, 171–84
individual, *see* individuation
struggle for, 520–2, 527–9
see also becoming